Study Guide

Psychology

NINTH EDITION

Douglas A. Bernstein
University of South Florida and University of Southampton

Louis A. Penner
Wayne State University and University of Michigan

Alison Clarke-Stewart
University of California, Irvine

Edward J. Roy
University of Illinois at Urbana-Champaign

Prepared by

Kelly Bouas Henry
Missouri Western State College

WADSWORTH
CENGAGE Learning™

Australia • Brazil • Japan • Korea • Mexico • Singapore • Spain • United Kingdom • United States

ISBN-13: 978-1-111-30156-9
ISBN-10: 1-111-30156-5

Wadsworth
20 Davis Drive
Belmont, CA 94002-3098
USA

Cengage Learning is a leading provider of customized learning solutions with office locations around the globe, including Singapore, the United Kingdom, Australia, Mexico, Brazil, and Japan. Locate your local office at: **www.cengage.com/global**

Cengage Learning products are represented in Canada by Nelson Education, Ltd.

To learn more about Wadsworth, visit **www.cengage.com/wadsworth**

Purchase any of our products at your local college store or at our preferred online store **www.cengagebrain.com**

CONTENTS

Preface
TO THE STUDENT

This *Study Guide* was designed to help you master the material in *Psychology,* Ninth Edition, by Bernstein/Penner/Clarke-Stewart/Roy. The *Study Guide* supplements the textbook but does not replace it. If used properly, the *Guide* should help you not merely to memorize but to *take command* of the key facts, concepts, and issues discussed in the text.

We, the authors, want you to succeed in your introductory psychology course. We also want to help you deepen your understanding of how psychological principles can illuminate and enrich your life.

Each *Study Guide* chapter corresponds to a text chapter and is divided into eight sections: Chapter, Outline, Key Terms, Fill-in-the-Blanks Key Terms, Learning Objectives, Concepts and Exercises, Critical Thinking, Personal Learning Activities, and Multiple-Choice Questions.

1. *Chapter Outline* The outline presents the major topics and ideas from the text chapter. It reveals in handy fashion the organizational logic underlying each chapter---that is, the way each chapter's components fit together. Reviewing the Chapter Outlines may prove especially useful before a quiz or an exam.

2. *Key Terms* Terms that are underlined in the Chapter Outlines are also defined in the Key Terms section. We have tried to help you fix these terms in your memory. For many of them, we provide an illustrative example. For others, we present an idea to help you remember the key term. You will also find a heading label in parentheses at the end of each definition to identify the page on which the term is first defined and explained in the text. *NOTE:* We urge you to create your own examples of key terms as part of your study program. If you do so successfully, you will have taken a giant step toward mastering the material.

3. *Fill-in-the-Blanks Key Terms* Following the Key Terms definition section in each chapter are fifteen fill-in-the-blanks questions. These exercises are designed to help you check your mastery of many of the key terms and to review this definitional information before going on to later sections. Reading the answer provided at the end of the section will reinforce your learning and deepen your understanding of chapter material as you work through later sections of the *Guide.*

4   *Learning Objectives* The Chapter Outline and Key Terms sections provide a basic overview of the contents of your textbook. The next section of each *Study Guide* chapter, Learning Objectives, will further strengthen your command of textbook material by focusing your attention on its specific goals: to be able to describe, compare, and explain the important information in each chapter. To help you master these learning objectives, we have identified the textbook sections to which each objective corresponds.

5. *Concepts and Exercises* This section will help you achieve selected learning objectives stated in the preceding section. The exercises apply key psychological concepts to situations from everyday life. You are asked to identify the concepts being applied. At the end of the exercises, we provide the correct answer to each exercise, along with an explanation of why the answer is correct.

6. *Critical Thinking* This section will help you sharpen your critical thinking skills by asking you to answer the five critical thinking questions presented in your text in relation to a particular situation or scenario. The five questions and their answers are stated in the answer

section. This section is introduced in the chapter on research in psychology, where critical thinking is first presented.

7. *Personal Learning Activities* Active involvement is an excellent way to improve your understanding of and memory for the psychological issues, principles, and concepts described in *Psychology*. We have included personal learning activities to help you practice using the new information contained in each chapter.

8. *Multiple-Choice Questions* Once you have carefully worked through the previous sections, you will be ready to test your comprehension of the material covered. Every *Study Guide* chapter contains two multiple-choice quizzes, each consisting of twenty questions. At the end of the chapter the correct answers are given, along with an explanation of *why* each is correct and why the alternatives are incorrect. If multiple-choice exams are part of your course, the multiple-choice quizzes in the *Study Guide* will provide a valuable way to prepare for them.

We suggest that you begin by taking Quiz 1. Next, check your answers against the answer key and fill in the number of items you answered correctly. For any you miss, turn to the section of the text listed by the answers and reread the relevant sections. Write down, in your own words, information that will help sections of the *Study Guide's* Chapter Outline and the appropriate Key Terms. Then you will understand why the correct answer is correct and why the others are not. Then take quiz 2 and score it, noting our explanations of right and wrong answers. Finally, restudy the textbook and *Study Guide* materials as necessary. By following this procedure, you will build incrementally toward mastery of the contents of the text.

Finally, turn to the table at the end of the *Study Guide* chapter and circle the item numbers that you answered correctly the first time through Quizzes 1 and 2. (Quiz 2 is shaded to help you distinguish between your first and second tries at mastering the material.) The table will provide you with valuable information to further guide your studying. Look for a pattern in your results. Are you answering most of the definitional items correctly, but not the comprehension or application questions? Is there a topic that you mastered and another for which no items are circled? Write in the number of items you answered correctly on the first and second quizzes. Did you improve?

As you can see, we have designed each chapter of this *Guide* as a sequenced program of study, and each section builds on the one before it. However, if you believe that a different sequencing of sections will work better for you, feel free to give it a try.

Here's to your success!

DEVELOPING YOUR CRITICAL THINKING SKILLS

If you were to memorize every fact in the textbook, you might still miss its essentials. Much as sports announcers often say that the statistics of a game don't begin to indicate the contribution of a certain player, so, too, the facts conveyed by a college textbook often represent only a small part of its message. Thus, even if you forget many pieces of information within a year or two, you may retain something far more valuable from your introductory course in psychology.

What is there beyond the facts? Psychology and other disciplines have certain methods for defining, uncovering, and interpreting facts; they have certain ways of thinking. More generally, psychology and other fields of study rely on the ability to think critically-to evaluate claims, ideas, and evidence. Learning these ways of thinking enriches your ability to understand the world long after you may have forgotten specific pieces of information.

At its simplest, thinking critically means evaluating information rather than merely accepting it because it is endorsed by some authority or because it flatters your prejudices. In 1986, for example, a U.S. government commission declared that pornography is dangerous; it linked pornography and crime. You might be inclined to accept this conclusion because of the authority behind the commission or because you find pornography repugnant. But if you think critically, neither reason will be sufficient. At a minimum, you will ask why the commission came to that conclusion. What was their evidence? Even beyond asking for the reasons behind a conclusion, however, critical thinking requires the ability to evaluate those reasons. Is the argument logical? What is the source of the evidence that backs up the argument? If it's an experiment, were the experimental methods sound? Learning how to ask and answer questions like these is a first step in becoming skillful at critical thinking.

Throughout the text, the authors' discussions provide examples of critical thinking, illustrating how to examine the assumptions underlying an assertion, to evaluate evidence for an assertion, and to draw reasonable conclusions. In addition, each chapter in the textbook includes a section, labeled "Thinking Critically," that is devoted to critical thinking about one specific topic or assertion. In each case, the section examines the issue by considering five questions:

1. What am I being asked to believe or accept?

2. What evidence is available to support the assertion?

3. Are there alternative ways of interpreting the evidence?

4. What additional evidence would help to evaluate the alternatives?

5. What conclusions are most reasonable?

These questions represent steps that you can apply in thinking about most assertions. As the textbook's chapter on research in psychology explains, you can think critically without using these specific steps, but they constitute one useful model for critical thinking. Take time to consider the "Thinking Critically" sections, not only for their content, but also as a model of a way of thinking.

For further practice at critical thinking, do the Critical Thinking exercises in each chapter of the *Study Guide*. These will help you understand the importance of the five critical thinking questions and how to apply them. When you come across an issue of particular interest in your reading of the text, try applying these five steps to the discussion. No textbook can examine every issue in depth. If some of the steps are not fully explored in the text, try doing further research to follow these steps yourself. Or take a very specific assertion implicit in the discussion and explore it further by applying the five steps to that assertion. Most of all, as you read, remember to think critically. Throughout the text, the authors have tried to stimulate your own thinking. Just as they examine the flaws in existing research and acknowledge the many psychological questions that remain unanswered, so, too, should you probe what the authors have written and ask your own questions about it.

Applying the authors' model of critical thinking during the course should bring you at least four benefits. First, it should reinforce the habit of thinking critically. Are you going to buy brand X based on the endorsement of Oprah Winfrey or Michael Phelps? Will you take melatonin because others claim it is good for you? We hope this course will help you strengthen the habit of questioning claims, and evaluating arguments for yourself. Second, the practice gained by applying the text's model of critical thinking should sharpen your critical thinking skills. These skills can help you in every phase of life---whether you are weighing a politician's promises, the advantages of taking a new job, searching for a new car or a way to reorganize a department. Third, going through this sequence of steps should lead you to a better understanding of the material and to wiser conclusions. Finally, thinking critically is likely to improve your memory of the material. As discussed in the textbook's chapter on memory, organizing and thinking about information makes that information easier to remember.

STUDYING LINKAGES

A first glance at your textbook might suggest that introductory psychology resembles a cafeteria, consisting of a series of unrelated topics. Here is a little chemistry of the brain, over there a little biology of reproductive systems, and for dessert, a description of social pressures. But unlike a cafeteria, the diversity of topics in the textbook reflects not an attempt to satisfy every taste, but an effort to analyze essential parts of a complex whole. The diversity is necessary because all of these topics are pieces of the puzzle of psychology. If you wanted to understand why a friend became addicted to alcohol, for example, you would want to explore not only the person's history but also his relationships and the effects of chemicals on his brain.

Obviously you cannot study all of these topics at once. You would examine them one at a time. So, too, the textbook focuses on one aspect of psychology at a time. Eventually, however, it helps to put the pieces together. Much as parts of a jigsaw puzzle may take on new meaning when you see where they fit, so, too, the pieces of psychology take on new dimensions once you see how they are related. For example, the chemical messengers used in the brain (introduced in the chapter on biology) are interesting in their own right, but your knowledge about them takes on new significance when you consider how these chemicals can be affected by drugs (discussed in the chapter on consciousness) and by certain treatments for psychological disorders (discussed in the chapter on disorders).

To help you see how the pieces of psychology fit together, the authors of *Psychology,* Ninth Edition, have paid special attention to the ties among the aspects of human psychology, among the different areas of psychological research, and among the chapters of the textbook. These ties are all forms of what the authors call *Linkages,* and the text highlights them in several ways. First, photographs, cross references, and discussions throughout the text point out how topics in one chapter are related to discussions that appear in other chapters. Second, a Linkages section in each chapter discusses in some depth one specific connection between subfields. Finally, near the end of each chapter, a Linkages diagram presents questions that illustrate a link between the current chapter and the topic of other chapters in the text. These questions are then repeated in the margin next to where they are explored. You could read the text profitably without paying special attention to the Linkage elements, but they can help you gain a clearer view of psychology as a whole, a deeper understanding of specific issues, and a framework on which you can build your knowledge of psychology. And when you organize your knowledge and relate one piece of information to another, you improve your ability to remember the information. The Linkages diagrams in particular can be used in many ways as tools for learning and remembering information. Here are some suggestions:

Before reading the chapter, read the questions in the Linkages diagram. They will give you' a feeling for the topic of the chapter and for the broader significance of specific issues. In each diagram, some of the questions are discussed in the current chapter and some in other chapters. Can you answer any of the questions? Do any of them concern a topic you have already read about in the text? If so, what do you remember about it? You might go to the section given after the question, look for the question in the margin on that page, and scan or read the discussion. This will refresh your memory for concepts or facts related to the material to be discussed in the current chapter.

After reading the chapter, you can use the diagram to check your memory and understanding of the chapter. Try writing answers to those questions in the diagram that were discussed in the chapter. Check your answers against the text discussions. (Again, the page numbers in the diagram indicate where the discussion occurs.)

The diagrams can also help you go beyond the textbook in gaining and organizing knowledge of psychology. Suppose you are studying for a final exam and want to check your understanding of the topic of learning. You might go first to the Linkages diagram in the learning chapter and check whether you can answer the questions. Then you might flip to the Linkages diagrams in other chapters, find questions tied to learning, and try to answer those questions. Also, keep in mind that the diagrams in the text provide only a sampling of linkages; there are many others. Finding additional linkages on your own can further your understanding of psychological issues and improve your memory of the material in the text. Finally, the questions in the Linkages diagrams or linkages that you find yourself may provide interesting topics for term papers.

READING A TEXTBOOK

Effective learners engage in a very deep level of processing. They are active learners, thinking of each new fact in relation to other material. As a result, they learn to see similarities and differences among facts and ideas, and they create a context in which many new facts can be organized effectively.

Based on what is known about memory, we suggest two specific guidelines for reading a textbook. First, make sure that you understand what you are reading before moving on. Second, use the *PQ4R method,* which is one of the most successful strategies for remembering textbook material (Anderson, 1990; Chastain & Thurber, 1989; Thomas & Robinson, 1972). PQ4R stands for the six activities that should be followed when you read a chapter: preview, question, read, reflect, recite, and review. These activities are designed to increase the depth to which you process the information you read.

1.   *Preview* One of the best ways to begin a new chapter is by *not* reading it. Instead, take a few minutes to skim the chapter. Look at the section headings and any boldface or italicized terms. Obtain a general idea of what material will be discussed how it is organized, and how its topics relate to one another and to what you already know. Some people find it useful to preview the entire chapter once and then preview each major section in a little more detail before reading it.

2.   *Question* Before reading each section, stop and ask yourself what content will be covered and what information should be extracted from it.

3.   *Read* Read the text, but think about the material as you read. Are the questions you raised earlier being answered? Do you see the connections between the topics?

4.   *Reflect* As you read your text, think of examples of the concepts that apply to your own life. Create visual images of the concept, and think about how the concept is related to other concepts in the chapter you are currently reading, and other chapters you have previously read.

5.   *Recite* At the end of each section, stop and recite the major points. Resist the temptation to be passive by mumbling something like "Oh, I remember that." Put the ideas into your own words.

6.   *Review* Finally, at the end of the chapter, review all the material. You should see connections not only within a section but also among the sections. The objective is to see how the author has organized the material. Once you grasp the organization, the individual facts will be far easier to remember.

At the end, take a break. Relax. Approach each chapter fresh. Following these procedures will not only allow you to learn and remember the material better but also save you considerable time.

CHAPTER 1

Introducing Psychology

OUTLINE

I.   THE WORLD OF PSYCHOLOGY: AN OVERVIEW
Psychology is the scientific study of behavior and mental processes. Positive psychology is the study of happiness, optimism, human strengths, and so forth.

A.   Subfields of Psychology
There are hundreds of topics available for the study of behavior and mental processes. Clusters of these topics are called subfields.

1.   The biological factors underlying our behavior are the concern of biological psychologists or physiological psychologists. How genetics, brain structures, and hormones affect our behavior are topics addressed by biological psychologists.
2.   Cognitive psychologists, or *experimental psychologists*, study processes underlying perception, motivation, emotion, memory, problem solving, and other aspects of human thought. Engineering psychologists study human factors in the use of equipment and work to design better versions of that equipment.
3.   Developmental psychologists explore the causes and effects of changes in behavior and mental processes over the life span. Developmental psychologists study children's friendships, parenting styles and outcomes, and changes in thinking abilities.
4.   Personality psychologists study the qualities that make people unique and explore relationships among personality characteristics, behavior, and mental processes.
5.   Clinical and counseling psychologists seek to understand the origins of behavior disorders and to help people deal with disorders. Community psychologists provide psychological services to people who often do not seek help and work to prevent disorders by trying to lessen stresses such as poverty. Health psychologists study the relation between behavior and health and work to promote healthy lifestyles.
6.   Educational psychologists investigate ways to improve student learning. School psychologists assess students' abilities and provide assistance when needed.
7.   Social psychologists focus on how people affect others' behavior and thinking. Social psychologists are interested in such subjects as advertising, prejudice, and interpersonal attraction.
8.   Industrial and organizational psychologists are interested in factors affecting work productivity and satisfaction, such as employee motivation and how to develop positive organizational behavior.
9.   Quantitative psychologists are interested in developing and using statistical tools to analyze data relevant to human behavior and mental process.
10.   Other subfields include sports psychology, forensic psychology, and environmental psychology.

B.   Linkages within Psychology and Beyond
Many psychologists are interested in several psychological subfields and may use more than one approach to study behavior and mental processes. Psychological research contributes to other disciplines such as neuroscience and uses theories from other disciplines (for example, physics and economics) to understand psychological phenomena.

C.   Research: The Foundation of Psychology
Psychologists use empirical research to collect and analyze information, rather than relying on speculation.

D.   A Brief History of Psychology
1.   *Wundt and the Structuralism of Titchener.* Wilhelm Wundt wanted to study consciousness using scientific methods. With his technique of introspection, he documented "quality" and "intensity" as elements of sensation. Edward Titchener further identified "clarity" as one of the dimensions of <u>consciousness</u>; his approach was called structuralism. Gestalt psychologists disagreed with Wundt's methods and suggested analyzing the whole conscious experience, not its elements.
2.   *Freud and Psychoanalysis.* Sigmund Freud developed a theory of personality based on the assumption that the unconscious could influence people's behavior.
3.   *William James and Functionalism.* William James investigated how consciousness works to help people adapt to their environments. Because James thought that the function of sensations, ideas, and memories was important, his view became known as functionalism.
4.   *John B. Watson and Behaviorism.* According to John B. Watson, psychologists should not study mental events but instead should observe people's behavioral reaction to stimuli without making inferences about consciousness. Watson inspired many psychologists to adopt behaviorism as the method of choice for scientific research in psychology.
5.   *Psychology Today.* Advances in technology have made it possible for psychologists to study the biological bases of mental activity. The study of consciousness has become more precise and objective.

II.   APPROACHES TO THE SCIENCE OF PSYCHOLOGY
Each theoretical approach makes different assumptions about the factors that cause behavior and mental processes, and what methods are most appropriate for studying those factors. Psychologists who use more than one approach are known as *eclectic.*

A.   *The Biological Approach.* According to the <u>biological approach</u>, physiological factors determine behavior and mental processes. A psychologist with this approach would note changes in brain activity during memory formation or decision making.
B.   *The Evolutionary Approach.* Psychologists taking the <u>evolutionary approach</u> believe that behavior results from evolution through <u>natural selection</u>. Researchers seek to understand the reasons a behavior has evolved. Why is it adaptive, and how has it been shaped by environmental conditions?
C.   *The Psychodynamic Approach.* Though less influential today, the <u>psychodynamic approach</u> states that behavior reflects unconscious internal conflict between inherited instincts and society's behavioral rules.
D.   *The Behavioral Approach.* The <u>behavioral approach</u> emphasizes learning in explaining behavior. For example, how do rewards and punishments shape, maintain, and change behavior? The cognitive-behavioral approach examines how learning influences thoughts and opinions, and how such cognitions influence observable behaviors.
E.   *The Cognitive Approach.* According to the <u>cognitive approach</u>, behavior is a result of information processing (for example, perception, memory, thought, judgment, and decision making). Cognitive scientists work with biologists, linguists, philosophers, computer scientists, and engineers to identify the components of thought that interact to produce behaviors.
F.   *The Humanistic Approach.* According to the <u>humanistic approach</u>, people choose how to behave based on their perceptions of the world to grow toward their unique potential. The

humanistic approach is less influential today because its ideas are difficult to test empirically.

III.   HUMAN DIVERSITY AND PSYCHOLOGY

Recently, women and minorities are earning a larger percentage of doctoral degrees in psychology. Psychologists are increasingly considering the influence of <u>sociocultural factors</u> such as gender, social class, and ethnicity in shaping human behavior and mental processes. <u>Culture</u>, the accumulation of values, religious belief, and so forth, is an organizing influence that determines much of behavior. Cultures can be classified as individualist or collectivist.

KEY TERMS

1.   **Psychology** is the science of behavior and mental processes. (see The World of Psychology: An Overview)

Example: Behavior is any action an organism performs, including those you can and cannot see (for example, jogging, laughing, heart rate, and blood pressure). Mental processes are activities involved in thinking (for example, remembering, dreaming, and forming opinions).

2.   **Positive psychology** is a field of research that focuses on people's positive experiences and characteristics, such as happiness, optimism, and resilience. (see The World of Psychology: An Overview)

Example: David studies the role of religious faith in promoting good coping skills.

3.   **Biological** or physiological psychologists study the biological factors influencing behavior and mental processes. (see Subfields of Psychology)

Example: Eating certain foods changes the chemical interactions within and between nerve cells in your brain, thereby possibly inducing drowsiness.

Example: How do people develop morals, social skills, and intellectual abilities?

4.   **Cognitive psychologists**, or **experimental psychologists**, study the mental processes underlying judgment, decision making, problem solving, imagining, and other aspects of human thought or cognition. (see Subfields of Psychology)

Example: Is the memory of how to tie shoes developed, stored, and retrieved in the same ways as the memory of a friend's telephone number?

5.   **Engineering psychology** is the field in which psychologists study human factors in the use of equipment and help designers create better versions of that equipment. (see Subfields of Psychology)

Example: An engineering psychologist might design an airplane cockpit so that it is easier for pilots to assimilate all the information without error.

6.   **Developmental psychologists** seek to understand, describe, and explore how behavior and mental processes change over a lifetime. (see Subfields of Psychology)

4.   **Personality psychologists** study the characteristics that make individuals similar to or different from one another. (see Subfields of Psychology)

Example: Why are some people consistently optimistic and others pessimistic?

5.   **Clinical and counseling psychologists** seek to assess, understand, and change abnormal behavior. (see Subfields of Psychology)

Example: Is schizophrenia hereditary? What therapy produces the best results with patients with schizophrenia?

6. **Community psychologists** work to obtain psychological services for people in need of help and to prevent psychological disorders by working for changes in social systems. (see Subfields of Psychology)

    Example: Some community psychologists examine the problems students have in making the transition from high school to college and design programs to lessen these problems.

7. **Health psychologists** study the effects of behavior and mental processes on health and illness and vice versa. (see Subfields of Psychology)

    Example: Health psychologists may investigate the connection between hostile attitudes and behavior and heart disease.

8. **Educational psychologists** study methods by which instructors teach and students learn and who apply their results to improving those methods. (see Subfields of Psychology)

    Example: Educational psychologists found that when students take notes in their own words, they recall the information better.

9. **School psychologists** test IQs, diagnose students' academic problems, and set up programs to improve students' achievement. (see Subfields of Psychology)

    Example: School psychologists identify students' academic strengths and problems, and tailor programs to meet students' needs.

10. **Social psychologists** are interested in how people influence one another's behavior and mental processes, individually and in groups. (see Subfields of Psychology)

    Example: How is behavior influenced by the type of group or situation a person is in? In a crowd, an anonymous person may be boisterous; however, when recognized as an individual (for example, in a classroom), the same person may be quiet and obedient.

11. **Industrial and organizational psychologists** study ways to increase efficiency, productivity, and satisfaction among workers and the organizations that employ them. (see Subfields of Psychology)

    Example: Researchers may examine whether relaxed dress-code days improve office workers' morale.

12. **Quantitative psychologists** develop and use statistical tools to analyze research data. (see Subfields of Psychology)

    Example: Quantitative psychologists have worked with industrial/organizational psychologists to analyze data about mental abilities, or intelligence. They helped industrial/organizational psychologists take large quantities of data related to intelligence and systematically break the data down into types, or factors, of intelligence so that those factors could be used more specifically to predict performance on various types of jobs.

13. **Sports psychologists** explore the relationships between athletic performance and such psychological variables as motivation and emotion. (see Subfields of Psychology)

    Example: Sports psychologists may work with athletes to restore their self-confidence after injury.

17. **Forensic psychologists** assist in jury selection, evaluate defendants' mental competence to stand trial, and deal with other issues involving psychology and the law. (see Subfields of Psychology)

    Example: Forensic psychologists may try to identify common characteristics across crime scenes to provide information about a killer's modus operandi.

18. **Environmental psychologists** study the effects of the physical environment on behavior, mental processes. (see Subfields of Psychology)

    Example: Environmental psychologists may study the interaction between the design of apartment buildings and neighborliness.

19. **Neuroscience** is the scientific study of all levels of the nervous system, including neuroanatomy, neurochemistry, neurology, neurophysiology, and neuropharmacology. (see Linkages within Psychology and Beyond)

    Example: A neuroscientist may study how brain damage in one area of the brain affects human performance, leading to particular loss of ability in one skill but not another.

20. **Consciousness** is the awareness of external stimuli and our own mental activity.

    Example: Darlene is at the amusement park with her kids. She is aware of watching them (external stimuli) and also aware of the fact that she is enjoying their excitement (her own mental activity).

21. The **biological approach** assumes that behavior and behavior disorders are the result of physical processes, especially those relating to the brain and to hormones and other chemicals. (see The Biological Approach)

    Example: People who are chronically depressed may have abnormal levels of certain chemicals important to mood.

22. **Natural selection** is the evolutionary mechanism through which Darwin said the fittest individuals survive to reproduce. (see The Evolutionary Approach)

    Example: Individuals who are friendlier tend to have a larger social support system that helps warn them of and protect them from danger. These individuals are more likely to survive longer, and thus friendliness as a trait is likely to be passed on to their offspring.

23. The **evolutionary approach** emphasizes the inherited, adaptive aspects of behavior and mental processes. (see The Evolutionary Approach)

    Example: Psychologists study the adaptive value of behavior (running away from threats); the anatomical and biological systems that make the behavior possible (muscular construction of limbs); and the environmental conditions that encourage or discourage it (a culture may not approve of people running away).

24. The **psychodynamic approach** emphasizes the interplay of unconscious mental processes in determining human thoughts, feelings, and behavior. (see The Psychodynamic Approach)

    Example: Freud might have said that surgeons express aggressive instincts in a manner that is approved of by society (performing surgery in an operating room rather than stabbing a stranger in a dark alley).

25. The **behavioral approach** emphasizes that human behavior is determined mainly by what a person has learned, especially from rewards and punishments. (see The Behavioral Approach)

    Example: Doctors become surgeons because they are rewarded by their salary, by the respect their position receives, or by the satisfaction they receive from healing.

26. The **cognitive approach** emphasizes research on how tthe brain takes in information, creates perceptions, forms and retrieves memories, processes information, and generates integrated patterns of action. (see The Cognitive Approach)

Example: A psychologist taking the cognitive approach might try to understand the decision processes of the passengers who decided to fight the terrorists hijacking their plane on September 11.

REMEMBER: Cognition means "thinking." The cognitive approach assumes that thoughts guide behavior.

27. The **humanistic approach** views behavior as controlled by the decisions that people make about their lives based on their perceptions of the world.. (see The Humanistic Approach)

Example: The innate tendency to grow toward one's unique potential is analogous to the development of a flower that will bloom if it receives adequate light, water, and nourishment. People, too, will achieve their potential if their environments provide the correct psychological and physical nourishment.

28. **Sociocultural factors** refer to social identity and other background factors, such as gender, ethnicity, social class, and culture. (see Human Diversity and Psychology)

Example: Women tend to produce more words per day than men do. This is an example of gender as a sociocultural factor that affects behavior.

29. A **culture** is the accumulation of values, rules of behavior, forms of expression, religious beliefs, occupational choice, and the like for a group of people who share a common language and environment. (see Human Diversity and Psychology)

Example: Some cultures tend to emphasize individual goals over the importance of group well-being (individualists), whereas other cultures emphasize group well-being over individual goals (collectivists).

FILL-IN-THE-BLANKS KEY TERMS

This section will help you check your knowledge of the key terms introduced in this chapter. Fill in each blank with the appropriate term from the list of key terms in the previous section.

1. _____ is the study of behavior and mental processes.

2. A developmental psychologist studying the relationship between brain development and changes in learning ability over the life span would be using the _____ approach.

3. Natural Selection is the evolutionary mechanism through which Darwin said the fittest individuals survive to reproduce.

4. A psychologist who attempts to find unconscious conflicts that have caused a psychological disorder is using the _____ approach.

5. A psychologist taking the _____ approach researches how rewards change people's actions.

6. A clinical psychologist who works to understand the unique feelings and perceptions of a depressed client would be using a(n) _____ approach.

7. The president of a campus student group interested in understanding how peer pressure affects student members' political views should consult a(n) _____ psychologist.

8. A(n) _____ psychologist would study the effect of a drug on brain activity and the resulting impact on emotional responses.

9. A teacher interested in understanding how students' individuality influences their behavior would consult a(n) ___School___ psychologist.

10. Trying to determine the best type of treatment for an alcoholic would be of interest to a(n) ___clinical___ psychologist.

11. You would expect a(n) ___developmental___ psychologist to compare and contrast changes in learning ability from infancy through childhood, adolescence, middle age, and old age.

12. A(n) ___cognitive___ psychologist would be interested in studying thought patterns underlying decision making in stressful situations.

13. A(n) _____ psychologist might develop programs to help integrate children with learning disabilities into regular classrooms.

14. The study of favorable human characteristics such as optimism, resilience, and happiness is known as _____.

15. A ___culture___ is the accumulation of values, rules, forms of expression, religious belief, and so forth for a people with a common language and environment.

Total Correct (See answer key) _____

LEARNING OBJECTIVES

1. Define *psychology*.

2. List and explain the major subfields of psychology.

3. Explain the influence of <u>positive psychology</u> on the kinds of problems psychologists study.

4. Explain how psychology is linked to other fields.

5. Describe the new field of neuroscience.

6. Explain the role of research in psychology.

7. Describe Wilhelm Wundt's approach to the study of <u>consciousness</u>.

8. Explain Edward Titchener's approach to the study of psychology. Explain why it became known as *structuralism*.

9. Discuss the perspective of the Gestalt psychologists.

10. Describe Sigmund Freud's ideas about the role of the unconscious mind.

11. Explain William James's *functionalism*, and discuss its relationship to Charles Darwin's theory of evolution.

12. Describe John B. Watson's ideas about how to develop psychology as a science. Explain why he called his approach *behaviorism*.

13. Describe B. F. Skinner's contributions to behaviorism. Explain the concept of the *functional analysis of behavior*.

14. Explain the basic ideas underlying the <u>biological approach</u> to psychology.

15. Explain the basic ideas underlying the <u>evolutionary approach</u> to psychology.

16. Explain the basic ideas underlying the *psychodynamic approach* to psychology.

17. Explain the basic ideas underlying the <u>behavioral approach</u> to psychology.

18. Explain the basic ideas underlying the <u>cognitive approach</u> to psychology.

19. Explain the basic ideas underlying the <u>humanistic approach</u> to psychology.

20. Describe how the diversity of people engaged in the science of psychology has changed over time.

21. Explain the importance of sensitivity to <u>sociocultural factors</u> in psychological science.

22. Define <u>culture</u>, and explain the difference between individualist and collectivist cultures.

23. Discuss how the multicultural nature of most societies affects how psychologists must approach new problems.

CONCEPTS AND EXERCISES

Research in a High School

Imagine you are a psychologist conducting research on violence at a local high school.

Identify which approach would be most likely to focus on each of the following to understand the students' behavior.

1.   Do negative consequences such as detentions and expulsions deter a person from acting in a violent way? _____

2.   Are certain types of decision-making styles more common among the violent students than the nonviolent students? _____

3.   Is violent behavior related to a student's inability to deny other impulses? _____

4.   Are the hormones associated with stress reactions at higher levels among students involved in violence? _____

   a.   Biological

   b.   Psychodynamic

   c.   Behavioral

   d.   Cognitive

   e.   Humanistic

The Problem of Depression

Match the subfields below with each of the following questions:

1.   Do depressed people have fewer or different quality social relationships than nondepressed? _____

2.   Is there a point over the life span when one is most likely to become depressed? _____

3.   Are there particular characteristics in a person that predict who will become depressed? _____

4.   Does depression co-occur with anxiety disorders? _____

5.   Which neurotransmitters are involved in causing depression? _____

   a.   Biological

   b.   Personality

   c.   Developmental

   d.   Clinical

   e.   Social

PERSONAL LEARNING ACTIVITIES

1.   In a recent newspaper or magazine find a report describing a psychological study. Does it give details of empirical research, or does it focus primarily on opinions, assumptions, and unsupported generalizations?

2.   How might psychology have been different if Freud had not presented his ideas about the unconscious? To get a better sense of this issue and others in the history of psychology, visit the following website: http://www.cwu.edu/~warren/today.html. Here, you can choose any date and find out what important events in the field of psychology occurred on that day.

3.   What is the difference between an approach to psychology and a subfield of psychology? If you are interested in a particular subfield, or psychology in general, consider exploring career options at the following site: http://www.apa.org/careers/resources/guides/careers.aspx. This site not only reviews what psychology is, but explains what sorts of jobs a psychologist might do, what the occupational outlook is for those careers, and includes many other pieces of useful information for career development in psychology.

4.   How might a psychologist from each of the approaches explain the motivation for people involved in terrorist activity? Do you think terrorist activity is more likely to originate in collectivist or in individualist cultures, or are both cultures equally likely to produce such behavior. Consider the following perspective offered by two social psychologists at: http://www.socialpsychology.org/pdf/chronicle04.pdf.

5.   Do you think personality is determined by genetics or by culture? To get an idea of how personality psychologists view the answer to this question, visit the following site to learn more: http://www.personalityresearch.org/bg.html. Here you can learn some of the research methods that personality psychologists use to try to understand this issue better.

MULTIPLE-CHOICE QUESTIONS

Quiz 1

1.   Psychology is the study of

   a.   the development of cultures, religions, and societies.
   b.   behaviors and mental processes.
   c.   earth, nations, plant life, and animals.
   d.   how people relate to each other.

2.   Understanding the factors that promote well-being in people would likely be a topic of study in

   a.   psychology.
   b.   positive psychology.
   c.   clinical psychology.
   d.   multiculturalism.

3. William James' interest in how images, sensations, memories, and other mental events make up our flowing stream of consciousness was integral to the historical approach to psychology known as

    a.   psychoanalysis.
    b.   behaviorism.
    c.   functionalism.
    d.   structuralism.

4. A psychologist who thinks current behavior is caused by unconscious conflicts was most likely trained in

    a.   behaviorism.
    b.   functionalism.
    c.   Gestalt psychology.
    d.   psychoanalysis.

5. Which of the following is NOT a historical approach to psychology?

    a.   Behaviorism
    b.   Gestalt
    c.   Structuralism
    d.   Evolutionary

6. Sometimes Janessa treats her clients with drugs, but at other times she tries to change the patterns of rewards and punishments the client receives. Janessa's approach can best be described as

    a.   behavioral.
    b.   biological.
    c.   eclectic.
    d.   humanistic.

7. Dr. Atilano says that behavior is caused by activity in the nervous system, genetic inheritance, and hormones. Dr. Atilano takes a _____ approach to psychological phenomena.

    a.   biological
    b.   psychodynamic
    c.   behavioral
    d.   cognitive

8. The idea of natural selection is MOST consistent with which of the following modern approaches to psychology?

    a.   Biological
    b.   Evolutionary
    c.   Cognitive
    d.   Humanistic

9. Deon believes that his friend Tom drives too fast on the interstate because Tom is unconsciously wishing for death. Deon suggests that Tom cannot admit he feels guilty about being independent from his family. Deon most likely has a _____ approach to psychology.

   a. behavioral
   b. biological
   c. cognitive
   d. psychodynamic

10. Mercedes often procrastinates when faced with a big assignment. A psychologist with a behavioral approach would be most likely to say that Mercedes procrastinates because she

   a. believes it helps her to get motivated later.
   b. perceives the assignment as unfair and overwhelming.
   c. is rewarded by the lighter workload during her early avoidance of the project.
   d. unconsciously desires to fail her assignment.

11. Psychologists who emphasize the role of mental processes in explaining behavior take a(n) _____ approach.

   a. evolutionary
   b. biological
   c. cognitive
   d. deterministic

12. Jonna is taking a graduate engineering program. She wants to be part of the development and design team to help make planes better protected from terrorists. One idea that has come up frequently is that the cockpit needs to be designed to be safer. To make the plane as a whole safer, what area of psychology should Jonna add to her graduate studies if she wants to understand how people interact with the technology inside and outside of a cockpit?

   a. Engineering psychology
   b. Cognitive psychology
   c. Industrial and organizational psychology
   d. Educational psychology

13. You are a biological psychologist interested in the emotional reactions of students to exams. Which of the following would be of most interest to you?

   a. Hormone levels
   b. How much support the student has from peers
   c. The dreams a student has before an exam
   d. Attitudes toward learning

14. Maria watches people to discover what unwritten rules for behavior they are following. Maria sees that people tend not to sit next to another person on the bus unless empty seats are limited. Maria's interests are most like those of psychologists in the _____ subfield.

   a. clinical
   b. developmental
   c. personality
   d. social

15. Michelle studies how sociable, conscientious, and anxious children are at age eight. She intends to see if she can predict differences in the number of years of school they have completed by age twenty-five. Michelle is most likely a _____ psychologist.
    a. community
    b. humanistic
    c. personality
    d. social

16. Which of the following is the best example of the work of a psychologist in the clinical subfield?
    a. Sadie observes how changes in playground equipment affect the interactions between children.
    b. Tad attempts to assist people who are extremely depressed.
    c. Val compares the IQ scores of sociable people with those of shy people.
    d. Vince wonders if people's hormones influence their thinking.

17. Dr. Li tests students at a grade school and makes recommendations about who may benefit from an accelerated program and who may need a specific type of tutoring. Dr. Li is most likely a(n) _____ psychologist.
    a. community
    b. industrial/organizational
    c. personality
    d. school

18. An industrial and organizational psychologist would be most interested in which of the following questions?
    a. How can we promote a stop-smoking campaign?
    b. What type of management style would generate the highest productivity?
    c. What mental steps are involved in perception and decision making?
    d. How do social skills evolve from the preschool years through old age?

19. Which of the following is NOT an example of a sociocultural factor?
    a. Gender
    b. Ethnicity
    c. Social class
    d. Blood type

20. Nia is an educational psychologist at a conference and meeting new colleagues. Someone asks her to say a little about herself. If Nia is from a collectivist culture, she will likely to say,
    a. "I got my Ph.D. in educational psychology from Harvard."
    b. "I love to play tennis and swim. Reading is one of my favorite hobbies, too."
    c. "I am really interested in studying how children respond to stereotype threat in a way no one else is investigating."
    d. "My family sacrificed a lot for me to get my education and develop my research program."

Total Correct (See answer key) _____

Quiz 2

Use this quiz to reassess your learning after taking Quiz 1 and reviewing the chapter.

1.   Which of the following questions would a psychologist most likely ask?

   a.   How does one's genetic makeup influence his or her risk for cancer?
   b.   Does God create people with antisocial personality?
   c.   Which ethical decision-making system is the best?
   d.   How do patterns of group development influence group productivity at work?

2.   Which of the following topics is LEAST relevant to studies in positive psychology?

   a.   Identifying factors that promote optimism
   b.   Studying how religious belief affects the development of good coping skills
   c.   Studying conditions that promote creativity
   d.   Determining factors that increase risk for depression

3.   After speculating that a noisy environment reduces helping behavior, a psychologist using empiricism will most likely

   a.   describe to talk-show viewers how noise affects us.
   b.   design research to test the idea.
   c.   try to reduce noise in the environment.
   d.   try to help someone in a noisy environment.

4.   Ming's research involves presenting participants with objects and asking them to report the sensations that they are experiencing. Ming is most likely a

   a.   functionalist.
   b.   structuralist.
   c.   behaviorist.
   d.   humanist.

5.   Roberto studies what people enjoy about listening to classical music. Roberto claims that it would be useless to isolate and listen to only a rhythm, a violin part, or any other single aspect of music, because it is the perception of the complete piece that is important. Roberto's emphasis on NOT dividing music into parts is most similar to

   a.   structuralism.
   b.   behaviorism.
   c.   Gestalt psychology.
   d.   psychoanalysis.

6.   Larry says that people act the way they learned to act. Larry believes that if others stop rewarding a person's annoying behaviors, those behaviors will lessen. Larry most likely has a(n) _____ approach to psychology.

   a.   behavioral
   b.   cognitive
   c.   evolutionary
   d.   humanistic

7.   Ruth is certain that her son is depressed because of some kind of chemical imbalance in him and that antidepressant medication would help. Laurence feels that his son is depressed because he is repressing memories of childhood abuse by a babysitter and that the son probably has not dealt with his anger about that abuse. Ruth takes the _____ approach to psychology, while Laurence takes the _____ approach.

    a.   biological; psychodynamic
    b.   psychodynamic; biological
    c.   evolutionary; behavioral
    d.   behavioral; evolutionary

8.   A cognitive psychologist investigating why students study regularly would be most interested in

    a.   the students' decisions about the advantages and disadvantages of putting off work.
    b.   the students' hidden internal conflicts.
    c.   how diet and exercise influence motivation level.
    d.   how past rewards and punishments have maintained this behavior.

9.   Marissa says that she often does not attend classes because she does not find her courses interesting. Her roommate, Leslie, claims that Marissa does not attend because her natural drive toward self-improvement has been blocked. Leslie's view is most similar to a psychologist with a _____ approach.

    a.   humanistic
    b.   psychodynamic
    c.   biological
    d.   cognitive

10.   Helen, a first-year college student, wants to become a biological psychologist. Her counselor will probably tell her to take which of the following courses?

    a.   Cognitive development
    b.   Physiology of behavior
    c.   The history of Freud
    d.   Community medical prevention programs

11.   Jenna's college roommate is driving her crazy! She's constantly complaining about how depressed she is and how worthless she feels. Jenna thinks that her roommate is "depressed" because it brings her attention. She believes her roommate is actually rewarded by most people for acting sad all the time. Jenna's thinking reflects the _____ approach to psychology.

    a.   biological
    b.   psychodynamic
    c.   behavioral
    d.   cognitive

12.   Brendan runs a diversity-training program that allows people to discuss stereotypes and become more accepting of people with different backgrounds. Brendan is especially interested in the effect his training has on the ability of employees to work together. Brendan is most likely a(n) _____ psychologist.

    a.   cognitive
    b.   community
    c.   industrial and organizational
    d.   personality

13. Rajesh is very concerned about meeting his parents' expectations. Rajesh does not want to attract attention to himself; therefore, when he is successful, he will usually emphasize the role his family played in helping him to achieve. Rajesh's behavior indicates he may be from a(n) _____ culture.
    a. collectivist
    b. communist
    c. democratic
    d. individualist

14. Alisha notices people in her classes becoming friends and wonders what attracts people to each other. Alisha's interests are most like those of psychologists in the _____ subfield.
    a. clinical
    b. developmental
    c. personality
    d. social

15. Jill wants to start a personal-service business offering nannies; an adolescent big-brother and big-sister program; and companions for the elderly. Jill must be able to teach her employees how to fulfill the psychological needs of every age group. Jill should study _____ psychology.
    a. biological
    b. psychodynamic
    c. developmental
    d. cognitive

16. On a bus you overhear a man talking to himself. The man appears to be getting angry and eventually starts pounding one fist into the other palm and shouting unintelligibly. Because he seems like he has a psychological disorder and may need help, you would want to recommend that someone call a _____ psychologist.
    a. clinical
    b. developmental
    c. personality
    d. social

17. A psychologist who wants to prevent disorders by ensuring children have proper nutrition and educational opportunities is most likely a(n) _____ psychologist.
    a. biological
    b. clinical
    c. community
    d. educational

18. The scientific study of all levels of the nervous system, including neuroanatomy, neurochemistry, neurology, neurophysiology, and neuropharmacology is known as
    a. evolutionary psychology.
    b. eclectic psychology.
    c. biological psychology.
    d. neuroscience.

19. Ethnic minorities earn approximately what percentage of new doctoral degrees in psychology each year?
    a.   25
    b.   50
    c.   67
    d.   75

20. Jerry is trying to decide which job offer to accept. He has one offer that is close to home and family, but the pay is just "okay," and the work is only marginally interesting to him. His other offer is for a fabulous job with excellent starting pay, but it is far from home, and his aging parents frequently benefit from his assistance. Jerry finally decides to take the fabulous job far from his folks, because "you've got to pursue your own dreams; no one will do it for you." Jerry's decision process suggests he is probably from a(n) _____ culture.
    a.   multicultural
    b.   individualist
    c.   collectivist
    d.   subcultural

Total Correct (See answer key) _____

ANSWERS TO FILL-IN-THE-BLANKS KEY TERMS

1. Psychology (see The World of Psychology: An Overview)

2. biological (see The Biological Approach)

3. Natural selection (see The Evolutionary Approach)

4. psychodynamic (see The Psychodynamic Approach)

5. behavioral (see The Behavioral Approach)

6. humanistic (see The Humanistic Approach)

7. social (see Subfields of Psychology)

8. biological (see Subfields of Psychology)

9. personality (see Subfields of Psychology)

10. clinical or counseling (see Subfields of Psychology)

11. developmental (see Subfields of Psychology)

12. cognitive (see Subfields of Psychology)

13. school (see Subfields of Psychology)

14. positive psychology (see The World of Psychology: An Overview)

15. culture (see Human Diversity and Psychology)

ANSWERS TO CONCEPTS AND EXERCISES

Research in a High School

1. The <u>behavioral</u> approach focuses on the consequences of behavior as an explanation for current behavior. (see The Behavioral Approach)

2. Psychologists with the <u>cognitive</u> approach would be most interested in knowing about beliefs, decision-making strategies, and perceptions. (see The Cognitive Approach)

3. The <u>psychodynamic</u> approach claims that people spend much of their energy trying to control their negative natural impulses. (see The Psychodynamic Approach)

4. A researcher with a <u>biological</u> approach would link behavior to hormone levels and other physiological differences such as brain activity, blood pressure, and muscle tension. (see The Biological Approach)

The Problem of Depression

1. <u>Social psychologists</u> try to see situational explanations for behavior and would look to see how social relationships and group dynamics might predict depression. (see Subfields of Psychology)

2. <u>Developmental psychologists</u> are interested in people's physical, behavioral, and mental growth over the life span, and might search for the point in life at which risk for depression is highest. (see Subfields of Psychology)

3. <u>Personality psychologists</u> are interested in studying personal traits and might use patterns of traits, or characteristics, to predict susceptibility to depression. (see Subfields of Psychology)

4. <u>Clinical psychologists</u> study psychological disorders and would be most interested in finding out whether depressed people tend to also have anxiety disorders. (see Subfields of Psychology)

5. <u>Biological psychologists</u> study the physiological factors that guide or control our behavior and would examine various neurotransmitters and how they explain behavior and experience, such as depression. (see Subfields of Psychology)

ANSWERS TO MULTIPLE-CHOICE QUESTIONS

Circle the question numbers you answered correctly.

Quiz 1

1. b is the answer.   Psychologists research the actions and thoughts of organisms. Psychologists also try to help people who have difficulty coping. (see The World of Psychology: An Overview)

   a. An anthropologist would probably study the development of societies.

   c. The focus of psychology is narrower; geography is the study of the earth and its many inhabitants.

   d. Psychology is much more than the study of human interaction; psychologists may study development, learning, memory, psychological disorders, and much more.

2. b is the answer.   Positive psychology focuses on people's positive experiences and characteristics. Well-being is a positive state of being. (see The World of Psychology: An Overview)

   a. Although it is true that the study of well-being is a topic of interest in psychology, this answer is too broad. Positive psychology is a more specific, and more correct, answer.

    c.   Clinical psychologists tend to study abnormal, and often more negative, experiences. Well-being is not abnormal.

    d.   Multiculturalism is a term used to describe how a country or other entity hosts many subcultures within its boundaries. The study of well-being is not inherent to understanding how multiple cultures merge within a single entity.

3.   c is the answer.   James was interested in how the experiences that comprise stream of conscious help people adapt, or function, in their environment. (see A Brief History of Psychology)

    a.   Psychoanalysis is built on Sigmund Freud's ideas that all behavior is a result of unconscious, largely conflicted, experience. He was not interested in stream of conscious and what comprises it.

    b.   Behaviorism is built on John Watson's ideas, which emphasize the study of overt behavior, not concepts such as consciousness, which are not directly observable.

    d.   Structuralism was founded by Titchener. Like James, he was interested in studying consciousness but focused more on the structure of consciousness than on its function.

4.   d is the answer.   Psychoanalysis is a treatment strategy that assumes that people are influenced by conflicts of which they are unaware. (see A Brief History of Psychology)

    a.   Behaviorists emphasize that people learn from the consequences of their behavior. The behavioral approach does not recognize the unconscious as an influence on people's behavior.

    b.   Functionalism wanted to understand how consciousness works but did not study the unconscious.

    c.   Gestalt psychology viewed consciousness as an experience that could not be divided into its parts; Gestalt psychologists did not concern themselves with the unconscious.

5.   d is the answer.   The evolutionary approach is a modern approach to psychology, not a historical one. However, you can see that James's functionalism's emphasis on the adaptive value of consciousness has had some impact on the modern evolutionary approach, which also considers the adaptive value of behavior more broadly. (see Approaches to the Science of Psychology)

    a, b, c. These are all historical approaches to psychology.

6.   c is the answer.   Many psychologists choose what they consider to be the best features of several approaches and use whatever feature or combination of features will be most helpful to a client. (see Approaches to the Science of Psychology)

    a.   A person with a behavioral approach would try to change the pattern of rewards and punishments but would not use drug therapy.

    b.   The biological approach would view drug treatment as a reasonable way to alter the chemical or hormonal imbalances that caused the problematic behavior, but it would not agree with altering the reward and punishment patterns.

    d.   A humanistic psychologist would be interested in a person's unique perceptions; therefore, a humanistic psychologist would not prescribe drugs or change the consequences of a client's behavior.

7.   a is the answer.   Biological psychologists assume that nervous-system activity, hormones, and genetic inheritance cause behavior. (see Approaches to the Science of Psychology)

    b.   The psychodynamic approach assumes that behavior results from our struggle to fulfill instinctive desires despite society's restrictions.

    c.   The behavioral approach assumes that behavior is caused by people's past experiences of rewards and punishments.

    d.   The cognitive approach assumes that behavior is caused by the thoughts involved with that behavior.

8.   b is the answer.   The evolutionary approach assumes that behavior and mental processes of animals and humans today are the result of natural selection. (see Approaches to the Science of Psychology)

    a.   The biological approach focuses on how behavior and mental processes are the result of current physical processes in the nervous system, endocrine system, and so forth. The biological approach does not make an assumption as to how these physical processes came to be.

    c.   The cognitive approach focuses on how our brain takes in information and manipulates it to create perceptions, memories, process information, and so forth; it does not assume that these cognitive processes were inherited through natural selection.

    d.   The humanistic approach focuses on how people's behavior is influenced by the decisions they make which are driven by their unique perceptions of the world. People are generally viewed as unique and no assumptions are made as to how those unique perceptions developed through any particular process.

9.   d is the answer.   The psychodynamic approach describes behavior as guilt-driven or unconsciously influenced. (see Approaches to the Science of Psychology)

    a.   The behavioral approach does not address unconscious motives.

    b.   To psychologists with the biological approach, the cause of behavior is physiological rather than intellectual.

    c.   The cognitive approach emphasizes conscious thoughts, memories, and decisions.

10.   c is the answer.   A psychologist with the behavioral approach would look to the consequences of procrastination for an explanation of why Mercedes waits to do an assignment. (see Approaches to the Science of Psychology)

    a.   Motivation is a cognitive factor not dealt with by the behavioral approach.

    b.   Beliefs and feelings are cognitive factors that would be addressed by the humanistic approach.

    d.   The unconscious is part of the psychodynamic approach.

11.   c is the answer.   Cognitive psychologists investigate thoughts and information processing. (see Approaches to the Science of Psychology)

    a.   The evolutionary approach is in agreement with Darwin's theory that adaptive behaviors will survive in a species, but it does not study current mental processes.

    b.   Mental processes are influenced by physiology, according to biological psychologists; therefore, physiology would be emphasized by biological psychologists.

    d.   The deterministic approach is not one of the major approaches to psychology.

12.   a is the answer.   Engineering psychology is the study of how people interact with tools and technology around them. (see Subfields of Psychology)

    b.   Cognitive psychology is the study of mental abilities such as sensation, perception, memory, learning, thought, and consciousness. Although cognitive psychologists' work can be applied to study how people interact with tools, such as those in a cockpit, those applications are more specifically called part of engineering psychology.

c.   Industrial/organizational psychology is the study of factors and processes that influence work behavior and experience, such as leadership, stress, and job satisfaction. Although the cockpit certainly holds people who are working, Jonna is not particularly interested in studying their work experience, rather in changing the environment to make work safer. Her interest is in the environment, not the employee.

d.   Educational psychology is the study of teaching and learning. Educational psychologists may be interested in classroom design and how it relates to both the teaching and learning that occurs in it, but this would not help Jonna design a better and safer cockpit.

13. a is the answer.   Psychologists who take a biological approach would emphasize the relationship between emotions and physiological factors such as nervous system and hormonal activity. (see Approaches to the Science of Psychology)

b.   Support from peers would be a concern of social psychologists.

c.   Dreams might be analyzed by a psychodynamic psychologist.

d.   Attitudes toward learning would interest cognitive psychologists.

14. d is the answer.   Social psychologists are interested in how people influence each other's behavior. (see Subfields of Psychology)

a.   Clinical psychologists study disorders and find ways to assist people in coping with disorders.

b.   A developmental psychologist researches the changes that take place in people as they age.

c.   Personality psychology documents individual differences but does not study how people are affected by others.

15. c is the answer.   A personality psychologist conducts research on long-lasting differences between people, much like Michelle's study of the association between a personality description and later behavior. (see Subfields of Psychology)

a.   Community psychologists work to prevent psychological disorders.

b.   A person with a humanistic approach would focus on immediate experience and current perceptions instead of looking for a relationship between early judgments and later behavior.

d.   Social psychologists look for general rules about how people interact.

16. b is the answer.   Clinical psychologists help people cope with stressors and psychological disorders. (see Subfields of Psychology)

a.   Sadie is a social psychologist.

c.   Val is a personality psychologist.

d.   Vince is a biological psychologist.

17. d is the answer.   School psychologists watch for learning disabilities and giftedness in order to arrange for special education if warranted. (see Subfields of Psychology)

a.   Community psychologists might be interested in keeping problems in academic achievement from occurring, but they would not be trained in educational testing and program placement.

b. Industrial/organizational psychology is the study of social behavior in the workplace.

c. Personality psychologists might research the influence of personality characteristics on student achievement, but they do not specialize in educational testing and placement as school psychologists do.

18. b is the answer. Industrial/organizational psychologists study social behavior, such as a supervisor's style of communication at work. (see Subfields of Psychology)

a. Health psychologists study promoting healthy lifestyles.

c. Cognitive psychologists study perception, learning, memory, judgment, and decision making.

d. Developmental psychologists research how and why behavior and mental processes change over the life span.

19. d is the answer. Blood type is not a sociocultural factor; it is a biological one. (see Human Diversity and Psychology)

a, b, c. Gender, ethnicity, and social class are all examples of sociocultural factors.

20. d is the answer. If Nia is from a collectivist culture, she is likely to see herself as part of a group (an interdependent self) rather than as separate from a group (independent self). So, when asked to say something about herself, she will probably couch her professional successes and interests in the context of her family or some other, social network. (see Human Diversity and Psychology)

a.. A person from a collectivist culture would probably see a comment about earning a Ph.D. from Harvard as bragging. It sounds like touting an achievement and one's independence, rather than emphasizing one's belongingness to a group.

b. Although there is nothing inherently good or bad about tennis, swimming, or reading, a response like this does not reflect one's interdependence on others. If Nia is from a collectivist culture, her response will probably reflect more interdependence, rather than independence.

c. This description of research focuses on uniqueness and being different from what others are doing. Persons from collectivist cultures may well study things in novel ways, but they are more likely to emphasize how what they do builds on the work and relationships they have with others than to emphasize their novelty.

Now turn to the quiz analysis table at the end of this chapter to find which areas you know well and which areas you need to work on. Circle the numbers in the table for items on Quiz 1 that you answered correctly.

Quiz 2

1. d is the answer. Psychologists are interested in human behavior and mental processes, and emphasize the use of empirical methods to study these matters. This is the only question that both deals with behavior and can be answered with empirical methods. (see The World of Psychology: An Overview)

a. Asking about the relationship between genetics and cancer might be a question a psychologist would ask, but he or she would probably be more likely to look for how genetics influences behavior, which in turn influences risk for cancer, rather than to explore a direct link.

    b.   Asking whether or not God creates persons with antisocial personality is an interesting question, but it is not something suitable for empirical investigation. This would be a question more likely to occur to a theologian or perhaps a philosopher, as those fields do not require empirical investigation of phenomena of interest.

    c.   Asking which system of ethics is best is again not suitable for empirical investigation. A psychologist would be more likely to ask how one's method of making ethical decisions in turn influences behavioral choices.

2.   d is the answer.   Depression is not a positive experience, so it is not the most relevant area of study in positive psychology. (see The World of Psychology: An Overview)

    a.   Optimism is a positive human experience and is a topic of study in positive psychology.

    b.   Good coping skills are a positive experience, so this is a topic of study in positive psychology.

    c.   Creativity is a positive human characteristic and thus is a topic in positive psychology.

3.   b is the answer.   After speculating that a noisy environment reduces helping behavior, Mathews and Canon designed research that indicated that stimulus overload makes people less likely to help. (see A Brief History of Psychology)

    a.   Before empiricists describe a phenomenon, they study it.

    c.   Trying to reduce noise in the environment before we know if it is the true cause of reduced helping behavior might be a waste of effort; therefore, empiricists see if their hunches are correct.

    d.   Helping someone in a noisy environment, while it is a nice thing to do, does not show whether noise influences most people's helping behavior.

4.   b is the answer.   Structuralists used the method of introspection to determine the elements of or the structure of consciousness. (see A Brief History of Psychology)

    a.   Functionalists studied consciousness, but they used a more experimental approach rather than introspection.

    c.   Behaviorists study behavior, not consciousness.

    d.   Humanists are interested in people's natural tendency toward growth, not in identifying elements of sensation.

5.   c is the answer.   Gestalt psychologists criticized other approaches for splitting up experience into its components rather than studying consciousness as a whole experience. (see A Brief History of Psychology)

    a.   Structuralism tried to identify the elements of sensation through introspection. People using introspection would often divide their experience into parts, such as quality, intensity, and clarity.

    b.   A behaviorist studies behaviors and the rewards and punishments that follow.

    d.   Psychoanalysis is a method for identifying hidden conflicts and memories that affect current behavior.

6.   a is the answer.   The behavioral approach emphasizes that people think and behave in ways that have been previously rewarded. (see Approaches to the Science of Psychology)

   b.   The cognitive approach emphasizes what people *think* about a situation and the consequences of their behavior, and emphasizes the way people process incoming information.

   c.   Evolutionists try to understand the environmental conditions that encourage (reward) behaviors; however, rather than trying to change the consequences, they emphasize that adaptive behaviors are passed on to future generations.

   d.   The humanistic approach emphasizes the role of a person's view of the situation.

7.   a is the answer.   Ruth's emphasis on a chemical explanation suggests the involvement of neurotransmitters in her son's depression, which reflects a biological approach. Laurence's emphasis on repressed, or unconscious, conflict regarding earlier abuse is consistent with the psychodynamic approaches' view that unconscious conflict is the root cause of behavior generally. (see Approaches to the Science of Psychology)

   b.   This is backwards. The psychodynamic approach emphasizes unconscious conflict, which is what Laurence's reasoning is based on. The biological approach emphasizes the role of nervous, endocrine, and other systems functions, which is what Ruth seems to be thinking.

   c.   The evolutionary approach emphasizes the adaptive value of behavior, not necessarily a chemical imbalance within one particular person. The behavioral approach emphasizes overtly observable explanations for behavior, not repression.

   d.   The behavioral approach emphasizes overtly observable explanations and generally does not focus on processes such as neurotransmission (or chemical imbalances) that are not directly observable. The evolutionary approach focuses on natural selection and adaptation processes, not on unconscious conflict.

8.   a is the answer.   Cognitive psychologists are interested in conscious decision making. (see Approaches to the Science of Psychology)

   b.   Internal conflicts are in the realm of psychodynamic psychologists.

   c.   Diet and exercise would most likely interest a biological psychologist.

   d.   Behavioral psychologists want to know what rewards and punishments maintain a behavior.

9.   a is the answer.   The humanistic approach stresses that people are basically good and will work toward improving themselves unless stopped by something major. (see Approaches to the Science of Psychology)

   b.   The psychodynamic approach downplays the role of positive impulses and plays up the role of unconscious conflicts and negative impulses.

   c.   Biological psychology emphasizes the importance of body chemistry in everyday life.

   d.   Cognitive psychology does not recognize a drive toward self-improvement.

10.   b is the answer.   Helen will learn which physiological processes affect behavior. (see Subfields of Psychology)

   a.   Cognitive development is the study of the development of thinking.

   c.   Clinical, personality, and developmental psychologists may be interested in discussing and testing Freud's ideas, but biological psychologists probably would not.

   d.   Community psychologists develop and operate prevention programs.

11. c is the answer.   The behavioral approach to psychology emphasizes overtly observable behaviors, with much attention given to how behavior changes based on reward contingencies. Jenna's thought that her roommate is reinforced for acting depressed is consistent with the behavioral approach. (see Approaches to the Science of Psychology)

   a.   The biological approach assumes that genetic inheritance, nervous system activity, and hormones cause behaviors. Jenna's explanation of her roommate's depressed behavior does not deal with these kinds of explanations.

   b.   The psychodynamic approach assumes that behavior is a result of our struggle to fulfill instinctive desires despite society's restrictions. Jenna's explanation of her roommate's depression focuses on reinforcement contingencies, not on struggling with conflict between instinct and society.

   d.   The cognitive approach emphasizes mental representation and processing of information, not on reward contingencies.

12. c is the answer.   Industrial and organizational psychologists research the influence of employee interactions and management structures on employee productivity. (see Subfields of Psychology)

   a.   Cognitive psychologists might study mental processes involved in prejudice; however, they would be unlikely to study the impact of diversity training on employee relations.

   b.   Community psychology attempts to reach people in need by providing affordable mental health care in the community.

   d.   Personality psychologists study how people differ from each other, but do not study employee interactions.

13. a is the answer.   People in collectivist cultures tend to try not to attract attention to themselves and are likely to credit their family or work group if they are successful. (see Human Diversity and Psychology)

   b.   A communist society may or may not be collectivist.

   c.   A democratic society may or may not be collectivist.

   d.   Individualist cultures emphasize individuality. If Rajesh were from an individualist culture, he would be likely to take credit for his success.

14. d is the answer.   Interpersonal attraction is a topic of interest to social psychologists. (see Subfields of Psychology)

   a.   Clinical psychology deals with psychological disorders.

   b.   A developmental psychologist would study differences in people as they age.

   c.   Personality psychology looks for similarities within an individual over time but does not study interpersonal attraction.

15. c is the answer   Developmental psychologists are interested in understanding how and why behavior and mental processes change over the life span. (see Subfields of Psychology)

   a.   Biological psychology would teach Jill the areas of the brain and the physiological processes that are involved in learning, but this knowledge would be difficult for her personnel to apply in their jobs.

   b.   Psychodynamic psychology would teach Jill that behavior is determined by the combination of unconscious internal conflicts and external (parents', peers', or society's) reactions to those conflicts. However, this approach would not help Jill fulfill changing needs for different age groups.

    d.   Cognitive psychology would help Jill understand certain useful principles of learning. However, she must understand how learning and many other behaviors and mental processes change over the life span in order to help people of all ages.

16.   a is the answer.   A clinical psychologist would be most qualified to work with a person who has a psychological disorder. (see Subfields of Psychology)

    b.   Developmental psychologists study age differences and do not provide counseling.

    c.   A personality psychologist might be interested in the person's unique personality but would not be able to offer counseling.

    d.   Social psychology is the study of how people influence one another; however, it does not study disorders or treatment.

17.   c is the answer.   Community psychology not only provides counseling service in the community but also works to reduce the number of risks that contribute to the appearance of disorders. (see Subfields of Psychology)

    a.   Biological psychology investigates the influence of physiological factors on behavior but does not seek to prevent disorders.

    b.   Clinical psychologists are trained to help people once they have a disorder.

    d.   Educational psychology focuses on learning and teaching strategies but would not address the prevention of disorders through nutrition.

18.   d is the answer.   Neuroscience is the study of all levels of the nervous system, including fields of neuroanatomy, neurochemistry, neurology, neurophysiology, and neuropharmacology. (see Linkages within Psychology and Beyond)

    a.   Evolutionary psychology studies how behavior and mental processes are influenced by the process of natural selection.

    b.   The eclectic approach to psychology blends a variety of approaches together, not just neuroscience.

    c.   Biological psychology is a subfield of psychology that focuses on biological processes and their influence on behavior and mental processes; however, it does not necessarily study the nervous system at all levels.

19.   a is the answer.   Members of ethnic minorities earn about 25 percent of new doctoral degrees in psychology each year. (see Human Diversity and Psychology)

    b, c, d.   These statistics are too high. Only 25 percent of the new doctoral degrees are awarded to members of ethnic minorities each year.

20.   b is the answer.   Individualist cultures emphasize the importance of being independent and separate from others. Jerry's thinking reflects a desire to pursue his own dreams, and self, rather than suggesting a more interdependent self construction. (see Human Diversity and Psychology)

    a.   Multicultural refers to the existence of more than one culture within a given geographic boundary, such as a country (Kenya) or a city (Los Angeles). Just from Jerry's thinking, it would be hard to tell if he was from a multicultural culture.

    c.   Collectivist cultures emphasize and reward behaviors that contribute to the success of the group. If Jerry were from a collectivist culture, he would probably have decided to stay with the job near his family, because membership in a family group would have been very important to his identity, more so than pursuing his dreams.

    d.   Subcultures are part of a multicultural society and would not be identifiable from one person's, like Jerry's, thought processes.

Now turn to the quiz analysis table at the end of this chapter to find which areas you know well and which areas you need to work on. Circle the numbers in the table for items on Quiz 2 that you answered correctly.

For each question you answered correctly, circle its number. (Quiz 1 numbers are not shaded; Quiz 2 numbers are shaded.) Are there patterns in the types of questions or the topics you got wrong that could direct your further study? Did you improve from Quiz 1 to Quiz 2?

QUIZ REVIEW

Topic	Type of Question		
	Definition	**Comprehension**	**Application**
The World of Psychology: An Overview	1	2	
			1, 2
Subfields of Psychology		13, 18	12, 14, 15, 16, 17
		10, 17	12, 14, 15, 16
Linkages within Psychology and Beyond			
	18		
A Brief History of Psychology	3	4, 5	
		3, 4, 8, 10	5
Approaches to the Science of Psychology	11	8	6, 7, 9, 10
		9	6, 7, 11
Human Diversity and Psychology		19	20
		19	13, 20

Total correct by quiz:

Quiz 1:
Quiz 2:

CHAPTER 2

Research in Psychology

OUTLINE

I. THINKING CRITICALLY ABOUT PSYCHOLOGY (OR ANYTHING ELSE)
Critical thinking is the process of assessing claims or assertions and making judgments about them on the basis of well-supported evidence. You can use the following set of questions to think critically about any topic:

- *What am I being asked to believe or accept? What is the hypothesis?*

- *What evidence is available to support the assertion?*

- *Are there alternative ways of interpreting the evidence?*

- *What additional evidence would help to evaluate the alternatives?*

- *What conclusions are most reasonable?*

A. Critical Thinking and Scientific Research
Psychologists investigate phenomena they are curious about by formulating hypotheses, which are testable propositions. Operational definitions provide the methods used in the research to test the hypothesis. They explain how variables are manipulated or measured in the research. The numbers or scores on the measured variables produce data. Data are evaluated as to their statistical reliability and statistical validity.

B. The Role of Theories
A theory is an integrated set of statements that explains, predicts, and suggests ways of controlling certain phenomena. The results of testing hypotheses are used to build or evaluate theories, which in turn create new hypotheses to be studied. As a result, theories are constantly being formulated, evaluated, revised, and evaluated again. In evaluating theories, psychologists are guided by the *law of parsimony*.

II. RESEARCH METHODS IN PSYCHOLOGY
Psychologists strive to attain four goals when researching a psychological phenomenon:

Describe the phenomenon by gathering information about it.

Make *predictions* and formulate hypotheses about the phenomenon.

Control variables to eliminate alternative hypotheses and establish cause and effect.

Explain the phenomenon.

A. Observational Methods: Watching Behavior
Psychologists use observational methods, like naturalistic observation, which is the process of watching behavior as it occurs in its natural environment.

B. Case Studies: Taking a Closer Look
A case study is an intensive examination of a phenomenon in a particular individual, group, or situation, often combining observations, interviews, tests, and analyses of written records. Case studies are used to describe phenomena in areas such as neuropsychology.

C.   Surveys: Looking at the Big Picture
Surveys involve asking people questions, in interviews or questionnaires, in order to obtain descriptions of behavior, attitudes, beliefs, opinions, and intentions.

D.   Correlational Studies: Looking for Relationships
Correlational studies examine relationships between variables in order to describe research data, test predictions, evaluate theories, and suggest hypotheses. Correlational studies do not involve manipulating variables, but rather measure numerous variables in tandem, and test for co-relations between them.

E.   Experiments: Exploring Cause and Effect
Psychologists use experiments to establish cause-effect relationships between variables and to help them choose among alternative hypotheses to explain a given phenomenon. Experiments have at least two groups of participants: the experimental group and the control group. The control group receives no treatment, thus providing a baseline against which to compare the experimental group.

Experiments allow researchers to manipulate or control one variable to observe the effect of that manipulation on another variable, while holding all other variables constant. In an experiment, the variable manipulated or controlled by the researcher is called the independent variable. The measurement of the consequences is called the dependent variable.

The experimental group experiences the independent variable. Any difference in the dependent variable between the control and experimental groups is caused by the independent variable.

Flaws in experimental control can reduce the validity of an experiment. Confounds are uncontrolled factors that might have affected the dependent variable and confused interpretation of the experimental data.

1.   *Random Variables.* Random variables are uncontrolled factors, such as differences in subjects' backgrounds, personalities, health, and so on, that might confound research results. Randomizing the way research participants are assigned to experimental and control groups reduces the impact of random variables on the results.
2.   *Participants' Expectations: The Placebo Effect.* A placebo is a treatment that contains no active ingredient but produces a change in the dependent variable because the experimental subject believes it will.
3.   *Experimenter Bias.* This occurs when experimenters unintentionally affect the dependent variable based on their expectations of experimental results. To prevent experimenter bias, psychologists use a double-blind design in which neither the experimenter nor the participants know which group received the independent variable.

F.   Selecting Human Participants for Research
Sampling is an important process used to select subjects for an experiment. Research results can be generalized (that is, said to be true of the entire population of interest) only if the sample of participants studied represents that population accurately. When choosing a sample, psychologists must consider the possible impact that variables such as age, gender, race, ethnicity, cultural background, socioeconomic status, sexual orientation, disability, and so on can have on the behavior or mental process being studied.

Psychologists must conduct representative sampling of participants who fairly represent the group their research intends to investigate. If every population member has an *equal* chance of being chosen for study, psychologists have engaged in random sampling; if all such chances are not equal, then <u>biased sampling</u> has occurred. Often, *convenience samples* are used instead of random, which limits the conclusions psychologists can draw from that data.

G. Linkages: Psychological Research Methods and Behavioral Genetics
Many psychologists, despite their subfield or area of interest, attempt to understand how nature (genetic makeup) and nurture (environment/experiences) interact to produce behavior and mental processes.

Researchers interested in <u>behavioral genetics</u> study the effect of heredity and the environment on behavioral tendencies in groups. Their work employs quasi-experimental methods such as *family*, *adoption*, and *twin studies*. The field of <u>epigenetics</u> studies how environmental influences alter the way genes function without altering the DNA sequence, itself.

III. STATISTICAL ANALYSIS OF RESEARCH RESULTS
Statistical analyses are used to interpret research results. <u>Descriptive statistics</u> describe data. <u>Inferential statistics</u> are used to draw conclusions and make inferences about what the data mean.

A. Descriptive Statistics
1. *Measures of Central Tendency.* Measures of central tendency are values that best describe a set of data. The <u>mode</u> is the most frequent score in a data set. The <u>median</u> score splits the data set in two; half the scores are above the median and half are below. The <u>mean</u> is the mathematical average. It is calculated by summing the values of all the scores and then dividing by the total number of scores.
2. *Measures of Variability.* Measures of variability indicate the dispersion or spread in a set of data. The <u>range</u> is calculated by subtracting the lowest score in a data set from the highest score. The <u>standard deviation (SD)</u> measures the average difference between each score and the mean of the data set.
3. *Correlation and Correlation Coefficients.* <u>Correlations</u>, even very strong ones, do not necessarily reflect cause-effect relationships between variables. The <u>correlation coefficient</u> is a mathematical calculation that describes the direction and strength of the relationship between two variables.
The sign (+ or −) of r describes a correlation's direction. A positive correlation (where the sign is +) describes a relationship in which two variables change in the same direction: as x increases, so does y (and vice versa). A negative correlation (where the sign is −) describes a relationship in which two variables change in opposite directions: As x increases, y decreases (and vice versa).

A correlation's numerical value (r) can vary from −1.00 to +1.00. The larger the absolute value of r (whether + or −), the stronger the relationship. In a perfect correlation, $r = +1.00$ or -1.00; knowing the value of one variable allows the exact prediction of the other variable.

B. Inferential Statistics
Inferential statistics are used to analyze research results. When inferential statistics demonstrate a high probability that research results are not due to chance, the results are said to have achieved <u>statistical significance</u>.

C. Statistics and Research Methods as Tools in Critical Thinking
Scientific evaluation of research requires the use of critical thinking to carefully assess the statistical and methodological aspects of even the most dramatic or desirable results.

IV. ETHICAL GUIDELINES FOR PSYCHOLOGISTS
Ethical guidelines and regulations exist for psychologists' use in treating patients and conducting research. Scientists must accurately report their results, minimize participant discomfort, and

prevent any long-term negative effects. Human participants must be fully informed about their participation before a given study and must be debriefed when the research is concluded. The obligation of psychologists to protect participants' welfare also extends to animals.

KEY TERMS

1. **Critical thinking** is the process of assessing claims and making judgments on the basis of well-supported evidence. (see Thinking Critically About Psychology (or Anything Else))

   Example: Consider the five steps of critical thinking: (a) What am I being asked to believe or accept? What is the hypothesis? (b) What evidence is available to support the assertion? Is it reliable and valid? (c) Are there alternative ways of interpreting the evidence? (d) What additional evidence would help to evaluate the alternatives? (e) What conclusions are most reasonable based on the evidence and the number of alternative explanations?

2. A **hypothesis** is a specific testable proposition, about a phenomenon. (see Critical Thinking and Scientific Research)

3. An **operational definition** is a statement that defines the exact operations or methods used in research. (see Critical Thinking and Scientific Research)

   Example: If we are conducting a study regarding the effects of caffeine on anxiety, we would have to decide exactly *how* we plan to measure anxiety. Our operational definition of anxiety might be changes in blood pressure or the subjects' answers to an anxiety questionnaire—whatever logically fits our research hypothesis.

   Example: If rats have access to toys, *then* they can practice behaviors similar to those used in running a maze and perform better than rats raised without access to toys.

4. **Variables** are factors or characteristics that are manipulated or measured in research. (see Critical Thinking and Scientific Research)

   Example: Marta is doing a study in which she investigates the impact of teaching style on learning. The variables in her study are "teaching style" and "learning."

5. **Data** are numbers that represent research findings and provide the basis for research conclusions. (see Critical Thinking and Scientific Research)

   Example: For a psychologist studying learning, a test score might represent an operational definition of the amount one has learned. Sets of test scores for classes that received different teaching methods are the data.

6. **Statistical reliability** is the degree to which test results or other research evidence occur repeatedly. (see Critical Thinking and Scientific Research)

   Example: When Mariah does a study showing a treatment for autism is successful, other scientists need to be able to repeat the study and find the same results to show the treatment is statistically reliable.

7. **Statistical validity** is the degree to which evidence from a test or other research method measures what it is supposed to measure. (see Critical Thinking and Scientific Research)

   Example: When a test says someone's IQ is high, we expect other measures of intelligence should also indicate the person is smart. This would demonstrate that the test measures what it claims to measure.

8. A **theory** is an integrated set of propositions that can be used to account for, predict, and even suggest ways of controlling certain phenomena. (see The Role of Theories)

Example: Finding that people under stress often overeat or drink more alcohol led to the theory that behaviors that appear self-destructive may be stress alleviators.

REMEMBER: Theories are not definitive; they are constantly amended as researchers collect and analyze new data.

9. **Observational methods** are procedures for systematically watching behavior in order to summarize it for scientific analysis. (see Observational Methods: Watching Behavior)

    Example: A researcher interested in measuring customer service might record customer service calls and analyze the sorts of problems that occur during the call.

10. **Naturalistic observation**, the process of watching without interfering, as a phenomenon occurs in the natural environment. (see Observational Methods: Watching Behavior)

    Example: A researcher interested in how much time children of different ages play alone could observe children at a playground.

    REMEMBER: A researcher *observes* a phenomenon in its *natural* environment.

11. **Case studies** are research methods involving the intensive examination of some phenomenon in a particular individual, group, or situation. (see Case Studies: Taking a Closer Look)

    Example: Biological psychologists cannot alter a person's brain in the laboratory for the purposes of study; therefore, they are interested in people who have suffered brain injuries in accidents. Researchers examine these patients intensively over long periods of time.

    REMEMBER: Case studies are particularly useful for studying rare or complex phenomena.

12. **Neuropsychology** is the study of the relationships among brain activity, thinking, and behavior. (see Case Studies: Taking a Closer Look)

    Example: Skip has a strange set of behaviors—he recognizes his wife on the phone, but when he sees her in person he cannot recognize her. Neuropsychologists might study what area of the brain might be damaged to create this strange circumstance.

13. **Surveys** involve giving people questionnaires or special interviews designed to obtain descriptions of their attitudes, beliefs, opinions, and intentions. (see Surveys: Looking at the Big Picture)

    Example: Social psychologists interested in learning what teenagers from families of varying income levels think of marriage can administer a questionnaire to a sample of teenagers.

14. **Correlational studies** are a research method that examines relationships between variables in order to analyze trends in data, test predictions, evaluate theories, and suggest new hypotheses. (see Correlational Studies: Looking for Relationships)

    Example: Surveys and naturalistic observation are examples of correlational studies.

    REMEMBER: Correlational studies do not allow researchers to discern cause-and-effect relationships.

15. An **experiment** is a situation in which the researcher manipulates one variable and then observes the effect of that manipulation on another variable, while holding all other variables constant. (see Experiments: Exploring Cause and Effect)

    REMEMBER: An experiment is a trial or test of a hypothesis. Experiments show causation.

    Example: Jenna believes alcohol consumption adversely affects reflex speed. To determine if this is the case, she constructs an experiment in which half the participants consume a small amount of alcohol and the other half consume a nonalcoholic beverage. She then gives them a test of reflex speed and compares their performance on it.

16. The **experimental group** in an experiment is the group that receives the experimental treatment. (see Experiments: Exploring Cause and Effect)

Example: In the experiment examining the effects of alcohol on reflex speed, the group who receives alcohol (the independent variable) is the experimental group.

17. The **control group** in an experiment is the group that receives no treatment or provides some other baseline against which to compare the performance or response of the experimental group. (see Experiments: Exploring Cause and Effect)

Example: In the experiment examining the effects of alcohol on reflex speed, the group who received the nonalcoholic beverage is the control group.

REMEMBER: This group is identical to the experimental group in every way *except* that these subjects *do not* receive the treatment. The control group provides the control in an experiment. Comparing the measure of the dependent variable in both the control and experimental groups indicates whether the independent variable is causing the changes in the dependent variable or whether these changes occurred by chance.

18. **Independent variables** are the variables manipulated by the researcher in an experiment. (see Experiments: Exploring Cause and Effect)

Example: An experiment is conducted to test the effects of alcohol on reflex speed. Two groups of subjects are randomly selected. One group, the experimental group, is given alcohol (alcohol is the independent variable), and the other group, the control group, is given a nonalcoholic beverage.

19. **Dependent variables** in an experiment are the factors affected by the independent variable. (see Experiments: Exploring Cause and Effect)

Example: In the experiment examining the effects of alcohol on reflex speed, the dependent variable is performance on the reflex speed test.

REMEMBER: The measure or value of the *dependent* variable *depends on* the independent variable.

20. **Confounds** in an experiment are any factors that affect the dependent variable, along with or instead of the independent variable. (see Experiments: Exploring Cause and Effect)

Example: Joe does an experiment to determine the effects of teaching style on student learning. He uses an interactive style with his 8 A.M. class and a lecture-only style with his noon class. He then measures their performance on exams. The noon class performs better on the exams, but Joe is unable to confidently assert that lecture-only is a better style of teaching for student learning because of the confounding variable—time of day for the class—that plagues his study. It is possible the noon class is more alert because they have had more sleep or have been awake longer and that this difference, rather than teaching style, accounts for the performance differences he observes.

REMEMBER: Examples of confounding variables include random variables, experimenter bias, and the placebo effect.

21. **Random variables** in an experiment are confounds in which uncontrolled or uncontrollable factors affect the dependent variable, along with or instead of the independent variable. (see Experiments: Exploring Cause and Effect)

Example: An experimenter wishes to test the effects of a teaching technique on test performance. The subjects are assigned to the control and experimental groups. The researcher does not know it, but most of the students in the experimental group are much brighter than the control group students. The data may suggest that the students who received the teaching technique scored higher than those who did not. In this case, however, intelligence is a random variable that, instead of the independent variable, could be responsible for the results.

22. **Randomizing** is assigning participants in an experiment to various groups through a random process to ensure that random variables are evenly distributed among the groups. (see Experiments: Exploring Cause and Effect)

    Example: Joe shows up for an experiment with two conditions. The experimenter flips a coin to determine which condition Joe will be in. Joe has been randomly assigned to the condition he is in for this experiment.

23. A **placebo** is a physical or psychological treatment that contains no active ingredient produces an effect because the person receiving it believes it will. (see Experiments: Exploring Cause and Effect)

    Example: In an experiment on the effects of alcohol, a researcher may find that people who have been given a nonalcoholic beverage behave as though they are drunk only because they *believe* they have been given an alcoholic drink.

24. **Experimenter bias** is a confound that occurs when an experimenter unintentionally encourages participants to respond in a way that supports the experimenter's hypothesis. (see Experiments: Exploring Cause and Effect)

    Example: An experimenter hypothesizes that an expert will be able to persuade a group of people that decision A is better than decision B. After the expert has spoken to the subjects, the researcher asks them which decision they prefer. She can ask in several ways. Asking, "Now, don't you think A is better than B?" will bias her data more than if she asks, "Which do you think is better, decision A or decision B?"

25. **Double-blind design** is a research design in which neither the experimenter nor the participants know who is in the experimental group and who is in the control group (see Experiments: Exploring Cause and Effect)

    Example: The experiment studying the effects of alcohol on reflex speed (described in relation to Key Term 15) is repeated using a double-blind design. Neither the participants nor the experimenter knows who has received alcohol and who has not. Thus, participants are prevented from changing their behavior simply because they think they have been given alcohol. At the same time, the experimenter is prevented from biasing observations of the subjects' behavior or mental processes.

26. **Sampling** is the process of selecting participants who are members of the population that the researcher wishes to study. (see Selecting Human Participants for Research)

    Example: If you are studying the behavior of gifted children, your sample should be drawn exclusively from this group.

27. **Representative sampling** is a process for selecting research participants whose characteristics fairly reflect the characteristics of the population from which they were drawn. (see Selecting Human Participants for Research)

    Example: A study that contained only people who were movie stars would not be a representative sample of the rest of the world population.

28. **Random sampling** is the process of selecting a group of research participants from a population whose members all had an equal chance of being chosen. If a sample is not random, it is said to be *biased*. (see Selecting Human Participants for Research)

    Example: A social psychologist is interested in studying the influence of parents on the career choice of first-year college students in the United States. If the sample is to be random, every first-year student must have an equal chance of being selected as a subject. The researcher thus draws the sample from lists of first-year college students in schools all over the United States, not just from the schools in one state.

29. **Biased sampling** is the process of selecting a group of research participants from a population whose members did not have an equal chance of being chosen. (see Selecting Human Participants for Research)

    REMEMBER: Experimental results obtained from a biased sample may not be generalizable to the population of interest. The results are *biased* by characteristics of the subjects, not by the independent variable.

30. **Behavioral genetics** is they study of how genes and environment work together to shape behavior. (see Linkages: Psychological Research Methods and Behavioral Genetics)

    Example: A behavioral genetics study might look for similarities in behavior among relatives. The children of a person who experiences depression, for example, might be more likely to develop depression than distant relatives or unrelated people.

31. **Epigenetics** is the study of potentially inheritable changes in gene expression that are caused by environmental factors that do not alter a cell's DNA. (see Linkages: Psychological Research Methods and Behavioral Genetics)

    Example: Sometimes people who have the same genes acquire a disease like Alzheimer's and sometimes they do not. Epigenetics explores how environmental influences can account for these differences in the same DNA structure.

32. **Descriptive statistics** are numbers that summarize a set of data. (see Statistical Analysis of Research Results)

    REMEMBER: Examples of descriptive statistics are measures of central tendency, measures of variability, and correlation coefficients.

33. **Inferential statistics** are a set of mathematical procedures that help psychologists make inferences about what their research data mean. (see Statistical Analysis of Research Results)

    REMEMBER: Inferential statistics allow psychologists to *infer* what the data mean.

34. The **mode** is a measure of central tendency that is the value or score that occurs most frequently in a data set. (see Descriptive Statistics)

    Example: In the data set 3, 12, 14, 16, 17, 18, 19, 22, 22, 22, 22, the mode is 22.

35. The **median** is a measure of central tendency that is the halfway point in a set of data: Half the scores fall above the median, and half fall below it. (see Descriptive Statistics)

    Example: In the data set, 3, 12, 14, 16, 17, 18, 19, 22, 22, 22, 22, the median is 18.

    REMEMBER: The *median* is "the score in the middle"—the score that divides the data set in half. When there is an even number of scores in a data set, the median is halfway between the *two* middle numbers.

36. The **mean** is a measure of central tendency that is the arithmetic average of the scores in a set of data. (see Descriptive Statistics)

Example: For the previous data set the mean is equal to $(3 + 12 + 14 + 16 + 17 + 18 + 19 + 22 + 22 + 22 + 22)/11 = 187/11 = 17.$

REMEMBER: This measure of central tendency takes into account all of the values of the scores in a data set. Therefore, even one extreme score can change the mean radically, possibly making it less representative of the data.

37. The **range** is a measure of variability that is the difference between the highest and the lowest scores in a data set. (see Descriptive Statistics)

Example: In the data set 2, 3, 4, 5, 5, 5, 6, 7, 8, 100, the range is $100 - 2 = 98$. If the extreme score (100) is dropped, the range is $8 - 2 = 6$. Extreme scores can radically affect the range of a data set.

38. The **standard deviation**, or **SD**, is a measure of variability that is the average difference between each score and the mean of the data set. (see Descriptive Statistics)

Example: Following are two data sets.

Data set 1: 1, 2, 3, 4, 5, 6, 7, 8, 9

Data set 2: 4, 4, 4, 4, 5, 6, 6, 6, 6

The mean of both data sets is 5. However, the scores in data set 1 are a greater distance from the mean. In other words, they are *more different* from the mean than the scores in data set 2. Therefore, the standard deviation (SD) in data set 1 is larger than the SD for data set 2.

REMEMBER: To *deviate* means to "differ." The standard deviation describes, overall, how *different* the scores in a data set are from the mean.

39. A **correlation** in research is the degree to which one variable is related to another. (see Descriptive Statistics)

Example: In a small English town, the seasonal appearance of a large number of storks is positively correlated with the number of human births; as x (the number of storks) increases, y (the number of births) increases. If correlations indicated causation, we could say that the storks cause babies to appear. But correlations *do not* imply causation, and storks do not bring babies.

REMEMBER: Correlations do not indicate causation.

40. A **correlation coefficient** is a statistic, r, that summarizes the strength and direction of a relationship between two variables. (see Descriptive Statistics)

Example: Brian conducts a correlational study to determine if a relationship exists between class attendance and grade in the class. Based on his data collection, he finds a correlation of $+.80$. The positive nature of the correlation indicates that the more a student attends class, the higher his or her grade is likely to be. The value of the correlation (.80) indicates that it is a relatively strong relationship, as it is close to the absolute value of 1.00.

REMEMBER: A correlation coefficient can range in value from -1.00 to +1.00. The sign (+ or −) indicates the direction of the relationship, whereas the absolute value indicates its strength.

41. **Statistical significance** refers to a correlation or difference between two groups that is larger than would be expected by chance. (see Inferential Statistics)

Example: If the difference between two group means is statistically significant, a researcher would conclude that the difference most likely exists in the population of interest. If the difference is not statistically significant, a researcher would conclude that the difference occurred by chance—possibly because of an unrepresentative sample or the presence of confounding variables.

FILL-IN-THE-BLANKS KEY TERMS

This section will help you check your knowledge of the key terms introduced in this chapter. Fill in each blank with the appropriate term from the list of key terms in the previous section.

1. The process of evaluating propositions or hypotheses and making judgments about them based on well-supported evidence is called _____.

2. A(n) _____ is a testable proposition about the relationship between two variables.

3. A description of the methods that will be used to measure a variable is called a(n) _____.

4. _____ are procedures for systematically watching behavior in order to summarize it for scientific analysis.

5. In an experiment, the variable manipulated by the experimenter is called a(n) _____.

6. The _____ group receives the treatment, or independent variable, in an experiment.

7. The main function of the _____ group in an experiment is to provide a comparison of the effects of the independent variable on the dependent variable.

8. Neither the experimenters nor the participants know who has received the independent variable in a(n) _____ design.

9. _____ are any factors other than the independent variable that introduce variation in the dependent variable.

10. A treatment that contains no active ingredient but can produce results simply because of a person's belief in its power is a(n) _____.

11. When a phenomenon is very rare, researchers use a(n) _____.

12. A sample is _____ if every person in the population has an equal chance of being selected as a study participant.

13. _____ is the degree to which test results or other research evidence occurs repeatedly.

14. Researchers must look at the _____ of their data to decide whether their results could have occurred by chance alone.

15. _____ is the study of the contributions of genetics and environmental factors to differences in the behavioral tendencies of groups.

Total Correct (See answer key) _____

LEARNING OBJECTIVES

1. Explain the importance of <u>critical thinking</u> in psychology, and list the five questions used by critical thinkers when evaluating information.

2. Define <u>hypothesis</u>, and explain the role of hypotheses in scientific research.

3. Explain what <u>operational definitions</u> are, and give examples of several.

4. Define what <u>variables</u> are, and give examples of variables that a psychologist might study.

5. Define the terms <u>statistical reliability</u> and <u>statistical validity</u>. Explain their importance in psychological research.

6. Explain the development and role of <u>theories</u> in psychological research.

7. Describe each of psychological science's goals of describing, predicting, controlling, and explaining psychological phenomena.

8. Explain how <u>observational methods</u> work, and give several examples of how psychologists might use <u>naturalistic observation</u> in conducting psychological research.

9. Explain how <u>case study</u> methods work, and give several examples of how psychologists might use case studies in conducting psychological research.

10. Explain how <u>survey</u> methods work, and give several examples of how psychologists might use surveys in conducting psychological research.

11. Explain how <u>correlational study</u> methods work, and give several examples of how psychologists might use correlational studies in conducting psychological research.

12. Explain how <u>experiments</u> work, and give several examples of how psychologists might use experiments in conducting psychological research.

13. Explain the relationship between <u>control groups</u> and <u>experimental groups</u> in psychological research.

14. Describe and explain the similarities and differences between <u>independent variables</u>, <u>dependent variables</u>, <u>random variables</u>, and <u>confounds</u>.

15. Explain why psychologists should <u>randomize</u> participants in their experiments.

16. Discuss the <u>placebo</u> effect.

17. Explain how the <u>double-blind design</u> for an experiment reduces the effects of <u>experimenter bias</u>.

18. Discuss the process of <u>sampling</u> in choosing participants for psychological research. Define <u>representative sampling</u>, <u>biased sampling</u>, and <u>random sampling</u>.

19. Explain how the field of <u>behavioral genetics</u> investigates psychological phenomena. Describe the use of family studies, twin studies, and adoption studies.

20. Define <u>epigenetics</u>.

21. Define the three measures of central tendency, the <u>mean</u>, <u>median</u>, and <u>mode</u>. Explain the importance of these <u>descriptive statistics</u> in describing <u>data</u> collected in psychological research.

22. Define the <u>range</u> and <u>standard deviation</u>, and explain how psychologists use these measures of variability.

23. Define the <u>correlation coefficient</u>, and discuss both its uses and limitations in psychological research.

24. Explain the use of <u>inferential statistics</u> in psychological research.

25. Describe the basic ideas behind ethical practices in psychological science. Explain the reasons why psychologists must engage in these practices.

26. Describe the main functions of *Institutional Review Boards*.

27. List some of the laws and guidelines that regulate research practices in psychology.

28. List some ethical dilemmas involved in psychological research, and discuss the ways in which psychological scientists may address them.

CONCEPTS AND EXERCISES

Research Methods

As a study aid for her final exam in a research methods course, Susan has made note cards listing the steps to be followed for conducting an experiment and descriptive research. Sitting down to study, she knocked the cards to the floor, and they scattered. Your job is to put the cards back in order. Ignore those cards that do not describe the steps in an experiment.

1. _____
2. _____
3. _____
4. _____
5. _____
6. _____
7. _____
8. _____

   a. Create an operational definition, if needed.

   b. Measure the dependent variable.

   c. Observe participants in their natural environment.

   d. Calculate a correlation coefficient.

   e. Identify the independent and dependent variables.

   f. Compare the measures of the dependent variables between the two groups of participants.

   g. Manipulate the independent variable.

   h. Administer a questionnaire.

   i. Assign participants randomly between two groups.

   j. Form a hypothesis based on previous descriptive and/or correlational data.

   k. Use inferential statistics to determine statistical significance.

Choose Your Method

From the list below, choose the best research method for obtaining the answer to each of the following questions.

1.   Does a lack of sleep cause changes in problem-solving ability? _____

2.   Throughout history, very young children have occasionally been lost in the wild and found several years later. Recently another such child was discovered. Has growing up in the wild affected his cognitive development? _____

3.   What is the average five-year-old's attention span at a playground? _____

4.   How do people residing near nuclear reactors feel about the nuclear arms race? Are their opinions different from those of people living far from nuclear facilities? _____

    a.   Survey

    b.   Experiment

    c.   Naturalistic observation

    d.   Case study

CRITICAL THINKING

Sam, a rookie police officer, has been assigned to Martina, an experienced detective who is going to show him the ropes. Martina smiled when Sam proudly told her that he had two college degrees and graduated with honors. "Sam," she said, "a college degree shows that you have learned many facts, but hopefully college has also helped you to think critically about those facts. The most important thing you need to do in this job is ask yourself five questions. If you know the answers, or at least how to go about finding the answers, you will solve most of your cases." Sam, doubting that a detective's entire method of crime solving could be distilled down to five questions, decided to humor Martina and play along. "OK, what are these five questions I have to ask myself?"

Help Martina by listing the five critical thinking questions as they might be used in a criminal investigation.

1.   _____

2.   _____

3.   _____

4.   _____

5.   _____

PERSONAL LEARNING ACTIVITIES

1.   In psychology, as in detective work, critical thinking is important, and naturalistic observation is a basic research method. Pretend you are a psychologist trying to gain information about yourself from your personal environment. Carefully examine a place in which you spend a lot of time (such as your car, bedroom, kitchen, computer station, garage). Compile a list of five specific features you observed in this environment. What inferences about your personality or habits could be made from these clues? Are all of the inferences clear-cut, or could the same observations be interpreted as an indication of something else?

2.   Take a survey and see if responses vary when you ask the same question in different ways. For example, many people are very wary of genetic engineering, particularly regarding their food

supply. You might ask some people if they would eat "genetically engineered" tomatoes. Ask others if they would eat "scientifically enhanced" tomatoes or tomato "clones." Think of some other ways of describing these tomatoes. If the answers you receive differ, what potential problems does this suggest with the use of surveys?

3. Design an experiment. To do so, you should outline your hypothesis, variables, operational definitions, and so on. For example, if your hypothesis is that rock music played during studying improves retention of material, then you should decide what rock music to play and what the control group(s) will hear during studying. You might operationally define memory improvement as a score increase of a certain size on a test of list learning or on a test of reading comprehension.

4. If you are interested in learning more about epigenetics, visit this website and explore some of the new evidence from this field: http://www.pbs.org/wgbh/nova/sciencenow/3411/02.html .

5. To see a video explaining why correlation does not imply causation with several examples, visit the following YouTube site: http://www.youtube.com/watch?v=VW1IEqKuf6s. Beyond a few simple examples, the video also explores some of the evidence that individuals often cite (based on correlational data) to suggest that vaccination causes autism. What is your opinion after watching this short clip? Does the video make a good case based on the critical thinking processes that your text proposes?

MULTIPLE-CHOICE QUESTIONS

Quiz 1

1. Which of the following is NOT one of the five questions associated with the critical thinking process described in your text?
   a. What am I being asked to believe or accept?
   b. What evidence is available to support the assertion?
   c. How can I best justify the conclusion I would like to reach?
   d. Are there alternative ways of interpreting the evidence?

2. Kara is charged with developing an assessment program for experiential learning activities at the university where she is employed. She interviews faculty members and students at the university, and determines that "experiential learning" includes study-abroad experiences, internships, clinical experiences, and service-learning experiences. She then develops an assessment tool for distribution in courses that, according to the college catalog, have one or more of those experiences embedded in the coursework. The operational definition guiding Kara's assessment is
   a. courses listed in the catalog as study-abroad, internship, clinical, or service-learning experiences.
   b. experiential learning.
   c. faculty and students.
   d. study-abroad, internships, clinical, and service-learning experiences.

3. Which of the following research questions is best suited to a correlational study design?
   a. Does smaller class size cause an increase in test scores for college students?
   b. Is daycare quality associated with the quality of the attachment a parent has to his or her child?
   c. Does diversity in a group lead to better performance of that group?
   d. None of these is suited to a correlational study design.

4. Dr. Dekka has collected data by doing case studies and naturalistic observation on a new phenomenon never studied before. The first goal of these studies is most likely
   a. to make predictions about the phenomenon of interest.
   b. to describe the phenomenon of interest.
   c. to exert control over the phenomenon of interest.
   d. to explain the phenomenon of interest.

5. Naturalistic observation is
   a. the intense observation of a single individual, group, or situation.
   b. giving people questionnaires or special interviews to obtain descriptions of their attitudes, beliefs, and intentions.
   c. the process of watching without interfering as a phenomenon occurs in its normal environment.
   d. a situation in which one manipulates one variable and then observes the effect of that manipulation on another variable, while holding all other variables constant.

6. Which of the following is a case study?
   a. Calling a random sample of people at home and asking them how they feel about riverboat gambling
   b. Watching an infant as it sleeps and counting the number of times it awakens throughout the night
   c. Intensive observation of a person with a rare psychological disorder
   d. Giving some people one antidepressant and others a placebo, and measuring their mood one month later

7. What is measured in an experiment?
   a. Random variables
   b. Confounding variable
   c. Independent variable
   d. Dependent variable

8. Which of the following threats to validity in a survey is most difficult to deal with?
   a. Proper wording of questions
   b. Getting a representative sample of the population being studied
   c. Controlling responses so they are not biased by socially acceptable standards
   d. All of the above

9. The experimental design that prevents experimenter bias from confounding a study's results is
   a. operational definition.
   b. naturalistic observation.
   c. random.
   d. double-blind design.

10. Akuba believes that group activities will result in better learning than lectures. She gives one of her introductory psychology classes lectures and the other class group activities. She then compares how they perform on exams. In this example, which class received lectures versus group activities is the _____ variable.

    a. confounding
    b. dependent
    c. independent
    d. placebo

11. Jeremy designed an experiment to test the effects of praise on the sharing behavior of children. Children in Group A will be praised after they share; children in Group B will only be observed. Group A is the _____ group.

    a. control
    b. experimental
    c. operational
    d. random

12. Susan wants to study the effects of peer pressure on study habits in first-year students at her university. She needs to obtain a random sample. How should she choose the participants for her experiment?

    a. Select one dormitory and ask all of the first-year students residing there to participate in the experiment
    b. Randomly select names from the introductory psychology course roster
    c. Randomly select names from the dormitory phone book
    d. Randomly select names from a list of all first-year students at the university

13. The question that puzzles Marianne is why some psychological problems seem to run in families. Marianne would like to discover whether it is nature or nurture that more strongly influences certain behaviors; therefore, she has an interest in

    a. behavioral genetics.
    b. genetic engineering.
    c. "pop" psychology.
    d. replicability.

14. Part of the data comparing the number of sharing behaviors for the two groups is listed here: Group A: 35, 12, 11, 9, 8, 6, 5; Group B: 9, 8, 7, 7, 6, 5, 4. Which of the following statistics would best represent the amount of sharing for the children in Group A?

    a. Mean
    b. Median
    c. Mode
    d. Range

15. Based on the data in question 14, which of the following statements about variability is most likely correct?

    a. Group A has a smaller range than Group B.
    b. Group A does not have a standard deviation.
    c. Group B has a smaller standard deviation than Group A.
    d. Group B has the same range as Group A.

16. Detective Brown observed that when he and his coworkers drank caffeinated tea while working on cases, they solved them faster. Brown conducted an experiment in which one group received caffeine pills and the other received inert sugar pills. Each person received a set of cases to solve, and Brown recorded the number of cases solved by people in the caffeine group versus people in the sugar pill group. The strongest evidence that caffeine pills improved the case solution rate would be

    a. a large mean for the caffeine group.
    b. a positive correlation between the number of cases solved by the caffeine and the sugar pill groups.
    c. a small range of scores in the sugar pill group.
    d. statistically different means for the caffeine and sugar pill groups.

17. Choose the strongest correlation coefficient from the following:

    a. +.75
    b. −.99
    c. +.01
    d. −.01

18. Neuropsychology is

    a. the study of the relationships among brain activity, thinking, and behavior.
    b. the study of potentially inheritable changes in gene expression caused by environment.
    c. the study of how genes and environment shape behavior.
    d. the study of behavior and mental processes.

19. Several states implemented laws requiring drivers and passengers to wear seat belts. Since the laws' implementation, the number of accident-related deaths has decreased. Therefore, a negative correlation exists, which indicates that

    a. wearing seat belts causes fewer car accidents.
    b. more laws result in fewer accident-related deaths.
    c. when the number of people wearing seat belts increases, the number of accident-related deaths decreases.
    d. enforcing the law causes fewer accidents to occur.

20. Because experimenters follow the ethical guidelines for psychologists, participants in psychological research can expect to be

    a. informed about the study before they agree to participate.
    b. offered counseling.
    c. psychoanalyzed.
    d. sent home without knowing they were deceived.

Total Correct (See answer key) _____

Quiz 2

Use this quiz to reassess your learning after taking Quiz 1 and reviewing the chapter.

1.   On a television program many people give testimony that they have never felt better than they have since they began using the Run-O-Sizer treadmill. Each person who is interviewed shows "before" and "after" photos depicting incredible weight loss and increased muscle tone. According to the critical thinking steps in your text, what should you do?

   a.   Look for alternative ways of interpreting the evidence that the Run-O-Sizer works.
   b.   Draw your conclusion about the worth of the Run-O-Sizer based on the strong testimonials.
   c.   Decide whether to order the treadmill based on the price.
   d.   Order only if they offer a money-back guarantee.

2.   The four scientific goals associated with research are

   a.   measurement, prediction, control, and explanation.
   b.   explanation, understanding, reasoning, and control.
   c.   description, critical thinking, control, and explanation.
   d.   description, prediction, control, and explanation.

3.   To document how the average first-year college student behaves during an exam, a researcher should conduct a(n)

   a.   case study.
   b.   experiment.
   c.   naturalistic observation.
   d.   survey.

4.   The Food and Drug Administration (FDA) has tested fluoxetine, a drug thought to decrease depression without causing weight gain. The experiment consisted of a random sample of depressed patients split into two groups. The experimental group received the drug; the control group received no treatment. The results were clear: those patients receiving fluoxetine experienced a decrease in depression without weight gain; those in the control group reported no change in depression or weight. Based on these results, should the FDA allow marketing of fluoxetine?

   a.   No, the results may have been due to the placebo effect.
   b.   No, the study should be repeated using a case study.
   c.   Yes, the experimental design is appropriate and the results are clear.
   d.   No, the results may have been due to incorrect sampling.

5.   In the experiment done by the FDA on fluoxetine, which variable needs an operational definition?

   a.   The independent variable
   b.   Fluoxetine
   c.   Depression
   d.   The placebo

6.   In the experiment done by the FDA on fluoxetine, the drug was the

   a.   independent variable.
   b.   dependent variable.
   c.   operational measure.
   d.   random variable.

7. A psychologist interested in maximizing control of variables in her research would use which of the following methods?
    a. Naturalistic observation
    b. Surveys
    c. An experiment
    d. A case study

8. Questionnaires or special interviews designed to obtain descriptions of people's attitudes, beliefs, opinions, and behavioral intentions are known as
    a. experiments.
    b. surveys.
    c. case studies.
    d. naturalistic observations.

9. Which of the following hypotheses should be tested with a case study?
    a. Thinking of examples of concepts while studying improves students' performance on tests.
    b. An unpleasant odor presented for one hour will cause a mild negative emotional reaction.
    c. Childhood abuse is associated with multiple personality disorder.
    d. All of the above

10. To understand the causal relationship between two variables, one must conduct which type of research study?
    a. Correlational study
    b. Experiment
    c. Naturalistic observation
    d. Survey

11. Which of the following is a possible random variable?
    a. Level of intelligence
    b. State of health
    c. Prior experience with the independent variable
    d. All of the above

12. Nicole was struck by lightning, and she now often runs down the street singing while wearing her underwear on the outside of her clothes. She cannot concentrate on her work for more than 10 minutes, nor can she understand the comics she used to enjoy so much. To understand Nicole's condition, a researcher should use a(n)
    a. case study.
    b. experiment.
    c. naturalistic observation.
    d. survey.

13. The placebo effect, or participant expectancy, is what type of variable in an experiment that failed to include a placebo condition?
    a. Independent variable
    b. Dependent variable
    c. Confounding variable
    d. Correlational variable

14. Statistical validity means that

    a. a test or evidence from a research method measures what it is supposed to measure.
    b. a test score or other research evidence occurs repeatedly.
    c. random assignment was used.
    d. a positive correlation was achieved.

15. Following is a data set: 10, 11, 12, 22, 12, 11, 10, 10, 10, 11, 13. The value of 10 is the

    a. mean.
    b. mode.
    c. median.
    d. range.

16. A positive correlation indicates the existence of a relationship between two variables such that

    a. one variable increases as the other decreases.
    b. one variable increases as the other increases.
    c. one variable causes an increase in the other.
    d. one variable causes a decrease in the other.

17. A recruiter has administered an intelligence test to a college graduating class. The test results are rather disappointing, however. The means, medians, and modes of all the classes are very similar and very low. The recruiter is determined to find the class with the brightest students to interview. What statistic could this recruiter look at to decide which one of the classes probably has the greatest number of high scores?

    a. The range
    b. The standard deviation
    c. A measure of central tendency
    d. An operational score definition

18. You are studying the effects of alcohol consumption on decision-making time. Your hypothesis states that as alcohol consumption increases, decision-making time will also increase. If your data describe a _____ correlation, your hypothesis will be supported.

    a. negative
    b. curvilinear
    c. positive
    d. statistically significant negative

19. Why do psychologists follow ethical guidelines?

    a. Psychologists would not want the cost of participating in an experiment to be too high in comparison to the information to be gained.
    b. The American Psychological Association has set standards for psychologists to follow when conducting research and treating patients.
    c. Stress and pain could act as confounding variables in an experiment.
    d. All of the above

20. A psychologist is planning to examine the contributions of heredity and environment to intelligence. Of the methods listed below, the psychologist is most likely to use a(n)
    a. adoption study.
    b. experiment.
    c. factor analysis.
    d. naturalistic observation.

Total Correct (See answer key) _____

ANSWERS TO FILL-IN-THE-BLANKS KEY TERMS

1. critical thinking (see Thinking Critically About Psychology (or Anything Else))

2. hypothesis (see Critical Thinking and Scientific Research)

3. operational definition (see Critical Thinking and Scientific Research)

4. Observational methods (see Observational Methods: Watching Behavior)

5. independent variable (see Experiments: Exploring Cause and Effect)

6. experimental (see Experiments: Exploring Cause and Effect)

7. control (see Experiments: Exploring Cause and Effect)

8. double-blind (see Experiments: Exploring Cause and Effect)

9. Confounds (see Experiments: Exploring Cause and Effect)

10. placebo (see Experiments: Exploring Cause and Effect)

11. case study (see Case Studies: Taking a Closer Look)

12. random (see Experiments: Exploring Cause and Effect)

13. Statistical reliability (see Critical Thinking and Scientific Research)

14. statistical significance (see Inferential Statistics)

15. Behavioral genetics (see Linkages: Psychological Research Methods and Behavioral Genetics)

ANSWERS TO CONCEPTS AND EXERCISES

Research Methods

1. j is the answer.   Experiments are usually tests of hypotheses based on descriptive and correlational data. Correlations, even very strong ones, do not demonstrate causation. Scientists do experiments to determine whether there is a causative relationship between strongly correlated variables. (see Correlation and Correlation Coefficients)

2. e is the answer.   Once scientists decide to do an experiment, they must identify and define the independent and dependent variables. (see Experiments: Exploring Cause and Effect)

3. a is the answer.   Sometimes an operational definition is needed to specify how one or more of the variables will be measured. (see Critical Thinking and Scientific Research)

4. i is the answer.   Experiments have two groups: experimental and control. Participants should be assigned randomly to these groups to reduce the effect of random variables. (see Experiments: Exploring Cause and Effect)

5. g is the answer.   In an experiment, researchers systematically manipulate the independent variable. (see Experiments: Exploring Cause and Effect)

6. b is the answer.   Then they measure the dependent variable. (see Experiments: Exploring Cause and Effect)

7. f is the answer.   Measurements of the dependent variable are compared for the experimental and control groups. (see Experiments: Exploring Cause and Effect)

8. k is the answer.   Statistical methods determine whether the differences between the dependent variables in the control and experimental groups occurred by chance. (see Inferential Statistics)

Choose Your Method

1. b is the answer.   <u>Experiments</u> indicate causation. The question here is whether sleep loss *causes* changes in problem-solving ability. None of the other methods listed shows causation. (see Experiments: Exploring Cause and Effect)

2. d is the answer.   This is a rare phenomenon, examination of which requires that a great deal of information be gathered about one person (the child). Researchers would conduct a <u>case study</u> in such circumstances. (see Case Studies: Taking a Closer Look)

3. c is the answer.   <u>Naturalistic observation</u> would provide the data necessary to answer this question. The researcher would *observe* the attention span of five-year-old children at the playground, rather than asking them about it. (see Observational Methods: Watching Behavior)

4. a is the answer.   <u>Surveys</u> are used to find out people's opinions. (see Surveys: Looking at the Big Picture)

ANSWERS TO CRITICAL THINKING

Martina lists the five critical thinking questions for Sam. Each of her questions is followed by its parallel question from the text.

1. What do I think happened? (*What am I being asked to believe or accept?*)

2. Why do I believe my hypothesis? (*What evidence is available to support the assertion?*)

3. Is there a solution to the crime that explains all the evidence? (*Are there alternative ways of interpreting the evidence?*)

4. What more do we need in order to prove I am right? (*What additional evidence would help evaluate the alternatives?*)

5. Can I be certain that I am right? (*What conclusions are most reasonable?*)

Throughout the remaining chapters, Sam and Martina have to solve a variety of cases. As you work through each case, sharpen your own critical thinking skills. Remember, critical thinking can be applied to every aspect of your life, not just to your psychology studies and exams.

ANSWERS TO MULTIPLE-CHOICE QUESTIONS

Circle the question numbers you answered correctly.

Quiz 1

1. c is the answer.   Asking, "How can I best justify the conclusion I would like to reach?" is not part of the five steps of critical thinking as outlined in your text. In fact, this question is diametrically opposed to the spirit of critical thinking. Critical thinking is the process of assessing claims and making judgments on the basis of well-supported evidence. This question seems more interested in supporting a particular conclusion, not evaluating the validity of it. (see Thinking Critically About Psychology(or Anything Else))

    a, b, d.   These questions are all part of the five steps of critical thinking outlined in your text.

2. a is the answer.   Kara uses the catalog listings of courses with study-abroad, internship, clinical, and service-learning experiences to operationally define experiential learning on her campus. (see Thinking Critically About Psychology (or Anything Else))

    a.   Experiential learning is the variable of interest, but it alone does not tell one what to measure or observe. Kara's specific definition of catalog descriptions does accomplish this operationalization.

    c.   Faculty and staff were the individuals questioned to help Kara begin to operationally define the construct of experiential learning, but they are not an operational definition.

    d.   These categories are part of Kara's operational definition, but many courses may have elements of clinical or service-learning experience that are not necessarily reflected in a catalog. Her operational definition limits the inclusion of courses that specifically list these elements in the course catalog. This is a good answer, but not the best one, given the description of Kara's research process.

3. b is the answer.   This question asks something that would not be ethical to address in a pure experimental design. It would not be ethical to randomly assign some children to poor-quality day care and others to high-quality day care just to see the effects of this on parent-child attachments. It would, however, be ethical to observe this as it naturally occurs, using either surveys or naturalistic observations. These are both correlational designs. Also, this question does not ask specifically about cause and effect, but about associations, which correlations can assess. (see Research Methods in Psychology)

    a, c.   Both of these research questions ask about cause-effect relations and therefore would require an experimental design.

    d.   b is the correct answer.

4. b is the answer.   Dr. Dekka must first describe the phenomenon before she can then make predictions, exert control, or explain it. (see Research Methods in Psychology)

    a.   This is likely to be her second goal. After describing the phenomenon, she will generate predictions about it.

    c, d.   Her first goal was probably not to control or explain the phenomenon, because she has chosen descriptive methods. If her goal had been to control or explain, she would have chosen an experiment.

5. c is the answer.   This is the definition of a naturalistic observation. (see Observational Methods: Watching Behavior)

    a.   This is the definition of a case study.

    b.   This is the definition of a survey.

    d.   This is the definition of an experiment.

6.   c is the answer. A case study is the intense observation of a single exemplar of a phenomenon of interest. It is best used when something is so rare that no other research methods would be viable. (see Case Studies: Taking a Closer Look)

   a.   This is a survey.

   b.   This is a naturalistic observation

   d.   This is an experiment.

7.   d is the answer.   Dependent variables are measured in an experiment. (see Experiments: Exploring Cause and Effect)

   a.   Random variables are confounding variables in which uncontrolled or uncontrollable factors affect the dependent variable, along with or instead of the independent variable.

   b.   Confounding variables are factors that, usually unintentionally, vary with the independent variable and thus could exert influence on the dependent variable, which is being measured.

   c.   The independent variable is manipulated, not measured.

8.   c is the answer.   This limitation of the survey method is very difficult to avoid, because there is no way to guarantee that people will not be influenced by what they think they *should* say on a survey. Although you can minimize the chance of this by assuring anonymity, response distortions may still be present for a variety of reasons. (see Surveys: Looking at the Big Picture)

   a.   Proper wording is difficult, but pilot-testing of item wordings can help reveal potential problems that can be solved before a full-scale survey is performed.

   b.   Although getting a representative sample is difficult, with careful study of the population of interest ahead of time, it can be very closely approximated.

   d.   c is the hardest threat to the validity of a survey to deal with because it involves controlling response bias (which is inherently out of the researcher's direct control), whereas wording and sampling are under the researcher's control.

9.   d is the answer.   In a double-blind experimental design, neither the subjects nor the experimenters know who has received the independent variable. The *experimenters cannot bias* the data in favor of their hypothesis, because they do not know which subjects received the independent variable. (see Experiments: Exploring Cause and Effect)

   a.   An operational definition is a statement of how a variable (for example, anxiety) is to be measured.

   b.   Naturalistic observation is a research method but not an experimental design.

   c.   Random refers to the means by which the subjects were selected for a study. It is not an experimental method.

10.   c is the answer.   Akuba manipulated, or determined, which class would receive which treatment. Therefore, receiving group activities versus lectures is the independent variable. (see Experiments: Exploring Cause and Effect)

   a.   A confounding variable would be a variable that could affect the dependent variable along with the independent variable.

   b.   The dependent variable in this study would be the test scores, because these were measured rather than manipulated.

   d.   A placebo is a treatment that contains no active effect but may produce an effect on the dependent variable through participant expectation.

11.   b is the answer.   The experimental group receives the independent variable. (see Experiments: Exploring Cause and Effect)

a.   The control group receives a placebo or no treatment.

c, d.   Operational groups and random groups are not part of experimental design; they do not exist.

12.   d is the answer.   Following this procedure will ensure that every student in the population Susan wishes to study (first-year students at her university) will have an equal chance of being selected for participation in the experiment. (see Selecting Human Participants for Research)

a.   The use of one dorm will not give every first-year student an equal chance of being selected. Also, a particular dorm might house a certain kind of student. For example, the majority of students living in a dorm located next to the College of Agriculture might be agriculture majors who live there because of the convenient location. But Susan is interested in *all* first-year students, not just agriculture students.

b.   Some first-year students may not take introductory psychology. Therefore, first-year students do not all have an equal chance of being selected for the study.

c.   Some first-year students may not have a phone or a listed phone number.

13.   a is the answer.   Behavioral genetics is the study of how genes (nature) and the environment (nurture) influence behavior. (see Linkages: Psychological Research Methods and Behavioral Genetics)

b.   Genetic engineering and the field of behavioral genetics are not the same thing. A genetic engineer, while interested in the role of genes in behavior, would use the results of genetics research to alter the gene set.

c.   "Pop" psychology is short for "popular" psychology, which offers answers that are easy rather than well-supported by research. A "pop" psychologist would be more likely to write an advice book than to conduct genetic research.

d.   Replicability means consistent results over many experiments. Replicating or repeating an outcome would most likely interest any scientist, but it does not describe the interest in problems that run in families.

14.   b is the answer.   The median is the middle score of a distribution and is a better description of a sample than the mean when the sample includes extreme scores. (see Descriptive Statistics)

a.   The mean would be affected by the extreme score to give the impression that there was typically more sharing than there truly was. (With the high score of 35, the Group A mean is about 12.3; without it the Group A mean would be 8.5, which is closer to most of the numbers.)

c.   There is no mode in Group A because no scores were repeated.

d.   The range is not a measure of central tendency; it would tell only the distance between the highest and lowest scores.

15.   c is the answer.   Group B scores are very close to one another; therefore, the standard deviation for Group B should be smaller than for Group A, which has an extreme score. (see Descriptive Statistics)

a.   The range for Group A would be 30; the range for Group B would be 5. Therefore, Group A's range is larger.

b.   A standard deviation could be calculated for Group A.

d.   Groups A and B do not have the same range.

16. d is the answer.   Statistically different means would show that the differences were unlikely to occur due to chance; this would be an indication that the experiment had an effect. (see Inferential Statistics)

  a.   A large mean for the caffeine group would be a small amount of evidence for the hypothesis; however, the sugar pill group could also have a large mean.

  b.   Correlations do not support a hypothesis that one group will be different from another; they would support a hypothesis that two variables are related.

  c.   A small range shows only that the subjects had similar scores (number of cases solved), not that the control group had lower scores.

17. b is the answer.   The strongest correlation coefficient possible is 1.00. No other coefficient listed is closer to a perfect correlation than −.99. (see Descriptive Statistics)

  a.   The strength and direction of a correlation are independent of each other. The positive or negative sign indicates the direction, and the number indicates the strength: the closer to 1.00, the stronger the correlation. As −.99 is closer to −1.00 than +.75 is to +1.00, −.99 is the stronger correlation.

  c, d.   You may have thought that a positive or negative .01 correlation coefficient represented a perfect correlation. However, a perfect correlation is +1.00 or −1.00.

18. a is the answer.   Neuropsychology is the study of the relationships among brain activity, thinking, and behavior. (see Case Studies: Taking a Closer Look)

  b.   This is the definition of epigenetics.

  c.   This is the definition of behavioral genetics.

  d.   This is the definition of psychology in general, not neuropsychology.

19. c is the answer.   A negative correlation tells us that as one variable (seat-belt use) increases, the other variable (accident-related deaths) decreases. (see Descriptive Statistics)

  a.   Correlations do not imply causation. Also, the variables here are the number of seat belts worn and the number of accident-related deaths, not the number of accidents.

  b.   This general statement does not follow from the information given and suggests causation. The information given specifies an inverse relationship between seat-belt laws and accident-related deaths.

  d.   Correlations do not imply causation. Also, the variable is the number of accident-related deaths, not the number of accidents.

20. a is the answer.   The ethical guidelines followed by psychologists require that researchers describe the study well enough for potential participants to give their informed consent to be involved. (see Ethical Guidelines for Psychologists)

  b.   Participants should not expect a psychologist conducting research to give them counseling. Perhaps if it became clear that a participant was in distress the researcher could recommend that he or she see a clinical or counseling psychologist, but not all researchers are trained in counseling.

  c.   Psychoanalysis would be the job of a psychodynamic therapist, not a researcher conducting a study.

  d.   If an experiment requires that participants be misled, the researcher is required to disclose fully the reasoning behind the study after it is completed.

Now turn to the quiz analysis table at the end of this chapter to find which areas you know well and which areas you need to work on. Circle the numbers in the table for items on Quiz 1 that you answered correctly.

Quiz 2

1.   a is the answer.   To think critically about the product offered, we should ask ourselves if there are other ways of interpreting the evidence. For example, were the people giving their testimonials because they were paid rather than because they used and benefited from the Run-O-Sizer? Are there other methods for achieving the same results? Could the photos have been altered to make the results look more dramatic? (see Thinking Critically About Psychology (or Anything Else))

   b.   Making your decision based on the testimonials would mean ignoring sources of information such as consumer magazines and fitness experts.

   c.   The price is important to consider, but it says very little about the product's effectiveness or safety, or the likelihood you would use it.

   d.   A guarantee might seem to make the purchase risk free, but if the product is not worthwhile, you will have wasted time trying it and may still lose money. Therefore, a critical thinker will evaluate the claims made about the Run-O-Sizer before examining the guarantee.

2.   d is the answer.   Science seeks to describe, predict, control, and explain. (see Research Methods in Psychology)

   a, b, c. Measurement, understanding, reasoning, and critical thinking are processes involved in pursuing scientific goals, but are not goals specific to research methods.

3.   c is the answer.   To record the behavior of people during their usual activities is naturalistic observation. (see Observational Methods: Watching Behavior)

   a.   A case study is used to describe a rare condition completely; therefore, it would not describe average behaviors.

   b.   A researcher would be unlikely to use an experiment, because behavior during a laboratory-simulated exam may be different from behavior during an actual exam.

   d.   Using a survey would be a good way to find out how students describe their behavior during an exam, but it would not show what they look like, the number of times they shifted in their seats, and so on. In addition, their description might not match their behavior.

4.   a is the answer.   The subjects in the experimental group may report less depression because they think fluoxetine has medicinal value. (see Experiments: Exploring Cause and Effect)

   b.   Before the FDA approves a drug, a clear cause-effect relationship between the drug and the desired effect (decreased depression) must be demonstrated with very few side effects. Case studies are not used to detect cause-effect relationships; they describe a phenomenon of interest.

   c.   The experimental design is incorrect. Both the experimental and the control groups should have been given pills. The experiment should be repeated using a double-blind design.

   d.   Random samples are excellent for use in experiments and other types of research.

5.   c is the answer.   An operational definition, which will describe how depression is measured, can help the FDA determine whether patients experienced a change in level of depression. To understand why an operational definition is necessary, consider the following scenario. Joe, a

subject in the experiment, is very, very depressed. After receiving the drug, he scores higher on the test. His test results show that he is still depressed, but not as depressed as he was prior to taking the drug. By using the test to operationally define depression, the FDA was able to measure a *change* in depression. If, however, the FDA had merely asked Joe how he felt, he might have responded that he was depressed both before and after taking the drug. (see Thinking Critically About Psychology (or Anything Else))

a, b.　The independent variable is fluoxetine. Measuring the amount of a drug administered to the subjects is easy. It does not require an operational definition.

d.　There was no placebo.

6.　a is the answer.　　The treatment administered to the experimental group is always the independent variable. (see Experiments: Exploring Cause and Effect)

b.　The dependent variable is depression.

c.　The operational definition of depression is a low score on a questionnaire.

d.　Because the sample used was purely random, the presence of random variables has been controlled.

7.　c is the answer.　　Experiments are used to conduct controlled research. Experimental and control groups are formed, and both groups are treated identically except the administration of the independent variable in the experimental group. At the end of the experiment, the dependent variable is measured in both groups. If there is a difference between the two groups on the dependent variable, that difference can only have been caused by the independent variable. (see Research Methods in Psychology)

a, b, d. Naturalistic observation, surveys, and case studies are all descriptive data collection methods.

8.　b is the answer.　　Surveys are used to collect descriptive data on people's attitudes, beliefs, opinions, and behavioral intentions. (see Surveys: Looking at the Big Picture)

a.　Experiments are controlled methods of establishing a cause-effect relationship.

c.　Case studies are used to collect descriptive information from a particular individual, group, or situation. Case studies usually combine several forms of data collection—observations, interviews, tests, and analyses of written records. Case studies provide a close-up, in-depth view of subjects, whereas surveys paint a broad portrait.

d.　Naturalistic observation is used to collect behavioral information from the subjects' natural environment.

9.　c is the answer.　　Multiple personality disorder is a rare problem, making a case study the most likely way to examine this hypothesis. (see Case Studies: Taking a Closer Look)

a.　Trying to improve students' study methods would not be something rare and could be studied with an experiment.

b.　Experiencing an unpleasant odor could be easily manipulated in the laboratory with few negative consequences; therefore, this hypothesis could be studied in an experiment.

d.　All of the above are not true.

10. b is the answer.   Experiments are used to study cause-effect relationships. (see Experiments: Exploring Cause and Effect)

   a.   A correlational study will describe the strength and quality of the relationship between two variables, but this description is not sufficient to determine if a causal relationship exists between the variables.

   c.   Because naturalistic observation involves watching people in their usual environments, it cannot be used to find out what changes a person's reaction to a negative event. Not only would the researcher be unable to wait for at least two negative events to occur for each subject, but he or she also could not determine which variables might have caused a change (or lack of change) in the subject's behavior.

   d.   A survey does not allow variables to be controlled to look for the effect on other variables.

11. d is the answer.   Suppose an experimenter finds significant differences between the experimental group and the control group. If random variables exist in the experimental group but not the control group, for example, the experimenter cannot be sure what caused his results—the independent or the random variables. Random variables are a problem because they are difficult to control; sometimes they cannot be controlled. All of the variables listed would be difficult or costly for an experimenter to quantify and control. (see Experiments: Exploring Cause and Effect)

12. a is the answer.   A person with a rare condition is best studied in depth through a case study. (see Case Studies: Taking a Closer Look)

   b.   An experiment could not be conducted to see if lightning causes unusual behavior; it would be wrong.

   c.   A researcher would not use naturalistic observation to gain understanding of a person with an unusual problem, because unobtrusively watching a person does not provide information about family background, health history, current physical condition, and so on.

   d.   To survey a person who is having trouble regulating her behavior and concentrating would be difficult, if not impossible. In addition, a survey includes more than one or a few participants because its purpose is to discover something about a group of people.

13. c is the answer.   Confounding variables are factors that affect the dependent variable along with, or instead of, the independent variable. When a researcher fails to include a placebo condition and observes an effect of a treatment, then the effect may be due to the treatment, or to participant expectancy, or both. The placebo effect of participant expectancy is a confounding variable. (see Experiments: Exploring Cause and Effect)

   a.   Independent variables are intentionally manipulated by the researchers. The placebo effect, or participant expectancy, is not.

   b.   The dependent variable is measured by the researchers. The placebo effect occurs when participants expect a treatment to have a particular effect, and the expectancy itself leads the effect to occur.

   d.   Though two variables may be correlated, there is no such thing as a "correlational variable."

14. a is the answer.   Statistical validity means that a test score or evidence from research measures what is claims it measures. (see Thinking Critically about Psychology (or Anything Else))

   b.   This is the definition of statistical reliability, not validity.

   c.   Randomization does not mean that results have statistical validity.

   d.   Positive correlations do not indicate statistical validity.

15. b is the answer.   10 is the most frequently occurring score. (see Descriptive Statistics)

   a.   The mean of this data set is 12. It is calculated by summing the values of all the scores and dividing by the number of scores.

   c.   The median of this data set is 11. It is the score that cuts the data set in half.

   d.   The range is 12. It is calculated by subtracting the lowest score from the highest score.

16. b is the answer.   In a positive correlation, both variables *vary* in the same direction together; as one increases so does the other (and vice versa). (see Descriptive Statistics)

   a.   A negative correlation tells us that as one variable increases, the other decreases.

   c, d.   Correlations do not imply causation. One can never conclude that one variable *causes* the other to change in any direction based on a correlation—regardless of its positive or negative value.

17. b is the answer.   The average test scores were very low. Because the recruiter wants to find students with the highest scores, he needs the data set with the greatest number of scores that are very distant from the mean. The standard deviation is a measure of variability; it describes the average distance from the mean in a data set. If the standard deviation is large, then there will be a large number of extreme scores; this, in turn, means there is a large probability that some scores are very high. Therefore, the recruiter should look at the data sets that have the largest standard deviations to find students who scored very high on the intelligence test. (see Descriptive Statistics)

   a.   The range is also a measure of variability. If the range is large, then the recruiter knows that at least one score in the data set is very low or very high. But the standard deviation takes into account more than two test scores and is a better measure of the probability that more than one high score exists in a data set.

   c.   The recruiter has already identified the mean, median, and mode—all measures of central tendency—for the data sets.

   d.   Operational definitions are used to describe ways of measuring a given variable (for example, anxiety).

18. c is the answer.   A positive correlation indicates that as one variable increases, the other variable increases. This type of relationship supports the data; as alcohol consumption increases, so does decision-making time. (see Descriptive Statistics)

   a, d.   A negative correlation indicates that as one variable increases, the other decreases. This relationship does not fit the data.

   b.   There is no such thing as a curvilinear correlation. Curvilinear correlations do not exist.

19. d is the answer.   Psychologists follow ethical guidelines because they want their studies to benefit society, because specific guidelines are set forth by several organizations, and because undue stress and pain might become confounding variables in an experiment. (see Ethical Guidelines for Psychologists)

   a.   Psychologists do not want the cost of participating in an experiment to be too high in comparison to the information gained. This is correct, but so are b and c, which makes "all of the above" the best answer.

   b.   The APA does set ethical standards for conducting research and treating patients, so this is correct, but so are a and c, which makes "all of the above" the best answer.

   c.   Stress and pain could be confounding variables in an experiment, so this is correct, but so are a and b, which makes "all of the above" the best answer.

20. a is the answer.   The studies used in such behavioral genetics research include adoption, family, and twin studies. (see Linkages: Psychological Research Methods and Behavioral Genetics)

   b.   An experiment would be a controlled study in which, for example, participants were assigned to families; therefore, it would not be ethical.

   c.   Factor analysis is a correlational method used to identify variables, such as personality traits, that tend to occur together. Factor analysis would not help in determining what the relative effects of environment and genetics are.

   d.   A psychologist using naturalistic observation would watch and record behaviors but could make no conclusions about the impact of heredity or environment on something like intelligence.

Now turn to the quiz analysis table at the end of this chapter to find which areas you know well and which areas you need to work on. Circle the numbers in the table for items on Quiz 2 that you answered correctly.

For each question you answered correctly, circle its number. (Quiz 1 numbers are not shaded; Quiz 2 numbers are shaded.) Are there patterns in the types of questions or the topics you got wrong that could direct your further study? Did you improve from Quiz 1 to Quiz 2?

QUIZ REVIEW

Topic	Type of Question		
	Definition	**Comprehension**	**Application**
Thinking Critically About Psychology (or Anything Else)		1	2
	14		1, 5
Research Methods in Psychology		3	4
	2	7	
Observational Methods: Watching Behavior	5		
			3
Case Studies: Taking a Closer Look	18		6
			9, 12
Surveys: Looking at the Big Picture		8	
	8		
Experiments: Exploring Cause and Effect	7	9	10, 11
		13	4, 6, 10, 11
Selecting Human Participants for Research			12
Linkages: Psychological Research Methods and Behavioral Genetics		13	
	20		
Statistical Analysis of Research Results			
Descriptive Statistics		17	14, 15 19
	16		15, 17, 18
Inferential Statistics			16
Ethical Guidelines for Psychologists			20
		19	

Total correct by quiz:

Quiz 1:
Quiz 2:

CHAPTER 3

Biological Aspects of Psychology

Biological psychology is the study of the physical and chemical factors that, either alone or through interaction with the environment, influence behavior and mental processes. The nervous system, one of the most important biological factors involved in behavior, receives input about the environment, processes it, and orchestrates outputs such as motor behavior and thought.

OUTLINE

I. THE NERVOUS SYSTEM
    A. Cells of the Nervous System
        1. Neurons are cells that are specialized to respond rapidly to signals and quickly send off signals of their own. Glial cells also serve a communication function by holding neurons in place, direct their growth and repair, and keep their chemical environment stable. Glial cells can also release and respond to chemicals from neurons.
            a) Common features of neurons include an outer membrane that acts as a fine screen, a cell body which contains a nucleus, and mitochondria which are structures that turn oxygen and glucose into energy.
            b) Neurons have special structural features. Axons are the fibers that carry signals away from the cell. Dendrites are the fibers that receive signals from nearby neurons. Each neuron usually has one axon but may have many dendrites. The neuron must also have an excitable surface membrane and communicate across synapses, the tiny gaps between the dendrite of one neuron and the axon of the next.
    B. Action Potentials
        1. The semipermeable membrane of the neuron keeps positively charged sodium and calcium ions from freely entering the axon through the gates or channels. As a result, the membrane becomes electrically polarized, such that the inside of the cell is more negatively charged than the outside. When an action potential occurs, some part of the axon membrane becomes depolarized, causing a sodium or calcium gate to open. Sodium rushes into the axon, causing the neighboring sodium gates to open as well, and more sodium rushes in. This chain of events occurs along the entire length of the axon.
        2. The neuron either fires or does not fire, in an all-or-none type of signal. The speed of the action potential is constant as it travels down the axon. If a neuron is larger or coated with myelin, action potentials will be faster. The length of the pause between action potentials is known as the refractory period and determines the rate or number of action potentials that occurs within a given time unit. Messages in the nervous system are coded by the speed and rate of action potentials.
    C. Synapses and Communication between Neurons
        Communication between neurons occurs at the synapse.
        1. *Neurotransmitters*. Communication at the synapse is chemical in nature. Neurotransmitters are chemicals that carry the signal across the synapse to the postsynaptic cell (usually a dendrite). When neurotransmitters bind to receptors (also called neural receptors) in the postsynaptic cell, a membrane potential is created.

2. *Excitatory and Inhibitory Signals.* When a postsynaptic cell is reached by a neurotransmitter, the postsynaptic membrane becomes depolarized or hyperpolarized, creating a postsynaptic potential, and the signal once again becomes electric in nature. A depolarized membrane will cause an excitatory postsynaptic potential (EPSP), and a hyperpolarized membrane will cause an inhibitory postsynaptic potential (IPSP). The combined impact of the many EPSPs and IPSPs will determine whether or not an action potential will occur.

D. Organization and Functions of the Nervous System
   1. Neurons in the brain and spinal cord are organized into groups called neural networks. Small networks are organized into bigger networks.
   2. The nervous system conveys information through the activity of groups of cells firing together in varying combination. The groups of cells that provide information about the environment are the sensory system, while the group that influences muscles and other organs to respond to the environment are called the motor system.
   3. The nervous system has two main divisions. The central nervous system (CNS) processes information and is encased in bone. The CNS is made up of the brain and spinal cord. The peripheral nervous system (PNS) extends throughout the body to relay information to and from the brain.

II. THE PERIPHERAL NERVOUS SYSTEM: KEEPING IN TOUCH WITH THE WORLD
The peripheral nervous system has two components: the somatic and autonomic systems.
   A. The Somatic Nervous System
      1. The somatic system carries information from the senses to the CNS and sends movement instructions back to the muscles.
      2. Sensory neurons bring information to the brain, while motor neurons carry information from the brain to direct motion.
   B. The Autonomic Nervous System
      1. The autonomic system contains the parasympathetic nervous system and the sympathetic nervous system.
      2. The sympathetic nervous system mobilizes the body for action, initiating the fight-or-flight response. The parasympathetic nervous system does the opposite: It slows organ and gland activity to conserve the body's energy.

III. CENTRAL NERVOUS SYSTEM: MAKING SENSE OF THE WORLD
The central nervous system (CNS) is made up of collections of neuronal cell bodies called nuclei and the fiber tracts or pathways that connect them.
   A. The Spinal Cord
      1. The spinal cord carries messages to and from the brain. Reflexes—quick, involuntary muscular responses (through efferent neurons) that are initiated on the basis of incoming sensory information (through afferent neurons)—occur in the spinal cord without instruction from the brain. The brain is informed of each reflex after it occurs.
      2. The spinal cord is an example of a feedback system, a process in which information about an action's results are conveyed back to the source of the action so that further adjustments to the activity can be made.
   B. The Brain
      1. A variety of modern brain-scanning techniques exist to help study the brain. PET scans can locate cell activity by locating where glucose and other fuels become concentrated, but is not good at providing structural information about the brain. MRI provides detailed structural information about the brain, and fMRI combines the benefits of both technologies. Newer techniques include Diffusion Tensor Imaging (DTI) and Transcranial Magnetic Stimulation (TMS).
      2. *The Hindbrain.* Hindbrain structures such as the medulla oblongata control vital functions (for example, blood pressure, heart rate, and breathing). The reticular

formation is a network of cells running throughout the hindbrain and into the midbrain that alters the activity of other brain structures. For example, the locus coeruleus, an area thought to be involved in the state of vigilance, is activated by the reticular formation. The cerebellum controls finely coordinated movements, including speech, as well as other processes such as our sense of timing.

3. *The Midbrain.* Located between the hindbrain and forebrain, the midbrain controls certain automatic behaviors. The substantia nigra is a midbrain structure that, together with the striatum, is involved in initiating smooth movement.

4. *The Forebrain.* The forebrain is the most highly developed part of the human brain. The thalamus lies deep within the brain and relays sensory signals. Below it lies the hypothalamus, which regulates basic drives. The suprachiasmatic nuclei, part of the hypothalamus, determines our biological rhythms. The amygdala and hippocampus are part of the limbic system, which plays an important role in regulating emotion and is involved in memory and other thought processes.

C. Thinking Critically: What Can fMRI Tell Us about Behavior and Mental Processes?
What am I being asked to believe or accept?
Scientists using fMRI can determine what parts of the brain cause various behaviors and mental processes.
Is there evidence available to support the claim?
When a participant in an fMRI experiment thinks or feels something, you can see the colors in the brain scan change.
Can the evidence be interpreted another way?
Sometimes the brain scan looks similar regardless of whether the person is actually doing the behavior in question or watching someone else do it (*mirror-image mechanisms*).
What evidence would help to evaluate the alternatives?
As the quality of fMRI improves, better images will result, but a greater understanding of correlation and causation in fMRI is needed. TMS may help sort out these differences.
What conclusions are most reasonable?
Although fMRI is a useful tool that offers detailed images of the brain structure and function, it will not likely explain how the brain creates behavior and mental processes on its own.

D. Focus on Research Methods: Manipulating Genes in Animal Models of Human Disease
To test hypotheses about the cause of Alzheimer's disease, experimenters implanted a gene in mice and found that it created brain damage similar to Alzheimer's. When these abnormalities are introduced into mice, the mice do tend to develop plaque in the brain, but not tangles, both of which are associated with Alzheimer's disease. Scientists are getting close to an animal model of this disease, but still have a way to go in completely understanding it.

E. The Cerebral Cortex
The cerebral cortex is the outer surface of the cerebrum or cerebral hemispheres. The frontal, parietal, occipital, and temporal lobes are used as physical landmarks for describing the cortex. The functional areas of the cortex include the sensory, motor, and association cortex.

1. *Sensory Cortex.* The sensory cortex receives sensory information.
2. *Motor Cortex.* The motor cortex neurons control the onset of voluntary movement.
3. *Association Cortex.* The association cortex receives information from more than one sense and combines sensory and motor information. Aphasia, a deficit in understanding and producing language, is caused by damage to Broca's area or Wernicke's area. Many areas of the brain are related to language; several are associated with specific semantic abilities.

F. The Divided Brain in a Unified Self
  1. <u>Lateral dominance</u> (<u>lateralization</u>) is the idea that each side of the brain might be specialized to perform specific functions.
  2. *Split-Brain Studies.* Split-brain (severed <u>corpus callosum</u>) data demonstrate that each hemisphere is superior in certain abilities. The left hemisphere controls spoken language, and the right controls recognition of faces and tasks dealing with spatial relations, such as drawing three-dimensional shapes. In addition, the left hemisphere controls the right side of the body, and the right hemisphere controls the left side.
  1. *Lateralization of Normal Brains.* Data collected from people with intact brains demonstrate the superiority of the left hemisphere in logical thinking and language abilities. The right hemisphere exhibits better spatial, artistic, and musical abilities. But keep in mind that, although the two halves of the brain may have lateralized abilities, the cerebral hemispheres work closely together.
G. Plasticity in the Central Nervous System
  1. <u>Neural plasticity</u> is the brain's ability to strengthen neural connections and establish new connections. Unfortunately, synaptic plasticity is somewhat limited. New neurons cannot be generated, and exact replication of the many synaptic connections prior to brain damage is almost impossible. However, old neurons do produce new axons and dendrites, which make new connections.
  2. Scientists are continually trying new methods to reproduce and grow nerve cells. Several methods for enhancing brain-damage recovery are under study, such as tissue transplants from a still-developing fetal brain into the brain of a mammal. This has shown promise, but is controversial because it uses tissue from aborted fetuses.
  3. Recent research has found some cell division in the CNS of adults, which led to the discovery of neural <u>stem cells</u> in the adult brain. This finding may abate the ethical controversy surrounding the use of embryonic stem cells if stem cells can be harvested from other sources in the adult.
H. Linkages: Human Development and the Changing Brain
  Patterns of behavioral development in infants are correlated with plastic changes in activity and structure in the developing brain. During development, the brain overproduces neural connections and, based on experience, establishes which connections are needed and then eliminates the extras. Even in adulthood, the number of connections is affected by experience: stimulating environments produce greater numbers of connections.

IV. THE CHEMISTRY OF PSYCHOLOGY
  A group of neurons that communicates with the same neurotransmitter is called a neurotransmitter system. Some neurotransmitter systems are responsible for certain behaviors or problems.
  A. Three Classes of Neurotransmitters
    1. *Small molecules* are found in both the CNS and PNS. Below are six examples of small molecules that function as neurotransmitters.
      a) <u>Acetylcholine</u> controls the contraction of muscles and is used by neurons in the parasympathetic nervous system. In the brain, cholinergic neurons are involved in movement and memory. A loss of cholinergic neurons is linked to Alzheimer's disease.
      b) Arousal is the main task of <u>norepinephrine</u>, which is also known as noradrenaline. Noradrenaline is used by neurons in the sympathetic nervous system and in the locus coeruleus.
      c) Sleep, moods, and appetite are influenced by <u>serotonin</u>. Antidepressants such as Paxil or Zoloft seem to work on serotonin systems.
      d) Problems with the <u>dopamine</u> system in the substantia nigra and striatum contribute to Parkinson's disease, which leads to difficulty in the initiation of movement. Dopamine is also involved in the experience of pleasure. Malfunctioning dopaminergic neurons may be partly responsible for schizophrenia, a psychological disorder characterized by distorted perception, emotion, and thought.

e)   Gamma-amino butyric acid, or GABA, is the major inhibitory transmitter of the central nervous system. Huntington's disease causes a loss of GABA-using neurons and results in uncontrollable movement of the arms and legs. GABA systems have also been implicated in epilepsy.

f)   The major excitatory neurotransmitter in the CNS is glutamate. Glutamate helps strengthen synaptic connections, which may be the origin of learning and memory.

2.   *Peptides* were discovered as scientists investigated opiates, substances derived from the poppy flower.

a)   Endorphins, natural opiate-like compounds, can reduce pain and cause sleep.

3.   *Gases* were most recently discovered to act as neurotransmitters.

a)   *Nitric oxide* and *carbon monoxide* are gases that function as neurotransmitters.

B.   Thinking Critically: Are There Drugs That Can Make You Smarter?

V.   THE ENDOCRINE SYSTEM: COORDINATING THE INTERNAL WORLD
The endocrine system, like the nervous system, influences a wide variety of behaviors. Glands secrete hormones, which travel via the bloodstream and affect coordinated systems of target tissues and organs, producing such responses as the fight-or-flight syndrome (also called the fight-flight reaction). A *negative feedback system* involving the brain regulates the amount of hormone released.

KEY TERMS

1.   **Biological psychology** is the psychological specialty focused on the physical and chemical changes that cause, and occur in response to, behavior and mental processes. (see introductory section)

Example: Changes in brain biochemicals are associated with depression.

REMEMBER: Biological psychology is the study of the *biological* factors that influence *psychological* phenomena.

2.   The **nervous system** is a complex combination of cells whose primary function is to allow an organism to gain information about what is going on inside and outside the body and to respond appropriately. (see introductory section)

Example: When we stand at the curb of a busy street, our nervous system receives sensory information about oncoming traffic, makes a decision to cross the street at a particular moment, and controls the movement (output) of stepping off the curb and crossing the street.

3.   **Neurons** are the fundamental units of the nervous system, nerve cells. (see Cells of the Nervous System)

REMEMBER: A neuron is similar to a computer in that information comes in, is processed, and is sent out.

4.   **Glial cells** are cells in the nervous system that hold neurons together and help them communicate with one another. (see Cells of the Nervous System)

REMEMBER: Glial means "glue"; part of the glial cells' job is to help "glue" neurons together and facilitate communication among them.

5.   **Axons** are fibers that carry signals from the body of a neuron out to communication with other neurons. (see Cells of the Nervous System)

REMEMBER: Axons create action potentials. Most of the time, the action potential travels from the cell body to the end of the axon. (See Key Term 8)

6. **Dendrites** are neuron fibers that receive signals from the axons of other neurons and carry those signals to the cell body. (see Cells of the Nervous System)

    REMEMBER: <u>De</u>ndrites <u>de</u>tect signals from other neurons.

7. **Synapses** are the tiny gaps between neurons across which they communicate. (see Cells of the Nervous System)

    The presynaptic cell sends a message and the postsynaptic cell receives that message. Typically, the axon is the presynaptic cell, and the dendrite is the postsynaptic cell. Neurotransmitters released from the presynaptic cell cross the synapse and fit snugly into the receptors on the postsynaptic cell.

    REMEMBER: Pre means "before." The presynaptic cell comes before the synapse. *Post* means "after." The postsynaptic cell comes after the synapse.

8. **Action potentials** are abrupt waves of electrochemical changes traveling down an axon when a neuron becomes depolarized. . (see Action Potentials)

    Opening one sodium gate causes the gate next to it to open, which causes the next one to open, and so forth, all the way down the length of the axon. Action potentials are all-or-nothing activities; the cell either fires at full strength or does not fire at all.

    REMEMBER: Electrical potentials occur when there is a difference in charge between the outside and inside of the cell. When an *active* change occurs in the electrical potential, such as depolarization, sodium rushes into the axon and makes the inside less negative, causing an *action potential*.

9. **Myelin** is a fatty substance that wraps around some axons and increases the speed of action potentials. (see Action Potentials)

    Example: When a stray object flies toward your face, the sensory nerves must quickly transmit this information to your brain, and the motor nerves must carry the signal to your muscles to move very rapidly. These sensory and motor nerves are covered with myelin.

10. A **refractory period** is a short rest period between action potentials. (see Action Potentials)

    Following one action potential, the axon must repolarize before another action potential can occur. The time required for the axon to repolarize is called a refractory period.

    REMEMBER: An axon <u>refrains</u> from firing an action potential during a <u>refractory</u> period.

11. **Neurotransmitters** are chemicals that assist in the transfer of signals from one neuron to another. (see Synapses and Communication Between Neurons)

    REMEMBER: Neuro refers to neuron. *Transmit* means to send something across space. Neurotransmitters *send* the signal or message *across* the space of the synapse to the postsynaptic *neuron*.

12. **Receptors (neural receptors)** are sites on the surface of a cell that allow only one type of neurotransmitter to fit into them, triggering a chemical response that may lead to an action potential. (see Synapses and Communication Between Neurons)

    REMEMBER: A <u>re</u>ceptor is something that <u>re</u>ceives. <u>Re</u>ceptors <u>re</u>ceive neurotransmitters.

13. **Postsynaptic potential** is the change in the membrane potential of a neuron that has received stimulation from another neuron. (See Key Terms 14 and 15.) (see Synapses and Communication Between Neurons)

14. An **excitatory postsynaptic potential (EPSP)** is a postsynaptic potential that depolarizes the neuronal membrane, making the cell more likely to fire an action potential. (see Synapses and Communication Between Neurons)

    REMEMBER: An *excitatory* postsynaptic potential *excites* the neuron that will cause it to fire. But also note that all the EPSPs and IPSPs that a dendrite receives combine to determine whether or not the axon of the postsynaptic cell will fire an action potential. If there are more EPSPs than IPSPs, the neuron will fire an action potential.

15. An **inhibitory postsynaptic potential (IPSP)** is a postsynaptic potential that hyperpolarizes the neuronal membrane, making a cell less likely to fire an action potential. (see Synapses and Communication Between Neurons)

    REMEMBER: An *inhibitory* postsynaptic potential *inhibits* or prevents the neuron from firing. But also note that all the EPSPs and IPSPs that a dendrite receives combine to determine whether or not the axon of the postsynaptic cell will fire an action potential. If there are more IPSPs than EPSPs, the neuron will not fire an action potential.

16. **Neural networks** are neurons that operate together to perform complex functions. (see Organization and Functions of the Nervous System)

17. The **peripheral nervous system** is the major division of the nervous system that is not housed in bone. (see Organization and Functions of the Nervous System)

    REMEMBER: Peri means "around." The peripheral nervous system is located *around* the center of your body. It has two major subdivisions, the somatic and autonomic nervous systems.

18. The **central nervous system (CNS)** is the major division of the nervous system encased in bone; specifically, the brain and the spinal cord. (see Organization and Functions of the Nervous System)

    REMEMBER: The brain and spinal cord are *centrally* located. Your spinal cord is in the *center* of your torso; the brain is *centered* over your shoulders. Therefore, the brain and spinal cord make up the *central* nervous system. The CNS's primary function is to process the information provided by the sensory systems and to decide on appropriate courses of action for the motor system.

19. The **somatic nervous system** is the subsystem of the peripheral nervous system that transmits information from the senses to the CNS and carries signals from the CNS to the muscles. (see The Somatic Nervous System)

    Example: When you dance, the somatic nervous system transmits the sound of the music to your brain and carries the signals from your brain to the muscles that move your arms and legs.

    REMEMBER: Soma means "body." The somatic nervous system is involved with taking sensory information from the body parts, such as the ears, and sending signals back to the body, such as movement instructions to coordinate dance steps.

20. **Sensory neurons** are cells in the nervous system that provide information to the brain about the environment. (see The Somatic Nervous System)

    Example: When you dance, the sensory neurons in the somatic nervous system transmit the sound of the music to your brain.

21. **Motor neurons** are cells in the nervous system that the brain uses to influence muscles and other organs to respond to the environment in some way. (see The Somatic Nervous System)

Example: When you dance, the motor neurons in the somatic nervous system carry the signals from your brain to the muscles that move your arms and legs.

17. The **autonomic nervous system** is a subsystem of the peripheral nervous system that carries messages back and forth between the CNS and the heart, lungs, and other organs and glands. (see The Autonomic Nervous System)

    Example: While you dance, your peripheral nervous system may alter the expansion of your lungs so that you can inhale more oxygen. Also, your heartbeat increases so that more blood reaches your muscles.

    REMEMBER: The *autonomic* nervous system regulates the *automatic* functions of your body, such as breathing and blood pressure. You do not normally think about these functions.

23. The **sympathetic nervous system** is the subsystem of the autonomic nervous system that readies the body for vigorous activity. (see The Autonomic Nervous System)

    Example: When Sarah thinks she is being followed to her car, her heart begins to pound, her pupils dilate, and she perspires. Her sympathetic nervous system initiated this reaction.

24. The **parasympathetic nervous system** is the subsystem of the autonomic nervous system that typically influences activity related to the protection, nourishment, and growth of the body. (see The Autonomic Nervous System)

    Example: When Sarah realizes that the person following her is her sister, just trying to tell her she forgot her house key, her heart slows down and she begins to breathe more normally and calmly because her parasympathetic nervous system shuts the initial reaction of fear off.

18. The **spinal cord** is the part of the central nervous system within the spinal column that relays signals from the peripheral senses to the brain and conveys messages from the brain to the rest of the body. (see The Spinal Cord)

    Example: The sensory information from feeling the fur on a kitten travels through the spinal cord's fiber tracts on its way to the brain. When your brain makes the decision to pick up the kitten, it sends signals through the fiber tracts in the spinal cord on the way to the muscles in your hands and arms.

19. **Reflexes** are involuntary, unlearned reactions in the form of swift, automatic, and finely coordinated movements in response to external stimuli. (see The Spinal Cord)

    Example: If you accidentally step on a pin embedded in your carpet, a withdrawal reflex occurs. The afferent sensory neurons will take the information from your foot to the spinal cord, and the efferent motor neurons will send the signal back to the foot to make it withdraw from the floor.

20. The **hindbrain** is an extension of the spinal cord contained inside the skull where nuclei control blood pressure, heart rate, breathing, and other vital functions. (see The Brain)

21. The **medulla oblongata** is an area in the hindbrain that controls blood pressure, heart rate, breathing, and other vital functions. (see The Brain)

    Example: A person with damage to her medulla would most likely need artificial life support to maintain breathing and perhaps would not survive the injury.

22. The **reticular formation** is a network of cells and fibers threaded through the hindbrain and midbrain that alters the activity of the rest of the brain. (see The Brain)

    REMEMBER: Reticular means "net-like." The cells of the reticular formation are not arranged in any distinct structure but, rather, thread throughout the hindbrain. The reticular formation is involved in arousal and attention.

23. The **locus coeruleus** is a small nucleus in the reticular formation that is involved in directing attention. (see The Brain)

    Example: The numerous branches of axons from the locus coeruleus contact other cells, perhaps causing a state of attention or change in mood.

24. The **cerebellum** is the part of the hindbrain whose main functions include controlling finely coordinated movements and storing memories about movement, but which may also be involved in impulse control, emotions, and language. (see The Brain)

    Example: Performing brain surgery requires delicate precision of movement so as to avoid damaging fragile tissue. A surgeon's cerebellum would be very active during an operation.

25. The **midbrain** is a small structure between the hindbrain and the forebrain that relays information from the eyes, ears, and skin and that controls certain types of automatic behaviors. (see The Brain)

    REMEMBER: Sensory information is integrated in the midbrain to produce the smooth initiation of movement.

26. The **substantia nigra** is an area of the midbrain involved in the smooth beginning of movement. (see The Brain)

    Example: Phil, a person with damage to his substantia nigra, is unable to reach out his arm to shake hands with a neighbor.

27. The **striatum** is a structure within the forebrain that is involved with the smooth beginning of movement. (see The Brain)

    Example: Many years ago, a surgical procedure called lobotomy was used to treat several types of mental disorders. The surgery involved destroying large parts of the forebrain. Patients on whom this surgery was performed were often unable to perform complex cognitive tasks afterward.

28. The **forebrain** is the most highly developed part of the brain; it is responsible for the most complex aspects of behavior and mental life. (see The Brain)

29. The **thalamus** is a forebrain structure that relays signals from most sense organs to higher levels in the brain and plays an important role in processing and making sense out of this information. (see The Brain)

    Example: Jane has damage to her thalamus. She has normal processing of visual images with her eyes but is unable to send that information on to be acted on further by the brain. In fact, Jane reports being totally unable to see.

30. The **hypothalamus** is a structure in the forebrain that regulates hunger, thirst, and sex drive. (see The Brain)

    Example: Destroying certain parts of the hypothalamus causes an animal to cease eating and drinking. It will eventually die if not force-fed.

31. The **suprachiasmatic nuclei** are nuclei in the hypothalamus that generate biological rhythms. (see The Brain)

    Example: Bob is used to getting up at 10:00 A.M. and working until about 2:00 A.M. Bob's suprachiasmatic nuclei have probably influenced him to be a "night person."

32. The **amygdala** is a structure in the forebrain that, among other things, associates features of stimuli from two sensory modalities. (see The Brain)

Example: When you eat ice cream, your amygdala is involved in your perception that the ice cream is both cold and sweet.

33. The **hippocampus** is a structure in the forebrain associated with the formation of new memories. (see The Brain)

    Example: Going to class every day would be a waste of time if your hippocampus was damaged. Although you would be able to understand everything the instructor said, you would not be able to form a memory for the new information.

34. The **limbic system** is a set of brain structures that play important roles in regulating emotion and memory. (see The Brain)

    Example: Grace has Alzheimer's disease, which causes not only memory lapses, but also emotional outbursts in which she falsely claims family members have taken advantage of her.

35. The **cerebral hemispheres** are the left and right halves of the rounded, outermost part of the brain. (see The Cerebral Cortex)

    REMEMBER: Hemi means "half." *Cerebral hemisphere* refers to *half of the cerebrum*, which is round like a *sphere*. To understand how the cerebrum is split into hemispheres, do the following: Place your finger right between your eyes, lift it straight over your forehead, and trace an imaginary part in the middle of your hair to the back of your head. The line that you have just traced is the dividing line of the two cerebral hemispheres.

36. The **cerebral cortex** is the outer surface of the brain. (see The Cerebral Cortex)

    REMEMBER: The cerebral hemispheres are divided into four lobes: frontal, parietal, occipital, and temporal. The cortex is also divided into three functional areas: the sensory cortex, the motor cortex, and the association cortex.

37. The **sensory cortex (sensory area)** is made up of the parts of the cerebral cortex that receive stimulus information from the senses. (see The Cerebral Cortex)

    Example: If you were to take a walk on the beach, your sensory cortex would be receiving various types of information in your lobes: occipital (the color of the water); parietal (the sandy feeling on your skin and the salt water on your face); and temporal (the sound of the surf).

38. The **motor cortex** is the part of the cerebral cortex whose neurons control voluntary movements in specific parts of the body. (see The Cerebral Cortex)

    Example: During that walk on the beach, your motor cortex would be sending information to your muscles to help you walk in the sand in a particular direction.

39. The **association cortex** pertains to the parts of the cerebral cortex that receive information from more than one sense or that combine sensory and motor information to perform complex cognitive tasks. (see The Cerebral Cortex)

    REMEMBER: Think of the *association* cortex as forming an *association* between many types of sensory and motor information.

47. **Lateral dominance (lateralization)** refers to the tendency for one cerebral hemisphere to excel at a particular function or skill compared with the other hemisphere. (see The Divided Brain in a Unified Self)

    Example: When Lynne reads, her left hemisphere is more activated than her right.

48. The **corpus callosum** is a massive bundle of fibers that connects the right and left cerebral hemispheres and allows them to communicate with each other. (see The Divided Brain in a Unified Self)

REMEMBER: Corpus callosum begins with two Cs. The corpus callosum connects the cerebral hemispheres.

40. **Neural plasticity** is the ability to create new synapses and to change the strength of synapses. (see Plasticity in the Nervous System)

    Example: New synapses are formed in your brain when you learn new material.

41. **Stem cells** are special cells in the nervous system that are capable of dividing to form new tissue, including new neurons. (see Plasticity in the Nervous System)

    Example: Rand's doctor is harvesting cells from his bone marrow that he hopes will be able to help form new tissue to heal him from the multiple myeloma he is fighting.

42. **Acetylcholine**, a neurotransmitter used by neurons in the peripheral and central nervous systems in the control of functions ranging from muscle contraction to digestion and memory. (see Three Classes of Neurotransmitters)

    Example: Grace's memory lapses are linked to a loss of cholinergic neurons in areas of her brain that store memories.

43. The neurotransmitter **norepinephrine** is involved in arousal, as well as in learning and mood regulation. (see Three Classes of Neurotransmitters)

    Example: Miguel's sympathetic nervous system has activated the fight-or-flight response by releasing norepinephrine to allow him to jump out of the way of an inexperienced cyclist.

44. **Serotonin** is a neurotransmitter used by cells in parts of the brain involved in the regulation of sleep, mood, and eating. (see Three Classes of Neurotransmitters)

    Example: Joyce finished a high-carbohydrate meal of macaroni and cheese; therefore, her desire for carbohydrates is being reduced by the release of serotonin.

45. The neurotransmitter **dopamine** is used in the parts of the brain involved in regulating movement and experiencing pleasure.. (see Three Classes of Neurotransmitters)

    Example: Nelson has Parkinson's disease, which is associated with a deterioration of dopamine cells. Nelson finds it increasingly difficult to move from a sitting to a standing position and is discouraged by his increasingly noticeable hand tremors.

46. **Gamma-amino butyric acid (GABA)** is a neurotransmitter that inhibits the firing of neurons. (see Three Classes of Neurotransmitters)

    Example: Huntington's disease has reduced the number of GABA-containing neurons in Victoria's striatum. Because her dopamine system is no longer inhibited by GABA, Victoria experiences uncontrollable movements of her arms and legs.

    REMEMBER: GABA is involved in a variety of behaviors and mental processes. Malfunctioning GABA systems are associated with severe anxiety, Huntington's disease, and epilepsy.

47. **Glutamate** is an excitatory neurotransmitter that helps strengthen synaptic connections between neurons. (see Three Classes of Neurotransmitters)

    Example: Craig believes he will one day be able to show evidence of learning through the tracking of glutamate's effects on synaptic connections.

48. **Endorphins** are a class of neurotransmitters that bind to opiate receptors and moderate pain. (see Three Classes of Neurotransmitters)

    Example: "Runner's high," or the absence of pain and the euphoric feeling that many runners report after covering long distances, may be caused by the release of endorphins.

49. The **endocrine system** is made up of cells that form organs called glands and that communicate with one another by secreting chemicals called hormones. (see The Endocrine System: Coordinating the Internal World)

    REMEMBER: A wide variety of behaviors and mental processes are influenced by this system. Hormones, traveling via the bloodstream, affect coordinated systems of target tissues and organs by producing such responses as the <u>fight-or-flight syndrome</u>.

50. **Glands** are organs that secrete hormones into the bloodstream. (see The Endocrine System: Coordinating the Internal World)

    Example: The pituitary, adrenals, testes, ovaries, pancreas, and thyroid are all glands of the endocrine system.

51. **Hormones** are chemicals secreted by a gland into the bloodstream, which carries them throughout the body. (see The Endocrine System: Coordinating the Internal World)

    Example: A woman's menstrual cycle is governed by the timed release of several different hormones from the pituitary and ovary glands.

52. The **fight-or-flight syndrome (fight-flight reaction)** is a physical reaction triggered by the sympathetic nervous system that prepares the body to fight or to run from a threatening situation. (see The Endocrine System: Coordinating the Internal World)

    Example: Any scary experience will induce the fight-or-flight syndrome. Hearing strange noises at night, giving your first speech in college, or almost being hit by a car can be very frightening. If you have been in any of these situations, you may recall how your heart suddenly thudded.

FILL-IN-THE-BLANKS KEY TERMS

This section will help you check your knowledge of the key terms introduced in this chapter. Fill in each blank with the appropriate term from the list of key terms in the previous section.

1. In most cases, _____ carry signals away from the cell body and _____ carry signals toward the cell body.

2. _____ occur when neurons become depolarized.

3. A neuron with a slow rate of firing would not have a(n) _____ coating.

4. A(n) _____ postsynaptic potential will cause a cell to become depolarized, whereas an _____ postsynaptic potential will cause a cell to become hyperpolarized.

5. The _____ nervous system is part of the peripheral nervous system and regulates "automatic" activity.

6. The medulla, reticular formation, and cerebellum are all part of the _____.

7. Very fine motor coordination is controlled by the _____.

8. The _____ is part of the forebrain and helps regulate hunger, thirst, and sex drive.

9. The _____ plays a significant role in forming new memories.

10. The idea of _____ refers to the brain's ability to strengthen existing connections at _____ and establish new ones.

11. The _____ and _____ are part of the limbic system and are located in the cerebrum.

12. The _____ connects the two cerebral hemispheres.

13. Neurotransmitters are to the nervous system what _____ are to the endocrine system.

14. Adrenal glands trigger the _____.

15. _____ communicate by releasing hormones.

Total Correct (See answer key) _____

LEARNING OBJECTIVES

1. Define biological psychology. (see introductory section)

2. Define the nervous system. Describe the three main components of information processing that the nervous system performs. (see introductory section)

3. Compare and contrast neurons and glial cells. (see The Nervous System)

4. Name and describe the functions of the neuronal parts that allow them to communicate with one another, including axons, dendrites, and the synapse. (see The Nervous System)

5. Describe the electrical and chemical changes that lead to an action potential. Define myelin and discuss its effects. (see Action Potentials)

6. Explain how polarization and refractory periods affect signal transduction in the nervous system. (see Action Potentials)

7. Define neurotransmitters and describe their roles in nervous system activity. (see Synapses and Communication Between Neurons)

8. Describe the role of receptors in the communication process between neurons. (see Neurotransmitters)

9. Define postsynaptic potentials and describe the difference between excitatory and inhibitory postsynaptic potentials. Describe their role in the creation of an action potential in the postsynaptic cell. (see Excitatory and Inhibitory Signals)

10. Describe how neural networks operate. (see Organization and Functions of the Nervous System)

11. Define sensory neurons and motor neurons. Describe their roles in two components of information processing: input and output. (see Organization and Functions of the Nervous System)

12. Name the two major divisions of the nervous system. (see Organization and Functions of the Nervous System)

13. Name the two components of the peripheral nervous system and describe their functions. (see The Peripheral Nervous System: Keeping in Touch with the World)

14. Name the two components of the autonomic nervous system and describe their functions. (see The Autonomic Nervous System)

15. Define nuclei and fiber tracts. (see The Central Nervous System: Making Sense of the World)

16. Name the type of neurons found in the spinal cord and describe their function. Define reflexes. (see The Spinal Cord)

17. Describe the techniques that scientists use to study the brain. (see The Brain)

18. Discuss what fMRI research had revealed about behavior and mental processes. (see Thinking Critically: What Can fMRI Tell Us About Behavior and Mental Processes?)

19. Name and define the structures in the hindbrain. Describe their functions. (see The Hindbrain)

20. Name and define the structures in the <u>midbrain</u>. Describe their functions. (see The Midbrain)

21. Name and define the structures in the <u>forebrain</u>. Describe their functions. (see The Forebrain)

22. Describe the experimental methods used by scientists in their study of Alzheimer's disease. (see Focus on Research Methods: Manipulating Genes in Animal Models of Human Disease)

23. Define <u>cerebral hemisphere</u> and <u>cerebral cortex</u>. Name the four lobes that make up the cortex and state their locations. (see The Cerebral Cortex)

24. Describe the functions of the <u>sensory cortex</u> and the <u>motor cortex</u>. (see The Cerebral Cortex)

25. Name and describe the role of the areas in the <u>association cortex</u> involved in understanding and producing language. (see The Association Cortex)

26. Describe split-brain studies and explain the function of the <u>corpus callosum</u>. (see The Divided Brain in a Unified Self)

27. Describe the <u>lateral dominance</u> (lateralization) of the cerebral hemispheres. (see Lateralization of Normal Brains)

28. Define <u>neural plasticity</u>. Explain why it is impossible for the brain to heal damaged neurons. Describe the methods used to help people recover from brain damage today. (see Plasticity: in the Central Nervous System)

29. Describe the changes that occur in the nervous system throughout development. (see Linkages: Human Development and the Changing Brain)

30. Define <u>neurotransmitter</u> systems. Name and describe the location of the seven major neurotransmitters. Discuss the behaviors and mental processes associated with each of them. (see The Chemistry of Psychology)

31. Define <u>endocrine system</u>, <u>glands</u>, and <u>hormones</u>. Compare and contrast the differences between the communication processes of the nervous and endocrine systems. (see The Endocrine System: Coordinating the Internal World)

32. Define the <u>fight-or-flight syndrome</u>. (see The Endocrine System: Coordinating the Internal World)

33. Define *negative feedback systems*. (see The Endocrine System: Coordinating the Internal World)

34. Describe the interaction of the immune, nervous, and endocrine systems. (see The Immune System: Defending the Body)

CONCEPTS AND EXERCISES

The Organization of the Nervous System

The organizational chart below is all mixed up. Correct the mistakes.

The Organization of the Nervous System

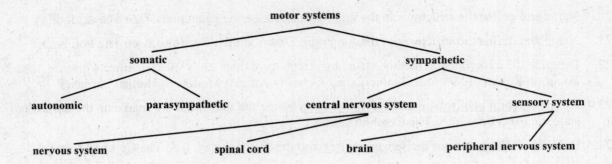

The Functions of the Brain

Match the symptoms of these patients with the area of the brain (from the list below) that may be damaged or malfunctioning. Answers may be used more than once or not at all.

1. Yolanda cannot form new memories. She can remember only events that occurred before her accident. _____

2. Cecil can no longer button his shirts. He has also developed a stutter. _____

3. Stan has lost all desire to have sexual relations with his partner. _____

4. Sara has constant memories that arouse intense feelings of fear. _____

5. Frank never feels satisfied and cannot stop eating. He is becoming seriously overweight. _____

6. Akbar is comatose—not responding to any sensory stimulation. _____

    a. amygdala

    b. cerebellum

    c. hippocampus

    d. hypothalamus

    e. reticular formation

    f. thalamus

CRITICAL THINKING

Sam and Martina are working on a murder case. The victim, a thirty-year-old male by the name of Jerry, was found dead in his office by his partner at 6:00 A.M. Jerry had multiple stab wounds. His girlfriend, Lisa, told Sam and Martina that she and Jerry had gone out to dinner. Jerry dropped her off at her apartment early, saying that he and his partner had to go back to the office and finish a presentation for the following day.

Lisa did have an alibi. She lived with her sister Susan in a high rise in the city. Susan said that she heard Lisa come in and go straight to bed at around 9:00 P.M.

The partner, Stephen, did not have an alibi. He said that Jerry was supposed to call and let him know whether the meeting was still on. If it was, then they were going to meet at 9:30 at the office. Stephen said he did not receive a phone call and assumed the meeting and presentation were called off. He stayed home and read until 10:00 P.M., and then went to bed.

Meanwhile, back at the office … Sam, with youthful enthusiasm, called the pathologist before the doctor could possibly have finished his report. Exasperated by Sam's impatience, the doctor told Sam what he knew so far. The cause of death was indeed the stabbing. Also, the man had a stomach full of undigested Chinese food.

Sam hung up the phone and grinned. "That's it," he said. "If the guy's stomach is still full, then he had to have been killed right after dinner. Let's say they get to the restaurant at 7:30. Let's say dinner takes an hour, they drive fifteen minutes to his office, and she kills him and takes a train home to the 'burbs."

Martina laughs to herself. She remembers that she made the same mistake that Sam was making today when she first started on the force. (They just didn't teach enough biology in school!) Martina knows that once the sympathetic nervous system is activated, as it is when an individual is really scared, the parasympathetic system ceases its activity.

Using the five critical thinking questions in your text, state Sam's original hypothesis and his evidence. Based on the clues in the story, what do you think Martina's alternative hypothesis is?

1.   What is Sam's hypothesis?

2.   What evidence does he have?

3.   What is Martina's probable alternative hypothesis?

4.   What is the evidence that supports her hypothesis? What else would you want to know if you were Martina?

5.   What conclusion can be drawn?

PERSONAL LEARNING ACTIVITIES

1.   Break the mechanism of neurotransmission into a series of steps. Begin with neurotransmitters binding to receptors of another neuron and end with neurotransmitters being released into the synapse. Now explain neurotransmission to someone, using these steps.

2.   Select a topic that particularly interests you from this chapter. Log onto the Internet. Using a World Wide Web browser, find a website concerned with the topic. Before you review the site, check its source. Make sure the author lists credentials that suggest that the information presented is likely to be correct. Does the website expand on material presented in your text? In what way did the site help you to understand the text material better?

3.   Make a chart that will help you remember the various brain structures. In the first column, list the brain structures. In the second column, list their location as in the hindbrain, midbrain, or forebrain. In the third column, write the function or purpose of the structure. In the fourth column, write down what would happen if that structure were damaged (e.g., if the hippocampus is damaged, you can no longer form new memories). Use the chart to study for quizzes and exams on this chapter.

4.   The precise nature and degree of lateralization vary quite a bit among individuals. If it were possible to use brain imaging techniques to discover specific individual differences in lateralized tasks, should this information be used in school placement and career planning? Provide reasons for and against this idea.

5.   To better understand the endocrine system, visit the following website: http://nhscience.lonestar.edu/biol/ap1int.htm#endocrine. Click on the endocrine link in the bottom right hand of the table at the top, and you will find a number of animations of processes in the

endocrine system. Seeing these processes in action can help you remember them better than still pictures might. What processes did you view? How did seeing them in action change your understanding of them?

MULTIPLE-CHOICE QUESTIONS

Quiz 1

1. Which of the following characteristics distinguishes neurons from other cells?

    a.   Mitochondria, which turn oxygen and glucose into usable energy
    b.   A nucleus that houses genetic information
    c.   A cell body
    d.   Axons and dendrites

2. Says one neuron to the next, "We seem to have a positively charged ion shortage around this place." The second neuron responds, "I know, I haven't been able to _____ at all lately, and I hate when I can't send my action potentials!"

    a.   demonstrate my synaptic plasticity
    b.   be myelinated
    c.   be depolarized
    d.   recover from my refractory period

3. Myelin serves what purpose in the nervous system?

    a.   It accelerates an action potential's movement.
    b.   It is a chemical that travels across the synapse.
    c.   It causes an inhibitory postsynaptic potential.
    d.   It causes an excitatory postsynaptic potential.

4. A fMRI is a technology that

    a.   provides a measure of electrical activity in the brain.
    b.   detects changes in blood flow that reflect ongoing changes in neuronal activity.
    c.   shows people's thoughts and feelings as they happen in the brain.
    d.   is no more than modern day phrenology.

5. While you are spying on a neuron neighbor, you see an equal number of excitatory and inhibitory postsynaptic potentials reach the cell body near the axon. You know this will

    a.   cause an action potential.
    b.   cause neurotransmitters to be released.
    c.   keep the neuron from sending a message.
    d.   keep the neuron from receiving a message.

6. If your sensory neurons were not functioning properly, which of the following would most likely be your symptom?

    a.   You would not be able to tell when things you touched were hot or cold.
    b.   You would not be able to form new memories.
    c.   You would not be able to walk any longer.
    d.   You would lose all interest in sex, eating, and other sensual pleasures.

7. Dr. Frankenstein has given up on creating a human and is trying to build King Kong's cousin. He forgot to install the motor neurons of the somatic system. What will Kong's kin be unable to do?

    a. Lift skyscrapers
    b. Hear people scream
    c. Digest skyscrapers
    d. See people run from him

8. Kalli finishes her exam and hurries home. When she arrives home, she slumps down on her bed to relax. As Kalli relaxes, her _____ nervous system becomes less active while her _____ nervous system becomes more active.

    a. central; somatic
    b. somatic; central
    c. parasympathetic; sympathetic
    d. sympathetic; parasympathetic

9. Our daily biological rhythms are governed by a structure called the

    a. substantia nigra.
    b. suprachiasmatic nuclei.
    c. striatum.
    d. thalamus.

10. The _____ is located in the hindbrain and helps to regulate blood pressure, breathing, and heart rate.

    a. medulla oblongata
    b. hypothalamus
    c. thalamus
    d. cerebellum

11. Kwan Li's auto accident caused her to have difficulty with her piano playing. She could no longer play pieces that she knew well. When the doctors tested her, she also had difficulty tracking with her eyes the movement of a finger held in front of her face and difficulty in tracing drawings with a pen. Damage to Kwan Li's _____ would most likely cause such motor skill difficulties.

    a. cerebellum
    b. thalamus
    c. parietal lobe
    d. occipital lobe

12. The inability to speak correctly is _____ aphasia; the inability to understand language is involved in _____ aphasia.

    a. Wernicke's; Broca's
    b. Broca's; Wernicke's
    c. hormonal; neural
    d. neural; hormonal

13. Derek has a tingling sensation in his left foot. Which area of the brain has most likely been affected?
    a.   Left temporal lobe
    b.   Left striatum
    c.   Right frontal lobe
    d.   Right parietal lobe

14. Which of the following is NOT a characteristic of our brains that would make complete recovery from brain damage difficult?
    a.   Adult brains generally do not generate new neurons.
    b.   The brain, prior to damage, has millions of neural connections.
    c.   Glial cells eliminate damaged neurons.
    d.   Neurons cannot change their functions.

15. For drafting class, Tasha must be able to draw three-dimensional views of various tools. Which cerebral hemisphere will most likely be activated while she completes this assignment?
    a.   Right
    b.   Left
    c.   Both
    d.   Cannot be determined

16. When her vision is blocked by a screen, Sue cannot name objects by using only the sense of touch with her left hand, but she can do so with her right hand. Sue can use the sense of touch to retrieve a previously held object from among several choices using the left hand only or the right hand only. Which part of Sue's brain was most likely damaged?
    a.   Hippocampus
    b.   Substantia nigra
    c.   Parietal lobe
    d.   Corpus callosum

17. Neural stem cell research is controversial because
    a.   people often think it is part of cloning an entire person.
    b.   it may someday be used to grow new cells that will replace damaged tissue in a person with a disease.
    c.   it requires the use of embryos, which links it to the abortion debate.
    d.   because it is linked to cloning an entire person and because it is linked to the abortion debate.

18. A nurse has mixed up some test results on neurotransmitter function in several patients at the hospital where you work. To help her out, you tell her that the Alzheimer patient's chart will show too little _____, and the Parkinson's patient's chart will show too little _____.
    a.   dopamine; norepinephrine
    b.   dopamine; acetylcholine
    c.   acetylcholine; dopamine
    d.   acetylcholine; norepinephrine

19. Ted is trying to make a study sheet to help him learn the differences between neurotransmitters and hormones. Which of the following statements on his list is NOT correct?

    a. Neurotransmitters travel via the bloodstream, and hormones travel across synapses.

    b. Both hormones and neurotransmitters stimulate only those cells and organs that have receptors for them.

    c. Hormones and neurotransmitters regulate complex behaviors and mental processes.

    d. Hormones are released by glands while neurotransmitters are released by neurons.

20. The system responsible for regulating functions ranging from stress responses through physical growth is which of the following?

    a. Central nervous system

    b. Endocrine system

    c. Immune system

    d. Reflexes

Total Correct (See answer key) _____

Quiz 2

Use this quiz to reassess your learning after taking Quiz 1 and reviewing the chapter.

1. One of the special features that enable neurons to communicate efficiently is

    a. their structure.

    b. their sensitive surface membranes.

    c. their synapses.

    d. All of these.

2. Following is a conversation between two axons. Fill in the blanks. *Axon No. 1:* "Life is so dull. I have not been _____ all day." *Axon No. 2:* "Don't complain. I have it rough, too. Even with all of this (these) _____ wrapped around me, I can't seem to get my signals to the synapse fast enough for the boss."

    a. depolarized; myelin

    b. depolarized; receptors

    c. polarized; sodium gates

    d. polarized; vesicles

3. Pretend your class is demonstrating the roles of various cells and structures of a neuron. If you are playing the role of a positive ion participating in an action potential, you should

    a. go in through an open gate in the axon.

    b. run from the cell body to the end of the axon.

    c. begin running from the cell body, but start slowing down at the end of the dendrite.

    d. float across the synapse and bind with a receptor.

4. Scientists have discovered a virus that binds to postsynaptic receptors and prevents the reception of neurotransmitter signals. On which parts of nerve cells would this virus most likely be found?

    a. Dendrites

    b. Axons

    c. Cell bodies

    d. All of the above

5. The neurotransmitter GABA reduces the likelihood that postsynaptic neurons will fire an action potential. GABA causes _____ postsynaptic potentials.

    a. excitatory
    b. inhibitory
    c. neutral
    d. increased

6. Sensory neurons are part of the _____ system.

    a. peripheral nervous
    b. sympathetic
    c. autonomic
    d. somatic

7. As you are waiting for a friend in a hospital waiting room, you overhear a doctor tell a worried spouse that her husband has a neurological problem. The nerves that carry signals to the muscles are not functioning. The _____ nervous system has been damaged.

    a. central
    b. autonomic
    c. somatic
    d. sympathetic

8. Sarah is playing volleyball. She is running, hitting the ball, and shouting encouragement to her teammates. As a consequence, her heart rate is high, her breathing is rapid, and she is sweating. Which subdivision of her autonomic nervous system is activated?

    a. Parasympathetic
    b. Peripheral
    c. Somatic
    d. Sympathetic

9. A reflex

    a. occurs without assistance from the brain.
    b. involves the activity of afferent and efferent neurons.
    c. is involuntary.
    d. All of these

10. People with severed spinal cords cannot receive sensory information from, or send signals to, the muscles below the level of damage, because

    a. the brain can no longer decipher incoming sensory information.
    b. the information going to and from the brain must travel through the spinal cord.
    c. the thalamus's relay station for sensory information always degenerates after spinal cord injuries.
    d. None of these is true.

11. Joe was walking along when his ex-girlfriend pelted him with an acorn she found lying on the ground. Unfortunately, the acorn embedded itself in his brain and had to be removed with a very risky surgery. Joe was lucky he survived the incident, but unlucky because some permanent damage was caused, and he is now not nearly as interested in sex as he was before the incident. What brain structure was most likely damaged?
    a. Substantia nigra
    b. Reticular formation
    c. Cerebellum
    d. Hypothalamus

12. Conchita can meet a person or read the same story over and over for months but will never recall either. Which part of Conchita's brain was most likely damaged?
    a. Cerebellum
    b. Hippocampus
    c. Medulla
    d. Hypothalamus

13. The occipital lobe receives sensory information concerning
    a. pain.
    b. body movement.
    c. vision.
    d. body temperature.

14. Large parts of the cerebral cortex perform higher-level cognitive tasks, even though they are not directly involved with any particular function. These parts are called the
    a. somatosensory cortex.
    b. limbic system.
    c. association cortex.
    d. homunculus.

15. When a participant in an fMRI study plans to reach for an object, certain areas of the brain "light up." When that same participant watches someone else reach for that object, the same areas light up. This phenomenon is known as
    a. neuroeconomics.
    b. diffusion tensor imaging.
    c. mirror neuron mechanisms.
    d. transcranial magnetic stimulation.

16. Which of the following is NOT true? The corpus callosum
    a. connects the two cerebral hemispheres.
    b. contains many fibers.
    c. is enlarged in cases of severe epilepsy.
    d. allows the brain to function as a whole.

17.   You have found an injured cat that cannot move the right side of its body very well. What kind of brain damage might explain the cat's condition?

   a.   A severed corpus callosum
   b.   Impaired functioning of the motor cortex in the left cerebral hemisphere
   c.   A dysfunctional hypothalamus
   d.   Impaired functioning of the somatosensory cortex in the right cerebral hemisphere

18.   Low levels of _____ are often found in the brains of suicide victims, suggesting this neurotransmitter's involvement in mood disturbances.

   a.   glutamate
   b.   dopamine
   c.   seratonin
   d.   nitric oxide

19.   When Mitch saw the woman who appeared to be drowning, he grabbed his life preserver ring and ran to save her. To prepare his body to run, Mitch's _____ released cortisol and other chemicals into his bloodstream.

   a.   glands
   b.   neurotransmitter systems
   c.   synapses
   d.   target organs

20.   Which of the following is NOT considered a sex hormone?

   a.   estrogen
   b.   androgens
   c.   testosterone
   d.   cortisol

Total Correct (See answer key) _____

ANSWERS TO FILL-IN-THE-BLANKS KEY TERMS

1.   axons; dendrites (see Cells of the Nervous System)

2.   Action potentials (see Action Potentials)

3.   myelin (see Action Potentials)

4.   excitatory; inhibitory (see Synapses and Communication Between Neurons)

5.   autonomic (see The Autonomic Nervous System)

6.   hindbrain (see The Brain)

7.   cerebellum (see The Brain)

8.   hypothalamus (see The Brain)

9.   hippocampus (see The Brain)

10.   neural plasticity; synapses or connections (see Plasticity in the Nervous System)

11. amygdala; hippocampus (see The Brain)

12. corpus callosum (see The Divided Brain in a Unified Self)

13. hormones (see The Endocrine System: Coordinating the Internal World)

14. fight-or-flight syndrome (see The Endocrine System: Coordinating the Internal World)

15. Glands (see The Endocrine System: Coordinating the Internal World)

ANSWERS TO CONCEPTS AND EXERCISES

The Organization of the Nervous System

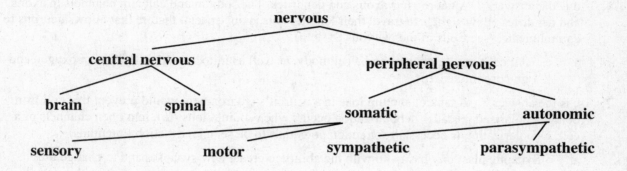

The Functions of the Brain

1. The <u>hippocampus</u> is involved in storing new memories. (see The Brain)

2. The <u>cerebellum</u> is involved in fine motor movements and in the integration of vocal sounds with lip and tongue movements in language production. (see The Brain)

3. The <u>hypothalamus</u> is involved in regulating hunger, thirst, and sex drives. (see The Brain)

4. The <u>amygdala</u> is involved in memory as well as in fear and other emotions. (see The Brain)

5. The <u>hypothalamus</u> is involved in regulating hunger. (see The Brain)

6. The <u>reticular formation</u> is important in arousal. If it is damaged, a person becomes comatose. (see The Brain)

ANSWERS TO CRITICAL THINKING

1. Sam's hypothesis is that Lisa killed Jerry.

2. The fact that Jerry's stomach is still full of Chinese food leads Sam to believe that the murder was committed right after dinner.

3. Martina knows that digestion (controlled by the parasympathetic nervous system) stops if the sympathetic nervous system is stimulated for any reason, such as onset of fear. She probably thinks that Stephen showed up at the office later that evening and killed Jerry.

4. If you were Martina, you would probably want to get the complete pathology report, which would include the time of death. Most likely, it was after 9:00 P.M. when Susan, Lisa's sister, heard Lisa come home and go to bed. (Martina might also want to check out Jerry and Stephen's relationship at the office.)

5. If the answer to Martina's continued investigation turns out the way she thinks it will, she will probably be able to conclude that Stephen killed Jerry. *NOTE:* Critical thinking is a constant process of hypothesizing, examining evidence, rehypothesizing, collecting more evidence, and so on. Martina may not be correct. Can you think of any other hypotheses that could explain this data?

ANSWERS TO MULTIPLE-CHOICE QUESTIONS

Circle the question numbers you answered correctly.

Quiz 1

1. d is the answer.   A neuron has axons and dendrites. The sodium and calcium channels in axons and dendrites allow signals to travel their length—this is one special feature that allows neurons to communicate. (see Cells of the Nervous System)

    a, b, c.   All cells have a nucleus and a cell body, as well as mitochondria, which turn oxygen and glucose into energy.

2. c is the answer.   A lack of sodium ions in a neuron's environment would prevent that cell from being depolarized, because depolarization occurs when sodium ions rush into open channels of a cell. Depolarization is necessary for action potentials to be sent. (see Action Potentials)

    a.   Synaptic plasticity has to do with the ability to create new synapses and to change the strength of synapses. It deals more with connections between neurons than with intracell activity. The neurons in this question are discussing intracell activity—the conditions under which they get to fire action potentials.

    b.   Myelin increases the speed of neural transmission by allowing an action potential to travel down an axon more swiftly. Myelin does not impact the amount of sodium ions available to a cell, or whether or not the cell can send an action potential in the first place.

    d.   Although a cell cannot fire an action potential again until it recovers from its refractory period, the refractory period itself does not correspond to the described "shortage" or sodium ions.

3. a is the answer.   (see Action Potentials)

    b.   A neurotransmitter travels across the synapse and fits into postsynaptic receptors.

    c, d.   Myelin does not influence the nature of the postsynaptic potential.

4. b is the answer.   The fMRI technology is capable of detecting changes in blood flow correspondent to neuronal activity, which provides deeper insight into brain structure and function. (see Thinking Critically: What Can fMRI Tell Us About Behavior and Mental Processes?)

    a.   EEG, not fMRI, is the technology that provides a measure of electrical activity in the brain.

    c.   Although some might claim the fMRI is capable of showing thoughts and feelings, this overstates the currently available evidence.

    d.   To equate fMRI to phrenology, as some have, understates what it has contributed to understanding behavior and mental processes.

5. c is the answer.   An equal number of excitatory and inhibitory signals will cancel each other out. (see Synapses and Communication Between Neurons)

a. An action potential will occur if enough excitatory signals reach the cell body. In this situation, not enough have reached the cell body to override the number of inhibitory signals.

b. Neurotransmitters are not released until an action potential occurs.

d. The neuron is receiving messages in the form of excitatory and inhibitory postsynaptic potentials.

6. a is the answer. The sensory neurons bring information from senses about the environment, such as vision, touch, pain, taste, hearing, and smell, to the brain. When they do not operate, you cannot receive "input" from your sensory organs. The only answer here that relies totally and solely on input from sensory neurons involves determining if something is hot or cold. This requires input from the sense of touch. (see Organization and Functions of the Nervous System)

b. This would involve improper function of the hippocampus, not the sensory neurons.

c. This would involve improper function of the motor system, not sensory neurons.

d. Although interest in sex and eating certainly depends in part on sensory neurons, it is also motivated by other factors, such as desire to survive, desire to connect with others, and so on. Improper function of sensory neurons would influence, but not eliminate, interest in these matters.

7. a is the answer. Without motor neurons to move the skeletal muscles, King Kong's cousin will not be able to move or pick up a rock, let alone lift a skyscraper. (see Organization and Functions of the Nervous System)

b. The somatic system's sensory neurons will be able to carry auditory information to the brain.

c. The autonomic nervous system will allow King Kong's cousin to digest skyscrapers. The autonomic system carries messages to the organs of the body, such as the stomach.

d. The somatic system's sensory neurons will be able to carry visual information to the brain.

8. d is the answer. The sympathetic nervous system is becoming less active now that Kalli is not hurrying or worrying. The parasympathetic system is responsible for conserving energy and relaxing a person, so it is becoming more active. (see The Autonomic Nervous System)

a, b. The central nervous system is no more activated when a person is relaxing than it is when the person is aroused. The somatic nervous system takes care of receiving information from the senses and sending instructions to the muscles.

c. The parasympathetic system is the part of the autonomic nervous system that calms a person, so it is becoming more active. The sympathetic system activates the person as in the fight-or-flight response.

9. b is the answer. The suprachiasmatic nuclei is part of the hypothalamus that acts as a type of biological clock, governing the timing of many recurring bodily processes. (see The Brain)

a. The substantia nigra is part of the midbrain concerned with smooth initiation of movement.

c. The striatum is also part of the midbrain and interacts with the substantia nigra.

d. The thalamus processes and relays sensory information to different parts of the brain.

10. a is the answer. The medulla oblongata, located in the hindbrain, helps to regulate breathing and blood pressure. (see The Brain)

b, c. The hypothalamus and the thalamus are located in the forebrain.

    d.   The cerebellum is located in the hindbrain, but it controls fine movement coordination and sense of timing.

11.   a is the answer.   The cerebellum controls well-rehearsed movements, such as piano playing, and assists the eyes in tracking a moving object, as well as processes such as our sense of timing. (see The Brain)

    b.   The thalamus relays sensory information to the appropriate parts of the cerebral cortex.

    c.   The parietal lobe receives information from the skin senses, but it would not account for difficulty in memories of rehearsed movements or difficulty in tracking.

    d.   The occipital lobe receives information from the eyes, but it would not account for difficulty in movement.

12.   b is the answer.   Broca's aphasia is the inability to produce language correctly, although one with it can understand language. Wernick's aphasia is the inability to properly understand language—language can be produced in a grammatically correct way, although lack of understanding often makes the production nonsensical. (see The Cerebral Cortex)

    a.   This is opposite of the correct answer. Wernicke's aphasia involves lack of understanding of language, whereas Broca's involves inability to produce language correctly.

    c, d.   There are no such things as neural or hormonal aphasias.

13.   d is the answer.   The right parietal lobe receives skin sense information from the body's left side. (see The Cerebral Cortex)

    a.   The left temporal lobe is the location of Wernicke's area. It is involved in hearing and language.

    b.   The striatum is part of the midbrain. Along with the substantia nigra, it is responsible for beginning a movement.

    c.   The right frontal lobe would control the muscles for the left side of the body.

14.   d is the answer.   Neurons *can* change their functions and make new connections with other neurons; therefore, this is not a characteristic that would make recovery from brain damage difficult. (see Plasticity in the Nervous System)

    a, b, c.   It is true that adult brain cells generally do not divide and generate new brain cells and that the brain has so many neural connections that exact replication following brain damage would be highly unlikely. Finally, glial cells do eliminate damaged brain cells before they have a chance to regenerate. Therefore, each of these *is* a characteristic making recovery from brain damage difficult.

15.   a is the answer.   The right hemisphere has better spatial and artistic abilities, which are important in a drafting assignment. (see The Divided Brain in a Unified Self)

    b.   The left hemisphere has better logic and language abilities.

    c, d.   The two hemispheres will not be equally activated in the completion of this task. Research has determined that certain tasks are performed more efficiently by one hemisphere than by another.

16.   d is the answer.   When the corpus callosum is cut, the two hemispheres are no longer joined. Without the corpus callosum, the information coming to the right side of Sue's brain (from her left hand) cannot reach the language centers on the left side of the brain. Sue can recognize the feel of the object because that task does not require help from the left hemisphere. (see The Divided Brain in the Unified Self)

a. The hippocampus is responsible for helping to store new memories. Sue could remember what the object was, as evidenced by her ability to choose it by touch.

b. The substantia nigra works with the striatum to help a person start moving. Sue does not have a problem with starting to move.

c. If Sue's parietal lobe were damaged, she would have trouble sensing touch, pressure, and temperature on her skin. Because she can choose the object, she must not have trouble with this lobe.

17. d is the answer.   Stem cell research is controversial both because it is linked to cloning and to the abortion debate. (see Linkages: Human Development and the Changing Brain)

a. Although stem cells are linked to cloning, part of the controversy is the connection to the abortion debate as well.

b. It is true that neural stem cells may someday be used to replace damaged tissue by cells created from a person's own body (e.g., stem cells harvested from bone marrow or some other accessible site). But this is an exciting application for persons suffering from disease that damages their brain tissue, not part of the controversy.

c. Although stem cells can be harvested from embryos, much of stem cell research focuses on harvesting them from a person's own bone marrow or some other accessible site. Further, the abortion debate is not the only controversy, as many people also believe stem cell research is connected to cloning an entire person.

18. c is the answer.   Degenerating acetylcholine neurons are associated with Alzheimer's disease, and low levels of dopamine are associated with Parkinson's disease. (see Three Classes of Neurotransmitters)

a, b, d. Decreased levels of dopamine are associated with Parkinson's disease; abnormal levels of norepinephrine are associated with depression; and degenerating cholinergic neurons are associated with Alzheimer's disease.

19. a is the answer.   Neurotransmitters travel across synapses, and hormones travel via the bloodstream; therefore, statement a is incorrect. (see The Endocrine System: Coordinating the Internal World)

b, c, d. All are true.

20. b is the answer.   The endocrine system regulates a variety of activity ranging from physical growth to stress response. (see The Endocrine System: Coordinating the Internal World)

a. The central nervous system guides all activity, but neurons in the CNS do not directly regulate physical growth.

c. The immune system finds and eliminate foreign cells, and will is not discussed in this chapter.

d. Although we do not have to consciously control our endocrine system in order for it to work, it is not a reflex. In a reflex, the spinal cord signals muscles to react to a stimulus; in immune system functioning, the cells locate and combat foreign cells.

Now turn to the quiz analysis table at the end of this chapter to find which areas you know well and which areas you need to work on. Circle the numbers in the table for items on Quiz 1 that you answered correctly.

Quiz 2

1.   d is the answer.   A neuron's structure, its "excitable" surface membrane, and the minute gap between neurons are the three unique features that enable efficient signal communication. (see Cells of the Nervous System)

    a, b, c.   Each contributes to efficient communication, but d is the correct answer.

2.   a is the answer.   When an axon is at rest, it is polarized. Depolarization leads to action potentials. The bored axon with no action is polarized. Myelin speeds the action potential on its way. The second neuron, despite the myelin wrapped around its axon, cannot seem to get action potentials down the length of the axon to the synapse fast enough for the boss. (see Action Potentials)

    b.   Axons have receptors, but they do not affect conduction speed.

    c.   An axon at rest is polarized. All axons have sodium gates. They do not affect the speed at which the action potential travels down the axon.

    d.   An axon at rest is polarized. Vesicles are located at the very tip of the axon and do not influence the speed of an action potential.

3.   a is the answer.   Positive ions depolarize an axon by entering through gates in a chain reaction from one end of the axon to the other. (see Action Potentials)

    b.   The sodium and calcium ions do not rush down the axon. Instead, like a line of dominoes pushed over, positive ions coming through one open gate cause the next gate to open (and the next, and the next) until one segment after another has been depolarized.

    c.   The postsynaptic potential does dissipate as it reaches the cell body, but an action potential starts and finishes at the same rate.

    d.   After an action potential has reached it, a neurotransmitter floats across a synapse to bind with a receptor.

4.   d is the answer.   Axons release neurotransmitters at synapses, and the most common arrangement is to have postsynaptic receptors on dendrites. However, postsynaptic receptors are also found on cell bodies and on axons (the axon of a second neuron can be postsynaptic to a presynaptic axon). (see Synapses and Communication Between Neurons)

5.   b is the answer.   An inhibitory postsynaptic potential (IPSP) makes it less likely the cell will fire. Because GABA makes the postsynaptic cell less likely to fire, we can say that it causes an IPSP. (see Synapses and Communication Between Neurons)

    a.   An excitatory postsynaptic potential (EPSP) makes it more likely that the cell following it will fire an action potential. GABA reduces the likelihood of firing in the postsynaptic cell.

    c.   *Neutral* is not a term associated with postsynaptic potentials. Although the *neutral* term might be interpreted to mean that the postsynaptic potential is unaffected, even this is incorrect, because GABA does affect postsynaptic potential.

    d.   *Increased* is not a term associated with postsynaptic potentials. Although it might imply that the postsynaptic potential was excitatory, even this is not correct, as GABA causes inhibitory postsynaptic potentials.

6.   d is the answer.   The somatic nervous system transmits information from the senses to the central nervous system (sensory neurons) and carries signals from the central nervous system to the muscles that move the skeleton (motor neurons). (see Organization and Functions of the Nervous System)

a. The peripheral nervous system includes the somatic nervous system, so this is partially correct, but the somatic nervous system is the more precise answer.

b. The sympathetic nervous system is part of the autonomic nervous system. Rather than relaying sensory information, the sympathetic nervous system is known primarily for initiating the fight-or-flight response.

c. The autonomic nervous system contains the sympathetic and parasympathetic nervous systems, not sensory neurons.

7. c is the answer.   The somatic nervous system carries information from the senses to the central nervous system and carries signals from the central nervous system to the muscles that move the skeleton. (see Organization and Functions of the Nervous System)

a. The central nervous system includes the brain and spinal cord. The brain makes decisions about how to move, but the somatic nervous system (part of the peripheral nervous system) carries these signals to the muscles.

b. The autonomic nervous system (part of the peripheral nervous system) carries messages back and forth between the central nervous system and the body's organs and glands.

d. The sympathetic nervous system is part of the autonomic system (it controls the automatic functions of the body, not voluntary skeletal muscle movement).

8. d is the answer.   The sympathetic nervous system is a division of the autonomic nervous system that activates the body. (see The Autonomic Nervous System)

a. The parasympathetic system of the autonomic nervous system calms the body.

b. The peripheral nervous system has two branches: the somatic and autonomic. It is not a subdivision of the autonomic.

c. The somatic nervous system is the branch of the peripheral nervous system controlling voluntary movement and receiving sensory information. It is not a subdivision of the autonomic.

9. d is the answer.   A reflex can occur entirely within the spinal cord; it involves afferent and efferent neurons; and it is involuntary. (see The Spinal Cord)

10. b is the answer.   Information about the environment travels through the spinal cord on its way to the brain. In addition, any directions that the brain sends to the skeletal muscles must pass through the spinal cord. If the spinal cord is severed, information cannot travel between the brain and any destination below the severed section of the spinal cord. (see The Spinal Cord)

a, c. Damage to the spinal cord will not injure the brain. The brain may not be as active because it does not receive as much information as it did prior to the spinal cord's injury, but it would still be capable of handling that information.

d. b is the answer.

11. d is the answer.   The hypothalamus is the correct answer. The hypothalamus influences basic motivated behavior, such as eating, sexual behavior, aggression, and fear. Joe's reduced interest in sex suggests that his hypothalamus was damaged. (see The Brain)

a. The substantia nigra is a structure of the midbrain involved in the initiation of movement, not in sexual behavior.

b. The reticular formation is a brain structure involved in attention and alertness, not sexual behavior.

   c.   The cerebellum is a part of the hindbrain involved in fine motor movement, not sexual behavior.

12. b is the answer   Damage to the hippocampus causes the inability to form new memories. Conchita cannot form new memories for people or stories. (see The Brain)

   a.   The cerebellum controls movement, not memory.

   c.   The medulla regulates vital functions, such as heart rate and breathing.

   d.   The hypothalamus regulates hunger, thirst, and sex drives, not memory.

13. c is the answer.   The sensory cortex found in the occipital lobe receives information concerning vision. (see The Cerebral Cortex)

   a.   The thalamus, found in the forebrain, relays pain signals from the spinal cord and the senses to upper levels in the brain.

   b.   The motor cortex, found in the frontal lobe, is involved in movement.

   d.   The parietal lobe receives information about temperature from the skin.

14. c is the answer.   The association cortex, involved in higher mental abilities, often receives information from more than one sense or combines sensory and motor information. (see The Cerebral Cortex)

   a.   The somatosensory cortex, in the parietal lobe, receives information about touch, pain, and temperature.

   b.   The limbic system is a series of interconnected structures that play an important role in regulating emotion and memory.

   d.   *Homunculus* is the term for the pattern of neighboring skin sensations corresponding to neighboring parts of the somatosensory cortex.

15. c is the answer.   Mirror neuron mechanisms occur when a neural response is the same when someone does something as it is when one observes the same thing. (see Thinking Critically: What Can fMRI Tell Us About Behavior and Mental Processes?)

   a.   Neuroeconomics is a new field focused on the neural processes underlying investment decisions.

   b.   Diffusion tensor imaging is a variant of fMRI technology which traces activity of axon pathways.

   d.   Transcranial magnetic stimulation is a technology that temporarily disrupts the function of a particular part of the brain.

16. c is the answer.   The corpus callosum, a massive bundle of fibers, connects the two cerebral hemispheres. It has been surgically severed, not enlarged, in cases of severe epilepsy, to decrease the spread of electrical seizures. (see Plasticity in the Nervous System)

   a, b, d.   All are true.

17. b is the answer.   The motor cortex in the left hemisphere controls the movement of the body's right side. (see The Divided Brain in a Unified Self)

   a.   A severed corpus callosum will only prevent the right hemisphere from communicating with the left hemisphere.

   c.   A damaged hypothalamus causes malfunction in eating, drinking, sex drives, and, possibly, emotional responses.

    d.   The right somatosensory cortex receives sensory information from the body's left side. Thus, motor functioning will not be impaired.

18. c is the answer.   Serotonin affects sleep and mood, and is indeed often found in lower amounts in the brains of suicide victims. (see The Endocrine System: Coordinating the Internal World)

    a.   The neurotransmitter glutamate is involved in memory, not mood.

    b.   The neurotransmitter dopamine is involved in movement and reward, not mood.

    d.   Nitric oxide, a gas that can act as a neurotransmitter, is involved in a variety of functions ranging from penile erection to the formation of memories. It has not been linked to mood, however.

19. a is the answer.   Glands release hormones such as cortisol into the bloodstream. (see The Endocrine System: Coordinating the Internal World)

    b.   Neurotransmitter systems are groups of neurons using the same neurotransmitter.

    c.   Synapses are the gaps between neurons; they do not release hormones into the bloodstream.

    d.   Target organs have cells with receptors for hormones. They receive, not send, the hormones.

20. d is the answer.   Cortisol is a stress hormone, not a sex hormone. (see The Endocrine System: Coordinating the Internal World)

    b, c, d.   Estrogen, androgens and testosterone are all examples of sex hormones.

Now turn to the quiz analysis table at the end of this chapter to find which areas you know well and which areas you need to work on. Circle the numbers in the table for items on Quiz 2 that you answered correctly.

For each question you answered correctly, circle its number. (Quiz 1 numbers are not shaded; Quiz 2 numbers are shaded.) Are there patterns in the types of questions or the topics you got wrong that could direct your further study? Did you improve from Quiz 1 to Quiz 2?

QUIZ REVIEW

Topic	Type of Question		
	Definition	**Comprehension**	**Application**
The Nervous System			
Cells of the Nervous System		1	
		1	
Action Potentials			2, 3
			2, 3
Synapses and Communication Between Neurons			5
			4, 5
Organization and Functions of the Nervous System		6	7
		6	
The Peripheral Nervous System: Keeping in Touch with the World			
The Somatic Nervous System			
			7
The Autonomic Nervous System			8
			8
Central Nervous System: Making Sense of the World			
The Spinal Cord			
	9	10	
The Brain	9, 10		11
			11, 12
Thinking Critically: What Can fMRI Tell Us About Behavior and Mental Processes?		4	
		15	
The Cerebral Cortex	12		13
	13	14	
The Divided Brain in a Unified Self			15, 16
			17
Plasticity in the Nervous System		14	
	16		
Linkages: Human Development and the Changing Brain		17	
The Chemistry of Psychology			
Three Classes of Neurotransmitters			18
		18	
The Endocrine System: Coordinating the Internal World	20	19	
		20	19

Total correct by quiz:

Quiz 1:	
Quiz 2:	

CHAPTER 4

Sensation

Our knowledge of the world comes through our senses; our senses translate information about the world into neural activity for interpretation by the brain. Messages received by the brain are called sensations.

OUTLINE

I. **SENSORY SYSTEMS**

    The first step in some systems occurs when the stimulus is modified by an accessory structure (the lens of the eye or the outer ear). Transduction, the transformation of incoming energy into neural activity, takes place at the neural receptors. Changes in stimuli produce the greatest receptor response; stimuli that remain at a constant level produce sensory adaptation. Neural receptors stimulate sensory neuron activity, which carries messages (except smell) to the thalamus and then to the cerebral cortex.

    A. The Problem of Encoding

        Encoding is the transformation of an object's distinguishing physical characteristics into a pattern of neural activity that precisely identifies those physical characteristics. According to the specific energy doctrine, each sensory system will produce codes for only that one sense. For example, *any* stimulation of the receptors in the eye, whether from light or eye pressure, will produce only the sensation of light. Codes for the physical attributes of an object can take different forms. *Temporal codes* cause changes in neural activity rates or timing; *spatial codes* are represented by the physical location of neural activity.

    B. Linkages: Sensation and Biological Aspects of Psychology

        Visual, auditory, and tactile information travels through the thalamus to a primary area of sensory cortex. The information is contralaterally represented and is mapped out in topographical representation. The density of neurons in the sense organ determines the extent of its representation in the brain. Regions of primary sensory cortex are divided into columns of cells that respond to similar stimuli in the environment. More complex processing of sensory information occurs in the association cortex.

II. **HEARING**

    Sound is a repetitive fluctuation in the pressure of a medium such as air. Vibrating objects create the fluctuations in air pressure that create sound. A repetitive fluctuation or change in pressure is a wave.

    A. Sound

        1. *Physical Characteristics of Sound*. Waves have three important characteristics: amplitude, wavelength, and frequency (frequency is described in units called hertz).

        2. *Psychological Dimensions of Sound*. The amplitude of the sound wave determines loudness; loudness is described in units called decibels. The frequency of the sound wave determines pitch, how high or low a tone is. Some individuals may have absolute pitch, often called perfect pitch. Complex waveforms added to the fundamental frequency that makes up a sound wave produce timbre, a sound's quality.

B. The Ear
    1. *Auditory Accessory Structures.* The pinna collects the sound waves, which then strike the tympanic membrane, which in turn produces a vibration that causes the malleus (hammer), incus (anvil), and stapes (stirrup) to vibrate.
    2. *Auditory Transduction.* Vibrations pass through the oval window and the fluid in the cochlea to move the basilar membrane, which stretches along the floor of the cochlea. Movement of the basilar membrane causes tiny hair cells that touch it to move. Hair-cell movement causes neuron activity in the acoustic nerve, which carries auditory information to the brain. This process is known as auditory transduction.
    3. *Deafness.* Deafness can be caused by problems with the bones in the inner ear (conduction deafness) or by problems with the auditory nerve or hair cells (nerve deafness).
C. Auditory Pathways, Representations, and Experiences
    Information from the right auditory nerve crosses to the left side of the brain and passes through the thalamus on its way to the auditory cortex.
    1. *Sensing Pitch.* Cells in the auditory cortex have preferred frequencies; they respond maximally to sounds of particular frequencies.
    2. *Locating Sounds.* A temporal code is used to localize sounds.
D. Coding Intensity and Frequency
    The firing rate of neurons within the auditory nerve increases as sound intensity increases. Frequency is coded in one of two ways:
    1. *Place Theory.* Place theory states that hair cells at a particular place on the basilar membrane respond most to the wave peak associated with a particular frequency of sound. High frequencies are coded exclusively by the place where the wave peaks.
    2. *Frequency-Matching Theory.* The firing rate of a neuron in the auditory nerve matches the frequency of a sound wave. The lowest frequencies are coded by frequency matching. Low to moderate frequencies are coded both by frequency matching and by the place on the basilar membrane where the traveling wave peaks. Firing together, neurons create a volley of firing at a combined frequency that is faster than any single neuron could achieve alone. The volley theory is another name for the frequency-matching theory.

III. VISION
A. Light
    Visible light is electromagnetic radiation that has a wavelength from about 400 to 750 nanometers. We cannot see electromagnetic radiation or light wavelengths that are outside of this range. Our sensation depends on light intensity and light wavelength.
B. Focusing Light
    Light waves pass through the cornea, the pupil, and the lens before being focused on the retina. The iris adjusts the size of the pupil opening. The cornea and the muscles that hold the lens in place focus the light on the retina through a process called ocular accommodation.
C. Converting Light into Images
    Visual transduction, the conversion of light energy into neural activity, takes place in the photoreceptors of the retina.
    1. *Photoreceptors.* The photoreceptors contain photopigments that break down in reaction to light and cause changes in photoreceptor membrane potentials. Dark adaptation, the gradually increasing ability to see in the dark, occurs as new photopigments are synthesized. Rods, one type of photoreceptor, contain the photopigment rhodopsin and are more sensitive to light but cannot discriminate between colors. Cones, the other type of photoreceptor, contain three varieties of iodopsin, which can detect color and

are more active in bright light. Cones are highly concentrated in the <u>fovea</u>, where <u>visual acuity</u> is greatest.

2. *Interactions in the Retina*. (Examination of Figure 4.10 in your text will greatly facilitate your understanding of this section.) Activity in the eye actually enhances the visual image. Light energy stimulates photoreceptor cells, which stimulate bipolar cells. Many photoreceptors converge on one bipolar cell. Photoreceptors also stimulate interneurons, which signal (usually in an inhibitory manner) surrounding bipolar cells. As a result, the photoreceptor that receives the greatest light energy stimulus will stimulate one bipolar cell and, through lateral inhibition (involving interneurons), decrease the stimulation of surrounding bipolar cells. As a result, the brain receives messages of light contrasts or comparisons from two bipolar cells that represent neighboring points in the visual field.

3. *Ganglion Cells and Their Receptive Fields*. Bipolar cells stimulate ganglion cells, whose axons form the optic nerve that extends into the brain. Most ganglion cells have center-surround <u>visual receptive fields</u>. Stimulation of <u>ganglion cells</u> enhances the sensation of variations, such as edges and small spots of light or dark.

D. Visual Pathways

The axons of all the ganglion cells combine to form the <u>optic nerve</u>, which travels to the brain. There are no photoreceptors at the point where the optic nerve leaves the eye, creating a <u>blind spot</u>. At the optic chiasm, fibers carrying information about the right side of the visual field cross over to the left side of the brain (see Figure 4.21 in your text). Beyond the <u>optic chiasm</u> the fibers synapse in the lateral geniculate nucleus (LGN); from the LGN, fibers go to the <u>visual cortex</u>, located in the occipital lobe. The cells in the cortex, arranged in columns, form topographical maps of the visual world. Larger areas of the cortex are devoted to areas of the retina that have many photoreceptors.

E. Visual Representations

1. *Parallel Processing of Visual Properties*. The LGN is organized into multiple layers of neurons; each layer contains a complete map of the retina. Each also responds to different aspects of visual stimuli: form, color, movement, and distance. There is no place in the cortex at which all of this information merges. Instead, each layer processes information in parallel (simultaneously) and communicates with the other layers.

2. *Hierarchical Processing of Visual Information*. Cells in the cortex that respond to specific features of objects are called <u>feature detectors</u>. Complex feature detectors are built out of simpler feature detectors.

F. Seeing Color

1. *Wavelengths and Color Sensation*. <u>Hue</u>, <u>color saturation</u>, and <u>brightness</u> are three psychological aspects of color sensation. Additive color mixing, the mixing of different wavelengths of light, always produces a lighter color. In subtractive color mixing, continued combinations of color (as in paints) will produce black.

2. *The Trichromatic Theory of Color Vision*. According to the <u>trichromatic theory</u>, there are three types of cones, each of which responds best to a different color (red, green, or blue) or wavelength.

3. *The Opponent-Process Theory of Color Vision*. The <u>opponent-process theory</u> states that the visual elements sensitive to color occur in three pairs and that the members of each pair inhibit each other. Each element signals one or the other color in a pair, but never both. The three element pairs, which contain complementary colors, are red-green, blue-yellow, and black-white.

4. *A Synthesis and an Update*. Together, the two theories of color vision can explain color vision. The existence of three types of cones that pick up information about red, green, and blue color conforms to trichromatic theory. And the center-surround receptive

fields of the ganglion cells are color-coded in pairs, which correspond to the three-element pairs of the <u>opponent-process theory</u>.

5. *Colorblindness*. People who are colorblind discriminate fewer colors than other people. Their cones lack the color-sensitive pigments for red, green, or blue, creating <u>colorblindness</u>.

G. Interaction of the Senses: Synesthesia

Various dimensions of vision interact, and vision can also interact with hearing and other senses in a process known as <u>synesthesia</u>. For example, some people experience certain letters, numbers, or sounds as being in certain colors.

IV. THE CHEMICAL SENSES: SMELL AND TASTE

A. Olfaction

<u>Olfactory perception</u>, or smell, occurs when airborne chemicals are detected by receptor cells in the upper part of the nose. Axons from the nose travel to the <u>olfactory bulb</u>, and from there axons spread to many areas of the brain, especially to the amygdala. Chemicals called <u>pheromones</u> can shape the behavior and physiology of animals. For instance, mammals lick the pheromones of others of their kind and pass them into a specialized portion of the olfactory system called the <u>vomeronasal system</u>. Although no solid evidence exists to suggest the action of pheromones in humans, it is known that people learn to associate smells with sexual activity or certain people.

B. Gustation

<u>Papillae</u> contain receptors for taste, which can detect only sweet, sour, bitter, salty, umami, and astringent flavors. Each taste bud in the papillae responds best to one or two of these categories but weakly to the other categories. This is how <u>taste perception</u> (also known as gustation), our sense of taste, operates.

C. Smell, Taste, and Flavor

Flavor is a combination of smell and taste. The temperature and texture of food, along with human nutritional states, can enhance flavor.

V. CUTANEOUS SENSES AND THE VESTIBULAR SYSTEM

The <u>cutaneous systems</u>, also known as the *somatic senses* or *somatosensory senses*, include the skin senses of touch, temperature, pain, and proprioception. Proprioceptive senses include kinesthesia and the sense of equilibrium.

A. Touch and Temperature

Survival would be extremely difficult without a sense of touch.

1. *Stimulus and Receptors for Touch*. There are many types of receptors in or somewhere near the skin that respond to mechanical deformation of the skin. The fingers, which have many receptors for touch, are the primary sensory apparatus for exploring by touch.

2. *Adaptation of Touch Receptors*. We are most sensitive to changes in touch. When in constant contact with a stimulus, the touch receptors show adaptation by decreasing the rate at which they fire.

3. *Encoding and Representation of Touch Information*. Information about the weight and vibration of a stimulus is coded by the number of nerves stimulated and the frequency at which individual nerves fire. Location is coded by the organization of the information, which is topographical and contralateralized; it tells the brain where you have been touched.

4. *Temperature*. Some skin receptors are sensitive to warmth and cold. Many receptors that respond to temperature also respond to touch.

B. Pain

1. *Pain as an Information Sense*. Painful stimuli cause the release of chemicals, causing pain nerves to fire. A-delta fibers and C fibers carry information about different types

of pain to the spinal cord, where they synapse with neurons that carry the pain signals to the thalamus and other brain areas.

2. *Emotional Aspects of Pain.* Specific pathways carry an emotional component of the painful stimulus to areas of the hindbrain and reticular formation, activating emotional responses. Our expectations of the onset and intensity of pain affect our evaluation of it.

3. *The Gate Control Theory of Pain.* According to the <u>gate control theory of pain</u>, pain can be blocked in several ways at the spinal cord. Other sensory information, aside from pain, can compete and take over pain pathways. The brain can produce <u>analgesia</u> by sending signals down the spinal cord.

4. *Natural Analgesics.* Serotonin and endorphins are naturally occurring substances that block synapses in fibers carrying pain signals. The body releases endorphins in painful situations: when experiencing labor pains during childbirth; when eating very hot, spicy food; and when people believe they are receiving a painkiller.

C.   Thinking Critically: Does Acupuncture Relieve Pain?

What am I being asked to believe or accept?

Acupuncturists assert that twirling a needle in the skin can relieve pain caused by just about any stimulus.

What evidence is available to support the assertion?

Well-controlled studies are surprisingly rare overall, and the results are contradictory. However, acupuncture does stimulate the release of endorphins, which are naturally occurring pain relievers.

Are there alternative ways of interpreting the evidence?

Endorphins can be activated by placebos, thus suggesting that acupuncture may not have an entirely physical basis for pain relief.

What additional evidence would help to evaluate the alternatives?

Placebo methodologies, such as the sham method, would help to sort out the claims of acupuncture's proponents. Researchers need to study the relationship between internal painkilling systems and external methods for stimulating them. In addition, an understanding of the types of pain for which acupuncture is most effective may lead to a better understanding of the possible physical effects of acupuncture.

What conclusions are reasonable?

Acupuncture does relieve certain types of pain, but we do not know why.

D.   Proprioception: Sensing Body Position

We know where we are and what each part of our body is doing through <u>proprioceptive senses</u>.

1. *Sense of Equilibrium.* The <u>sense of equilibrium</u>, often called the <u>vestibular sense</u>, tells the brain about the head and body's position in space as well as about general movement. Fluid and <u>otoliths</u> within the <u>vestibular sacs,</u> and fluid within the <u>semicircular canals</u> located near the inner ear, shift as our position changes; the resulting movement of hair cells stimulates neurons. The vestibular system has connections to the cerebellum, parts of the autonomic nervous system, and the eyes.

2. *Kinesthetic Perception.* The ability to know where the parts of your body are with respect to one another is called the <u>kinesthetic sense</u>. It operates through information sent from joint and muscle-fiber receptors called <u>proprioceptors</u> to the thalamus and then to the somatosensory cortex and the cerebellum.

E.   Focus on Research Methods: The Case of the Mysterious Spells

Linda was studied by Jozsef Janszky, a neurologist, for recurring spells that began with orgasmic sensations, followed by a staring, unresponsive state. Using EEG and MRI technology, Janszky found that Linda had abnormal tissue in her right temporal lobe which made seizures likely to occur there. After removing the tissue surgically, her seizures in that area stopped. It may be that the right temporal cortex is important in creating the sensory experience of orgasm.

KEY TERMS

1. A **sense** is a system that translates information from outside the nervous system into neural activity. (see introductory section)

    Examples: Vision, hearing, olfaction, touch, and taste

2. **Sensations** are messages from the senses that make up the raw information that affects many kinds of behavior and mental processes. (see introductory section)

    Example: Feeling a touch on your mouth is a sensation. Knowing that you have been kissed—instead of, say, scratched—and by whom is a perception.

    REMEMBER: Sensation is the message that is sent to the brain about an object's characteristics. Perception is the brain's interpretation of what is sensed. For example, your senses may tell your brain that there is a bright light filling the top half of your visual system and that the light energy has many different wavelengths. Your brain interprets these messages and perceives a sunset.

3. **Accessory structures** are structures, such as the lens of the eye, that modify a stimulus. (see Sensory Systems)

    Example: The lens in the eye bends light before it is picked up by photoreceptors in the retina and transduced into neural activity.

4. **Transduction** is the process of converting incoming energy into neural activity. (see Sensory Systems)

    Example: Photoreceptors in the eye pick up information about light and change it into neural energy, which tells the brain about what is in the visual field.

5. **Neural receptors** are specialized cells that detect certain forms of energy and transduce them into nerve cell activity. (see Sensory Systems)

    REMEMBER: Just as a receptionist *receives* people, the neural receptors in the sensory systems *receive* information about the world.

6. **Sensory adaptation** is the process through which responsiveness to an unchanging stimulus decreases over time. (see Sensory Systems)

    Example: Try to feel your underwear. You probably had to concentrate to feel it against your skin, if you felt it at all. The reason is that the skin receptors in contact with your underwear may have fired rapidly when you got dressed this morning, but now have decreased their activity.

7. **Encoding** is translating the physical properties of a stimulus into a pattern of nerve cell activity that specifically identifies those properties. (see The Problem of Encoding)

    Example: Someone has just touched your cheek. How do the neurons communicate to the brain that your face has been caressed and not slapped? Encoding must convey the intensity of the stimulus to your brain so that it can interpret the touch as a caress or a slap.

    REMEMBER: Your brain interprets messages or sensations as if they were a type of Morse *code*.

8. **Specific energy doctrine** is the discovery that stimulation of a particular sensory nerve provides codes for that sense, no matter how the stimulation takes place. (see The Problem of Enoding)

    Example: Putting pressure on your eyeballs, thereby stimulating sensory nerves with touch, generates the sensation of light. This happens because the receptors in the eye will always transmit a message about light, no matter what type of stimulus is experienced.

9. **Sound** is a repetitive fluctuation in the pressure of a medium, such as air. (see Hearing)

   Example: When an object (such as a violin string) vibrates, molecules in the air move, causing temporary changes in air pressure that stimulate the ear.

10. **Amplitude** is the difference in the peak and the baseline of a waveform. (see Sound)

    REMEMBER: When you amplify something, you make it greater. The greater the amplitude of the sound wave, the greater the loudness of the sound.

11. **Wavelength** is the distance from one peak to the next in a waveform.. (see Sound)

    REMEMBER: Long wavelength and low pitch both begin with *l*.

12. **Frequency** is the number of complete waveforms, or cycles, that pass a given point in space every second. (see Sound)

    REMEMBER: Frequency means "how often." The frequency of a sound wave tells you how often a complete wave or cycle passes a given point in one second. As the wave's frequency increases, so does the sound's pitch. Frequency is described in a unit called hertz.

13. **Loudness** is a psychological dimension of sound determined by the *amplitude* of a sound wave. (see Sound)

    Example: People using a sound system in an auditorium control the loudness of the sound coming from the speakers by adjusting the *amplitude* of the sound waves with their equipment.

    REMEMBER: Loudness is measured in decibels

14. **Pitch**—how high or low a tone sounds. (see Sound)

    Example: Spanky sang a note of the wrong pitch, so his friend told him to sing a slightly higher note. When the frequency of the sound waves coming from Spanky's mouth increased, his friend sensed a higher note.

    REMEMBER: Pitch is determined by the *frequency* of sound waves

15. **Absolute pitch** is the ability to identify the musical notes associated with specific sound frequencies. (see Sound)

    Example: Connor listens to the lawn mower and comments to his mom, "The hum of the motor is a G on the piano!" Connor has absolute, or perfect, pitch.

16. **Timbre** is the mixture of frequencies and amplitudes that make up the quality of sound. (see Sound)

    Example: The next time you listen to music, try to identify the instruments that you hear. The sound of each instrument has a unique timbre. A note played on the piano has a much different sound than the same note played on the cello.

17. The **tympanic membrane** is a membrane in the middle ear that generates vibrations that match the sound waves striking it. (see The Ear)

    REMEMBER: The tympanic membrane is stretched tightly across the end of the ear canal, just like the skin stretched tightly across the head of a <u>drum</u>. The tympanic membrane is also called the ear<u>drum</u>.

18. The **cochlea** is a fluid-filled spiral structure in the ear in which auditory transduction occurs. (see The Ear)

    REMEMBER: The cochlea is like a coiled <u>hose</u>; it contains <u>fluid</u> that moves when sound <u>waves</u> come in.

19. The **basilar membrane** is the floor of the fluid-filled duct that runs through the cochlea. (see The Ear)

REMEMBER: The basilar membrane, which runs along the base of the cochlea, moves the hair cells to create a neural signal. Imagine placing your thumb over the bristles on a toothbrush. The bristles bend when you press on them, much like the hair cells are moved when the basilar membrane reacts to the sound wave going through the fluid. Your thumb represents the pressure from the basilar membrane, and each bristle represents a hair cell that will now translate the pressure into neural activity.

20. The **acoustic nerve** is the bundle of axons that carries stimuli from the hair cells of the cochlea to the brain. (see The Ear)

REMEMBER: The acoustic nerve receives signals from the hair cells and carries them to the thalamus. From the thalamus, the signals are relayed to the auditory cortex in the temporal lobe of the brain.

21. **Auditory cortex** is the area in the brain's temporal lobe that is first to receive information about sounds from the thalamus. (see Auditory Pathways, Representations, and Experiences)

22. **Place theory** states that hair cells at a particular place on the basilar membrane respond most to a particular frequency of sound. (see Coding Intensity and Frequency)

REMEMBER: In your mind, create an image of the basilar membrane all curled up inside the cochlea. Along the length of the membrane, mentally write the names of musical notes. Each place on the membrane is associated with one note or pitch.

23. **Volley theory** is the view that some sounds are coded by matching the frequency of neural firing. (see Coding Intensity and Frequency)

REMEMBER: The frequency of the neuron's firing *matches* the frequency of the sound wave. Together, neurons create a *volley* of firing at a combined frequency that no single neuron could manage alone.

24. **Visible light** is electromagnetic radiation that has a wavelength of approximately 400 to 750 nanometers. (see Light)

25. **Light intensity** is a physical dimension of light waves that refers to how much energy the light contains; it determines the brightness of light. (see Light)

REMEMBER: Just as a higher-amplitude sound wave is experienced as a louder sound, a higher light intensity is experienced as a brighter light.

26. **Light wavelength** is the distance between peaks in light waves. (see Light)

Example: A light wavelength of about 500 nanometers is perceived as green.

27. The **cornea** is the curved, transparent, protective layer through which light rays enter the eye. (see Focusing Light)

REMEMBER: Like plastic wrap covers a bowl, your cornea covers the opening to your eye, yet it allows light to pass through.

28. The **pupil** is an opening in the eye, just behind the cornea, through which light passes. (see Focusing Light)

29. The **iris** is the colorful part of the eye, which constricts or relaxes to adjust the amount of light entering the eye. (see Focusing Light)

30.   The **lens** is the part of they eye behind the pupil that bends light rays, focusing them on the retina. (see Focusing Light)

31.   The **retina** is the surface at the back of the eye onto which the lens focuses light rays. (see Focusing Light)

      REMEMBER: The retina is where transduction of light rays happens. Transduction is the process of converting incoming energy (wavelengths of light) into neural activity.

32.   **Ocular accommodation** is the ability of the lens to change its shape and bend light rays so that objects are in focus. (see Focusing Light)

      REMEMBER: Think of the muscles (when they change the curvature of the lens) as helping the eyes to accommodate to the distance of the object they are looking at.

33.   The **photoreceptors** are specialized cells in the retina that code light energy into nerve cell activity. (see Converting Light into Images)

      REMEMBER: Photo means "light," and *receptors* "receive." Photoreceptors receive light from the visual environment.

34.   **Photopigments** are chemicals in photoreceptors that respond to light and assist in converting light into nerve cell activity. (see Converting Light into Images)

      REMEMBER: When light strikes a photoreceptor, these chemicals break apart and cause changes in the photoreceptor's membrane potential. Photopigments are necessary to the transduction process.

35.   **Dark adaptation** is the increasing ability to see in the dark as time in the dark increases. (see Converting Light into Images)

      REMEMBER: In the dark, photoreceptors synthesize more photopigments, and people can begin to see more clearly. The cones adapt to dark more quickly than the rods do (complete adaptation occurs in about forty-five minutes) and allow us to see with greater acuity in dim light.

      Example: When Rakesh first sat in the darkened auditorium to watch the school play, he could not read the title on the program. After about half an hour, he had no trouble seeing the title.

36.   **Rods** are highly light-sensitive but color-insensitive photoreceptors in the retina that allow vision even in dim light. (see Converting Light into Images)

      Example: The program for Rakesh's school play had pages of different colors, but while in the dark Rakesh could not tell the difference.

37.   **Cones** are photoreceptors in the retina that help us distinguish colors. (see Converting Light into Images)

      REMEMBER: Cones, as compared to rods, are less sensitive to light. Thus, they need more light to be stimulated. When you are in the dark, the lack of light decreases cone stimulation, which in turn decreases your ability to see color. The *c* in cones reminds us of color.

38.   The **fovea** is a region in the center of the retina where cones are highly concentrated. (see Converting Light into Images)

      REMEMBER: Use the following sentence to help you remember the definition of fovea: FOcusing Very Easy in this Area.

39.   **Visual acuity** is visual clarity, which is greatest in the fovea because of its large concentration of cones. (see Converting Light into Images)

      Example: When you take a vision test, your visual acuity is being assessed.

40. **Ganglion cells** are the cells in the retina that generate action potentials. (see Converting Light into Images)

    REMEMBER: Rods and cones transduce light and send the information to bipolar cells and interneurons, which send their information to ganglion cells, which send their information to the brain.

    REMEMBER: A <u>gang</u> of <u>gang</u>lion cell axons reaches from the retina to the brain.

41. A ganglion's **visual receptive field** is the portion of the retina, and the visual world, that affects a given ganglion cell. (see Converting Light into Images)

42. The **optic nerve** is a bundle of fibers composed of axons of ganglion cells that carries visual information to the brain. (see Visual Pathways)

43. The **blind spot** is the light-insensitive point at which axons from all of the ganglion cells converge and exit they eyeball. (see Visual Pathways)

    REMEMBER: It is termed "blind" because it has no photoreceptors and is therefore insensitive to light.

44. The **optic chiasm** is part of the bottom surface of the brain where half of each optic nerve's fibers cross over to the opposite side of the brain. (see Visual Pathways)

    REMEMBER: Chiasm means "cross."

45. The **visual cortex** is an area at the back of the brain to which neurons in the lateral geniculate nucleus relay visual input. (see Visual Pathways)

46. **Feature detectors** are cells in the cortex that respond to a specific feature of an object. (see Visual Representations)

    REMEMBER: Cortical cells detect features, so they are called <u>feature detectors</u>.

47. **Hue** is the essential "color," determined by the dominant wavelength of light. (see Seeing Color)

    Example: Red and green are two different hues with two different wavelengths. (See also Key Term 48.)

    REMEMBER: Black, white, and gray are not considered colors because they do not have their own dominant wavelengths.

48. **Color saturation** is the purity of a color. (see Seeing Color)

    Example: The next time you go to a fast-food restaurant, compare the pictures of food on the wall with the actual food you buy. The colors or hues are the same. However, the pictures appear to be more vibrant. The reason is that the pictures are saturated with wavelengths of similar lengths, whereas the food reflects a broad variety of wavelengths.

49. **Brightness** is the overall intensity of all of the wavelengths that make up light. (see Seeing Color)

50. **Trichromatic theory** is a theory of color vision identifying three types of visual elements, each of which is most sensitive to different wavelengths of light. (see Seeing Color)

    REMEMBER: Tri means "three" and *chromo* means "color." The <u>trichrom</u>atic theory is concerned with the sensation of three colors.

51. The **opponent-process theory** is a theory of color vision stating that color-sensitive visual elements are grouped into red-green, blue-yellow, and black-white elements. (see Seeing Color)

    Example: One ganglion cell may have a red-green center-surround receptive field. If red light causes the center to be stimulated, the surround is inhibited. If green light causes the surround to be stimulated, the center is inhibited. If both the center and the surround are stimulated, we see gray because the opponent colors cancel each other out.

REMEMBER: The color in the center and the color in the surround of a ganglion cell receptive field are *opponents*; they are competing.

52. **Colorblindness** is a condition in which lack of certain photopigments leave a person unable to sense colors. (see Seeing Color)

    Example: Kenny cannot tell the difference between green and red.

53. **Synesthesia** is a blending of sensory experience that causes some people to "see" sounds or "taste" colors, for example. (see Interaction of the Senses: Synesthesia)

    Example: Someone might "taste" the color green as being tart.

54. **Olfactory perception** is the sense of smell. (see The Chemical Senses: Smell and Taste)

    REMEMBER: Olere means "to smell," and *facere* means "to make." *Olfaction* literally means "to make a smell." You can use the following story to help you remember this word. The grandfather of one of the authors worked in a paper mill that was very old and produced an incredibly awful smell. Just remember that the ol' factory smells.

55. **Taste perception** (gustatory perception) refers to the sense of taste. (see The Chemical Senses: Smell and Taste)

    REMEMBER: The first letters of the words in the following sentence spell gustation: Gus's Uncle Sam Tasted All The Indian's Onions.

56. The **olfactory bulb** is a brain structure that receives messages regarding smell. (see Olfaction)

    Example: The axons that synapse in Tyrone's olfactory bulb signaled that a flowery odor was being experienced. The information went on to Tyrone's amygdala, where memories of a friend who wore the same flower-scented perfume were activated.

    REMEMBER: Neural connections from the olfactory bulb travel to many parts of the brain, especially the amygdala.

57. **Pheromones** are chemicals released by one animal and detected by another that shape the second animal's behavior or physiology. (see Olfaction)

    Example: Female pigs immediately assume a mating stance after smelling a pheromone called "androsterone" in a boar's saliva.

58. The **vomeronasal system** is a portion of the mammalian olfactory system that is sensitive to pheromones. (see Olfaction)

59. **Papillae** are structures on the tongue containing groups of taste receptors, or taste buds. (see Gustation)

    Example: The combination of signals from Maggie's papillae results in a salty and sweet taste, which Maggie perceives as caramel corn.

60. The **cutaneous senses** are the senses of touch, temperature, pain, and kinesthesia. (see Cutaneous Senses and the Vestibular System)

    *REMEMBER: Cut*aneous senses would feel if someone *cut* you.

61. The **gate control theory of pain** suggests that a functional "gate" in the spinal cord can either let pain impulses travel upward to the brain or block their progress. (see Pain)

     REMEMBER: The nervous system can use the spinal cord as a gate that will allow only so much information to go through it in either direction. To better understand this concept, think of what happens when a movie lets out. There are so many people coming *out* the doors that nobody can get *into* the theater for a few minutes. Similarly, to prevent pain information from reaching its destination, the brain sends information *down* the spinal cord that blocks the pain signals from *ascending* the spinal cord.

62. **Analgesia** is the absence of pain sensations in the presence of a normally painful stimulus. (see Pain)

     Example: Aspirin is an analgesic drug. Our bodies make chemicals called natural analgesics that can reduce pain sensation. Endorphins are natural analgesics. Serotonin, a neurotransmitter, also plays a role in blocking pain sensation.

63. **Proprioceptive senses** are the sensory systems that allow us to know about where we are and what each part of our body is doing. (see Proprioception: Sensing Body Position)

     Example: Your sense of equilibrium is an example of a proprioceptive sense.

64. The **sense of equilibrium (vestibular sense)** is the proprioceptive sense that provides information about the position of the head (and hence the body) in space and about its movements. (see Proprioception: Sensing Body Position)

     Example: Doing something as simple as a handstand requires vestibular information. If your vestibular senses were not working, you would not know if you were upside down or right-side up.

65. **Vestibular sacs** are organs in the inner ear that connect the semicircular canals and the cochlea and contribute to the body's sense of balance. (see Proprioception: Sensing Body Position)

66. **Otoliths**, also called ear stones, are small crystals in the fluid-filled vestibular sacs of the inner ear that, when shifted by gravity, stimulate nerve cells that inform the brain of the position of the head. (see Proprioception: Sensing Body Position)

67. **Semicircular canals** are tubes in the inner ear whose fluid, when shifted by head movements, stimulates nerve cells that tell the brain about those movements. (see Proprioception: Sensing Body Position)

68. **Kinesthetic perception** is the proprioceptive sense that tells you where the parts of your body are with respect to one another. (see Proprioception: Sensing Body Position)

     Example: You must know where your head is in relation to your hands to be able to touch the tip of your finger to your nose while your eyes are shut.

69. **Proprioceptors** are the receptors in muscles and joints that provide information to the brain about movement and body position. (see Proprioception: Sensing Body Position)

FILL-IN-THE-BLANKS KEY TERMS

This section will help you check your knowledge of the key terms introduced in this chapter. Fill in each blank with the appropriate term from the list of key terms in the previous section.

1. The sensory process in which physical energy is converted into neural energy is _____.

2. In the _____ process, neurons fire at different rates to translate and represent specific sensations to the brain.

3. When examining a sound waveform, one can determine loudness by measuring the _____ of the wave.

4. The quality of a sound by which you can tell it apart from other sounds of the same pitch is called _____.

5. The part of the ear that physically vibrates in response to sound waves is the _____.

6. The hair cells in the ear send neural signals to the brain via the _____.

7. _____ states that the firing rate of a neuron matches the number of sound waves that occur in a second.

8. The color that one perceives is a function of _____.

9. The ability to change the shape of the lens in order to focus images on the retina is called _____.

10. Photoreceptors in the retina that detect color are called _____.

11. The sense of taste is known as _____.

12. The senses of touch, temperature, pain, and kinesthesia are called _____.

13. When sensory receptors decrease their firing in response to a constant stimulus, _____ is said to have occurred.

14. A person who feels no pain in the presence of pain-producing stimuli is experiencing _____.

15. The sense that tells you where your body parts are in relation to one another is called _____.

Total Correct (See answer key) _____

LEARNING OBJECTIVES

1. Define <u>sense</u> and <u>sensation</u>. Be able to explain the differences between sensation and perception. (see introductory section)

2. Define <u>accessory structure</u>, <u>transduction</u>, and <u>neural receptor</u>. (see Sensory Systems)

3. Define adaptation and give an example. (see Sensory Systems)

4. Define <u>encoding</u>, temporal coding, and spatial coding. Explain why sensory information must be coded before it reaches the brain. (see The Problem of Coding)

5. Define the doctrine of specific nerve energies. (see The Problem of Coding)

6. Describe the six characteristics of sensory representation for vision, hearing, and the skin senses. Define topographical representation and primary cortex. (see Linkages: Sensation and Biological Aspects of Psychology)

7. Define <u>sound</u>. Describe the physical characteristics of sound, including <u>amplitude</u>, <u>wavelength</u>, and <u>frequency</u>. (see Sound)

8. Describe the psychological characteristics of sound, including <u>loudness</u>, <u>pitch</u>, and <u>timbre</u>. (see Sound)

9. Name and describe the <u>accessory structures</u> of the ear. (see The Ear)

10. Describe the roles of the <u>cochlea</u>, <u>basilar membrane</u>, hair cells, and <u>acoustic nerve</u> in the process of auditory transduction. Name and describe the types of deafness. (see The Ear)

11. Describe how information is relayed to the <u>auditory cortex</u> and how the cortex codes the frequency and location of sounds. (see Auditory Pathways, Representations, and Experiences)

12. Describe the process of coding auditory information. Discuss the relationship between <u>place theory</u> and <u>volley theory</u> in frequency coding. (see Coding Intensity and Frequency)

13. Define <u>visible light</u>. (see Light)

14. Define <u>light intensity</u> and <u>wavelength</u>. Describe how both are related to what you sense. (see Light)

15. Define and describe the accessory structures of the eye, including the <u>cornea</u>, <u>iris</u>, <u>pupil</u>, and <u>lens</u>. (see Focusing Light)

16. Define <u>retina</u> and explain how <u>ocular accommodation</u> affects the image on the retina. (see Focusing Light)

17. Define <u>photoreceptors</u> and <u>photopigments</u>. Describe how these structures are involved in transduction and <u>dark adaptation</u>. (see Converting Light into Images)

18. Define <u>rods</u>, <u>cones</u>, and <u>fovea</u>. Explain why <u>visual acuity</u> is greatest in the fovea. (see Converting Light into Images)

19. Define lateral inhibition and describe the interactions in the retina that produce it. (see Converting Light into Images)

20. Describe the center-surround <u>visual receptive field</u> of <u>ganglion cells</u>. (see Converting Light into Images)

21. Describe the path that visual information follows on its way to the brain, including the roles of the <u>optic nerve</u>, the <u>optic chiasm</u>, the lateral geniculate nucleus, and the primary <u>visual cortex</u>. Know what creates the <u>blind spot</u>. (see Visual Pathways)

22. Describe parallel processing of visual properties and hierarchical processing of visual information using <u>feature detectors</u>. (see Visual Representations)

23. Define <u>hue</u>, <u>color saturation</u>, and <u>brightness</u>. (see Seeing Color)

24. Describe the <u>trichromatic</u> and <u>opponent-process theories</u> of color vision. Discuss the phenomena each explains, including complementary colors. (see Seeing Color)

25. Describe the physical problem that causes <u>colorblindness</u>. (see Seeing Color)

26. Explain <u>synesthesia</u> and discuss possible explanations for such sensory interactions (see Interaction of the Senses: Synesthesia)

27. Define <u>olfactory perception</u>. Describe the transduction process in the olfactory system. Discuss the path that olfactory information follows to the brain. Define <u>pheromones</u> and the <u>vomeronasal organ</u>. Explain the role of pheromones in humans. (see Olfaction)

28. Define <u>taste</u> and <u>papillae</u>. Describe the relationship among taste, smell, and flavor. (see Gustation; see also Smell, Taste, and Flavor)

29. Define <u>cutaneous senses</u> Describe the transduction process in the skin senses, including touch, temperature, and pain. (see Somatic Senses and the Vestibular System)

30. Describe the <u>gate control theory of pain</u>. Define <u>analgesia</u>. Know the names of the body's natural analgesics. (see Pain)

31. Describe the evidence concerning acupuncture and the conclusions that are most reasonable. (see Thinking Critically: Does Acupuncture Relieve Pain?)

32. Name the proprioceptive senses and explain how they differ from other sensory systems. (see Proprioception: Sensing Body Position)

33. Describe the types of information that the sense of equilibrium (vestibular sense) provides. Discuss the role of the vestibular sacs, otoliths, and semicircular canals in the sensation of vestibular information. (see Proprioception: Sensing Body Position)

34. Define kinesthetic perception. Name the source of kinesthetic information. Explain what went wrong with Linda, who was the subject of a case study. (see Proprioception: Sensing Body Position; see also Focus on Research Methods: The Case of the Mysterious Spells)

CONCEPTS AND EXERCISES

Dr. Roley's Vision

Dr. Roley has only his peripheral vision. Which of the following is true about Dr. Roley?

1. T F   Dr. Roley will not be able to read because he lacks central vision.

2. T F   Dr. Roley will be able to see in color, but only in his periphery.

3. T F   Dr. Roley will not be able to see well in the dark because the photoreceptors that are light sensitive are in central vision.

4. T F   Dr. Roley is functionally blind because the optic nerve depends on central vision, not peripheral, to exit the retina.

5. T F   Dr. Roley's eyes will rely a lot on the photopigment rhodopsin but will not be able to much use iodopsins.

Processes in Sensation

Name the sensory process demonstrated in each of the following incidents.

1. Lori has just stepped into the shower with her watch on. She did not realize the watch was on her arm until it got wet. _____

2. Dr. Malpeli is recording the activity of interneurons and bipolar cells in the retinas of cats. Whenever he places a figure with many contrasting features in the cat's visual field, the recordings show a large increase in neuronal firing. _____

3. In general, the faster a neuron fires, the more intense the stimulus is. _____

4. Jill is six years old. She awakens with a bad dream in the middle of the night. She decides to play with her crayons and coloring book. She becomes frustrated, however, because she cannot see the colors in the dim light. _____

CRITICAL THINKING

Sam and Martina have been called to Marsh Landing, a resort-like residential neighborhood. Recently, several jewelry robberies have occurred in this area. The thief apparently knows his trade very well. He steals only the "good stuff." Mr. and Mrs. Fletcher, who live in Marsh Landing, reported a robbery last night—the seventh in the past two weeks.

Sam and Martina talk to the Fletchers about what happened. They gave Sam and Martina a list of the items that were stolen: a ring, a bracelet, several pairs of cuff links, and a brooch.

Martina continues to ask questions. "Did you see the thief, Mr. Fletcher?"

"Oh, yeah, he woke me up when he came into the room. I was too scared to say anything, though. I didn't know if he was dangerous. Besides, it took him all of five minutes to locate our jewelry box and take our things. He tiptoed out of the bedroom, and I think he went out through the back door."

"Well, what did he look like?" Martina asked.

"He was about six feet tall, and he was wearing a pink T-shirt and olive-green khakis. I think he had black hair. I also noticed that he stood very straight; he had great posture."

"Is the jewelry insured, Mr. Fletcher?"

Mrs. Fletcher piped up, "Oh yes—my goodness, dear, that jewelry was quite expensive. We took out a special policy on it last year."

Sam turns to Martina and says, "This has to be the same guy. Only the *valuable* jewelry is gone. And, as in every other hit, nothing but jewelry has been taken."

Martina just shakes her head. Sam was jumping to conclusions again.

"Mr. Fletcher, do you have a night-light in your room? And if so, is it located near the jewelry box?"

"No, Martina, we don't," Mr. Fletcher replied.

Using the five critical thinking questions in your text, state Sam's original hypothesis and describe his evidence. Based on the clues in the story, what do you think Martina's alternative hypothesis is?

1.   What is Sam's original hypothesis?

2.   What evidence does he have?

3.   What is Martina's probable alternative hypothesis?

4.   What is the evidence that supports her hypothesis? What else would you want to know if you were Martina?

5.   What conclusions can Martina draw?

PERSONAL LEARNING ACTIVITIES

1.   Your textbook says that rods are located in the periphery of the retina and that rods are not sensitive to color. This suggests that you should not be very good at seeing color in your peripheral vision. Do an experiment on yourself to test this idea. Get a batch of colored pencils or markers and lay them in front of you on a table. Without looking at the color, reach down and grab one and hold it far into your peripheral vision. Can you correctly identify the color? Repeat this multiple times and note your percentage correct.

2.   Take a survey of people you know. How many are colorblind? How many wear hearing aids, corrective lenses, or other aids to sensation?

3. To see some interesting color afterimages based on opponent process theory, visit the following website: http://www.colorcube.com/illusions/aftrimge.htm. Does the website expand on the discussion in the text? In what way did the site help you to understand the text material on color vision better? To learn more about the sense of pain on the web, try this site, too: http://faculty.washington.edu/chudler/pain.html. Can you find other sites on the internet that help explain and illustrate the material in your text?

4. Test your taste perception by having someone prepare foods for you to taste without the help of your senses of smell or vision. Without olfactory or visual cues, can you tell the difference between an apple and a potato or between mixtures of salt water and sugar water? Will taste alone distinguish between tapioca pudding and cottage cheese?

5. Experiment on the cues you use to maintain your balance. In a place with room to move, stand without touching anything, close your eyes, and then lift one foot. Lead a blindfolded friend around a building, being careful to indicate obstacles, steps, and turns. Have the friend report on the experience of moving without benefit of sight.

MULTIPLE-CHOICE QUESTIONS

Quiz 1

1. When Ali first had corrective braces put on his teeth, the pressure and tension were very uncomfortable. Now, however, he barely notices his braces. Why?
   a. Because the pressure is constant, his neural receptors have adapted.
   b. Stimulation of a sensory nerve provides codes for only one sense.
   c. There are no free nerve endings in Ali's mouth.
   d. His transduction has been altered by the introduction of the braces.

2. Which is NOT necessary for sound?
   a. Airborne chemicals
   b. A medium, such as air
   c. Fluctuations in the pressure of a medium
   d. Vibrations of an object

3. Ashanti cannot hear. All of the structures in his hearing system work, except for those that transduce the sound waves. Ashanti's _____ do not work; therefore, he has _____ deafness.
   a. hair cells; nerve
   b. hammer, anvil, and stapes bones; conduction
   c. semicircular canals; conduction
   d. tympanic membranes; nerve

4. Place theory proposes a _____ code for sensing pitch; volley theory proposes a _____ code.
   a. temporal; spatial
   b. spatial; temporal
   c. spatial; spatial
   d. temporal; temporal

5.   Contralateral representation in sensation means
    a.   that the world is represented laterally.
    b.   that the cortex builds sensory representations of the opposite side of the world.
    c.   that the cortex contains maps of each sense.
    d.   none of these.

6.   Which of the following structures is NOT necessary for the transduction of light energy?
    a.   Photoreceptors
    b.   Rods and cones
    c.   Visual cortical cells
    d.   Photopigments

7.   A villain is trying to obliterate the visual system of his opponent. If he destroys
    _____, the opponent will be unable to see color.
    a.   rhodopsin
    b.   rods
    c.   iodopsin
    d.   photoreceptors outside the fovea

8.   Which of the following would cause the least amount of lateral inhibition to occur?
    a.   Looking at a spider web covered with dew in the morning sun
    b.   Looking at a zebra's black and white stripes
    c.   Looking at a green refrigerator's surface
    d.   Looking at the pattern of light coming through window blinds

9.   While Becky watched a basketball game on TV, Cindy asked her, "Is this OK for dinner?" Becky did not look away from the game and thought, based on her peripheral vision, that Cindy held up a TV dinner, so she said, "Sure." Only when Cindy served Becky a plate of Brussels sprouts did Becky realize that her visual acuity was not very good because she was relying primarily on
    _____.
    a.   bipolar cells
    b.   cones
    c.   ganglion cells
    d.   rods

10.   Women are more likely than men to have four distinct photopigments, which means that women
    a.   with all four photopigments will have a poorer experience of color than people who do not.
    b.   will always have a poorer experience of color than men.
    c.   will always have a richer experience of color than men.
    d.   with all four photopigments will have a richer experience of color than people who do not.

11. A projection-screen TV has a separate box that aims green, red, and blue lights at the screen. Because the TV shows a full range of colors by combining the green, red, and blue lights in differing amounts, it fits best with the _____ theory of color vision.

     a.   convergence
     b.   frequency-matching
     c.   opponent-process
     d.   trichromatic

12. Roxanne is responsible for teaching a new student how to do the stage lighting for their school's play. What should Roxanne tell the student?

     a.   Mixing colors for lights is identical to the process used for mixing paint.
     b.   Mixing two different colors of light produces a darker color.
     c.   Mixing two different colors of light is called subtractive color mixing.
     d.   Mixing all possible colors of lights produces a white light.

13. When Julia says that the color red tastes tart and the color pink tastes sweet to her, she is describing her sense of

     a.   gustation.
     b.   kinesthesia.
     c.   synesthesia.
     d.   olfaction.

14. Which sense does not send information through the thalamus on its way to the cortex?

     a.   Hearing
     b.   Vision
     c.   Olfaction
     d.   Touch

15. The taste sensation that enhances other tastes is known as

     a.   salty.
     b.   sour.
     c.   astringent.
     d.   umami.

16. In a biology class, Samantha rated solutions on how salty, sweet, or sour each was. Samantha most likely has taken a test of

     a.   analgesia.
     b.   gustation.
     c.   kinesthesia.
     d.   vestibulation.

17. The nerves that signal what is touching Gary's face are firing very, very rapidly. Which of the following most likely happened?

     a.   He was just punched in the mouth.
     b.   He was just kissed on the cheek.
     c.   He just took a drink of water.
     d.   A fly just landed on his nose.

18. Marina hit her elbow on the doorway. According to the gate control theory of pain, in order to reduce the amount of pain she is feeling, Marina should

    a. use the image of a closing gate to give herself the expectation that the pain will end.
    b. rub the sore area.
    c. think about anything other than the pain.
    d. do any of these.

19. Ally has lost her kinesthetic sense. Ally will most likely be unable to

    a. be sure her hand is raised without looking at it.
    b. detect the flavor of her ice cream cone.
    c. feel the warmth of the sun on her face.
    d. respond to pain.

20. In Focus on Research Methods in this chapter, the study described used which methodology?

    a. Experiment
    b. Naturalistic observation
    c. Survey
    d. Case study

Total Correct (See answer key) _____

Quiz 2

Use this quiz to reassess your learning after taking Quiz 1 and reviewing the chapter.

1. Ben is undergoing an experimental treatment that electrically stimulates the hair cells on the organ of Corti. According to the specific energy doctrine,

    a. Ben's auditory neurons will fire at one specific rate.
    b. Ben's proprioceptive nerves will be activated.
    c. Ben will feel a touch.
    d. Ben will hear sounds.

2. For the auditory sense, the physical dimension of wave amplitude corresponds to the psychological experience of _____; the physical dimension of wave frequency corresponds to the psychological experience of _____.

    a. loudness; pitch
    b. pitch; loudness
    c. brightness; color
    d. hue; timbre

3. When Adriana pushes forward on the backs of her pinnas near her scalp, she notices that she can no longer tell where a high-pitched sound is coming from. Adriana's action has directly affected her

    a. accessory structures.
    b. cochlea.
    c. timbre.
    d. transduction mechanisms.

4. Conduction deafness is related to problems with the
   a. hair cells of the basilar membrane.
   b. acoustic nerve.
   c. malleus (hammer), incus (anvil), and stapes (stirrup).
   d. pinna.

5. Which theory suggests that pitch is determined by the location of movement along the basilar membrane?
   a. Place theory
   b. Characteristic-frequency theory
   c. Frequency-matching theory
   d. Volley theory

6. It is too dim for Carly to see what she is reading; therefore, she should _____ by turning on a lamp.
   a. increase the light intensity
   b. increase the light wavelength
   c. decrease the light intensity
   d. decrease the light wavelength

7. Rhoda, who is visiting her sister, just turned out the bathroom light and has to grope along the wall to feel her way back to the bedroom. After being in bed again for about forty-five minutes, she realizes that she can see well. Why?
   a. Ganglion cells have been activated.
   b. Enough photopigments in her rods have been synthesized.
   c. The muscles that control her lenses have adapted to the dark.
   d. The dendrites in her optic nerve have finally resynthesized.

8. People who are colorblind
   a. are blind to all color.
   b. see the world as shades of black, white, and gray.
   c. have cones that contain only two of the three color-sensitive pigments.
   d. see all the same colors as people who are not colorblind, they just mismatch them.

9. The process of lateral inhibition allows the brain to see
   a. color.
   b. black and white.
   c. more distinct contrasts in stimuli.
   d. movement.

10. A villain is working feverishly in his laboratory to devise a way of preventing visual transduction. Which of the following methods would work?
    a. Destroy all the photopigments in a person's eye.
    b. Remove the lateral geniculate nucleus.
    c. Uncross the optic nerve at the optic chiasm.
    d. All of these will prevent transduction.

11. Evelyn tried on a pair of sunglasses with red lenses. After wearing them for a few minutes, Evelyn took them off and realized that everything she looked at now had a green tint. The cells directly responsible for this afterimage were Evelyn's
    a. cones.
    b. bipolar cells.
    c. ganglion cells.
    d. rods.

12. The theory that best explains the afterimage seen by Evelyn is the _____ theory.
    a. computational
    b. opponent-process
    c. trichromatic
    d. volley

13. Joe is walking across campus when he sees his roommate's girlfriend, once again, dressed in an orange top and hot pink skirt with white stripes on it. He comments to his pal, "I can't stand how she dresses. I mean, look at that outfit. It's just screaming at us!" Joe's sense that the outfit's appearance was "loud" illustrates the mixing of senses in
    a. analgesia.
    b. synesthesia.
    c. vestibulation.
    d. proprioception.

14. The brain structure through which each eye's optic nerve crosses over to the opposite side of the brain is the
    a. lateral geniculate nucleus.
    b. optic chiasm.
    c. blind spot.
    d. visual cortex.

15. Neural activity concerning an object that Maria has in her visual field has reached her lateral geniculate nucleus (LGN). A neuron in her LGN is most likely responding to the incoming information by
    a. sending a different message to indicate which side of the visual field the object is in.
    b. sending information to ganglion cells.
    c. combining information about types of lines, colors, and the distance of the object into one message.
    d. sending information about one aspect of the object, such as its depth.

16. When Pete bought a hot dog and fries at a street festival, the smell suddenly brought back memories of playing baseball for his adoring fans. The memory was most likely activated because his nose
    a. sends its messages to the thalamus, which is connected to the olfactory network.
    b. sends its messages to the olfactory bulb, which is connected to the amygdala.
    c. causes papillae to become activated.
    d. causes the basilar membrane to become activated.

17. Andre's papillae do not work. Which of the following statements is Andre most likely to make?
    a. "I miss the feeling of a hot shower on my skin."
    b. "Green and red both look gray to me."
    c. "I couldn't smell the toast burning."
    d. "Nothing tastes right anymore."

18. There is a new website advertising a pheromone product for men that "will have women making eye contact, flirting with, and even coming up and introducing themselves to you!" This product would most likely be a
    a. tape of music with hidden messages.
    b. drug that could be slipped into someone's drink.
    c. gas that would alter a man's voice.
    d. cologne that a man would put on his body.

19. At a track and field competition, Paige pulls a muscle on her best discus throw of the season, but in all the excitement of her school's win, she does not experience much pain from the injury. Paige's lessened pain could be due to
    a. activated A-delta fibers.
    b. activated C fibers.
    c. a higher-than-usual naloxone level.
    d. a higher-than-usual endorphin level.

20. The vestibular sense can be most influenced which of the following other issues in a sensory system?
    a. Eye infection
    b. Ear infection
    c. Skin infection
    d. Canker sore

Total Correct (See answer key) _____

ANSWERS TO FILL-IN-THE-BLANKS KEY TERMS

1. transduction (see Sensory Systems)

2. encoding (see The Problem of Encoding)

3. amplitude (see Sound)

4. timbre (see Sound)

5. tympanic membrane (see The Ear)

6. acoustic nerve (see The Ear)

7. Frequency matching or Volley theory (see Coding Intensity and Frequency)

8. light wavelength (see Light)

9. ocular accommodation (see Focusing Light)

10. cones (see Converting Light into Images)

11. taste perception, or gustation (see The Chemical Senses: Smell and Taste)

12. cutaneous senses (see Cutaneous Senses and the Vestibular System)

13. sensory adaptation (see Sensory Systems)

14. analgesia (see Pain)

15. kinesthetic perception (see Proprioception: Sensing Body Position)

ANSWERS TO CONCEPTS AND EXERCISES

Dr. Roley's Vision

1. *False* Dr. Roley will be able to read using his peripheral vision by holding books or papers with writing on them in his peripheral vision. Although it is challenging to do, people have learned this skill.

2. *False* Dr. Roley will not be able to see in color using his peripheral vision. The photoreceptors that are responsible for color vision are located primarily in the fovea—where central vision occurs. Without central vision, Dr. Roley will be unable to use those photoreceptors, or cones. He will have only the photoreceptors known as rods, which are in the periphery of the retina. Rods detect black and white, but not color.

3. *False* Dr. Roley will see very well in the dark. Because he relies on his peripheral vision and because the photoreceptors in the periphery of the retina, or rods, are extremely light sensitive, Dr. Roley will see well in the dark.

4. *False* Dr. Roley will not be functionally blind. Although the optic nerve does exit the retina in a more central location than the periphery, the axons from the ganglion cells in the periphery go to that exit point and bundle together with those axons from the fovea. Axons from the periphery will still be part of the optic nerve in spite of the fact that Dr. Roley has lost his central vision.

5. *True* Dr. Roley will rely heavily on the photopigment rhodopsin, because that is the photopigment in rods, which are the photoreceptors in the periphery. Iodopsins are photopigments in the cones, which are the photoreceptors in the fovea (where central vision occurs), so Dr. Roley will not rely on these.

Processes in Sensation

1. Your inability to feel a watch on your wrist is due to the sensory adaptation process. When you put on your watch, the cells in the skin begin to fire rapidly and then decrease their activity back to a baseline rate. When Lori stepped into the shower, the cells that would detect the presence of her watch had long ago returned to a baseline firing rate. If you think about it, you will realize that the process of sensory adaptation is very necessary. For just a moment, make yourself notice everything that is touching you. Without sensory adaptation, all of the information would feel as though it were new—as if you had just put on all of your clothes, had just sat down, and had just put on your makeup and jewelry. Without it, we would be overloaded with sensory information. (see Sensory Systems; see also Cutaneous Senses and the Vestibular System)

2. Stimuli with contrasting features—light, dark, edges, or lines—cause bipolar cells and interneurons to engage in lateral inhibition so that the brain receives exaggerated information regarding these contrasts. The exaggerated information makes it easier for the brain to "see." (see Converting Light into Images)

3.   A neuron's firing rate tells the brain how intense a stimulus is. This process is an example of temporal coding. (see The Problem of Encoding)

4.   Jill is experiencing dark adaptation. Her cone and rod cells have adapted so that she can see shapes and images. However, the rods, which work best in dim light, cannot pick up color information. That is why Jill cannot see the colors of her crayons. (see Converting Light into Images)

ANSWERS TO CRITICAL THINKING

1.   Sam hypothesizes that the same jewelry thief who has been in the neighborhood for the past several weeks is also the culprit in the Fletcher burglary.

2.   The fact that the Fletchers live in Marsh Landing and that the thief took only the good jewelry supports Sam's hypothesis.

3.   Martina believes that the Fletchers made the whole thing up so they could claim the insurance money.

4.   Martina knows that, because rods are more active in the dark, Mr. Fletcher would not be able to tell what colors the thief was wearing (hence the night-light question). Martina should also find out if the Fletchers are having money troubles. Financial problems may have been their motive for faking the crime.

5.   Martina probably cannot conclude anything just yet, but she is well on her way to supporting her hypothesis. *NOTE:* Critical thinking is a constant process of hypothesizing, examining evidence, rehypothesizing, collecting more evidence, and so on. Martina may not be correct. Can you think of any other hypotheses that could explain the data?

ANSWERS TO MULTIPLE-CHOICE QUESTIONS

Circle the question numbers you answered correctly.

Quiz 1

1.   a is the answer.   A constant level of stimulation usually produces sensory adaptation, a process through which responsiveness to an unchanging stimulus decreases over time. (see Sensory Systems)

 b.   This statement is true, but it refers to the idea that specific sensory nerves serve specific senses.

 c.   Many types of nerve endings are involved in the cutaneous senses.

 d.   Transduction is the process of converting environmental signals into neural signals. Braces would not interfere with transduction; they would just produce another sensation to be transduced.

2.   a is the answer.   Airborne chemicals are detected by the olfactory sense, the sense of smell. (see Sound)

 b, c, d.   Together these form the definition of sound. Sound is the result of repetitive fluctuations in the pressure of a medium, such as air, produced by the vibrations of an object.

3.   a is the answer.   Hair cells are the transduction mechanisms for hearing; if they or the auditory nerve malfunction, nerve deafness results. (see The Ear)

 b.   The hammer (malleus), anvil (incus), and stirrup (stapes) are accessory structures. If these middle-ear bones are fused, conduction deafness results.

c. The semicircular canals are the parts of the inner ear used for the vestibular sense.

d. Tympanic membranes (eardrums) send vibrations to the bones of the middle ear; they do not transduce sound waves.

4. b is the answer.   Place theory proposes that different sound frequencies cause waves to move down the basilar membrane which peak in different places. The place in space on the basilar membrane where the wave peaks corresponds to a particular pitch sensation, according to place theory. This is a spatial code. Volley theory, however, proposes that for low-pitch sounds (which are low frequency) the frequency of the sound is matched by the firing rate of auditory nerve fibers. Thus, the temporal speed of the neural firing is the code. (see Coding Intensity and Frequency)

a, c, d.   Place theory proposes a spatial coding process, whereas frequency-matching theory proposes a temporal coding process.

5. b is the answer.   Contralateral representation means that each side of the cortex builds a sensory representation for the opposite side of the world. (see Linkages: Sensation and Biological Aspects of Psychology)

a..   Contralateral representation refers to representation across the different sides of the cortex.

c.   Cortical maps of the senses are called *topographical representation,* not contralateral representation.

d.   b is the answer.

6. c is the answer.   Transduction is the conversion of stimulus energy into neural energy. This process occurs before information reaches the central nervous system. Therefore, the visual cortical cells in the brain receive already-transduced information about the world. (see Converting Light into Images)

a, b, d.   Visual transduction takes place at the photoreceptors (rods and cones) in the retina. Photopigments in the rods and cones break apart when stimulated by light, causing changes in membrane potential. A change in membrane potential is the first step toward neural activity.

7. c is the answer.   Iodopsin is the photopigment in cones that initiates the transduction process. If this substance were destroyed, transduction would not occur and color vision would be impossible. (see Converting Light into Images)

a, b.   Rods contain the photopigment rhodopsin. Rods detect black and white. Destroying rhodopsin would not destroy color vision.

d.   The photoreceptors outside of the fovea are rods, which detect black and white.

8. c is the answer.   Lateral inhibition occurs when there are many contrasts in visual stimuli, such as stripes or patterns of light and dark. The surface of a refrigerator does not feature much contrast. (see Converting Light into Images)

a.   The edges of the lines in the web would be seen as differences between light and dark, causing a great deal of lateral inhibition.

b.   The edges of a zebra's stripes would be seen as differences between light and dark, causing a great deal of lateral inhibition.

d.   The pattern of light coming through the blinds would create strips of dark next to strips of light. The contrast would cause a great deal of lateral inhibition.

9.   d is the answer.   Rods are predominant in the periphery of the retina. If Becky uses peripheral vision, her acuity will be poorer. (see Converting Light into Images)

   a, c.   Bipolar and ganglion cells receive information from the rods and cones; the lack of information from the cones causes the poor vision.

   b.   Cones are located primarily in the fovea, or center, of the retina and are responsible for its high visual acuity.

10. d is the answer.   Women who have all four photopigments have a richer experience of color than people who do not have all four. Men who have all four would also have a richer experience of color than people who do not. (see Seeing Color)

   a, b.   Having all four distinct photopigments leads to a richer, not poorer, experience of color.

   c.   Having all four distinct photopigments does lead to a richer experience of color, and women are more likely to have this. However, it is the presence of the four distinct photopigments, not gender per se, that causes the richer experience. So it is not true to say that women will always have a richer experience of color than men.

11. d is the answer.   The trichromatic theory proposes that combining three colors of light will produce any other color. (see Seeing Color)

   a.   Convergence is the arrangement whereby bipolar cells receive information from many photoreceptors; it is not a theory of color vision.

   b.   Frequency-matching theory is a theory of hearing which states that the firing rate of a neuron will match the frequency of a sound wave.

   c.   The opponent-process theory of color vision proposes that colors in pairs inhibit each other. Therefore, if red is activated in one pair, green will be inhibited in that pair.

12. d is the answer.   Mixing lights is called additive color mixing. The more colors of light you add, the closer the resulting color is to white. (see Seeing Color)

   a.   Mixing paint is called subtractive color mixing. The more colors of paint you add, the darker the color becomes. This occurs because the two paints absorb, or subtract, more wavelengths of light than either color can alone.

   b.   Mixing two colors of light will always produce a lighter, not a darker, color.

   c.   Mixing paint, not light, is called subtractive color mixing.

13. c is the answer.   Synesthesia is the unusual mixing of senses reported in some people. These people experience colors or sounds as touches or shapes, or they may experience some other mixing of the senses. Julia's description mixes color with taste, which illustrates synesthesia. (see Interaction of the Senses: Synesthesia)

   a.   Gustation is the sense of taste alone, not taste mixed with sensation of color.

   b.   Kinesthesia is the sense of knowing where one part of your body is with respect to another, not the mixing of senses.

   d.   Olfaction is the sense of smell, not the mixing of sensations.

14. c is the answer.   Nerves that carry information about smell leave the nose and travel to the olfactory bulb. Axons leaving the olfactory bulb travel to many parts of the brain, especially to the amygdala. (see Olfaction)

   a, b, d.   Nerves carrying information about hearing, vision, and touch do travel through the thalamus.

15. d is the answer.   Umami is the taste sensation that enhances other tastes. (see Smell, Taste, and Flavor)

    a, b, c.   Salty, sour, and astringent are taste sensations, but they are not known for enhancing other tastes.

16. b is the answer.   Gustation is the sense of taste. (see Gustation)

    a.   Analgesia is the lack of a pain sensation in response to a usually painful stimulus.

    c.   Kinesthesia is our sense of where our body parts are in relation to one another.

    d.   Vestibulation is not a term. You may have been thinking of the vestibular sense, but that sense provides information about our head position, not taste.

17. a is the answer.   The intensity or heaviness of an object touching the skin is coded by the number of active neurons as well as by the speed with which they are firing. Many of Gary's neurons are firing rapidly, so the touch must be heavy. Getting punched in the mouth is the heaviest touch among the choices. (see Touch and Temperature)

    b, c, d.   A kiss on the cheek, the feel of a glass against one's lips, and the feel of a fly on one's nose would cause only a few neurons to be active, and they would not fire very rapidly.

18. b is the answer.   According to the gate control theory of pain, other sensations can compete with the pain sensations for the pathways to the brain. If Marina rubs her elbow, the rubbing may overpower some of the pain sensations and thereby reduce her pain. (see Pain)

    a.   An image of a closing gate might help Marina reduce her pain, but visualizations are not covered in the gate control theory. The gate control theory states that signals coming up the spinal cord or down from the brain may block the pain sensations.

    c.   Thinking about something else may reduce Marina's pain, but the gate control theory does not address this.

    d.   Only b is correct.

19. a is the answer.   Kinesthesia gives us knowledge of the position of our body parts by sending information from our muscles and joints. (see Proprioception: Sensing Body Position)

    b.   Gustation and olfaction would allow Ally to detect ice cream flavors.

    c, d.   The feeling of warmth on skin and responding to pain are part of the cutaneous senses but are not kinesthetic senses.

20. d is the answer.   The study described focused intensely on the experiences of a single individual. This is the hallmark of a case study. (see Focus on Research Methods: The Case of the Mysterious Spells)

    a.   Difficulty judging distances might occur if the visual system were affected.

    c.   Incorrect feedback from joints and tendons would indicate that the kinesthetic sense is malfunctioning.

    d.   Overarousal of the autonomic nervous system would not result from vestibular stimulation. The autonomic nervous system activates or calms the automatic processes in the body such as heart rate and digestion. Overstimulation might result in some arousal, but not overarousal.

Now turn to the quiz analysis table at the end of this chapter to find which areas you know well and which areas you need to work on. Circle the numbers in the table for items on Quiz 1 that you answered correctly.

Quiz 2

1.   d is the answer.   The specific energy doctrine states that a sensory nerve can code information only for that sense. The hair cells on the organ of Corti transduce sound waves; therefore, any stimulation will be perceived as sounds. (see The Problem of Encoding)

   a.   The auditory neurons might fire at different rates, depending on how much stimulation they are receiving.

   b, c.   The proprioceptive and touch senses are unrelated to the hair cells on the organ of Corti.

2.   a is the answer   Wave amplitude corresponds to the experience of loudness, whereas wave frequency corresponds to the experience of pitch. (see Sound)

   b.   This is reversed. Wave amplitude corresponds to the experience of loudness, whereas wave frequency corresponds to the experience of pitch.

   c.   These terms refer to the psychological experience of light, not sound. The question refers to the auditory, not the visual, system.

   d.   Hue is a description for the psychological experience of the essential color determined by the dominant wavelength in the light and thus refers to the visual, not the auditory, system. Timbre is an auditory experience, but it is the quality of sound, which is determined by complex wave patterns that are added onto the lowest frequency of a sound. Sometimes timbre is referred to as the quality of a sound.

3.   a is the answer.   The pinnas (outer ears) are accessory structures; they modify the sound waves entering the ears. (see The Ear)

   b.   The cochlea is in the inner ear and would not be directly affected by Adriana's action.

   c.   Timbre is a quality of sound not related to the pinnas.

   d.   The transduction mechanisms for hearing are in the cochlea and would not be directly affected by movement of the pinnas.

4.   c is the answer.   Conduction deafness is caused by improper vibration in the malleus (hammer), incus (anvil), and stapes (stirrup). Onset usually occurs with increasing age when the bones begin to fuse together, preventing their movement. (see The Ear)

   a.   Damage to the hair cells of the basilar membrane results in nerve deafness.

   b.   Damage to the acoustic nerve results in nerve deafness.

   d.   Depending on its severity, damage to the pinna may not harm hearing.

5.   a is the answer.   According to the place theory, the location of movement along the basilar membrane determines the pitch that we hear. (see Coding Intensity and Frequency)

   b.   There is no such thing as the characteristic-frequency theory.

   c, d.   The frequency-matching or volley theory suggests that the rate of neuronal firing in the auditory nerve matches the frequency of the sound.

6.   a is the answer.   Light intensity determines brightness. Carly should increase intensity to increase brightness. (see Light)

   b, d. Wavelength determines color.

   c.   Decreasing light intensity would dim the light.

7.   b is the answer.   The rods, which are photoreceptors in the retina, allow us to see well in the dark. When the lights are first turned out, the rods must synthesize photopigments. This process takes between a half-hour and forty-five minutes. (see Converting Light into Images)

   a.   Ganglion cells receive information from both rods and cones, but it is the rods that are responsible for dark adaptation.

   c.   The muscles of the lenses do help us to focus on objects in the environment. However, the level of light in the environment does not affect the efficiency of these muscles.

   d.   Dendrites are fibers that are permanent fixtures. They do not have to be resynthesized in any way.

8.   c is the answer.   Colorblind persons have cones with only two of three color-sensitive pigments. They are not blind to all color, but they discriminate fewer colors than other people. (see Seeing Color)

   a.   Colorblind people are not blind to all color; they just discriminate fewer colors than others.

   b.   Colorblind people see more color than just black, white and gray, though they do discriminate fewer colors than others.

   d.   Colorblind people do not see all of the colors that others see—they discriminate fewer colors.

9.   c is the answer.   Lateral inhibition occurs when a cell with the greatest stimulation (cell number one) causes a reduction in activity in the surrounding cells (cells two through five). This will cause the brain to receive information indicating that the receptive field of cell one contains much more light than the receptive fields of cells two through five—in other words, that there is a light region next to a dark region. Therefore, lateral inhibition codes for contrast in the environment. (see Converting Light into Images)

   a.   Cones detect color information.

   b.   Rods detect black-and-white information.

   d.   Specialized cells in the cortex detect movement.

10. a is the answer.   Visual transduction occurs at the retina's receptors, called rods and cones. Photopigments in the rods and cones break apart when stimulated by light and cause changes in membrane potential. (see Converting Light into Images)

   b.   Removal of the lateral geniculate nucleus would impair vision but not the transduction process.

   c.   Uncrossing the optic nerve at the optic chiasm would change the way we see the world, but it would not impair transduction.

   d.   Only a is the answer.

11. c is the answer.   Ganglion cells have a center-surround receptive field that responds to opponent colors. Red or green, blue or yellow, and white or black are the opposing colors, only one of which can be signaled at a time. After one stops being stimulated, the other is activated, which creates afterimages. (see Seeing Color)

   a.   Cones are responsible for color vision but are not set up in opposing pairs to create afterimages.

   b.   Bipolar cells receive information from rods and cones but do not have receptive fields responding to opponent colors.

   d.   Rods are responsible for black-and-white differentiation and cannot create afterimages.

12. b is the answer.   The opponent-process theory explains afterimages. When one color in a pair has been inhibited, it will "overreact" and become activated when the other color is no longer stimulated. (see Seeing Color)

   a.   There is no such thing as a computational theory of color vision.

   c.   Trichromatic theory cannot explain afterimages; it describes how three colors can be combined to create all colors.

   d.   Volley theory is another term for the frequency-matching theory of hearing.

13. b is the answer.   Synesthesia is the mixing of senses such that one might associate a taste with a shape or a sound with a color. Joe's sense that a color combination can be associated with a loud sound is reminiscent of this sort of mixing of senses. (see Interaction of the Senses: Synesthesia)

   a.   Analgesia is the absence of pain sensation in the presence of a normally painful stimulus, not the mixing of sensations.

   c.   The vestibular sense is the sense of balance.

   d.   The proprioceptive senses are the sense of balance and of kinesthesia—senses in which the input is from the body, not an external source.

14. b is the answer.   The optic chiasm is the criss-cross structure through which half the fibers from each eye's optic nerve cross over to the opposite side of the brain. (see Visual Pathways)

   a.   The lateral geniculate nucleus (LGN) contains neurons that provide visual input to the primary visual cortex. Visual information goes to the LGN after the optic chiasm.

   c.   The blind spot in the eye occurs where the nerve exits the eyeball, before reaching the optic chiasm.

   d.   The primary visual cortex is in the occipital lobe, to which visual information travels after the optic chiasm and LGN.

15. d is the answer.   The LGN consists of layers of neurons that respond to different types of stimuli. Separate aspects of visual information are handled by parallel processing systems. Therefore, one neuron is responsible for depth information, another is responsible for color, and so on, and all work simultaneously. (see Visual Pathways)

   a.   The LGN has a complete map of the retina and hence the visual field. Neighboring cells respond to neighboring areas of the retina; therefore, they do not need to send another type of signal to indicate the area to which they are responding.

   b.   The ganglion cells send information to the thalamus, specifically the region known as the LGN.

   c.   There does not appear to be a place in the LGN or elsewhere in the brain where all streams of visual information are combined.

16. b is the answer.   Axons from the nose synapse in the olfactory bulb, which makes connections to the amygdala and many other brain areas. The amygdala is involved in emotion, which may explain why some smells activate memories. (see Olfaction)

   a.   Olfaction does not relay signals through the thalamus.

   c.   Papillae are the structures containing taste buds; they are not activated by smells.

   d.   The basilar membrane is in the cochlea of the inner ear.

17. d is the answer.   Papillae contain taste buds. (see Gustation)

   a.   Feeling a hot shower is the responsibility of the somatosensory system.

   b.   If green and red appear the same, one type of iodopsin, the photopigment in cones, may be missing.

   c.   Olfaction does not receive information from taste buds.

18. d is the answer.   Pheromones are sexual chemical signals usually detected by the olfactory system. A cologne would fit this definition. (see Olfaction)

   a, c.   Both a tape of music and an alteration of voice concern hearing, not olfaction.

   b.   This describes an illegal date-rape drug. It has no relation to pheromones or olfaction.

19. d is the answer.   Endorphins can reduce a person's sense of pain. (see Pain)

   a, b.   Activated A-delta fibers indicate sharp pain; activated C fibers indicate dull aches.

   c.   Naloxone is a drug that can block the pain-reducing effects of endorphins.

20. b is the answer.   The inner ear connects to the organs for the vestibular sense. An ear infection can influence the movement of fluid in the semicircular canals, which influences the sense of balance. see Proprioception: Sensing Body Position)

   a, c, d.   Problems in the eye, on the skin, or in the mouth will not influence the vestibular sense as much as problems in the ear, as they are less directly connected to that sense than the ear is.

Now turn to the quiz analysis table at the end of this chapter to find which areas you know well and which areas you need to work on. Circle the numbers in the table for items on Quiz 2 that you answered correctly.

For each question you answered correctly, circle its number. (Quiz 1 numbers are not shaded; Quiz 2 numbers are shaded.) Are there patterns in the types of questions or the topics you got wrong that could direct your further study? Did you improve from Quiz 1 to Quiz 2?

QUIZ REVIEW

Topic	Type of Question		
	Definition	Comprehension	Application
Sensory Systems			1
The Problem of Encoding			
		1	
Linkages: Sensation and Biological Aspects of Psychology	5		
Hearing			
Sound		2	
		2	
The Ear		3	
		4	3
Coding Intensity and Frequency		4	
	5		
Vision			
Light			
			6
Converting Light into Images		6	7, 8, 9
	9		7, 10
Visual Pathways			
	14	15	
Seeing Color		10	11, 12
	8	12	11, 13
Interaction of the Senses: Synesthesia			13
			13
The Chemical Senses: Smell and Taste			
Olfaction		14	
			16, 18
Gustation			16
			17
Smell, Taste, and Flavor	15		
Cutaneous Senses and the Vestibular System			
Touch and Temperature			17
Pain			18
			19
Proprioception: Sensing Body Position			19
			20
Focus on Research Methods: The Case of the Mysterious Spells		20	

Total correct by quiz:

| Quiz 1: |
| Quiz 2: |

CHAPTER 5

Perception

<u>Perception</u> is the process by which we take raw sensations from the environment and interpret them, using knowledge and understanding of the world, so that they become meaningful experiences.

OUTLINE

I.   THE PERCEPTION PARADOX
    The fundamental paradox of perception is that what seems so easy for the perceiver is exceedingly difficult for psychologists to understand and explain. In order to function so effectively and efficiently, perceptual systems must be extremely complex. To help understand perception, scientists draw attention to perceptual failures.

II. THREE APPROACHES TO PERCEPTION
    The <u>computational model</u> argues that neural activity transforms sensory stimulation into our experience of reality, much as a computer would do computations. The <u>constructivist approach</u> argues that the perceptual system must often make a reality out of fragments of sensory information. According to the <u>ecological approach</u> to perception, we perceive most clues from the environment directly, without interpretation.

III. PSYCHOPHYSICS
    <u>Psychophysics</u> is the study of the relationship between the physical energy of the environmental stimuli and the psychological experience that those stimuli produce.
    A.   Absolute Thresholds: Is Something Out There?
         <u>Absolute threshold</u> is the minimum amount of energy that can be detected 50 percent of the time. <u>Subliminal stimulation</u> refers to stimuli that fall below this threshold and are usually not detected. <u>Supraliminal stimulation</u> refers to stimuli that are detected because they are above the threshold. Absolute thresholds can be amazingly low.
    B.   Thinking Critically: Can Subliminal Stimuli Influence Your Behavior?
         What am I being asked to believe or accept?
         There are claims that humans can be influenced or persuaded by subliminal messages, which are detected, perceived, and overtly acted upon without conscious awareness.
         What evidence is available to support the assertion?
         Some research studies on subliminal priming show that subliminal information can have a temporary impact on judgment and emotion.
         Are there alternative ways of interpreting the evidence?
         One alternative explanation of the supposed success of subliminal stimuli is the possibility that only research supporting the idea of subliminal perception has been reported. Another possibility is that positive expectations of subliminal stimuli (such as with self-help tapes) are more important than the content of the subliminal messages; therefore, the findings may be due to the placebo effect.
         What additional evidence would help to evaluate the alternatives?
         Double-blind, placebo-controlled experiments would provide empirical research results that could offer insight into the extent of the influence of subliminal perceptions.
         What conclusions are most reasonable?
         The evidence available to date suggests that subliminal perception does occur, but that it has no potential for "mind control."

C.   Signal-Detection Theory

Signal-detection theory is a mathematical model that describes what determines whether a person perceives a near-threshold stimulus. Sometimes a person perceives noise (spontaneous random neural firing) that is always present, even without stimulation, as a perceptual experience. Whether a person determines a perception is noise or noise-plus-stimulus depends on sensitivity, the person's physical ability to detect a stimulus, and on response criterion, the person's willingness or reluctance to say that a stimulus is present. If a person expects a stimulus to be present, then his or her response criterion will be lowered. In other words, as expectations of stimuli increase, the amount of stimulus energy necessary to trigger perception is lowered. Signal-detection theory has led to improvement in the accuracy of people who are responsible for signal-detection tasks.

D.   Judging Differences: Has Anything Changed?

Just-Noticeable Difference (JND). The minimum detectable difference between two stimuli, the difference threshold or just-noticeable difference (JND), depends on the initial magnitude or intensity of the stimuli and on which sense is being stimulated. Weber's law states that the JND is a fixed proportion (symbolized by the letter K) of the intensity of the stimulus. K is different for each of the senses. With age, we tend to become less sensitive to stimulus differences.

E.   Magnitude Estimation: How Intense Is That?

Magnitude estimation is about how our perception of stimulus intensity relates to the actual strength of the stimulus. Fechner observed that constant increases in physical energy will produce progressively smaller increases in perceived stimulus size, an idea known as *Fechner's law.* Stevens's power law describes the relative changes in perception of size for stimuli that Fechner's law doesn't cover.

IV. ORGANIZING THE PERCEPTUAL WORLD

A.   Basic Processes in Perceptual Organization

Perceptual organization is the task performed by the perceptual system to determine what edges and other stimuli go together to form an object. It is a process by which order is imposed on the information received by your senses by organizing elements into *subjective contours,* or imaginary connecting lines. Two basic processes guide perceptual organization.

1.   *Figure-Ground Discrimination.* Using figure-ground discrimination, our perceptual processes actively try to assign some stimuli to the foreground (figure) and some to the meaningless background (ground).

2.   *Grouping.* According to *Gestalt psychologists*, we see a figure via principles of *grouping.* These principles are proximity, similarity, continuity, closure, texture, simplicity, common fate, synchrony, common region, and connectedness. The *likelihood principle* says that we tend to perceive objects in the way that experience tells us is the most likely arrangement.

B.   Perception of Location and Distance

1.   *Two-Dimensional Location.* This ability lets us determine whether a stimulus is coming from the right or left, from above or below. According to the computational approach, this is accomplished visually by the brain calculating an estimate of where an image strikes the retina with information about the movement of one's eyes and head. In terms of sound, localization is determined by differences in the information received by each of the ears. When vision and sound produce conflicting information about the location of the sound, vision tends to be more dominant in the final determination.

2.   *Depth Perception.* Depth perception allows us to experience the world in three dimensions. Stimulus depth cues include interposition, *relative size, height in the visual field,* linear perspective, *reduced clarity, color, light and shadow,* and the gradient of texture. Depth cues from moving objects include motion parallax, the phenomenon in which near objects seem to move faster than objects in the distance.

There are also cues based on properties of the visual system. These are <u>ocular accommodation</u>, <u>eye convergence</u>, and <u>retinal disparity</u>.

C.   Perception of Motion

Our brain decides whether something is moving by evaluating movement cues in the retinal image, eye and head movement, and vestibular and tactile cues.

<u>Looming</u> is the rapid expansion in the size of an image on the retina. You interpret this as an approaching stimulus.

<u>Stroboscopic illusion</u> occurs when we perceive continual movement from a series of separate still images moving across the retina. It enables us to perceive movement in films and videos.

D.   Perceptual Constancy

<u>Perceptual constancy</u> is the ability to perceive sameness even when the image on the retina changes.

1.   *Size Constancy.* Our perception of an object's size is based on the size of our retinal image and how far away we think the object is. We interpret the retinal image in relation to its perceived distance.

2.   *Shape Constancy.* The brain automatically puts together information about retinal images and distance as movement occurs. Take a square object, turn it in many different directions (movement and distance cues), and see if you perceive anything other than a square.

3.   *Brightness Constancy.* How bright we perceive an object to be is based on real-world knowledge and on the brightness of that object relative to its background.

V.   RECOGNIZING THE PERCEPTUAL WORLD

Perception is a result of <u>top-down processing</u> and <u>bottom-up processing</u>.

A.   Bottom-up Processing

We can recognize an object because we perform feature analysis using *feature detectors* in the visual cortex. Our sensory systems analyze stimuli into basic features before higher centers of the brain recombine them to create a full perceptual experience. Color, motion, spatial orientation, and patterns of light and darkness are some of the features that our visual systems analyze.

B.   Top-down Processing

In top-down processing, our knowledge, motivations, and expectations influence perception. You may have observed this in *pareidolia*, a process in which you perceive a specific object in an ambiguous stimulus. Schemas are mental representations of our knowledge and expectations, and can create a *perceptual set*, which is a predisposition to perceive a stimulus in a certain way. Such expectancies are influenced by context and past experience. Motivation—that is, the way we want to perceive—can also alter perceptions.

C.   Network Processing

Network processing is the extensive interaction and communication among the various feature analyzers detecting and sending sensation messages to the brain. *Neural network models* can explain findings such as the *object superiority effect* in which we are able to identify a feature faster when it is embedded in a three-dimensional object than in a random pattern of lines, as well as the *word superiority effect* (the ability to detect target letters if they are in a word than in a nonword string of letters). According to <u>parallel distributed processing (PDP)</u> models, recognition occurs as a result of simultaneous (parallel) operation of connected units in the brain that are activated by stimulus features. Other units are excited or inhibited by the connections that exist between units.

D.   Culture, Experience, and Perception

Different experiences affect perception by creating differing expectations and other top-down processes. When people from different cultures are exposed to substantially different visual environments, they respond differently to the same visual stimuli. People from cultures that are not westernized often do not see depth cues in visual stimuli as Westerners.

E. Linkages: Perception and Human Development

Psychologists use inborn patterns of *habituation* and *dishabituation* to study infant perception. The study of newborns has helped psychologists identify innate perceptual processes, such as feature analysis. Infants quickly become good at face discrimination. At three months, infants begin to use retinal disparity and relative motion depth cues. They do not begin to use textual gradients or linear perspective until they are about three years old. Visual experience is necessary to develop these perceptual abilities.

VI. ATTENTION

Attention is the process of directing and focusing certain psychological resources, usually by voluntary control, to enhance perception, performance, and mental experience. Attention improves mental processing, requires effort, and has limited resources. Attention may be directed *overtly* or *covertly*.

A. Focus on Research Methods: An Experiment in "Mind Reading"

Psychologists wondered whether perceptual systems might become more sensitive to stimuli where people have covertly shifted their attention. Volunteers watched a fixation point on a computer screen where a symbol indicated the likely location of the target. When the fixation point cue gave correct information about the location of the stimulus, the participants covertly directed their attention to that area and detected the target significantly faster.

B. Divided Attention

Attention is *selective,* and control over it can be *voluntary* or *involuntary*. Voluntary control is usually driven by top-down processing, while involuntary is more a bottom-up process.

B. Ignoring Information

Sometimes attention can be so focused that it results *in inattentional blindness*, a failure to detect or identify normally noticeable stimuli.

D. Directing Attention

Multitasking involves dividing attention in a way that allows one to perform more than one task. Sometimes this is easier than others, usually because of the degree of *automaticity* in the tasks. If one task is fairly automatic, that frees up attention to divert to another task. If the two tasks require different types of attentional resources, this also helps successful multitasking.

C. Attention and Automatic Processing

Parallel processing is the ability to search a number of locations rapidly and automatically for targets.

D. Attention and the Brain

MRI and PET scans show that blood flow and neural activity increase to and in areas of the brain associated with the mental processing necessary for the task. When attention is divided, the blood flow is also divided. There is no single area of the brain responsible for attention, although certain regions of the brain are responsible for momentary lapses in attention.

VII. APPLICATIONS OF RESEARCH ON PERCEPTION

A. Aviation Psychology

Some landing scenarios decrease a pilot's ability to rely on top-down and bottom-up processing. To compensate, engineers have developed cockpit displays that represent a realistic three-dimensional image of the flight environment. In addition, visual displays have been developed that minimize reliance on auditory cues. But auditory perception research has also contributed to help promote effective communication with air traffic controllers.

    B.   Human-Computer Interaction
        Engineering psychologists employ perception principles in designing computer displays.
        The displays use depth perception cues, attention-getting stimuli, and simple visual images
        to make computers easier to operate.

    C.   Traffic Safety
        Research on divided attention is being applied to help understand the potential dangers of
        driving while using various kinds of mobile phones. Research suggests that dividing
        attention between driving and talking on a mobile phone impairs the driver significantly,
        even if the driver is using a hands-free device. Some research suggests that a driver using a
        mobile phone is more impaired than a driver who is legally drunk (but not on a mobile
        phone).

KEY TERMS

1.   **Perception** is the process through which people take raw sensations from the environment and
interpret them, using knowledge, experience, and understanding of the world, so that the
sensations become meaningful experiences. (see introductory section)

    Example: After being in school for years, you will recognize the sign +. You know what it is and
what it is used for. However, at your first birthday, you would have been unable to understand this
sign.

2.   The **constructivist approach** is taken by those who argue that the perceptual system uses
fragments of sensory information to construct an image of reality. (see Three Approaches to
Perception)

    Example: Many children's books contain connect-the-dots tasks. On the page are a series of dots
and some features, such as eyes, ears, or a mouth. A constructivist would say that we can make
good guesses as to what the picture is going to be by putting together all the bits of information
from the dots and the features. Because eyes and ears go with a face, the completed drawing will
probably have a person in it.

3.   The **computational model** focuses on how computations by the nervous system translate raw
sensory stimulation into an experience of reality. (see Three Approaches to Perception)

    Example: To identify an object as a red ball, each of the neurons in our visual cortex responds to
one aspect, such as the color, curved edges, or texture, and other neurons join the information to
create our perception.

4.   The **ecological approach** to perception maintains that humans and other species are so well
adapted to their natural environment that many aspects of the world are perceived without
requiring higher-level analysis and inferences. (see Three Approaches to Perception)

    Example: As Margie walks across the street she needs only look around to perceive the visual and
auditory cues that traffic is coming.

5.   **Psychophysics** is an area of research focusing on the relationship between the physical
characteristics of environmental stimuli and the psychological experiences those stimuli produce.
(see Psychophysics)

    REMEMBER: <u>Psych</u> is part of the word *psychological*, and <u>physics</u> is part of the word *physical*.
<u>Psychophysics</u> is the study of the relationship between perception's <u>psych</u>ological and <u>physic</u>al
aspects.

6.   **Absolute threshold** is the minimum amount of stimulus energy that can be detected 50 percent of
the time. (see Absolute Thresholds: Is Something Out There?)

7. **Subliminal stimulation** is stimulation that is too weak or too brief to be perceived. (see Absolute Thresholds: Is Something Out There?)

8. **Supraliminal stimulation** is stimulation that is strong enough to be consistently perceived. (see Absolute Thresholds: Is Something Out There?)

9. **Sensitivity** is the ability to detect a stimulus. (see Signal-Detection Theory)

    Example: In the chapter on sensation, you learned how age can affect the ability of the three bones in the inner ear to conduct sound. A person with a decrease in bone conductivity would be less sensitive to external auditory stimuli.

    REMEMBER: In contrast to the response criterion (influenced by a person's motivation and expectancies), sensitivity reflects physical changes in the nervous system, sensory system, or stimulus. This capacity is influenced by internal neural noise, the intensity of the stimulus, and how well a person's nervous system is working.

10. The **response criterion** is the internal rule a person uses to decide whether or not to report a stimulus. (see Signal-Detection Theory)

    Example: Dr. Charles, a cancer specialist, sees cancer patients who have been referred to him by other physicians. Therefore, when he looks at patients' x-rays for the first time, he *expects* to perceive cancerous shadows. Therefore, he is likely to perceive even faint shadows as cancer when, in reality, none may exist.

11. **Signal-detection theory** is a mathematical model of what determines a person's report that a near-threshold stimulus has or has not occurred. (see Signal-Detection Theory)

12. A **just-noticeable difference (JND),** or difference threshold, is the smallest detectable difference in stimulus energy. (see Judging Differences: Has Anything Changed?)

    Example: During a power outage, your roommate lights twenty candles while you are in the basement coping with the fuse box. When you get back, you tell her that the room is still too dark and ask her to light another candle. She replies that she will have to light several more candles before you can "just notice the difference" in the light in the room.

13. **Weber's law** states that the smallest detectable difference in stimulus energy is a constant fraction of the intensity of the stimulus. (see Judging Differences: Has Anything Changed?)

    Example: Imagine that a book weighing ten pounds is in your knapsack. You notice a change in the weight of your knapsack after adding two pounds of books. According to Weber's law, if you started out with twenty pounds of books, you would need to add four pounds of books before you would notice a difference. The proportion of 2 to 10 is the same as the proportion of 4 to 20.

14. **Perceptual organization** is the task of determining what edges and other stimuli go together to form an object. (see Organizing the Perceptual World)

    REMEMBER: It is guided by figure-ground processing. The figure is that part of the visual field that has meaning and stands out from the rest of the stimulus. The rest of the visual field is the ground. Perceptual organization is also guided by grouping.

15. **Figure-ground discrimination** is the ability to organize a visual scene so that it contains meaningful figures set against a less relevant ground. (see Basic Processes in Perceptual Organization)

    Example: Kiernan is looking at a basketball game being played. He focuses on the players as the figure, and the crowd beyond him in the opposite side of the stands as the background.

16. **Depth perception** is the ability to perceive distance. (see Perception of Location and Distance)

    Example: Being able to determine how far a car in front of you is from your automobile is an example of depth perception.

17. **Interposition** is a depth cue whereby closer objects block one's view of things farther away. (see Perception of Location and Distance)

    Example: Stand in your driveway and look at your residence. You know that the bushes in front of your house, dorm, or apartment are closer to you than the building is because they block your complete view of the building.

18. **Linear perspective** is a depth cue whereby objects closer to the point at which two lines appear to converge are perceived as being at a greater distance. (see Perception of Location and Distance)

    Example: Stand in the middle of railroad tracks and look far into the distance. The tracks seem to come together to make a point. Objects that are close to that point appear far away.

19. The **gradient of texture** is a graduated change in the texture, or grain, of the visual field, whereby objects with finer, less detailed textures are perceived as more distant. (see Perception of Location and Distance)

    Example: Try to find the biggest, steepest classroom on campus. Go to the front of the class and look up at the empty seats. Your view should form a texture. As you look toward the back of the classroom, you will notice that the texture is gradually changing as the chairs get smaller and smaller. The amount of change in texture indicates how far away the chairs are.

20. **Motion parallax** is a depth cue whereby a difference in the apparent rate of movement of different objects provides information about the relative distance of those objects. (see Perception of Location and Distance)

    Example: The next time you ride in a car, notice that objects close to you whiz by but those farther away seem to move more slowly.

21. **Ocular accommodation** is the ability of the lens of the eye to change its shape and bend light rays so that objects are in focus. (see Perception of Location and Distance)

22. **Eye convergence** is a depth cue involving the rotation of the eyes to project the image of an object on each retina. (see Perception of Location and Distance)

    Example: Try to focus on the end of your nose. You will feel your eyes strain as they attempt to "find" your nose. Slowly shift your focus to an object across the room, and you will feel your muscles relax.

23. **Retinal disparity** is a depth cue based on the difference between the two retinal images of the world. (see Perception of Location and Distance)

    Example: Hold your arm straight out in front of your face and focus on the tip of one finger. To see the disparity in the two images that your eyes see, look at your finger first with one eye and then with the other. Now focus on an object at the far end of the room. Again, shut one eye and then the other. There should be a greater difference between the images your eyes saw when you focused on your finger than between those your eyes saw when you focused on the object far away from you.

24. **Looming** is a motion cue involving a rapid expansion in the size of an image so that it fills the retina. (see Perception of Motion)

    Example: Ted is in a fight on the playground. He knows that the fist that is quickly getting bigger and bigger is moving toward his face. He does not perceive the fist as simply growing in size.

25. **Stroboscopic illusion** is an illusion of motion that is created when we see slightly different images or slightly displaced lights flashed in rapid succession. (see Perception of Motion)

    Example: We perceive motion pictures from a series of snapshots presented at a rate of 24 per second.

26. **Perceptual constancy** is the perception of objects as constant in size, shape, color, and other properties despite changes in their retinal image. (see Perceptual Constancy)

    Example: At a concert, you end up sitting very far from the stage. As you look at the members of the band, you perceive them as being adults rather than children because of the constancy of their size.

27. **Top-down processing** refers to aspects of recognition that are guided by higher-level cognitive processes and psychological factors such as expectations. (see Recognizing the Perceptual World)

    Example: Jill's friend says that the cloud looks like a soda can with a straw sticking out of it. When Jill first looks at it, she sees a soda can and straw, although the cloud looks as much like a candle, cup, or piece of candy as it does a can.

28. **Bottom-up processing** refers to aspects of recognition that depend first on the information about the stimulus that comes to the brain from the sensory receptors. (see Recognizing the Perceptual World)

    Example: When presented with an image of the letter "A", feature detectors for "/", "–", and "\" are activated, and then the features are recombined to create the perception of "A."

29. **Parallel distributed processing (PDP)** models are theoretical models of object recognition in which various elements of the object are thought to be simultaneously analyzed by several widely distributed but connected neural units in the brain. (see Network Processing)

    REMEMBER: A stimulus activates a network of feature detectors that work concurrently (in parallel) in various areas of the brain (distributed) to identify the object.

31. **Attention** is the process of directing and focusing psychological resources to enhance perception, performance, and mental experience. (see Attention)

    Example: Sonia leans forward and listens intently to the speaker.

FILL-IN-THE-BLANKS KEY TERMS

This section will help you check your knowledge of the key terms introduced in this chapter. Fill in each blank with the appropriate term from the list of key terms in the previous section.

1. The _____ approach emphasizes that perception is strongly influenced by expectations and past experiences.

2. Increased expectations of perceiving a stimulus will lower the _____.

3. The smallest difference in stimulus energy that can be detected is called the _____.

4. _____ are too weak or brief to be perceived.

5. The amount of stimulus energy required for a person to perceive a stimulus 50 percent of the time is called the _____.

6. The graduated changed in the grain of the visual field with distant objects having less detailed textures is known as _____.

7. The brain uses information from muscles that control the inward turning of the eyes, a cue called _____, to judge the distance of a visual stimulus.

8. _____ is a depth cue in which the brain compares the differing retinal images from the eyes to create a three-dimensional image.

9. _____ calculates the amount of stimulus change required for a person to perceive change.

10. People who hold the _____ view argue that perception is an automatic process based on information found in the environment.

11. _____ is a stimulus cue for depth perception in which objects that block a complete view of another object are perceived as closer.

12. Our ability to perceive objects as remaining the same even though the image on our retina varies is explained by the principle of _____.

13. The recognition of stimuli that is guided by knowledge, expectations, and motivation is referred to as _____.

14. The process of directing psychological resources to enhance information processing is called _____.

15. When the brain recognizes a stimulus based first on incoming sensory information, it is said to be employing _____.

Total Correct (See answer key) _____

LEARNING OBJECTIVES

1. Define perception. Compare and contrast perception and sensation. (see introductory section)

2. Discuss the debate among the computational, constructivist, and ecological viewpoints as to how perception works. (see Three Approaches to Perception)

3. Define psychophysics and absolute threshold. (see Psychophysics)

4. Define subliminal and supraliminal stimuli. Discuss the debate about the degree to which people's behavior can be influenced by subliminal perception. (see Absolute Thresholds: Is Something Out There? see also Thinking Critically: Can Subliminal Stimuli Influence Your Behavior?)

5. Describe how sensitivity to stimuli and response criterion factor into signal-detection theory. Describe how information can change a person's response criterion. (see Signal-Detection Theory)

6. Define difference threshold or just-noticeable difference (JND). Describe Weber's law and explain the equation JND = KI. (see Judging Differences: Has Anything Changed?)

7. Describe Fechner's law. Explain how Stevens's power law can account for a wider array of stimuli. (see Magnitude Estimation: How Intense Is That?)

8. Describe the two basic principles of perceptual organization: *figure-ground organization* and *grouping*. Define and give examples of proximity, similarity, continuity, closure, common region, common fate, synchrony, and connectedness. Discuss the roles of *likelihood* and *simplicity principles* in explaining perceptual organization. (see Basic Processes in Perceptual Organization)

9. Define and describe depth perception. (see Perception of Location and Distance)

10. Describe the stimulus cues that influence depth perception. Your answer should include interposition, relative size, height in the visual field, texture gradients, linear perspective, and motion parallax. (see Perception of Location and Distance)

11. Describe the cues to depth provided by <u>accommodation</u>, <u>convergence</u>, and <u>binocular disparity</u>. (see Perception of Location and Distance)

12. Describe the cues used to perceive motion. Your answer should include <u>looming</u>, the brain's ability to sense the position of the eyes and head, and the illusion called <u>stroboscopic motion</u>. (see Perception of Motion)

13. Define <u>perceptual constancy</u>. Give examples of size, shape, and brightness constancy. (see Perceptual Constancy)

14. Compare and contrast <u>bottom-up processing</u> and <u>top-down processing</u>. (see Recognizing the Perceptual World)

15. Explain how feature analysis works in bottom-up processing. (see Bottom-up Processing)

16. Discuss the influences on top-down processing. Your answer should include expectancy, <u>schemas</u>, and motivation. (see Top-down Processing)

17. Define network processing. Explain the <u>parallel distributed processing (PDP) models</u> of pattern recognition. (see Network Processing)

18. Describe the impact of culture on perception. (see Culture, Experience, and Perception)

19. Describe an infant's perceptual abilities. (see Linkages: Perception and Human Development)

20. Define <u>attention</u>. Describe *overt* and *covert orienting*, including the research on the covert shifting of attention. (see Attention; see also Focus on Research Methods: An Experiment in "Mind Reading")

21. Describe the influences that determine the ease of directing or dividing our attention. (see Directing Attention; see also Divided Attention)

22. Explain parallel processing. (see Attention and Automatic Processing)

23. Discuss how neural activity underlies the directing of attention. (see Attention and the Brain)

24. Describe the influence of perceptual studies on aviation psychology, human-computer interactions, and traffic safety. (see Applications of Research on Perception)

CONCEPTS AND EXERCISES

James Bond's Psychological Secrets

James Bond needs to have some weapons and equipment made for a new assignment. He has hired you to make them. After reading the description of each, decide whether you will need to know the absolute threshold or difference threshold to make the device.

1. A lipstick with a deadly poison in it

2. A poison that can be added to spice

3. A pen that is really a silent gun

4. An alcoholic drink containing a powerful tranquilizer

5. A watch that is really a radio that beeps a little louder than usual when Bond's accomplices are trying to get in touch with him

Perception on the Playground

Many childhood activities and games require the ability to perceive figure-ground, grouping, and depth. Match the grade-school activities listed below with the appropriate cues or principles of perception from the list that follows. Answers may be used once or not at all. Each problem may have more than one answer.

1. Yolanda knows that players on the other side of the soccer field appear smaller than players next to her because they are farther away from her. _____

2. As Alice runs to get in the line progressing back into the building, she sees a *line* of students instead of separate individuals. _____

3. As Brian looks down the road at Sam cycling away, he knows his friend is getting more distant because Sam seems to be closing in on the point where the road converges. _____

4. Sally is calling to Penny and Ali, who are across the playground. She knows that Ali is closer because she is blocking part of Penny from Sally's view. _____

5. Marcel is looking at a flock of birds flying south together for the winter. He perceives them as a flock, rather than as 347 birds. _____

6. Children play a game called "Duck, Duck, Goose." Everyone stands in a circle. One or two people are chosen to leave the circle. They walk around the circle, touching each person as they go and saying, "Duck." Eventually, they touch someone and say, "Goose." The "goose" must chase the person all the way around the circle and try to catch him or her. Even though there are always two to four individuals missing from the circle, everyone still perceives a circle. _____

7. Consuela likes to ride on the merry-go-round. She loves to try looking at the objects that are close to the merry-go-round because they seem to move so fast. _____

    a. Similarity

    b. Closure

    c. Proximity

    d. Common fate

    e. Continuity

    f. Linear perspective

    g. Motion parallax

    h. Interposition

    i. Relative size

CRITICAL THINKING

Sam and Martina are investigating a bomb that exploded at a rock concert. They are curious as to how this could have happened, because all the doors have sensors that are extremely sensitive to any materials that could be used in any type of bomb or electronic weapon. None of the ushers or security guards at the theater noticed anything amiss that night. There were no clues that a bomb had either entered the theater or was going to explode while the theater was full.

Sam pulls in all the theater personnel for questioning. He is convinced that one of the sensor monitors (people who watch the sensors to see if anyone is carrying anything suspect into the theater) was a partner in the crime. He thinks that whoever carried in the bomb made an arrangement with a sensor monitor to let the bomb remain undetected.

Sam discovers that one of the sensor monitors knows the bomb suspect. Sam is sure he has found the guilty party.

Martina joins the questioning of Sam's suspects for about an hour. Finally she tells Sam to let the sensor monitor go home. Frustrated, Sam asks, "How can you do that? He's the only clue we have."

Martina replies, "Sam, just send him home. Then get me a list of all the employees who have worked there for a couple of years and anybody who was working a double shift that night."

Using the five critical thinking questions in your text, the clues in the story, and what you have just learned about perception, answer the following:

1.   What is Sam's hypothesis?

2.   What is the evidence in support of Sam's hypothesis?

3.   What is Martina's alternative hypothesis?

4.   What is the evidence in support of Martina's hypothesis?

PERSONAL LEARNING ACTIVITIES

1.   Try to approximate your absolute threshold for tastes. You could have someone prepare several glasses, some of which are plain water, the rest of which have varying amounts of salt or sugar in them. How much must be there before you notice it? Does the amount change if you try the experiment at another time of day?

2.   Conduct an experiment on judging differences between stimuli. For example, to test your perception of weight differences, you could close your eyes and have a friend place one magazine or notebook on your hand. How many sheets of paper can the friend add before you just notice a difference? How much must be added before you believe it is twice as heavy as it was originally? If you start with a textbook, how many magazines or notebooks are needed for you to notice a difference or to judge it to be twice as heavy?

3.   If your living space permits it, see if you can use the principles of perception described in this chapter to change the way one of your rooms looks. Can you move objects around so that the room looks smaller or bigger?

4.   Log onto the Internet. There are a number of great websites featuring animated, three-dimensional optical illusions, as well as some interesting auditory illusions. Using a World Wide Web browser, locate some of these sites, such as http://www.michaelbach.de/ot/. How do they expand on illusions presented in the text? In what way did the sites increase your understanding of the material presented in your text?

5.   Visit the following website: http://www.youtube.com/watch?v=2pK0BQ9CUHk. It will provide you with a surprising illustration of how much less effective you can be at a task when your attention is divided or misplaced. Why do you think this particular video clip is so likely to produce the perceptual error that it does? What implication does this raise for the issue of talking on the phone or texting while driving?

MULTIPLE-CHOICE QUESTIONS

Quiz 1

1. J. D. looks up in the clouds and says, "I see a horse." His mother looks at the same cloud and says, "What are you talking about? That looks like a car!" The _____ approach to perception would best be able to explain the discrepancy between J. D.'s and his mother's perception of the same stimulus.

    a. ecological
    b. computational
    c. constructivist
    d. deconstructionist

2. Vicki is sailing toward shore. Her expectation of seeing shore soon will _____ her response criterion for perceiving land.

    a. increase
    b. decrease
    c. have no effect on
    d. delay

3. Dante raises his hand each time he hears a tone over headphones in an experiment. The tone gets quieter and quieter until Dante misses hearing it half the time. After repeating the same procedure many times, the researcher concludes the experiment, because she has found Dante's

    a. absolute threshold.
    b. difference threshold.
    c. internal noise.
    d. response criterion.

4. Which of the following would NOT affect a person's sensitivity?

    a. The level of internal noise in the nervous system
    b. The person's motivation
    c. The condition of the person's sensory system
    d. The intensity of the stimulus

5. Participants in a study are watching a computer screen, which displays randomly appearing dots of different colors. Each time participants see a red light, they are to press the "Enter" key. When participants are told they will be given $1 each time they correctly indicate they have seen a red light, their number of _____ will increase.

    a. thresholds
    b. correct rejections
    c. false alarms
    d. misses

6. The experimenters in Question 5 used money to alter participants'

    a. difference threshold.
    b. internal noise.
    c. response criterion.
    d. sensitivity.

7.   Stimuli that are above the absolute threshold are _____; stimuli that are below the absolute threshold are _____.

   a.   subliminal; supraliminal
   b.   supraliminal; subliminal
   c.   hits; misses
   d.   misses; hits

8.   What is the difference between just-noticeable differences (JNDs) and magnitude estimations?

   a.   The ability to detect a JND does not vary across senses. Magnitude estimation laws vary according to the specific senses being stimulated.
   b.   JND refers to the smallest detectable difference between stimuli. Magnitude estimation laws refer to specific amounts of difference between stimuli.
   c.   JND refers to specific amounts of difference between stimuli. Magnitude estimation laws refer to the smallest detectable difference between stimuli.
   d.   There is no difference. These terms are synonymous.

9.   Four swimmers practicing their synchronized swimming routine are perceived as a group because they are performing the same movements at the same speed. This is an example of the grouping principle

   a.   closure.
   b.   common fate.
   c.   orientation.
   d.   interposition.

10. Harriet Greene is going to take her Brownie troop on a field trip to Chicago. She wants all the children to wear the same T-shirt. That way, a stray child will still be recognized as part of the troop. This demonstrates the principle of

   a.   similarity.
   b.   proximity.
   c.   orientation.
   d.   the gradient of texture.

11. Knowing that an object is closer to you because it blocks out part of the background is called

   a.   linear perspective.
   b.   reduced clarity.
   c.   interposition.
   d.   motion parallax.

12. A Cyclops has only one eye. What depth cue based on the properties of her visual system would a Cyclops NOT have?

   a.   Linear perspective
   b.   Motion parallax
   c.   Eye convergence
   d.   Reduced clarity

13. As Cliff exits his front door using a garbage can lid as a shield, he sees a snowball coming straight for him. Although the size of the snowball on his retina is enlarging, he realizes the snowball is approaching, not getting larger, because of
    a. induced motion.
    b. looming.
    c. motion parallax.
    d. reduced clarity.

14. As Maura looks at her television from different vantage points in her room, the actual image of the screen projected onto her retina changes. However, Maura continues to interpret the shape of the television screen as unchanging because of
    a. closure.
    b. interposition.
    c. proximity.
    d. shape constancy.

15. Bottom-up processing is congruent with the _____ approach to perception, and top-down processing is congruent with the _____ approach to processing.
    a. computational; ecological
    b. constructivist; computational
    c. computational; constructivist
    d. constructivist; ecological

16. As soon as Jocelyn stepped on a tack, she reflexively pulled her foot up from its sharp point. Jocelyn used primarily _____ processing to sense and react reflexively.
    a. bottom-up
    b. parallel
    c. network
    d. top-down

17. Which of the following does NOT contribute to the creation of a perceptual set?
    a. Context
    b. Expectancy
    c. Past experience
    d. Sensitivity

18. A huge fire burned the local town hall, leaving smoke scars on the buildings near it in Jonah's hometown. A few people feel like they see the Virgin Mary in the markings left on one of the buildings. Jonah did not see this image at first, but once he heard about it, he did see the image. This phenomenon is known as
    a. bottom-up processing.
    b. pareidolia.
    c. network processing.
    d. Stevens's law.

19. As strings of letters were flashed on the screen, Carrie recognized the letter *t* more quickly in the word *met* than in the nonsense letter string *lgt*. Carrie's brain was faster at recognizing the *t* in *met* because its features, *m, e,* and *t,* have more connections due to Carrie's experience. _____ processing was most responsible for the differences in recognition speed.
    a. Bottom-up
    b. Network
    c. Relative
    d. Serial

20. An architect wants to make his building look taller than it actually is. What should he do?
    a. Make the windows exactly the same size on successively higher floors.
    b. Make the windows progressively larger on successively higher floors.
    c. Make the windows progressively smaller on successively higher floors.
    d. Use no windows at all.

Total Correct (See answer key) _____

Quiz 2

Use this quiz to reassess your learning after taking Quiz 1 and reviewing the chapter.

1. The _____ viewpoint is best at explaining our use of the grouping principle closure.
   a. computational
   b. constructivist
   c. ecological
   d. signal-detection

2. Expecting to see a stimulus will _____ the response criterion.
   a. increase
   b. decrease
   c. not influence
   d. be influenced by

3. Joe is studying how to train airport security guards to identify terrorists attempting to board commercial aircraft. Specifically, he wants to increase the number of hits and reduce the number of false alarms. Joe should study
   a. signal-detection theory.
   b. subliminal stimuli.
   c. optical acuity theory.
   d. Weber's law.

4. LaKisha has an ear infection that muffles the sounds presented to her during a signal-detection experiment. Because LaKisha's hearing is poor, she responds to very few of the tones. Her lowered _____ is causing an increase in _____.
   a. absolute threshold; false alarms
   b. difference threshold; misses
   c. response criterion; false alarms
   d. sensitivity; misses

5. You are in charge of advertising an event for the campus Multicultural Studies Center. You want to improve the chance that people will come to the event. Your friend tells you that you should create a subliminal advertisement for the event, using an Internet pop-up connected to the campus web page. The pop-up would happen so quickly that people would not even know they had seen it, but they would still be influenced to come. What should you tell your friend?
   a. "Great idea! That will definitely work."
   b. "That's a good idea, but I should probably print up some actual fliers to go with the pop-up."
   c. "Subliminal advertising like that works best with supraliminal advertising, not instead of it."
   d. "It would probably be better to use a supraliminal strategy than subliminal."

6. The just-noticeable difference depends on
   a. extremes in the weakness or intensity of the stimulus.
   b. the particular type of stimuli being compared.
   c. genetic differences in a person's sensory system sensitivity.
   d. how much of the stimulus there was to begin with and which sense is being stimulated.

7. Jake is a detective. He is usually very good at his job but has been making mistakes lately. Last night, he was on a stakeout and let a suspect slip away. Which of the following explanations would point to inadequate sensitivity as the reason for Jake's mistake?

    a.   Jake was sure that the suspect was going to sleep that night instead of making a break for it.
    b.   Jake fell asleep in the car at about 5:00 A.M.
    c.   Jake knew that the suspect's partner was across the street aiming a gun at Jake. If Jake had made a move, he would have been shot.
    d.   Jake knows that he is going to retire soon; a few mistakes will not mar his record.

8. When you arrive at a party, you are distressed to discover that people have already paired off. Although couples are just talking while sitting near to each other, you think that no one is available to talk to. The perceptual grouping principle most likely causing your perception of the party attenders as several pairs of people rather than as individuals is

    a.   closure.
    b.   continuity.
    c.   figure-ground.
    d.   proximity.

9. Baby Molly is in her bouncy seat. The television screen, which was off when she was first put in her seat, is turned on. Suddenly Molly starts looking at the screen because it is offering change in stimuli. This is an example of

    a.   habituation.
    b.   dishabituation.
    c.   inattentional blindness.
    d.   multitasking.

10. Stanley gazed down at his new grandson and saw the "spitting image" of his son, Hank. But when Edna first saw her grandson (the same baby), he looked just like her daughter at that age. This bias in perception exhibited by these proud grandparents demonstrates

    a.   top-down processing.
    b.   perceptual constancy.
    c.   feature detection.
    d.   the perception paradox.

11. A Persian cat bounds across the yard after a mouse, only to watch it crawl under the fence. The cat steps up to the fence and peers through a hole with one eye. He realizes that the mouse is already far away because it looks very small. This is an example of

    a.   eye convergence.
    b.   retinal disparity.
    c.   relative size.
    d.   looming.

12. Clint sculpts a figure of a penguin out of clay and photographs it. He makes a subtle change in the penguin's feet and photographs it again. Clint continues to subtly change and photograph the penguin until the figure has made a complete step. Clint develops the fifty photographs, puts them in order of occurrence, and flips through them. He perceives the penguin actually going through the movement of taking a step. This perceptual phenomenon is known as
    a. the motion parallax.
    b. the stroboscopic illusion.
    c. retinal disparity.
    d. eye convergence.

13. _____ allows us to perceive an object as being the same size despite a change in the size of the retinal image.
    a. Looming
    b. Proximity
    c. Size constancy
    d. Motion parallax

14. Mental representations of what we know and have come to expect, about the world are known as
    a. schema.
    b. images.
    c. illusions.
    d. gradients.

15. Which region of the brain has been identified by positron emission tomography (PET) scans as being the primary site where mental processing associated with attention takes place?
    a. Right hemisphere
    b. Left hemisphere
    c. Reticular formation
    d. No single brain region has been identified as the attention center.

16. People from cultures in which pictures and photographs are not used to represent reality will have a(n) _____ time judging differences shown in pictures.
    a. more difficult
    b. similarly difficult
    c. easier
    d. longer

17. When Lou looks at a lily, her brain matches its features (stem, petals, fragrance, and color) to the perceptual category "flower." Such feature analysis is characteristic of _____ processing.
    a. bottom-up
    b. ecological
    c. illusory
    d. top-down

18.   Sasha is reading her textbook chapter while watching an engrossing program on television. Can Sasha devote attention to her book and the TV simultaneously?

   a.   Yes, attentional resources are unlimited.
   b.   Yes, because each task is tapping into the same kind of attentional resource.
   c.   No, attentional resources are limited.
   d.   No, because each task is tapping into a different kind of attentional resource.

19.   Although Alan appears to be listening as Rich talks about his new clothes, vacation plans, and exercise routine, Alan is thinking through his list of errands to run. Alan has

   a.   covertly shifted attention.
   b.   overtly shifted attention.
   c.   used parallel distributed processing.
   d.   used serial processing.

20.   According to the available research, using a mobile phone while driving is

   a.   not dangerous in any way.
   b.   safe as long as you have a hands-free phone.
   c.   safe as long as you have a hands-free phone and voice-controlled dialing.
   d.   unsafe.

Total Correct (See answer key) _____

ANSWERS TO FILL-IN-THE-BLANKS KEY TERMS

1.   constructivist (see Three Approaches to Perception)

2.   response criterion (see Signal-Detection Theory)

3.   just-noticeable difference (see Judging Differences: Has Anything Changed?)

4.   Subliminal stimuli (see Absolute Thresholds: Is Something Out There?)

5.   absolute threshold (see Absolute Thresholds: Is Something Out There?)

6.   the gradient of texture (see Perception of Location and Distance)

7.   eye convergence (see of Perception of Location and Distance)

8.   Retinal disparity (see Perception of Location and Distance)

9.   Weber's law (see Judging Differences: Has Anything Changed?)

10.   ecological (see Three Approaches to Perception)

11.   Interposition (see Perception of Location and Distance)

12.   perceptual constancy (see Perceptual Constancy)

13.   top-down processing (see Recognizing the Perceptual World)

14.   attention (see Attention)

15.   bottom-up processing (see Recognizing the Perceptual World)

ANSWERS TO CONCEPTS AND EXERCISES

James Bond's Psychological Secrets

1. *Absolute threshold.* You would need to know the absolute threshold for the taste of the poison so that the person using the lipstick would not be able to taste the poison. (see Absolute Thresholds: Is Something Out There?)

2. *Difference threshold.* Spices already have a flavor. Therefore, you would need to know how much poison you could add before someone just noticed a difference in the taste. (see Judging Differences: Has Anything Changed?)

3. *Absolute threshold.* You would have to know the absolute threshold for the sound of the gunshot. The amount of auditory stimulus that the gunshot would make would have to be *below* the absolute threshold so that nobody could hear it. (see Absolute Thresholds: Is Something Out There?)

4. *Difference threshold.* Most alcohol already has a taste. You would have to find out what amount of tranquilizer you could add before someone would just notice a difference. (see Judging Differences: Has Anything Changed?)

5. *Difference threshold.* Bond would have to be able to just notice a difference in the amplitude of the beep of the watch/radio. (see Judging Differences: Has Anything Changed?)

Perception on the Playground

1. *Relative size.* This is a stimulus cue for depth perception. Players on the other side of the soccer field will appear to be smaller than players on the side of the field closest to Yolanda. (Perception of Location and Distance)

2. *Continuity.* This is a grouping principle. We perceive sensations that appear to create a continuous form (a line) as belonging together. (see Basic Processes in Perceptual Organization)

3. *Linear perspective.* This is a stimulus cue for depth perception. The parallel lines of a road that stretch out into the distance will seem to converge at the horizon. So, the closer Sam gets to this convergence point, the farther away he will appear to Brian. (see Perception of Location and Distance)

4. *Interposition.* This is a depth cue. Objects that block the view of other objects are closer to us. Ali is blocking the view of Penny; therefore, Ali is closer to Sally. (see Perception of Location and Distance)

5. *Common Fate.* This is a Gestalt principle of perception, stating that when objects move in the same direction at the same speed, they will be perceived as a group. (see Basic Processes in Perceptual Organization)

6. *Closure.* This is a grouping principle. Even though parts of the circle are missing, the children still perceive the group as a circle. Their perceptual abilities allow them to fill in the gaps. (see Basic Processes in Perceptual Organization)

7. *Motion parallax.* This is a depth cue. Consuela knows that the objects that are closer to her seem to be moving much faster than those objects that are farther away. (see Perception of Location and Distance)

ANSWERS TO CRITICAL THINKING

1. Sam's hypothesis is that one of the sensor monitors is the bomb suspect's partner.

2. Sam believes his hypothesis because the sensor monitor knows the bomb suspect.

3. Martina hypothesizes that someone missed the sensor's signal, probably because of an altered response criterion or inadequate sensitivity.

4. In asking Sam to get a list of employees, Martina suspects the culprit to be someone who has worked on the job for a long time. Working at the theater for several years and never seeing a monitor get tripped might have increased that person's response criterion. (*NOTE:* A new employee would probably have a very low response criterion and have several false alarms. Someone working there for a long time would have probably thought that night was going to be like every other boring night and would not have expected to see a bomb. This would have resulted in the monitor's missing the alerting sensor signal.) Martina also wants to know who had a double shift; anyone who was very tired might not have been sensitive enough to detect the stimulus.

ANSWERS TO MULTIPLE-CHOICE QUESTIONS

Circle the question numbers you answered correctly.

Quiz 1

1. c is the answer. The constructivist approach emphasizes that perceptions are individually constructed, and that various persons may construct different perceptions from the same stimulus. (see Three Approaches to Perception)

   a. The ecological view emphasizes that there is sufficient information in the environment for perception to occur.

   b. The computational approach emphasizes the steps, or computations, one goes through in turning sensations into perceptions.

   d. There is no such thing as the deconstructionist approach to perception.

2. b is the answer Vicki's expectations of seeing a light on shore soon will decrease her response criterion. This means that she will need less of the stimulus (light) to perceive that she is seeing a shore light. (see Signal-Detection Theory)

   a. Increasing Vicki's response criterion means that she will be less likely to perceive a stimulus.

   c. b is the answer.

   d. The response criterion is the willingness or reluctance to respond to a stimulus; therefore, it is not something that can be delayed.

3. a is the answer. The absolute threshold is the point at which you perceive a stimulus half the time. (see Absolute Thresholds: Is Something Out There?)

   b. The difference threshold is the amount of change required before a person will just notice a difference in a stimulus.

   c. Internal noise is not something that can be seen or heard by a researcher, but it can interfere with a person's perception if it is too high. Internal noise is the automatic, random firing of cells in the nervous system.

   d. Expectancies and motivation affect our response criterion, which is our willingness or hesitancy to react to a stimulus.

4.   b is the answer.   Sensitivity is the ability to detect a stimulus. Motivation affects whether we do perceive a stimulus, but it does not affect our ability to perceive a stimulus. (see Signal-Detection Theory)

   a.   A very high level of internal noise may be mistaken for a very faint stimulus. This will alter sensitivity.

   c.   The sensory system's physical health can affect its ability to perceive a stimulus. For example, a person with burned fingertips will be unable to detect slight pressure very well.

   d.   The intensity of a stimulus will affect our ability to detect it. If the stimulus is below absolute threshold, it will be undetectable.

5.   c is the answer.   Because the participants have something to gain from seeing a stimulus, they are more likely to say that they have seen one when it did not actually appear. (see Signal-Detection Theory)

   a.   You may have been thinking of a change in the level of absolute or difference thresholds, but the number of these would not change.

   b.   The participants will not increase their number of correct rejections, because they are more motivated to see the light than not to see it.

   d.   Misses will decrease, because participants are motivated by money to watch carefully.

6.   c is the answer.   The criterion was lowered by the chance to gain money. (see Signal-Detection Theory)

   a.   Difference thresholds are the smallest noticeable change in a stimulus and depend on the intensity of the stimulus, not factors in the participants.

   b.   Internal noise is the random firing of neurons and is not affected by motivation.

   d.   Sensitivity is related to the abilities of the sensory systems and the amount of internal noise.

7.   b is the answer.   Stimuli that are above the absolute threshold—stimuli consistently perceived—are referred to as supraliminal. Stimuli that are below the absolute threshold are referred to as subliminal. (see Thinking Critically: Can Subliminal Stimuli Influence Your Behavior?)

   a.   This is reversed. Stimuli above the absolute threshold are supraliminal; stimuli below it are subliminal.

   c.   Although stimuli above the absolute threshold are perceived more consistently than those below, and consequently are more likely to be hits in terms of signal-detection theory, they still may be missed from time to time. Stimuli below the absolute threshold are certainly more likely to be missed, but from time to time they will be recognized.

   d.   Misses are stimuli that should have been perceived but were not; hits are stimuli that should have been perceived and were. This question does not compare what should have been perceived with what was perceived.

8.   b is the answer.   Just-noticeable differences refer to detection of any difference, whereas magnitude estimation laws specify a difference or amount of change. (see Judging Differences: Has Anything Changed?)

   a.   One of the factors that affects detection of a JND is which sense is being stimulated. Magnitude estimation laws refer more to features of the stimuli being compared.

   c.   This is the reverse of the correct answer.

   d.   There is a difference.

9. b is the answer.   Objects (or people) moving at the same rate and in the same direction are perceived as a group. (see Basic Processes in Perceptual Organization)

   a.   Closure would be filling in the gaps of a still object.

   c.   Orientation is one aspect of a stimulus that relates to texture, not movement.

   d.   Interposition is a depth perception cue.

10. a is the answer.   Harriet Greene wants to be sure that all her Brownies look alike so that people will perceive them all as members of the same group. (see Basic Processes in Perceptual Organization)

   b.   If one child wanders away from the rest of the Brownies, she will *not* be close enough to be perceived as part of the group.

   c.   Even if one child strays from the group, she will still be in the same orientation (standing up) as everyone else in the museum. Her orientation will not distinguish her as one of Harriet Greene's Brownies.

   d.   The gradient of texture is a depth cue, not a principle of grouping.

11. c is the answer.   Interposition is a depth perception cue. (see Perception of Location and Distance)

   a.   Linear perspective is a depth cue. As parallel lines get farther and farther away, they seem to converge at a point.

   b.   Reduced clarity is a depth cue. As objects get very far away, we see them less clearly.

   d.   Motion parallax is a depth cue. As you move forward—for example, in a car—the objects that are close to you seem to go by more quickly than those that are far away.

12. c is the answer.   The brain receives and processes information from the eye muscles about the amount of muscular activity. The eyes must converge, or rotate inward, to project the image of an object on each retina. The closer the object is, the greater the convergence is, and thus the greater is the muscular activity reported to the brain. The brain of a Cyclops would receive no information about eye convergence, because a Cyclops has only one eye. (see Perception of Location and Distance)

   a.   Linear perspective is a depth cue that can be seen with one eye.

   b.   Motion parallax is a depth cue that can be seen with one eye.

   d.   Reduced clarity is a depth cue that can be seen with one eye.

13. b is the answer.   (see Perception of Motion)

   a.   Induced motion is not a term used in your text, but it is the feeling that we are moving when something on either side of us moves. For example, when sitting in a car in a parking lot, if both cars next to you back out, you may feel for a moment as if you are moving forward, although your car is still.

   c.   Motion parallax is the difference in the *apparent* movement of objects, which occurs as we move by them.

   d.   Reduced clarity is the depth cue in which less clear images are perceived as farther away.

14. d is the answer.   Shape constancy is our knowledge and experience that tells us that most objects do not suddenly change shape. Maura's knowing that her television screen does not change shape is guiding her perception of its shape as constant. (see Perceptual Constancy)

    a.   Closure is a grouping principle that helps us fill in gaps in the perceptual scene that we observe.

    b.   Interposition is a depth cue that tells us that closer objects block the view of things farther away. No one is described as blocking Jean's view of her husband in this question.

    c.   Proximity is a grouping principle that automatically organizes objects that are close together into a group.

15.   c is the answer.   Both bottom-up processing and the computational approach rely on neural activity as the basis of perception. In bottom-up processing, neural cells analyze and recombine features of a stimulus to create the perceptual experience. The computational approach explains how manipulations within the nervous system transform sensory stimulation into perceptual experience. Both top-down processing and the constructivist approach suggest that expectations and inferences based on past experiences and prior knowledge strongly influence perception. (see Three Approaches to Perception)

    a.   The computational approach would be congruent with bottom-up processing. However, the ecological approach discounts inferences and expectations and suggests that information supplied by the environment is primary in our perception of the world.

    b.   This is the reverse of the correct answer.

    d.   The computational approach and bottom-up processing rely on neural activity as the basis of perception. The constructivist approach and top-down processing are concerned with interpretation of stimuli. The ecological approach considers the environment to be key in perception.

16.   a is the answer.   Bottom-up processing is the reaction of cells in the nervous system to aspects of a stimulus. Each of the cells processes one characteristic, and eventually the characteristics are combined to make a whole stimulus perception. In a reflexive action, sensory neurons send the pain information to the spinal cord, which sends a "pull away" message to the muscles. (see Bottom-up Processing)

    b, c.   Parallel and network processing are used when a person is scanning the environment for a stimulus. Network processing refers to how units in a network operate in parallel—all at once, making certain targets easier to recognize in particular contexts.

    d.   Top-down processing is influenced by motivation and expectation.

17.   d is the answer   A perceptual set is a readiness to perceive a stimulus in a certain way. Sensitivity is the ability to perceive an object *at all,* not an indication of *how* we perceive it. (see Top-down Processing)

    a.   Context can change the way we perceive an object. For example, the sound of "reed" means two different things depending on the context of the sentence. Compare "The oboe contains a reed" and "I like to read."

    b.   Our expectations, based on past experience and context, can create a perceptual set.

    c.   Our past experiences can create perceptual sets. A person who does not have children may take some time to realize that children's bloodcurdling screams may not always signify pain. Anyone who has been around children for any length of time knows that they sometimes scream while they play and that alarm is not always the necessary response.

18.   b is the answer.   Pareidolia is the perception of a specific image, such as the Virgin Mary, in an ambiguous stimulus array. The smoke scars are ambiguous, but the perception of some townspeople is specific. (see Top-down Processing)

a. Bottom-up processing would have meant everyone saw and interpreted the smoke scars similarly, regardless of whether they had been told about the image of the Virgin Mary or not. Jonah did not see the image until he had been told about it, which suggests top-down processing underlying pareidolia.

c. Network processing is based on connections between various units in a cognitive network. This question does not describe any such connections.

d. Stevens's law involves estimating magnitude, not interpreting ambiguous stimulus arrays.

19. b is the answer.   Network processing causes the word superiority effect that Carrie experienced. The neural links between letters previously seen together in a word are stronger than those between letters not previously shown together as a word. (see Network Processing)

a. Perception cannot occur without bottom-up processing, the reaction of nervous system cells to features of the stimulus, but the effect Carrie experienced was related to the networks of information in Carrie's brain.

c. Relative is not a processing type.

d. Serial processing occurs when a person must scan the environment carefully, examining several characteristics before deciding whether the target has been found.

20. c is the answer.   By making the windows progressively smaller on successively higher floors, the architect will create the illusion that the top of his building is farther away and thus higher, than if the windows are the same size as the floors go up. (see Applications of Research on Perception)

a. Windows of equal size will not make the building look larger or smaller than its actual dimensions.

b. If the windows get larger on successively higher floors, this will make the building seem shorter, not taller, than its actual dimensions.

d. Having no windows will not make the building look taller.

Now turn to the quiz analysis table at the end of this chapter to find which areas you know well and which areas you need to work on. Circle the numbers in the table for items on Quiz 1 that you answered correctly.

Quiz 2

1. b is the answer.   The constructivist viewpoint is that we piece together a perception from fragmented parts of sensory information by using our experience and knowledge. In closure, missing gaps are filled in to create a perception of a whole, based on our experience of how the whole perception should appear. (see Three Approaches to Perception)

a. A computational view is one that explains that features of the environment are formed into complete perceptions through the actions of nervous system structures and mechanisms.

c. The ecological view asserts that everything needed for perception is present in the environment; we only have to attend to the important aspects.

d. Signal-detection theory does not address why someone would use the grouping principle of closure.

2. b is the answer.   Response criterion determines the amount of physical energy needed for a person to justify reporting that a stimulus is present. Expecting to see a stimulus decreases, or lowers, the response criterion. (see Signal-Detection Theory)

a. Expecting to see the stimulus does not increase, or raise, the response criterion. In other words, when the response criterion is decreased, we are more likely to report seeing a stimulus because we know it is coming.

c, d. Expectations do influence the response criterion, and the response criterion does not influence expectations.

3. a is the answer. Signal-detection theory addresses the factors that influence whether we will perceive a stimulus. In this case, the stimulus is a terrorist. (see Signal-Detection Theory)

b. By definition, subliminal stimuli are *not* detectable. Here, Joe is concerned about the guard's identification of a terrorist (hits) and misidentification of nonterrorists (false alarms)—part of signal-detection theory.

c. Optical acuity theory is not a term.

d. Weber's law addresses the perception of differences between stimuli, not stimulus detection itself.

4. d is the answer. An ear infection's muffling sounds has affected the capacity of LaKisha's sensory systems, one influence on sensitivity. LaKisha does not hear many of the tones; in other words, she misses them. (see Signal-Detection Theory)

a. Absolute threshold is the point at which a stimulus is perceived on half of its presentations; false alarms are saying stimuli were presented when they were not.

b. The experiment is not testing whether LaKisha can notice a difference between two stimuli, and her difference threshold is not affected.

c. Nothing is said about LaKisha's response criterion; therefore, we do not know if she lowered it; she did not have any false alarms because she was barely responding to any tones.

5. d is the answer. Subliminal perception does not control behavior, so a subliminal advertisement probably would not help much. It would be better to rely on supraliminal perception—an advertisement that someone is actually aware that they saw. (see Thinking Critically: Can Subliminal Stimuli Influence Your Behavior?)

a. This is not a great idea, because subliminal perception does not control behavior, and its effects are small and short-lived. You need an effect that will last long enough to make people want to leave their dorm and go to the event.

b, c. Although subliminal perception does occur, its effects are brief and small. It would be much better to focus on supraliminal perception in advertising your event.

6. d is the answer. These are the two factors that determine the ability to detect a difference in the amount of stimulation received. (see Judging Differences: Has Anything Changed?)

a. Extremes in stimuli are handled by the magnitude estimation laws, not by Weber's law.

b. Particular types of stimuli are covered by magnitude estimation laws

c. Individual differences are addressed in signal-detection theory, not by the general formula for just-noticeable differences in Weber's law.

7. b is the answer. Changes in internal noise, stimulus intensity, or the workings of the sensory system alter sensitivity. If Jake is asleep, his visual sensory system is not working. Jake's eyes must be open before he can see the suspect creep by the car. (see Signal-Detection Theory)

a.   If Jake thought that the suspect was in for the night, then his expectations of activity would decrease. This would increase the necessary response criterion but would not affect sensitivity.

c.   If Jake thought that the suspect's partner was aiming a gun at him, then his motivation to grab the suspect might have been lowered. Jake may think he is too close to retirement to take chances. This would affect Jake's motivation, not his sensitivity.

d.   If Jake is not concerned about his record, he may not be as attentive at work. This would lower his response criterion (he is probably a bit reluctant to hear the suspect) and increase his absolute threshold (the amount of noise required before Jake hears the suspect).

8.   d is the answer.   The people closer to each other are seen as groups. (see Basic Processes in Perceptual Organization)

a.   The grouping principle closure fills in gaps.

b.   Continuity groups seemingly unbroken forms.

c.   Figure-ground would assign some figures to the foreground and others to the background, but it would not account for your perception of pairs of people at the party.

9.   b is the answer.   Dishabituation occurs when a person resumes looking at something when the stimulus appears to be different than it was. (see Linkages: Perception and Human Development)

a.   Habituation occurs when a person stops looking at an object that is not changing.

c.   Inattentional blindness occurs when the spotlight of your attention is voluntarily or involuntarily focused on one part of the environment, making you blind to the other parts of your environment.

d.   Multitasking involves doing more than one thing at a time.

10.   a is the answer.   Top-down processing is guided by expectations and motivations. Stanley, the proud grandparent, expected to see the features of his side of the family, and Edna, equally proud, expected to see the features of her side of the family. (see Top-down Processing)

b.   Perceptual constancy is the perception of objects as constant in size, shape, and color, despite changes in their retinal image. It does not explain the difference between Stanley's and Edna's perceptions.

c.   Feature detection refers to the activity of particular cells in the cortex corresponding to particular features of stimuli in the environment.

d.   The perception paradox refers to the idea that because the perceptual system functions efficiently and effectively, it is a very complex system and thus difficult to study.

11.   c is the answer.   Although several of the alternatives are depth cues, the reduced or relative size of the mouse tells the cat that his quarry is far away. (see Perception of Location and Distance)

a.   Eye convergence is a depth cue, but it requires a visual image from both eyes. The cat is peering through the fence with only one eye.

b.   Retinal disparity is a depth cue, but it requires a visual image from both eyes. The cat is peering through the fence with only one eye.

d.   Looming is a motion cue. Objects are perceived as moving closer as they take up more and more of our retinal space.

12. b is the answer.   The stroboscopic illusion, a motion illusion, enables us to interpret motion from a series of still images flashed in rapid succession. (see Perception of Motion)

    a.   Motion parallax is a visual depth cue in which near objects seem to move faster across the visual field than objects in the distance.

    c.   Retinal disparity provides information about the distance of objects. It is the difference between the two retinal images of an object.

    d.   Eye convergence is another depth cue. The more eyes converge inward, the closer the object.

13. c is the answer.   Due to size constancy, we perceive objects as retaining their same size despite changes in retinal size. (see Perceptual Constancy)

    a.   Looming is a motion cue. Objects fill the entire retinal space as they get closer and are perceived as moving.

    b.   Proximity is a grouping principle. The closer objects are, the more likely we are to perceive them as part of the same group.

    d.   Motion parallax helps us perceive depth.

14. a is the answer.   Schema refers to the mental representations of what we know, and have come to expect, about the world. (see Top-down Processing)

    b.   Images are visual representations in the mind. Schemas refer to more general representations than merely visual ones.

    c.   Illusions are perceptual errors.

    d.   A gradient refers to a change. In this chapter, one of the depth cues is the gradient, or change, in texture as an object becomes more distant.

15. d is the answer.   Particular patterns of blood flow have been observed in different areas of the brain, depending on the type of attentional process that was active. (see Attention and the Brain)

    a, b, c.   No single brain region has been identified as the attention center.

16. a is the answer.   People from cultures that do not use pictures or photographs to represent reality will have a more difficult time judging distances in pictures compared to people from cultures that do use pictures and photographs. (see Culture, Experience, and Perception)

    b, c.   It will be harder, not easier or similarly difficult, for people from cultures without pictures or photographs to judge distances in pictures because their experience set will not have prepared them to do so with any regularity or accuracy.

    d.   It will be harder to judge distances for one from a culture that doesn't use pictures or photographs. While it is possible that this difficulty may increase how long these judgments take, this is not necessarily true.

17. a is the answer.   Feature analysis is part of bottom-up processing. It is usually followed by top-down processing, but that is not described in the item. (see Bottom-up Processing)

    b.   There is no such thing as ecological processing; you may have been thinking of the ecological view of perception.

    c.   Illusory processing is a made-up term.

    d.   Top-down processing and bottom-up processing work together. Lou's top-down processing probably started as soon as the perceptual category "flower" was activated, but her inference that, for example, the flower was given to her by someone who likes her is not described in the question.

18. c is the answer.   Attentional resources are limited, particularly when tasks involve the same type of attentional resources. This would be applicable in Sasha's case because both reading and following the TV program involve perceiving incoming stimuli. (see Attention)

   a, b, d. Attentional resources are *not* unlimited. If the same resource is being tapped by two different tasks, as is the case here, only one task can be performed. If two different attentional resources are being tapped, it might be possible to perform them simultaneously.

19. a is the answer,   Covert orienting is a shift of attention that is not possible for the casual observer to see. (see Attention)

   b.   An overt attention shift would be turning away from Rich to stare at an approaching person.

   c, d. Parallel and serial processing are types of searches.

20. d is the answer.   Existing research suggests that using a mobile phone while driving is dangerous not only because it can take your eyes of the road and hands off the wheel, but also because the conversation itself competes for attentional resources needed to drive safely. (see Applications of Research on Perception)

   a.   Driving while talking on a mobile phone is dangerous.

   b, c. Although hands-free phones and voice-controlled dialing address the problems of taking one's eyes off the road to dial and hands off the wheel to hold the phone, these features do not deal with the problem of the conversation itself taking attention away from the road.

Now turn to the quiz analysis table at the end of this chapter to find which areas you know well and which areas you need to work on. Circle the numbers in the table for items on Quiz 2 that you answered correctly.

For each question you answered correctly, circle its number. (Quiz 1 numbers are not shaded; Quiz 2 numbers are shaded.) Are there patterns in the types of questions or the topics you got wrong that could direct your further study? Did you improve from Quiz 1 to Quiz 2?

QUIZ REVIEW

Topic	Type of Question		
	Definition	**Comprehension**	**Application**
Three Approaches to Perception			1, 15
			1
Psychophysics			
Absolute Thresholds: Is Something Out There?			3
Thinking Critically: Can Subliminal Stimuli Influence Your Behavior?	7		
			5
Signal-Detection Theory		4	2, 5, 6
		2	3, 4, 7
Judging Differences: Has Anything Changed?		8	
		6	
Organizing the Perceptual World			
Basic Processes in Perceptual Organization			9, 10
			8
Perception of Location and Distance	11		12
			11
Perception of Motion			13
			12
Perceptual Constancy			14
	13		
Recognizing the Perceptual World			
Bottom-up Processing			16
			17
Top-down Processing		17	18
	14		10
Network Processing			19
Culture, Experience, and Perception			
			16
Linkages: Perception and Human Development			
			9
Attention			
			18, 19
Attention and the Brain			
		15	
Applications of Research on Perception			20
		20	

Total correct by quiz:

Quiz 1:	
Quiz 2:	

CHAPTER 6

Learning

<u>Learning</u> is the adaptive process of modification through experience of pre-existing behavior and understanding.

OUTLINE

I.   LEARNING ABOUT STIMULI
     <u>Habituation</u> is considered a simple form of adaptive learning; organisms stop paying attention to stimuli that are often repeated and that do not signal any important environmental events. Instead, we focus on novel stimuli. Habituation is complemented by *dishabituation*. Another simple form of learning is *sensititzation*.
     According to the opponent-process theory, habituation to repeated stimuli causes two processes. The first process is an almost reflexive increase or decrease in some response. The second process causes an opposite or opposing response. The opponent-process theory has been used to explain drug-tolerance development.

II. CLASSICAL CONDITIONING: LEARNING SIGNALS AND ASSOCIATIONS
     A.   Pavlov's Discovery
          1.   Ivan Pavlov's experiment was the first demonstration of <u>classical conditioning</u>. Pavlov's experiment had three phases. During the first phase, a natural reflex and a neutral stimulus were established. During the second phase, the neutral stimulus and the stimulus causing the natural reflex were repeatedly paired. During the third phase, the neutral stimulus alone caused some form of the natural reflex to occur.
          2.   In classical conditioning, a neutral stimulus is paired with a stimulus that elicits a reflex or other response until the formerly neutral stimulus alone elicits a similar response. The stimulus that causes the natural reflex is called the <u>unconditioned stimulus (UCS)</u>; the reflex itself is designated the <u>unconditioned response (UCR)</u>. The neutral stimulus that is paired with the UCS is the <u>conditioned stimulus (CS)</u>, and the learned response to the conditioned stimulus is the <u>conditioned response (CR)</u>.
     B.   Conditioned Responses over Time: Extinction and Spontaneous Recovery
          The CS will continue to elicit a CR only if the UCS continues to appear at least some of the time. If the CS and UCS are unpaired (that is, the CS is not followed by the UCS), the CR gets weaker and weaker and undergoes <u>extinction</u>. However, the learned relationship between the CS and the UCS is not completely forgotten, as is demonstrated by <u>reconditioning</u> and <u>spontaneous recovery</u>. In reconditioning, the relationship between the CS and the UCS is relearned as the stimuli are paired once again. This time the CS will elicit the CR much more quickly. Spontaneous recovery occurs when, after no presentation of either the CS or the UCS for a period of time, a single presentation of the CS elicits the CR.
     C.   Stimulus Generalization and Discrimination
          <u>Stimulus generalization</u> occurs when a stimulus similar but not identical to the original stimulus also elicits a response. <u>Stimulus discrimination</u> is a complementary process through which organisms learn to differentiate between stimuli that are similar but not identical to the CS.

D.   The Signaling of Significant Events
In classical conditioning, the CS acts as a signal that the UCS is about to appear. Situations that highlight and strengthen the CS-UCS relationship will produce stronger CRs.
1.   *Timing*. Classical conditioning produces the strongest CRs when the CS precedes the UCS by no more than a few seconds. This is known as *forward conditioning*. *Backward conditioning* and *simultaneous conditioning* are less effective.
2.   *Predictability*. A strong CR will be developed if a very noticeable CS is reliably followed by the UCS.
3.   *Signal Strength*. The relationship between the CS and the UCS is learned faster as the salience or intensity of the CS and UCS increases.
4.   *Attention*. Often, more than one CS is associated with a UCS. The CS that is most attended to will be the best predictor of the UCS.
5.   *Biopreparedness*. Humans and animals may be innately likely or biologically "prepared" to learn certain adaptive associations. Nausea is likely to be a conditioned response to an internal stimulus such as taste (conditioned taste aversion), and pain is likely to be a conditioned response to an external stimulus such as noise.
6.   *Higher-Order Conditioning*. Higher-order conditioning occurs when a conditioned stimulus acts like an unconditioned stimulus, creating conditioned stimuli out of events associated with it.
E.   Some Applications of Classical Conditioning
1.   *Phobias*. Phobias are fears of objects or situations that are not harmful. Classical conditioning can both produce (via stimulus generalization) and eliminate (through *systematic desensitization*) phobias.
2.   *Predator Control*. Some ranchers have set out mutton laced with lithium for wolves and coyotes. The dizziness and severe nausea (UCR) caused by the lithium becomes associated with the smell and taste of mutton (CS), thus making sheep an undesirable meal.
3.   *Detecting Explosives*. Insects can detect explosive material. By repeatedly pairing the taste of sugar water with the smell of chemicals used in some explosives, wasps develop a conditioned response to the smell alone, displaying an attraction to it.
III.   OPERANT CONDITIONING: LEARNING THE CONSEQUENCES OF BEHAVIOR
People learn more than just an association between neutral and unconditioned stimuli. For many behaviors, the stimuli that follow an action are important. In other words, people learn to respond in a way that brings about positive consequences.
A.   From the Puzzle Box to the Skinner Box
According to the law of effect, if a response made in the presence of a particular stimulus is followed by a reward, that response is more likely to be made the next time the stimulus is encountered. Responses that are "instrumental," meaning that they help produce some rewarding or desired effect, are learned; therefore, Thorndike called this learning *instrumental conditioning*. Skinner's emphasis on how an organism learns to "operate on" its environment to produce a positive effect led him to rename instrumental conditioning to operant conditioning.
B.   Basic Components of Operant Conditioning
1.   *Operants and Reinforcers*. An operant is a behavioral response that has some effect on an organism's environment. In operant conditioning, people learn the relationship between operants and their consequences. A reinforcer is a consequence that increases the probability that a behavioral response will occur again. Two types of reinforcers exist. Positive reinforcers are positive stimuli that act like rewards. Negative reinforcers are negative stimuli that, once removed, encourage or reinforce behavior. Reinforcement is the process by which by which a behavior is strengthened (either through removal of an unpleasant consequence or delivery of a pleasant consequence).

2. *Escape and Avoidance Conditioning.* Negative reinforcements are used in escape and avoidance conditioning. In <u>escape conditioning</u>, an organism learns behaviors that lead to an escape from an unpleasant situation (negative reinforcement). In <u>avoidance conditioning</u>, an organism learns behaviors that allow it to completely avoid an unpleasant situation (negative reinforcement). Avoidance conditioning is very strong and may prevent an organism from learning new behaviors. Avoidance conditioning has also increased researchers' focus on cognitive processes in learning.

3. *Discriminative Conditioned Stimuli and Stimulus Control.* <u>Discriminative conditioned stimuli</u> signal to an organism that reinforcement is available if a certain response is made. This response is said to be under *stimulus control*. Stimulus generalization, recognizing a stimulus similar to the original stimulus that signaled reinforcement, also occurs in operant conditioning.

C.   Forming and Strengthening Operant Behavior

1. *Shaping.* Creation of new responses never before displayed can be accomplished through <u>shaping</u>, or reinforcing successive approximations (more and more like the desired response) of the desired behavior.

2. *Secondary Reinforcement.* Often, operant conditioning will begin with <u>primary reinforcers</u>—events or stimuli that are intrinsically rewarding, such as food. A <u>secondary reinforcer</u> is a previously neutral stimulus that, if paired with a stimulus that is already reinforcing, will itself take on reinforcing properties.

3. *Delay and Size of Reinforcement.* Operant conditioning is strongest when the delay in receiving a reinforcer is short and when the reinforcer is large.

4. *Schedules of Reinforcement.* <u>Continuous reinforcement</u> involves rewarding *every* correct response every time it occurs. <u>Partial reinforcement</u> involves reinforcing only some of the behaviors some of the time. Different <u>reinforcement schedules</u> result in different patterns of extinction.
   a) <u>Fixed-ratio (FR) reinforcement</u> gives a reward after a fixed number of responses.
   b) <u>Variable-ratio (VR) reinforcement</u> gives a reward after an average number of responses.
   c) <u>Fixed-interval (FI) reinforcement</u> rewards the first response displayed after a fixed time interval.
   d) <u>Variable-interval (VI) reinforcement</u> rewards the first response displayed after a varying time interval.

5. *Schedules and Extinction.* Eliminating reinforcers for behavioral responses eventually causes the behavioral response to cease (<u>extinction</u>). The <u>partial reinforcement effect</u> demonstrates that it is more difficult to extinguish an operant behavior learned under a partial rather than a continuous reinforcement schedule.

D.   Why Reinforcers Work

Primary reinforcers are items that fulfill basic needs or are inherently rewarding experiences, such as relief from pain.

Premack's principle asserts that each person has a hierarchy of behavioral preferences and that the higher an activity is in that hierarchy, the greater its reinforcement power.

The *response deprivation hypothesis* contends that any activity can become a reinforcer if access to it has been restricted for a time.

Biological psychologists have found that stimulation of "pleasure centers" in the brain is a powerful reinforcer, suggesting a physiological component to reinforcement.

E.   Punishment
     <u>Punishment</u> presents an aversive stimulus or removes a pleasant stimulus to decrease the frequency of a behavior. Punishment has several disadvantages. First, it does not eliminate learning; it merely suppresses a behavior. If an organism knows that punishment is unlikely, then the behavior is repeated. Second, punishment is not effective unless it immediately follows the undesired behavior. Third, punishment may be associated with the punisher so that eventually the punisher is feared. Fourth, the organism being punished may learn to relate to others in an aggressive manner. Fifth, punishment may escalate into abuse. Finally, punishment makes clear what behaviors are incorrect, but it doesn't provide any demonstration of desired behaviors.
     Punishment can work if used wisely. One should punish the behavior, not the person; punish immediately; use a severe enough punishment to eliminate the behavior; and explain and reinforce more appropriate behaviors.

F.   Some Applications of Operant Conditioning
     Operant conditioning can be used to teach people the "rules" of social behavior and to eliminate problematic behavior and reinforce positive, desired behavior in people afflicted with mental retardation, autism, and other behavior disorders. Operant conditioning principles can also be used to help people understand the stimuli that trigger behaviors they want to eliminate (such as smoking or overeating). Understanding and avoiding discriminative conditioned stimuli can reduce the undesired behavior. Stimulus control has been applied in the treatment of insomnia.

G.   Linkages: Neural Networks and Learning
     As the chapters on perception and memory suggest, neural networks likely play an important role in storing and organizing information. Psychologists have developed models of how these associations that occur in learning might be established as neural connections. These *parallel distributed processing models* suggest that knowledge is distributed throughout a network of associations. They focus on how these connections develop through experience. The weaker the connection between two items, the greater the increase observed in connection strength when they are experienced together.

IV. COGNITIVE PROCESSES IN LEARNING
     Cognitive processes, such as how people store, represent, and use information, can influence learning.

A.   Learned Helplessness
     Humans and animals placed in situations that eliminate their control over the environment tend to give up any effort to exert control over their environment in new situations. They learn to be helpless. <u>Learned helplessness</u> is a tendency to give up any effort to control the environment.

B.   Focus on Research Methods: An Experiment on Human Helplessness
     In this experiment, the dependent variable—the degree to which participants acted to control noise—could be affected by two independent variables: prior experience with noise and expectation about the ability to influence the noise. People tend to feel less able to control a situation if they previously could not control it or if they are told they are powerless. These experiences may give rise to negative thinking or *pessimistic explanatory styles*, which may affect performance and mental health. Repeated experience with successful control may develop an *optimistic cognitive style*.

C.   Latent Learning and Cognitive Maps
     Learning that is not immediately evident in an organism's behavior is known as <u>latent learning</u>. <u>Cognitive maps</u> are mental representations of the environment.

D.   Insight and Learning
The cognitive process of <u>insight</u> involves understanding the global organization of a problem.

E.   Observational Learning: Learning by Imitation
A series of experiments by Albert Bandura demonstrated that people learn by watching others, which is termed <u>observational learning</u> or <u>social learning</u>. In observational learning, a person learns new behaviors by watching others' behavior. In <u>vicarious experience</u>, a type of observational learning, a person learns new behaviors by observing the consequences (reinforcement or punishment) of someone else's behavior. Both are powerful in the *socialization* process.

F.   Thinking Critically: Does Watching Violence on Television Make People More Violent?
What am I being asked to believe or accept?
Watching violence on television causes violent behavior in viewers.
What evidence is available to support the assertion?
Anecdotes and case studies describe incidents of violence among children after watching violence on TV. Many studies show a positive correlation between watching and committing violence. Controlled experimental studies also show increases in violent behavior following violent visual stimulation.
Are there alternative ways of interpreting the evidence?
Anecdotal evidence and correlational evidence do not prove causation. It may be possible that the dependent variables used in the controlled studies are not similar enough to violence in everyday life.
What additional evidence would help to evaluate the alternatives?
More controlled studies are needed to better understand the relationship between viewing violence and committing violent acts. However, ethical considerations prohibit these types of studies.
What conclusions are most reasonable?
The large number of studies done in this area make it reasonable to conclude that watching TV violence may be one cause of violent behavior.

V.   USING RESEARCH ON LEARNING TO HELP PEOPLE LEARN
A.   Classrooms Across Cultures
Studies show that the average academic performance of U.S. students tends to lag behind that of students in other countries. Suggested causes include static classroom formats and less time spent on practice.

B.   Active Learning
Active learning exercises improve memory of material and make classrooms more enjoyable. Active learning is a more elaborate process in which students solve problems in groups, think about how material relates to what they know, and answer every question asked by the teacher.

C.   Skill Learning
Practice is the most critical component of skill learning. Practice should continue until the skill can be performed automatically for perceptual-motor skills. For cognitive skills, practice should focus on retrieval of information from memory.
Feedback lets the learner know if she or he is correct and may provide understanding of the cognitive and physical processes used in the skill. Feedback should be given after a learner is finished practicing and should not be so detailed that the learner does not have to learn from his or her own mistakes.

KEY TERMS

1.   **Learning** is the modification through experience of preexisting behavior and understanding. (see introductory section)

     REMEMBER: People learn primarily by identifying relationships between events and noting the regularity in the surrounding world.

2.   **Habituation** is the process of adapting to stimuli that do not change. (see Learning About Stimuli)

     Example: When Jason first had corrective braces affixed to his teeth, he reported tension and discomfort. After about a week, these complaints decreased because Jason had adapted to the sensations.

3.   **Classical conditioning** is a procedure in which a neutral stimulus is repeatedly paired with a stimulus that elicits a reflex or other response until the neutral stimulus alone comes to elicit a similar response. (see Pavlov's Discovery)

     Example: Cat owners who feed their cats canned food and use an electric can opener know that just the sound of the opener will cause the cat to come running into the kitchen and salivate. The sound of the opener (an originally neutral stimulus) is paired with food (a stimulus that elicits a reflexive response such as salivation or other behavioral responses such as running into the kitchen) until the sound alone elicits the response. This occurs because the sound of the electric opener predicts the presence of food.

     REMEMBER: Throughout the chapter, the word *response* is used. It is equivalent to a behavior or mental process. If you become confused by the use of this word, simply substitute the terms *mental process* or *behavior*, and the sentence's meaning should become clear.

4.   An **unconditioned stimulus (UCS)** is a stimulus that elicits a response without conditioning. (see Pavlov's Discovery)

     Example: In the cat example in Key Term 3, food is the unconditioned stimulus; it naturally causes the cat to salivate.

     REMEMBER: Unconditioned means "unlearned." Cats do not have to learn about food every time in order to respond to food.

5.   An **unconditioned response (UCR)** is the automatic or unlearned response to a stimulus. (see Pavlov's Discovery)

     Example: In the cat example in Key Term 3, salivation is an unconditioned response. This behavior or response is reflexive or unlearned and occurs in the presence of the unconditioned stimulus (food).

6.   A **conditioned stimulus (CS)** is the originally neutral stimulus that, through pairing with the unconditioned stimulus, comes to elicit a conditioned response. (see Pavlov's Discovery)

     Example: In the cat example in Key Term 3, the sound of the can opener is the conditioned stimulus because it initially elicited no response from the cat (as a neutral stimulus). Only when the sound of the opener was paired with the presentation of food did the sound predict the presence of food (UCS) and cause the cat to run to the kitchen and salivate.

     REMEMBER: Conditioned means "learned." The conditioned stimulus is originally neutral; the organism must learn that it predicts the presence of the UCS.

7.   A **conditioned response (CR)** is the response that the conditioned stimulus elicits. (see Pavlov's Discovery)

Example: In the cat example in Key Term 3, the cat's response of running to the kitchen and salivating when it hears the can opener is the conditioned response.

8.   **Extinction** is the gradual disappearance of a conditioned response when a conditioned stimulus is no longer followed by an unconditioned stimulus. (see Conditioned Responses over Time: Extinction and Spontaneous Recovery)

Example: The story "The Boy Who Cried Wolf" is an example of extinction in classical conditioning. Shepherds learned that hearing someone cry, "Wolf!" (CS) meant that a wolf (UCS) had appeared, and consequently they would run (CR) for help. When one little boy repeatedly cried, "Wolf!" for no reason, the other shepherds stopped responding (CR) to his cry (CS) because it no longer predicted the presence of a wolf (UCS).

REMEMBER: To become *extinct* means to "no longer exist." In the above example, the CR (running) no longer exists when the cry of "Wolf!" (CS) is heard.

9.   **Reconditioning** is the quick relearning of a conditioned response following extinction. (see Conditioned Responses over Time: Extinction and Spontaneous Recovery)

REMEMBER: Conditioning involves the association of two stimuli such that one (CS) begins to predict the occurrence of the other (UCS). Reconditioning is simply repeating this process.

10.   **Spontaneous recovery** is the reappearance of the conditioned response after extinction and without further pairings of the conditioned and unconditioned stimuli. (see Conditioned Responses over Time: Extinction and Spontaneous Recovery)

Example: Pavlov's dogs were conditioned to salivate (CR) in response to the sound of a bell. After extinction (hearing the bell without receiving food), the dogs no longer responded. If, after a long time following extinction, the dogs heard the sound of the bell again, they would most likely salivate. The conditioned response would have spontaneously "recovered."

REMEMBER: Spontaneously means "suddenly" or "without planning." In spontaneous recovery, the CR occurs suddenly or immediately after only *one* presentation of the CS (bell).

11.   **Stimulus generalization** is a phenomenon in which a conditioned response is elicited by stimuli that are similar but not identical to the conditioned stimulus. (see Stimulus Generalization and Discrimination)

Example: Nguyen was very curious as a child. He had never seen a spider (CS) before the time he picked up a big reddish-brown one to investigate it closely. Eventually, the spider bit him (UCS), causing him to become ill (UCR) for several days. Nguyen is now an adult and avoids (CR) all spiders, not just reddish-brown ones. He is reacting to stimuli that are similar but not necessarily identical to the original conditioned stimulus (reddish-brown spiders).

12.   **Stimulus discrimination** is a process through which individuals learn to differentiate among similar stimuli and respond appropriately to each one. (See Key Term 23 for more information about discrimination in operant conditioning.) (see Stimulus Generalization and Discrimination)

Example: Raoul the dog receives an injection (UCS) at the veterinarian's every four months. Raoul usually loves to ride in the car. However, whenever his owner drives Raoul to the veterinarian's (CS), Raoul whimpers (CR) for most of the ride. Raoul has learned to discriminate between the route to the veterinarian's and the route to other places.

13. **Higher-order conditioning** is a phenomenon in which a conditioned stimulus acts as an unconditioned stimulus, creating conditioned stimuli out of events associated with it. (see The Signaling of Significant Events)

    Example: If Pavlov had turned on the light in the room before ringing the bell (CS) and the dogs eventually began to salivate (CR) as soon as he turned on the light, higher-order conditioning would have occurred.

14. The **law of effect** states that if a response made in the presence of a particular stimulus is followed by satisfaction, that response is more likely the next time the stimulus is encountered. (see From the Puzzle Box to the Skinner Box)

    REMEMBER: The law of effect means the law of being effective. If an organism learns that a behavior produces a desired effect, such as good grades or money, the organism will repeat the behavior. If the behavior is ineffective (it does not produce anything or it produces bad effects, such as a scolding), it will not be repeated.

15. **Operant conditioning** is a process through which an organism learns to respond to the environment in a way that produces positive consequences and avoids negative ones. (see From the Puzzle Box to the Skinner Box)

16. An **operant** is a response that has some effect on the world. (see Basic Components of Operant Conditioning)

    REMEMBER: Operant responses are behaviors that operate in the world in some way.

17. A **reinforcer** is a stimulus event that increases the probability that the response that immediately preceded it will occur again. (see Basic Components of Operant Conditioning)

18. **Positive reinforcers** are stimuli that strengthen a response if they follow that response. (see Basic Components of Operant Conditioning)

    Example: If Rover gets a bone (a positive reinforcer) every time he rolls over, he will probably roll over frequently.

    REMEMBER: A reinforcer always encourages the repetition of the behavior that it follows. A pleasant stimulus (+) is added (+) to the environment. You can remember this by thinking that a positive number times a positive number yields a positive number.

19. **Negative reinforcers** are unpleasant stimuli, such as pain, that, strengthen a response if they are removed following that response. (see Basic Components of Operant Conditioning)

    Example: Hunger pains are unpleasant stimuli. Eating causes them to go away. People learn the habit of eating when they experience hunger pains because the pains disappear (negative reinforcers).

    REMEMBER: A reinforcer always encourages the repetition of the behavior that it follows. In negative reinforcement, a negative stimulus (−) is subtracted from (−) the environment. You can remember this by thinking that a negative number times a negative number always yields a positive number.

20. **Reinforcement** is the process through which a particular response is made more likely to recur. see Basic Components of Operant Conditioning)

    Example: Claudia is rewarded by her parents for coming home early with extra computer privileges at home. Claudia is now more likely to come home early in the future.

21. **Escape conditioning** is a type of learning in which an organism learns to make a particular response in order to terminate an aversive stimulus. (see Basic Components of Operant Conditioning)

    Example: Lydia has recently set up a computer at home and now does most of her work there. Her cat, Spooky, has begun to sit next to the terminal and cry until Lydia gets up to feed him. Lydia has learned that her response of feeding the cat will remove the distracting sound of his cries.

    REMEMBER: Escape and avoidance conditioning are sometimes confused. In order for escape conditioning to occur, the organism must first be in trouble.

22. **Avoidance conditioning** is a type of learning in which an organism responds to a signal in a way that prevents exposure to an aversive stimulus. (see Basic Components of Operant Conditioning)

    Example: Leslie has learned that by accepting most men's invitations for dates she avoids the awkwardness of explaining that she is not interested in them.

    REMEMBER: Escape and avoidance conditioning can be confused. In avoidance conditioning, the organism avoids ever getting into trouble. In escape conditioning, the organism learns how to get out of trouble.

23. **Discriminative conditioned stimuli** are stimuli that signal whether reinforcement is available if a certain response is made. . (see Basic Components of Operant Conditioning)

    Example: Alicia knows that her business partner is in a good mood if she is smiling, is not wearing her suit jacket, and has opened the blinds. These discriminative conditioned stimuli inform Alicia that she can approach her partner with a new idea (Alicia's particular response) and expect her partner to be supportive (reinforcement). Alicia's behavior is under stimulus control because Alicia will not approach her partner unless the discriminative conditioned stimuli are present.

    REMEMBER: Such a response is said to be under *stimulus control* because the response is usually made when only the discriminative stimulus is present.

24. **Shaping** is the process of reinforcing responses that come successively closer to the desired response. (see Forming and Strengthening Operant Behavior)

    Example: Trainers at Sea World want to teach a whale to jump through a hoop. Because wild whales do not normally perform this behavior, the trainers must shape it. They might begin by rewarding the whale for jumping out of the water. Then they reward the whale for jumping toward a hoop and eventually for touching it. Each of these behaviors is a successive approximation of jumping through a hoop. Eventually, the entire behavior pattern will be learned and rewarded.

    REMEMBER: To *shape* means to "mold into something." In shaping, the behavior must be gradually molded.

25. **Primary reinforcers** are reinforcers that meet an organism's basic needs, such as food and water. (see Forming and Strengthening Operant Behavior)

    Example: Food and water are primary reinforcers if you are hungry.

26. A **secondary reinforcer** is a reward that people or animals learn to like. (see Forming and Strengthening Operant Behavior)

    Example: Before people used money in exchange for goods, they worked to produce or exchange life's basic necessities, such as food. Money, because it allows people to buy food and has therefore become associated with food, is a secondary reinforcer.

27. **Continuous reinforcement** is a pattern in which a reinforcer is delivered every time a particular response occurs. (see Forming and Strengthening Operant Behavior)

    Example: Every time Martine sets the table, her mother offers her a soda with dinner.

28. **Partial**, or *intermittent*, **reinforcement** is a pattern in which a reinforcer is administered only some of the time after a particular response occurs. (see Forming and Strengthening Operant Behavior)

    REMEMBER: Any reinforcement schedule other than a continuous one is an example of this.

29. **Reinforcement schedules** in operant conditioning are rules that determine how and when certain responses will be reinforced. (see Forming and Strengthening Operant Behavior)

    Example: Kelli decides to reinforce her son every time he cleans his room. This particular reinforcement schedule is a fixed-ratio schedule.

30. **Fixed-ratio (FR) reinforcement** schedules are partial reinforcement schedules that provide reinforcement following a fixed number of responses. (see Forming and Strengthening Operant Behavior)

    Example: Phil, a real estate broker, receives a bonus for every ten houses he sells.

    REMEMBER: The word *fixed* in a schedule always means "set"; the word *ratio* always means "behavior." A fixed-ratio schedule indicates that a reward is given after a set number of behaviors.

31. **Variable-ratio (VR) reinforcement** schedules are partial reinforcement schedules that provide reinforcement after a varying number of responses. (see Forming and Strengthening Operant Behavior)

    Example: Joycelyn's parents will reward her with a gift of her choice when she gets one to three good report cards.

    REMEMBER: The word *variable* means "changing"; the word *ratio* means "behavior." A reward is presented after a varying number of behaviors—in other words, after some variable number of responses.

32. **Fixed-interval (FI) reinforcement** schedules are partial reinforcement schedules that provide reinforcement for the first response that occurs after some fixed time has passed since the last reward. (see Forming and Strengthening Operant Behavior)

    Example: Levar, a graduate teaching assistant, gets paid once a month.

    REMEMBER: The word *fixed* in a schedule means "set"; the word *interval* in a schedule means "time period." An organism is rewarded for the first behavior after a set time period.

33. **Variable-interval (VI) reinforcement** schedules are partial reinforcement schedules that provide reinforcement for the first response after varying periods of time. (see Forming and Strengthening Operant Behavior)

    Example: Students who study a little every day in order to be prepared for surprise quizzes given at various times throughout the semester are on a variable-interval schedule.

    REMEMBER: The word *variable* in a schedule means "changing." The word *interval* means "time period." An organism is rewarded at changing periods of time.

34. **Extinction** is the gradual disappearance of operant behavior due to the elimination of rewards for that behavior. (see Forming and Strengthening Operant Behavior)

    Example: Jason's mom used to reward him every time e said please, so he always said it. Now she no longer praises him when he says please so he is saying it less and less.

35. The **partial reinforcement effect** is a phenomenon in which behaviors learned under a partial reinforcement schedule are more difficult to extinguish than behaviors learned on a continuous schedule. (see Forming and Strengthening Operant Behavior)

    REMEMBER: To extinguish an operant behavior, reinforcement is no longer given following a response. On a partial reinforcement schedule, an organism will have to perform a response more than once or wait for a period of time before realizing that responses are no longer being rewarded. An animal on a continuous reinforcement schedule can know after only one response that reinforcement has been withdrawn.

36. **Punishment** is the presentation of an aversive stimulus or the removal of a pleasant stimulus. (see Punishment)

    Example: For people who want to break their nail-biting habit, there is a fingernail polish with a bad taste. When people wearing this polish bite their nails, they are punished with an aversive stimulus (the taste of the polish). This is done to decrease the behavior (nail biting) immediately preceding the taste.

    REMEMBER: Punishment has several side effects.

37. **Learned helplessness** occurs when an organism learns that responses do not affect consequences, resulting in failure to try to exert control over the environment. (see Learned Helplessness)

    Example: Children may develop learned helplessness if they find that no matter how much or how little they try to learn, failing grades always result. At that point they may no longer feel that it is worth trying to achieve at school.

    REMEMBER: Organisms learn to be helpless.

38. **Latent learning** is learning that is not demonstrated at the time that it occurs. (see Latent Learning and Cognitive Maps)

    Example: You discover that you enjoy your psychology class. However, you do not demonstrate the knowledge that you learned during the first lecture until the first test several weeks later.

    REMEMBER: Latent means "not visible." What you have learned is not visible until a later time.

39. **Cognitive maps** are mental representations of the environment. (see Latent Learning and Cognitive Maps)

    Example: When he was at college, Dale lost his sight in a car accident. When he got out of the hospital, he still knew how to get around the campus because he had a mental representation (or cognitive map) of the campus.

40. **Insight** is a sudden understanding about what is required to solve a problem. (see Insight and Learning)

41. **Observational learning (social learning)** is learning how to perform new behaviors by watching others. (see Observational Learning: Learning by Imitation)

    Example: Suppose you found a being from another planet on your doorstep. Charlie the alien is intelligent and looks just like a human being. That night, Charlie watches you brush your teeth. Then he picks up the toothbrush and imitates your behavior. This is not because he knows you get great checkups at the dentist. He is merely learning a behavior by watching you do it.

42. **Vicarious experience**, or vicarious conditioning, refers to conditions that allow us to learn by watching what happens to others. (see Observational Learning: Learning by Imitation)

    Example: Tara is the youngest of six children. By watching her brothers and sisters, she learns which behaviors her parents reward and which behaviors they punish.

FILL-IN-THE-BLANKS KEY TERMS

This section will help you check your knowledge of the key terms introduced in this chapter. Fill in each blank with the appropriate term from the list of key terms in the previous section.

1. _____ is a phenomenon in which organisms respond to a stimulus that they have learned will predict the occurrence of another stimulus.

2. In classical conditioning, the stimulus that elicits a reflexive response is called the _____.

3. In classical conditioning, learned responses that are made to a once-neutral stimulus are called _____.

4. If a CS is repeatedly presented without the UCS, _____ is likely to occur.

5. During _____, an organism learns the relationship between the conditioned stimulus and the unconditioned stimulus more quickly.

6. When an organism responds to a stimulus that is similar to the conditioned stimulus, this is called _____.

7. A(n) _____ is a behavior that brings about a positive or negative consequence.

8. Something that increases the chances that a behavior will be repeated is called a(n) _____.

9. _____ are unpleasant stimuli that, if removed following a behavior or response, will increase the likelihood of that behavior's future occurrence.

10. When an organism learns that it can prevent certain consequences from occurring by behaving in a certain way, this is called _____.

11. Rewarding successive approximations of a behavior is called _____.

12. Operant responses that are rewarded every time they occur are on a(n) _____ schedule of reinforcement.

13. Knowledge that comes through watching the behavior of others being reinforced or punished is called _____.

14. When an organism learns that its behavior has no bearing on the consequences of its actions, this is called _____.

15. _____ are mental representations of the environment.

Total Correct (See answer key) _____

LEARNING OBJECTIVES

1. Define <u>learning</u>. Describe the difference between nonassociative learning and associative learning. (see introductory section)

2. Define <u>habituation</u> and *sensitization*. Explain why they are examples of nonassociative learning. (see Learning About Stimuli)

3. Define <u>classical conditioning</u>, <u>unconditioned stimulus</u>, <u>unconditioned response</u>, <u>conditioned stimulus</u>, and <u>conditioned response</u>. Describe how classical conditioning works by using the stimuli and responses in an example. (see Pavlov's Discovery)

4. Describe the processes of <u>extinction</u>, <u>reconditioning</u>, and <u>spontaneous recovery</u>. Give an example of each. (see Conditioned Responses over Time: Extinction and Spontaneous Recovery)

5. Define and give an example of <u>stimulus generalization</u> and <u>stimulus discrimination</u>. Describe the adaptive balance between these two phenomena. (see Stimulus Generalization and Discrimination)

6. Describe the role that timing, predictability, and strength of signals play in the speed and strength of conditioned response development. Indicate which type of conditioning produces the strongest type of conditioned response. (see The Signaling of Significant Events)

7. Explain how biopreparedness influences taste-aversion learning. Explain why it is a special case of classical conditioning. (see The Signaling of Significant Events)

8. Discuss how attention influences which stimulus is linked to the unconditioned stimulus. Define and give an example of higher-<u>order conditioning</u>. (see The Signaling of Significant Events)

9. Describe the relationship between classical conditioning and phobias, predator control, detecting explosives, and diagnosis of Alzheimer's disease. (see Some Applications of Classical Conditioning)

10. Define the <u>law of effect</u>. (see From the Puzzle Box to the Skinner Box)

11. Define <u>operant conditioning</u> and explain how it differs from classical conditioning. (see From the Puzzle Box to the Skinner Box)

12. Define the components of operant conditioning: <u>operants</u> and <u>reinforcers</u>. (see Basic Components of Operant Conditioning)

13. Define <u>positive</u> and <u>negative reinforcers</u> and give examples of each. (see Basic Components of Operant Conditioning)

14. Define <u>escape conditioning</u> and <u>avoidance conditioning</u>. Give an example of each that demonstrates their similarities and differences. (see Basic Components of Operant Conditioning)

15. Define <u>discriminative conditioned stimuli</u> and *stimulus control*. Give an example of stimulus control. Explain how *stimulus discrimination* and *stimulus generalization* can work together. (see Basic Components of Operant Conditioning)

16. Define <u>shaping</u>. Explain when it is used in operant conditioning. (see Forming and Strengthening Operant Behavior)

17. Discuss the differences between <u>primary</u> and <u>secondary reinforcers</u>. (see Forming and Strengthening Operant Behavior)

18. Define <u>continuous</u> and <u>partial reinforcement</u> schedules. Compare and contrast the <u>fixed-ratio</u>, <u>variable-ratio</u>, <u>fixed-interval</u>, and <u>variable-interval</u> reinforcement schedules; include a description of their effect on the intensity of operant responses and the <u>partial reinforcement effect</u>. (see Forming and Strengthening Operant Behavior)

19. Explain why activity preference and physiological factors influence the efficiency of reinforcement. (see Why Reinforcers Work)

20. Define <u>punishment</u> and describe its role in operant conditioning. Discuss the disadvantages of and guidelines for using punishment. (see Punishment)

21. Discuss how operant conditioning can be used to treat problematic behavior. (see Some Applications of Operant Conditioning)

22. Discuss networks of learning and how parallel-distributed processing and connectionist models provide insight into how associations are stored in the brain. (see Linkages: Neural Networks and Learning)

23. Define <u>learned helplessness</u> and give an example of it. Describe the experiments used to study learned helplessness and the results. (see Learned Helplessness; see also Focus on Research Methods: An Experiment on Human Helplessness)

24. Define and give an example of <u>latent learning</u> and a <u>cognitive map</u>. (see Latent Learning and Cognitive Maps)

25. Define <u>insight</u>. Discuss the differences in what is learned in classical conditioning, instrumental conditioning, and insight. (see Insight and Learning)

26. Define <u>observational learning</u> and <u>vicarious experience</u>. Discuss their similarities and differences. (see Observational Learning: Learning by Imitation)

27. Describe the research on the effects of television violence. State what conclusions are most reasonable, based on the evidence available. (see Thinking Critically: Does Watching Violence on Television Make People More Violent?)

28. Describe differences in classrooms across cultures. Define *active learning* and give an example. (see Classrooms Across Cultures; see also Active Learning)

29. Describe the roles of practice and feedback in skill learning. (see Skill Learning)

CONCEPTS AND EXERCISES

Learning in Advertising: Take 1

Advertising is all around you: television, magazines, radio, billboards, pencils, the backs of cabs, matchbooks, just about anywhere you look. The people who create these ads often use learning principles to persuade you to buy their products. In the following exercise, you are the ads' creator. It is your job to tell your boss the learning principle behind each of the following ad descriptions. Choose from the list at the end of each exercise. Answers may be used more than once or not at all.

Television spot, thirty seconds.

(Scene: The counter at a Brand X dry cleaner. An anxious-looking woman enters carrying a yellow dress with chocolate stains on it.)

Customer: I need to have this dress cleaned by noon.

Counter clerk: Don't worry; it'll be ready at noon.

Customer: I hope so. I really have to have the dress by noon.

Counter clerk: We'll have it by noon. No problem.

(Shift of scene: customer is at home, smiling as she talks on the phone.)

Customer: Hi. I dropped a dress off there earlier—to be ready at noon. Can I pick it up now?

(Pause. Customer's smile abruptly turns to a frown.)

Narrator: Why take chances? Speedy Dry Clean guarantees that your clothes will always be ready on time.

1. This is an example of _____ conditioning.

2. The dress failing to be ready illustrates the use of _____ for the behavioral response of using a dry-cleaning service other than Speedy.

3. The service guarantee that states, "Your clothes will always be ready on time" is an example of a(n) _____ reinforcement schedule.

4. How many times do you think Speedy Dry Clean can break the service guarantee before its customers will go to another dry cleaner? _____

    a.   Operant

    b.   Positive reinforcement

    c.   Negative reinforcement

    d.   Punishment

    e.   Classical

    f.   Conditioned stimulus

    g.   Conditioned response

    h.   Unconditioned stimulus

    i.   Unconditioned response

    j.   Extinction

    k.   Continuous

    l.   Fixed interval

    m.   Once

    n.   Ten times

    o.   One hundred times

Learning in Advertising: Take 2

Television spot, thirty seconds.

(Scene: Mother checking on sleeping child. Mother speaks very quietly.)

Mother: Jennifer went to the doctor today to get the stitches taken out of her knee. Before we went to the Stone Clinic, just mentioning the word *doctor* made her cry for fear of getting a shot. But the doctors and nurses at the Stone Clinic understand a child's needs; they're gentle, soothing, kind, and thoughtful. That makes Jennifer happy. I know that the Stone Clinic staff are experts in their fields, and as a mother (mother looks lovingly at Jennifer) that makes me very happy.

(Mother leans over, smoothes Jennifer's hair, kisses her on the forehead, and tiptoes out of room.)

1. This is an example of _____ conditioning.

2. The doctors are a(n) _____.

3. Jennifer's old fear of doctors is a(n) _____.

4. What conditioning process caused Jennifer to lose her fear of doctors? _____

    a.   Instrumental

    b.   Positive reinforcement

c. Negative reinforcement

d. Punishment

e. Classical

f. Conditioned stimulus

g. Conditioned response

h. Unconditioned stimulus

i. Unconditioned response

j. Extinction

k. Continuous

l. Fixed interval

m. Once

n. Ten times

o. One hundred times

Teaching an Alien

To discover the prevalence of learning in our everyday lives, read the following story of Sam and Gufla, an alien. You will find many of the basic learning principles embedded in the plot. Afterward, answer the questions using the list of terms at the end of the exercise. Answers may be used more than once.

One day while playing in the park, Sam met someone he thought was a boy his own age. Thinking the boy was human, Sam began a conversation. Even though the stranger spoke perfect English, Sam soon realized that he was from another planet and had landed here by accident. Eight-year-old Sam was more curious than afraid and invited the alien home for dinner.

The trip home was eventful. Sam, worried about being late, decided to take a shortcut that one of his pals had told him about earlier. As the two boys entered a backyard, a snarling German shepherd charged them. Sam quickly figured out that the dog's chain could not reach to the fence. He and the alien, whom he had named Gufla, ran along the fence until they were out of the yard.

After slowing down and catching his breath, Sam realized that he would have to tell Gufla a few things about the family and how to behave, so that Sam's mother would not suspect anything. Most important, Sam knew that he could not share his discovery with his sister, who would tell his mother.

Gufla asked Sam what eating felt like. How would he recognize food? Sam replied that anything that smelled good was edible. Gufla promptly picked a rose from a garden they were passing and ate it. Sam laughed, but Gufla was holding his stomach because the rose, which had fertilizer on it, made him feel ill. Gufla vowed never to go near a rose again.

Sam told Gufla that any time Sam nodded his head, Gufla could eat whatever his fork was touching. Any time Sam shook his head, Gufla was not to eat whatever his fork was touching. Sam tried to explain that food, not napkins or salt and pepper shakers, tastes good, which is a pleasant feeling. By the time they reached Sam's driveway, Sam realized that there was not enough time to teach Gufla all the behaviors he would need to know, so Sam told Gufla to imitate Sam's behavior whenever he felt confused. Sam said that because it was Friday night, his mother might let them stay up and watch the late-night horror movie, a special treat, if all went well.

1. Sam's mother had probably successfully used _____ to decrease his tardiness.

2. Sam was using a _____ to follow a shortcut home. This was also a case of _____, because Sam had never taken this shortcut before, even though he had known about it before that day.

3. Sam decided not to tell his sister about his find. This illustrates _____. Sam did not want his sister to tell his mother about Gufla.

4. Gufla became ill after eating the rose, probably because it had fertilizer on it. This is an example of learning a _____.

5. Gufla knew that the direction in which Sam moved his head would be a _____, because this would let Gufla know if what he put in his mouth (the behavior) would taste good or bad. Good food in this case is a _____.

6. Gufla will watch and imitate what Sam does even though he will not really understand why he is doing it or if it will bring him any sort of pleasure. This is an example of _____.

7. Sam and Gufla may be allowed to watch a late-night movie if they behave well at dinner. This illustrates the use of a _____.

   a. Primary

   b. Secondary

   c. Avoidance conditioning

   d. Escape conditioning

   e. Punishment

   f. Positive reinforcer

   g. Taste aversion

   h. Discriminative conditioned stimulus

   i. Observational learning

   j. Cognitive map

   k. Latent learning

CRITICAL THINKING

Sam and Martina have just dropped a teenager, Rose, off at juvenile hall. She has been in trouble on and off for the past two years. They are discussing the causes of her delinquency.

Sam fumes, "Do you realize that's the fifteenth time she's been hauled down there in the past two years?"

Martina mumbles, "Hmmm."

Sam continues, "And do you realize that every time she does something, it's the same old thing? She waits till her dad comes back from a business trip, she tells him what she has done, they have a huge fight, and he brings her to us."

Martina mumbles again, "Hmmm."

Sam finally decries, "She's just a bad apple. She probably has an antisocial personality disorder."

Martina finally says, "Nope, I think Rose is a good kid at heart. Based on the pattern you describe, I think she has just learned to be bad."

Using the five critical thinking questions in your text, the clues in the story, and what you have learned in this chapter, answer the following:

1. What is Sam's hypothesis?

2. What is the evidence in support of Sam's hypothesis?

3. What is Martina's alternative hypothesis?

4. What is the evidence in support of Martina's hypothesis?

PERSONAL LEARNING ACTIVITIES

1. Consider the following website: http://frontpage.wiu.edu/~mfjtd/Matt%20Lybarger.html. It has a great discussion of the use of classical conditioning in advertising, along with some links that illustrate the use of this type of learning in marketing and advertising. Now watch some commercials that are current on television or the web. What elements of classical conditioning can you identify there?

2. Recall a time when someone tried to punish you. What emotional and behavioral reactions did you have? Did it, in fact, behave as a punishment and decrease your behavior, or was it somehow reinforcing?

3. Visit the following website to see one interesting application of the use of discriminative conditioned stimuli: http://www.youtube.com/watch?v=fmx5YgxmCdw. Here, you can learn the story of the dolphin, Winter, who lost her tail when she was caught in a crab trap. After losing her tail, she taught herself to swim using a side-to-side motion (like a fish) instead of the up-and-down tail action a dolphin usually uses. Her trainers had to teach Winter that when she wore a prosthetic tail, she should switch to the up-and-down tail action instead of the side-to-side motion. The tail became a discriminative conditioned stimulus. What discriminative conditioned stimuli can you identify in your life?

4. Have someone use observational learning to master a skill that you have. For instance, if you make a delicious casserole or know how to skate backwards, you could attempt to pass on those talents. What problems did you encounter? Was there a particular demonstration or explanation that made things clearer for your volunteer? Based on your first lesson, how much practice do you think will be required before the person masters the skill? What type of feedback was most helpful to the person?

5. Use active learning when working with a classmate to understand material. For example, if you are studying with a psychology classmate, you could work on this chapter by comparing what elements of classical conditioning you identified in current commercials (see Personal Learning Activity 1, which is an active learning exercise).

MULTIPLE-CHOICE QUESTIONS

Quiz 1

1. In classical conditioning, an organism learns

    a. an association between the unconditioned stimulus and the conditioned response.
    b. that the conditioned stimulus is a substitute for the unconditioned stimulus.
    c. that the conditioned stimulus predicts the occurrence of the unconditioned stimulus.
    d. an association between the unconditioned response and the conditioned response.

2. Spontaneous recovery follows
   a. reconditioning.
   b. extinction.
   c. stimulus control.
   d. stimulus degradation.

3. Pavlov used _____ conditioning in his classic study in which dogs were classically conditioned to salivate in response to a bell that predicted the arrival of meat powder.
   a. forward
   b. backward
   c. simultaneous
   d. None of the above

4. Reconditioning refers to
   a. the appearance of a conditioned response following extinction.
   b. the elimination of the association between the conditioned stimulus and the unconditioned stimulus.
   c. the occurrence of spontaneous recovery.
   d. relearning the connection between the conditioned stimulus and the unconditioned stimulus after extinction.

5. Marsha reads aloud a list of words and shoots a puff of air at Kat's eye. It is only after Marsha says "nice" that she blasts Kat's eye with air to make her wink. Eventually Kat winks even when Marsha says "nice" and does not shoot the puff of air into her eye. If Kat undergoes extinction, she will
   a. be unable to wink at anything.
   b. feel she is being punished.
   c. wink when she hears the word *night*.
   d. not wink when she hears the word *nice*.

6. The fact that you did not notice the feeling of your underwear until you read this sentence is an example of
   a. habituation.
   b. hypothalamic stimulation.
   c. stimulus discrimination.
   d. spontaneous recovery.

7. The idea behind Premack's Principle is that
   a. when you have not done something for a while, it will be reinforcing to do that thing.
   b. any activity that is preferred over another can be used as a reinforcer.
   c. if you have done something a lot lately, it will not be as reinforcing to get to do it again.
   d. reinforcers are biologically determined.

8. Manuel has learned that every time he cleans his room, his mother makes his favorite dessert. This is an example of
   a. classical conditioning.

b.   negative reinforcement.

c.   operant conditioning.

d.   association of stimuli.

9.   In operant conditioning, negative reinforcers are

     a.   pleasant stimuli presented following a response.

     b.   unpleasant stimuli that are removed following a response.

     c.   methods of decreasing a response.

     d.   rewards considered basic to survival, such as food and drink.

10.   Ten minutes before a movie starts, the theater is filled with people who are talking or laughing. As soon as the lights go out, everyone becomes quiet. A few people, who continue to laugh out loud and prevent the audience from hearing the show, are booed and hissed until they are quiet. Turning off the lights serves as a _____ in this example of operant conditioning.

     a.   positive reinforcer

     b.   negative reinforcer

     c.   punishment

     d.   discriminative conditioned stimulus

11.   Sometimes Amy hits her sister, Zoë, in the arm until Zoë says, "I give," and then Amy stops. Because Amy stops hurting Zoë when she says, "I give," Zoë says it whenever she is being hit. In this example of _____, the operant is _____.

     a.   negative reinforcement; Zoë saying, "I give"

     b.   positive reinforcement; Amy stops hitting Zoë

     c.   punishment; Zoë saying, "I give"

     d.   punishment; Amy stops hitting Zoë

12.   In operant conditioning, if a reinforcer is on a fixed-ratio schedule it is presented after a(n)

     a.   fixed amount of time.

     b.   fixed number of responses.

     c.   average number of responses.

     d.   average amount of time.

13.   Which reinforcement schedule produces the fastest extinction rate?

     a.   Fixed ratio

     b.   Primary

     c.   Variable ratio

     d.   Variable interval

14.   Every fifth time Russell washes the dishes, his mom gives him a candy bar, and he now washes them every day. Susan's dad gives her reinforcement for washing the dishes every Friday, and she also washes them every day. What schedules of reinforcement are Russell and Susan on, respectively?

     a.   Fixed interval; variable interval

     b.   Fixed ratio; fixed interval

     c.   Variable ratio; fixed interval

     d.   Variable interval; fixed ratio

15. Caden is at the store with his mom. He starts kicking his legs against the cart because he is bored. His mom says, "Hey, stop it." Caden then kicks the cart harder. His mom says, "Caden, I'm warning you. …" Caden then really starts clobbering the cart with his feet. His mother again threatens, "I mean it, Caden. You better stop it!" Because his mother was not firm in the first place, Caden is demonstrating

    a. the effectiveness of negative reinforcers.
    b. stimulus discrimination.
    c. the escalation effect.
    d. the partial reinforcement extinction effect.

16. In learned helplessness, an organism believes that

    a. behavior is unrelated to consequences.
    b. certain behaviors always result in negative consequences.
    c. positive consequences are rare.
    d. certain behaviors provide escape from negative stimuli.

17. Gertrude's grandfather came to visit her recently for the first time. In the middle of the night he got up to use the bathroom. Half asleep, he took a wrong turn and walked into a wall. This is an example of

    a. use of an incorrect cognitive map.
    b. reverse insight.
    c. latent learning.
    d. vicarious learning.

18. According to research on neural networks, in classical conditioning the connections between the nodes characterizing the CS and the nodes characterizing the UCS will show the greatest increase in strength

    a. during the first few learning trials.
    b. during the middle learning trials.
    c. during the final learning trials.
    d. equally across learning trials.

19. Cathy is afraid of dogs. She watches a number of people petting and playing with a dog, and decides that dogs are not just scary and mean. The next day at her neighbor's house she pets their dog. She has learned to pet a dog through

    a. classical conditioning.
    b. operant conditioning.
    c. vicarious experience.
    d. dishabituation.

20. Which of the following is NOT one of the types of evidence that supports the claim that watching violent television programs increases violent behavior, according to the Thinking Critically section of this chapter?

    a. Case studies
    b. Correlational studies
    c. Experiments
    d. Naturalistic observations

Total Correct (See answer key) _____

Quiz 2

Use this quiz to reassess your learning after taking Quiz 1 and reviewing the chapter.

1. Paul switches his cat from dry food to canned food. He always uses an electric can opener to open the can. At first, his cat does nothing in response to the noise of the can opener. After a few days of the new food, though, that kitty comes running every time she hears the can opener running. Before the cat was running in response to the can opener, the can opener was an example of a(n)

    a. neutral stimulus.
    b. conditioned stimulus.
    c. unconditioned stimulus.
    d. conditioned response.

2. Letitia's first experience at the dentist was a traumatic one. During that first visit, the dentist used no anesthetic before drilling her teeth. Now, just sitting in the waiting room and hearing the whirring sound of the drill make Letitia nauseated. This is an example of what kind of conditioning?

    a. Classical conditioning
    b. Negative reinforcement
    c. Operant conditioning
    d. Positive reinforcement

3. When Antonio rode the Ferris wheel at the amusement park for the first time, he became very dizzy. Now when Antonio sees an advertisement for amusement parks, he feels nauseated. In this case, the unconditioned stimulus is

    a. the Ferris wheel ride.
    b. the feeling of dizziness.
    c. nausea.
    d. the sight of an amusement park.

4. In this case of Antonio's feelings about Ferris wheels, the conditioned response is

    a. dizziness.
    b. the Ferris wheel ride.
    c. the sight of an amusement park.
    d. nausea.

5. In the case of Antonio's feelings about Ferris wheels, the conditioned stimulus is

    a. dizziness.
    b. the Ferris wheel ride.
    c. the sight of an amusement park.
    d. nausea.

6. Higher-order conditioning is

    a. operant conditioning.
    b. learning to pair a neutral stimulus with an unconditioned stimulus.
    c. a phenomenon in which a conditioned stimulus acts like an unconditioned stimulus.
    d. predicting that a behavior will be followed by a particular type of consequence.

7.   In September, Jefferson High School's fire alarm sounded, and students ran from the building to escape the flames. For the next few weeks, the school experienced a rash of false alarms, and people began to ignore the sound. The alarms were repaired and did not sound for the next few months. Then in December, a fire alarm sounded, and students ran from the building in panic. What phenomenon was responsible for the students' renewed fear?

   a.   Reconditioning
   b.   Spontaneous recovery
   c.   Stimulus control
   d.   Stimulus generalization

8.   After a lab rat was exposed to repeated pairings of a dark blue light and electrical shock, it became very nervous whenever a turquoise light was flashed in its cage. This phenomenon is called stimulus

   a.   generalization.
   b.   discrimination.
   c.   degradation.
   d.   control.

9.   Which of the following types of conditioning produces the strongest conditioned response?

   a.   Spontaneous conditioning
   b.   Forward conditioning
   c.   Simultaneous conditioning
   d.   Backward conditioning

10.   When Tanya was given chemotherapy, she developed a conditioned response to the food that she ate just prior to feeling nauseated. Tanya developed an aversion to the food rather than to the song she heard on the radio due to

   a.   biopreparedness.
   b.   generalization.
   c.   simultaneous conditioning.
   d.   signal strength.

11.   In operant conditioning, discriminative conditioned stimuli

   a.   automatically trigger a conditioned response.
   b.   indicate the presence of reinforcement if a response is made.
   c.   are successive approximations of a desired response.
   d.   are similar but not identical to the conditioned stimulus.

12.   Punishment is

   a.   the presentation of an aversive stimulus.
   b.   the removal of a pleasant stimulus.
   c.   a means to decrease the occurrence of an undesired response.
   d.   all of these.

13. Neural network models propose that knowledge of specific information in the brain is
    a. located in a single spot in the brain.
    b. distributed in several spots that are unconnected.
    c. distributed in several locations in the brain that are connected.
    d. isolated from other information.

14. Anne is angry with her boss and would like to tell him exactly how she feels about him. But the last time Anne did something similar, she was fired. So, in order not to lose her job, Anne keeps her temper under control. What kind of learning does this represent?
    a. Escape conditioning
    b. Classical conditioning
    c. Avoidance conditioning
    d. Discriminative conditioned stimuli

15. Shaping is used when the conditioned response
    a. is physically difficult to perform.
    b. is to be decreased.
    c. has never been displayed before.
    d. is reflexive.

16. Dr. Velagati is paid on the last day of the month. Regardless of how many patients she saw, she receives the same amount at the end of the month. Dr. Velagati is on a _____ schedule of reinforcement.
    a. fixed-interval
    b. fixed-ratio
    c. variable-interval
    d. variable-ratio

17. Two patients are recovering from surgery. Patient A is given an injection every six hours. Patient B is hooked up to a machine that delivers pain medication whenever he presses a button. Who is on a continuous reinforcement schedule?
    a. Patient A
    b. Patient B
    c. Both Patient A and Patient B
    d. Neither Patient A nor Patient B

18. Jeana is trying to figure out how to put her new baby crib together. She is really stumped. She stares at all the parts lying around her and studies the directions. Suddenly, she understands, and the crib is put together in under thirty minutes flat. Jeana has demonstrated which type of learning.
    a. Insight
    b. Learned helplessness
    c. Latent
    d. Vicarious

19. Which type of feedback leads to better skill learning?
    a. Constant feedback so the learner knows how they are doing
    b. Very little feedback to promote independent learning
    c. Feedback that comes after a person has had a chance to work on the skill independently
    d. Any type of feedback helps.

20. Jimmy's parents tell him not to hit his sister. Jimmy watches a cartoon in which one character clocks his little sister in the head for borrowing his stuff. Based on the research discussed in the Thinking Critically section of your text, what is likely to occur the next time Jimmy experiences a conflict with his little sister?
    a. Jimmy will probably not hit her, because his parents do not allow it.
    b. Jimmy will probably hit her because of what he saw modeled on TV.
    c. Jimmy will probably not hit her, because television violence is more likely to increase violent behavior in girls than in boys.
    d. Although watching the cartoon increases Jimmy's likelihood of hitting his sister, what he may do in a specific situation is based not only on the television he watches, but also the way he interprets it, his parents' rules, and his peer and other environmental influences, which are not addressed in this question.

Total Correct (See answer key) _____

ANSWERS TO FILL-IN-THE-BLANKS KEY TERMS

1. Classical conditioning (see Pavlov's Discovery)

2. unconditioned stimulus (see Pavlov's Discovery)

3. conditioned responses (see Pavlov's Discovery)

4. extinction (see Conditioned Responses over Time: Extinction and Spontaneous Recovery)

5. reconditioning (see Conditioned Responses over Time: Extinction and Spontaneous Recovery)

6. stimulus generalization (see Stimulus Generalization and Discrimination)

7. operant (see Basic Components of Operant Conditioning)

8. reinforcer (see Basic Components of Operant Conditioning)

9. Negative reinforcers (see Basic Components of Operant Conditioning)

10. avoidance conditioning (see Basic Components of Operant Conditioning)

11. shaping (see Forming and Strengthening Operant Behavior)

12. continuous reinforcement schedule (see Forming and Strengthening Operant Behavior)

13. vicarious experience or vicarious conditioning (see Observational Learning: Learning by Imitation)

14. learned helplessness (see Learned Helplessness)

15. Cognitive maps (see Latent Learning and Cognitive Maps)

ANSWERS TO CONCEPTS AND EXERCISES

Learning in Advertising: Take 1

1. *Operant.* The customer is learning a relationship between a behavior (using a dry cleaner other than Speedy) and its consequence (clothes that are not cleaned on time). (see From the Puzzle Box to the Skinner Box)

2. *Punishment.* The dress not being ready will cause the customer problems and is therefore aversive. (see Punishment)

3. *Continuous.* Every time a behavior (going to Speedy Dry Clean versus any other dry cleaner) occurs, it is rewarded or reinforced (getting clothes back on time). (see Forming and Strengthening Operant Behavior)

4. *Once.* Behaviors learned on a continuous reinforcement schedule are very easy to extinguish. (see Forming and Strengthening Operant Behavior)

Learning in Advertising: Take 2

1. *Classical.* Jennifer has learned that one stimulus (the doctor) predicts another (activities that cause pain). (see Pavlov's Discovery)

2. *Conditioned stimulus.* Jennifer was not always afraid of doctors; originally they were a neutral stimulus. When neutral stimuli begin to predict the presence of another stimulus, such as an injection, they become conditioned stimuli. (see Pavlov's Discovery)

3. *Conditioned response.* Because Jennifer had to learn to be afraid of doctors, this is a conditioned (or learned) response. (see Pavlov's Discovery)

4. *Extinction.* The association between the CS (doctors) and the UCS (activities that cause pain) has been eliminated or at least greatly diminished. The CR (fear of doctors) has also been eliminated. (see Pavlov's Discovery)

Teaching an Alien

1. *Punishment.* Sam has decreased his behavior of being late for dinner. Punishment decreases the occurrence of the behavior it follows. When Sam was late, he was probably punished. (see Punishment)

2. *Cognitive map; latent learning.* Sam learned a shortcut by representing the information in his mind in the form of a map. We know that he learned the shortcut before he demonstrated his knowledge of it. (see Latent Learning and Cognitive Maps)

3. *Avoidance conditioning.* Sam learned to avoid having his sister inform his mother of his doings by simply not telling her what he did. (see Basic Components of Operant Conditioning)

4. *Taste aversion.* Gufla learned that roses (CS) predict the presence of fertilizer (UCS). Fertilizer causes stomachaches (CR). Gufla will stay away from (CR) all roses (CS) in the future. (see The Signaling of Significant Events)

5. *Discriminative conditioned stimulus; primary positive reinforcer.* The direction in which Sam nodded his head would be a discriminative conditioned stimulus, or signal, that would let Gufla know when to make a response (eating whatever his fork touched) in order to receive the reinforcement of eating food. Food is a pleasant stimulus and basic to survival. Therefore, it is a primary positive reinforcer. (see Basic Components of Operant Conditioning; see also Forming and Strengthening Operant Behavior)

6. *Observational learning.* Gufla will attend to what Sam is doing, retain the information, and reproduce it because Sam has told him to. Gufla is not performing each specific behavior to obtain a reward. (see Observational Learning: Learning by Imitation)

7. *Secondary positive reinforcer.* Watching a movie, although not basic to survival, is a pleasant stimulus. Therefore, this is an example of secondary positive reinforcement. (see Basic Components of Operant Conditioning; see also Forming and Strengthening Operant Behavior)

ANSWERS TO CRITICAL THINKING

1. Sam hypothesizes that Rose has an antisocial personality.

2. Rose's history of being in trouble lends some support to his hypothesis.

3. Martina's probable hypothesis is that Rose has learned that she will be rewarded with her father's attention when she misbehaves. She probably has to go to extremes to get his attention because he is apparently so busy.

4. Martina will probably want to find out more about Rose's family situation.

ANSWERS TO MULTIPLE-CHOICE QUESTIONS

Quiz 1

1. c is the answer.   The conditioned stimulus predicts the occurrence of the unconditioned stimulus. (see Pavlov's Discovery)

    a. There is no relationship between the UCS and the CR. The UCS causes a natural reflexive response (UCR); only the conditioned (learned) stimulus causes a conditioned (learned) response.

    b. If the CS was merely a substitute for the UCS, the conditioned response would always be identical to the unconditioned response (UCR). This is not the case.

    d. No relationship between the UCR and the CR is learned.

2. b is the answer.   For a conditioned response to recover, it must first have undergone extinction. (see Conditioned Responses over Time: Extinction and Spontaneous Recovery)

    a. Reconditioning once again pairs the conditioned stimulus and the unconditioned stimulus. The conditioned response is relearned. Spontaneous recovery is just that, spontaneous. No relearning is necessary.

    c. Stimulus control is associated with operant conditioning. Spontaneous recovery is a phenomenon in classical conditioning.

    d. There is no learning phenomenon called stimulus degradation.

3. a is the answer.   Because the conditioned stimulus preceded the unconditioned stimulus in time in Pavlov's study, the conditioning was forward in nature. (see The Signaling of Significant Events)

b. Backward conditioning occurs when the conditioned stimulus follows the unconditioned stimulus during the conditioning process.

c. Simultaneous conditioning occurs when the conditioned stimulus occurs at the same time as the unconditioned stimulus during the conditioning process.

d. a is the answer.

4. d is the answer.   Reconditioning is a repetition of the conditioning process. This occurs after extinction; if extinction had not already occurred, there would be no need for reconditioning. (see Conditioned Responses over Time: Extinction and Spontaneous Recovery)

a, c. The occurrence of a conditioned response after extinction is called spontaneous recovery.

b. The process of extinction removes the association between the CS and the UCS so that the CS no longer predicts the presence of the UCS. Reconditioning restores the association between the CS and the UCS.

5. d is the answer.   A person's conditioned response is extinguished when a long time passes without the unconditioned stimulus's appearing with the conditioned stimulus. (see Conditioned Responses over Time: Extinction and Spontaneous Recovery)

a. Kat will be able to wink at things if she undergoes extinction. She will just be less likely to wink at "nice" than she was before.

b. A feeling of being punished would not happen as a result of discontinuing the pairing of the CS and UCS.

c. Winking upon hearing the word *night* is an example of generalization.

6. a is the answer.   In habituation, an organism stops responding to repeated stimuli that do not signal a change in the environment. When you put your underwear on in the morning, you feel it. However, after a few minutes, your body begins to ignore the sensation (see Learning About Stimuli)

b. Hypothalamic stimulation has nothing to do with habituation.

c. In classical conditioning, organisms discriminate among stimuli when they can make finer and finer distinctions among them. For example, if the CS is a red ball, an organism may not respond to a green ball. Stimulus discrimination does not play a role in the process of habituation.

d. Spontaneous recovery occurs when a CS that has not been paired with a UCS for some time elicits a conditioned response.

7. b is the answer.   Premack's principle argues that any activity can serve as a reinforcer for any other activity that is less preferred at the moment. (see Why Reinforcers Work)

a, c. These statements correspond to the disequilibrium hypothesis, not Premack's principle.

d. Premack's principle does not argue that reinforcers are biologically determined.

8. c is the answer.   Operant conditioning involves learning that behaviors have consequences. When Manuel cleans his room (the operant), his mom makes his favorite dessert (the consequence). (see From the Puzzle Box to the Skinner Box)

a, d. Classical conditioning involves making an association between stimuli such that one (CS) comes to predict the presence of the other (UCS). This example involves learning that a behavior (cleaning the room) will bring about a reinforcer (dessert) and is therefore an example of operant conditioning.

b. A negative reinforcer is an unpleasant stimulus that is removed following a desired response. In this case, a positive reinforcer (a pleasant stimulus: dessert) is being presented following a desired behavior (cleaning the room).

9. b is the answer. In operant conditioning, reinforcers always produce a positive effect and work to increase a behavior. A negative reinforcer is a negative stimulus that is removed after the organism displays a desired response. (see Basic Components of Operant Conditioning)

a. Positive reinforcers are pleasant stimuli that are presented after an organism displays a desired response.

c. Punishment and extinction are used to decrease the occurrence of a response. (You may be confusing punishment and negative reinforcers.) Remember, reinforcements (both positive and negative) increase the occurrence of a desired behavior.

d. Rewards that are basic to survival are primary reinforcements.

10. d is the answer. A discriminative conditioned stimulus tells the people in the theater that if they are quiet (the response), they will be rewarded by seeing a movie (the reinforcement). Those who do not pay attention to the light (those who are not under the control of the light stimulus) are punished by being booed and hissed at. (see Basic Components of Operant Conditioning)

a. The lights are not turned off to reward the audience for its behavior.

b. The turned-off lights do not represent the removal of an unpleasant stimulus following the display of a desired behavior. Lights that are on are not unpleasant, and the audience did not display any behaviors in order to get the lights to go out.

c. Turning off the lights does cause a decrease in the behavior that preceded it, but turned-off lights are not aversive, so they cannot be considered punishment.

11. a is the answer. Zoë is being negatively reinforced for saying, "I give." When she says it, Amy removes the unpleasant stimulus (hitting her arm). (see Basic Components of Operant Conditioning)

b. Amy is not rewarded for stopping her hitting.

c. If Zoë were punished for saying, "I give," she would be less likely to say it in the future.

d. If Amy were punished for stopping her hitting, she would be less likely to stop hitting in the future.

12. b is the answer A fixed ratio schedule of reinforcement involves reinforcing the behavior following a fixed (predictable) number of responses. (see Forming and Strengthening Operant Behavior)

a. This is called a fixed-interval schedule.

c. This is called a variable-ratio schedule.

d. This is called a variable-interval schedule.

13. a is the answer. A fixed-ratio schedule of reinforcement produces the fastest rate of extinction because the organism realizes very quickly that reinforcements have ceased to be presented and that after the appropriate number of responses has been made, the reinforcement should be there. A continuous schedule of reinforcement, which is a type of fixed-ratio schedule, produces the fastest rate of extinction possible. (see Forming and Strengthening Operant Behavior)

b. There is no such thing as a primary reinforcement schedule. Primary reinforcers are events or stimuli that are inherently rewarding, like treats for animals.

c, d.   Organisms on a variable schedule of reinforcement cannot predict when the reinforcement will appear. They therefore take longer to realize that the reinforcement is missing once the extinction process has begun.

14.   b is the answer.   A fixed number of behaviors must be exhibited by Russell to receive reinforcement. Susan must wait a fixed amount of time before receiving reinforcement for her actions. (see Forming and Strengthening Operant Behavior)

    a.   Russell does not have to wait a set amount of time before reinforcement. If he washed dishes twice a day while company was around, he could have his reinforcement (after five operants) in a day and a half. If he skipped a day of washing dishes, he would still get rewarded after the fifth operant, but it might take six days. Susan does not have to wait differing amounts of time; she is reinforced every Friday.

    c, d.   Russell is on a fixed-ratio schedule, and Susan is on a fixed-interval schedule.

15.   c is the answer.   The escalation effect occurs when caregivers are not firm enough in initially dealing with misbehavior. This results in children's becoming habituated to mild reproof, leading the parent to have to use more severe punishment than they might have had to if they had dealt with the issue in the first place. (see Punishment)

    a.   Negative reinforcers are the removal of negative stimuli following a desired behavior, not the delivery of a (mildly) punishing remark following an undesired behavior.

    b.   Stimulus discrimination is found in classical conditioning scenarios. This is an example of operant conditioning, and punishment that is not being used effectively.

    d.   The partial reinforcement extinction effect involves behaviors learned under a partial reinforcement schedule—such behaviors are more difficult to extinguish than behavior learned on a continuous schedule. This question asks about the use of mild punishment, not reinforcement.

16.   a is the answer.   In learned helplessness, an organism learns that its behaviors are unrelated to the consequences that occur. It learns that it is helpless or unable to control its circumstances. (see Learned Helplessness)

    b.   If an organism learns that certain behaviors always result in negative consequences, then it is not helpless; it can avoid doing those behaviors.

    c.   Learning that positive consequences are rare is not learned helplessness. In learned helplessness, an organism learns that its behaviors are unrelated to the consequences that occur.

    d.   In learned helplessness, an organism learns the opposite: that no behavior provides escape from negative stimuli or consequences.

17.   a is the answer.   Gertrude's grandfather used a cognitive map of his own house when he sleepily tried to find his way to the bathroom in hers. (see Latent Learning and Cognitive Maps)

    b.   There is no such thing as reverse insight.

    c.   Latent learning occurs when an organism learns something but does not overtly demonstrate this new knowledge until later. If Gertrude's grandfather had successfully learned a cognitive map and made it to the bathroom without walking into a wall, this would have been an example of latent learning.

    d.   To learn a response vicariously, an organism must watch someone else display that response and be rewarded or punished for it.

18. a is the answer.   The strength of the connection increases the most when the CS and UCS are first being paired together. (see Linkages: Neural Networks and Learning)

    b, c.   The middle and latter trials will show slower increases in strength than the first few trials.

    d.   The increase in connection strength is not equivalent across trials in classical conditioning.

19. c is the answer.   Cathy watched others petting a dog and learned from it. Learning through vicarious experience involves just this—watching others to see what happens and then imitating their behavior a future time. (see Observational Learning: Learning by Imitation)

    a.   Classical conditioning is the pairing of unconditioned stimuli with neutral stimuli.

    b.   In operant conditioning, a person's behavior is followed by a consequence. According to the story, Cathy only watched people; she was not rewarded.

    d.   Dishabituation involves reorienting to a stimulus that one has previously habituated to after it changes in some way.

20. d is the answer.   Naturalistic observation is neither specifically mentioned nor described as one of the methods used to determine whether television violence increases violent behavior. Although naturalistic observation is a form of a correlational study (which is mentioned), the descriptions of the correlational studies are not exemplars of naturalistic observation. (see Thinking Critically: Does Watching Violence on Television Make People More Violent?)

    a, b, c.   These three methods are specifically mentioned as providing evidence that supports the claim that watching violent television programs increases violent behavior.

Now turn to the quiz analysis table at the end of this chapter to find which areas you know well and which areas you need to work on. Circle the numbers in the table for items on Quiz 1 that you answered correctly.

Quiz 2

Circle the question numbers you answered correctly.

1. a is the answer.   A neutral stimulus becomes a conditioned stimulus (CS) and elicits a conditioned response (CR) only after it is paired with an unconditioned stimulus (UCS). Before the cat paired the can opener with the food, the can opener was a neutral stimulus. (see Pavlov's Discovery)

    b.   The can opener was a conditioned stimulus *after* the cat started running toward its sound in anticipation of food, not before.

    c.   The food was the unconditioned stimulus, not the can opener. An unconditioned stimulus is one that elicits a reflexive response in an organism.

    d.   The conditioned response was the cat's running to the can opener, not the can opener itself. A conditioned response is a behavior. A can opener is not a behavior.

2. a is the answer.   The conditioned stimulus is the sound of the drill. The unconditioned stimulus is the use of the drill on the teeth. The unconditioned response is the pain that the drill causes. The conditioned response is nausea, which is elicited by the CS, the sound of the drill. (see Pavlov's Discovery)

    b, d.   Reinforcement, both positive and negative, is used in operant conditioning.

    c.   Operant conditioning involves learning an association between a behavior and its consequences. Letitia is learning an association between two stimuli: the sound of the drill and the feeling of the drill on her teeth.

3. a is the answer. The Ferris wheel ride is the unconditioned stimulus. It automatically made Antonio feel dizzy with no learning involved. *Unconditioned* implies "unlearned" or "automatic." (see Pavlov's Discovery)

   b. The feeling of dizziness is a response, not a stimulus. Feeling dizzy is an unconditioned response when it occurs reflexively in response to the movement of the Ferris wheel, and it is a conditioned response when it occurs in response to the sight of an amusement park. In this example, the conditioned response becomes exaggerated to actual nausea—beyond mere dizziness.

   c. The nausea in response to the sight of an amusement park is an example of a conditioned response. Antonio is not naturally nauseated by the sight of amusements parks but has learned that response by associating the sight of amusement parks as a predictor of the dizziness he felt on the Ferris wheel ride.

   d. The sight of the amusement park is the conditioned stimulus.

4. d is the answer. Nausea is the conditioned response. Antonio does not automatically feel nauseated in response to the sight of the amusement park. He learns this response only after associating the park with the dizziness he felt on the Ferris wheel ride. (see Pavlov's Discovery)

   a. The dizziness is the unconditioned response to the movement of the Ferris wheel.

   b. The Ferris wheel ride is the unconditioned stimulus.

   c. The sight of the amusement park is the conditioned stimulus.

5. c is the answer. The sight of the amusement park is the conditioned stimulus, because Antonio learned to associate it as a predictor of the dizziness he would later feel on the Ferris wheel. (see Pavlov's Discovery)

   a. The dizziness is the unconditioned response to the movement of the Ferris wheel.

   b. The Ferris wheel ride is the unconditioned stimulus.

   d. The nausea is the conditioned response to the sight of the amusement park.

6. c is the answer. Higher-order conditioning occurs when a conditioned stimulus acts like an unconditioned stimulus, creating conditioned stimuli out of events associated with it. (see The Signaling of Significant Events)

   a. Operant conditioning is a process in which one learns the consequences of various behaviors, repeats behaviors that earn desirable consequences, and fails to repeat those behaviors that earn undesirable consequences.

   b. This describes basic classical conditioning. Higher-order conditioning builds on that, rather than simply starting with a reflexive relationship.

   d. This is part of the process of operant conditioning. Higher-order conditioning builds on classical conditioning.

7. b is the answer. Spontaneous recovery is the recurrence of a conditioned response following extinction in the absence of reconditioning. (see Conditioned Responses over Time: Extinction and Spontaneous Recovery)

   a. Reconditioning is the re-pairing of the CS and the UCS after extinction. The fire alarm (CS) would have to be paired repeatedly with fire (UCS) again for reconditioning to occur.

   c. Operant conditioned responses are under stimulus control. This is an example of classical conditioning. The CS is the fire alarm, and the UCS is the fire.

    d.   If stimulus generalization had occurred, the students would have run out of the building in response to an alarm (CS) that was similar but not identical to the original fire alarm. The students heard the same fire alarm in December and September.

8.   a is the answer.   The rat has been classically conditioned to a dark blue light. When it reacts to a turquoise light, it is generalizing its response to a different, but similar, stimulus. (see Stimulus Generalization and Discrimination)

    b.   If the rat had learned to discriminate between stimuli, then it would not react to any stimulus other than the one that originally predicted the electric shock.

    c.   There is no stimulus degradation in this example.

    d.   Stimulus control occurs with the use of operant conditioning.

9.   b is the answer.   Forward conditioning produces the strongest conditioned responses. The CS is presented prior to the UCS, so it becomes a good predictor of the UCS. (see The Signaling of Significant Events)

    a.   There is no such thing as spontaneous conditioning per se. (You may be thinking of spontaneous recovery, in which the conditioned response is elicited after extinction.) But remember, even the spontaneous conditioned response is not very strong.

    c.   In simultaneous conditioning, the CS and the UCS are presented simultaneously. This is not the strongest conditioning scenario, because the CS does not predict the UCS, and the organism is probably paying more attention to the reflex-producing UCS.

    d.   In backward conditioning, the CS is presented after the UCS. Again, this order of events does not allow the CS to become a good predictor of the UCS.

10.   a is the answer.   Biopreparedness is a natural tendency to make certain associations, such as between food and nausea rather than between a sound and nausea. (see The Signaling of Significant Events)

    b.   Tanya did not generalize from one food to another; she associated the food with the nausea.

    c.   In simultaneous conditioning, the CS and UCS arrive at the same time. Tanya did not experience chemotherapy and food at the same time.

    d.   High signal strength causes more rapid learning but does not explain why she had a conditioned response to the food rather than to the song.

11.   b is the answer.   Discriminative conditioned stimuli allow the organism to discriminate between situations that will produce a consequence—a reinforcer or punishment—and those that will not. (see Basic Components of Operant Conditioning)

    a.   Discriminative conditioned stimuli let an organism know when to make a response; they do not cause a response. Conditioned stimuli elicit or cause a conditioned response. There are no conditioned stimuli in operant conditioning.

    c.   Shaping involves rewarding successive approximations of a behavior (behaviors that come closer and closer to the desired response).

    d.   Stimulus generalization in classical conditioning is when a conditioned response is made to a stimulus similar to the conditioned stimulus.

12.   d is the answer.   (see Punishment)

    a, b, c.   These are all true. Punishment is not pleasant for the organism. It is accomplished by presenting an aversive stimulus (getting fired) or taking away a positive stimulus (the privilege of going out on the weekend). Punishment is used to decrease the occurrence of the behavior that precedes it.

13. c is the answer.   Neural network research, also known as parallel distributed processing models, propose that knowledge is distributed throughout the brain through a series of associations (see Linkages: Neural Networks and Learning)

   a, d.   Neural network research does not propose that knowledge is in a single spot nor that it is isolated.

   b.   Although neural network research does propose that knowledge is distributed, it does not argue that it is unconnected.

14. c is the answer.   Anne is not going to tell her boss how she feels about him, because she wants to avoid being fired. (see Basic Components of Operant Conditioning)

   a.   Escape conditioning involves learning to respond in order to get away from an already-present aversive stimulus. Anne does not refrain from telling her boss what she is feeling in order to escape anything. She is trying to avoid the possibility of an aversive stimulus (getting fired) in the future.

   b.   This is an example of operant, not classical, conditioning. Anne avoids making a behavioral response because she has learned that the consequence of that response is getting fired. She has not learned that one stimulus (CS) predicts the occurrence of another (UCS).

   d.   Discriminative conditioned stimuli let an organism know when to respond in order to avoid punishment or receive reinforcement. There are no stimuli in the environment that let Anne know when not to tell her boss that she is angry. She simply knows that she should not yell at her boss. A discriminative conditioned stimulus in this question would have been some clue that her boss was in a good mood and therefore more receptive to hearing what she had to say.

15. c is the answer.   A behavior must occur before it can be reinforced. If an organism has never performed the desired behavior, behaviors that are successive approximations of the desired response are reinforced until the whole behavior appears. For an example of successive approximation, see the example of teaching your dog to "shake" in your text. (see Forming and Strengthening Operant Behavior)

   a.   Behaviors that are shaped are not always difficult to perform. For example, it is not physically difficult for a dog to roll over, but if the dog has never done so, its behavior must be shaped.

   b.   Shaping is the creation of a new behavior, not the decreasing of an existing behavior.

   d.   Shaping allows an organism to learn a new behavior. Reflexive behaviors are not new. Also, conditioned responses are learned, not reflexive.

16. a is the answer.   A fixed-interval schedule is reinforcement after a predictable amount of time passes. Dr. Velagati gets paid each month, which is a temporal marker, not a behavioral one. (see Forming and Strengthening Operant Behavior)

   b.   On a fixed-ratio schedule, reinforcement occurs after a predictable number of behaviors, not amount of time.

   c.   A variable-interval schedule involves reinforcement after an unpredictable, not a predictable, amount of time passes.

   d.   A variable-ratio schedule involves reinforcement after an unpredictable number of behaviors.

17. b is the answer.   Patient B will receive a reinforcer—pain medication—every time he presses a button. The reinforcement will be continuously under his control. (see Forming and Strengthening Operant Behavior)

    a.   Patient A is reinforced after a fixed interval of time, every six hours.

    c, d.   Patient B's situation fulfills the criteria for a continuous reinforcement schedule, but Patient A's does not.

18. a is the answer.   Insight is a sudden understanding of how to solve a problem. (see Insight and Learning)

    b.   Learned helplessness occurs when one learns that his or her responses do not affect consequences and then quits trying to control his or her environment.

    c.   Latent learning is learning that is not demonstrated at the time it occurs.

    d.   Vicarious conditioning is a type of observational learning. By watching others and observing the rewards and punishments they experience, one can learn the rewards and punishments that will apply to oneself, and act accordingly.

19. c is the answer.   Feedback that comes after a person has had a chance to focus on their independent effort in learning a skill is usually most helpful. (see Using Research on Learning to Help People Learn)

    a.   Constant feedback, particularly when it comes too quickly after an action, can impair performance because it diverts attention from how the action was achieved and what it felt like to perform it.

    b.   Little feedback is not necessarily helpful. If the feedback is too little, then the person learning the skill will be unable to learn to assess their performance level.

    d.   It is not true that any feedback at all is helpful. Feedback that is well-timed and controlled in volume so as to promote independent skill learning is the best.

20. d is the answer.   Although watching violent TV increases the likelihood of violent behavior in general, it is not possible to predict individual behavior without knowing more information about Jimmy's peers and other environmental influences. (see Thinking Critically: Does Watching Violence on Television Make People More Violent?)

    a.   We cannot predict that he will not hit her based solely on his parents' instructions, particularly given the programming to which he has been exposed.

    b.   Although watching violence on TV increases Jimmy's likelihood of engaging in violent behavior, we cannot predict this without more information.

    c.   Violence on television actually has more impact on boys than on girls, in general. Thus Jimmy would be more susceptible because of his gender, not less.

Now turn to the quiz analysis table at the end of this chapter to find which areas you know well and which areas you need to work on. Circle the numbers in the table for items on Quiz 2 that you answered correctly.

For each question you answered correctly, circle its number. (Quiz 1 numbers are not shaded; Quiz 2 numbers are shaded.) Are there patterns in the types of questions or the topics you got wrong that could direct your further study? Did you improve from Quiz 1 to Quiz 2?

QUIZ REVIEW

Topic	Type of Question		
	Definition	Comprehension	Application
Learning About Stimuli			6
Classical Conditioning: Learning Signals and Associations			
Pavlov's Discovery	1		
			1, 2, 3, 4, 5
Conditioned Responses over Time: Extinction and Spontaneous Recovery	2, 4		5
			7
Stimulus Generalization and Discrimination			
			8
The Signaling of Significant Events			3
	6	9	10
Operant Conditioning: Learning the Consequences of Behavior			
From the Puzzle Box to the Skinner Box			8
Basic Components of Operant Conditioning	9		10, 11
	11		14
Forming and Strengthening Operant Behavior	12	13	14
		15	16, 17
Why Reinforcers Work		7	
Punishment			15
	12		
Linkages: Neural Networks and Learning		18	
		13	
Cognitive Processes in Learning			
Learned Helplessness	16		
Latent Learning and Cognitive Maps			17
Insight and Learning			
			18
Observational Learning: Learning by Imitation			19

Thinking Critically: Does Watching Violence on Television Make People More Violent?		20	
		20	
Using Research on Learning to Help People Learn			
		19	

Total correct by quiz:

Quiz 1:	
Quiz 2:	

CHAPTER 7

Memory

OUTLINE

I. THE NATURE OF MEMORY
    A. Basic Memory Processes
        The process of putting information into memory is called <u>encoding</u>. Codes for <u>auditory memory</u> (also known as <u>acoustic memory</u>) represent information as sequences of sounds. Codes for <u>visual memory</u> represent information in the form of images. Codes for semantic memory represent the general meaning of the experience. Holding information in memory over time is called <u>storage</u>. Pulling information out of memory and into consciousness after it has been stored is called <u>retrieval</u>.

    B. Types of Memory
        There are at least three basic types of memory, each of which is named for the type of information it handles. Any memory of a specific event that happened while you were present is an <u>episodic memory</u>. <u>Semantic memory</u> contains generalized knowledge of the world that does not involve memory of a specific event. <u>Procedural memory</u> (skill memory) represents knowledge of how to perform physical tasks, and is also known as <u>procedural knowledge</u>.

    C. Explicit and Implicit Memory
        <u>Explicit memory</u> is the process of deliberately trying to remember something; <u>implicit memory</u> is the unintentional influence of prior experiences. Explicit memory processes are much more negatively affected by the passing of time than are implicit memory processes.

    D. Focus on Research Methods: Measuring Explicit vs. Implicit Memory
        1. To document the difference between explicit and implicit memory, participants studied a word list and were tested on it an hour later and a week later. For the explicit memory test, participants picked which words on a new list had been on their study list. For the implicit memory test, they solved word fragment problems.

        2. Explicit memory decreased between the two tests, but implicit memory hardly changed. This research showed that time differentially affects explicit and implicit memory, and supports the notion of dissociation between implicit and explicit memory.

        3. Research now is considering if implicit social cognitions could influence our judgments about groups of people. Research needs to distinguish what mechanisms are differentially responsible for implicit versus explicit processes, and functional neuroimaging will help in that endeavor.

    E. Models of Memory
        Currently, there are four models of memory that attempt to explain what and how well items such as processes, episodes, and general information are remembered.

        1. *Levels of Processing.* The <u>levels-of-processing model of memory</u> suggests that what and how well we remember are a function of how deeply information is processed or rehearsed and encoded when first experienced. <u>Maintenance rehearsal</u> is simply repeating an item over and over. <u>Elaborative rehearsal</u> is building associations or

linkages between new and old information. Elaborative rehearsal requires a deeper level of processing; hence these memories are stronger than those encoded with maintenance rehearsal.

2. *Transfer-Appropriate Processing*. The transfer-appropriate processing model of memory suggests that the most important memory determinant is how well the encoding process matches what is retrieved.

3. *Parallel Distributed Processing (PDP)*. Parallel distributed processing (PDP) models of memory suggest that new facts change our knowledge base by altering interconnected networks, facts, and associations. These networks allow us to quickly and efficiently draw inferences and generalizations about new and old information. They are very connected to our understanding of neural networks.

4. *Multiple Memory Systems*. The multiple memory systems model suggests that the brain contains several separate memory systems, each of which resides in a different area and serves a different purpose.

5. *Information Processing*. The information-processing model of memory states that there are three stages of mental processing required before information can be permanently stored in memory: sensory, short-term, and long-term memory. It is the earliest, and most influential, model of memory.

II.   STORING NEW MEMORIES
   A.   Sensory Memory
   Sensory memory holds information from all the senses in sensory registers for a fraction of a second. It helps us experience a constant flow of information. For example, each visual scene we view is held in our iconic memory for a second so that all the small eye movements we make seem to flow together. Selective attention, which focuses mental resources on only part of the stimulus field, controls which information in the sensory registers is actually perceived and transferred to short-term and working memory.

   B.   Short-Term Memory and Working Memory
   Short-term memory (STM) receives the information that was perceived and selectively attended to in sensory memory or retrieved from long-term memory. Short-term memory stores information for a very limited amount of time. Working memory allows us to mentally work with information held in short-term memory, making short-term memory a component of working memory. Working memory has two components: maintenance and manipulation.

   1. *Encoding in STM*. People tend to use acoustic codes to encode information into short-term memory. Visual codes tend to decay faster than acoustic codes.

   2. *Storage Capacity of STM*. The immediate memory span is the number of items you can recall perfectly after one presentation of a stimulus. It is usually seven plus or minus two chunks of information. Chunks are meaningful groupings of information produced by the cognitive process of chunking.

   3. *The Power of Chunking*. STM can be noticeably improved by creating bigger and bigger chunks of information. Although the capacity of STM is 7 (plus or minus two) chunks of information, the size of those chunks can vary dramatically.

   4. *Duration of STM*. Research using the Brown-Peterson distractor technique indicates that, unless rehearsed, material stays in STM for about eighteen seconds. This is adaptive, as it clears STM from clutter.

   C.   Long-Term Memory
   1. *Encoding in LTM*. Encoding information into long-term memory (LTM) is the result of a deep level of conscious processing and usually involves some form of semantic coding. Visual codes are also used to encode long-term memories. The dual coding

theory states that information is remembered better if both semantic and visual codes are used.

2. *Storage Capacity of LTM*. Most theorists believe that there is no limit to the amount of information that can be stored in long-term memory. However, long-term memories are likely to be distorted. Flashbulb memories, for example, seem to be detailed recollections but can be inaccurate.

D. Distinguishing Between Short-Term and Long-Term Memory
Psychologists disagree about the differences between short-term and long-term memory. Some believe that short-term memory and long-term memory are different systems.

1. *Experiments on Recall*. Serial position curves show a tendency to recall both the first and last parts of a list (primacy and recency effects) when memory is immediately tested. The primacy effect may occur because of rehearsal that moved the words to long-term memory, while the recency effect may be because the last few words on a list are still in short-term memory when the recall task begins.

III. RETRIEVING MEMORIES
Retrieval is the ability to bring a memory into consciousness.

A. Retrieval Cues and Encoding Specificity
Retrieval cues help retrieve information from long-term memory. According to the encoding specificity principle, these cues are more efficient when they tap into information that was encoded at the time of learning (consistent with transfer-appropriate processing).

B. Context and State Dependence
When people remember more material while in a physical location that is similar to the one where the material was originally learned, it is called context-specific memory (also known as context-specific learning). In state-dependent memory (also known as state-dependent learning), people remember better when their psychological state is the same as it was when the information was encoded. In the *mood congruency effect*, information processing is facilitated if a person's emotional state is similar in tone to the information being processed.

C. Retrieval from Semantic Memory
1. *Semantic Networks*. One theory states that semantic memories are represented in a dense network of hierarchical associations. Strong associations and/or those at the top of the hierarchy are quickly retrieved. Semantic network theory suggests that information is retrieved through a spreading activation process; for example, thinking about concept A spreads neural activity to all other features, attributes, and concepts associated with concept A.

2. *Retrieving Incomplete Knowledge*. In a phenomenon called incomplete knowledge (as in the *tip-of-the-tongue phenomenon*), we often retrieve features and attributes of a concept but cannot access the entire concept. For example, we may feel that we would recognize the answer to a trivia question if we were presented several options (*feeling-of-knowing experience*).

D. Constructing Memories
People construct memories from their existing knowledge to fill in gaps in new information that is being encoded.

1. *Relating Semantic and Episodic Memory: PDP Models*. PDP models allow us to increase our general knowledge of the world by accessing a network of facts and associations. A note of caution: PDP models can facilitate *spontaneous generalizations* of networks that are based on limited or biased information. Prejudice can result from such generalizations, although unprejudiced people recognize this and can consciously ignore or suppress the generalizations.

2. *Schemas*. According to PDP models, the generalized knowledge contained in <u>schemas</u> provides the basis for making inferences about incoming information during the encoding stage.

E. Linkages: Memory, Perception, and Eyewitness Testimony

1. Witnesses can accurately report what they have seen or heard but can be biased by the manner in which questions are asked and relevant occurrences are discussed.

2. This *misinformation effect* can occur in several ways. First, new information may make it hard to retrieve older information. Second, new information can be integrated into an older memory, making it impossible to determine what was observed and what was heard later. A final way this may manifest itself is through assumptions that if a police officer or lawyer says something happened or was at the crime scene, the eyewitness may be more likely to report having seen it.

3. Jurors may rely too heavily on *how* witnesses present evidence, such as reporting a great deal of detail or appearing very confident of what they are reporting. Eyewitness testimony confidence is often much higher than the accuracy of the testimony.

IV. FORGETTING

A. How Do We Forget?
Hermann Ebbinghaus's contributions to psychology included demonstration of the <u>relearning method</u> and the shape of the forgetting curve. The forgetting curve, which depicts how much and when people forget, stays relatively constant regardless of the type of information learned.

B. Why Do We Forget? The Roles of Decay and Interference

1. <u>Decay theory</u> sees forgetting as the gradual erosion of a memory. Decay plays the main role in forgetting from short-term memory.

2. <u>Interference</u> causes forgetting by interrupting the encoding or retrieval process through the presence of other information. In short-term memory, new information displaces old information because of the limited number of spaces available. However, in long-term memory, space is not the issue; rather, as the number of stored memories increases, it becomes more and more difficult to "find" one particular memory among the huge number of memories.

3. Interference, the main cause of forgetting in long-term memory, can be due to <u>retroactive inhibition</u> or <u>proactive inhibition</u>.

C. Thinking Critically: Can Traumatic Memories Be Repressed, Then Recovered?
What am I being asked to believe or accept?

Some people claim that subconscious processes such as repression could keep a person from recalling a memory. Such memories are known as <u>repressed memories</u>.

What evidence is available to support the assertion?

Research supports that mental activity can occur outside of awareness, that implicit memories can influence people, and that the use of retrieval cues can allow people to access buried memories. In addition, people may be motivated to forget especially unpleasant events. Fourth, retrieval cues can help people recall memories that previously were inaccessible. Finally, many recovered memories are reported with such confidence that some argue they must be real.

Are there alternative ways of interpreting the evidence?

Even vivid retrieved memories may have been constructed. A person might be led by books or therapists to construct false memories. Research shows that false memories can be as vivid as accurate, real memories and held with great confidence. People who are prone to fantasy, who easily confuse real and imagined stimuli, and have lapses in attention and memory are more likely to report false memories.

What additional evidence would help to evaluate the alternatives?

If we knew how frequently people repress traumatic memories, it would be easier to evaluate such reports. Knowledge of the process leading to repressed memories and a method for distinguishing between genuine memories and constructed memories would also help evaluate the alternatives.

What conclusions are most reasonable?

Although people do forget unpleasant events and remember them later, they also may distort their memories. For now, people should neither uncritically accept nor reject a report of a recovered memory, but should investigate the evidence for and against the claim. People may be able to repress and recover memories, but a false memory is also possible.

V. BIOLOGICAL BASES OF MEMORY
Networks of brain cells change as memories are formed and stored.

A. The Biochemistry of Memory
Two types of synaptic changes occur during memory formation: New synapses are formed, and communication at existing synapses is improved. As existing synapses are sensitized, *long-term potentiation* has occurred. Neurotransmitters, such as glutamate and *acetylcholine*, are involved in memory processes.

B. Brain Structures and Memory
The hippocampus and the thalamus are important in the formation of new memories. Memories are stored in many different areas of the cortex. However, no single brain structure or neurotransmitter is exclusively involved in memory formation or storage.

1. *The Impact of Brain Damage.* Hippocampal brain damage often results in anterograde amnesia, a loss of memory of events occurring after the injury. Patients cannot transfer new experiences from short-term memory to long-term memory. This limitation does not apply to implicit memory, however. Retrograde amnesia is the loss of memory of events prior to an injury. Although many injury patients regain most of their memories, few can recall the events just prior to the injury. As a result of the injury, the short-term memories of what happened were never transferred to long-term memory and *consolidated.* Memory deficits in several medical conditions (e.g., *Korsakoff's psychosis*) support the theory that short-term memory and long-term memory are distinct storage systems.

2. *Multiple Storage Areas.* Long-term memories are stored in and around the cortex, but not all in one place. Multiple sensory and motor systems are involved in memory, and some evidence suggests the sensory and motor areas involved in formation of a memory are activated at retrieval. So, memories are both localized and distributed throughout the brain.

VI. APPLICATIONS OF MEMORY RESEARCH
A. Improving Your Memory
1. *Mnemonics.* Mnemonic strategies place information in an organized framework to remember it more easily. The *method of loci* associates well-known locations with information to be remembered.

2. *Guidelines for More Effective Studying.* Create a context, such as an outline, for organizing information. Elaborate the new information and associate it with related knowledge you already possess. Remember that <u>distributed practice</u> is more effective than <u>massed practice</u>, and practice retrieving information yourself by repeated testing, not just looking over information that is freely available.

3. *Reading a Textbook.* Make sure you understand what you are reading before you go on. Use the PQ4R method of preview, question, read, reflect, recite, and review.

4. *Lecture Notes.* Focus on creating a framework for facts (outline) and expressing major ideas in relatively few words. Finally, work to see and understand the relationship between facts and concepts. Review your notes as soon as possible after a lecture and fill in the gaps.

B. Design for Memory
The scientific study of memory has influenced the design of electronic and mechanical devices that play important roles in our lives.

KEY TERMS

1. **Encoding** is the process of acquiring information and entering it into memory. (see Basic Memory Processes)

Example: Sherra is studying for her final exam. She keeps repeating material to herself and trying to generate examples of it. She is encoding the course material both acoustically (by repeating it) and semantically (by generating examples).

REMEMBER: There are three types of encoding: acoustic, visual, and semantic.

2. **Auditory memory (acoustic memory)** consists of mental representations of information as a sequence of sounds. (see Basic Memory Processes)

Example: Think of your favorite song and hum it to yourself. The memory of how the melody sounds is an acoustic memory code.

3. **Visual memory** is the representation of information as images. (see Basic Memory Processes)

Example: If you think of a Christmas tree or the car you would buy if you had enough money, you will most likely see images of these things in your mind. You do so because you have visual memory codes for them.

4. **Storage** is the process of maintaining information in memory over time. (see Basic Memory Processes)

Example: Memories of your kindergarten class, your second-grade teacher, or the first home you lived in are old memories. They have been stored for quite some time.

5. **Retrieval** is the process of recalling information stored in memory. (see Basic Memory Processes)

Example: Whenever you remember anything, you are retrieving that memory from storage. Some memories are retrieved so quickly that you are unaware of the process. Answer the following questions: How old are you? How many people have been president of the United States? Both questions require you to retrieve information, but the retrieval process is much easier for the first question than for the second.

6. **Episodic memory** is memory of an event that happened while one was present. (see Types of Memory)

Example: The memory of your first pony ride, a surprise birthday party that you held for a friend, or your first day of college is an episodic memory.

REMEMBER: Episodic memories are episodes that involved you.

7. **Semantic memory** is a type of memory containing generalized knowledge of the world. (see Types of Memory)

    Example: Knowing that the freezing point is 32 degrees Fahrenheit, that red lights mean "stop," and that the capital of the United States is Washington, D.C., are all examples of semantic memory. You probably cannot remember the specific time or episode during which you learned these facts.

8. **Procedural knowledge**, also known as **procedural memory**, is a type of memory containing information about how to do things. (see Types of Memory)

    Example: Knowing how to waltz, do a somersault, tie a tie, and drive a car are all procedural memories.

9. **Explicit memory** is the process of intentionally trying to remember something. (see Explicit and Implicit Memory)

    Example: While you are taking an exam, you are using explicit memory to retrieve information regarding the questions.

10. **Implicit memory** is the unintentional influence of prior experiences. (see Explicit and Implicit Memory)

    Example: Although you do not understand why, you are nervous whenever you wait for a bus on a specific corner. Stored unintentionally is the memory of a frightening event from your childhood in which a stranger approached you at that corner and you ran away.

11. The **levels-of-processing model of memory** holds that how well something is remembered depends on the degree to which incoming information is mentally processed. (see Models of Memory)

    REMEMBER: Maintenance rehearsal does not require much processing and is effective for encoding information into short-term memory. Elaborative rehearsal requires a great deal of processing and is effective for encoding into long-term memory.

12. **Maintenance rehearsal** is repeating information over and over to keep it active in short-term memory. (see Models of Memory)

    Example: Kan arrives in New York to visit his cousin Zhou but loses Zhou's phone number. Kan calls directory assistance and the operator tells him the number. Kan repeats it over and over to himself while he inserts coins for the call.

    REMEMBER: Maintenance rehearsal maintains information in short-term memory.

13. **Elaborative rehearsal** is a memorization method that involves thinking about how new information relates to information already stored in long-term memory. (see Models of Memory)

    Example: Ursula is a world-class shopper. She has a mental image of all the major cities she has shopped in and images of the locations of all her favorite stores on each street. When Ursula wants to store information about a new store, she uses her mental image and places the new store on its street. She thinks about the new store in relationship to the stores surrounding it. Ursula is not just repeating the address of the new store but is also relating it to the addresses of all the other stores that she knows.

    REMEMBER: New information is elaborated with information already in long-term memory. The new address is elaborated by relating its location to all the old addresses of stores already in long-term memory.

14. The **transfer-appropriate processing model of memory** is a model that suggests that a critical determinant of memory is how well the retrieval process matches the original encoding process. (see Models of Memory)

Example: Samantha studied for an auto mechanics test by spending many weekends with her head under the hood of a car. However, much to her surprise, when it came time to take the test, the professor handed out a multiple-choice exam. Samantha, who felt that she had really learned the material, scored poorly. According to the transfer-appropriate processing model, Samantha did not do well because she encoded the material by applying what she had learned from the text, but the exam asked her only to retrieve specific facts. Samantha's encoding process was not appropriate for the retrieval process required by the exam.

REMEMBER: Think of this model as stating that the encoding process that transfers information into long-term memory must be appropriate for (match) the retrieval cues.

15. **Parallel distributed processing (PDP) models of memory** are memory models in which new experiences change one's overall knowledge base. (see Models of Memory)

Example: Zoë's knowledge that the term neonate means "newborn" is linked to her memory of seeing a premature infant taken to a neonatal unit. Both neonate and neonatal are connected to her memory that *neo* means "new." When Zoë thinks of *neonate,* an image of her nephew as a newborn is also readily accessible. This background made it easier for her to understand that a *neo-Freudian* is a person who developed a new version of Freud's theory.

REMEMBER: Tapping into any connection (via a memory process) provides us with access to all the other connections in the network.

16. The **information-processing model** is a memory model in which information is seen as passing through sensory memory, short-term memory, and long-term memory. (see Models of Memory)

17. **Sensory memory** is a type of memory that holds large amounts of incoming information very briefly, but long enough to connect one impression to the next. (see Sensory Memory)

Example: When Julie is interrupted in a conversation by her daughter, she is still able to hear the last statement fragment enough to reorient to the conversation quickly after telling her daughter to stop interrupting. She is able to do this because her auditory sensory memory is holding the information briefly on-line.

REMEMBER: If the information is attended to and recognized, perception takes place, and the information can enter short-term memory.

18. **Sensory registers** are memory systems that hold incoming information long enough for it to be processed further. (see Sensory Memory)

REMEMBER: There is a sensory register for each sense.

19. **Iconic memory** is the sensory register for visual information. (see Sensory Memory)

Example: When you see a sparkler "drawing", you aren't really seeing the light of the sparkler at all those points, but iconic memory of all of those points of light as the sparkler is waved through the air.

20. **Selective attention** is the focusing of mental resources on only part of the stimulus field. (see Sensory Memory)

Example: Imagine going to New York's Times Square for New Year's Eve. The crowd is immense. Suddenly, you see someone waving a sparkler in front of you. Even though your eyes and ears are being hit with a variety of stimuli, your sensory registers will retain information about the person with the sparkler because you "selected" that particular set of stimuli to "attend" to.

21. **Short-term memory (STM)** is the maintenance component of working memory, which holds unrehearsed information for a limited time. (see Short-Term Memory and Working Memory)

    Example: If you look up a phone number and repeat it to yourself until you finish dialing, you will have kept it active in your short-term memory. However, it is likely that you will have forgotten it by the time you get off the phone, because you were using your working memory to process the new information coming in during the conversation.

22. **Working memory** is the part of the memory system that allows us to mentally work with, or manipulate, information being held in short-term memory. (see Short-Term Memory and Working Memory)

    Example: When you have a conversation with someone, you think about what they are saying and use that information to frame a response. You are using your working memory to do this.

23. An **immediate memory span** is the maximum number of items a person can recall perfectly after one presentation of the items. (see Short-Term Memory and Working Memory)

    Example: Use a telephone book to help you test your own immediate memory span. Read the first two names at the top of the page, look away, and then try to recall them. Then read the next three names, look away, and try to recall them. Continue this process, using a longer list each time, until you cannot repeat the entire list of names. The number of names that you can repeat perfectly is your immediate memory span.

    REMEMBER: Most people have an immediate memory span of five to nine items.

24. **Chunking** is organizing individual stimuli so that they will be perceived as larger units of meaningful information. (see Short-Term Memory and Working Memory)

    Example: During her first night as a waitress, Bridget needed all five to nine chunks in short-term memory to remember one order for one person. For example, a drink before dinner, a drink with dinner, a main dish, a type of salad dressing, a type of potato, and whether the customer wanted cream, sugar, or both with coffee made up five to nine chunks of information. After two years of waitressing, Bridget can easily hold in memory four to eight people's complete food and drink orders. Each person's order had become one chunk of information.

    REMEMBER: Chunks can be anything—letters, numbers, words, names, or locations—just to list a few. The more information you can condense or group into one chunk, the more information you can hold in short-term memory.

25. The **Brown-Peterson distractor technique** is a method for determining how long unrehearsed information remains in short-term memory. (see Short-Term Memory and Working Memory)

    Example: Juan is participating in a study where he is trying to remember as many words from a list as he can. Instead of being allowed to repeat them over and over, the experimenter tells him to count backwards from one hundred by intervals of seven. This prevents Juan from rehearsing the list to remember.

26. **Long-term memory (LTM)** is a relatively long-lasting stage of memory whose capacity to store new information is believed to be unlimited. (see Long-Term Memory)

    Example: You can easily remember and recognize your grade school classmate from many years ago.

27. The **primacy effect** is a characteristic of memory in which recall of the first two or three items in a list is particularly good. (see Distinguishing Between Short-Term and Long-Term Memory)

    REMEMBER: Primacy means "being first." The primacy effect is the remembering of the first words in a list better than other words in the list.

28. The **recency effect** is a characteristic of memory in which recall of the last few items in a list is particularly good. (see Distinguishing Between Short-Term and Long-Term Memory)

    Example: After hearing all her students' names once, Leslie tries to recite them one by one. She remembers the names of students in the first two rows (primacy effect) and the names of the students in the last two rows (recency effect), but she has difficulty recalling the names of students in the middle two rows.

    REMEMBER: Recency means "that which occurred most recently." The last items of a list are presented most recently.

29. A **retrieval cue** is a stimulus that aids the recall or recognition of information stored in memory. (see Retrieval Cues and Encoding Specificity)

    Example: On a multiple-choice exam, the answer appears somewhere in the question. Some of the words in the correct answer should jog your memory and allow you to answer the question correctly.

30. The **encoding specificity principle** states that the ability of a cue to aid retrieval depends on the degree to which it taps into information that was encoded at the time of the original learning. (see Retrieval Cues and Encoding Specificity)

31. **Context-specific memory** (also known as **context-specific learning**) is memory that can be helped or hindered by similarities or differences between the context in which it is learned and the context in which it is recalled. (see Context and State Dependence)

    Example: When taking his exam in his regular classroom, Leon's memory for lecture information is improved by glancing around at the chalkboard, peeling paint, and lecturer's desk. Although he does not realize it, he recalls the discussion of the opponent-process theory of color vision better because he is among familiar classmates and surroundings. Unfortunately, he does not remember as much of the information he studied in his room with the stereo blaring, because few of the retrieval cues associated with that learning exist in the quiet classroom environment where he is taking the exam.

    REMEMBER: The environment acts as a retrieval cue. This means that it is easier to remember information when you are in the location (context) where you originally learned that information.

32. **State-dependent memory** (also known as **state-dependent learning**) is memory that is aided or impeded by a person's internal state. (see Context and State Dependence)

    Example: In the evening when she studied psychology, Lydia had several cups of coffee to keep her alert. The next morning, she did not do well on the quiz. Later, when drinking coffee with some friends, she was in the same state as when she studied for the quiz, and to her amazement, she remembered some of the material that had escaped her during the quiz.

    REMEMBER: When you are trying to remember, if you are in the same psychological state you were in at the time of learning, you will retrieve more material.

33. **Spreading activation** is a principle that explains how information is retrieved in semantic network theories of memory. (see Retrieval from Semantic Memory)

    Example: When Jane thinks about pizza, this activates other concepts such as food, delivery, cost, and so on.

    REMEMBER: Whenever a question is asked, neural activation spreads from those concepts contained in the question down all paths related to them.

34. **Schemas** are mental representations of categories of objects, events, and people. (see Constructing Memories)

Example: If your schema for a classroom is a square room filled with desks, upon seeing people seated on pillows in a round room you might be likely to classify it as a lounge.

35. The **relearning method** is a way to measure forgetting by comparing the number of repetitions needed to learn, and after a delay, relearn the same material. (see How Do We Forget?)

    Example: If it took a subject twenty repetitions to learn a list of items but only five repetitions to relearn the list a semester later, there would be a savings of 75 percent.

    REMEMBER: The relearning method was introduced by Hermann Ebbinghaus.

36. **Decay theory** is a description of forgetting as the gradual disappearance of information from memory. (see Why Do We Forget? The Roles of Decay and Interference)

    Example: Marissa learned Spanish but has not tried to speak it in years. When Marissa tries to say, "Hello, how was your day?" to her roommate, she cannot remember the necessary vocabulary.

37. **Interference** is the process through which either the storage or retrieval of information is impaired by the presence of other information. (see Why Do We Forget? The Roles of Decay and Interference)

38. **Retroactive inhibition** is a cause of forgetting in which new information placed in memory interferes with the ability to recall information already in memory. (see Why Do We Forget? The Roles of Decay and Interference)

    REMEMBER: Retro means "back." New information goes back and inhibits recall of old information.

39. **Proactive inhibition** is a cause of forgetting in which information already in long-term memory interferes with the ability to remember new information. (see Why Do We Forget? The Roles of Decay and Interference)

    Example: If you have ever learned something incorrectly and then tried to correct it, you may have experienced proactive interference. Young children who take music lessons once a week experience this. They learn an incorrect note, and at their lesson the next week, their teacher points out the mistake. However, it is very difficult to play the correct note, because the old memory of the wrong note interferes with the new memory of the correct note.

    REMEMBER: Pro means "forward." Old information goes forward and inhibits recall of new information.

40. A **repressed memory** is a painful memory that is said to be kept out of consciousness by psychological processes. (see Thinking Critically: Can Traumatic Memories Be Repressed, then Recovered?)

    Example: Nathan was injured in a terrible car accident as a child, but he has no memory of the event because it is too horrible to even think about.

41. **Anterograde amnesia** is a loss of memory for any event that occurs after a brain injury. (see Brain Structures and Memory)

    Example: People with anterograde amnesia will not be able to remember the new people they meet, because they are unable to form new memories.

    REMEMBER: Anterograde amnesia is a loss of memory for the future, or after some point in time.

42. **Retrograde amnesia** is a loss of memory for events prior to a brain injury. (see Brain Structures and Memory)

    REMEMBER: Retro means "backward." The memory loss goes back in time.

43. **Mnemonic strategies** are methods for placing information in an organized context in order to remember it. (see Improving Your Memory)

    Example: To remember the name "Hathaway," you might picture the person coming "half the way" to you.

44. **Distributed practice** involves the spacing of study sessions over days or weeks. (see Improving Your Memory)

    Example: Hank practices pitching for one hour each day. His practice is distributed across days of the week.

45. **Massed practice** involves a long period of concentrated study ("cramming"). (see Improving Your Memory)

    Example: Connor practices pitching only the day before the game but he practices most of the day.

FILL-IN-THE-BLANKS KEY TERMS

This section will help you check your knowledge of the key terms introduced in this chapter. Fill in each blank with the appropriate term from the list of key terms in the previous section.

1. Memories that contain general, factual knowledge are called _____.

2. Sequences of sounds that we perceive are represented as _____ codes.

3. Incoming stimuli from the world are held in _____ until they are processed or decay.

4. Information in _____ memory will be lost within eighteen seconds if it is not further processed.

5. When new information interferes with the remembering of old information, this phenomenon is called _____.

6. Repeating information over and over as a way to remember it is called _____.

7. The _____ is a way to measure forgetting by comparing the number of repetitions needed to learn, and relearn after a delay, the same material.

8. Methods that can improve your memory by increasing encoding efficiency are called _____.

9. _____ is the phenomenon in which people's memory is enhanced if they are in the same situation as when they learned the material.

10. Practicing material to remember in a single long session is known as _____.

11. When a person remembers the last few items on a list better than others, this is called the _____ effect.

12. _____ rehearsal is an effective method for encoding information into long-term memory.

13. The _____ model holds that differences in remembering information are based on the degree to which the information is mentally analyzed.

14. Retrieval cues help us recall information from _____ memory.

15. The inability to remember any information before a certain point in time is called _____.

Total Correct (See answer key) _____

LEARNING OBJECTIVES

1. Define and give an example of <u>encoding</u>, acoustic encoding, visual encoding, semantic encoding, <u>storage</u>, and <u>retrieval</u>. Discuss the importance of encoding, storage, and retrieval in memory processes. (see Basic Memory Processes)

2. Define and give an example of <u>episodic</u>, <u>semantic</u>, and <u>procedural memory</u>. (see Types of Memory)

3. Define and give an example of <u>explicit</u> and <u>implicit memory</u>. Discuss the series of experiments on explicit and implicit memory. (see Explicit and Implicit Memory)

4. Define the <u>information-processing model</u> of memory. Name the three stages of processing. (see Models of Memory)

5. Define the <u>levels-of-processing model</u> of memory. Describe the role of rehearsal in this memory model. Define <u>maintenance</u> and <u>elaborative rehearsal</u>. (see Models of Memory)

6. Define the <u>transfer-appropriate processing model</u>. Describe the role of encoding and retrieval processes in this memory model. (see Models of Memory)

7. Define the <u>parallel distributed processing (PDP) model</u> of memory. Describe the role of association networks in drawing inferences and making generalizations. (see Models of Memory)

8. Explain the multiple memory systems approach and how it accounts for each of the memory models. (see Models of Memory)

9. Define <u>sensory memory</u> and <u>sensory registers</u>. Discuss the amount of information and the length of time it stays in sensory memory. (see Sensory Memory)

10. Explain why <u>selective attention</u> is important in determining which information is transferred to short-term memory from sensory memory. (see Sensory Memory)

11. Define <u>short-term memory (STM)</u>. Discuss the relationship between short-term memory and <u>working memory</u>. (see Short-Term Memory and Working Memory)

12. Describe short-term memory encoding. (see Short-Term Memory and Working Memory)

13. Define <u>immediate memory span</u> and <u>chunking</u>. Discuss the role of long-term memory in the chunking process. (see Short-Term Memory and Working Memory)

14. Define the <u>Brown-Peterson distractor technique</u>. Describe the importance of rehearsal in maintaining information in short-term memory. (see Short-Term Memory and Working Memory)

15. Define <u>long-term memory (LTM)</u> and discuss the importance of semantic encoding in long-term memory. Describe the storage capacity of LTM. Discuss how long-term memories, including flashbulb memories, can become distorted. (see Long-Term Memory)

16. Describe the controversy over the differences between short-term and long-term memory. Define <u>primacy</u> and <u>recency effects</u>. (see Distinguishing Between Short-Term and Long-Term Memory)

17. Define <u>retrieval cues</u> and explain why their use can increase memory efficiency. Define the <u>encoding specificity principle</u>. (see Retrieval Cues and Encoding Specificity)

18. Explain how memory is both <u>context dependent</u> and <u>state dependent,</u> and give examples of each. Explain the *mood congruency effect*. (see Context and State Dependence)

19. Describe the semantic network theory of memory. Explain the process of spreading activation in memory. (see Retrieval from Semantic Memory)

20. Define the *tip-of-the-tongue phenomenon* and the *feeling-of-knowing experience*. Explain how these are related to the semantic network theory of memory. (see Retrieval from Semantic Memory)

21. Define *constructive memory*. Describe how PDP memory models explain the integration of semantic and episodic memories in memory construction. (see Constructing Memories)

22. Explain how PDP models produce spontaneous generalizations and why they help explain the operation of schemas. (see Constructing Memories)

23. Discuss the use of eyewitness testimony in the courtroom. (see Linkages: Memory, Perception, and Eyewitness Testimony)

24. Define Ebbinghaus's relearning method. Explain his discoveries and why they are important to memory research. (see How Do We Forget?)

25. Compare and contrast the decay and interference theories regarding forgetting information stored in long-term memory. Define retroactive and proactive inhibition. (see Why Do We Forget? The Roles of Decay and Interference)

26. Discuss the controversy surrounding repressed memory. Describe *motivated forgetting*, *false memories*, and *flashbulb memories*. (see Thinking Critically: Can Traumatic Memories Be Repressed, Then Recovered?)

27. Describe the synaptic activity associated with forming new memories. Describe the role of the hippocampus in episodic and procedural memory formation. (see The Biochemistry of Memory)

28. Explain the debate concerning the localized versus distributed nature of memory processes in the brain. Define anterograde and retrograde amnesia, and discuss what information brain damage has provided to address this debate. (see Brain Structures and Memory)

29. Define mnemonic strategies and explain why they improve memory. Give an example of the *method of loci*. (see Improving Your Memory)

30. Explain why distributed practice is more effective than massed practice. Describe the *PQ4R method* and its use. Describe the best method of taking notes in a lecture. (see Improving Your Memory)

CONCEPTS AND EXERCISES

Memory Cues

There has been a robbery at a local bank. For questioning, the police have placed the witnesses in the locations they occupied during the robbery. Indicate what type of memory, encoding, or process is responsible for each statement. Draw your answers from the list following the exercise. Answers may be used more than once or not at all.

1. Police: We are questioning you here at the bank because we think it will improve your recall of the robbery. _____ What was the suspect wearing?

2. Teller 1: I know he had a coat on, but I don't remember the color. _____

3. Teller 2: I remember. It was green. _____

   Police (to Teller 3): Where were you when the robbery took place?

4. Teller 3: I was standing in the manager's office when the man approached me and told me to unlock the door to the safe. _____

Police: Did you have to look up the combination to the safe?

5. Teller 3: No, sir. The manager had just given me the new combination for the day ten seconds before the man approached me. I just grouped the numbers into a date so I'd remember them for the few minutes it would take me to walk from the office to the safe. _____ Just as I'd finished thinking about the combination, the gunman was there ordering me to unlock the safe.

Police: Did the man have any unusual speech characteristics?

6. Teller 2: Yes, he did. I remember hearing him slur his *S*s. _____

Police (to Teller 1): Please demonstrate the steps you follow in order to sound the alarm.

7. Teller 1: I have to step on this foot pedal like this. _____

Police: Why did it take you so long to sound the alarm?

8. Teller 1: Well, sir, I've just started working at this bank. The alarm at my last job sounded at the push of a button. I guess I panicked a bit. I was looking for the button for a few seconds before I realized that here I have to push a foot pedal. _____

Police: Thank you, everyone. That will be all for now.

a. Acoustic encoding

b. Procedural memory

c. Context-specific memory

d. Chunking

e. Semantic encoding

f. Visual encoding

g. Episodic memory

h. Proactive inhibition

i. Retroactive inhibition

Learning How to Study

Below are descriptions of study methods that need improvement. Use the information you have learned in this chapter to fill in the blanks following the descriptions.

1. Rodney is taking a vocabulary improvement class. He is learning to recognize the roots of words and their meanings. He tries to memorize the material by repeating it to himself over and over again. Instead of doing this, he should probably try using _____.

2. Ginny is a college freshman. She is taking a course in biology, a subject she never had in high school. When she takes notes, she desperately tries to write down every word the instructor says. Instead, she should _____ the information.

3. Carin hates to read. She wants to get it over with quickly, so she reads large amounts of material at a time. Then she complains that she can never remember what she has just read. She should try using the _____ method.

CRITICAL THINKING

Sam is very frustrated. He had to release a suspect he was sure was guilty because the only witness could not remember what happened.

Sam had found the witness next to the scene of the crime about fifteen minutes after it happened. The witness was an old man who lived on the corner at the scene of the crime. He spent most of his time drinking and was in pretty bad shape. Sam pulled the witness in and let him sleep in jail, figuring that if the witness got a good, warm, safe night's sleep, a hot meal, and a chance to sober up, he would be willing to talk. However, Sam's efforts were to no avail. The witness just could not remember what he had seen. In fact, all he wanted to do was get back to his corner so that he could get a drink.

Sam, crestfallen, tells Martina that he failed and had to let the witness go.

Martina says, "All may not be lost. Grab your coat and let's go."

"Where are we going?" asks Sam.

Martina replies, "First we are going to the liquor store, and then back to the scene of the crime."

Using the five critical thinking questions in your text, the clues in the story, and what you have just learned about memory, answer the following:

1.   What is Sam's hypothesis?

2.   What is the evidence in support of Sam's hypothesis?

3.   What is Martina's alternative hypothesis?

4.   What evidence must Martina gather to support her hypothesis?

5.   What conclusions can Martina draw if the evidence she needs to collect supports her hypothesis?

PERSONAL LEARNING ACTIVITIES

1.   Describe your earliest memories of several family members and see how well they match your relatives' recollections of the same events.

2.   Do an experiment to see the effects of maintenance versus elaborative rehearsal. One way to do this would be to read a list of about twenty words or names and repeat them several times. Then write down the time of day, your full name, address, and phone number (to clear the words from your short-term memory). Without looking at the list, write as many as you can. Next, study a list of twenty words or names by associating an image with each, clear your short-term memory, and then write as many as you can. Was there a difference? Does the size of any difference depend on what type of information you are trying to learn?

3.   Do you think your memory has improved with increasing age? Why or why not? What factors do you think most influence whether you will recall a phone number, an appointment, someone's name, or lecture information?

4.   Because our memory is set up in parallel distributed processing networks, we construct memories, and we may generalize from scanty information. Visit a new store, restaurant, or library. After your visit, answer these questions: What spontaneous generalizations did you make? Were they based on your earlier experiences in similar places? How could limited or biased prior experience have influenced your opinions of this new place? What implications can you see for ethnic stereotyping and prejudice?

5.   Visit the Memory Exploratorium at http://www.exploratorium.edu/memory/lectures.html to see lectures from some of the scholars who are cited in this chapter of your textbook. If you navigate around the site a bit further, you will find some fun memory games to play, as well.

MULTIPLE-CHOICE QUESTIONS

Quiz 1

1. Steven heard his instructor say, "Remember to read the short stories by Christie, Cheever, Porter, and Sayers for next week." Because Steven is not familiar with the names, he remembers them as "Krissy, Cleever, Porter, and Savers." Steven most likely used _____ encoding.

    a. acoustic
    b. episodic
    c. semantic
    d. visual

2. The memory for how to perform a physical action is called _____ memory.

    a. episodic
    b. procedural
    c. semantic
    d. short-term

3. Which of the following is an example of an episodic memory?

    a. Recalling what you did the night you graduated from high school
    b. Remembering how to touch-type (type without looking at the keyboard)
    c. Remembering the capitals of the fifty states in the United States
    d. Remembering how to play a piano recital piece from memory

4. Nathan does not consciously think about an incident from his childhood when a red-haired neighbor gave him candy and comforted him after he skinned his knee. Due to the unintentional influence of that memory, however, Nathan tends to react positively to any red-haired people he meets; therefore, he is being influenced by his _____ memory.

    a. episodic
    b. explicit
    c. implicit
    d. procedural

5. Raquel was still studying ten minutes before her test. As she entered the classroom, she kept repeating the last sentence she had read: "One meter equals approximately 39.37 inches." This is an example of

    a. elaborative rehearsal.
    b. maintenance rehearsal.
    c. a mnemonic strategy.
    d. retrieval.

6. At the same time that Reepal is listening to her father tell about the party the family is planning, Reepal smells popcorn, hears her radio, sees lightning, and feels hot. Reepal is able to transfer the information about the party to her short-term memory primarily because of

    a. elaborative rehearsal.
    b. implicit memory cues.
    c. selective attention.
    d. transfer-appropriate processing.

7. An immediate memory span is the number of items that
    a.   can be held in the sensory registers.
    b.   are stored in long-term memory.
    c.   can be held in semantic codes.
    d.   can be recalled in perfect order following one presentation of a stimulus.

8. The capacity of short-term memory is generally described by the "magic number":
    a.   3.
    b.   5.
    c.   7.
    d.   10.

9. Which of the following sentences would require the most chunks in short-term memory if you only knew how to speak English?
    a.   John has many friends.
    b.   *Ich liebe dich.*
    c.   *Je ne sais pas.*
    d.   –.–.–.–..–..–.– (Morse code)

10. What feature of long-term memory is of the greatest help to money counterfeiters?
    a.   People usually ignore details and encode the general, underlying meaning of information.
    b.   The dominant type of encoding in long-term memory is visual encoding.
    c.   The capacity of long-term memory is limited.
    d.   Long-term memory is dependent on retrieval cues.

11. Vinnie is exasperated. He has gone to the library to look up a book for class. Even though he checked his class notes before he left, he cannot remember the name of the book. What could account for his memory lapse?
    a.   Inefficient storage in sensory memory
    b.   Information's not getting transferred to long-term memory
    c.   Problems with selective attention
    d.   Proactive inhibition

12. The patient H. M. described in your text suffered from _____ amnesia.
    a.   retrograde
    b.   anterograde
    c.   proactive
    d.   retroactive

13. Multiple-choice questions are easier to answer than essay questions because multiple-choice questions
    a.   cause more interference.
    b.   contain more retrieval cues.
    c.   use only semantic memory.
    d.   use only procedural memory.

14. Better recall of the first few words of a list from long-term memory is called the _____ effect.

    a. primacy
    b. recency
    c. fatigue
    d. parallel position

15. Alberta is a night owl. She loves to stay up late and study. However, she has so many classes this semester that she is forced to take her calculus class and study calculus in the morning when she is sluggish and a bit sleepy. Alberta's calculus teacher has given the class a take-home test. Alberta should take the test

    a. in the evening.
    b. in the afternoon.
    c. in the morning.
    d. whenever she feels like it.

16. To answer a question like "How many legs do spiders have?" a person will most likely use _____ memory.

    a. episodic
    b. semantic
    c. sensory
    d. short-term

17. An officer shows Sarah a box of office supplies believed to have been stolen from her store and then puts them at the back of the room. When Sarah is asked whether the staplers appear to be those stolen from her store, she thinks for a minute about the staplers she recalls seeing in the box and says they are like the ones stolen. To Sarah's surprise, the officer then shows her that there are no staplers in the box! Sarah must have used _____ memories to answer the question.

    a. constructive
    b. elaborative
    c. generalized
    d. implicit

18. Shorty is studying for her biology test. She is trying to remember the biological classifications kingdom, phylum, class, order, genus, and species. To help her remember, she uses the sentence "King Phillip Came Over for Good Soup" because the first letters of the words of the sentence correspond to the first letters of the different terms she needs to remember. What tool is Shorty using to improve her memory?

    a. Method of loci
    b. Mnemonic strategies
    c. Distributed practice
    d. PQ4R

19. Christy is trying to help her sixteen-year-old son with his algebra homework. It has been years since she worked on algebra, and she is having trouble remembering how to do it herself, much less be able to help him. The type of forgetting that Christy is experiencing is

    a. amnesia.
    b. decay.
    c. retroactive inhibition.
    d. proactive inhibition.

20. Cody is studying for his psychology class. He skims the chapter and thinks about what content he expects to be covered in each section. Then he reads the text, thinking of his own examples and creating visual images as he goes along. He recites the major points after each section. Which step of PQ4R has Cody skipped?

    a. preview
    b. question
    c. reflect
    d. review

Total Correct (See answer key) _____

Quiz 2

Use this quiz to reassess your learning after taking Quiz 1 and reviewing the chapter.

1. Which of the following is semantic encoding?

    a. Encoding that a movie you went to was called *Avatar*
    b. Encoding that the movie you went to had a lot of blue people
    c. Encoding that a movie you went to was about a another planet with a threatened habitat
    d. None of these

2. Colleen frequently loses her keys. To find them, she always has to sit and remember where she had them last. This is an example of

    a. semantic memory.
    b. procedural memory.
    c. episodic memory.
    d. acoustic memory codes.

3. As Kaliina completes a personal history questionnaire, she recalls her birth date, names of schools she has attended, and relatives' names. Suddenly she feels hot, flushed, and embarrassed but does not know why. Kaliina's mom realizes that Kaliina unintentionally remembers the time she filled out a similar form and then fainted. When Kaliina tries to remember her personal information, she is using _____ memory; when she feels embarrassed, she is using _____ memory.

    a. episodic; semantic
    b. semantic; episodic
    c. implicit; explicit
    d. explicit; implicit

4. Which of the following would be most effective for encoding information into long-term memory?
   a. Chunking
   b. Maintenance rehearsal
   c. Elaborative rehearsal
   d. Serial rehearsal

5. As Laura reads her psychology textbook, the image of each word is stored long enough to be processed and understood. Laura's _____ memory holds the images just long enough to allow stimulus identification to begin.
   a. long-term
   b. semantic
   c. sensory
   d. short-term

6. Ever since her accident, Rita has to constantly remind herself of what she is doing, or she forgets. For instance, when driving she has to post a note on her dashboard with her destination. Without these notes, she forgets where she is going and has to stop until she remembers again. Rita's _____ memory was damaged in the accident.
   a. sensory
   b. working
   c. long-term
   d. procedural

7. The encoding specificity principle states that
   a. newly learned information can go back and interfere with the recall of previously learned information.
   b. previously learned information can interfere with learning new information.
   c. the ability of a cue to aid retrieval depends on the degree to which it taps into information that was encoded at the time of original learning.
   d. you are most likely to recall items that are first or last on a list, but not in the middle.

8. In the case discussed in your text, H. M. (whose hippocampus is damaged) is impaired on tests of explicit, but not implicit, memory. The fact that these two memory systems seem to be supported by different regions of the brain and perform different function supports the _____ model of memory.
   a. information-processing
   b. levels-of-processing
   c. PDP
   d. multiple memory systems

9. To increase the capacity of your short-term memory, you should utilize
   a. chunking.
   b. the Brown-Peterson distractor technique.
   c. the PQ4R method.
   d. the method of loci.

10. Ted showed his third-graders pictures of famous presidents. To quiz them, he gave them clues about what these people looked like. For example, "He wore a big black hat; enjoyed reading by the fireplace; was very, very tall; and had a black beard." These clues will function as

    a. retrieval cues.
    b. primacy cues.
    c. contextual codes.
    d. acoustic memory codes.

11. Context-specific memory means that information is easier to remember when

    a. it is organized—for example, in an outline.
    b. people are in the same place they were when they learned the material.
    c. people are in the same psychological state of mind as when they learned the material.
    d. a mnemonic strategy is used.

12. Shelly is talking with Eric at an office party. He asks her about her opinion—whom she plans to vote for in the next presidential election. Shelly says she is not sure, but she usually votes for whoever will have the policies that are best for her financially. Then she says, "Oh! That reminds me. … Did you hear that the company isn't giving us our end-of-year bonus this year?" That Shelly's discussion of financial policies jogs her memory to bring up the bonus they aren't getting illustrates the concept of _____ in semantic networks.

    a. constructive memory
    b. primacy
    c. spreading activation
    d. relearning

13. If you lost the ability to retrieve any information from long-term memory, you would not be able to

    a. chunk information.
    b. recognize information in sensory memory.
    c. use the method of loci.
    d. do any of these things.

14. Marcie was in a really bad mood when she recalled the day of her graduation from college. What will she be most likely to remember?

    a. Mostly negative incidents
    b. Mostly positive incidents
    c. Negative and positive incidents equally
    d. She will have trouble recalling much of anything.

15. Which of the following statements is NOT supported by recent research in the area of false memories?

    a. It is fairly easy to create false memories of events.
    b. False memories can be as vivid as accurate ones.
    c. People may be more likely to forget unpleasant events than to forget pleasant events.
    d. People are less confident of false recovered memories than of accurate memories.

16. Retroactive inhibition occurs when
    a. new information interferes with the ability to recall old information.
    b. old information interferes with the learning of new material.
    c. old information decays.
    d. new information decays.

17. When Robin moved to a new state, her new teacher told her that the class was learning the names of all the presidents. Robin was horrified. She had painstakingly memorized all those names the year before and could not remember very many of them. To her surprise, however, learning them the second time took much less time than it had the first time. This is an example of
    a. mnemonics.
    b. release from proactive inhibition.
    c. savings.
    d. state dependence.

18. Jen has hippocampus damage; therefore, she has memory problems. Which of the following will she most likely be unable to do?
    a. Learn how to solve a puzzle
    b. Remember the names of new people she met ten minutes ago
    c. Remember a childhood birthday party
    d. Remember how to ride a bike

19. Connor has a big chemistry exam next week. He thinks he probably needs to study for about twelve hours for the exam, and it is seven days away. He decides that if he studies different sections of the text an hour and a half each night, reviewing as he goes along, he should be all right. Connor is using
    a. the method of loci.
    b. mnemonic strategies.
    c. massed practice.
    d. distributed practice.

20. Jacques was so involved in his social life his first semester that he almost flunked out. At the beginning of second semester, he asked his friends for their advice. Which friend should he NOT listen to?
    a. Friend 1: "Read the material a second time."
    b. Friend 2: "Create an outline for your lecture notes. You need to mentally organize the material somehow."
    c. Friend 3: "Ask yourself questions about the material as you read, and then look for the answers in the text."
    d. Friend 4: "Try to relate the material to information you already know."

Total Correct (See answer key) _____

ANSWERS TO FILL-IN-THE-BLANKS KEY TERMS

1. semantic memories (see Types of Memory)

2. auditory (or acoustic) memory (see Basic Memory Processes)

3.   sensory registers (see Sensory Memory)

4.   short-term (see Short-Term Memory and Working Memory)

5.   retroactive inhibition (see Why Do We Forget? The Roles of Decay and Interference)

6.   maintenance rehearsal (see Models of Memory)

7.   relearning method (see How Do We Forget?)

8.   mnemonic strategies (see Improving Your Memory)

9.   Context-specific memory (see Context and State Dependence)

10.   massed practice (see Improving Your Memory)

11.   recency (see Distinguishing Between Short-Term and Long-Term Memory)

12.   Elaborative (see Models of Memory)

13.   levels-of-processing (see Models of Memory)

14.   long-term (see Long-Term Memory)

15.   retrograde amnesia (see Brain Structures and Memory)

ANSWERS TO CONCEPTS AND EXERCISES

Memory Cues

1.   *Context-specific memory.* The context, in this case the bank, acts as a retrieval cue and helps the witnesses remember as much as possible about the robbery. (see Context and State Dependence)

2.   *Semantic encoding.* Teller 1 remembers that the robber had a coat on but does not have a visual code containing the color of the coat. (see Basic Memory Processes)

3.   *Visual encoding.* Teller 2 does have a visual memory code of the robber, which includes the color of the robber's coat. (see Basic Memory Processes)

4.   *Episodic memory.* Teller 3 is remembering an event (or episode) in which he was a participant. (see Types of Memory)

5.   *Chunking.* Teller 3 has used chunking to remember the combination to the safe. He has grouped the numbers into one meaningful unit of information: a date. (see Short-Term Memory and Working Memory)

6.   *Acoustic encoding.* Teller 2 has an acoustic memory code for the sound of the robber's voice. (see Basic Memory Processes)

7.   *Procedural memory.* Teller 1 has a procedural memory for how to sound the alarm. (see Types of Memory)

8.   *Proactive inhibition.* The old information, how to sound the alarm in the bank that Teller 1 used to work at, is interfering with her ability to remember how to sound the alarm at her present job. (see Why Do We Forget? The Roles of Decay and Interference)

Learning How to Study

1.   *Elaborative rehearsal.* Classical mnemonics are good tools for memorizing long lists of words, as Rodney has to do. Maintenance rehearsal is a good method for keeping information in short-term memory. However, it will not help Rodney place the information in long-term memory. (see Levels of Processing)

2. *Summarize.* Ginny should think about the lecture when she hears it in order to build a framework or overall organization for the material. She should write down only summaries of basic ideas. (see Improving Your Memory)

3. *PQ4R.* The PQ4R method is a series of six steps that will increase the amount of information Carin remembers from her reading assignments. (see Improving Your Memory)

ANSWERS TO CRITICAL THINKING

1. Sam's hypothesis is that the witness simply cannot remember what happened.

2. Support for Sam's hypothesis is the fact that after a hot meal, a good night's sleep, and the opportunity to sober up, the witness cannot remember.

3. Martina remembers the concepts of context-specific memory and state-dependent memory. She hypothesizes that if the witness goes back to the corner where he lives (same context) and has a drink (same state), he will be better able to remember.

4. Martina needs to carry out her hypothesis—that is, question the witness on his corner after he has had a drink and see if he can remember.

5. Martina cannot really draw any conclusions even if the man does remember. He could lie just to ensure that he is allowed to drink. Therefore, Martina can only follow up the clues that the old man provides and hope that his memory is accurate and that he is telling the truth. (*NOTE:* Critical thinking is a constant process of hypothesizing, examining evidence, rehypothesizing, and collecting more evidence. Can you think of any other hypotheses to explain the situation?)

ANSWERS TO MULTIPLE-CHOICE QUESTIONS

Circle the question numbers you answered correctly.

Quiz 1

1. a is the answer.   When acoustic memory codes are used, the errors likely to be made are errors in remembering the sound of the words. (see Basic Memory Processes)

    b.   Episodic memories are those of events you witnessed, but episodic is not a type of encoding.

    c.   Semantic encoding represents the meaning of the information. If Steven had used semantic encoding, he might have remembered something about the meaning of the names (assuming he was familiar with them, which he was not), such as the titles of the stories or the homelands of the authors.

    d   Visual encoding would require a visual stimulus or image, but the instructor said just the names.

2. b is the answer.   Remembering how to do something is procedural memory. (see Types of Memory)

    a.   Episodic memories are memories of events that occurred while you were present, such as the memory of your first day at school.

    c.   Semantic memories are memories of generalized knowledge, such as remembering the tribal names of the Plains Indians.

    d.   Remembering how to do something is not necessarily a short-term memory. It could be in long-term memory.

3.   a is the answer.   An episodic memory is memory for an event or series of events—an episode in your life. Remembering where you went and with whom on the night of high school graduation is recalling such an episode in your personal history. (see Types of Memory)

   b, d.   These are examples of procedural memories.

   c.   This is an example of a semantic memory.

4.   c is the answer.   Implicit memories are not intentionally recalled but do influence behavior. (see Explicit and Implicit Memory)

   a.   Episodic memories are memories of events, but Nathan has not recalled the childhood event; therefore, it is not what is influencing him.

   b.   Explicit memories are those we purposely try to remember. Nathan has not tried to remember the childhood incident, nor has he remembered it.

   d.   Procedural memories are skill memories. Nathan is not recalling a skill such as bike riding; he is being influenced by a subconscious childhood memory.

5.   b is the answer.   Maintenance rehearsal is a method of keeping information in short-term memory. Raquel is trying to keep in short-term memory the most recently read information. (see Models of Memory)

   a.   Elaborative rehearsal occurs when new information is related to old information in long-term memory. If Raquel tried to integrate the number of inches in a meter with other information about the metric system, she would have been using elaborative rehearsal.

   c.   A mnemonic strategy organizes material in order to improve recall later. Raquel was not doing anything other than repeating the information. She did not use mental imagery or the method of loci, for example.

   d.   Raquel was trying to keep the information in storage, not trying to retrieve it.

6.   c is the answer.   Selective attention allows the most important information processed by the sensory registers to be retained in short-term memory. (see Sensory Memory)

   a.   Reepal is not described as having used elaborative rehearsal. Elaborative rehearsal would be relating new information to old information.

   b.   Implicit memory is the unintentional recall and influence of prior experiences, but there is no such thing as an implicit memory cue.

   d.   Transfer-appropriate processing is when encoding method matches retrieval method.

7.   d is the answer.   An immediate memory span or the capacity of short-term memory is that amount of information a person can remember after one presentation of a stimulus. (see Short-Term Memory and Working Memory)

   a.   An unlimited amount of information can be stored in sensory memory, but only for a short time.

   b.   There is no span or limit on the amount of information that can be stored in long-term memory.

   c.   Items in memory can take the form of a semantic code, but items are not stored in semantic code.

8.   c is the answer.   7 is the magic number describing the capacity of short-term memory. (see Short-Term Memory and Working Memory)

a, d.   7 is the magic number describing most people's short-term memory capacity, not 3 or 10.

b.   This is a better answer than 3 or 10, but not as good as 7. The magic number describing the capacity of most people's short-term memory is 7, plus or minus 2, which makes a range of 5 to 9. 5 is in the range, but the "magic number" is actually 7.

9.   d is the answer.   Morse code uses a different "alphabet" than English does. A person who does not know Morse code would not have any information in long-term memory that would help put more than one symbol into one chunk. Therefore, the Morse code statement (which translates as the one-word sentence "No") would require the greatest number of chunks in short-term memory. (see Short-Term Memory and Working Memory)

a.   The entire sentence could be one chunk for a native English speaker.

b, c.   Both French and German use the same alphabet as English. Therefore, each word would be a chunk because information stored in long-term memory would help recognize the letters as words. However, each dot or dash of a Morse code letter would be one unit of new information, causing that statement to require a greater number of chunks.

10.   a is the answer.   Because semantic encoding is the dominant form of encoding in long-term memory, people often encode the general meaning of visual stimuli rather than specific details. Therefore, people will tend to recognize the monetary significance of a $20 bill but may miss the fine visual differences between fake $20 bills and authentic bills. (see Long-Term Memory)

b.   Semantic encoding is dominant in long-term memory. If visual encoding were dominant, counterfeiters would have a more difficult time passing off fake bills.

c.   The capacity of long-term memory is unlimited. This feature would be a hindrance to counterfeiters because people can recall previous information they received on distinguishing real bills from fake bills.

d.   Retrieval cues can aid recall, but long-term memory is not totally dependent on such cues. Even if it were, this could still be a hindrance to a counterfeiter. A slightly different feel or look to a bill could be a cue that might help people recognize that a bill is different and suspicious.

11.   b is the answer.   When Vinnie remembered what it was he needed, he put that information into short-term memory. He then probably became distracted before the memory was transferred into long-term memory. (see Long-Term Memory)

a, c.   If Vinnie checked his class notes before he left for the library, information had probably already been processed and transferred from sensory to short-term memory. Selective attention determines what is held in the sensory registers for further processing.

d.   Proactive inhibition occurs when old information in long-term memory interferes with remembering new information. In Vinnie's case, there is no suggestion of interference; he just cannot remember.

12.   b is the answer.   Anterograde amnesia is the inability to form new long-term memories. H. M. had hippocampal damage that occurred when he was twenty-seven years old and has not been able to form new episodic memories since that time. (see Brain Structures and Memory)

a.   Retrograde amnesia is the inability to remember what happened before damage or injury. H. M. was not able to form new memories but could remember events from before the hippocampal damage occurred.

c, d.   There is no such thing as proactive or retroactive amnesia. (You are probably thinking of proactive and retroactive interference.)

13. b is the answer.   The answer to a multiple-choice question is listed on the page. It will act as a retrieval cue by helping you recognize information stored in long-term memory. (see Retrieval Cues and Encoding Specificity)

   a.   Answering multiple-choice questions actually creates less interference. Retrieval cues decrease the effect of interference.

   c.   A good answer to an essay question would require more extensive semantic memory than would a multiple-choice answer.

   d.   Neither multiple-choice questions nor essay questions use only procedural memories.

14. a is the answer.   Better recall of the first few words of a list from long-term memory is called the primacy effect. (see Distinguishing Between Short-Term and Long-Term Memory)

   b.   Better recall of the last few words of a list from short-term memory is called the recency effect.

   c.   There is no such thing as the fatigue effect.

   d.   There is no such thing as the parallel position effect.

15. c is the answer.   Taking the test in the morning lets Alberta's state of mind act as a retrieval cue (utilizes state-dependent memory). (see Context and State Dependence)

   a, b, d.   At any other time of the day, Alberta would not be in the same psychological state as she was when she learned the material.

16. b is the answer.   Semantic memory contains general knowledge that is not linked to a particular event. (see Types of Memory)

   a.   Episodic memory would not answer a question about facts that are not related to a personally experienced event.

   c.   A person uses sensory memory to hear or read a question, but in order to answer the question the person must draw on information in the semantic memory.

   d.   Short-term memory lasts only eighteen seconds; therefore, it would be unlikely to contain the answer to a question of general knowledge.

17. a is the answer.   Constructive memories can be very vivid. Sarah probably thought that staplers would be likely to be in the box of office supplies and accidentally created a memory of their image. (see Constructing Memories)

   b.   There is no such thing as elaborative memories. *Elaborative rehearsal* is the term for linking new information to old information. Sarah was probably not rehearsing the information about what was in the box.

   c.   *Generalized memories* is not a term. You may have been thinking of semantic memories, but Sarah was not using her semantic memory to create the memory of a stapler.

   d.   Implicit memories are actual memories that we have not tried to retrieve but that affect us anyway. Because there were no staplers in the box, Sarah could not have an implicit memory of them.

18. b is the answer.   Shorty is using a mnemonic strategy known as an acronym. (see Improving Your Memory)

   a.   Although the method of loci is a mnemonic, this answer is too specific. The method of loci involves remembering items on a list by associating them with familiar locations.

    c.   This question provides no information about the timing and spacing of Shorty's studying. Distributed practice occurs over time, with smaller study sessions.

    d.   PQ4R involves a strategy for studying a textbook by previewing, questioning, reading, reflecting, reciting, and reviewing. This question does not describe Shorty's using this method.

19.   **b is the answer.**   Decay is the gradual disappearance of a memory. Christy has not used her algebra skills for years, and they have gradually decayed over time. (see Why Do We Forget? The Roles of Decay and Interference)

    a.   Amnesia is abnormal forgetting due to brain injury or some other kind of trauma. Forgetting algebra skills that you have not used in years is not an unusual kind of forgetting.

    c.   For retroactive inhibition to be the correct answer, learning new skills would have had to have made it difficult for Christy to recall her algebra skills. This question does not describe newly acquired memories' interfering with Christy's recall; rather, it describes a gradual decay over time from lack of use.

    d.   Proactive inhibition occurs when the process of remembering new information is disrupted by the presence of old information. For proactive inhibition to have occurred, the question would have needed to describe how learning something prior to learning algebra made it difficult for Christy to remember her algebra skills.

20.   **d is the answer.**   Cody has failed to *review* the entire chapter after reading the whole thing. (see Improving Your Memory)

    a.   Cody did preview the chapter by skimming it before starting.

    b.   Cody did question, by asking himself what content would be covered in each section as he previewed it.

    c.   Cody did reflect as he read by thinking of his own examples and creating visual images.

Now turn to the quiz analysis table at the end of this chapter to find which areas you know well and which areas you need to work on. Circle the numbers in the table for items on Quiz 1 that you answered correctly.

Quiz 2

1.   **c is the answer.**   Semantic encoding is a meaning code. Remembering what the movie was about deals with the meaning of the movie, not what the title sounded like or the movie looked like. (see Basic Memory Processes)

    a.   This is an example of an acoustic memory code.

    b.   This is an example of a visual memory code.

    d.   c is the correct answer.

2.   **c is the answer.**   Colleen has to remember where she was when she last had her keys. This is episodic memory; she will be present in the remembered event. (see Types of Memory)

    a.   Semantic memories are of general knowledge. Because Colleen is trying to remember an incident or episode that involves her presence, this cannot be the answer.

    b.   Procedural memories are of how to do something. Colleen is trying to remember an episode, not a procedure.

    d.   Acoustic memory codes represent sequences of sound. Colleen is trying to remember where she left her keys, not what sound they made.

3.   d is the answer.   Trying to recall personal information is using explicit memory; accidentally being influenced by an unintentional memory is an effect of implicit memory. (see Explicit and Implicit Memory)

    a, b.   Kaliina is not remembering an episode from her life or from general knowledge.

    c.   Implicit memories unintentionally influence us; they are not the intentional recall of personal information. (See d.)

4.   c is the answer.   Elaborative rehearsal, which is relating the new information to be remembered to information in long-term memory, is an effective way of encoding information into long-term memory. (see Models of Memory)

    a.   Chunking is an effective method for storing information in short-term memory.

    b.   Maintenance rehearsal is an effective method for retaining information in short-term memory.

    d.   There is no such thing as serial rehearsal.

5.   c is the answer.   Sensory memory lasts about a second; then the information is transferred to short-term memory or lost. (see Sensory Memory)

    a.   Long-term memory can last for years; it is not a sensory register.

    b.   Semantic memory is part of long-term memory. A network links information.

    d.   Short-term memory is involved in reading, but it is not a sensory register.

6.   b is the answer.   Short-term or working memory uses information in the immediate present (eighteen seconds). Rita cannot keep information in her working memory long enough to accomplish a task, such as making correct judgments in order to reach her destination. (see Short-Term Memory and Working Memory)

    a.   Sensory memory holds information only long enough for it to be processed further and recognized. Laura recognizes her surroundings; she just forgets why she is there.

    c.   Laura's long-term memory is fine. When she stops and thinks about it, she is able to recall her destination and how to get there.

    d.   Laura's procedural memory, her skill memory, appears to be fine—she is driving.

7.   c is the answer.   The encoding specificity principle suggests that the effectiveness of cues aiding memory retrieval depends on the degree to which they tap into information that was first encoded. (see Retrieval Cues and Encoding Specificity)

    a.   This is the definition of retroactive interference.

    b.   This is the definition of proactive interference.

    d.   This describes primacy and recency effects.

8.   d is the answer.   Multiple memory systems is a model of memory that proposes that the brain contains relatively separate memory systems based in different parts of the brain and having different functions. (see Models of Memory)

    a.   Information-processing models of memory describe how sensory, short-term, and long-term memory constantly interact and "share" information as it is encoded and retrieved. This question does not describe information moving through these memory stages.

b.   The levels-of-processing model of memory argues that the most important determinant of memory is how extensively information is encoded when it is first received. This question does not describe an encoding strategy.

c.   PDP models of memory focus on how knowledge is integrated in a network. This question does not describe a network.

9.   a is the answer.   Chunking is the ability to group information into a meaningful unit that can be stored in short-term memory. By grouping information meaningfully, you increase the capacity of your short-term memory. (see Short-Term Memory and Working Memory)

b.   The Brown-Peterson distractor technique is used to determine how long unrehearsed information remains in short-term memory. It in fact interferes with short-term memory rather than increasing capacity.

c.   The PQ4R method is a way to read a textbook by previewing, questioning, reading, reflecting, reciting, and reviewing. It would help your long-term memory, but probably not your short-term memory.

d.   The method of loci is a mnemonic strategy. It would help your long-term memory, not your short-term memory.

10.   a is the answer.   Ted has listed features that should help his students recognize the correct information stored in long-term memory: the name Abraham Lincoln. (see Retrieval Cues and Encoding Specificity)

b.   Primacy cue is not a term. You may have been thinking of primacy effect.

c, d.   When Ted's students hear his question, the clues will enter sensory memory as acoustic memory codes and then, after further processing, will enter short-term memory. However, the students will use the clues in short-term memory, not the acoustic codes, as retrieval cues to help them pull information out of long-term memory. There is no such thing as contextual coding. You may have been thinking of context-specific memory.

11.   b is the answer.   It is easier to remember material when you are in the place where you originally learned it. The surrounding environment acts as a retrieval cue. (see Context and State Dependence)

a.   Organizing material in an outline is one way to remember it more easily later on, but context-specific memory does not refer to this.

c.   State-dependence occurs when people find it easier to recall material when they are in the same psychological state of mind as they were when they learned the information. A psychological state acts as a retrieval cue.

d.   Using mnemonic strategies can improve your memory, but this is not the same thing as context-specific memory.

12.   c is the answer.   Semantic networks are links of related information. When a person recalls information from one node of the network, it can feel as if the person is very close to accessing the information needed in the next node. When that happens in the form of neural energy, it is called spreading activation. Shelly's talking about finance and politics was close to the idea of her bonus (both are related to money) in her semantic network. (see Retrieval from Semantic Memory)

a.   Constructive memory is a fabricated, but seemingly real, recollection. This question says nothing about fabricating memory.

b.   Primacy is the tendency to recall items at the beginning of a list (or anything else you are trying to remember) better than things in the middle or end.

d.   The relearning method is a way of measuring forgetting. This question is about why Shelly remembered one thing and then another, closely related thing in sequence, not about forgetting.

13.   d is the answer.   In order to chunk, you must use the information in long-term memory to help you group items into one chunk in short-term memory. The ability to recognize something in sensory memory involves retrieving a similar pattern of information or material from long-term memory. In order to use the method of loci, you must retrieve knowledge about a specific location or loci stored in long-term memory. (see Long-Term Memory)

14.   a is the answer.   We tend to remember incidents congruent with our moods. (see Context and State Dependence)

b.   Marcie would be more likely to recall positive events if she were in a positive mood, not a negative mood.

c.   Our memories tend to correspond to our moods.

d.   Our moods tend to elicit memories similar to them. Our moods do not impair memories.

15.   d is the answer.   Part of the controversy surrounding recovered memories is that people are extremely confident of their memories because they are so vivid, even though these memories may be inaccurate. To date there is no incontrovertible way to distinguish the experience of a true memory from the experience of a false memory. (see Thinking Critically: Can Traumatic Memories Be Repressed, Then Recovered?)

a, b, c.   All of these statements are supported by research on false memories.

16.   a is the answer.   The presence of new information displaces old information in short-term memory. (see Why Do We Forget? The Roles of Decay and Interference)

b.   Proactive inhibition occurs when old information disrupts the learning of new information.

c, d.   Decay is the gradual disappearance of memories.

17.   c is the answer.   Ebbinghaus discovered that relearning took much less time than learning. Savings is the difference between learning and relearning time. (see How Do We Forget?)

a.   A mnemonic strategy involves placing information in an organized context. In this question, Robin did not use any strategies or methods to relearn the names of the presidents.

b.   Release from proactive interference occurs when new information differs so greatly from old information that the old information interferes less with the learning of the new information. Robin is trying to relearn exactly the same information. There is no new information with which the old information can interfere.

d.   Because state dependence means that cues from your physical state help you to remember, Robin would have to be in the same state (mood, arousal level, and so on) she was when she first learned the names of the presidents. Not only is this not mentioned specifically in the description of her situation, but it also is unlikely that a person would be in one state when learning such a large amount of information.

18. b is the answer.   Hippocampal damage usually results in anterograde amnesia, which is the inability to form new memories. Procedural memory formation and recall appear to be unaffected, however. (see Brain Structures and Memory)

    a, d. Both of these are procedural memories. She could learn to solve a puzzle or could remember how to ride her bike.

    c.   Recall of a childhood event would be unaffected by anterograde amnesia.

19. d is the answer.   By spacing his studying over time, Connor is using distributed practice. (see Improving Your Memory)

    a.   Method of loci involves visualizing familiar places and then imagining items on a list in those places.

    b.   Mnemonic strategies organize information. Connor has focused on how to organize his time, but not on the information.

    c.   Massed practice involves cramming the entire study time into a single block of time. Connor has not done this.

20. a is the answer.   Just rereading the material is not an effective way to learn information from a text. (see Improving Your Memory)

    b, c, d. These are all good study habits to adopt.

For each question you answered correctly, circle its number. (Quiz 1 numbers are not shaded; Quiz 2 numbers are shaded.) Are there patterns in the types of questions or the topics you got wrong that could direct your further study? Did you improve from Quiz 1 to Quiz 2?

QUIZ REVIEW

Topic	Type of Question		
	Definition	Comprehension	Application
The Nature of Memory			
Basic Memory Processes			1
			1
Types of Memory	2		3, 16
			2
Explicit and Implicit Memory			4
			3
Models of Memory			5
		4	8
Storing New Memories			
Sensory Memory			6
			5
Short-Term Memory and Working Memory	7	8	9
		9	6
Long-Term Memory		10	11
			13
Distinguishing Between Short-Term and Long-Term Memory	14		
Retrieving Memories			
Retrieval Cues and Encoding Specificity		13	
	7		10
Context and State Dependence			15
	11		14
Retrieval from Semantic Memory			
			12
Constructing Memories			17
Forgetting			
How Do We Forget?			
			17
Why Do We Forget? The Roles of Decay and Interference			19
	16		
Thinking Critically: Can Traumatic Memories Be Repressed, Then Recovered?			
		15	

	Type of Question		
Topic	**Definition**	**Comprehension**	**Application**
Biological Bases of Memory			
Brain Structures and Memory		12	
			18
Applications of Memory Research			
Improving Your Memory			18, 20
			19, 20

Total correct by quiz:

Quiz 1:	
Quiz 2:	

CHAPTER 8

Cognition and Language

OUTLINE

<u>Cognitive psychology</u> is the study of mental processes by which the information humans receive from their environment is modified, made meaningful, stored, retrieved, used, and communicated to others. Cognitive psychologists' collaboration with neuroscience has led to the field of *cognitive neuroscience*, which helps us understand the relationship between the mind and brain.

I. BASIC FUNCTIONS OF THOUGHT
    A. The Circle of Thought
        The five core functions of human thinking—describe, elaborate, decide, plan, and guide action—form a circle of thought. An <u>information-processing system</u> receives information, represents the information with symbols, and then manipulates those representations. <u>Thinking</u> is the manipulation of mental representations.

    B. Measuring Information Processing
        1. *Mental Chronometry.* Researchers study the time it takes to go through the stages of information processing, or mental chronometry. <u>Reaction time</u> is the time elapsed between the presentation of a stimulus or information and a response. Several factors influence reaction time in quick decisions: complexity, stimulus-response compatibility, expectancy, and speed-accuracy tradeoff.
        2. *Evoked Potentials.* <u>Evoked potentials</u> are used to analyze mental events and their timing. Evoked potentials are changes in voltage on an electroencephalogram (EEG) as the brain responds to specific events.
        3. *Neuroimaging.* PET scans and fMRI technologies help scientists image the brain, and cognitive neuroscientists can watch what happens during information processing. When a task is new and difficult, frontal lobe activity is higher than when the task is well learned. At the point a task is well learned, activation is greater in the hippocampus, suggesting the task is performed from memory.

II. MENTAL REPRESENTATIONS: THE INGREDIENTS OF THOUGHT
    A. Concepts
        <u>Concepts</u> are categories of objects, events, or ideas with common properties, such as the way they look or the subjects they contain.

        1. *Types of Concepts.* Formal concepts can be defined by a set of characteristics that all members have and no nonmembers have. <u>Natural concepts</u> (also known as a <u>natural category</u>) are concepts whose members do not have fixed, defined sets of features but must have at least some typical characteristics that define the concept. <u>Prototypes</u> are objects or events that best represent a natural concept by containing all or most of the characteristic features of the concept.
    B. Propositions
        A <u>proposition</u> is a mental representation that expresses a relationship between concepts. Propositions can be either true or false.

    C. Schemas, Scripts, and Mental Models
        <u>Schemas</u> are our general knowledge about categories of objects, places, events, and people.

1. *Scripts.* Scripts are schemas about familiar sequences of activity.
2. *Mental Models.* Representations of particular situations or arrangements of objects that guide our thinking about them are called mental models. When our mental models are incomplete, we tend to make mistakes.

D. Images and Cognitive Maps
Thinking is sometimes based on visual image manipulation, such as rotation of a mental image of an object. Mental images may be called *analogical representations*. Cognitive maps are mental models of the spatial arrangements in familiar parts of the world.

III. THINKING STRATEGIES
Reasoning is the process by which we generate arguments, evaluate them, and reach conclusions.

A. Formal Reasoning
The mental procedures that yield a valid conclusion are known as formal reasoning. Algorithms are systematic methods that always reach a correct result. Rules of logic provide a set of statements that are a formula for drawing valid conclusions about the world. Logical arguments contain two or more premises known as syllogisms. The conclusion is an inference based on these premises and uses deductive reasoning. Logic errors include belief bias and limits on working memory.

1. Belief bias occurs when what we already know biases our reasoning processes. It is related to the more general problem of confirmation bias in which we tend to seek evidence and conclusions that are consistent with our existing beliefs.

2. If a logical task requires that you keep more information in your short-term memory than its capacity will allow, then logical errors may ensue.

B. Informal Reasoning
Informal reasoning involves inducing a conclusion on the basis of specific facts or examples and is known as inductive reasoning. For example, people tend to use heuristics, or mental shortcuts, rather than algorithms, which always yield a correct solution. These shortcuts are generally easy to use and work well, although they can bias thinking and result in error. Research has revealed a *dual process model* indicating that we sometimes use the quicker intuitive thinking systems that rely on such shortcuts, and other times use the more taxing rational analysis.

1. *The Anchoring Heuristic.* The anchoring heuristic (also known as the anchoring bias) occurs when one estimates the probability of an event not by starting from scratch, but by adjusting an earlier estimate.
2. *The Representativeness Heuristic.* The representativeness heuristic occurs when people decide whether an example belongs in a certain class on the basis of how similar it is to other items in that class, while ignoring base rates.
3. *The Availability Heuristic.* The availability heuristic involves judging the likelihood of an event or the correctness of a hypothesis based on how easily the hypothesis or examples of that event come to mind.

IV. PROBLEM SOLVING
A. Strategies for Problem Solving
1. *Incubation.* Incubation involves setting a problem aside for a while and thinking about other things. This allows you to forget incorrect ideas that may have been blocking you from a solution. Incubation alone may not be sufficient, however.
2. *Means-end analysis.* Means-end analysis involves continuously asking where you are in relation to your final goal, and then deciding on the means by which you can get one step closer to it. This process of identifying smaller subgoals that lead to the solution is known as *decomposition*.

3. *Working Backward. Working backward* is a problem-solving strategy that involves starting with the solution and working backward from it to determine what you need to generate or obtain that solution.

4. *Using Analogies.* Using *analogies* involves trying to find similarities between the present problem you are trying to solve and other problems you have encountered before.

B. Focus on Research Methods: Locating Analogical Thinking

To study the relationship between brain activity and analogical mapping, researchers used PET scans and asked participants to perform two tasks in succession. The tasks made similar demands on the brain with the exception that one of the tasks required analogical thinking, whereas the other did not. Psychologists then "subtracted" the brain activity recorded for the task without analogical demands from the activity recorded for the task requiring participants to make analogies. Areas that remained "active" after the subtraction—mainly the left frontal and parietal lobes—were taken as evidence of the source of analogical thinking. Future research is necessary to determine whether these areas are activated in all analogical thinking or only in certain types of analogical thinking.

C. Obstacles to Problem Solving

1. *Multiple Hypotheses.* Testing the incorrect hypothesis first when more than one hypothesis exists can delay problem solving.

2. *Mental Sets.* A <u>mental set</u> is the tendency for old patterns of problem solving to persist, even when better strategies might be available. <u>Functional fixedness</u>, the inability to use objects in new ways, can also impede problem solving and is related to mental sets in that experience works against thinking of novel ways to use objects.

3. *Ignoring Negative Evidence.* We do not use the *lack* of evidence as often as we should when testing a hypothesis.

4. *The <u>Confirmation Bias</u>.* Once we choose a hypothesis, we tend to interpret available information as confirming it. This is like the anchoring heuristic, in which we anchor on our first explanation and are reluctant to disconfirm it and let it go.

D. Building Problem-Solving Skills

Experts efficiently use old information to organize new material into smaller, more meaningful units and use their experience as a guide. However, experts need to beware of mental sets, functional fixedness, and confirmation biases. There is a fine line between using an expert experience base and being trapped by it.

E. Problem Solving by Computer

<u>Artificial-intelligence (AI)</u> scientists develop computer systems that imitate the products of human perception and thought. These computerized *expert systems* can perform as well as, and sometimes better, than humans.

1. *Symbolic Reasoning and Computer Logic.* Expert systems are computer programs that solve very specific problems. But these systems require an extensive knowledge base and an inference engine. Unfortunately, the computer's expertise in one area cannot be easily transferred to a different domain or area. They are not able to use analogical thinking the way humans can. Finally, these systems rest on a series of if-then statements, and it can sometimes be difficult to get the computer to recognize the "if" conditions.

2. *Neural Network Models.* Many AI specialists have begun to use a connectionist or neural network approach because much of intelligent diagnostics and problem solving depends on recognition and classification of conditions and patterns. The capacities of such systems, though, still fall short of human neural networks.

3. *Computer-Assisted Problem Solving.* Computer-human combinations are increasingly being used to solve problems more efficiently than either could do alone. Computers can reduce error by keeping track of findings from previous tests, listing possible tests yet to be tried, and indicating that a certain sequence of tests should be tried.

V. DECISION MAKING

Risky decisions are decisions made when the result is uncertain.

A. Evaluating Options

Multiattribute decision making involves choosing between options that have both positive and negative features, or attributes.

1. *Comparing Attributes.* Multiattribute decisions can be difficult because comparisons of many attributes must be made despite the limited storage capacity of working memory. Utility is the subjective, personal value of each attribute. The positive and negative utilities of each attribute must be weighed in a decision.

2. *Estimating Probabilities.* Good decisions maximize expected value. People must take into account the probabilities of certain outcomes and the outcome value in decision making.

B. Biases and Flaws in Decision Making

People do not always maximize expected values for several reasons.

1. *Gains, Losses, and Probabilities.* Positive utilities are not mirror images of negative utilities; people feel worse about losing a certain amount than they feel good about gaining the same amount, a phenomenon known as *loss aversion.* Most people see large losses as disproportionately more serious than small losses. They also evaluate gains differently depending on what the starting point was. People also assess the probability of a decision incorrectly because they tend to estimate incorrectly the probability of rare or frequent events. They may also think that the probability of a future event is influenced by a pattern of past events, a bias known as the *gambler's fallacy.* Finally, people tend to have too much confidence in their own predictions.

2. *How Biased Are We?* Psychologists are not sure how to answer this question. Do people make too many decision-making mistakes because they are attempting to satisfy criteria other than expected value? For example, it is hard to quantify the "value" of saving a human life, even if the cost to do so is great.

C. Linkages: Group Processes in Problem Solving and Decision Making

Groups tend to begin problem solving by polling the stated preferences of group members, with majority factions having a greater influence than smaller, more extreme factions, on the group decision.

Yet, group interaction shapes decision-making processes. Group discussions follow a consistent pattern. Various options are proposed and debated until a minimally acceptable solution is agreed on. This option is staunchly defended against all newer options and is likely to become the group's decision. The outcomes of group decisions may be more extreme than individual decisions—a phenomenon called *group polarization.*

When a correct solution can be easily demonstrated to all members, groups usually outperform individuals. On less clear-cut problems, though, the best group member may outperform the group. Because of *social loafing* and *groupthink* a group may well underperform its ostensible capabilities.

A critical element in successful group problem solving is the sharing of individual members' unique information and expertise. *Brainstorming* groups in particular struggle to outperform individuals, although special instructions or interacting electronically can remediate this problem.

VI. LANGUAGE
  A. The Elements of Language
     A language has two basic elements: symbols and grammar.

     1. *From Sounds to Sentences.* Phonemes are the smallest unit of sound with meaning. Morphemes are the smallest unit of language with meaning. Words are made of morphemes, which in turn consist of phonemes. Rules of syntax determine the ways in which words are combined to form sentences. Semantics are rules that govern the meanings of words and sentences.
     2. *Surface Structure and Deep Structure.* The surface structure of a sentence (the string of words) may have more than one meaning, or deep structure.
  B. Understanding Speech
     1. *Perceiving Words and Sentences.* The gaps we hear between spoken words are not real but are perceived because of top-down processing. Syntax, memories, and knowledge of the world help us comprehend and remember verbal and written communication.
     2. Understanding speech is also guided by nonverbal cues.

  C. The Development of Language
     1. *The First Year.* At about four months of age, babies begin repeating simple syllables, called infant vocalizations, or babblings. At about nine months, babies stop uttering sounds that are not part of the language to which they are exposed. At twelve to eighteen months, babies utter their first real words, which usually are proper names and object words. In the one-word stage, children tend to use one word at a time and overextend its use to mean more than one object.
     2. *The Second Year.* This one-word stage of speech lasts for about 6 months. Then, these appear at about eighteen to twenty-four months of age as two-word pairs. These first sentences are *telegraphic*: brief and to the point. Next are three-word sentences that use subject-verb-object sequences. Word endings begin to appear, but at first are used incorrectly. Finally, adjectives and auxiliary verbs are added. By age five, children have acquired most of the syntax of their native language.
     3. *The Third Year and Beyond.* At about age three, children begin to use auxiliary verbs, question words, and clauses.
  D. How Is Language Acquired?
     1. *Conditioning, Imitation, and Rules.* Conditioning, imitation, and rules do not fully explain the development of language in children. However, when adults provide correct revisions of a child's conversation, the learning process is enhanced.
     2. *Biological Bases for Language Acquisition.* Noam Chomsky suggests that children possess an innate *universal grammar* that helps them learn the complexities of language. Some children display *Specific Language Impairment.* There appears to be a *critical period* for language development.
     3. *Bilingualism.* Children in a bilingual environment prior to the end of the critical period show enhanced language performance. Those children with similar mastery of two languages, or *balanced bilinguals*, may have more cognitive flexibility and creativity.
  E. Thinking Critically: Can Nonhumans Use Language?
     What am I being asked to believe or accept?

     Some researchers believe that nonhumans can use language.

     What evidence is available to support the assertion?

     Research with chimpanzees and gorillas suggests that animals can learn to use words and adopt a crude grammar. They are able to use words to refer to things not present, to master up to 500 words, and enjoy their communication skills, using them to interact spontaneously with their caretakers. Grammatical sensitivity has also been observed in dolphins.

Are there alternative ways of interpreting the evidence?

Other researchers argue that chimps' very short sentence structure and lack of spontaneous and creative use of language mean that they are incapable of language. The so-called language learned is argued to be little different from a dog begging for table scraps. Animals tend not to point, while humans do from a very early age. In addition, experimenter bias may explain some of the "language-learning" results seen in chimpanzees.

What additional evidence would help to evaluate the alternatives?

Studies in the area are few in number. More studies using more subjects need to be done. In addition, researchers need to examine the limiting capacity of nonhuman working memory and its effects on animals' use of language. Research on how nonhumans acquire language through listening and observing would also be helpful.

What conclusions are most reasonable?

Psychologists are still not in full agreement on this issue. The communication displayed by animals is much more limited than human children's language. And the level of language produced by chimps so far falls short of matching their very high levels of intelligence. But the evidence does suggest that under the right conditions, animals can learn language-like skills.

F. Culture, Language, and Thought
Research across cultures and within North American culture suggests that language does not determine what we can think about, but it does influence how we think, solve problems, and make decisions. Whorf called this *linguistic determinism*. Rosch's research failed to support this notion in total, leading to a weaker version of Whorf's hypothesis being more widely accepted. Language can affect thinking, and this is clearly demonstrated in *framing effects*.

KEY TERMS

1. **Cognitive psychology** is the study of the mental processes by which information from the environment is modified, made meaningful, stored, retrieved, used, and communicated to others. (see introductory section)

Example: Ginny is studying how people process text messages, and what the emotional impact of text messages is compared to verbal language.

2. An **information-processing system** is made up of mechanisms for receiving information, representing it with symbols, and manipulating it. (see The Circle of Thought)

REMEMBER: Psychologists consider people similar to information-processing systems in the way they take in information, pass it through several stages, and finally act on it.

3. **Thinking** is the manipulation of mental representations. (see The Circle of Thought)

4. A **reaction time** is the time between the presentation of a stimulus and an overt response to it. (see Measuring Information Processing)

Example: Susan and several of her friends are standing in her office looking for her keys. Suddenly, Dave calls out, "Hey!" and throws her the keys. The reaction time is the time it takes Susan to look up and get ready to catch the keys after hearing Dave call out.

5. An **Evoked potential** is a small, temporary change in EEG voltage in the brain that is caused by some stimulus. (see Measuring Information Processing)

Example: About 300 milliseconds after a stimulus is presented, a large positive peak—the P300—occurs. The timing can be affected by how long sensory processing and perception take.

REMEMBER: Evoke means to "cause" or "produce." Stimuli evoke, or produce, small changes in the brain. Psychologists have instruments that allow them to record these changes for study.

6.   **Concepts** are categories of objects, events, or ideas that have common properties. (see Concepts)

7.   **Natural concepts** (or **natural categories**) are concepts that have no fixed set of defining features, but have a set of characteristic features. (see Concepts)

Example: The concept of vegetable is a natural concept. There are no rules or lists of features that describe every single vegetable. Many vegetables are difficult to recognize as such because this concept is so "fuzzy." Tomatoes are not vegetables, but most people think they are. Rhubarb is a vegetable, but most people think it is not.

8.   A **prototype** is a member of a natural concept that possesses all or most of its characteristic features. (see Concepts)

Example: Try this trick on your friends. Have them sit down with a pencil and paper. Tell them to write down all the numbers that you will say and the answers to three questions that you will ask. Recite about fifteen numbers of at least three digits each, and then ask your friends to write down the name of a tool, a color, and a flower. About 60 to 80 percent of them will write down "hammer," "red," and "rose" because these are common prototypes of the concepts tool, color, and flower. Prototypes come to mind most easily when people try to think of a concept.

9.   **Propositions** are mental representations of the relationships between concepts. (see Propositions)

Example: "Carla (concept) likes to buy flowers (concept)" is a proposition that shows a relationship between two concepts. "Dogs bark" is a proposition that shows a relationship between a concept (dog) and a property of that concept (bark).

10.   **Schemas** are generalizations about categories of objects, events, and people. (see Schemas, Scripts, and Mental Models)

Example: Dana's schema for books is that they are a bound stack of paper with stories or other information written on each page. When her fifth-grade teacher suggests that each student read a book on the computer, Dana is confused until she sees that the same information could be presented on a computer screen. Dana has now revised her schema for books to include those presented through electronic media.

11.   **Scripts** are mental representations of familiar sequences of activity. (see Schemas, Scripts, and Mental Models)

Example: As a college student, you have a script of how events should transpire in the classroom: students enter the classroom, sit in seats facing the professor, and take out their notebooks. The professor lectures while students take notes, until the bell rings and they all leave.

12.   **Mental models** are representations of particular situations or arrangements of objects that guide our interaction with them. (see Schemas, Scripts, and Mental Models)

Example: There is a toy that is a board with different types of latches, fasteners, and buttons on it. As children play with it, they form a mental model of how these things work. Then, when they see a button, perhaps a doorbell, they will have an understanding of how it works.

13.   **Images** are mental representations of visual information. (see Images and Cognitive Maps)

Example: Kiernan can picture, or visualize, the mountains he stayed at on vacation last year. When someone talks about mountains, this image comes into his mind.

14.   **Cognitive maps** are mental models of familiar parts of the environment. (see Images and Cognitive Maps)

Example: Lashon's friend asks, "How do you get to the mall from here?" To answer the question, Lashon pictures the roads and crossroads between their location and the mall and is able to describe the route for his friend to travel.

15.   **Reasoning** is the process by which people generate and evaluate arguments and reach conclusions about them. (see Thinking Strategies)

16.   **Formal reasoning** (also called logical reasoning) is the process of following a set of rigorous procedures for reaching valid conclusions. (see Formal Reasoning)

17.   **Algorithms** are systematic procedures that cannot fail to produce a correct solution to a problem if a solution exists. (see Formal Reasoning)

Example: To solve the math problem $3{,}999{,}999 \times 1{,}111{,}111$ using an algorithm, you would multiply the numbers out:

$$
\begin{array}{r}
3{,}999{,}999 \\
\times \quad\quad 1{,}111{,}111 \\
\hline
4{,}444{,}442{,}888{,}889
\end{array}
$$

This computation takes a long time. You could, however, use a heuristic to solve the problem: round the numbers to $4{,}000{,}000 \times 1{,}000{,}000$, multiply 4×1, and add the appropriate number of zeros ($000{,}000{,}000{,}000$). Although simpler and faster, this heuristic approach yields a less accurate solution than that produced by the algorithmic approach.

18.   **Logic** is a system of formulas for drawing valid conclusions. (see Formal Reasoning)

19.   A **syllogism** is an argument made up of two propositions, called premises, and a conclusion based on those premises. (see Formal Reasoning)

Example: Here is an incorrect syllogism: All cats are mammals (premise), and all people are mammals (premise). Therefore, all cats are people (conclusion).

20.   **Confirmation bias** is the tendency to pay more attention to evidence in support of one's hypothesis than to evidence that refutes that hypothesis. (see Formal Reasoning)

Example: Brady is sure that the reason his car isn't running is because his battery isn't working. He doesn't think to disconfirm this hypothesis by noticing that his light turns on when he gets out of the car.

21.   **Informal reasoning** is the process of evaluating a conclusion, theory, or course of action based on the believability of evidence. (see Informal Reasoning)

7.   **Heuristics** are time-saving mental shortcuts used in reasoning. (see Informal Reasoning)

Example: You are trying to think of a four-letter word for "labor" to fill in a crossword puzzle. Instead of thinking of all possible four-letter combinations (an algorithmic approach), you think first of synonyms for labor—job, work, chore—and choose the one with four letters.

8.   The **anchoring heuristic** is a mental shortcut that involves basing judgments on existing information. (see Informal Reasoning)

Example: Jean is getting ready to move to the city. Her parents lived there ten years ago and were familiar with the area that she wants to move into now. Ten years ago it was an exceedingly dangerous neighborhood. Since that time, however, many changes have taken place, and the area now has one of the lowest crime rates in the city. Jean's parents think that the crime rate may have improved a little, but, despite the lower crime rate, they just cannot believe that the area is all that safe.

9. The **representativeness heuristic** is a mental shortcut that involves judging whether something belongs in a given class on the basis of its similarity to other members of that class. (see Informal Reasoning)

   Example: After examining a patient, Dr. White recognizes symptoms characteristic of a disease that has a base-rate frequency of 1 in 22 million people. Instead of looking for a more frequently occurring explanation of the symptoms, the doctor decides that the patient has this very rare disease. She makes this decision based on the similarity of this set of symptoms (example) to those of the rare disease (a larger class of events or items).

10. The **availability heuristic** is a mental shortcut in which judgments are based on information that is most easily brought to mind. (see Informal Reasoning)

    Example: A friend of yours has just moved to New York City. You cannot understand why he has moved there, because the crime rate is so high. You hear from a mutual acquaintance that your friend is in the hospital. You assume that he was probably mugged, because this is the most available information in your mind about New York City.

11. A **mental set** is the tendency for old patterns of problem solving to persist, even when they might not be the best ones available. (see Obstacles to Problem Solving)

    Example: The last time his CD player door would not open, Del tapped the front of it and it popped open. This time when it will not open, Del does the same thing—not noticing that the power isn't even on!

12. **Functional fixedness** is a tendency to think about familiar objects in familiar ways that may prevent using them in other ways. (see Obstacles to Problem Solving)

    Example: Lisa is very creative in her use of the objects in her environment. One day she dropped a fork down the drain of the kitchen sink. She took a small refrigerator magnet and tied it to a chopstick. She then put the chopstick down the drain, let the fork attach itself to the magnet, and carefully pulled the fork out of the drain. *If* Lisa had viewed the magnet as being capable only of holding material against the refrigerator and the chopstick as being useful only for eating Chinese food, she would have experienced functional fixedness.

28. **Artificial intelligence (AI)** is the field that studies how to program computers to imitate the products of human perception, understanding, and thought. (see Problem Solving by Computer)

    Example: Lydia plays chess against a computer that has been programmed with rules, strategies, and outcome probabilities.

29. **Utility** is a subjective measure of value. (see Evaluating Options)

    Example: Juan prefers large classes because he likes the stimulation of hearing many opposing viewpoints. In choosing courses, Juan decides whether the positive utility of the preferred class size is greater than the negative utility of the inconvenient meeting time.

30. **Expected value** is the total benefit to be expected if a decision were to be repeated several times. (see Evaluating Options)

    Example: Sima does not have enough money for this month's rent. She knows that going on a shopping spree would be a wonderful stress reliever in the short run, but the increase in her amount of debt would outweigh the enjoyment in the long run.

31. **Language** is composed of symbols and a set of rules for combining them that provide a vehicle for communication. (see The Elements of Language)

Example: The German and English languages use the same symbols (Roman characters), but each has a different set of rules for combining those symbols. The Russian language has different symbols (Cyrillic characters) as well as different rules of grammar.

32. **Grammar** is a set of rules for combining the words used in a given language. (see The Elements of Language)

33. **Phonemes** are the smallest units of sound that affect the meaning of speech. (see The Elements of Language)

    Example: Phonemes are sounds that make a difference in the meaning of a word. By changing the beginning phoneme, the meanings of the following words are changed: <u>b</u>in, <u>th</u>in, <u>w</u>in.

    REMEMBER: Phono means "sound." Phonemes are sounds that change the meaning of a word.

34. **Morphemes** are the smallest units of language that have meaning. (see The Elements of Language)

    Example: Any prefix or suffix has meaning. The suffix -<u>s</u> means "plural," as in the words bat<u>s</u> or flower<u>s</u>. The prefix <u>un</u>- means "not," as in <u>un</u>happy or <u>un</u>rest. <u>S</u> and <u>un</u> are morphemes for the words *bat, flower, happy,* and *rest.*

35. **Syntax** is the set of rules that govern the formation of phrases and sentences in a language. (see The Elements of Language)

    REMEMBER: Syn means "together" (as in *synchronized*). Syntax is the set of rules that determines the order of words when they are put together.

36. **Semantics** is the rules governing the meaning of words and sentences. (see The Elements of Language)

    Example: The sentence "Wild lamps fiddle with precision" has syntax but incorrect semantics.

37. **Surface structure** is the order in which words are arranged in sentences. (see The Elements of Language)

    Example: The sentence "You are killing me!" is a particular order of words that may have several meanings (deep structure) depending on the context and verbal cues that accompany its utterance.

38. **Deep structure** is an abstract representation of the underlying meaning of a given sentence. (see The Elements of Language)

    Example: "The eating of the animal was grotesque." The surface structure of this sentence is the order of the words. The deep structure contains at least two meanings: The way the animal is eating could be grotesque, and the way people are eating the animal could be grotesque.

39. **Infant vocalizations**, or **babblings,** are the first sounds infants make that resemble speech. (see The Development of Language)

    Example: While Patrick plays, he says, "Ba-ba-ba."

13. The **one-word stage** is a stage of language development during which children tend to use one word at a time. (see The Development of Language)

    Example: When McKelvey wants the kitchen lights turned on, she points to the light and says, "Lah-ee" rather than a full sentence.

FILL-IN-THE-BLANKS KEY TERMS

This section will help you check your knowledge of the key terms introduced in this chapter. Fill in each blank with the appropriate term from the list of key terms in the previous section.

1. The most commonly given example of a natural concept is a(n) _____.

2. A small, temporary change in EEG voltage in the brain that is brought on by a particular stimulus is called a(n) _____.

3. Cognitive representations of how things work are called _____.

4. _____ are representations of familiar patterns of human activities.

5. An argument made up of two assertions and a conclusion is called a(n) _____.

6. A shortcut in problem solving is called a(n) _____.

7. The _____ is a method of estimating the probability of an outcome based on initial information without appropriate adjustment for later information.

8. _____ are systematic procedures that always produce solutions to problems.

9. The set of rules that dictates the order in which words should be put together to form a sentence is called _____.

10. _____ is a term used to describe the stage of speech for twelve-to-eighteen-month-old infants.

11. _____ are the first speech-resembling sounds that infants make, starting at about four months of age.

12. The meaning of a sentence is expressed in its _____.

13. Even though a suffix is not a word, a suffix is considered a(n) _____, because it carries meaning.

14. When people are unable to solve a problem because they cannot recognize how they could use a familiar tool in a new way, this is called _____.

15. A _____ exists when old solutions interfere with a person's ability to solve a new problem.

Total Correct (See answer key) _____

LEARNING OBJECTIVES

1. Define <u>cognitive psychology</u>. (see Basic Functions of Thought)

2. Describe the core functions that form a *circle of thought*. (see The Circle of Thought)

3. Define <u>information-processing system</u> and <u>thinking</u>. Discuss the relationship between information-processing systems and decision making in humans. (see The Circle of Thought)

4. Define *mental chronometry* and <u>reaction time</u>. Describe how *complexity, stimulus-response compatibility, expectancy,* and *speed-accuracy tradeoff* influence reaction time. (see Measuring Information Processing)

5. Define <u>evoked potentials</u>. Discuss the use of evoked brain potentials in the study of mental chronometry. (see Measuring Information Processing)

6. Describe neuroimaging techniques and how they are useful in studying information-processing. (see Measuring Information Processing)

7. Define <u>concept</u>. Describe the difference between formal and <u>natural concepts,</u> and give an example of each. Explain the role of <u>prototypes</u> in natural concepts. (see Concepts)

8.   Define <u>propositions</u>, <u>schemas</u>, <u>scripts</u>, and <u>mental models,</u> and describe their role in the thinking process. (see Propositions; see also Schemas, Scripts, and Mental Models)

9.   Describe the manipulation of mental <u>images</u>. Define <u>cognitive maps</u> and discuss their use and the biases that distort them. (see Images and Cognitive Maps)

10.   Define <u>reasoning</u>, <u>formal reasoning</u>, <u>algorithms</u>, rules of <u>logic</u>, and <u>syllogisms</u>. Discuss the causes of errors in logical reasoning. (see Thinking Strategies; see also Formal Reasoning)

11.   Define <u>informal reasoning</u> and <u>heuristics</u>. Describe and give an example of the <u>anchoring</u>, <u>representativeness</u>, and <u>availability</u> heuristics. (see Informal Reasoning)

12.   Describe the problem-solving strategies: *incubation*, *means-end analysis, working backward*, and *analogies*. (see Strategies for Problem Solving)

13.   Explain why multiple hypotheses, <u>mental sets</u>, <u>functional fixedness</u>, <u>ignoring negative evidence</u>, and <u>confirmation bias</u> can hinder problem solving. Give an example of each. (see Obstacles to Problem Solving)

14.   Explain why an expert is better at solving problems. Explain why experts use chunking more efficiently than novices do. Discuss the dangers of being an expert when solving problems. (see Building Problem-Solving Skills)

15.   Define <u>artificial intelligence (AI)</u>, symbolic reasoning, and neural networks. Describe how expert systems can be used. (see Problem Solving by Computer)

16.   Give an example of *multiattribute decision making*. Define <u>utility</u> and <u>expected value</u>, and explain their role in the decision-making process. (see Evaluating Options)

17.   Describe the sources of bias and flaws in decision making in regard to perceptions of utilities, losses, and probabilities. Be sure to include *loss aversion* and *gambler's fallacy*. (see Biases and Flaws in Decision Making)

18.   Describe the impact of groups on decision making. Outline the typical discussion patterns in groups trying to make a decision. Define group polarization and list the factors that improve or impair group decision making. (see Linkages: Group Processes in Problem Solving and Decision Making)

19.   List the components of language. Define <u>language</u> and <u>grammar</u>. (see The Elements of Language)

20.   Define <u>phoneme</u>, <u>morpheme</u>, and word. Give an example of the phonemes and morphemes in a word. (see The Elements of Language)

21.   Define <u>syntax</u> and <u>semantics</u>. Explain how syntax and semantics help us comprehend language. (see The Elements of Language)

22.   Define <u>surface structure</u> and <u>deep structure</u>. Describe the surface and deep structures of a particular sentence. (see The Elements of Language)

23.   Discuss the role of *bottom-up processing, top-down processing*, and nonverbal cues in the comprehension of language. (see Understanding Speech)

24.   Describe language development in children. Define <u>babblings</u>, the <u>one-word stage</u>, *telegraphic* speech, and complex sentences. (see The Development of Language)

25.   Discuss the roles of conditioning, imitation, nature, and nurture in language development. (see How Is Language Acquired?)

26.   Describe the impact of a bilingual environment on the development of language abilities. (see How Is Language Acquired?)

27. Discuss the controversy surrounding the question: Can nonhumans use language? and describe what conclusions are reasonable given the evidence so far. (see Thinking Critically: Can Nonhumans Use Language?)

28. Discuss the relationship among language, culture, and perception. Explain Whorf's *linguistic determinism* and how Rosch's study has led to a modified view of Whorf's hypothesis. (see Culture, Language, and Thought)

CONCEPTS AND EXERCISES

Approaches to Problem Solving

Below are several problems. Read the description of each problem and answer the questions following it.

1. Viola's parents have just moved to a suburb of Chicago. She is home for a visit for the first time since they moved. To her embarrassment, she is always getting lost because she has not yet learned the organization of the streets.

    What is Viola trying to develop?

2. Although it was a stormy night, it was perfect for a cozy and romantic meal. Pete brought in the pasta and salad while Erin put on some CDs and dimmed the overhead light. As they sat down to eat, the light went out. Pete jumped up, yelling that lightning must have struck the power lines. Erin watched Pete's tirade while tapping her foot to the beat of the music.

    Why did Erin *not* get upset?

    What was Pete's error?

3. Al is lost somewhere in Paris. He wants to get to a museum that a friend told him to visit, but he has no idea where he is. He stops someone on the street and asks for directions. The Parisian says that she can give Al either a tricky shortcut or a very long set of directions that will be easy to follow. Al decides to take the long way because it will guarantee his arrival at the museum, even though it will take a bit longer.

    What two choices did the Parisian offer Al?

    Which one did Al choose?

4. Carlotta, a color analyst at a paper mill, is upset because something is wrong with the paper's color as it comes off the machine. She and the people who work with her have thought about all the previous color problems they have encountered, but they cannot find a solution. Carlotta decides to bring in a person who has just started to work in the paper room and ask him what he thinks.

    What might be preventing Carlotta from solving the problem?

Structures of Language

Below are two sentences. Identify the structures of language as indicated. (*HINT:* When you look for morphemes, use a dictionary to discover the prefixes, suffixes, and roots of words.)

1. *The husband's dinner was terrible.* Underline all the morphemes and identify at least two deep structures.

2. *My friend painted me in his backyard.* Underline all the morphemes and identify at least two deep structures.

CRITICAL THINKING

Sam and Martina are just arriving at the scene of what promises to be a media event. Sylvia Star, a famous ninety-eight-year-old gossip columnist, has been found dead in her bed. Sylvia has a long list of enemies, and Sam, eager for action, immediately decides that she has been murdered. While Martina stands calmly in the bedroom doorway surveying the room, Sam scurries around looking for evidence of foul play.

In his search, Sam finds a glass of water on the bedstand. Smugly, he turns toward Martina and beckons her closer. "When I was in the academy," Sam said, "I read about this real rare drug case. The drug dissolves in water and can't be traced in the water or the body. I bet one of the people the old bird was writing about dumped some in this glass or paid off the maid to do it. No Sylvia, no bad press. Everybody knew she was an elderly woman with a heart problem. The murderer probably figured it would look like a heart attack. We should check her notes for her next column and find out who was here today! And we should check out the maid!"

Martina, looking slightly bemused, takes a drink from the glass of water and says, "I couldn't disagree with you more on this one!"

Using the five critical thinking questions in your text, the clues in the story, and what you have just learned in this chapter, answer the following.

1. What is Sam's hypothesis?

2. What evidence supports Sam's hypothesis?

3. What is Martina's alternative hypothesis?

4. What evidence supports Martina's hypothesis?

PERSONAL LEARNING ACTIVITIES

1. Consider some natural concepts—such as "home," "family," "love," "justice," "games," or "success"—and decide on a prototypical example of each. Think of other examples of the concepts. How are the examples similar to and different from the prototypes? When is an example too far away to fall within the category? How do you know this? How might these variations of the same concept affect communication among individuals and groups?

2. Consider the role of the media in the availability heuristic by watching the following video: http://www.youtube.com/watch?v=KOzAxhu6w2s. How does the media make errors in thinking more likely based on the availability heuristic?

3. Think of all the uses you can for a backpack, paper bag, and paper clip. Were you at first held back from creative uses by functional fixedness?

4. Imagine that you are planning to purchase some piece of equipment, such as a computer, sound system, or cellular phone. Approach it as a multiattribute decision. Look at newspaper advertisements or visit a store to get information on the product. For each brand or model, list all the features you would need to consider, such as cost, accessories, power or speed, reputation, whether any important upgrades are expected within the next year, and so on. Then rank all these features according to their importance to you. You now have a good idea of what is on the market and what is important to you. You could make an informed decision if you decided to buy.

5. Watch a young relative or observe children in a daycare center to see what early language use is like. Are the children at an age when babbling is most common, or are they forming words and/or sentences? If you hear errors, what sort are they?

MULTIPLE-CHOICE QUESTIONS

Quiz 1

1. When Dr. Lowry tries to figure out what is wrong with his patient, he examines the patient and then connects what he sees in the patient's symptoms to what he has learned from his schooling. When Dr. Lowry engages in that connective thinking, he is in the _____ phase of the circle of thought.

   a. describe
   b. elaborate
   c. plan
   d. action

2. Halle watches mayonnaise jars going by on an assembly line and is supposed to grab any jars with crooked lids or two labels. Halle's reaction time will most likely decrease if she

   a. also has to look for underfilled jars or crooked labels.
   b. does not know when the defective jars come by.
   c. tries to be extremely careful not to grab a good jar.
   d. only has to watch for crooked lids.

3. A _____ is a mental representation of familiar parts of your world.

   a. cognitive map
   b. reconstructive memory
   c. directional bias
   d. proposition

4. Propositions

   a. are the basic components of words.
   b. show the relationships among concepts.
   c. are always true.
   d. show the relationship among mental models.

5. Determine the name of the natural concept to which the following four items belong, and then choose the prototypical example of that concept.

   a. Ferret
   b. Gerbil
   c. Dog
   d. Tropical bird

6. An algorithm

   a. is a shortcut to the solution of a problem.
   b. will sometimes yield a correct answer to a problem.
   c. will always yield a correct answer to a problem.
   d. is subject to bias from the availability heuristic.

7. If the temperature falls below 32 degrees Fahrenheit, any precipitation that falls will be in the form of snow. Then, if it is now 37 degrees Fahrenheit outside and about to storm, we should expect rain. These statements are an example of

    a. formal reasoning.
    b. a counterfactual argument.
    c. the confirmation bias.
    d. informal reasoning.

8. In the classic fairy tale, when the prince wants to find Cinderella after she runs from the ball at midnight, he first uses a(n) _____ strategy and checks only estates in the kingdom where women of her beauty and refinement would most likely live. When that does not work, he uses a(n) _____ strategy and conducts a house-to-house search.

    a. schematic; heuristic
    b. algorithmic; heuristic
    c. heuristic; algorithmic
    d. schematic; algorithmic

9. Many senior citizens lose thousands of dollars each spring because they place unwarranted trust in neatly dressed, clean-cut, polite young men who come to their house and advise them that they need roof repairs. The seniors put down a substantial deposit for work to be done, only to realize later that the men are not going to return and no work was actually needed. They fall prey to this scam because of the

    a. confirmation bias.
    b. anchoring heuristic.
    c. availability heuristic.
    d. representativeness heuristic.

10. Which of the following is an example of using an analogy to assist in problem solving?

    a. Using my new e-mail system is a lot like my old one—there is a check mail function, transfer function, and so one. They are just called different things.
    b. To learn how to use my new e-mail system, I am going to first break down the menu into all of its categories. Then I am going to work through each category until I understand it.
    c. When I use my new e-mail system, the main thing I want to do is check and send mail. So first I will figure out how to check and then I will figure out how to send.
    d. None of these is an analogy.

11. Functional fixedness occurs when a person

    a. uses old solutions to solve new problems.
    b. looks only for information that will confirm a hypothesis.
    c. ignores negative evidence.
    d. cannot think of novel uses for familiar objects in order to solve a problem.

12. While trying to balance equations in a chemistry assignment, Luna uses the same method of working through the first ten problems. On the eleventh problem, however, a completely different approach is necessary and Luna cannot figure out what it is. Luna most likely developed

    a. an algorithm.
    b. functional fixedness.
    c. a mental model.
    d. a mental set.

13. Luna (see Question 12) decides to forget about the problem for a while at dinner. When she returns to her room, she realizes how to solve the problem. Luna used _____ to solve the problem.

    a. deep structures
    b. expert systems
    c. incubation
    d. prototypes

14. Raymond recently won $500 in a lottery drawing. He will not buy any more tickets at the store that sold him his winning ticket because he thinks he has used up his luck at that store. This is an example of

    a. the gambler's fallacy.
    b. loss aversion.
    c. ignoring negative evidence.
    d. the confirmation bias.

15. Loss aversion in decision making refers to

    a. the likelihood of that choice's being the actual outcome.
    b. someone feeling worse about losing a certain amount than they would feel good had they gained the same amount.
    c. someone feeling better about gaining a certain amount than they would feel bad had they lost the same amount.
    d. the tendency to believe that future events in a random process will be changed by past events.

16. The deep structure of a sentence is

    a. the sequence of words in the sentence.
    b. the meaning of the sentence.
    c. the syntax of the sentence.
    d. a reflection of the complexity of the sentence.

17. Every Sunday morning, Juan and his roommate jogged to the Hotcake House, where they ate a leisurely breakfast while reading the Sunday *New York Times*. When Juan's roommate was called out of town for two weeks, disrupting their normal routine, Juan lost track of what day of the week it was. What aspect of Juan's Sundays was affected?

    a. His schema
    b. His script
    c. His mental model
    d. His image

18. Context can alter the interpretation of a sentence. Which of the following would NOT be considered a part of context?

    a. A person's knowledge of the world based on experience
    b. The situation in which the communication is taking place
    c. The inflection of a person's voice when communicating
    d. All of these contribute to the context of a situation.

19. Whorf's idea that language determines how we think is known as

    a. mental chronometry.
    b. deep structure.
    c. telegraphic speech.
    d. linguistic determinism.

Total Correct (See answer key) _____

Quiz 2

Use this quiz to reassess your learning after taking Quiz 1 and reviewing the chapter.

1. The manipulation of mental representations defines

    a. an information processing system.
    b. mental chronometry.
    c. cognitive psychology.
    d thinking.

2. When Sheila goes to a theater, she expects someone to take her ticket, offer to seat her, and hand her a program. This is an example of a

    a. proposition.
    b. schema.
    c. script.
    d. cognitive map.

3. Cliff has just stopped his car at a red light when the light changes to green. Which of the following will affect his reaction time?

    a. Cliff is driving a stick shift for the first time.
    b. Cliff did not expect the light to change to green so quickly.
    c. Five roads intersect at this light. Cliff can turn onto one of these roads or go straight ahead.
    d. All of these.

4. The smallest segments of knowledge that can stand as individual assertions are called

    a. schemas.
    b. propositions.
    c. syllogisms.
    d. scripts.

5. Natural and formal concepts differ in that
    a. formal concepts provide a way to classify objects, whereas natural concepts do not.
    b. natural concepts provide a way to classify objects, whereas formal concepts do not.
    c. formal concepts are fuzzy and sometimes difficult to define, whereas natural concepts are rigidly defined.
    d. natural concepts are fuzzy and sometimes difficult to define, whereas formal concepts are rigidly defined.

6. When Bobbie walks around her neighborhood, she knows how to find her way around using an image of the neighborhood in her head. Bobbie is using a(n)
    a. cognitive map.
    b. proposition.
    c. evoked potential.
    d. algorithm.

7. You would use a _____ when thinking about how to record on a VCR.
    a. schema
    b. script
    c. mental model
    d. proposition

8. Clinton is really frustrated. His uncle has been beating him at checkers all night. He is going to play another game, but this time he is going to base his strategy on an algorithm, not a heuristic. What problem will this cause?
    a. Clinton still may not win the game.
    b. Clinton and his uncle may be playing the same game of checkers for a very long time.
    c. Clinton is ignoring overall probabilities.
    d. The representativeness heuristic will bias Clinton's choice of strategy.

9. Cindy is 100 percent positive of her ability to find an advertising job in New York City. When she gets to New York, she reads in the paper that jobs are extremely scarce because of the large number of recent corporate mergers. Despite this, she is still 90 percent sure that, with her qualifications, she will land a job. Which heuristic is responsible for her reasoning?
    a. The anchoring heuristic
    b. The availability heuristic
    c. The representativeness heuristic
    d. The base-rate information heuristic

10. Many companies are reporting an inability to staff their foreign offices in Europe. Employees previously interested in overseas work are frightened of the terrorist activity they keep hearing about in the news. They are sure that something disastrous will happen to their family if they move to Europe. Which heuristic are the employees using to assess the incidence of terrorist activities?
    a. The availability heuristic
    b. The representativeness heuristic
    c. The anchoring heuristic
    d. The syllogistic heuristic

11. Artificial intelligence is
    a. someone's pretending to know a solution when they really do not.
    b. a field that seeks to develop computers that imitate human perception and thought processes.
    c. the study of neural network models.
    d. heuristic, not algorithmic, thinking.

12. The representativeness heuristic causes us to
    a. ignore overall probabilities.
    b. give improper weight to contradictory evidence when making a decision.
    c. focus on solutions that are easily brought to mind.
    d. consider only those hypotheses with which we are the most familiar.

13. Mike and Cal are marketing executives working as a team for a Fortune 500 company. They have been given an extremely difficult project: They are to design a new consumer product. Mike wants to review all the market research on consumer needs, identify what the product must do to solve those needs, and then see if his company can build it. Cal wants go to the library and look up case histories of other companies in similar situations noted for developing brilliant new products. Mike wants to use a(n) _____ process to solve the problem, and Cal is trying to use a(n) _____ to solve the problem.
    a. analogy; decomposition
    b. working backward; analogy
    c. analogy; visual representation
    d. incubation; visual representation

14. Winnie, a teacher, has been told that the test scores of one of her new students, Nelson, suggest that he is very bright. The principal has asked her to keep an eye on Nelson and let him know what she thinks of Nelson's intelligence. All through the first six weeks of the semester, she finds many examples that seem to show that Nelson is indeed very bright. However, during the seventh week, she finds out that the records have been mixed up. Nelson's actual test scores show him as being strictly average. What explains Winnie's observations during the first six weeks?
    a. Confirmation bias
    b. Functional fixedness
    c. Mental set
    d. Decomposition

15. Emmeline works as a lab technician in a neurobiological laboratory. She has just received an announcement that must be posted in the lab immediately. Because she cannot find any thumbtacks, she uses the ends of hypodermic needles to attach the announcement to the bulletin board. What pitfall in problem solving has Emmeline just avoided?
    a. Functional fixedness
    b. Confirmation bias
    c. Ignoring of negative evidence
    d. Faulty hypothesis testing

16. Going to college is something Tyson really values. His brother, Daniel, does not value going to college at all. Tyson and Daniel have different _____ for going to college.

    a. propositions
    b. prototypes
    c. mental sets
    d. utilities

17. The newspaper headline reads, "Campus police start operation to run down jaywalkers." This statement has two

    a. deep structures.
    b. surface structures.
    c. morphemes.
    d. phonemes.

18. Which of the following is correct?

    a. Phonemes make up morphemes, which make up words.
    b. Morphemes make up phonemes, which make up words.
    c. Words make up morphemes, which make up sentences.
    d. Words make up phonemes, which make up morphemes.

19. Which of the following sentences would be the easiest to memorize? (1) A grickly aftla hicktored the bubla. (2) Oftla grick hickt bubla.

    a. The first sentence
    b. The second sentence
    c. Both would be equally easy to memorize.
    d. The answer cannot be determined.

20. In Tarzan movies, a husband, his wife, and their baby are shipwrecked. The baby survives and is raised by apes until a doctor finds him twenty years later. The doctor takes the wild man out of the jungle, teaches him to speak French and English, and introduces him to society. Although the wild man's accents are not perfect, he manages to live in England for some time before choosing to go back to the jungle. Why are these movies unrealistic?

    a. A language acquisition device needs to be learned.
    b. A critical period may exist for language acquisition.
    c. The wild man should have been able to learn proper French and English accents.
    d. All of the above

Total Correct (See answer key) _____

ANSWERS TO FILL-IN-THE-BLANKS KEY TERMS

1. prototype (see Concepts)

2. evoked potential (see Measuring Information Processing)

3. mental models (see Schemas, Scripts, and Mental Models)

4. Scripts (see Schemas, Scripts, and Mental Models)

5. syllogism (see Formal Reasoning)

6.   heuristic (see Informal Reasoning)

7.   anchoring heuristic (see Informal Reasoning)

8.   Algorithms (see Formal Reasoning)

9.   syntax (see The Elements of Language)

10.   One-word stage (see The Development of Language)

11.   Babblings or infant vocalizations (see The Development of Language)

12.   deep structure (see The Elements of Language)

13.   morpheme (see The Elements of Language)

14.   functional fixedness (see Obstacles to Problem Solving)

15.   mental set (see Obstacles to Problem Solving)

ANSWERS TO CONCEPTS AND EXERCISES

Approaches to Problem Solving

1.   Viola is trying to develop a cognitive map, and she is being affected by rectangular bias. (see Images and Cognitive Maps)

2.   Erin realized that if the CDs were still playing, the problem was just a blown light bulb. Pete, on the other hand, was ignoring negative evidence—evidence that needed to be present for his hypothesis to be true: If lightning had taken out the power lines, the CD player should have shut down at the same time the light went out. (see Obstacles to Problem Solving)

3.   The Parisian offered Al a choice between a heuristic (the shortcut) and an algorithm (the sure but longer way to get to the museum). Al chose the algorithm. (see Formal Reasoning; see also Informal Reasoning)

4.   Carlotta has realized that being an expert has caused her to have a mental set. Therefore, she is bringing in someone who doesn't have old answers that will get in the way of thinking of new answers. (see Obstacles to Problem Solving)

Structures of Language

1.   The morphemes (meaningful units) are as follows: the, husband, s (after an apostrophe means a possessive), dinner, was, and terrible. Two possible deep structures are as follows: The dinner that the husband cooked was impossible to eat, and the meal that the husband was eating was prepared poorly. (see The Elements of Language)

2.   The morphemes are as follows: my, friend, paint, ed, me, in, his, back, and yard. Two possible deep structures are as follows: My friend created a painting depicting me in his backyard, and my friend and I were in his backyard, where he was painting my portrait. Can you think of others? (see The Elements of Language)

ANSWERS TO CRITICAL THINKING

1.   Sam hypothesizes that Sylvia Star was murdered by a rare drug.

2.   The evidence includes the following facts: Sylvia had lots of enemies, old and current; a drug could have been slipped into her drink; Sam knows a crime like that has been committed before; and there could be a connection between Sylvia's visitors that day and her current writing subjects.

3.   Martina hypothesizes that the woman died of old age.

4.   The probability of a death resulting from natural causes is the evidence Martina uses to support her hypothesis.

ANSWERS TO MULTIPLE-CHOICE QUESTIONS

Circle the question numbers you answered correctly.

Quiz 1

1.   b is the answer.   When Dr. Lowry connects his observations to his knowledge base, he is elaborating on the information. (see The Circle of Thought)

    a.   Describing is the first stage of the circle of thought. When Dr. Lowry examines the patient, he is gathering information to describe the problem.

    c.   The planning phase occurs after Dr. Lowry has made a decision and develops a plan to implement it.

    d.   Action is the phase that follows the decision, when Dr. Lowry actually implements his plan of action.

2.   d is the answer.   If the task were less complex, Halle's reaction time would decrease. (see Measuring Information Processing)

    a.   If she needed to look for two additional problems, Halle's reaction time would increase or lengthen.

    b.   If Halle did not know when to expect the jars, her reaction time would increase. People who anticipate stimuli can respond more quickly.

    c.   Halle would be making the speed-accuracy tradeoff if she tried to be very careful not to grab a good jar.

3.   a is the answer.   A cognitive map is a mental representation, or picture, of familiar parts of your world, such as your neighborhood. (see Images and Cognitive Maps)

    b.   Reconstructive memory is the process of filling the gaps in our memories with information that has been stored in long-term memory.

    c.   There is no such thing as directional bias with regard to cognitive maps.

    d.   Propositions are statements that describe the relationship between concepts.

4.   b is the answer.   (see Propositions)

    a.   Propositions are made up of words. (You may be thinking of phonemes and morphemes.)

    c.   Propositions can be true or false.

    d.   Mental models are made up of propositions, not the other way around. Propositions show the relationship between concepts or the relationship between a property or characteristic and a concept.

5.   c is the answer.   The concept is "pet," and a dog is the best example of a pet. (see Concepts)

    a, b, d.   Although ferrets, gerbils, and tropical birds all can be pets, they are not the prototypical example of a pet. A prototype is something that possesses all or nearly all of the characteristic features of a category.

6. c is the answer.   An algorithm will always produce a solution if one is available. (see Formal Reasoning)

    a.   A heuristic, not an algorithm, is a shortcut to the solution of a problem.

    b.   An algorithm always produces a correct answer.

    d.   An algorithm is not subject to bias.

7. a is the answer.   These statements are examples of formal reasoning because they follow logic by providing a formula for drawing valid conclusions about the world. (see Formal Reasoning)

    b.   A counterfactual argument consists of currently untrue "what if" statements and does not apply here.

    c.   The confirmation bias is an obstacle to problem solving that involves attending only to confirming information.

    d.   Informal reasoning is used when the evidence is weighed to judge the credibility of a conclusion. It does not apply here.

8. c is the answer.   In a heuristic strategy, the prince concludes that because Cinderella was dressed in finery and was at the ball, she must be the daughter of one of the kingdom's noblemen. When that strategy does not work, he uses an algorithmic strategy that, if followed, cannot fail to produce a correct answer if it exists. (see Informal Reasoning)

    a, d.   You might have been thinking of schemas. There is no such thing as a schematic strategy.

    b.   This choice is a reversal of the correct answer.

9. d is the answer.   The con men look and act like the seniors' stereotype of trustworthy and hard-working young men. The seniors therefore decide that these men belong to that classification without processing more information about the situation. (see Informal Reasoning)

    a.   Confirmation bias is a form of the anchoring heuristic.

    b.   The anchoring heuristic is based on inadequate adjustments to first impressions as a result of new information. There is no comparison to new information here; the problem is jumping to a conclusion based only on the first impression.

    c.   The availability heuristic involves judging how true a hypothesis is by how easily it or examples of it come to mind. If the question had included a statement that a neighbor had just had roof repairs done, the idea that roof repairs were needed might be judged more likely to be true because it would easily come to mind.

10. a is the answer.   This is an example of an analogy, because it likens the current problem to how one dealt with a similar problem—learning the previous e-mail system. (see Strategies for Problem Solving)

    b.   This is an example of decomposition. Decomposition is breaking apart a problem into subproblems and working on each.

    c.   This is an example of working backward. The person started with the desired end result and then worked backward to determine how to get there.

    d.   a was an example of an analogy.

11. d is the answer.   Many objects designed for a particular purpose can be used to solve other types of problems. However, when people can think of an object as serving only its intended purpose, they are victims of functional fixedness. (see Obstacles to Problem Solving)

   a.   A mental set causes people to use old solutions to solve new problems instead of looking for simpler solutions.

   b.   Confirmation bias occurs when people look only at information that will confirm a hypothesis.

   c.   Ignoring negative evidence means that people do not consider the lack of symptoms when testing a hypothesis.

12.   d is the answer.   Getting stuck in one way of solving a problem is a mental set. (see Obstacles to Problem Solving)

   a.   An algorithm is a formal reasoning procedure that always results in a correct answer.

   b.   Functional fixedness is being unable to think of a novel use for an object.

   c.   A mental model is a description of how something works.

13.   c is the answer.   In incubation, the problem is set aside for awhile. (see Strategies for Problem Solving)

   a.   Deep structure is the meaning of a sentence.

   b.   Expert systems are computer programs that are capable of solving problems in a specific area.

   d.   Prototypes are the most typical example of a natural concept.

14.   a is the answer.   The gambler's fallacy is the belief that events in a random process will correct themselves—will configure themselves to fit some purpose. Raymond figured that somehow the lottery machine would "know" that he had won and would not give him any more winning numbers. (see Biases and Flaws in Decision Making)

   b.   People with loss aversion usually feel worse about losing an amount of money than they would feel good about gaining the same amount.

   c.   Ignoring negative evidence is the practice of overlooking absent symptoms that might eliminate a hypothesis.

   d.   People with a confirmation bias are likely to ignore information that is inconsistent with their hypothesis.

15.   b is the answer.   Loss aversion occurs when someone feels worse about losing a certain amount than they feel happy about gaining the same amount. (see Biases and Flaws in Decision Making)

   a.   The likelihood of a choice being the outcome deals more with expected value, which takes into account the probability of an outcome and its perceived benefits and costs.

   c.   This is the opposite of loss aversion and is not something psychologists generally observe in decision making.

   d.   This is the gambler's fallacy.

16.   b is the answer.   Deep structure is the underlying meaning of a string of words. (see The Elements of Language)

   a.   Surface structure is the sequence of the words.

   c.   The syntax of the sentence is the set of rules that govern the way the words are strung together.

   d.   Deep structure refers to the meaning of a sentence, not to its complexity.

17. b is the answer.   The sequence of activities Juan usually followed was disrupted, interfering with his perception of time. (see Schemas, Scripts, and Mental Models)

    a.   Schemas are knowledge structures. They are categories containing *all* of our knowledge about particular concepts, not just the specific series of events described in this question. This is not the *best* answer.

    c.   A mental model is one's idea about how something works. Juan's ideas of Sunday were those pertaining to a chain of events. Juan would have a mental model of how his muscles worked together when he jogged.

    d.   An image is a visual mental representation. Juan could, for example, mentally picture Sunday mornings as stacks of hotcakes, sausages, and steaming coffee.

18. c is the answer.   Semantics is the set of rules governing the meanings of words and sentences. The words *no va* have a particular meaning in Spanish, but this particular combination of letters has no meaning in English. (see The Elements of Language)

    a.   Syntax is a set of rules governing the way words are put together.

    b.   A language acquisition device is an innate ability to understand the regularities of speech and the fundamental relationships between words.

    d.   The surface structure is the sequence in which words are strung together.

19. d is the answer.   (see Understanding Speech)

    a, b, c.   Each option is only one part of the contextual information that will influence the interpretation of a sentence.

20. d is the answer.   Linguistic determinism is the notion that language actually determines how we think. (see Culture, Language and Thought)

    a..   Mental chronometry is the study of the timing of mental events.

    b.   Deep structure refers to the underlying meaning of the surface structure of language.

    c.   Telegraphic speech refers to the statements children make as they acquire language which are brief and to the point, like a telegram.

Now turn to the quiz analysis table at the end of this chapter to find which areas you know well and which areas you need to work on. Circle the numbers in the table for items on Quiz 1 that you answered correctly.

Quiz 2

1.   d is the answer.   Thinking is the manipulation of mental representations. (see The Circle of Thought)

    a.   An information-processing system is what receives, represents, and manipulates the representations, but it is not the actual process of doing so.

    b.   Mental chronometry is the timing of mental events.

    c.   Cognitive psychology is the study of the mental processes by which humans receive information from their environment, and modify it, make it meaningful, store, retrieve, use and communicate it.

2.   c is the answer.   A script is a mental representation of a sequence of events. This question describes Sheila's expectation for the sequence of events when going to a theatre (see Schemas, Scripts, and Mental Models)

    a.   A proposition is the smallest unit of knowledge that can stand as an assertion. They describe the relations between concepts. This question does not describe relations between concepts.

    b.   A schema is a generalization about categories of objects, events, and people. Although this question does describe Sheila's generalizations about events at a restaurant and is an example of a schema, the better answer is script. A script is a type of schema that involves mental representation of a sequence of events. Script is more precise than schema in this case.

    d.   A cognitive map is a mental representation of a familiar setting. The question describes an expected sequence of events—not a map of the setting.

3.   d is the answer.   Cliff will need more time to respond to the green light (the stimulus) because he is driving a stick shift for the first time, which requires a starting procedure different from that of an automatic. Also, the light turned green sooner than he expected, and unexpected stimuli lengthen reaction time. Finally, an increase in the complexity of the decision will lengthen reaction time. Cliff has more than the usual number of streets to choose from when the light turns green. (see Measuring Information Processing)

4.   b is the answer.   Propositions are the smallest segment of knowledge that can stand as individual assertions. (see Propositions)

    a.   Schemas are collections of information about the world that influence how we remember and store information.

    c.   Syllogisms are basic arguments that consist of two premises.

    d.   Scripts contain knowledge about sequences of human activity.

5.   d is the answer.   Natural concepts are fuzzy, while formal concepts are more rigid. (see Concepts)

    a, b.   Both natural and artificial concepts provide a way to classify objects.

    c.   Artificial concepts have rigid definitions. If an object does not meet all the specifications, then it is not part of that particular artificial concept. Natural concepts are fuzzy. For example, an ostrich is a bird even though it does not meet all the criteria for "bird"—that is, it cannot fly.

6.   a is the answer.   A cognitive map is a mental representation of a familiar setting, such as a neighborhood. (see Images and Cognitive Maps)

    b.   A proposition is a statement that describes a relationship between concepts. This question does not describe usage of a relationship between concepts, but of a mental map of a familiar setting.

    c.   An evoked potential is a small, temporary change in voltage on an EEG. This question does not mention EEGs.

    d.   An algorithm is a systematic search for a solution that will always produce a solution if one exists. Bobbie is not searching for a solution in this question.

7.   c is the answer.   Mental models are clusters of propositions that represent people's understanding of how things (usually physical things) work. (see Schemas, Scripts, and Mental Models)

    a.   Schemas serve as general representations of a large set of more specific examples that generate expectations of the world. Schemas are broader than mental models.

b.   Scripts are mental representations of what is supposed to happen during sequences of events, such as weddings or parties. Mental models are clusters of propositions about how things or objects work.

d.   A proposition is the smallest unit of knowledge that can stand alone. A mental model is made up of many propositions.

8.   b is the answer.   An algorithm will always produce the correct answer, which in this case is winning the game. However, Clinton and his uncle will be playing for a very long time. Clinton will have to evaluate the consequences of every possible move he can make each time it is his turn. (see Formal Reasoning)

a.   Algorithms always produce a correct answer.

c, d.   People usually ignore overall probabilities when using a representativeness heuristic. Clinton is using an algorithm, not a heuristic.

9.   a is the answer.   Cindy starts out being 100 percent sure that she will get a job. After reading the paper, she should realize that her chances are very slim. Instead, she is still very sure; she is anchored in her hypothesis that she will get a job. (see Informal Reasoning)

b.   People use the availability heuristic when they judge the probability of an event by how easily examples of that event come to mind. If Cindy had thought of all her many friends who had gotten jobs in the city, this would have been the correct answer.

c.   If Cindy were using the representativeness heuristic, she would have focused on the representative information (the paper) instead of her original estimate.

d.   There is no such thing as the base-rate information heuristic. (You may be thinking of the representativeness heuristic. Ignoring base-rate frequencies results in the use of this heuristic.)

10.   a is the answer.   Employees are judging the probability of terrorism based on the information that is most available to them. This bias is due to the availability heuristic. (see Informal Reasoning)

b.   Employees are not trying to determine whether an example is part of a class of objects, as they would do when using the representativeness heuristic.

c.   Employees are not adjusting their hypothesis to match new information. They have made a decision about the degree of terrorist activity based on the information available to them.

d.   There is no such thing as the syllogistic heuristic.

11.   b is the answer.   Artificial intelligence is the study of how to develop computers that imitate the processes of human thought and perception. (see Problem Solving by Computer)

a.   Pretending to know something you do not is not artificial intelligence.

c.   Neural network models are studied by those interested in artificial intelligence but are not artificial intelligence itself.

d.   Artificial intelligence would involve both algorithmic and heuristic strategies, as both are parts of human thought and perception.

12.   a is the answer.   The representativeness heuristic leads us to look at an example and compare it to a larger class of items. We focus on the similar appearances of the example and the larger class of items, ignoring information on how often the larger class of items occurs (overall probability). (see Informal Reasoning)

b.   The anchoring heuristic causes us to give improper weight to contradictory evidence in making a decision.

c, d.   The availability heuristic causes us to focus on the solutions that are most easily brought to mind and that are therefore most familiar. These are usually the hypotheses that have occurred most frequently in the past.

13.   b is the answer.   Mike wants to start with what the product has to do (an end point) and work backward to the solution of what the product will be. Cal wants to use an analogy: employing the same techniques that other companies employ in trying to solve the same kind of problem. (see Strategies for Problem Solving)

a.   Cal, not Mike, wants to employ an analogy by looking at other companies' solutions to the same problem. Decomposition is breaking a problem into its subparts.

c.   Mike is trying to develop his own strategy, not use a strategy that has worked for anyone else facing a similar problem.

d.   Mike is not letting the problem incubate by laying it aside for awhile.

14.   a is the answer.   Winnie has a hypothesis that Nelson is very smart. She takes into consideration only the evidence that supports her hypothesis and ignores evidence that Nelson is only average. (see Formal Reasoning)

b.   Winnie is testing a hypothesis, not trying to find a solution involving the use of an object.

c.   A mental set means using the solutions to old problems to try to solve new ones. Winnie is not using old solutions to test her hypothesis about Nelson's intelligence.

d.   Decomposition is a way to simplify problem solving by breaking a problem into smaller subproblems. Winnie is not engaged in this activity.

15.   a is the answer.   If Emmeline had thought of the hypodermics as being useful only for giving injections, she would have experienced functional fixedness. Instead, she used them for something other than their traditional function and solved her problem. (see Obstacles to Problem Solving)

b, d.   Confirmation bias occurs because people always try to confirm, rather than refute, their hypotheses. Emmeline is not testing a hypothesis, so neither of these alternatives is correct.

c.   People ignore negative evidence when looking for explanations of some event. Emmeline is not looking for an explanation but, rather, for a way to solve a problem.

16.   d is the answer.   Utility is the subjective value one attaches to an outcome. Tyson really values college, whereas Daniel does not. They differ in the utility they attach to college education. (see Evaluating Options)

a.   A proposition is a mental representation of relations between concepts.

b.   A prototype is a concept exemplar that has all or nearly all of the defining characteristics of that concept category.

c.   A mental set is an obstacle to problem solving. No problem or attempt to solve it is described in this question.

17.   a is the answer.   The sentence has two meanings. The police are probably trying to catch jaywalkers, but it sounds as if they could be running them down with a vehicle! (see The Elements of Language)

b.   The sentence has only one surface structure, because that is the string of words.

c.   More than two morphemes make up the sentence. For example, <u>campus</u>, <u>police</u>, and <u>start</u> are all morphemes.

d.   More than two phonemes make up the sentence. For example, campus has six: *c, a, m, p, u,* and *s*.

18.   a is the answer.   Phonemes (sounds that affect the meaning of a word) make up morphemes (the smallest units of meaning in a language), which make up words. (see The Elements of Language)

b.   This is the reverse of what is correct. Phonemes are sounds that affect the meaning of a word, and morphemes are the smallest units of meaning in a language which make up words.

c.   This is incorrect because morphemes make up words, not the other way around.

d.   This is incorrect, because words do not make up phonemes; phonemes are part of morphemes which make up words. Phonemes do not make up words by themselves.

19.   a is the answer.   The words *a* and *the*, as well as the *-ly* and *-ed* suffixes, make it easier for us to chunk the nonsense syllables in short-term memory, because of the similarity to English usage. The sentence also has syntax similar to English. (see The Elements of Language)

b.   There are no words or suffixes that help us chunk information in the second sentence. It is more difficult to remember, even though it is shorter than the first sentence.

c.   If one sentence is easier than the other, then both cannot be equally easy.

d.   The answer can be determined.

20.   b is the answer.   Many cases support the idea that a critical period exists for language development. The wild man was found when he was in his twenties and was past the critical period for language development. Therefore, he should not have been able to learn any language. (see How Is Language Acquired?)

a.   The language acquisition device Chomsky proposed is innate.

c.   When people learn a second language after the age of twelve to fifteen, they usually cannot speak with a flawless accent.

d.   Only b is the answer.

Now turn to the quiz analysis table at the end of this chapter to find which areas you know well and which areas you need to work on. Circle the numbers in the table for items on Quiz 2 that you answered correctly.

For each question you answered correctly, circle its number. (Quiz 1 numbers are not shaded; Quiz 2 numbers are shaded.) Are there patterns in the types of questions or the topics you got wrong that could direct your further study? Did you improve from Quiz 1 to Quiz 2?

QUIZ REVIEW

Topic	Type of Question		
	Definition	**Comprehension**	**Application**
Basic Functions of Thought			
The Circle of Thought			1
	1		
Measuring Information Processing			2
			3
Mental Representations: The Ingredients of Thought			
Concepts			5
		5	
Propositions		4	
	4		
Schemas, Scripts, and Mental Models			17
			2, 7
Images and Cognitive Maps	3		
			6
Thinking Strategies			
Formal Reasoning	6		7
			8, 14
Informal Reasoning			8, 9
		12	9, 10
Problem Solving			
Strategies for Problem Solving			10, 13
			13
Obstacles to Problem Solving	11		12
			15
Problem Solving by Computer			
	11		
Decision Making			
Evaluating Options			
			16
Biases and Flaws in Decision Making	15		14
Language			
The Elements of Language	16		18
		18	17, 19
Understanding Speech		19	
How Is Language Acquired?			
			20
Culture, Language, and Thought	20		

Total correct by quiz:

Quiz 1:	
Quiz 2:	

CHAPTER 9

Consciousness

<u>Consciousness</u> is the awareness of your own thoughts, actions, feelings, sensations, perceptions, and other mental processes.

OUTLINE

I.   ANALYZING CONSCIOUSNESS
     Scientists who study consciousness sometimes call their work *cognitive science* or *cognitive neuroscience*. Today, three questions dominate the study of consciousness. First, what is the relationship between the conscious mind and the physical brain—are they different (*dualism*) or the same (*materialism*)? Secondly, is consciousness a unified phenomenon (*theatre* view) or several different phenomena (*parallel distributed processing models*)? Finally, are conscious and unconscious mental activities related to each other?

   A.   Some Functions of Consciousness
        Consciousness produces the best current interpretation of sensory information in light of past experience and makes this interpretation available to the part of the brain that plans voluntary actions and speech.

   B.   Levels of Consciousness
        Mental activity that you are aware of occurs at the <u>conscious level</u> of experience. However, mental activity can occur outside of consciousness at the <u>nonconscious level,</u> or cognitive unconscious, levels. At the nonconscious level, physiological processes that you cannot consciously monitor without the aid of biofeedback occur. The cognitive unconscious includes the <u>preconscious level</u> and <u>unconscious level</u> (or <u>subconscious level</u>). The preconscious level contains everything that can easily be brought into consciousness. Other mental activities that can alter thoughts, feelings, and actions but that are more difficult to bring into awareness are said to be in the unconscious.

   C.   Mental Processing Without Awareness
        Research on *priming* indicates that many important mental operations, such as learning, can occur without awareness. Visual processing without awareness may also occur in a condition known as *blindsight*. These sorts of studies indicate that unconscious processing does not operate as Freud thought—to protect us from painful or frightening material—but to help us more effectively carry out more mundane daily activities.

   D.   Focus on Research Methods: Subliminal Messages in Popular Music
        To investigate whether backward masked messages could be perceived, understood, and influence behavior when music plays forward, researchers recorded readings of the 23rd Psalm and Jabberwocky. The researchers then played them backwards. Participants were unable to discern messages in the backward versions, and no evidence was found to show that backward masked messages could influence behavior. Research should now focus on why the myth of backward masked messages influence on behavior persists.

   E.   The Neuropsychology of Consciousness
        Brain damage can impair consciousness. When on has *prosopagnosia*, individuals cannot consciously recognize faces, although they show autonomic nervous system responses to

familiar faces that they do not show to unfamiliar faces. With anterograde amnesia, individuals can learn new skills although they do not consciously recall the practice sessions that led to those skills.

F.   Consciousness States
Consciousness state refers to the characteristics of consciousness at any particular moment. Possible states range from deep sleep to alert wakefulness, with many gradations in between. Significant changes in behavior and mental processes are characteristic of altered states of consciousness. The value of altered states of consciousness varies from culture to culture.

II.   SLEEPING AND DREAMING
Early researchers thought that sleep was a time of mental inactivity. Modern research shows, however, that sleep is actually a very active, complex state.

A.   Stages of Sleep
1.   Sleep researchers use an *electroencephalograph* (EEG) to measure how brain waves differ during different states of sleep.
2.   *Non-REM Sleep*. Stages 1 through 4 are progressively deeper stages of non-REM (or NREM) sleep. The last two stages—3 and 4—are slow-wave sleep. Each stage has an EEG pattern characterized by slow brain waves and accompanied by deep breathing; calm, regular heartbeat; and reduced blood pressure.
3.   *REM Sleep*. REM (rapid eye movement) sleep, or paradoxical sleep, is a paradoxical state in which brain waves and other physiological functions resemble those of a person who is awake, but muscle tone resembles that of paralysis.
4.   *A Night's Sleep*. Most people travel through the five stages of non-REM and REM sleep four to six times each night. REM sleep is most frequent during the second half of the night. The amount of time spent in stages 1 to 4 and REM sleep varies with age.

B.   Why Do People Sleep?
2.   *Sleep as a Circadian Rhythm*. Humans have a built-in biological clock that is entrained to light and dark environmental cues, but will even continue without such external cues. Human circadian rhythms (or human biological rhythms) are "clocked" in a part of the hypothalamus called the suprachiasmatic nucleus. Jet lag and its accompanying symptoms of fatigue and irritability are examples of what happens when the sleep-wake cycle is interrupted.
3.   *The Value of Sleep*. The value of sleep can be understood by studying what happens when one is sleep deprived. Errors and accidents increase when one is sleep deprived. Sleep is necessary for resting and restoring the body, particularly non-REM sleep. REM sleep may help maintain the activity of neurons that use norepinephrine. It may also be a time for developing, checking, and expanding the brain's nerve connections. Finally, REM sleep may help consolidate what has been learned during the day.

C.   Sleep Disorders
1.   Insomnia, fatigue resulting from little sleep or difficulty falling asleep, is the most common sleep disorder and is correlated with mental distress. Relaxation training and cognitive behavioral therapy are approaches that can decrease insomnia. Short daytime naps and moderate evening exercise can also help.
2.   People with narcolepsy fall, without warning, into REM sleep from an active waking state. Napping and some drugs can help alleviate narcolepsy.
3.   Sleep apnea is a disorder in which people stop breathing momentarily while they sleep. Apnea episodes can occur hundreds of times per night, thus leaving the victim feeling tired during the day. Treatments include weight loss, CPAP mask, and in severe cases surgery.

4. <u>Sudden infant death syndrome (SIDS)</u> is a disorder, affecting primarily infants two to four months old, in which a baby stops breathing and dies. Doctors now recommend that babies sleep on their back to keep them from accidentally suffocating in soft bedding.

5. <u>Nightmares</u> are frightening dreams that can occur during REM sleep. <u>Sleep terror disorder</u> (also known as <u>night terrors)</u> occur during stage 4 and are characterized by horrific images, screaming upon wakening, and difficulty in calming down afterward.

6. <u>Sleepwalking</u>, which is most common among children, is walking during non-REM sleep. <u>REM behavior disorder</u>, a condition similar to sleepwalking, occurs during REM sleep. In this condition, the normal paralysis that occurs during REM sleep is absent, and the person acts out his or her dreams.

B. Dreams and Dreaming

<u>Dreaming</u> involves a story-like sequence of images, sensations, and perceptions. In <u>lucid dreaming</u>, people know when they are dreaming and may be able to direct some of the dream content. Some theories suggest that dreaming helps mammals process and consolidate information of great personal significance or survival value. Psychodynamic theory suggests that dreams express unconscious wishes. The *activation-synthesis theory* suggests that dreams represent efforts to make sense of random signals sent to the cortex.

III. HYPNOSIS

<u>Hypnosis</u> is an altered state of consciousness brought on by special techniques and characterized by responsiveness to suggestions for changes in experience and behavior.

A. Experiencing Hypnosis

1. Individuals vary in their <u>hypnotic susceptibility</u>. Hypnotically susceptible people are more imaginative, have a tendency to fantasize, can focus their attention for long periods, are able to process information quickly and effortlessly, and have a positive expectation for hypnosis.

2. Under hypnosis, people respond to suggestions and can appear to forget their names or even display age regression. *Posthypnotic suggestions* affect behavior after hypnosis has ended. Some people experience *posthypnotic amnesia*, which is an inability to remember what happened under hypnosis. Hypnotized people exhibit reduced planfulness (the ability to initiate action on their own), redistributed attention, increased ability to fantasize, reduced reality testing, and enhanced ability to role play.

B. Explaining Hypnosis

Two major categories theories attempt to explain hypnosis. According to <u>state theories of hypnosis</u>, hypnotized people experience an altered state of consciousness. According to <u>nonstate theories of hypnosis</u>, hypnosis does not involve an altered state. *Role theorists*, for example, argue that hypnotized individuals merely comply with social demands associated with hypnosis. Another nonstate theory is *dissociation theory*, which blends role and state theories to argue that consciousness is split under hypnosis such that one agrees to share control with they hypnotist.

C. Applications of Hypnosis

Hypnosis has been used to decrease pain from surgery, childbirth, headaches, and cancer. More controversially, it has been used in attempts to enhance memory.

D. Linkages: Meditation, Health, and Stress

Meditation is intended to create an altered state of consciousness characterized by inner peace, calmness, and tranquility. Most types of meditation share common characteristics, including a method for focusing, a quiet environment, a comfortable position, a mental device to organize attention, and a passive attitude. Physiological effects include decreases in respiration rate, heart rate, muscle tension, blood pressure, and oxygen consumption, along with the appearance of alpha-wave activity. People who meditate regularly report experiencing decreases in stress-related problems such as anxiety and high blood pressure. How meditation works its effects is unclear, although it may be through effects on dopamine activity.

IV.   PSYCHOACTIVE DRUGS
Psychoactive drugs cause psychological changes by altering the functioning of the brain. Psychopharmacology is the study of psychoactive drugs.

A.   Psychopharmacology
Psychoactive drugs or substances influence the interaction between neurotransmitters and receptors. These drugs get into the brain through the blood supply when they pass the blood-brain barrier. Drugs that act as agonists mimic the effects of neurotransmitters, whereas those acting as antagonists prevent neurotransmitters from binding with receptors and inhibit neurotransmitter activity.

B.   The Varying Effects of Drugs
Drug abuse is a pattern of drug use that causes the user to have significant impairment or distress or serious social, legal, or interpersonal problems. *Psychological dependence* occurs when a person continues to use the drug to gain a sense of well-being even when the drug produces adverse consequences. Physical dependence, or drug addiction, exists when there is an altered physiological state in which continued use of the drug is required to prevent the onset of drug withdrawal. Drug tolerance may develop with prolonged use of a drug. Physical dependence can develop easily and without conscious awareness as the drug acts on the brain on dopamine and other neurotransmitters in the brain's pleasure centers.

1.   *Expectations and Drug Effects.* People who think they have taken a drug but really have not may display the effects of the drug because they expect to be affected by it. The learned *expectations* regarding a drug's effect vary from culture to culture.

C.   CNS Depressant Drugs
CNS depressant drugs reduce central nervous system activity. Many depressants increase GABA neurotransmitter activity.

1.   *Alcohol.* Alcohol has an impact on the dopamine, norepinephrine, serotonin, endorphin, endocannibinoids, glutamate, and GABA neurotransmitters. Genetics influences people's tendency toward alcohol dependency. It affects specific brain regions, particularly reducing activity in the locus coeruleus which may produce the relaxation of cultural inhibitions we see in drunken states.

2.   *Barbiturates.* Also called downers or sleeping pills, barbiturates cause relaxation, some euphoria, and diminished attention, among other effects.

3.   *GHB.* GHB is a naturally occurring substance similar to GABA and has recently become a popular "club drug." Because it is associated with loss of consciousness, it is among the drugs considered "date rape" drugs.

D.   CNS Stimulating Drugs
CNS stimulating drugs increase behavioral and mental activity.

1.   *Amphetamines.* Commonly known as uppers or speed, amphetamines increase the release of and decrease the removal of norepinephrine and dopamine at synapses, resulting in increased receptor activity. Amphetamines stimulate the brain and sympathetic nervous system, raising heart rate and blood pressure and constricting blood vessels. In some extreme cases, abuse of these drugs produces symptoms very similar to paranoid schizophrenia.

2. *Cocaine*. This drug's effects are similar to but more rapid than those of amphetamines. Additionally, the effects of cocaine are short-lived, which may help explain why this drug is especially addictive both psychologically and physiologically.

3. *Caffeine*. This drug decreases drowsiness, makes thought more rapid, increases physical work capacity, and raises urine production. Caffeine can cause physical dependence, but has few negative effects.

4. *Nicotine*. Nicotine enhances the action of acetylcholine, and stimulates the autonomic nervous system. Regular nicotine use can cause psychological and/or physiological dependence.

5. *MDMA*. Also called Ecstasy, MDMA is similar to both stimulants and psychedelics. It increases the activity of dopamine neurons. Although MDMA does not appear to be physically addictive, it does cause permanent brain damage and other psychological dysfunction.

E. Opiates

Opiates, which include opium, morphine, heroin, and codeine, induce sleep and relieve pain. These drugs are quite addictive and act as agonists for endorphins. They also stimulate glutamate receptors, altering the neuron so the drug is required for proper function.

F. Hallucinogens

Hallucinogenic drugs, sometimes referred to as *psychedelics*, cause a loss of contact with reality and induce changes in emotion, perception, and thought.

1. *LSD*. Lysergic acid diethylamide (LSD) is one of the most powerful psychedelics. LSD is not addictive, but tolerance does develop.

2. *Ketamine*. Ketamine is used in veterinary medicine, and has hallucinogenic properties when used in humans. Its use can lead to enduring memory impairment due to damage of the hippocampus.

3. *Marijuana*. The active ingredient in cannabis sativa is tetrahydrocannabinol (THC). It is absorbed quickly by many organs, including the brain.

G. Thinking Critically: Is Marijuana Dangerous?

Some say marijuana usage is dangerous, illegal, and wrong. Others contend that marijuana should be decriminalized and used for medicinal purposes.

What am I being asked to believe or accept?

Marijuana is a dangerous drug. It is addictive, it leads to "hard drug" use, it endangers the user and others, and if used long term, it has adverse effects on health and behavior.

What evidence is available to support the assertion?

Some people become at least psychologically dependent on marijuana. One study indicated a possibility of addiction. Marijuana interacts with the same receptors as heroin, suggesting that it could lead to the use of more addictive drugs. Marijuana disrupts memory formation and motor coordination. One study showed that long-term use impairs intellectual functioning. It appears to reduce creativity and increase risk for later appearance of anxiety, depression, and other mental disorders.

Are there alternative ways of interpreting the evidence?

The studies referred to earlier provide incomplete information. The same receptors activated by marijuana and heroin are also activated by sex and chocolate, which would not be considered criminal. The correlation between marijuana use and hard drug use could be due to the environment more than to properties of the drug. Studies of long-term effects on memory and reasoning are correlational. There is no evidence of a cause-effect relationship.

What additional evidence would help evaluate the alternatives?

More definitive evidence on marijuana's short- and long-term effects is needed.

What conclusions are most reasonable?

There is no hard evidence that marijuana is any more harmful than alcohol or tobacco. But though less dangerous than cocaine or heroin, marijuana is not totally harmless, and it is illegal. Scientists must objectively study all of marijuana's effects—positive and negative.

KEY TERMS

1. **Consciousness** is the awareness of external stimuli and one's own mental activity. (see introductory section)

    Example: At this moment, you are aware of the words printed on this page. You may also be aware of noises around you, such as a radio playing or a jet flying overhead.

2. The **conscious level** of consciousness is the level at which mental activities that people are normally aware of occur. (see Levels of Consciousness)

    Example: You are conscious of the words you are reading at this moment.

3. The **nonconscious level** is a level of mental activity that is inaccessible to conscious awareness. (see Levels of Consciousness)

    Example: Your brain is sensing the amount of sugar in your blood, but you cannot consciously experience this activity, even if you try to attend to it.

    REMEMBER: Training in techniques such as biofeedback can make you conscious of them indirectly.

4. The **preconscious level** is a level of mental activity that is not currently conscious but of which we can easily become conscious. (see Levels of Consciousness)

    Example: Before reading this sentence, you probably did not feel your socks or your underwear on your skin. But now that you are attending to them, you can feel these physical sensations. They were at the preconscious level but were easily brought into consciousness, in this case by a shift in attention.

5. The **unconscious level** or **subconscious level** is a level of mental activity that influences consciousness but is not conscious. (see Levels of Consciousness)

    Example: In studies of priming, people could not remember having seen certain words on a study list but could solve anagrams of those words faster than words they had not seen. The influence of having studied the words was subconscious and inaccessible.

6. **Consciousness state** refers to the characteristics of consciousness at any particular moment. (see Consciousness States)

7. An **altered state of consciousness** is a condition in which changes in mental processes are extensive enough that a person or others notice significant differences in psychological and behavioral functioning. (see Consciousness States)

8. **Non-REM** or **NREM sleep** consists of sleep stages 1, 2, 3 and 4; they are accompanied by gradually slower, deeper breathing, a calm and regular heartbeat, reduced blood pressure, and slower brain waves. (Stages 3 and 4 are called *slow-wave sleep*.) (see Stages of Sleep)

    REMEMBER: These stages are called quiet sleep because, in comparison to REM sleep, body and brain activity are relatively calm and quiet.

9. **REM (rapid eye movement) sleep** is a stage of sleep in which brain activity and other functions resemble the waking state but that is accompanied by rapid eye movements and virtual muscle paralysis. (see Stages of Sleep)

10. **Circadian rhythms**, or **human biological rhythms**, are cycles, such as waking and sleeping, that repeat about once a day. (see Why Do People Sleep?)

11. **Jet lag** is a syndrome of fatigue, irritability, inattention, and sleeping problems caused by air travel across several time zones. (see Why Do People Sleep?)

    Example: Holly flies to London from Chicago. She arrives in London around 10:00 A.M., but to her body 4:00 A.M. She is tired and has trouble staying awake the rest of the day. It takes her several days to adjust to her new time zone.

12. **Insomnia** is a sleep disorder involving difficulty falling asleep or staying asleep at night. (see Sleep Disorders)

    REMEMBER: The Latin *in* means "no," "not," or "without." *Somnus* means "sleep." Therefore, *insomnia* means "without sleep."

13. **Narcolepsy** is a daytime sleep disorder in which a person shifts abruptly from an active, often emotional waking state into several minutes of REM sleep. (see Sleep Disorders)

    Example: Joe is working on a stressful math problem with his study group and slumps over, asleep, in the middle of the group's heated discussion. He appears unable to move, and his muscles go slack. Joe has narcolepsy.

14. **Sleep apnea** is a sleep disorder in which people briefly but repeatedly stop breathing during the night. (see Sleep Disorders)

    Example: Kirk's wife complains about his snoring and says he seems to gasp for air several times in the night. Kirk goes to do a sleep study, and the results reveal that he stops breathing on average forty times an hour as he sleeps. Kirk has sleep apnea.

15. **Sudden infant death syndrome (SIDS)** is a disorder in which a sleeping baby stops breathing and suffocates. (see Sleep Disorders)

16. **Nightmares** are frightening dreams that take place during REM sleep. (see Sleep Disorders)

    Example: Molly has terrible dreams that a monster is under her bed.

17. **Sleep terror disorder (night terrors)** are the occurrence of horrific dream images during stage 4 sleep, followed by rapid awakening in a state of intense fear. (see Sleep Disorders)

    Example: Connor wakes up in the night screaming his head off. When his parents come running into his room, he is absolutely terrified that bad people are trying to take him away from home. He remains afraid for the next thirty minutes, unwilling to let his parents leave his side.

18. **Sleepwalking** is a phenomenon primarily occurring in non-REM sleep in which people walk while asleep. (see Sleep Disorders)

    Example: Kirby sleepwalks into her sister's room and talks to her about playing Barbie dolls. The next morning, Kirby has no recollection of her nocturnal wanderings.

    REMEMBER: Awakening a sleepwalker is not dangerous.

19. **REM behavior disorder** is a sleep disorder in which a person does not lose muscle tone during REM sleep, allowing the person to act out dreams. (see Sleep Disorders)

Example: Joe's wife complains that he thrashes about at night, kicking her constantly. He says that he has dreams that he is playing football and is the team's kicker. A sleep study reveals that Joe is kicking his wife while he is in REM sleep.

20. **Dreaming** is the experience of story-like sequences of images, sensations, and perceptions occurring mainly during REM sleep. (see Dreams and Dreaming)

10. **Lucid dreaming** is awareness that a dream is a dream while it is happening. (see Dreams and Dreaming)

REMEMBER: The word *lucid* means "clear" or "readily understood." Lucid dreamers clearly know while still asleep that they are dreaming.

11. **Hypnosis** is a phenomenon brought on by special induction techniques and characterized by varying degrees of responsiveness to suggestions for changes in experience and behavior. (see Hypnosis)

Example: Jenna is attending a stage hypnotist's show on campus. She is selected to be hypnotized on stage and listens to the hypnotist's voice, gradually focusing on only it. Her friends tell her she did some crazy things during the show, but she has no memory of it.

REMEMBER: Some people are more susceptible to hypnosis than others. Hypnotic effects can last for days through posthypnotic suggestions, instructions given during hypnosis. People who experience posthypnotic amnesia cannot recall what happened during hypnosis.

12. **Hypnotic susceptibility** is the degree to which a person responds to hypnotic suggestions. (see Experiencing Hypnosis)

Example: Augie wants to be hypnotized, but has trouble doing so. He has low hypnotic susceptibility.

13. **State theories of hypnosis** propose that hypnosis is an altered state of consciousness. (see Explaining Hypnosis)

Example: Moira claims that when she is hypnotized, it is like being asleep—really a totally altered state of consciousness.

14. **Nonstate theories of hypnosis** are theories, such as role theory, proposing that hypnosis does not create an altered state of consciousness. (see Explaining Hypnosis)

Example: Terri thinks that the people who are hypnotized are just going along with what the hypnotists says, not that anything special is going on in their minds. They are just pretending to be hypnotized and following the hypnotist's directions—playing the role that is called for.

15. **Psychoactive drugs** are substances that act on the brain to cause some psychological effect. (see Psychoactive Drugs)

Example: LSD, a psychedelic, changes the perception of sensory information and drastically alters thought processes.

16. **Psychopharmacology** is the study of psychoactive drugs and their effects. (see Psychoactive Drugs)

Example: Emmie is studying the role of the dopamine system in opium addiction. She is a psychopharmacologist.

17. The **blood-brain barrier** is a feature of blood vessels supplying the brain that allows only certain substances to leave the blood and interact with brain tissue. (see Psychopharmacology)

18. **Agonists** are drugs that mimic the effects of the neurotransmitter that normally binds to a neural receptor. (see Psychopharmacology)

    Example: Agonists for endorphins stimulate endorphin receptors, resulting in the same mood-elevating response that an endorphin would cause.

19. **Antagonists** are drugs that bind to receptors and prevent the normal neurotransmitters from binding. (see Psychopharmacology)

    Example: Naloxone, an endorphin antagonist, keeps endorphins from binding with receptors, thereby preventing a "high."

20. **Drug abuse** is the self-administration of psychoactive drugs in ways that deviate from cultural norms and cause serious problems for the user. (see The Varying Effects of Drugs)

    Example: Jeff has a case of beer with him no matter where he goes. He regularly drinks and drives and has received multiple citations for doing so. In fact, he has lost his license and has trouble getting to work because of his drinking.

32. **Addiction** is the development of a physical need for a psychoactive drug. (see The Varying Effects of Drugs)

    Example: Carol's addiction to a barbiturate became evident when, after attempting to quit using the drug, she experienced restlessness, violent outbursts, convulsions, and hallucinations.

33. **Drug withdrawal** is a set of symptoms associated with discontinuing the use of a habit-forming substance. (see The Varying Effects of Drugs)

    Example: Neil is trying to quit using caffeine. He had a bad headache, is shaky, and can't stop thinking about his morning cup of coffee.

34. **Drug tolerance** is a condition in which increasing large drug doses are needed to produce a given effect. (see The Varying Effects of Drugs)

    Example: After using cocaine daily for several weeks, Jesse began to need more and more of the drug to achieve the same "high" he had initially experienced.

35. **CNS depressant drugs** are psychoactive drugs that inhibit the functioning of the central nervous system. (see CNS Depressant Drugs)

    REMEMBER: Depressants create feelings of relaxation, drowsiness, and, sometimes, depression.

36. **CNS stimulating drugs** are psychoactive drugs that have the ability to increase behavioral and mental activity. (see CNS Stimulating Drugs)

    Example: Sally has a cup of coffee in the morning to wake herself up and get going.

37. **Opiates** are psychoactive drugs, such as opium, morphine, and heroin, that produce sleep-inducing and pain-relieving effects. (see Opiates)

    REMEMBER: In the chapter on biological aspects of psychology, you learned that your brain produces a class of neurotransmitters called endorphins, which have effects similar to those of morphine.

38. **Hallucinogenic drugs** are psychoactive drugs that alter consciousness by producing a temporary loss of contact with reality and changes in emotion, perception, and thought. (see Hallucinogens)

    REMEMBER: Because many of these changes are similar to symptoms of psychotic forms of mental illness, these drugs are also called psychedelics, meaning that they mimic psychosis.

FILL-IN-THE-BLANKS KEY TERMS

This section will help you check your knowledge of the key terms introduced in this chapter. Fill in each blank with the appropriate term from the list of key terms in the previous section.

1. When consciousness is characterized by changes from normal waking thought and behavior, a person is said to be in a(n) _____.

2. Physiological processes of which we are unaware, such as brain activity and blood pressure, occur at the _____ level of consciousness.

3. Stages of sleep characterized by slow brain waves are called _____.

4. People who report not being able to go to sleep have _____.

5. _____ occurs when infants die because they did not awaken from an accidental interruption of their breathing.

6. Acting out dreams during REM sleep is characteristic of a person who suffers from _____.

7. The sleep-wake cycle that occurs in humans during a twenty-four-hour period is called a(n) _____.

8. People who involuntarily fall directly into REM sleep, even while engaging in activities, suffer from _____.

9. The awareness of the fact that one is having a dream while it is occurring is called _____.

10. _____ are drugs that block a neurotransmitter's receptors.

11. The theory that suggests that hypnotism is a phenomenon in which subjects voluntarily act as they believe hypnotized people should act is called a _____.

12. A person with a physical need for a drug is experiencing _____.

13. _____ are drugs that reduce central nervous system activity.

14. Drugs that are highly addictive and produce pain relief belong to the class called _____.

15. _____ can cause hallucinations and changes in thought, perception, and emotion.

Total Correct (See answer key) _____

LEARNING OBJECTIVES

1. Define <u>consciousness</u>. Describe the work of cognitive scientists and cognitive neuroscientists. (see introductory section; see also Analyzing Consciousness)

2. Describe the three main questions that dominate the psychological study of consciousness today. Be sure to include *dualism* and *materialism*, the *theater* view versus the *parallel distributed processing (PDP) models* of consciousness, and the link between mental activity and conscious awareness. (see Analyzing Consciousness)

3. Distinguish among the various levels of conscious activity: <u>conscious</u>, <u>nonconscious</u>, <u>preconscious</u>, and <u>unconscious</u>. Give an example of each. (see Levels of Consciousness)

4. Describe priming. (see Mental Processing Without Awareness)

5.   Discuss the research on subliminal messages in rock music. (see Focus on Research Methods: Subliminal Messages in Rock Music)

6.   Describe the effects of *prosopagnosia* and anterograde amnesia on consciousness. (see The Neuropsychology of Consciousness)

7.   Define state of consciousness and altered state of consciousness. (see States of Consciousness)

8.   Compare and contrast slow-wave and REM sleep. Explain the differences in the EEGs of each sleep stage. Discuss the physiological changes that occur during REM sleep. (see Stages of Sleep)

9.   Describe a night's sleep and the changes in sleeping patterns that occur across the lifespan. Discuss the role of culture, society, and the individual in sleep pattern differences. (see Stages of Sleep)

10. Discuss the symptoms and causes of the following sleep disorders: insomnia, narcolepsy, sleep apnea, sudden infant death syndrome (SIDS), nightmares, sleep terror disorder, sleepwalking, and REM behavior disorder. Indicate during which stages of sleep they occur. (see Sleep Disorders)

11. Discuss jet lag and other effects of interfering with the human body clock. Define circadian rhythms and explain their role in sleep patterns. (see Why Do People Sleep?)

12. Discuss the various hypotheses on the reasons for slow-wave and REM sleep. Define REM rebound. (see The Functions of Sleep)

13. Define dreams and lucid dreaming. (see Dreams and Dreaming)

14. Discuss the various theories that explain why people dream, including *wish fulfillment* and *activation-synthesis theory*. (see Dreams and Dreaming)

15. Define hypnosis and describe *hypnotic susceptibility*, *age regression*, *posthypnotic suggestions*, and *posthypnotic amnesia*. (see Hypnosis; see also Experiencing Hypnosis)

16. Describe the five main changes people experience during hypnosis. (see Experiencing Hypnosis)

17. Compare and contrast the role, state, and dissociation theories of hypnosis. (see Explaining Hypnosis)

18. List some of the applications of hypnosis. (see Applications of Hypnosis)

19. Define *meditation*. List the common characteristics of meditation techniques and describe their effects. (see Linkages: Meditation, Health, and Stress)

20. Define psychoactive drugs and psychopharmacology. Explain the function of the blood-brain barrier and discuss how agonist and antagonist drugs work. (see Psychoactive Drugs; see also Psychopharmacology)

21. Define substance abuse, psychological dependence, and physical dependence or addiction. Explain the mechanisms of withdrawal syndrome and tolerance. (see The Varying Effects of Drugs)

22. Explain the role of *learned expectations* in the influence of drugs on behavior. (see The Varying Effects of Drugs)

23. Define depressant. Describe the effects of alcohol and barbiturates on the nervous system and behavior. (see Depressants)

24. Define stimulant. Describe the effects of amphetamines, cocaine, caffeine, nicotine, and MDMA on the nervous system and behavior. (see Stimulants)

25. Define <u>opiates</u>. Describe the effects of opium, morphine, codeine, and heroin on the nervous system. (see Opiates)

26. Define <u>hallucinogens</u>. Describe the effects of LSD, ketamine, and marijuana on the nervous system and behavior. (see Hallucinogens)

27. Discuss research on the level of danger associated with marijuana use. (see Thinking Critically: Is Marijuana Dangerous?)

CONCEPTS AND EXERCISES

Types of Consciousness

Several types of activities are described in the following list. Decide whether these activities are conscious, preconscious, nonconscious, or unconscious. Answers may be used more than once or not at all.

1. Belinda, enjoying the taste of her favorite food, thanks her mother for preparing it.
    _____

2. Paul is putting an adhesive bandage on a cut. He cannot feel the neural activity in his brain that is directing his hand movements. _____

3. Leslie Anne has been in a car accident. She is so busy helping people that she does not feel the pain from her broken collarbone. _____

Stages and Disorders of Sleep at a Slumber Party

Joanna's daughter is having a slumber party. The noise died down about an hour ago. Joanna decides to see if everyone is asleep. Match the listed stages of sleep or sleep disorders with the description of what Joanna finds when she checks on the girls. Answers may be used more than once or not at all.

1. LaVonne is perfectly still except for a few twitches of her face and hands. Joanna notices that the girl's eyes are moving rapidly back and forth even though they are closed.

    _____

2. Joanna spies Isabella in the corner of the room all curled up but clearly still awake. She tells Joanna that it is always hard for her to fall asleep, no matter what the time.

    _____

3. Suddenly Brenda sits up in her sleeping bag. Staring straight ahead, she lets out a bloodcurdling scream. It takes Joanna half an hour to calm her. What has Brenda just experienced?

    _____

4. Joanna counts only six girls in the room. She knows that there should be seven. She makes a quick search of the house and finds Juliette stumbling around the living room, still asleep.

    _____

    a. Narcolepsy

    b. Insomnia

    c. Sleep terror disorder

    d. Nightmares

    e. REM sleep

    f. Stage 1 sleep

    g. Sleepwalking

CRITICAL THINKING

Sam and Martina have been put on a case involving a robbery at a house in the country. The thieves left no marks on any doors or windows. Sam assumes, given the rural location, that the owners did not lock the house every night and asks the husband what their habits are regarding the doors and windows. The owner, named Jack, says, "We used to live in the city where we locked our doors every night. When we moved out here, we just kept up the habit. I lock up every night while Leona's gettin' ready for bed. And, no, we haven't given a key to anyone else." Sam, however, is convinced that Jack must have given keys to someone else and then forgotten about it.

Meanwhile, Martina and Leona are chatting like long-lost friends and eating pie in the kitchen. Leona is describing a hypnosis demonstration in which she has just participated. The hypnotist told her that for two weeks she would go outside and howl at the moon like a dog. She laughs and says, "For the first couple of nights, Jack came out just to see if I would do it, but now he sleeps right through the noise. I still don't believe it myself." Martina asks, "Who gets up first in the morning, you or Jack?" "Oh, I don't know; it varies, I guess," Leona replies.

Sam comes grumpily into the kitchen and motions Martina over to the door for a private consultation. "I'm sure these folks just gave the wrong kind of neighbor a key. We should go question all the neighbors in the vicinity."

Martina shakes her head slowly and tells Sam to have some pie. She says that Jack and Leona did not give a key to anyone and that even if they did, that person did not rob the house.

Using the five critical thinking questions in your text, the clues in the story, and what you have learned in this chapter, answer the following:

1.   What is Sam's hypothesis?

2.   What evidence supports Sam's hypothesis?

3.   What is Martina's alternative hypothesis?

4.   What evidence supports Martina's hypothesis?

PERSONAL LEARNING ACTIVITIES

1.   Examine your own behavior for habits that occur at the preconscious level of consciousness. For example, do you bite your nails or twist your hair without realizing it, until someone brings it to your attention?

2.   Evaluate your amount of sleep. Do you sleep more or less on weekends? Can you tell a difference in your motivation level on days after you have had less sleep? Dr. James Maas, who has done an enormous amount of research on sleep debt, has an interesting website on these topics to explore: http://www.powersleep.org/. There, you will also find a link to a "Sleep IQ" test. Did you learn anything you could use to improve your sleep habits and well-being?

3.   Keep a note pad next to your bed to write down your dreams as soon as you awaken and record daily events and hopes on a calendar. For example, if you have an exam, a date, or a major assignment due, write down how it went. After a week of jotting down the images from your dreams and the events and hopes from your waking life, try to see if there is a connection between the two.

4.   There are numerous websites devoted to meditation, including http://www.learningmeditation.com/. Visit this site and see if you get any ideas for how meditation might help promote stress reduction and well-being. How do you think it is different from other, more traditional, spiritual forms such as prayer?

5. While you watch a few of your favorite television programs, make a note of any statements or actions that relate to drug use. Are there misperceptions about the effects of any drugs? Do people casually mention that they "have" to get a cup of coffee or an alcoholic drink? Do the "popular" characters habitually smoke or drink alcohol? What sort of message do the media send about drug use? Does the message change as the hour of the evening gets later?

MULTIPLE-CHOICE QUESTIONS

Quiz 1

1. Kelly and Juanita are having an argument. Kelly believes that consciousness is separate from the mind, whereas Juanita believes that consciousness and the mind are the same thing. Kelly believes in _____, and Juanita believes in _____.
   a. materialism; dualism
   b. dualism; materialism
   c. the PDP view; materialism
   d. dualism; the PDP view

2. Thad needs to track his blood-sugar level to keep his diabetes under control. Because blood-sugar level is at the _____ level of consciousness, he must use a blood test to check it.
   a. nonconscious
   b. unconscious
   c. subconscious
   d. preconscious

3. Max was in an accident that took away his vision. He says he cannot see anything. But in an experiment, when the experimenter insists that Max try to locate a visual target, he is able to do so. Max is experiencing
   a. priming.
   b. blindsight.
   c. activation synthesis.
   d. a backward masked message.

4. A man with brain damage learns how to play golf, but when asked about his game, he has no conscious recollection that he has ever played golf in his life. This man appears to be suffering from
   a. prosopagnosia.
   b. anterograde amnesia.
   c. an altered state.
   d. posthypnotic amnesia.

5. Lisa can never seem to remember to take off her watch before she steps into the shower. This is probably because the sensation of the watch on her arm occurs at the _____ level.
   a. nonconscious
   b. preconscious
   c. subconscious
   d. unconscious

6.   Slowed brain waves, deep breathing, a calm heartbeat, and low blood pressure are prime indicators of
    a.   REM sleep.
    b.   hypnosis.
    c.   slow-wave sleep.
    d.   lucid dreaming.

7.   EEG readings show different types of brain waves. Alpha waves indicate _____, and delta waves indicate _____.
    a.   alertness; relaxation
    b.   alertness; deep sleep
    c.   relaxation; deep sleep
    d.   deep sleep; alertness

8.   Functional paralysis occurs in which of the following stages of sleep?
    a.   REM
    b.   Stage 4
    c.   Stage 2
    d.   Stage 1

9.   Sleep apnea refers to
    a.   vivid recurrent nightmares.
    b.   breathing problems during sleep.
    c.   excessive daytime sleepiness.
    d.   sudden sleep attacks.

10.   REM sleep is most prevalent during
    a.   infancy.
    b.   puberty.
    c.   young adulthood.
    d.   old age.

11.   Kirk Hinrich has just flown back to Chicago from a basketball game halfway around the world, and he is concerned about jet lag. What is the *most* effective thing he can do to reset his biological clock?
    a.   Get as much sleep as possible after arriving
    b.   Sleep as little as possible after arriving
    c.   Spend as much time as possible outdoors after arriving
    d.   Take a sleeping pill to suppress REM sleep

12. Maryann had the oddest dream last night. She dreamed that her mentor at work, who is an older man, made a pass at her and the she was actually receptive to him. She wonders if maybe the dream is a sign that she is unconsciously attracted to this man. Which theory of dreaming is consistent with Maryann's explanation of her dream?
    a. Activation-synthesis theory
    b. Circadian theory
    c. Problem-solving theory
    d. Wish fulfillment theory

13. Khalid's therapist suggests that they use hypnosis to help him to quit smoking. During hypnosis, the therapist puts Khalid under and then suggests that cigarettes will make him feel nauseated. When the session is over, Khalid remembers nothing that occurred while he was hypnotized. Khalid lack of memory for the hypnotic session is an example of
    a. age regression.
    b. posthypnotic suggestion.
    c. posthypnotic amnesia.
    d. enhanced ability to fantasize.

14. Herman was dreaming of competing in the Boston Marathon. He did not like how he was progressing, so he changed his position in the race. Herman was most likely
    a. hypnotized.
    b. meditating.
    c. experiencing lucid dreaming.
    d. under the influence of psychoactive drugs.

15. If Eli is pretending that he is on a Caribbean beach, it is only because the situation provided him with a socially acceptable reason for seeing things that do not exist. This statement supports the _____ theory of hypnosis.
    a. dissociation
    b. lucid
    c. role
    d. state

16. Norman has found himself a quiet spot, settled into a comfortable position, focused on the sound of his breathing, and assumed a passive attitude. He is about to
    a. start meditating.
    b. develop awareness of his nonconscious.
    c. go to sleep.
    d. start daydreaming.

17. Tolerance is
    a. a need for larger and larger amounts of a drug to achieve the same effect.
    b. a physical need for a drug.
    c. dependence on a drug in order to function.
    d. a drug buildup that prevents overdosing.

18. Stena's endorphin receptors were blocked by the drug she took while in a food-tasting experiment. As a result, when Stena eats spicy, hot chili peppers (which she usually loves), she is extremely uncomfortable and reports not liking the chili pepper. The drug she took prior to eating the chili peppers can be described as a(n)

    a. antagonist.
    b. agonist.
    c. hypnagogic.
    d. psychedelic.

19. Shauna was sexually assaulted and is being seen in the ER. She says that she believes something was slipped into her drink at a party, and she cannot remember everything that happened. She appears to have taken some form of a depressant. Most likely it was

    a. GHB.
    b. an amphetamine.
    c. ketamine.
    d. a barbiturate.

20. Which of the following is true about the consumption of alcohol?

    a. Eating prior to excessive drinking will prevent you from getting drunk.
    b. It is impossible to overdose on alcohol.
    c. Alcohol is a stimulant.
    d. Alcohol can cause memory problems, poor motor coordination, and reduced inhibitions.

Total Correct (See answer key) _____

Quiz 2

Use this quiz to reassess your learning after taking Quiz 1 and reviewing the chapter.

1. Materialism is to the theater view as dualism is to _____.

    a. PDP models
    b. the mind-body problem.
    c. cognitive neuroscience.
    d. prosopagnosia.

2. Following brain damage, Miranda is back to normal awareness in all respects except one: She cannot recognize faces, even those of her family. But when her doctors ask her to listen to voices, she can accurately discern those of her family members. Miranda's brain damage has caused

    a. anterograde amnesia.
    b. an altered state of consciousness.
    c. implicit memories.
    d. prosopagnosia.

3. Material that can be easily brought into consciousness is at the _____ level.

    a. nonconscious
    b. preconscious
    c. subconscious
    d. unconscious

4. Jennifer is at the movies. During the previews, one of the frames flashes "Drink Coca-Cola," but it is so brief she is not even aware she saw it. According to research on subliminal perception, what is most likely to occur?

    a. Jennifer will suddenly feel very thirsty.
    b. Jennifer will continue to sit in her chair and watch the previews.
    c. Jennifer will immediately get up and go buy a Coca-Cola.
    d. Jennifer will think about it long enough and realize what she saw on the screen.

5. Which of the following is the best example of a process operating at the nonconscious level?

    a. Alice names all her teachers from kindergarten to the present.
    b. Juan accidentally calls his sister "creepy" instead of "sleepy" because he dislikes her, although he is not consciously aware of it.
    c. Chris now likes country music but does not realize that it is due to hearing it at work.
    d. Derek uses biofeedback to help him control his blood pressure.

6. Which of the following statements about hypnosis is *true*?

    a. Memories of hypnotized individuals may be less accurate than those of nonhypnotized individuals.
    b. Anyone can be hypnotized.
    c. Hypnosis is actually a stage of sleep.
    d. There is no such thing as posthypnotic suggestion.

7. Altered states of consciousness are characterized by

    a. increased reality testing.
    b. changes in perception.
    c. increased self-control.
    d. planfulness.

8. If you have no circadian rhythms, you probably

    a. cannot dance.
    b. are dead.
    c. cannot sleep.
    d. are overly sensitive to norepinephrine.

9. Kirk is sleeping so deeply that he does not even hear his alarm going off. It goes off for twenty minutes before he hears it and awakens. When the alarm started to go off, Kirk was probably in which stage of sleep.

    a. REM
    b. Stage 1
    c. Stage 2
    d. Stage 3

10. Delta just awakened from a very strange dream of a faceless man chasing her with a knife. The dream became very scary, but because it took place in REM sleep, she often had the feeling that she could not move or scream. Delta's dream would be classified as a

    a.   REM behavior disorder.
    b.   narcoleptic vision.
    c.   nightmare.
    d.   night terror.

11. Ruby has had a terrible evening. Just as her boyfriend, Kato, started to propose to her, he fell asleep. Ruby would feel better if she knew that Kato has

    a.   hypersomnia.
    b.   narcolepsy.
    c.   insomnia.
    d.   sleep terror disorder.

12. Which of the following people would most likely have the greatest amount of REM sleep?

    a.   A person who goes to bed and gets up at exactly the same time each day
    b.   A person on vacation
    c.   A student who has been studying constantly for three days and three nights
    d.   A person with REM behavior disorder

13. Hypnosis has been used to reduce

    a.   nausea due to chemotherapy.
    b.   surgical bleeding.
    c.   pain.
    d.   all of these.

14. A post-hypnotic suggestion is

    a.   the inability to remember what occurred while under hypnosis.
    b.   a suggestion made under hypnosis to have impact after the hypnotic session has ended.
    c.   the theory that consciousness is split while one is under hypnosis.
    d.   the theory that one plays a role during hypnosis but is not actually experiencing an altered state of consciousness.

15. Brendan believes during hypnosis that he cannot see. Later, Brendan tells you that he felt like he was sharing control over his actions with the hypnotist. But also it was as if his ability to see was not part of him while he was hypnotized. Brendan's description of his experience agrees most with the _____ theory of hypnosis.

    a.   dissociation
    b.   lucid
    c.   role
    d.   state

16. A mantra is

    a.   a person trained in meditation.
    b.   a soothing word or phrase.
    c.   the position a person assumes when meditating.
    d.   a special form of meditation.

17. A molecule that fits into a receptor and blocks neurotransmitters from binding is a(n)

　　a.　agonist.
　　b.　antagonist.
　　c.　placebo.
　　d.　cytoblocker.

18. Schizophrenia is a disease that may involve overactivity of the neurotransmitter dopamine. If this is so, then it would be important for drug treatments of schizophrenia to *exclude* dopamine

　　a.　agonists.
　　b.　antagonists.
　　c.　stimulants.
　　d.　depressants.

19. Which of the following is a hallucinogen?

　　a.　Ketamine
　　b.　GHB
　　c.　Morphine
　　d.　MDMA

20. During Cleo's sixteenth birthday party, the rumor spread that someone had spiked the punch (added alcohol to it). This was not the case, but

　　a.　those who believed the rumor became intoxicated when they drank the punch.
　　b.　everyone who drank the punch became intoxicated.
　　c.　no one who drank the punch became intoxicated.
　　d.　those who heard the rumor became intoxicated when they drank the punch.

Total Correct (See answer key) _____

ANSWERS TO FILL-IN-THE-BLANKS KEY TERMS

1. altered state of consciousness (see Consciousness States)

2. nonconscious (see Levels of Consciousness)

3. non-REM sleep (see Stages of Sleep)

4. insomnia (see Sleep Disorders)

5. Sudden infant death syndrome (see Sleep Disorders)

6. REM behavior disorder (see Sleep Disorders)

7. circadian rhythm (see Why Do People Sleep?)

8. narcolepsy (see Sleep Disorders)

9. lucid dreaming (see Dreams and Dreaming)

10. Antagonists (see Psychopharmacology)

11. nonstate theory (see Explaining Hypnosis)

12. addiction (see The Varying Effects of Drugs)

13. CNS depressant drugs (see CNS Depressant Drugs)

14. opiates (see Opiates)

15. Hallucinogens (see Hallucinogens)

ANSWERS TO CONCEPTS AND EXERCISES

Types of Consciousness

1. *Conscious.* Belinda is aware of the taste of the food in her mouth. (see Levels of Consciousness)

2. *Nonconscious.* Paul is not and cannot become aware of the neural activity in his motor cortex. (see Levels of Consciousness)

3. *Preconscious.* Leslie Anne has her attention focused on the people who need her help. Once she attends to the pain in her collarbone, it will easily come into consciousness. (see Levels of Consciousness)

Stages of Sleep at a Slumber Party

1. *REM sleep.* LaVonne is not moving because muscle tone decreases to near-paralysis during this stage. The eyes move rapidly back and forth. (see Stages of Sleep)

2. *Insomnia.* This sleep disorder is characterized by an inability to fall asleep. (see Sleep Disorders)

3. *Sleep terror disorder.* Sleep terror disorder is characterized by vivid and terrifying dreams that occur during stage 4 sleep. It often takes quite a while to calm people after they have a sleep terror disorder experience. (see Sleep Disorders)

4. *Sleepwalking.* Juliette is taking a tour of the house, but she is still asleep. This is sleepwalking. (see Sleep Disorders)

ANSWERS TO CRITICAL THINKING

1. Sam's hypothesis is that someone used a key to get into the house.

2. The evidence in support of the hypothesis is that none of the doors or windows had marks on them typical of forcible entry. Sam also believes that Jack has just forgotten that he gave a key to someone.

3. Martina believes that Leona has probably gone out every night since her hypnosis escapade to "howl at the moon." She probably has not remembered to lock the doors when she comes back in because that has been Jack's responsibility for years. Therefore, any passing burglar could have just walked into the house.

4. The evidence supporting Martina's hypothesis is that if either Jack or Leona consistently got up first and left the house each morning, one of them would probably have noticed the unlocked door. However, if the first person up varied, then each probably assumed the other had unlocked the door on the way out of the house.

ANSWERS TO MULTIPLE-CHOICE QUESTIONS

Circle the question numbers you answered correctly.

Quiz 1

1. b is the answer.   (see Analyzing Consciousness)

    a.   Materialists believe that consciousness and the mind are the same thing, whereas dualists believe that consciousness is separate from the mind.

    c.   A PDP view of consciousness holds that conscious experience is made up of parallel streams of information.

    d.   Juanita may take a PDP view of consciousness, but this does not address her belief that the mind and consciousness are the same thing.

2. a is the answer.   Blood sugar is at the nonconscious level, so Thad cannot become directly aware of it without a physical test. (see Levels of Consciousness)

    b.   Unconscious mental activity cannot be easily brought to conscious awareness. Bodily processes below conscious awareness are categorized as being nonconscious.

    c.   Subconscious is a synonym for unconscious.

    d.   Preconscious activities can easily be brought to conscious awareness.

3. b is the answer.   Blindsight occurs when damage occurs to the primary visual cortex, but surviving pathways permit visual processing without awareness. (see Mental Processing Without Awareness)

    a.   Priming involves mental processing without awareness, as occurs in blindsight, but involves presentation of stimuli to someone with normal sensory processes at a speed faster than permits awareness. Blindsight is a state involving abnormal sensory processes.

    c.   Activation synthesis is a theory of dreaming.

    d.   A backward message is a message that can be heard by playing a recording backward.

4. b is the answer.   Although people with anterograde amnesia have no memory of new information, they can learn new skills. (see The Neuropsychology of Consciousness)

    a.   Prosopagnosia is the inability to recognize faces.

    c.   An altered state of consciousness is a noticeable change from normal conscious functioning. This man just cannot remember his newly acquired skills.

    d.   Posthypnotic amnesia is lack of recall of being hypnotized.

5. b is the answer.   Physical sensations and memories that we can easily access are at the preconscious level of activity. When Lisa stepped into the shower, the sensation of her watch on her arm was at the preconscious level of activity. (see Levels of Consciousness)

    a.   Nonconscious activities are those that cannot reach consciousness. Lisa did feel the watch on her arm, even if she was a bit late in doing so.

    c.   Subconscious activity cannot be easily brought into consciousness. The feeling of water between watch and skin is very easy to bring into consciousness.

    d.   Unconscious activity cannot be easily brought into consciousness. The unconscious is the level to which Freudians suggest our socially unacceptable desires, impulses, and wishes are banished.

6. c is the answer.   These are all indicators of non-REM sleep. (see Stages of Sleep)

    a.   REM sleep is active sleep, much like the waking state of consciousness.

    b.   Hypnosis has characteristics similar to the waking state of consciousness.

d.   In lucid dreaming, individuals are asleep but are aware that they are dreaming. These features are not the prime indicators of lucid dreaming.

7.   c is the answer.   An EEG reading for a relaxed person with closed eyes shows alpha waves, and that of someone in deep sleep shows delta waves. (see Stages of Sleep)

a, b, d.   Only c is correct.

8.   a is the answer.   Functional paralysis occurs during REM sleep. (see Stages of Sleep)

b, c, d.   Functional paralysis does not occur in non-REM sleep. Stages 1, 2, and 4 are all non-REM stages of sleep.

9.   b is the answer.   People suffering from sleep apnea stop breathing hundreds of times each night, waking up each time long enough to resume breathing. (see Sleep Disorders)

a.   Recurrent nightmares are nightmares. They have nothing to do with breathing difficulties unless that is the subject of the nightmare.

c.   Excessive daytime sleepiness can be the result of insomnia, the inability to sleep at night.

d.   Sudden sleep attacks are a prime feature of narcolepsy.

10.   a is the answer.   An average infant sleeps sixteen hours a day; about eight hours of that is spent in REM sleep. (see Why Do People Sleep?)

b, c, d.   As people get older, they spend less and less time asleep. Most of the loss is a decrease in REM sleep.

11.   c is the answer.   Kirk Hinrich needs to readjust to altered light-dark cycles, and staying in the natural light will be the fastest way to do so. (see Why Do People Sleep?)

a.   He does not need more sleep. He needs to readjust to the light-dark cycles of Chicago. Sleeping may make his jet lag worse if it is daytime in Chicago.

b.   He does not need less sleep. He needs to readjust to the light-dark cycles of Chicago. Not sleeping may make his jet lag worse if it is the middle of the night in Chicago.

d.   REM sleep is not a primary factor in jet lag. Altered light-dark cycles are the problem.

12.   d is the answer.   Maryann's explanation is consistent with wish fulfillment theory, which suggests that dreams reflect our unconscious urges. (see Dreams and Dreaming)

a.   Activation synthesis theory suggests that dreams are the mind's attempt to make sense of random brain activity during sleep.

b.   There is no such thing as circadian theory about dreaming.

c.   Research does not support the notion that dreams are attempts to solve everyday problems, so this is not a current theory explaining dreaming; nor does Maryann's explanation focus on problem solving.

13.   c is the answer.   Post-hypnotic amnesia is the inability to recall the events that occurred while under hypnosis. (see Experiencing Hypnosis)

a.   In age regression, the person seemingly returns to childhood in thoughts or actions while hypnotized.

b.   Posthypnotic suggestion is a suggestion made under hypnosis that is to have an impact after hypnosis. The therapist's suggestion that cigarettes will nauseate Khalid is an example of this.

d. A characteristic of people who are hypnotized is enhanced ability to fantasize. Khalid may be better able to fantasize, but this question says nothing about this matter.

14. c is the answer. In lucid dreaming, Herman is aware that he is dreaming and may be able to intentionally direct the dream content. (see Dreams and Dreaming)

a. If Herman were hypnotized, the hypnotist would control Herman's progress in the marathon.

b. If Herman were meditating, he would not be dreaming but would be trying to attain inner peace and tranquility.

d. Dreaming occurs during sleep. Although psychoactive drugs can lead to sleep, they also have many other effects. This is too general an answer for the question.

15. c is the answer. Eli is acting in accordance with the social role of being a hypnosis subject; therefore, he is not in a different state. (see Explaining Hypnosis)

a. The dissociation theory states that people will experience changes in mental processes if enough control is relinquished to the hypnotist.

b. This is not a theory of hypnosis. You may have been thinking of lucid dreaming.

d. State theorists would argue that hypnosis causes an altered state of mental activity, not compliance with a social role.

16. a is the answer. Norman is about to start meditating. Finding a quiet spot, assuming a comfortable position, focusing on one thing, and taking a passive attitude are all elements of meditation methods. (see Linkages: Meditation, Health, and Stress)

b. The nonconscious is totally removed from conscious awareness. Without biofeedback training, Norman cannot become aware of it.

c. Use of one attentional focus and a passive attitude is more likely to be a method of meditation than sleep inducement.

d. Daydreaming does not necessarily require a quiet spot, nor does it require a focus.

17. a is the answer. (see The Varying Effects of Drugs)

b. When there is a physical need for a drug, the person is addicted or physically dependent. Physical dependence can lead to tolerance, but they are not the same phenomenon.

c. Psychological dependence occurs when the drug user relies on a drug in order to function every day. Not taking the drug may cause psychological discomfort.

d. No matter how long people use a drug, they can still overdose if the amount is large enough.

18. a is the answer. An antagonist blocks neurotransmitters from entering, and stimulating, a receptor site. (see Psychopharmacology)

b. An agonist binds with a receptor and stimulates it as a usual neurotransmitter would.

c. Hypnagogic state is the transition from wakefulness into sleep, not a drug type.

d. A psychedelic is another term for a hallucinogen.

19. a is the answer. GHB is a depressant that can cause loss of memory and is also one form of "date rape" drugs. (see CNS Depressant Drugs)

b. Amphetamines are stimulants, not depressants.

    c.   Ketamine is a hallucinogen, not a depressant.

    d.   Barbiturates are not typically considered likely suspects in date rape drugs.

20.   d is the answer.   (see CNS Depressant Drugs)

    a.   Eating prior to drinking may slightly delay the absorption of alcohol and therefore delay its effects, but it does not prevent them from occurring.

    b.   It is possible to overdose on alcohol. The alcohol first affects the frontal cortex, then the midbrain, and finally the hindbrain.

    c.   Alcohol is a depressant, which inhibits central nervous system activity.

Now turn to the quiz analysis table at the end of this chapter to find which areas you know well and which areas you need to work on. Circle the numbers in the table for items on Quiz 1 that you answered correctly.

Quiz 2

1.   a is the answer.   Materialism and dualism are different answers to the mind-body problem. Materialism emphasizes the mind and body as one, whereas dualism sees them as separate. The theater view is a perspective on the question of whether consciousness is a unified phenomenon. The theater view sees it as a single point in mental processing. Thus, materialism and the theater view answer questions of consciousness focusing on units of one, whereas dualism and the PDP model focus on consciousness as more than singular. (see Analyzing Consciousness)

    b.   The mind-body problem asks the relationship between the mind and the physical brain.

    c.   Cognitive neuroscience is the area of psychology that studies consciousness.

    d.   Prosopagnosia is the inability to recognize faces.

2.   d is the answer.   Prosopagnosia is characterized by an inability to recognize faces. (see Mental Processing Without Awareness)

    a.   Anterograde amnesia is the inability to form new memories.

    b.   An altered state occurs when changes in mental processes are great enough that significant differences in functioning are noted. Miranda is in the waking state of consciousness in all respects except for her inability to recognize faces.

    c.   Implicit memories (see the chapter on memory) influence us without our awareness, but incoming information is not a memory.

3.   b is the answer.   Preconscious memories can be recalled easily. (see Levels of Consciousness)

    a.   Nonconscious processes are those physiological activities that people cannot become directly aware of.

    c.   Subconscious activity includes thought processes that cannot easily be brought into consciousness, such as priming and mere exposure. This label is used by those who disagree with Freud's theory about the unconscious.

    d.   Unconscious processes are also not easily brought into consciousness. Freud suggested that socially unacceptable urges are kept in the unconscious.

4.   b is the answer.   Although Jennifer has been primed with the "Drink Coca-Cola" frame—meaning she perceived it without awareness—the impact of priming on behavior is weak and short-lived. It is unlikely to cause any real change in her behavior in this setting. If Coca-Cola were being offered at her seat, she might be more likely to take some, but to get up and leave the

theater as the movie is starting would take a more significant impact than priming usually causes. (see Mental Processing Without Awareness)

    a.   It is unlikely that the message will influence her thirst. Jennifer might be more receptive to Coca-Cola offered to her, but that is the extent of the typical priming effect.

    c.   It is unlikely that a priming message would cause someone to get out of his or her seat and leave the movie to purchase a drink, as priming effects tend to be weak and short-lived.

    d.   Priming effects tend to be short-lived. The longer she sits, the less likely she is to be aware of or affected by the frame.

5.   d is the answer.   Nonconscious activity is not available to our conscious awareness. In biofeedback training, a machine would indicate Derek's blood pressure, but he could not feel it. (see Levels of Consciousness)

    a.   Alice is using her conscious memories to name her teachers.

    b.   Juan may have an unconscious dislike of his sister.

    c.   Chris may be experiencing the mere-exposure effect, which occurs at the unconscious level of consciousness.

6.   a is the answer.   Memories of past events reported by hypnotized, age-regressed individuals are less accurate than those of nonhypnotized individuals. (see Experiencing Hypnosis)

    b.   Not everyone can be hypnotized. About 10 percent of adults are very difficult or impossible to hypnotize.

    c.   Brain waves of hypnotized individuals are very similar to the waking state of consciousness, not to a sleep state.

    d.   Hypnotic effects can last for days through posthypnotic suggestions—instructions about behavior to take place after hypnosis has ended.

7.   b is the answer.   People in an altered state of consciousness experience a change in mental processes significant enough for others to notice. Perceptions are altered and inhibitions are weakened. (see Consciousness States)

    a.   Reality testing is decreased in individuals who are in altered states of consciousness.

    c.   Self-control is decreased in altered states.

    d.   Planfulness, the ability to initiate action on one's own, is decreased in altered states.

8.   b is the answer.   Circadian rhythms are the cycles of behavior and physiology that repeat about every twenty-four hours. If you did not have them, your body would not function, and you would be dead. (see Why Do People Sleep?)

    a.   It is not that kind of rhythm.

    c.   Without circadian rhythms, if you slept you would probably never wake because you would follow no light-dark cycles.

    d.   A certain amount of sensitivity to norepinephrine is needed for alertness. This has no direct connection to circadian rhythms, but it may concern REM sleep.

9.   d is the answer.   Stages 3 and 4 of non-REM sleep are the deepest stages of sleep. It is hardest to rouse someone from sleep in these stages. (see Stages of Sleep)

    a.   REM sleep is not particularly hard to awaken from.

b, c.   Stages 1 and 2 of non-REM sleep are lighter stages of sleep and are not particularly hard to awaken from.

10.   c is the answer.   Nightmares are frightening dreams that take place during REM sleep. (see Sleep Disorders)

a.   REM behavior disorder is a sleep disorder characterized by lack of muscle paralysis during REM sleep. The fact that Delta could not move eliminates this option.

b.   Narcolepsy is the abrupt switch from a waking state into REM sleep. Narcoleptic vision is not a term.

d.   Sleep terror disorder occurs during stage 4 sleep. It involves horrifying images that cause a person to become extremely frightened. The person may wake up with a scream and be difficult to soothe.

11.   b is the answer.   People who have narcolepsy often fall asleep in the middle of an active waking state. They immediately shift into REM sleep. Ruby would feel much better if she knew that Kato had fallen asleep because of narcolepsy, and not because he was bored with the thought of their engagement. (see Sleep Disorders)

a.   People with hypersomnia sleep longer than most people at night, feel tired during the day, and take one or more naps during the daytime. However, they do not fall asleep in the middle of an active waking state.

c.   If Kato had insomnia, he would not be able to fall asleep at all.

d.   Sleep terror disorder occurs during stage 4. Ruby is worried about why Kato fell asleep, not about what happened while he was asleep.

12.   c is the answer.   When people go without REM sleep, they have more REM periods than usual when they finally do sleep. (see Why Do People Sleep?)

a.   People who go to sleep and get up at the same time every day will not have their REM periods interrupted. Therefore, their REM periods will not increase in number or length.

b.   A person on vacation would probably not be doing anything to require more REM sleep.

d.   People with REM behavior disorder spend plenty of time in REM sleep. However, they do not experience the muscle paralysis typical during REM sleep.

13.   d is the answer.   Hypnosis has been used to help people reduce nausea from chemotherapy, surgical bleeding, and pain. (see Applications of Hypnosis)

a, b, c.   These are all uses of hypnosis, but not the only uses.

14.   b is the answer.   Posthypnotic suggestions are given during hypnosis but are followed after hypnosis. (see Experiencing Hypnosis)

a.   Post-hypnotic amnesia is the inability to remember what occurred during hypnosis once one is no longer hypnotized.

c.   This is the dissociation theory of hypnosis.

d.   This is the role theory of hypnosis.

15.   a is the answer.   The dissociation theory states that people will experience changes in mental processes if enough control is relinquished to the hypnotist. (see Explaining Hypnosis)

b.   This is not a theory of hypnosis. You may have been thinking of lucid dreaming.

    c.   The role theory of hypnosis says that people are complying with a social role and are not in a different state.

    d.   State theorists would argue that hypnosis causes an altered state of mental activity, but they do not include releasing control to the therapist and a dissociation of abilities (like sight) from central control.

16.   b is the answer.   (see Linkages: Meditation, Health, and Stress)

    a.   There is no special name for a person well versed in meditation.

    c.   Many different types of positions have been used to meditate. Their only common characteristic is that they are comfortable.

    d.   Several different techniques of meditation exist, but none of them is called a mantra.

17.   b is the answer.   Antagonists bind to a receptor but do not trigger action potentials. (see Psychopharmacology)

    a.   An agonist binds with a receptor but activates it as the neurotransmitter would.

    c.   A placebo is not a molecule.

    d.   Cytoblocker is a made-up name. There is no such thing.

18.   a is the answer.   Agonists are drugs that mimic the effects of neurotransmitters. If a person with schizophrenia has too much dopamine activity already, he or she does not need more. (see Psychopharmacology)

    b.   The drug that would help a person with schizophrenia would be a dopamine antagonist, one that would prevent dopamine activity.

    c.   *Stimulants* is the name for a general class of drugs that increase behavioral and mental activity. Stimulants do not apply specifically to the effect of dopamine in schizophrenia.

    d.   *Depressants* is the name for a general class of drugs that reduce central nervous system activity. Depressants do not apply specifically to the effect of dopamine in schizophrenia.

19.   a is the answer.   Ketamine is the only of these drugs classified as a hallucinogen. (see Hallucinogens)

    b.   GHB is classified as a depressant.

    c.   Morphine is classified as an opiate.

    d.   MDMA is classified as a stimulant.

20.   a is the answer.   The drug itself does not necessarily have to be present to alter people's behavior. Learned expectations also play a role. So, those who believed there was alcohol in the punch would expect to be affected by it and would behave accordingly. (see The Varying Effects of Drugs)

    b.   Only those who believed alcohol was in the punch would expect to become drunk.

    c.   Learned expectations will influence those who think the punch is spiked.

    d.   Again, only those who believed the rumor would expect to become drunk. Merely hearing the rumor would not affect behavior.

Now turn to the quiz analysis table at the end of this chapter to find which areas you know well and which areas you need to work on. Circle the numbers in the table for items on Quiz 2 that you answered correctly.

For each question you answered correctly, circle its number. (Quiz 1 numbers are not shaded; Quiz 2 numbers are shaded.) Are there patterns in the types of questions or the topics you got wrong that could direct your further study? Did you improve from Quiz 1 to Quiz 2?

QUIZ REVIEW

Topic	Type of Question		
	Definition	Comprehension	Application
Analyzing Consciousness		1	
			1
Levels of Consciousness			2, 5
	3		5
Mental Processing Without Awareness			3
			2, 4
The Neuropsychology of Consciousness			4
Consciousness States			
	7		
Sleeping and Dreaming			
Stages of Sleep	7	6, 8	
			9
Why Do People Sleep?		10	11
			8, 12
Sleep Disorders		9	
			10, 11
Dreams and Dreaming		12	14
Hypnosis			
Experiencing Hypnosis			13
	14	6	
Explaining Hypnosis			15
			15
Applications of Hypnosis			
		13	
Linkages: Meditation, Health, and Stress			16
	16		
Psychoactive Drugs			
Psychopharmacology			18
	17		18
The Varying Effects of Drugs	17		
			20
Drugs: CNS Depressant Drugs, CNS Stimulating Drugs, Opiates, and Hallucinogens		20	19
		19	

Total correct by quiz:

Quiz 1:	
Quiz 2:	

CHAPTER 10

Cognitive Abilities

<u>Cognitive ability</u> is the capacity to perform the higher mental processes of reasoning, remembering, understanding, solving problems, and making decisions.

OUTLINE

I. TESTING FOR INTELLIGENCE
    Many psychologists agree that three characteristics encompass <u>intelligence</u>: abstract reasoning or thinking ability, problem solving abilities, and the capacity to acquire knowledge.

    A. A Brief History of Intelligence Tests
        Alfred Binet's original test included a series of age-graded items that demonstrated differences among children in reasoning, judgment, and problem-solving abilities and measured their <u>mental age</u>. Children who answered questions at their age level were considered of "regular" intelligence. Louis Terman developed the <u>Stanford-Binet Intelligence Scale</u>, devised a scoring method known as the intelligence quotient (IQ), and created the IQ test, which included questions for adults. Despite cultural biases, IQ tests were given to screen immigrants and to place soldiers in appropriate assignments. David Wechsler developed a new test that was made up of several subtests. Wechsler's test reduced the extent to which answers depended on a certain culture and had some subtests that had little or no verbal content and created a profile of abilities.

    B. Intelligence Tests Today
        The Wechsler test, which is designed to be administered individually, includes the *verbal scale* and the *performance scale.*

        The average result obtained by people at each age level is assigned an <u>intelligence quotient</u>, or <u>IQ</u>, of 100. Each individual's score is compared to the average for his or her age level in order to compute an IQ. Therefore, an IQ score is a relative measurement.

    C. Aptitude and Achievement Tests
        These two types of tests are closely related to intelligence tests. <u>Aptitude measures</u> are designed to gauge a person's ability to learn or do certain things. <u>Achievement measures</u> assess how much a person already knows in a certain area.

II. MEASURING THE QUALITY OF TESTS
    <u>Tests</u> have two advantages over other means of evaluation: They are standardized so that different people's performances can be compared, and they are quantifiable (which allows the calculation of <u>norms</u>).

    A. Statistical Reliability
        If a test has <u>statistical reliability</u>, a person will receive about the same score when tested on different occasions. There are three methods of checking the reliability of a test: *test-retest*, *alternate-form*, and *internal consistency* (usually calculated as *split-half reliability*). If the *correlation coefficient* between two scores is high and positive, the test is considered reliable.

B.   Statistical Validity
A test has <u>statistical validity</u> to the degree that its scores are interpreted properly and used appropriately. There are several measures of validity, including *content validity*, *criterion validity*, *predictive validity*, and *construct validity*.

III.   EVALUATING INTELLIGENCE TESTS
A.   The Statistical Reliability and Validity of Intelligence Tests
1.   *How Reliable Are Intelligence Tests?* IQ tests usually provide consistent results. However, test-retest reliability can be low if the initial testing is done prior to seven years of age. The testing conditions and the person's motivation when taking the test can also affect results.
2.   *How Valid Are Intelligence Tests?* The validity of IQ tests is difficult to measure, in part because intelligence itself is difficult to define. IQ tests do a reasonably good job of predicting academic and job success. Few other psychological tests show the reliability and validity that intelligence tests do.
3.   *How Fair Are IQ Tests?* Controversy about the fairness of IQ tests continues, especially in terms of cultural factors. Although many of the technical problems in IQ tests have been solved, the social consequences of testing should be evaluated.
B.   Linkages: Emotionality and the Measurement of Cognitive Abilities
People tend to perform at their best when their arousal level is moderate. Too much or too little arousal will result in decreased performance. Those whose arousal inhibits their performance in testing are said to suffer from *text anxiety*. Concern over negative stereotypes about the mental abilities of the group to which they belong can impair test performance of some members of ethnic minorities, a phenomenon known as *stereotype threat*. In sum, people who are severely anxious about testing will not perform to the best of their ability.

C.   Innate and Environmental Influences on IQ
The influences of heredity and the environment interact to produce intelligence, leading intelligence to be viewed as a *developed ability*. Correlational studies with twins suggest that heredity influences the development of IQ. However, the environment also exerts a strong influence on IQ. Previously underprivileged children placed in homes that provide an enriching intellectual environment have shown moderate but consistent increases in IQ. Yet an impoverished environment does more to limit intelligence than an enriching one does to develop it. About half the variability in IQ among a group of people is due to heredity, while the other half is due to both environment and measurement error.

D.   Group Differences in IQ
An examination of the differences among group means on IQ tests does not provide information about specific individuals in those groups. A person in the low-score group may have an individual score that is much higher than a person from the high-score group. In addition, inherited features may be influenced by the environment.

1.   *Socioeconomic Differences.* There is a positive correlation between socioeconomic status and IQ scores. A child's ability is influenced by genetic factors and perhaps by the effects of the parents' occupation and education on the home environment. Also, higher-income families may encourage a higher level of motivation to succeed, leading to greater effort put forth in a testing situation.
2.   *Ethnic Differences.* There is variation in average IQ scores between ethnic groups, but more variation within groups. Research indicates that differences in IQ among ethnic groups may be due to differences in socioeconomic environment, parental education, nutrition, health care, and schools. Also, people in some cultures may be more or less

motivated during testing, depending on the value their cultures place on education or intelligence.

E.   Conditions That Can Raise IQ

Enrichment programs such as Head Start can cause at least temporary gains in IQ scores. Spending time in projects such as Head Start may cause a child to be more motivated and have a better attitude toward school. Yet the gains often do not last, fading after about two years. This may be because children graduate from such enrichment programs and then enter substandard schools that serve the poor. The primary benefit of enrichment programs probably lies in improving children's attitudes toward school.

F.   IQ in the Classroom

IQ scores may influence teachers' expectations about the abilities of their students. In turn, these expectancies may influence students' performance, but this relationship is fairly complex. Although IQ scores are criticized as informing teacher expectancy, they may also help correct errors, revealing that a student has ability that a teacher failed to recognize. IQ tests can also help educators identify student strengths and weaknesses, and offer a curriculum that will best serve the students.

G.   Thinking Critically: Are Intelligence Tests Unfairly Biased Against Certain Groups?

What am I being asking to believe or accept?

Intelligence tests are biased against some minority groups.

What evidence is available to support the assertion?

Differences in IQ scores may reflect motivation and a person's trust in the test administrator, or other non-cognitive factors. Some tests are not "culture fair" and make assumptions about knowledge of middle class culture in the United States. People may interpret the test questions intelligently but differently than the defined "right" answer.

Are there alternative ways of interpreting the evidence?

Intelligence tests may be biased in assessing general intelligence, but they may still be good predictors of who will do well in school or on the job.

What additional evidence would help to evaluate the alternatives?

If the problem of test bias is really a reflection of group differences, then it is important to conduct research on interventions that will reduce those differences. At the same time, continuing to search for better tests that minimize those differences without a loss of predictive validity would be helpful, as well.

What conclusions are most reasonable?

Current tests, although not completely culture fair, can be useful as predictors of success in the culture in which they are administered. Probably no culture-free test of intelligence exists, as intelligence is defined by the behaviors that a culture values. Psychologists have turned to focus more energy on how to help people develop the abilities required for success in a particular culture.

IV.   UNDERSTANDING INTELLIGENCE

A.   The Psychometric Approach

Standardized intelligence tests are associated with <u>psychometrics</u>, the scientific study and measurement of knowledge, ability, attitudes, personality, and other psychological characteristics. The <u>psychometric approach</u> tries to describe the structure of intelligence by examining the correlations among scores on various tests. Charles Spearman postulated two types of intelligence that account for test scores: general intelligence or *g*; and special intelligences, or _s_, which are the specific skills and knowledge needed to answer the questions on a particular test. L. L. Thurstone disagreed. He used factor analysis, a statistical technique, to find several independent primary mental abilities, including numerical ability, reasoning, verbal fluency, spatial visualization, perceptual ability, memory, and verbal comprehension. Later, Raymond B. Cattell argued that _g_ exists and that it consists of <u>fluid intelligence</u> and <u>crystallized intelligence</u>. Most psychologists agree that there is _g_. They just do not agree on what _g_ is.

B. The Information-Processing Model
Psychologists using the <u>information-processing model</u> have tried to understand intelligence by examining the mental processes involved in intelligent behavior. Research suggests that those with greater intellectual ability have more attentional resources available when performing a task and greater working memory resources.

C. The Triarchic Theory of Intelligence
Robert Sternberg proposed the <u>triarchic theory of intelligence</u>: _analytic, creative_, and _practical_. Analytic intelligence refers to the sort of intelligence that traditional IQ tests measure. Creative intelligence is what you would use to complete a generative task, such as composing music. Practical intelligence refers to one's "common sense," or ability to solve practical problems in life, such as determining what to do if you are stranded in a blizzard. The theory is important because it extends intelligence into everyday life but has been criticized for being so broad that it is difficult to test.

D. Multiple Intelligences
In his theory of <u>multiple intelligences</u>, Howard Gardner proposed that certain abilities are relatively independent of one another and that individuals may develop some "intelligences" more highly than others. Gardner suggested eight different intelligences: _linguistic, logical-mathematical, spatial, musical, body-kinesthetic, intrapersonal_ (self-knowledge), _interpersonal_ (social skills), and _naturalistic_. Other researchers have described _emotional_ intelligence. Gardner's views are welcome by some because they allow everyone to be intelligent in at least one way, but critics say it dilutes the value of the intelligence concept.

E. Focus on Research Methods: Tracking Cognitive Abilities over the Life Span
Age-related changes in mental abilities can be examined through _cross-sectional_ and _longitudinal studies_. The _cross-sequential with resampling design_ combines cross-sectional and longitudinal studies. Results show that crystallized intelligence may continue to grow into old age. Fluid intelligence remains stable in adulthood and then declines in late life. Specifically, problems in working memory, processing speed, problem-solving strategy organization, flexibility, and control of attention appear late in life. What is still unclear is why these age-related changes occur.

V. DIVERSITY IN COGNITIVE ABILITIES
A. Creativity
<u>Creativity</u> is often assessed by tests of <u>divergent thinking</u>, which measure the ability to generate many different but plausible responses to a problem. Expertise in the field, a set of creative skills, and intrinsic motivation are necessary for creativity. External rewards can deter creativity. The correlation between IQ scores and creativity is fairly modest, but positive. IQ tests measure <u>convergent thinking</u>, whereas creativity is characterized by divergent thinking. The combination of intelligence and creativity in one person has been labeled _wisdom_.

B. Unusual Cognitive Ability
1. _Giftedness._ People who have remarkably high levels of accomplishment in particular domains (or show promise of accomplishment) are categorized as <u>gifted</u>. Those with

extremely high IQs do not necessarily become creative geniuses. They do, however, usually become very successful in their society or culture.

2. *Intellectual Disability.* This label, or others (including *developmentally disabled, cognitively disabled,* or *mentally challenged*), is applied to people whose IQs are 70 or below and who fail at daily living skills. Mental retardation sometimes has very specific causes, such as *Down syndrome.* In most cases of cultural familial intellectual retardation, there is no specific cause. Psychologists believe <u>cultural familial intellectual disability</u> results from an interaction between heredity and the environment, and most are what we would call mildly intellectually disabled. These children differ from other children in three ways: They perform certain mental operations more slowly, they know fewer facts about the world, and they are not very good at using particular mental strategies in learning and problem solving. *Mainstreaming* intellectually disabled individuals who are higher functioning may provide some benefit to those students.

3. *Learning Disabilities.* People with <u>learning disabilities</u> have academic performance that does not measure up to their measured intelligence. People with *dyslexia* see letters as distorted or jumbled. *Dysphasia* is difficulty in understanding spoken words. In *dysgraphia* a person has trouble writing, and in *dyscalculia* a person has trouble with arithmetic. Most researchers describe learning disabilities in terms of dysfunctional information processing. Diagnosing a learning disability requires one to rule out alternative explanations for the poor academic performance and alternative diagnoses.

KEY TERMS

1. **Cognitive ability** is the capacity to reason, remember, understand, solve problems, and make decisions. (see introductory section)

2. **Intelligence** describes personal attributes that center around skill at information processing, problem solving, and adapting to new or changing environments. (see Testing for Intelligence)

    REMEMBER: Psychologists do not agree on an exact definition of intelligence.

3. **Mental age** is a score corresponding to the age level of the most advanced items a child could answer correctly on Alfred Binet's first intelligence test. (see A Brief History of Intelligence Tests)

    Example: Cheri is 7 years old and is able to answer the same questions that most other 7-year-olds can. Her mental age matches her chronological age.

4. The **Stanford-Binet Intelligence Scale** is a test for determining a person's intelligence quotient, or IQ. (see A Brief History of Intelligence Tests)

    Example: Mark's IQ has been tested. Although he is only twelve, he answered questions designed for children up to fourteen years of age. The following steps are used to determine his IQ:

    a. Mark's mental age is fourteen.

    b. Mark's chronological age is twelve.

    c. $14/12 = 1.16$

    d. $1.16 \times 100 = 116$.

    e. Mark's IQ is 116.

REMEMBER: It was a revised version of Binet's original test of cognitive abilities. Each set of age-graded questions could be answered correctly by a substantial majority of the children in that age group. Children were above average if they could correctly answer questions above their age grade. The score received, called mental age, was divided by chronological age and then multiplied by 100, resulting in an IQ.

5. **Intelligence quotient (IQ)** is an index of intelligence that reflects the degree to which a person's score on an intelligence test deviates from the average score of others in the same age group. (see Intelligence Tests Today)

6. **Aptitude measures** are tests designed to measure a person's capacity to learn certain things or perform certain tasks. (see Aptitude and Achievement Tests)

7. **Achievement measures** are tests designed to measure what a person has accomplished or learned in a particular area. (see Aptitude and Achievement Tests)

8. **Tests** are systematic procedures for observing behavior in a standard situation and describing it with the help of a numerical scale or a category system. (see Measuring the Quality of Tests)

   Example: To give a test in a standard situation, the directions, setting, and scoring methods used are the same regardless of the people involved. An example of a numerical scale would be the calculation of an IQ.

9. **Norms** are descriptions of the frequency at which particular scores occur, allowing scores to be compared statistically. (see Measuring the Quality of Tests)

10. **Statistical reliability** is the degree to which a test can be repeated with the same results. (see Statistical Reliability)

    Example: Each time Connie takes an intelligence test, she scores at the mean for her age group.

11. **Statistical validity** is the degree to which test scores are interpreted correctly and used appropriately. (see Statistical Validity)

    Example: Defining a list of words is a valid test of vocabulary but may not be a valid test of intelligence.

12. **Psychometrics** is the scientific study and measurement of knowledge, abilities, attitudes, personality, and other psychological characteristics. (see The Psychometric Approach)

    REMEMBER: Psych means "mental." *Metric* means to "measure."

13. The **psychometric approach** is a way of studying intelligence that emphasizes analysis of the products of intelligence, especially scores on intelligence tests. (see The Psychometric Approach)

    Example: Ray uses factor analysis to identify what "factors" go into intelligence. He thinks there are three main factors to measure.

14. General intelligence, called g, is a general intelligence factor that Charles Spearman postulated as accounting for positive correlations between people's scores on all sorts of cognitive ability tests. (see The Psychometric Approach)

15. s, is a group of special abilities that Charles Spearman saw as accompanying general intelligence (g). (see The Psychometric Approach)

    Example: A person with a high level of g might still answer a mathematics question incorrectly if the person lacked the necessary s-factors.

16. **Fluid intelligence** is the basic power of reasoning and problem solving. (see The Psychometric Approach)

Example: To be a good detective, you must be able to look at all the available clues and deduce "who done it." The powers of deduction and reasoning represent fluid intelligence. (Read the example of crystallized intelligence, Key Term 17, to understand the difference between the two types.)

17. **Crystallized intelligence** is the specific knowledge gained as a result of applying fluid intelligence. (see The Psychometric Approach)

    Example: Detectives who have been working for a long time have gained specific knowledge about how to read clues and people. An experienced detective may be able to examine the scene of a crime and notice clues that tell her when the crime took place. This specific knowledge (crystallized intelligence) gained from previous experience (previous applications of fluid intelligence) will increase her overall chances of solving the crime.

18. The **information-processing model** is an approach to the study of intelligence that focuses on mental operations, such as attention and memory, that underlie intelligent behavior. (see The Information-Processing Model)

    Example: A psychologist using this approach to study intelligence would ask the following types of questions: What influence does effective chunking ability have on intelligent behavior? Does being able to rapidly access information in long-term memory increase the ability to behave intelligently? (Chunking and accessing long-term memory are ways of processing information.)

19. The **triarchic theory of intelligence** is Robert Sternberg's theory that describes intelligence as having analytic, creative, and practical dimensions. (see The Triarchic Theory of Intelligence)

    REMEMBER: Analytic intelligence is traditional, academically oriented ability. Creative intelligence is the ability to produce novel but effective solutions to problems or situations. Practical intelligence deals with adapting to or shaping the environment when correct answers may not necessarily exist.

20. The **multiple intelligences** are eight semi-independent kinds of intelligence postulated by Howard Gardner. (see Multiple Intelligences)

    REMEMBER: According to multiple intelligence theory, people have linguistic, logical-mathematical, spatial, musical, body-kinesthetic, intrapersonal, interpersonal, and naturalistic intelligences.

21. **Creativity** is the ability to produce new, high-quality ideas or products. (see Creativity)

    Example: LaKisha is making a stuffed roast, and the recipe calls for kitchen twine to tie the roast together. She does not have the twine, but she figures out that she can use the dental floss (unflavored, of course) that she does have, to serve the same purpose.

22. **Divergent thinking** is the ability to think along many alternative paths to generate many different solutions to a problem. (see Creativity)

    Example: Consider the following question: What can you use a newspaper for? Answers that relate to gaining information or news represent convergent thinking. Answers that are examples of divergent thinking include using newspapers to create a papier-mâché object, to light a fire, to pad a package, to cover oneself for warmth, to provide insulation from noise, to stuff shoes so that they keep their shape, to make a higher seat for a short child, to make a toy for a cat, to make an airplane, to wrap a box, to train a puppy, to humidify the air (by draping wet newspapers over a radiator), to make a ransom note (by cutting out letters from a newspaper), and to soak up water (by putting newspapers in wet shoes).

23. **Convergent thinking** is the ability to apply logic and knowledge to narrow down the number of possible solutions to a problem or perform some other complex cognitive task. (see Creativity)

Example: Linda is taking a test in which she has to find the correct answer to an algebra problem. She is engaged in convergent thinking.

24.   **Gifted** is a term referring to people who show remarkably high levels of accomplishment, or promise for such accomplishment in particular cognitive domains. (see Unusual Cognitive Ability)

Example: Abby has scored very highly on measures of cognitive ability—she has been placed into her school district's gifted program.

25.   **Cultural familial intellectual disability** refers to cases of mild cognitive disability for which there is no obvious genetic or environmental cause. (see Unusual Cognitive Ability)

Example: Kylie has an IQ of 69. Her parents have IQs in the normal range and provide a typical environment. She has no identifiable genetic problems. She is slow at reasoning and knows fewer facts about the world than most children her age.

26.   **Learning disabilities** are conditions which may account for a significant discrepancy between a person's measured intelligence and academic performance. (see Unusual Cognitive Ability)

Example: Sydney has difficulty writing, which adversely affects his school grades. However, when he takes a standardized intelligence test, he has very high intelligence. The writing problems mask his intelligence in school academic performance.

FILL-IN-THE-BLANKS KEY TERMS

This section will help you check your knowledge of the key terms introduced in this chapter. Fill in each blank with the appropriate term from the list of key terms in the previous section.

1.   The capacity to perform processes such as reasoning is called _____.

2.   Information necessary to decide how a person's test score compares to the scores of others comes from _____.

3.   A(n) _____ is a systematic procedure for observing behavior in a standard situation.

4.   If a person achieves a high score on an IQ test the first time but a very low score the second time he or she takes it, the test has low _____.

5.   A test that actually measures what it is designed to measure is said to be _____.

6.   The _____ reflects relative standing on a test within a population of the same age group.

7.   According to Cattell, the basic power of logical thought is _____.

8.   Psychologists who seek to describe and understand intelligence by analyzing data from intelligence tests take the _____ approach.

9.   A psychologist who takes the _____ approach examines intelligence by studying the mental operations that underlie intelligent behavior.

10.   _____ is the ability to come up with new or unusual but viable solutions to a problem.

11.   A(n) _____ test is designed to measure a person's capacity to learn certain things or perform certain tasks.

12.   A person adept at _____, or capable of thinking along many paths when generating problem solutions, is considered to be creative.

13. _____ is the ability to apply rules, logic, and knowledge to reduce the number of possible solutions to a problem.

14. Conditions which account for significant discrepancy between a person's measured intelligence and academic performance are called _____.

15. Cattell believed that intelligence involving specific knowledge gained through reasoning and problem solving is called _____.

Total Correct (See answer key) _____

LEARNING OBJECTIVES

1. Define <u>cognitive ability</u>. (see introductory section)

2. Define <u>intelligence</u>. Discuss the reasons that intelligence is so difficult to define. (see Testing for Intelligence)

3. Explain the scoring methods used in the Binet test and <u>Stanford-Binet Intelligence Scale.</u> Discuss the history of intelligence test, or IQ test, construction. (see A Brief History of Intelligence Tests)

4. Discuss the use and abuse of intelligence testing in the United States in the early 1900s. (see A Brief History of Intelligence Tests)

5. Describe Wechsler's intelligence test. Explain why it is different from tests that were used previously. Explain the components of the verbal and performance scales. (see Intelligence Tests Today)

6. Describe the process of IQ test scoring used today to yield an <u>intelligence quotient,</u> or <u>IQ</u>. (see Intelligence Tests Today)

7. Describe the differences between an <u>aptitude measure</u> and an <u>achievement measure</u>. (see Aptitude and Achievement Tests)

8. Define <u>test</u>. Describe the advantages of tests over other evaluation methods. Explain the usefulness of norms. (see Measuring the Quality of Tests)

9. Define <u>statistical reliability</u>. Describe the process of assessing reliability using *test-retest*, *alternate-forms*, and *split-half reliability* methods. Give an example of each. (see Reliability)

10. Define <u>statistical validity</u> as well as *content, criterion, predictive,* and *construct validity*. (see Validity)

11. Describe the results of checks on IQ test reliability. Describe studies of the validity of IQ tests. (see The Reliability and Validity of IQ Tests)

12. Discuss the evidence for and against the argument that IQ tests are culturally biased. Define culture-fair tests. (see The Reliability and Validity of IQ Tests)

13. Describe how emotional arousal affects the measurement of mental abilities. Define *test anxiety* and *stereotype threat*. (see Linkages: Emotionality and the Measurement of Cognitive Abilities)

14. Discuss the possible interpretations of evidence from correlational twin studies on the role of heredity and the environment in the development of intelligence. (see IQ Scores as a Measure of Innate Ability)

15. Explain why a group intelligence score tells you nothing about the individuals in the group. Discuss the variables that affect group intelligence scores. (see Group Differences in IQ Scores)

16. Describe the conditions that can raise IQ scores. Explain why a teacher's expectancies can affect students' classroom performance and improvement. (see Conditions That Can Raise IQ Scores; see also IQ Scores in the Classroom)

17. Discuss the evidence of group bias in intelligence tests and what reasonable conclusions can be drawn for creating a culture-fair intelligence test. (see Thinking Critically: Are Intelligence Tests Unfairly Biased Against Certain Groups?)

18. Describe the psychometric approach to studying intelligence. Define *g*, *s*, *group factors*, *primary mental abilities*, fluid intelligence, and crystallized intelligence. Give an example of each. (see The Psychometric Approach)

19. Describe the information-processing approach to studying intelligence. Describe the role of attention in intelligent behavior. (see The Information-Processing Approach)

20. Describe the triarchic theory of intelligence. Define *analytic intelligence, creative intelligence,* and *practical intelligence*. (see The Triarchic Theory of Intelligence)

21. Explain Gardner's theory of multiple intelligences. List the eight types of intelligences he proposed. (see Multiple Intelligences)

22. Explain the differences between *cross-sectional* and *longitudinal studies* as tools for examining age-related changes in intelligence. Describe the *cross-sequential with resampling design* and the confounds for which it corrects. (see Focus on Research Methods: Tracking Cognitive Abilities over the Life Span)

23. Describe the types of changes in intelligence that occur with aging. (see Focus on Research Methods: Tracking Cognitive Abilities over the Life Span)

24. Discuss the relationship between creativity and intelligence. Define divergent and convergent thinking. (see Creativity)

25. Describe the correlation between giftedness and success in our society. Define intellectual disability and *cultural familial intellectual disability*. (see Unusual Cognitive Ability)

26. Define *learning disability*. Describe the types of learning disabilities and their possible causes. (see Learning Disabilities)

CONCEPTS AND EXERCISES

Defining Intelligence

Following is a conversation among several professors who want to found a new university. They are arguing about what admission requirements would ensure that only the brightest students attended their school. Determine which approach each professor would use to study intelligence and who generated the original ideas behind those approaches. Choose your answers from the list following the conversations. Answers can be used more than once.

1. *Pedro:* I think we should have several tests: one for language, one for musical abilities including dancing, one for analytical skills, and one for personal knowledge. (Pedro would follow the _____ approach as suggested by _____.)

2. *Pam:* How many engineers do you know who can do the polka? I think we should give prospective students a general intelligence test and look at the correlations among the various subscales to see how high their *g* is. (Pam would follow the _____ approach as suggested by _____.)

3.   *Steve:* g doesn't explain all the available data. Besides, we could end up admitting someone with a high g who doesn't have many of the primary mental abilities, such as reasoning, spatial visualization, perceptual ability, memory, and verbal fluency and comprehension. (Steve would follow the _____ approach as suggested by _____.)

4.   *Elena:* Let's get down to what counts. I know primary mental abilities are necessary for success, but that's not all there is to it. We should look for students who can approach problems with fresh, new ideas and who can adapt and function in the real world when there may be no readily available "right" answers. (Elena would follow the _____ approach as suggested by _____.)

5.   *Leigh:* We really need to find people who can think creatively. I know a ton of dull but brilliant people. Let's ask students to produce a film on what would happen if all higher-level education were banned by the government and decide on the basis of that. (Leigh wants to test for _____.)

   a.   Sternberg

   b.   Divergent thinking

   c.   Gardner

   d.   Psychometric theory

   e.   Spearman

   f.   Thurstone

   g.   Multiple intelligences

   h.   Triarchic theory

The Testing Business

Sean Dorgan has recently begun a testing service. Following are some descriptions of his activities. Fill in the blank with the correct term by either choosing from the list at the end of the exercise or recalling the appropriate information from your reading. Answers can be used more than once.

1.   Dorgan has just received information on a new test on the market. He has ordered a sample copy of the test and plans to divide the test into two sections that are roughly equivalent, and then correlate the scores on the two sections. Dorgan is using the _____ method to check for statistical reliability.

2.   Dorgan has just received a new achievement test. He knows that it has already been successfully tested for statistical reliability. Because the test is reliable, does Dorgan have to test it for validity? _____

3.   Dorgan wants to attract newcomers from foreign countries as clients. Can Dorgan develop a culture-fair test? _____

4.   Dorgan has just issued a memo to all his employees saying that all tests are to be administered in exactly the same way, given in the same room, and scored in exactly the same way. Dorgan wants to ensure that all of his tests are _____.

5.   Dorgan has just received a new test of mathematical ability. He is confused because there are no math problems on the test. What kind of validity is he worried about? _____

   a.   Standardized

   b.   Culture-fair

c. Achievement test

d. Predictive validity

e. Criterion validity

f. Content validity

g. Reliability

h. Test-retest

i. Alternate forms

j. Split-half

CRITICAL THINKING

Sam and Martina, who work in New York, are trying out a new lie detector test that requires no equipment. The test was designed in South Carolina. Supposedly, if a suspect looks down when answering a question, she or he is lying. If the suspect looks up and to the right, she or he is considering all possible responses. If the suspect looks up and to the left, she or he is simply trying to pull information out of long-term memory.

Sam and Martina have tested quite a number of people in New York City and are not happy with the results. Some people who were innocent were unable to pass the test. Consequently, Sam has decided that the test has no validity. Martina, however, thinks she knows why some people could not pass the test.

Using the five critical thinking questions in your text, the clues in the story, and what you have learned about mental abilities and testing, answer the following.

1. What is Sam's hypothesis?

2. What evidence supports Sam's hypothesis?

3. What is Martina's alternative hypothesis?

4. What evidence would Martina need to collect to support her hypothesis?

PERSONAL LEARNING ACTIVITIES

1. List behaviors and abilities that you consider intelligent. Now write your own definition of intelligence. Design a test that will measure intelligence as you have defined it. Create two or three sample tasks or items that could differentiate between people of varying levels of ability and give them to volunteers. How did your volunteers perform on your test? How culturally fair do you think your test is? To take a test that my feel culturally "unfair" to you (depending on where in the world you are from), visit the following website: http://wilderdom.com/personality/intelligenceOriginalAustralian.html. Take the test, then go to the score sheet, and see how you did. Does this experience inform your judgment of whether or not your own items are culturally fair or not?

2. Read the list, definition, and items you wrote for Personal Learning Activity 2, and identify the approach you took to intelligence. Was your theory more similar to the psychometric approach, information-processing model, triarchic theory, or multiple intelligences theory?

3. Based on the information on the reliability, validity, and impact of IQ testing presented in your text, do you think the testing should continue? Why or why not? Describe the advantages and disadvantages of assigning people IQ scores. To learn more, read the following article online:

http://www.apa.org/monitor/feb03/intelligent.aspx. It describes issues related to the usage of intelligence testing that might inform you opinion.

4.   What impact do you think computers have had on intelligence scores? Are people smarter now than they were in the past? Do you think differential access to computers and the stimulation and instant information they provide may further divide people into haves and have-nots? To learn more about how IQ scores have changed over time, and possible explanations for why, visit the following website: http://www.indiana.edu/~intell/flynneffect.shtml.

5.   For fun, visit the following website to try out some divergent thinking puzzles: http://www.aimsedu.org/Puzzle/categories/divergent.html. They are rated for difficulty from 1 star to 5 stars. Do you think that they are good measures of divergent thinking? Would they predict creativity? How do these problems differ from the sort of academic work you generally engage in?

MULTIPLE-CHOICE QUESTIONS

Quiz 1

1.   Which of the following tests was first to have verbal and performance subscales?

   a.   ACT
   b.   Wechsler's Adult Intelligence Scale-III
   c.   The Stanford-Binet Intelligence Scale
   d.   The Binet

2.   An average man has taken a modern intelligence test. His IQ score is most likely

   a.   100.
   b.   90.
   c.   the result of his mental age divided by his chronological age multiplied by 100.
   d.   IQ scores are no longer used to rank individual mental ability.

3.   Today, IQ scores are relative scores. This means that your IQ will tell you

   a.   your *g*.
   b.   how many primary mental abilities you possess.
   c.   how intelligent you are in comparison to other people your age.
   d.   how creative you are.

4.   Lonnie wants to design a test that will accurately measure mathematics aptitude. According to the text, what characteristics should Lonnie's test have?

   a.   Standardized conditions
   b.   Qualitative descriptions
   c.   Written questions
   d.   All of these

5.   Which of the following is an example of predictive validity?

   a.   A teacher spends half the class time talking about one topic, and half of the quiz questions over that class period are on that topic.
   b.   The ACT correlates with high school GPA for high school juniors.
   c.   The ACT correlates positively with first semester college GPA.
   d.   None of these

6.   A newly developed intelligence test was given to the same group of people twice. The large positive correlation between the two scores was significant; therefore, the test has
   a.   test-retest reliability.
   b.   split-half reliability.
   c.   high construct validity.
   d.   low predictive validity.

7.   Which of the following is true with respect to reliability and validity?
   a.   A reliable test is always valid.
   b.   A valid test must have a substantial level of reliability.
   c.   There is no relationship between reliability and validity.
   d.   Reliability and validity are the products of standardization procedures.

8.   What factors explain the *inability* of an IQ test to perfectly predict academic performance?
   a.   Academic success is not wholly determined by intelligence.
   b.   IQ tests may be culturally biased.
   c.   IQ tests may measure factors other than intelligence which do not influence academic success.
   d.   All of these could explain the imperfect correlation between IQ and academic performance.

9.   Randy's students are very upset with him. He told them that he was going to give a quiz on the principles of learning, but instead he asked about the principles of memory. The students told him that his quiz had no _____ validity.
   a.   test-retest
   b.   predictive
   c.   content
   d.   criterion

10.   Which of the following statements is true of intelligence tests for adults in general?
   a.   They are neither reliable nor valid.
   b.   They are valid but not reliable.
   c.   They are reliable but not valid.
   d.   They are both reliable and valid.

11.   The green species has an average IQ score that is ten points higher than the purple species. Given this information, which is the most accurate statement about the intelligence of any one member of green and any one member of purple?
   a.   The green individual is smarter than the purple individual.
   b.   We cannot draw any conclusions about their intelligence.
   c.   There is no difference in their intelligence.
   d.   The purple individual is smarter than the green individual.

12. Janice has been given an assignment: She is to devise a way to test the validity of intelligence tests. Why is her task so difficult?

    a. She cannot find a group of people to give the same test to twice.
    b. Some controversy still exists over the definition of intelligence.
    c. Intelligence covers a narrow range of qualities and abilities, whereas most IQ tests test a broad range of abilities.
    d. None of these

13. Which of the following is true about how the interaction between heredity and environment affects intelligence?

    a. A favorable environment can improve a child's performance, even if the inherited influences on that child's IQ are negative.
    b. Inherited characteristics are fixed, but environmentally determined features are changeable.
    c. The environment has very little impact on a person's intelligence.
    d. Inherited characteristics have very little impact on a person's intelligence.

14. Devon is a ten-year-old from an inner-city culture. He is taking an IQ test that requires him to match patterns. Devon most probably

    a. has mental retardation.
    b. is taking a culture-fair test.
    c. is taking a culture-free test.
    d. is taking a mathematical achievement test.

15. Longitudinal research on intelligence suggests that _____ intelligence is more likely to decline than _____ intelligence over the life span.

    a. fluid; crystallized
    b. crystallized; fluid
    c. interpersonal; intrapersonal
    d. intrapersonal; interpersonal

16. An educator believes the information-processing model would look to which of the following to explain a student's poor performance on an aptitude test?

    a. The student's g-factor
    b. The student's attentional skills
    c. The student's IQ
    d. The environment in which the student was raised

17. Chuck says that intelligence is a general characteristic, meaning that a person capable in one area is also capable in another area. Chuck believes that testing people will support his hypothesis; therefore, he has a(n) _____ approach to intelligence.

    a. information-processing
    b. multiple intelligences
    c. psychometric
    d. triarchic

18. Nettie gets lost while hiking. However, she is able to find water and build shelter until the park rangers find her. She is even able to forage for food and build a fire to keep herself safe and warm. According to the triarchic theory of intelligence, Nettie is high on _____ intelligence.
    a. analytic
    b. practical
    c. creative
    d. kinesthetic

19. Shlomo and Jaime are both twelve years old. They were given identical boxes and told to open them. Shlomo finds the latch and pushes it up, down, and then sideways. Even though he cannot get the latch to open, he persists in his efforts. Jaime realizes that the latch is not going to open the box, so he looks at it from many different angles, trying to find another way to open it. Shlomo is thinking _____, and Jaime is thinking _____.
    a. convergently; divergently
    b. divergently; convergently
    c. convergently; convergently
    d. divergently; divergently

20. Jack has a lot of trouble with speaking. He cannot understand speech easily and has a lot of difficulty generating his own speech. Jack probably has
    a. cognitive complexity.
    b. dysphasia.
    c. dysgraphia.
    d. cultural familial intellectual retardation.

Total Correct (See answer key) _____

Quiz 2

Use this quiz to reassess your learning after taking Quiz 1 and reviewing the chapter.

1. The first mental abilities test is generally attributed to
    a. Lewis Terman.
    b. Alfred Binet.
    c. Jonathan Stanford.
    d. David Wechsler.

2. The strongest evidence of the role of heredity in determining intelligence is provided by the fact that the IQ scores of
    a. identical twins raised separately are more similar than those of fraternal twins raised together.
    b. fraternal twins are more similar than those of ordinary siblings.
    c. identical twins raised together are more similar than those of identical twins raised apart.
    d. unrelated children raised in different homes are less similar than those of unrelated children raised in the same home.

3. Which of the following would you NOT find on the performance scale of an intelligence test?
    a. Block design
    b. Maze solving
    c. Picture completion
    d. Mathematical word problems

4. Which of the following could jeopardize the standardization of a test?
    a. Individual variations in how the instructions are read to test takers
    b. Changes in the way the test is scored
    c. Variations in the environment in which the test is taken
    d. All of these

5. Consuela is giving a test that she has devised to the same group of people twice. She is testing for
    a. statistical reliability.
    b. statistical validity.
    c. norms.
    d. none of these.

6. Lola is a seventy-eight-year-old woman. She stays active mentally and physically. In which of the following areas is Lola most likely to experience a decline in her cognitive abilities?
    a. Knowing the capitals of the fifty states, which she learned and has remembered since childhood
    b. Being able to learn a lot of new names at a cocktail party and retain them all
    c. Being able to remember the names of all her friends at the country club
    d. Age will not affect any of these areas of ability for Lola.

7. A test is valid if it
    a. produces scores that are interpreted appropriately and used properly.
    b. is standardized.
    c. yields consistent and stable results.
    d. None of the above

8. Joel believes that knowledge of introductory psychology material is positively related to future success on the GRE test. Joel uses his students' combined midterm and final exam scores (called "exam total") as his measure of introductory psychology knowledge. He correlates exam total with the later obtained GRE scores of his students. Joel is trying to determine whether his introductory psychology "exam total" has
    a. criterion validity.
    b. predictive validity.
    c. content validity.
    d. split-half reliability.

9. Joel shows his midterm and final exams to the other psychology instructors to find out if the items fairly assess knowledge of introductory psychology material. By getting the other instructors' opinions, Joel is evaluating his tests'
   a. alternate-form reliability.
   b. split-half reliability.
   c. content validity.
   d. criterion validity.

10. You know that Jake is a member of a race that on average scores lower on measures of cognitive ability. You know that Jennifer is a member of a race that on average scores higher on measures of cognitive ability. What can you say about Jake and Jennifer?
    a. Jake is from a poorer family than Jennifer.
    b. Jennifer is smarter than Jake.
    c. Jake is less motivated than Jennifer when he takes IQ tests.
    d. Nothing

11. One factor that does NOT help explain why higher family income results in higher IQ scores for children is that
    a. the parents' jobs and status may be related to innate intelligence that is passed on to their children.
    b. income affects experience and environment.
    c. children of upper-income families may have greater motivation to succeed and to excel academically.
    d. upper-income families live in neighborhoods with a genetically similar population.

12. Following are questions from an intelligence test for adults. The instructions, test environment, and scoring are the same for all test takers. What color is the sun? How many fingers are on each hand? How many biological mothers do you have? The weather in summer is usually _____. What's wrong with this test?
    a. This test has no reliability.
    b. This test has no validity.
    c. This test is not standardized.
    d. What is wrong cannot be determined from the information given.

13. Ana has developed a new test for engineering students. She is delighted because people's scores on her new test correlate highly with their scores on other engineering tests used to successfully measure their skill in this area. This demonstrates that her test has _____ validity.
    a. alternate-forms
    b. predictive
    c. content
    d. criterion

14. Studying scores on intelligence tests in order to understand the structure of intelligence is using the _____ approach.
    a. psychometric
    b. information-processing
    c. triarchic
    d. divergent-convergent

15. On *American Idol,* Melinda continuously "wows" the judges with great musical performances that tell a story. According to the triarchic theory of intelligence, Melinda probably has high _____ intelligence.

    a.   analytic
    b.   creative
    c.   practical
    d.   performance

16. Lee Ann is about to take a math test. Her teacher says, "Good luck, because most women don't do as well on this test as men do." Lee Ann frets about her teacher's comment and consequently does worse on the exam. Lee Ann has experienced

    a.   test anxiety.
    b.   stereotype threat.
    c.   multiple intelligences.
    d.   creativity.

17. Kirby is really a fast thinker. She can read an executive summary at the office rapidly and apply it to solve problems in a matter of minutes. Kirby is probably very intelligent, based on what the _____ model says about intelligence.

    a.   psychometric
    b.   multiple intelligences
    c.   information-processing
    d.   triarchic

18. Corrina agrees with the multiple intelligences approach to mental abilities. *Unlike* people with any other approach, Corrina would be interested in hearing about a person's

    a.   athletic ability.
    b.   attention level.
    c.   spatial visualization.
    d.   vocabulary.

19. Which of the following statements about people with mild intellectual disability is NOT accurate?

    a.   They perform certain mental operations more slowly than other people do.
    b.   They know fewer facts about the world than other people know.
    c.   They tend to forget information from working memory at a faster rate than other people do.
    d.   They are less able than others to use particular mental strategies that may be important in learning and problem solving.

20. If scientists ever capture an alien, they will want to check its creativity. Which of the following would be the best way to do that?

    a.   See how fast it learns to speak English
    b.   Administer a verbal scale of the Wechsler
    c.   Administer a performance scale of the Wechsler
    d.   Administer a test of divergent thinking

Total Correct (See answer key) _____

ANSWERS TO FILL-IN-THE-BLANKS KEY TERMS

1. cognitive ability (see introductory section)

2. norms (see Measuring the Quality of Tests)

3. test (see Measuring the Quality of Tests)

4. statistical reliability (see Statistical Reliability)

5. statistically valid (see Statistical Validity)

6. intelligence quotient (see Intelligence Tests Today)

7. fluid intelligence (see The Psychometric Approach)

8. psychometric (see The Psychometric Approach)

9. information-processing (see The Information-Processing Model)

10. Creativity (see Creativity)

11. aptitude (see Aptitude and Achievement Tests)

12. divergent thinking (see Creativity)

13. Convergent thinking (see Creativity)

14. learning disabilities (see Unusual Cognitive Ability)

15. crystallized intelligence (see The Psychometric Approach)

ANSWERS TO CONCEPTS AND EXERCISES

Defining Intelligence

1. Pedro would follow the <u>multiple intelligences</u> approach as suggested by <u>Gardner</u>. (see Multiple Intelligences)

2. Pam would follow the <u>psychometric approach</u> as suggested by <u>Spearman</u>. (see The Psychometric Approach)

3. Steve would follow the <u>psychometric approach</u> as suggested by <u>Thurstone</u>. (see The Psychometric Approach)

4. Elena would follow the <u>triarchic approach</u> as suggested by <u>Sternberg</u>. (see The Triarchic Theory of Intelligence)

5. Leigh would test for <u>divergent thinking</u>. (see Creativity)

The Testing Business

1. *Split-half.* (see Statistical Reliability)

2. *Yes.* A test may be reliable but invalid because it does not test the correct abilities, cannot be interpreted, or may be used inappropriately. (see Measuring the Quality of Tests)

3. *No.* There is probably no such thing as a culture-fair test. However, Dorgan can determine what skills are valued for success, how intelligence is defined differently across cultures, and design or purchases tests that suit those varying definitions. (see Thinking Critically: Are Intelligence Tests Unfairly Biased Against Certain Groups?)

4. *Standardized.* (see Measuring the Quality of Tests)

5. *Content validity*. He is worried about whether the questions on the test are related to the skills that the test is supposed to assess. (see Statistical Validity)

ANSWERS TO CRITICAL THINKING

1. Sam hypothesizes that the test is not a good measure of whether someone is lying.

2. That not everyone they tested in New York could pass the test is evidence supporting his hypothesis.

3. Martina, realizing that the test was designed and tested in South Carolina, hypothesizes that the test is culturally biased. (In some cultures, for example, looking down when being asked a question is a demonstration of respect.)

4. Martina would have to discover the cultural impact on people's head movements of answering questions, especially when under stress or when questioned by the police.

ANSWERS TO MULTIPLE-CHOICE QUESTIONS

Circle the question numbers you answered correctly.

Quiz 1

1. b is the answer.   The WAIS-III was the first test to have verbal and performance subscales. (see Intelligence Tests Today)

    a, c.   Both the Stanford-Binet and the ACT use subscales but were not first to introduce their use.

    d.   There is no such test as The Binet.

2. a is the answer.   The arbitrary number 100 is assigned to the average score obtained by people at a particular age level. Other IQ numbers reflect how much the scores deviate from the average. (see Intelligence Tests Today)

    b.   A score of 90 would indicate that the person scored below the age-group average.

    c.   This formula was the scored method used early in the twentieth century by Lewis Terman.

    d.   As long as there is testing for differential abilities, there will be scoring and ranking.

3. c is the answer.   An IQ score tells how smart you are *relative* to other people your age. If your IQ is 100, then you are average with respect to others your age. A higher IQ means you scored higher than others your age. (see Intelligence Tests Today)

    a.   Spearman concluded that intelligence is a combination of general mental ability, *g*, and a group of special intelligences, *s*. Neither *g* nor *s* provides comparative information about IQ.

    b.   Thurstone suggested that intelligence is made of primary mental abilities. An IQ score may tell you about these abilities, but more important, the score tells about them relative to other people.

    d.   An IQ score will not tell you how creative you are. IQ scores are not highly correlated with creativity.

4. a is the answer.   An advantage of using a test is that the administration, scoring, and interpretation are standardized. (see Measuring the Quality of Tests)

    b.   Quantifiable terms allow norms to be calculated. Qualitative descriptions would not be numerical.

    c.   A test does not have to be written. Lonnie could have people listen to a problem and use tokens to show a number answer.

    d.   Only a is correct.

5.   c is the answer.   Predictive validity is a high positive correlation between a test and an outcome that had to be measured in the future. (see Statistical Validity)

    a.   This is content validity.

    b.   This is criterion-related validity.

    d.   c is the answer.

6.   a is the answer.   (see Statistical Reliability)

    b.   Split-half reliability is checked by comparing answers on half of the items on a test to the other half.

    c, d.   Validity is not determined by administering the same test twice. Construct validity is based on a theory about the concept. Predictive validity compares scores on a test to a criterion later.

7.   b is the answer.   If a test is valid, it must be reliable. If a test produces scores that vary from one test occasion to another, there is no way that the test would correlate highly enough with a criterion to establish validity. (see Statistical Reliability)

    a.   A test that is reliable is not necessarily valid.

    c.   There is a relationship between reliability and validity, whereas a reliable test yields the same results repeatedly. A valid test must have a substantial level of reliability.

    d.   If a test is valid, it measures what it is supposed to measure. This is not dependent on standardization procedures. Standardization does not guarantee validity.

8.   d is the answer.   Cultural bias, other factors affecting academic success, and the fact that IQ tests may measure factors other than intelligence (such as motivation) all contribute to the imperfect correlation between IQ scores and academic success. (see Statistical Validity)

9.   c is the answer.   The questions on the quiz did not assess the knowledge they were supposed to test. (see Statistical Validity)

    a.   Test-retest is not a type of validity. It is a type of reliability.

    b.   Using a test to predict the ability to carry out some later endeavor successfully, such as a job or major in school, requires the test to have predictive validity.

    d.   The correlation of a test score with some other measure of the ability tested is the test's criterion validity.

10. c is the answer.   Intelligence tests for adults are generally fairly stable in the results they produce, which means that they are reliable. However, because people cannot agree on what intelligence is, validity can be determined only for specific purposes. (see The Statistical Reliability and Validity of Intelligence Tests)

    a.   Intelligence tests for adults are generally quite reliable.

    b.   A test cannot be valid without first being reliable.

    d.   Intelligence tests for adults are generally reliable, but their validity extends only to specific purposes and is not generally accepted for broad decisions.

11. b is the answer.   A group score is an average of the scores of a large number of people; it says nothing about a particular individual. (see Group Differences in IQ)

    a, c, d.   A group average tells us nothing about individual members of a group.

12. b is the answer.   It is very difficult to tell whether a test is measuring what it is supposed to measure when the tester cannot define what is supposed to be measured. (see Statistical Validity)

    a.   This is an example of not being able to check test-retest reliability.

    c.   Intelligence covers a broad range of qualities and abilities, whereas most IQ tests test a narrow range of abilities.

    d.   b is the answer.

13. a is the answer.   The quality of the environment can cause children's IQ scores to increase. (see Innate and Environmental Influences on IQ)

    b.   The opposite is true: inherited characteristics are not necessarily fixed, and environmentally determined features are not necessarily changeable.

    c, d.   Neither of these statements is true. Both genetics and the environment have a large impact on the development of intelligence.

14. b is the answer.   Devon is taking a test that does not rely heavily on education and verbal abilities. This test is attempting to measure intelligence instead of the effect of cultural advantages, such as an education. (see Statistical Reliability; see also Statistical Validity)

    a.   Many normal children—not just those with mental retardation—take IQ tests.

    c.   There is no such thing as a culture-free test.

    d.   Devon is being asked to match patterns, not to do mathematical tasks. Additionally, an achievement test measures what has already been learned; Devon is taking an IQ test, which attempts to measure intelligence, not knowledge.

15. a is the answer.   Fluid intelligence is more likely to decline over the life span, particularly in the areas of working memory, processing speed, organization, flexibility, and control of attention. Crystallized intelligence may even continue to grow well into old age. (see Focus on Research Methods: Tracking Cognitive Abilities over the Life Span)

    b.   This is the opposite—crystallized intelligence tends to remain stable or increase with age, whereas fluid intelligence is more likely to decrease.

    c, d.   These are types of intelligence from Gardner's theory of multiple intelligences. Neither has been studied in a longitudinal design at this point.

16. b is the answer.   Within the information-processing model, effective intellectual functioning is related to competence in basic mental processes. An educator would look at these skills to explain poor performance on an aptitude test. (see The Information-Processing Model)

    a.   The analysis of a general intelligence, or *g*, centers on the correlations among various measures of mental abilities. The information-processing model is not concerned with final scores, but with the various skills involved in achieving them.

    c.   Because this model focuses on attentional resources, speed of access to memory, and other processes of intelligent behavior, the product of that intelligence (one test score) would not explain poor performance on another measure.

    d.   Examining the influence of environmental factors on intelligence is not a component of the information-processing model.

17. c is the answer.   The psychometric approach looks for a general factor of intelligence by using tests. (see The Psychometric Approach)

    a.   The information-processing model emphasizes the influence of attention skills and processes of sensation, perception, and memory.

    b.   Multiple intelligences is the approach emphasizing that people could have a high level of one ability (musical intelligence) and a low level of another (logical-mathematical intelligence).

    d.   The triarchic theory focuses on components and adaptation to the environment.

18. b is the answer.   Nettie's ability to figure out what to do in the wilderness illustrates her ability to adapt to the environment and solve practical problems that present themselves to her. (see The Triarchic Theory of Intelligence)

    a.   Analytic intelligence is the sort measured on a typical intelligence test.

    c.   Creative intelligence is the sort that you use when you are generating music or drawing a painting.

    d.   The triarchic theory does not have kinesthetic intelligence as part of it.

19. a is the answer.   Shlomo is thinking convergently, but Jaime, by imagining all the possible ways to open the box, is thinking divergently. (see Creativity)

    b, c, d.   Only a is correct.

20. b is the answer.   Dysphasia is a learning disability in which people have trouble understanding spoken words or recalling the words needed for effective speech. (see Unusual Cognitive Ability)

    a.   Cognitive complexity assists people in thinking about many aspects of a problem.

    c.   Dysgraphia is a learning disability in which people have trouble with writing.

    d.   Cultural familial intellectual retardation is usually mild and results from an interaction of genetic and environmental influences. Mary Beth is of average or slightly above-average intelligence; she does not have any form of retardation.

Now turn to the quiz analysis table at the end of this chapter to find which areas you know well and which areas you need to work on. Circle the numbers in the table for items on Quiz 1 that you answered correctly.

Quiz 2

1.   b is the answer.   The first test of mental abilities was developed by Alfred Binet in France. (see A Brief History of Intelligence Tests)

    a.   Lewis Terman was the first American to convert Binet's test for use in the United States.

    c.   There is no such person in the history of intelligence testing. The "Stanford" in the Stanford-Binet test refers to Stanford University, where Lewis Terman conducted his research.

    d.   David Wechsler has authored several modern intelligence tests, not the first test of mental abilities.

2.   a is the answer.   If the IQ scores of twins who have the same genes but are raised in different environments are more similar than the scores of twins with different genes who are raised in the same environment, we can conclude that the similarity of genes was also responsible for the similarity of IQ scores. (see Innate and Environmental Influences on IQ)

b.   This is evidence for environmental influence. Fraternal twins and ordinary siblings both develop from separate eggs and thus have different genes. The scores of fraternal twins may be more similar because their environment may be more similar: They were born at approximately the same time and they share many experiences.

c, d.   This is evidence for environmental influence. Children raised in the same environment will be more similar than children raised in different environments.

3.   d is the answer.   Although math skills in general do not require a great deal of language ability, mathematical word problems do. The test taker must be able to read, interpret, and set up the problem using language skills as well as mathematical reasoning in order to arrive at the solution. (see Intelligence Tests Today)

a, b, c.   Block design, mazes, and picture completion are all problems that require no verbal skills.

4.   d is the answer.   Variations in administration, scoring, or the test-taking environment could jeopardize the standardization of a test. (see Measuring the Quality of Tests)

5.   a is the answer.   A reliable test is one that gives stable and consistent answers. If a test is given twice and yields consistent results, it is considered reliable. (see Statistical Reliability)

b.   Giving the same test twice is a test of reliability, not validity. To check validity, you must make sure that the content of the questions relates to the skills or knowledge being tested or that the test scores are correlated with scores on other tests relating to the same constructs or criteria.

c.   Norms are descriptions of the frequency of particular scores. In order to test for this, the same test would have to be given to a very large number of people, not the same people twice.

d.   a is the answer.

6.   b is the answer.   Learning a lot of new names all at once at a party relies on good working memory skills. This is one of the aspects of fluid intelligence that is somewhat likely to decline with age. (see Focus on Research Methods: Tracking Cognitive Abilities over the Life Span)

a, c.   These are examples of crystallized intelligence, which tends to remain stable or increase with age.

d.   Age does affect fluid intelligence adversely.

7.   a is the answer.   (see Statistical Validity)

b.   Standardization refers to the use of the same methods every time the test is given.

c.   A reliable test yields consistent and stable scores over several test sessions.

d.   a is the answer.

8.   b is the answer.   Predictive validity involves determining whether the test in question predicts future criteria of interest. Joel is determining whether his introductory psychology exam totals predict GRE performance. (see Statistical Validity)

a.   Criterion validity is similar to predictive validity, but it does not involve actual prediction. Concurrent scores are correlated to determine whether the test in question is related to other measures of the ability.

c.   Content validity involves determining whether your test measures the appropriate substantive content.

  d. Split-half reliability involves determining whether the test in question is internally consistent by correlating two separate but equivalent halves of the test.

9. c is the answer. Asking other psychology instructors about the items on his test will evaluate the content validity. (see Statistical Validity)

  a, b. Alternate-form reliability and split-half reliability both involve comparing two sets of scores (two tests or two halves of a test, respectively). Joel is only asking for opinions.

  d. Criterion validity is evaluated by comparing a new test to an accepted measure of the same construct.

10. d is the answer. Group scores on tests of cognitive ability tell you nothing about individual scores on those tests. (see Group Differences in IQ)

  a. Although lower socioeconomic status is associated with lower scores on tests of cognitive ability, group scores do not tell you about individuals.

  b. Group scores are not diagnostic of individuals' performance on tests.

  c. Although lower motivation is associated with lower scores on tests of cognitive ability, knowing Jake's group membership does not tell you about Jake in particular. Likewise for Jennifer.

11. d is the answer. The ethnicity of a neighborhood has nothing to do with why high income leads to children with higher IQs. Lower-class communities have lower average IQs than are found in upper-class communities of the same ethnic makeup. Many high-income neighborhoods are populated by a variety of ethnic groups. (see Group Differences in IQ)

  a, b, c. All of these factors influence the relationship between IQ and socioeconomic status.

12. b is the answer. Most people could answer these questions. Therefore, this test will not tell you how people differ in intelligence. (see Statistical Validity)

  a. This test is very reliable. You would give exactly the same answers every time you took it.

  c. This test is standardized; it is administered and scored in exactly the same way every time for everyone.

  d. What is wrong can be determined.

13. d is the answer. The correlation of a test score with some other measure of the ability tested evaluates the test's criterion validity. (see Statistical Validity)

  a. When two alternate, but substantively equivalent, versions of a test are highly correlated, the test has alternate forms reliability. Alternate forms is not a type of validity.

  b. Using a test to predict the ability to carry out some later endeavor successfully, such as a job or a major in school, requires the test to have predictive validity.

  c. When a test measures the knowledge "content" it is supposed to measure, the test has content validity.

14. a is the answer. Psychologists who seek to understand the structure of intelligence by examining the correlations among scores on IQ tests are following the psychometric approach. (see The Psychometric Approach)

  b. The information-processing model studies the mental processes underlying intelligent behavior, such as the speed of information transfer from short-term to long-term memory.

c.   The triarchic approach involves specific knowledge components and metacomponents: the ability to know how to set up a problem in order to solve it.

d.   There is no such thing as the divergent-convergent approach to studying intelligence.

15.   b is the answer.   Creative intelligence is used when one is creating something new, such as painting a picture or performing a song. (see The Triarchic Theory of Intelligence)

a.   Analytic intelligence is the sort typically measured on a traditional intelligence test. Melinda's performances do not tell us about her analytic intelligence.

c.   Practical intelligence is the kind of "street smarts" one uses to solve problems in one's environment to adapt effectively. We do not know about this sort of ability from Melinda's performances.

d.   Performance intelligence is not part of the triarchic theory. You may be thinking of the Performance Scale on the Wechsler tests.

16.   b is the answer.   Stereotype threat is the idea that priming of a stereotype about a group's lower ability in comparison to others will distract members of that group so that they may become anxious and fail to perform at the level of their ability. Lee Ann received this kind of priming. (see Linkages: Emotionality and the Measurement of Cognitive Abilities)

a.   Test anxiety is anxiety over testing situations in general. Although Lee Ann is anxious about the test, it is only because her teacher raised the issue of her membership in the category of "women" as being a reason for her to worry.

c.   Multiple intelligences are various types of intelligence proposed by Howard Gardner.

d.   Creativity is the ability to produce novel ideas or products. This question does not suggest Lee Ann is taking a test of creativity.

17.   c is the answer.   The information-processing approach emphasizes the importance of attentional resources and processing speed in intelligence. Kirby is a fast thinker, which is high processing speed. (see The Information-Processing Model)

a.   The psychometric approach does not emphasize processing speed as essential to intelligence.

b.   Multiple intelligences does not emphasize processing speed as a form of intelligence.

d.   The triarchic theory of intelligence does not emphasize processing speed as part of intelligence.

18.   a is the answer.   According to the multiple intelligences approach, athletic ability is body-kinesthetic intelligence. (see Multiple Intelligences)

b.   Attention level is important to an information-processing theorist.

c.   Spatial intelligence is part of the multiple intelligences approach, but it is also measured by psychometric theorists.

d.   Vocabulary is not part of the multiple intelligences approach. People with a psychometric approach are interested in language comprehension; therefore, it may be an interest of theirs.

19. c is the answer.   People with mild intellectual disability are just as proficient as others in recognizing simple stimuli, and they do not tend to forget information from working memory at a faster rate. (see Unusual Cognitive Ability)

   a.   People with mild mental retardation do perform certain mental operations more slowly.

   b.   People with mild mental retardation do tend to know fewer facts about the world.

   d.   People with mild mental retardation do have difficulty using some mental strategies that are important in learning and problem solving.

20. d is the answer.   Tests of divergent thinking measure creativity. (see Creativity)

   a.   The ability to learn a new language is not correlated with creativity.

   b, c.   IQ scores do not correlate highly with creativity.

Now turn to the quiz analysis table at the end of this chapter to find which areas you know well and which areas you need to work on. Circle the numbers in the table for items on Quiz 2 that you answered correctly.

For each question you answered correctly, circle its number. (Quiz 1 numbers are not shaded; Quiz 2 numbers are shaded.) Are there patterns in the types of questions or the topics you got wrong that could direct your further study? Did you improve from Quiz 1 to Quiz 2?

QUIZ REVIEW

Topic	Type of Question		
	Definition	Comprehension	Application
Testing for Intelligence			
A Brief History of Intelligence Tests			
		1	
Intelligence Tests Today	1	2, 3	
		3	
Measuring the Quality of Tests			4
		4	
Statistical Reliability			6, 7
			5
Statistical Validity		5, 8	9, 12
	7		8, 9, 12, 13
Evaluating Intelligence Tests			
The Statistical Reliability and Validity of IQ Tests		10	14
Linkages: Emotionality and the Measurement of Cognitive Abilities			
			16
Innate and Environmental Influences on IQ		13	
			2
Group Differences in IQ			11
		11	10
Understanding Intelligence			
The Psychometric Approach		17	
		14	
The Information-Processing Model			16
			17
The Triarchic Theory of Intelligence			18
			15
Multiple Intelligences			
			18
Focus on Research Methods: Tracking Cognitive Abilities Over the Life Span		15	
			6
Diversity in Cognitive Abilities			
Creativity			19
			20
Unusual Cognitive Ability			20
		19	

Total correct by quiz:

Quiz 1:	
Quiz 2:	

CHAPTER 11

Motivation and Emotion

Motivation can be defined as the influences that account for the initiation, direction, intensity, and persistence of behavior. Motivation influences emotion.

OUTLINE

I. CONCEPTS AND THEORIES OF MOTIVATION
    A motive, acting as an *intervening variable*, may provide a single reason for the occurrence of many different behaviors and may explain fluctuations in behavior over time.

    A. Sources of Motivation
        Four factors can serve as sources of motivation: physiological, emotional, cognitive, and social.

    B. Instinct Doctrine and Its Descendants
        Instinctive behaviors are automatic, involuntary behavior patterns that are triggered by particular stimuli. They were once thought to be a major factor in motivation. The instinct doctrine, however, may provide a description, rather than an explanation, of behavior. In addition, the instinct doctrine failed to accommodate the role of learning in human behavior.

        The Instinct Doctrine and Mate Selection. The evolutionary approach suggests that inborn desires to pass on our genes cause women to focus on men's dependability, emotional stability, intelligence, and earning power (important for creating a positive environment for children). This greater investment in finding a mate causes women to be choosier. Men tend to be less choosy as they have less invested in the mating process, which may explain men's more casual attitudes about sex. Instead, men focus more on physical beauty (a signal to good health and fertility) as a way of trying to have as many offspring as possible. These evolutionary perspectives are "modern" takes on the instinct doctrine. Surveys have supported this hypothesis; however, mate selection patterns may reflect social and economic influences, not innate biological needs.

    C. Drive Reduction Theory
        According to drive reduction theory, drives reduce biological needs caused by an imbalance in homeostasis. Primary drives are produced by physical needs, while secondary drives are learned through experience.

    D. Arousal Theory
        Arousal theory states that people are motivated to maintain their optimal level of physiological arousal, increasing arousal when it is too low and decreasing it when it is too high. Optimal arousal levels vary from person to person, and for each person across time.

    E. Incentive Theory
        According to incentive theory, behavior is goal-directed; we behave in ways that allow us to attain desirable stimuli and avoid negative stimuli. *Wanting* is the process of being attracted to incentives; *liking* is the immediate evaluation of how pleasurable a stimulus is. The value of an incentive is influenced by biological and social factors.

II. HUNGER AND EATING
  A. Biological Signals for Hunger and Satiety
    1. <u>Hunger</u> is the general state of wanting to eat. <u>Satiation</u> is the satisfaction of hunger. Satiation leads to <u>satiety</u>, the state of no longer wanting to eat.
    2. *Signals from the Gut.* The stomach may partially control the hunger motive, but the cues may operate primarily when people are very hungry or very full.
    3. *Signals from the Blood.* The brain monitors blood content for the presence of nutrients (glucose, fatty acids, and amino acids) and hormones whose presence communicates hunger or satiety.
       a. *Cholecystokinin (CCK)* is a hormone that affects short-term intake—known as a satiety factor.
       b. *Glucose* is also monitored by the brain and affects eating both directly and indirectly through *insulin* production.
       c. Long-term regulation of fat stores is accomplished with the hormone *leptin*. When leptin levels are low, hunger increases.

  B. Hunger and the Brain
      The *lateral* and *ventromedial hypothalamus* and the *paraventricular nucleus (PVN)* play roles in the regulation of hunger and eating, but control of eating is more complicated than that alone. The hypothalamus may be involved in the homeostatic maintenance of a *set point*. Neurotransmitter activity in the PVN may selectively motivate eating of different kinds of foods. *Neuropeptide Y* motivates carbohydrate eating while *serotonin* suppresses it. *Galanin* motivates high-fat consumption while *enteristatin* suppresses it. These are just two examples, and neurotransmitter activity alone cannot fully account for eating behavior.

  C. Flavor, Sociocultural Experience, and Food Selection
      Flavor and variety are important in initiating eating. More food will be eaten when a variety of tastes is offered. *Appetite,* or desire to seek foods pleasures, can also override blood-borne hormonal signals. Classical conditioning (pairing the taste with the nutritional value) influences the preference for a variety of foods. The sight of food can elicit conditioned responses (the secretion of saliva, gastric juices, and insulin) that are associated with eating. *Specific hungers*, the desire for certain foods at certain times, may reflect the biological need for a nutrient found in those foods. Finally, social cues tell people what and how much are appropriate to eat in certain social situations and in particular *food cultures*.

  D. Unhealthy Eating
    1. *Obesity*.
       a. <u>Obesity</u> is a condition of severe overweight and is defined by a body mass index (BMI) of greater than 30. It can contribute to diabetes, high blood pressure, certain cancers, and increased risk of heart attack.
       b. Obesity is on the rise and may contribute to a shortened life expectancy in the coming years. Obese people tend to eat too much high-fat, tasty food and less low-calories, nutritious food. They tend to be less active than people of a normal weight.
       c. Genetic factors may include low sensitivity to leptin. Psychological factors include having seen poor eating habits modeled by parents.
       d. For most people it is easier to gain weight than lose weight, perhaps because thrifty genes were evolutionarily adaptive in certain environments.
       e. Many treatments for obesity exist, but the best ones focus on long-term components like reduction of intake, change in attitude toward food, and increase in exercise. Prevention is the real solution to work towards.

2. *Anorexia Nervosa.* This is an eating disorder characterized by a preoccupation with food and self-starvation and dramatic weight loss. Physical causes are unknown, but psychological factors that contribute to anorexia nervosa include a preoccupation with thinness. Anorexia can have serious long-term health consequences that are irreversible. Drugs, hospitalization, and therapy have all been used to treat anorexia nervosa.

3. *Bulimia (bulimia nervosa).* This eating disorder is characterized by binging and purging and is usually not life-threatening. The victim may be thin, normal weight, or overweight. Bulimia appears to be caused by cultural factors, emotional problems, and possibly malfunctioning biological mechanisms. Bulimics tend to see their eating as problematic whereas anorexics do not. Individual and group therapy and sometimes antidepressant drugs have been used with success to treat bulimia.

III. SEXUAL BEHAVIOR

A. Focus on Research Methods: A Survey of Human Sexual Behavior
The National Health and Social Life Survey used face-to-face interviews with a representative sample of people aged eighteen to fifty-nine in the United States. The survey found that most people have sex once a week in monogamous relationships and that about a third have had sex only a few times or not at all in the past year. People in committed monogamous relationships had the most frequent and the most satisfying sex.

B. The Biology of Sex
Masters and Johnson's in-depth study of sexual arousal resulted in a description of the sexual response cycle. Although all sex hormones circulate in both males and females, some predominate in each sex: female hormones include estrogens (estradiol) and progestational hormones (progestins); male hormones are androgens (e.g., testosterone). Sex hormones have both brain structure organization and behavioral activation effects. Organizational effects tend to occur around the time of birth, sculpting mammals' brains into male-like or female-like structures. In terms of behavioral activation, estrogen and androgens affect female interest in sex, while androgens alone seem to affect male interest in sex.

C. Social and Cultural Factors in Sexuality
Sexual motivation and behaviors are learned as part of gender roles, early relationships with nurturing adults, and cultural expectations. Women and men differ in what they find sexually arousing. These factors interact with physiology to produce our sexuality.

D. Sexual Orientation
Sexual orientation can be heterosexuality, bisexuality, or homosexuality. The prevalence of gay, lesbian, and bisexual orientations is difficult to estimate, but is probably somewhere between 2 to 20 percent of the population.

E. Thinking Critically: What Shapes Sexual Orientation?
What am I being asked to believe or accept?

Perhaps genes dictate sexual orientation.

What evidence is available to support the assertion?

In a study of homosexual men with brothers, 52 percent of the identical twin brothers were homosexual or bisexual; however, only 22 percent of the nonidentical and 11 percent of the adoptive brothers were homosexual or bisexual. Similar results are found for male identical twins reared apart. Prenatal hormonal influences may affect sexual orientation. Finally, the sexual orientation of children's caregivers doesn't appear to have a significant effect on the children's subsequent orientation.

Are there alternative ways of interpreting the evidence?

Remember, although a correlation exists between genetics and sexual orientation, it does not prove that one caused the other. Possibly, the shared genes determined other nonsexual behavior, which due to *environmental factors* resulted in homosexual or bisexual behavior. Also, almost 50 percent of the identical twins had different sexual orientations. Finally, the internal and external physical differences could be the result of their behavior and not just genetics.

What additional evidence would help to evaluate the alternatives?

Researching sexual orientation should extend beyond the study of genetic characteristics to compare and contrast personality, cognitive, social, and developmental attributes of people with different orientations.

What conclusions are most reasonable?

Sexual orientation results from the complex interplay of both genetic and nongenetic mechanisms.

IV.   ACHIEVEMENT MOTIVATION
We work because of *intrinsic* and *extrinsic motivation*. The desire for approval, admiration, and other types of positive evaluation from ourselves and others motivates our behavior.

A.   Need for Achievement
People with a high need achievement are motivated to master tasks and take great pride in doing so.
   1.   *Individual Differences.* People with a high <u>achievement motivation</u> set challenging but realistic goals that have clear outcomes. They like feedback from competent critics. In contrast, people with low achievement needs seem to enjoy success because they have avoided failure. Differences also appear in people's goals, which can be *learning* or *performance goals*.
   2.   *Development of Achievement Motivation.* The need for achievement appears to be largely learned from parents and other cultural arenas. Parents who encourage children to try difficult tasks, give praise and reward for success, encourage the child to find ways to succeed, and prompt the child to go on to the next challenge tend to foster achievement motivation.

B.   Goal Setting and Achievement Motivation
Goals influence motivation, especially the amount of effort, persistence, attention, and planning we devote to a task. Clear, specific, and realistic but challenging goals seem to be most effective.

C.   Achievement and Success in the Workplace
Workers tend to be more satisfied and productive if they are encouraged to participate in decision making, given problems to solve on their own, taught more than one skill, given individual responsibility, given public recognition, and allowed to set and achieve goals. Effective goals are those that are personally meaningful, specific, set by the employees, and rewarded.

D.   Achievement and Well-Being
Psychologists who study *positive* psychology tend to find that people have a characteristic level of happiness, or <u>well-being</u> (or subjective well-being), which is not necessarily related to the attainment of money, status, or other material goods. This seems to be related to temperament. Social ties, religious faith, and sufficient basic resources are related to happiness levels. A *deficiency orientation* is associated with lower subjective well-being.

V.   RELATIONS AND CONFLICTS AMONG MOTIVES
Abraham Maslow proposed that there are five levels of motives, or needs, arranged in a hierarchy: biological, safety, belongingness and love, esteem, and self-actualization. According to Maslow, we must satisfy needs or motives low on the hierarchy before we are motivated to satisfy needs at the next level. However, the ordering of these needs is not as rigid as Maslow proposed, varying with cultural and temporal factors. Alderfer reduced the number of categories to three (existence, relatedness, and growth needs) and argued that they may rise and fall in importance over time.

A.   Linkages: Conflicting Motives and Stress
Several motives that act at the same time complicate life and can be a source of stress. Four basic types of motivational conflicts are approach-approach, avoidance-avoidance, approach-avoidance, and multiple approach-avoidance. These may be difficult to resolve and contribute to stress levels.

B.   Opponent Processes, Motivation, and Emotion
According to *opponent-process theory*, any reaction to a stimulus is automatically followed by an opposite reaction, called the opponent process. After repeated exposure to the same stimulus, the initial reaction weakens, and the opponent process becomes stronger. We are motivated to seek a pleasurable opponent process (such as relief) or to avoid a negative one by quickly repeating exposure to the initial stimulus (such as bungee jumping). Often, the opponent process is an emotional response.

VI.   THE NATURE OF EMOTION
A.   Defining Characteristics
Emotions have several defining features. Emotions are transitory (not constant). They are either positive or negative. They are partially dependent on your cognitive appraisal or interpretation of a situation. They tend to alter thought processes such as attention. They create a tendency toward certain actions. However, they are passions, not actions, because you can decide to act, but passions happen whether you want them to or not. Emotions are also felt as happening to the self. The objective aspects of emotion include learned and innate *expressive displays* and *physiological responses*.

B.   The Biology of Emotion
1.   *Brain Mechanisms.* Activity in the limbic system is important to the experience of emotion. Voluntary and involuntary facial expressions are controlled by two different areas of the brain: the pyramidal motor system and the extrapyramidal motor system, respectively. Most researchers agree that the right hemisphere is activated during emotions and contributes more to facial expressions than the left does. However, some investigators purport that the left hemisphere is more active than the right in experiencing positive emotions.
2.   *Mechanisms of the Autonomic Nervous System.* Signals from the autonomic nervous system (ANS) modify the ongoing activity of the organs and glands in the body. The ANS is made up of two branches—the sympathetic nervous system and the parasympathetic nervous system—both of which communicate with all the organs and glands in the body. Because of different neurotransmitters used at the target organs, the two branches have opposite effects. The parasympathetic nervous system initiates activity related to the nourishment and growth of the body. The sympathetic nervous system prepares the body for vigorous activity and stimulates the adrenal medulla to release norepinephrine and epinephrine into the bloodstream, which in turn stimulates all the target organs of the sympathetic system. The result is the fight-flight reaction (fight-or-flight syndrome). Although you are not conscious of ANS activity, you can consciously alter it.

VII. THEORIES OF EMOTION
    A.   James's Peripheral Theory
        1.   *Observing Peripheral Responses*. According to this theory, people experience emotion based on observations of their own physical behavior and peripheral responses. It is known as the *peripheral theory* of emotion or the *James-Lange theory*.
        2.   *Evaluating James's Peripheral Theory*. If the James theory is correct, there should be a unique peripheral physiological response for every emotion, and people who cannot feel their peripheral responses should not experience emotion. According to the facial-feedback hypothesis, those incapable of feeling peripheral responses can get all the physiological information necessary to perceive an emotion from facial expressions.
        3.   *Lie Detection*. The use of a *polygraph* as a lie detector is based upon the assumption that there is a link between lying and emotions and that patterns of physiological arousal will distinguish true from false statements. However, polygraph results are not 100 percent accurate. Scientists now are investigating lie detection that focuses more on brain activity and brief facial "microexpressions" rather than a link between deception and autonomic nervous system activity.
    B.   Cannon's Central Theory
        According to *Cannon's Central theory* (or the Cannon-Bard theory), emotion starts in the thalamus and is then passed simultaneously to the cerebral cortex, where it becomes conscious, and to the autonomic nervous system. Recent evidence suggests that the thalamus does not produce the direct central experience of emotion but that different parts of the central nervous system (for example, the amygdala) may be activated for different emotions and for different aspects of the total emotional experience.

    C.   Cognitive Theories of Emotion
        1.   Schachter's modification of James's theory, known as the *Schachter-Singer theory* of emotion, suggests that emotions are produced both by feedback from peripheral responses and by a cognitive appraisal of what caused those responses. Cognitively appraising, a process known as <u>attribution,</u> the source of arousal to a specific cause dictates the specific emotion you experience. If you attribute physiological arousal to a nonemotional cause, your experience of emotion should be reduced. If you experience artificially produced arousal, you should experience emotion and attribute it to the situation at hand.
        2.   <u>Excitation transfer theory</u> explains that arousal from one experience can carry over to an independent emotional situation. People sometimes attribute prior arousal to the new situation at hand, thereby intensifying their present emotion.
        3.   Schachter argued that the cognitive interpretation focused on the bodily response, but more recently Lazarus's *cognitive appraisal theory* sees the interpretive process as focused on the events themselves. Reactions will be positive or negative depending on how an event is interpreted as impacting progress to our own goals. Even more recent work has focused on how to incorporate culture and language into understanding our emotional experiences.
VIII. COMMUNICATING EMOTION
        Facial movements and expressions play the primary role in communicating human emotions.

    A.   Innate Expressions of Emotion
        Two types of evidence support a Darwinian proposal that states that certain emotions are innate: Infants show facial expressions appropriate to their current state, and people of all cultures show similar facial responses to show certain similar emotional stimuli.

    B.   Social and Cultural Influences on Emotional Expression
        Culture affects the ways in which emotions are expressed.

1. *Learning About Emotions*. People begin to communicate some emotions by learning *emotion cultures* and by undergoing operant shaping.
2. *Social Referencing*. People use *social referencing* in an ambiguous situation to determine how to react.

KEY TERMS

1. **Motivation** is defined as the influences that account for the initiation, direction, intensity, and persistence of behavior. (see introductory section)

   Example: What causes us to initiate the movements necessary to get up from the couch and get something to drink? What causes us to persist in our work, sometimes to the point of staying up all night? Why do some people exert intense effort and others no effort at all? These are the kinds of questions asked by people studying motivation.

2. A **motive** is a reason or purpose for behavior. (see Concepts and Theories of Motivation)

   Example: A woman drives a Jaguar, wears expensive sports clothes, and joins a country club. Her motive is to demonstrate that she belongs to a specific group of people who are quite wealthy.

3. **Instinctive behaviors** are innate, automatic dispositions toward responding in a particular way when confronted with a specific stimulus. (see The Instinct Doctrine and Its Descendants)

   Example: In some species of birds, baby birds instinctively respond to the striped beak of the adult birds by opening their mouths.

4. **Instinct doctrine** is a view that explains human behavior as motivated by automatic, involuntary, and unlearned response sets. (see The Instinct Doctrine and Its Descendants)

   Example: The instinct doctrine would say that Nancy wants to have children because she has a reproductive instinct.

5. **Drive reduction theory** is a theory of motivation stating that motivation arises from imbalances in homeostasis. (see Drive Reduction Theory)

   Example: Oscar hasn't had anything to drink for hours. He has a need for fluids, which has caused a drive to find something to drink.

6. A **drive** is a psychological state of arousal created by an imbalance in homeostasis that prompts an organism to take action to restore the balance and reduce the drive. (see Drive Reduction Theory)

7. **Needs** are biological requirements for well-being that are created by an imbalance in homeostasis. (see Drive Reduction Theory)

   Example: Because we cannot live without food and water, they are excellent examples of needs.

8. **Homeostasis** is the tendency for organisms to keep their physiological systems at a stable, steady level by constantly adjusting themselves in response to change. (see Drive Reduction Theory)

   Example: Suppose that you had to walk outside in bitterly cold weather. Your body would sense this change in an external stimulus (the cold) and would begin taking action to maintain your temperature. Shivering, an adjustment that generates body heat, would help keep your temperature from dropping.

9. **Primary drives** are drives that arise from basic, biological needs. (see Drive Reduction Theory)

   Example: A sex drive or hunger drive arises from basic biological needs.

10. **Secondary drives** are drives that arise through learning and can be as motivating as primary drives. (see Drive Reduction Theory)

    Example: Money is not biologically important, but we learn through experience that it will be helpful in addressing biological needs. A drive to earn money would be a secondary drive.

11. **Physiological arousal** is a general level of activation that is reflected in several physiological systems. (see Arousal Theory)

    Example: After the announcement about the pop quiz, Paola's heart rate, muscle tension, and brain activity increased.

12. **Arousal theory** is a theory of motivation stating that people are motivated to behave in ways that maintain what is for them an optimal level of arousal. (see Arousal Theory)

    Example: Jorge is sitting in his office after a twelve-hour day, unhappy and bored. His level of arousal is too low. He decides to take a vacation in a country he has never visited. Toward the end of his vacation, he begins to look forward to getting back to work. Now Jorge's level of arousal is too high. He wants to go back to a well-known environment where his arousal level will decrease.

13. **Incentive theory** is a theory of motivation stating that behavior is directed toward obtaining desirable stimuli and avoiding unwanted stimuli. (see Incentive Theory)

    Example: When Joanna and David were first married, they saved money to buy a house (incentive). Now their mortgage is paid, and buying a house is no longer an incentive that guides their behavior. Instead, they save money to take vacations in Europe.

14. **Hunger** is the general state of wanting to eat. (see Biological Signals for Hunger and Satiety)

    REMEMBER: Stomach cues, signals carried by the blood, and hypothalamus activity indicate when we should eat.

15. **Satiation** is the satisfaction of a need such as hunger. (see Biological Signals for Hunger and Satiety)

    Example: Kent has eaten to his fill. He is now experiencing satiation.

16. **Satiety** is the condition of no longer wanting to eat. (see Biological Signals for Hunger and Satiety)

17. **Obesity** is a condition in which a person is severely overweight, as measured by a body mass index greater than 30. (see Unhealthy Eating)

    Example: Dena has a BMI of 35. She is considered obese.

    REMEMBER: Obesity can contribute to diabetes, high blood pressure, and increased risk of heart attack.

18. **Anorexia nervosa** is an eating disorder characterized by self-starvation and dramatic weight loss. (see Unhealthy Eating)

    Example: Cara thinks about food all the time, but will only eat about 600 calories per day. She exercises constantly, and has lost 30 percent of her body weight, when she was normal-sized to begin with.

    REMEMBER: Psychological factors associated with anorexia include a preoccupation with thinness and a distorted body image.

19. **Bulimia** is an eating disorder that involves eating massive amounts of food and then eliminating the food by self-induced vomiting or the use of strong laxatives. (see Unhealthy Eating)

Example: Marla eats a box of Oreos, a tub of ice cream, a bag of chips, and a whole pizza. She then feels guilty and induces vomiting to rid herself of the food.

20.   **Sexual arousal** is shown by physiological responses that arise from sexual contact or erotic thoughts. (see The Biology of Sex)

Example: David is thinking about the woman he saw at the pool and starts to get an erection.

21.   The **sexual response cycle** is the pattern of physiological arousal during and after sexual activity. (see The Biology of Sex)

Example: Dana and her boyfriend are making out and eventually have sex. Dana initially feels sexual arousal which plateaus for a while, and then she eventually reaches orgasm. She could repeat the cycle, but her boyfriend has a refractory period in his cycle.

22.   **Sex hormones** are chemicals in the blood of males and females that have both organizational and activational effects on sexual behavior. (see The Biology of Sex)

23.   **Estrogens** are sex hormones that circulate in the bloodstream of both men and women; more estrogens circulate in women than in men. (see The Biology of Sex)

24.   **Progestational hormones** or (*progestins*) are sex hormones that circulate in the bloodstream of both men and women, also known as progestins; more progestins circulate in women than in men. (see The Biology of Sex)

25.   **Androgens** are sex hormones that circulate in the bloodstream in both sexes; more androgens circulate in men than in women. (see The Biology of Sex)

26.   **Sexual orientation** is the nature of a person's enduring emotional, romantic, or sexual attraction to others. (see Sexual Orientation)

27.   **Heterosexuality** is sexual motivation that is focused on people of the other sex. (see Sexual Orientation)

Example: Sarah is attracted to men and only has sex with them, not women.

28.   **Bisexuality** is sexual motivation that is focused on members of both sexes. (see Sexual Orientation)

Example: Holly is attracted to both men and women, although right now she is in a committed relationship with a man.

29.   **Homosexuality** is sexual motivation that is focused on members of one's own sex. (see Sexual Orientation)

Example: Jane is attracted to women and only has sex women.

30.   **Achievement motivation** is the degree to which a person establishes specific goals, cares about meeting those goals, and experiences feelings of satisfaction by doing so. (see Need for Achievement)

Example: During grade school, Kelly chose to join an after-school math activity program that had regular tests in addition to projects. Kelly knew that she was good in math and wanted something new to challenge her.

31.   **Well-being** refers to a combination of a cognitive judgment of satisfaction with life, the frequent experiencing of positive moods and emotions, and the relatively infrequent experiencing of unpleasant moods and emotions; also known as *subjective well-being*. (see Achievement and Well-Being)

Example: Jules is generally happy with her life and rarely feels upset or angry. Jules probably has high subjective well-being.

32. **Emotions** are transitory positive or a negative experiences that are felt as happening to the self, are generated in part by cognitive appraisal of a situation, and are accompanied by both learned and innate physical responses. (see Defining Characteristics)

    Example: Imagine that your boss unjustly says your work is worthless. Rage wells up inside you because you have worked very hard. The involuntary experience of negative emotion just happens; you do not make it happen. Your cognitive appraisal of the situation is also important. You have determined that your boss is not kidding but is very serious. When in a rage, you may feel your face flush and your heart rate increase (reflexive physical responses).

33. The **sympathetic nervous system** is the subsystem of the autonomic nervous system that usually prepares the organism for vigorous activity. (see The Biology of Emotion)

34. The **parasympathetic nervous system** is the subsystem of the autonomic nervous system that typically influences activity related to the protection, nourishment, and growth of the body. (see The Biology of Emotion)

    Example: Coleman is happily relaxing after a long day of classes. As he watches a comedy on TV, his heart rate slows, but digestion activity increases.

35. The **fight-flight reaction** (also called **fight-or-flight syndrome**) is the physical reaction initiated by the sympathetic nervous system that prepares the body to fight or to run from a threatening situation. (see The Biology of Emotion)

    Example: A fire alarm startles Coleman. In the fight-or-flight response activated by the sympathetic nervous system, his heart rate and breathing increase. Although he can't feel the difference as he walks to the stairway, his digestive activity has slowed and his blood sugar has increased.

36. **Attribution** is the process of explaining the causes of an event. (see Cognitive Theories of Emotion)

    Example: Felicia was smiling as she studied. When she noticed it, she attributed it to her happiness about a trip she was planning for the weekend.

37. **Excitation transfer theory** is the theory that physiological arousal stemming from one situation is carried over to and enhances emotional experience in an independent situation. (see Cognitive Theories of Emotion)

    Example: You have just run to class. Just outside the door of the classroom, one of the people working on your group project tells you that she could not finish her part of the paper that is due this period. Normally you would be angry, but your increased arousal from the run intensifies your emotion. You are not just angry; you are furious.

FILL-IN-THE-BLANKS KEY TERMS

This section will help you check your factual knowledge of the key terms introduced in this chapter. Fill in each blank with the appropriate term from the list of key terms in the previous section.

1. _____ theory holds that motivation arises out of an imbalance in homeostasis.

2. A purpose for behavior is called a(n) _____.

3. _____ are innate, automatic dispositions for responding to specific stimuli.

4. The tendency of organisms to keep their physiological systems at a stable level by adjusting in response to change is _____.

5. _____ theory proposes that people behave in ways that are necessary to maintain a certain internal activation level.

6. _____ is an eating disorder characterized by a preoccupation with thinness and self-starvation.

7. In _____, a person consumes large quantities of food and then attempts to remove the food by vomiting or using laxatives.

8. _____ are a general name for male hormones.

9. _____ is the sexual orientation of a person who is sexually active with persons of both sexes.

10. Sex hormones that are more predominant in females are _____ and _____.

11. _____ is the sexual orientation of a person who is sexually active with people of the same sex.

12. When people label their physiological arousal based on various information in their environment, this is called _____.

13. When physiological arousal carried over from one situation influences one's interpretation of a new situation, this is called _____.

14. Experiences that include both learned and reflexive physical responses that are generated by a person's appraisal of a situation are _____.

15. _____ is the state of no longer wanting to eat.

Total Correct (See answer key) _____

LEARNING OBJECTIVES

1. Define motivation. Discuss the types of behaviors that motivation may help to explain. (see introductory section)

2. Define motive and *intervening variables*, and explain the latter's role in understanding motivation. (see "Concepts and Theories of Motivation")

3. Describe the sources of motivation. (see "Sources of Motivation")

4. Define instinct. Discuss how instinct doctrine explains behavior. Explain why instinct theory failed. Describe the evolutionary approach and its views of mate selection. (see "Instinct Theory and Its Descendants")

5. Define homeostasis, need, drive, and drive reduction theory. Explain what behaviors drive theory can and cannot account for. (see "Drive Reduction Theory"; see also "Optimal Arousal Theory")

6. Define arousal. Describe the arousal theory of motivation. Discuss the role of an optimal level of arousal in motivation and the impact of more or less than an optimal level of arousal on performance. (see "Optimal Arousal Theory")

7. Define incentive theory. Describe incentive theory's attempt to explain behavior and distinguish *wanting* from *liking*. (see "Incentive Theory")

8. Define <u>hunger</u> and <u>satiety</u>. List the nutrients and hormones that the brain monitors in the bloodstream as it regulates hunger and eating. Explain the role of the *ventromedial nucleus*, *lateral hypothalamus*, and *paraventricular nucleus* in hunger and eating. Define *set point*. (see "Hunger and Eating")

9. Specify the role of *flavor* and learning in the regulation of eating. Define *appetite*. Describe the mechanisms controlling *specific hungers*. Give examples of the effects of a *food culture*. (see "Flavor, Cultural Learning, and Food Selection")

10. Define <u>obesity</u>, <u>anorexia nervosa</u>, and <u>bulimia</u>. Describe the behaviors, causes, health dangers, and treatments associated with each of these eating disorders. (see "Eating Disorders")

11. Describe the survey of human sexual behavior and discuss its findings. Describe the <u>sexual response cycle</u>. Name the three prominent <u>sex hormones</u>. Explain their organizational and activational effects. (see "The Biology of Sex")

12. Discuss the social and cultural influences on sexual motivation. Define <u>heterosexuality</u>, <u>homosexuality</u>, and <u>bisexuality</u>. Describe the evidence on the extent to which genes may determine sexual orientation. (see "Social and Cultural Factors in Sexuality"; see also "Sexual Orientation"; see also "Thinking Critically: What Shapes Sexual Orientation?")

13. Define <u>achievement motivation</u>. Describe the characteristics of achievement motivation and the factors that can affect its development. (see "Need for Achievement")

14. Describe the extrinsic and intrinsic factors that affect job satisfaction and dissatisfaction. Give an example of a job that has been designed to increase satisfaction and motivation. (see "Achievement and Success in the Workplace")

15. Discuss the relation between achievement and <u>well-being</u>. (see "Achievement and Well-Being")

16. Describe Maslow's hierarchy of needs. Give examples of each kind of need. Explain how the *existence, relatedness, growth (ERG) theory* addresses some of the problems with Maslow's theory. (see "Relations and Conflicts Among Motives")

17. Describe the four types of motivational conflicts, and explain the relationships between motivation and stress. (see "Linkages: Conflicting Motives and Stress")

18. Discuss the opponent-process theory of motivation. Give an example of the kinds of behavior it explains. (see "Opponent Processes, Motivation, and Emotion")

19. Describe the defining characteristics of the subjective experience of <u>emotion</u>. (see "Defining Characteristics")

20. Describe the role of the brain in emotion and facial expressions. Describe how the <u>parasympathetic nervous system</u> and <u>sympathetic nervous system</u> are involved in emotional experience, including the <u>fight-flight reaction</u>. (see "The Biology of Emotion")

21. Discuss James' peripheral theory of emotion. Give an example of how an emotion would occur, according to this theory. (see "James's Peripheral Theory")

22. Discuss the research that evaluates James' theory. Describe the *facial-feedback hypothesis*. Discuss the assumptions upon which a lie detector test is based. (see "Evaluating James's Theory"; see also "Lie Detection")

23. Describe Cannon's *central theory* of emotion and discuss how this theory has been updated following new research findings. (see "Cannon's Central Theory")

24. Describe the *Schachter-Singer theory* as a modification of James' peripheral theory of emotion. Define <u>attribution</u> and give an example. (see "Cognitive Theories")

25. Discuss the research stimulated by the Schachter-Singer theory, including <u>excitation transfer theory</u> and Lazarus' *cognitive appraisal theory*. (see "Cognitive Theories")

26. Compare and contrast the key elements of the theories of emotion. (see "In Review: Theories of Emotion")

27. Discuss the role of facial movements in expressing human emotion. Describe Darwin's theory of innate basic facial expressions. Discuss the research that supports this theory. (see "Communicating Emotion"; see also "Innate Expressions of Emotion")

28. Describe the social and cultural factors involved in communicating emotion. Describe the role and sources of learning in human emotional expression. Define *emotion culture* and *social referencing*. (see "Social and Cultural Influences on Emotional Expression")

CONCEPTS AND EXERCISES

Theories of Motivation

Below is a list of several different behaviors. Which theory would best explain the motivation underlying each behavior?

1. Bill says he cannot help but wear gold necklaces and earrings because he was born that way. _____

2. Veteran video-game players seek out new games that offer new challenges and higher levels of difficulty. _____

3. Some taverns believe it's good business to serve extremely salty free snacks to their customers. _____

4. Kelly was terrified the first time she used the high-diving board at the pool. But when she successfully completed her dive, she felt a sense of exhilaration. Now when Kelly dives, she feels much less fear, but she still enjoys the invigorating feelings that accompany her dives.

   _____

5. Eight-year-old Simon is given coveted *Star Wars* stickers when he successfully completes his homework. _____

Emotions at the Prom

Following are some of the experiences of Franklin High students at their school dance. After each description, choose from the following list of options the phenomenon or theory of emotion that best matches the experience. Each answer may be used more than once or not at all.

1. Joya, after dancing a slow dance with Ted, walks back to where her friends are standing. She is smiling, a little breathless, and has a quickened heartbeat and shaky knees. Joya realizes that these responses indicate that she is happy. _____

2. Helen arrived at the dance twenty minutes late. She ran all the way from the parking lot to the school. She spent several minutes talking with her friends in the bathroom, brushing her hair, and putting on new lipstick. Just as she stepped into the gym to survey the crowd, she tripped and fell, ripping her dress. Absolutely furious, she yelled at the boy who tried to help her up, "You idiot, look what you made me do!" What could explain her intense emotional reaction?

   _____

3. Cecelia is dancing with her boyfriend. She simultaneously realizes how much she loves him and notices how fast her heart is beating and that she has butterflies in her stomach. _____

    a.   James' peripheral theory

    b.   Schachter-Singer theory

    c.   Cannon's central theory

    d.   Excitation transfer

CRITICAL THINKING

Sam and Martina and another friend of theirs, Pete, are arguing about the reasons for a crime. A mobster named Joey killed Tony, a member of a rival family.

Sam starts the conversation by saying, "Look, Martina, Joey has been part of the mob for years. He probably thought he had to knock Tony off before Tony killed him. The guy had a plain and simple goal—to live."

Martina returns, "You have to wonder why some guys become 'soldiers' in the mob in the first place. Lots of people think these guys are violent by nature. But sometimes I think maybe they just want the security of being part of a group. They were probably really scared the first time they killed someone and only felt relief when it was over and everyone in the group was being supportive. Now, I'll bet the fear is short-lived and they feel more elation at their accomplishment. Every time they kill someone, they are 'worthy' of even more protection from the group."

Pete rubs his jaw and says, "I think he was just bored. There hasn't been a lot happening in the streets lately. I bet he just wanted a little fun. That's why he killed Tony."

Using the five critical thinking questions in the text, the clues in the story, and what you have learned about motivation, answer the following.

1.   What is Sam's hypothesis? What theory of motivation would support his hypothesis?

2.   What is Martina's hypothesis? What theory of motivation would support her hypothesis?

3.   What is Pete's hypothesis? What theory of motivation would support his hypothesis?

PERSONAL LEARNING ACTIVITIES

1.   Why do you study psychology? List the reasons you study this subject. Try to identify whether your explanations fit with a particular theory of motivation. For example, if you wrote "curiosity," which theory would be best at explaining this motive? Which reasons would incentive theory explain? Is achievement motivation a factor?

2.   *New York Times* science reporter, Gina Kolata, wrote a book on the weight loss industry called *Rethinking Thin* that is heavily grounded in ideas about set point. To hear her present some of her ideas, visit the following site for a short video: http://abcnews.go.com/Health/video?id=3181905. After hearing her thoughts, what are your own thoughts on the obesity epidemic? Does set point theory allow us to just disregard obesity or should we still try to address it?

3.   If you enjoy psychological research, you might like to try to participate in research on subjective well-being and emotion. Visit the following website to see if any studies are running that you might be interested in participating in: http://swbresearch.netfirms.com/. How are the researchers measuring well-being? How does the way the measure it affect what level of well-being you report? If you are interested in learning more, then visit the Positive Psychology Center website at: http://www.ppc.sas.upenn.edu/index.html.

2.   Think about the times you have experienced motivational conflicts—for example, when you had to decide whether to participate in an activity that had positive and negative aspects. Was it an approach-approach, approach-avoidance, avoidance-avoidance, or multiple approach-avoidance

conflict? After you decided to participate (or not), did the positive or the negative features become more prominent?

3. A notion called "misattribution of arousal" is related to the idea of excitation transfer presented in this chapter. To see an interesting experiment that investigates the role of excitation transfer in romantic attraction, visit the following YouTube site: http://www.youtube.com/watch?v=P0aMEkGlcQE. After watching the video, can you think of times when you started dating someone who you met in an arousing situation (dangerous or exciting)?

MULTIPLE-CHOICE QUESTIONS

Quiz 1

1. Motivation is considered an intervening variable because
   a. it is a stimulus that causes a response.
   b. motives or needs are causes of behavior.
   c. it helps explain the relationship between stimuli and responses.
   d. motives or needs are responses to external stimuli.

2. Drive reduction theory is based on the concept of
   a. incentives.
   b. subjective well-being.
   c. level of arousal.
   d. homeostasis.

3. Stewart desperately wants a job in the computer field. He has just finished an interview during which he was aggressive about his thoughts and ideas. An incentive theorist would say that Stewart
   a. has a strong aggressive instinct.
   b. thinks that being aggressive will land him the job.
   c. has a very high optimal level of arousal.
   d. is worried about having enough money to live on.

4. Which of the following is the best evidence that differences in what men and women look for in mates are more cultural than biological?
   a. Men in the United States are more ambitious than men in Canada.
   b. Most men look for an attractive mate.
   c. Most women try to look younger.
   d. Zulu women are expected to be physically strong, ambitious, and mature.

5. Dwayne enjoys spending quiet evenings at home, watching old movies. To best explain his motivation for this behavior using the arousal theory, we should say that Dwayne
   a. is rewarded by his enjoyment of the movies.
   b. has hectic, busy days and wants some peace and quiet in the evenings.
   c. has an emotional need fulfilled by watching the movies.
   d. has met his physiological needs and therefore can seek arousal.

6.   Cholecystokinin is involved in the regulation of
   a.   eating.
   b.   thirst.
   c.   sex.
   d.   arousal.

7.   Madison is extremely obese. Her doctor does some tests and determines that her body does not make a hormone, and the lack of it is causing her to eat more food than she needs. He puts her on a hormone treatment and she begins to eat more normally and approach normal size. What hormone does Madison's body not make?
   a.   Androgen
   b.   Leptin
   c.   Progestin
   d.   Glucose

8.   One survey of sexual behavior in the United States found that
   a.   single people report having the most frequent and satisfying sex.
   b.   people tend to be attracted to and have sex with many partners in their lifetime.
   c.   people in committed, monogamous relationships have the most frequent and satisfying sex.
   d.   most people have sex an average of three times a week.

9.   Kate has a high achievement motivation. Kate's parents most likely
   a.   encouraged her to try new challenges and rewarded her successes.
   b.   always got involved with her work and even helped her finish assignments.
   c.   told her to quit torturing herself and give up when things got tough.
   d.   did not praise Kate very much because they did not want her to become satisfied and quit trying new things.

10.   The main difference between ERG theory and Maslow's hierarchy of need is that
   a.   ERG theory specifies no particular order in which needs should be met.
   b.   ERG theory places more importance on self-actualization.
   c.   ERG theory places less emphasis on belongingness.
   d.   ERG has more categories of needs than Maslow.

11.   The first time a group of military parachutists jumped out of a plane, some were so frightened that they involuntarily urinated on themselves. Once they landed safely, they felt relief and excitement. After repeated jumps, the initial fear response subsided and the feelings of euphoria intensified. Which theory of motivation best explains this behavior?
   a.   Arousal
   b.   Drive reduction
   c.   Incentive
   d.   Opponent-process

12. Caitlin is not sure what she should do. She has been asked to go to a fraternity winter formal by a guy she really likes. She has also been invited to go with her family on a ski trip at a fabulous resort the same weekend. She can't do both—she has to choose. Caitlin is experiencing a(n)
    a. approach-avoidance conflict.
    b. approach-approach conflict.
    c. avoidance-avoidance conflict.
    d. multiple approach-avoidance conflict.

13. The Hanley brothers became addicted to a type of video game because a pleasure center in the brain was stimulated each time they scored. Eventually, the Hanleys played the game nearly constantly and simultaneously experienced a pleasurable emotion and a physiological reaction. This is most supportive of which of the following?
    a. Schachter-Singer theory
    b. Cannon's central theory
    c. James' peripheral theory
    d. Arousal theory

14. Kurt, who is about to take a lie detector test, has sneakily put a tack in his shoe. Kurt should jam the tack into his toe to show an increase in physiological response after
    a. questions about his alibi.
    b. control questions.
    c. relevant questions.
    d. questions about his age, education, and income.

15. Matt is very interested in a woman he met at the gym. When would be the best time for him to approach her to talk?
    a. As she is warming up before her workout
    b. During her workout
    c. When she is toweling off right after her workout
    d. In the parking lot after a shower

16. When people are scared to do something, they are said to have cold feet. Fear really is associated with a decrease in blood flow to the feet and hands, which supports _____ of emotion.
    a. Cannon's central theory
    b. James' peripheral theory
    c. the incentive theory
    d. Schachter-Singer theory

17. Ian is very happy with his life and relationships. He generally feels good about his work and is rarely moody. Ian probably scores high on measures of
    a. achievement motivation.
    b. subjective well-being.
    c. emotion culture.
    d. social referencing.

18. Gloria went to the doctor for her usual anti-allergy shots. The nurse mistakenly gave her a shot of epinephrine, which caused a great deal of physiological arousal. As Gloria sailed out of the office, she decided that she was feeling shaky from drinking too much caffeinated coffee. Her lack of emotion despite physiological arousal can be explained by which of the following?

    a. Darwin's theory
    b. James's peripheral theory
    c. Schachter-Singer theory
    d. Cannon's central theory

19. When Michele heard someone trying to open her car door while she was stopped at a light, she felt her heart race. A few seconds later, without consciously considering her situation, she knew her physical response was fear. Michele's experience supports which of the following?

    a. Optimal arousal theory
    b. Cannon's central theory
    c. James' peripheral theory
    d. Schachter-Singer theory

20. Connor is playing with his friend, Jake. He thinks it will be funny to hang onto the back of Jake's bike to slow him down, but when he sees Jake roll his eyes at him, he realizes he should stop. Connor is using

    a. facial feedback.
    b. social referencing.
    c. attribution.
    d. excitation transfer.

Total Correct (See answer key) _____

Quiz 2

Use this quiz to reassess your learning after taking Quiz 1 and reviewing the chapter.

1. Which of the following is the best illustration of motivation as an intervening variable?

    a. A bell causes a rat to salivate.
    b. When a person passes a candy machine, she doesn't get candy unless she is hungry.
    c. A relative calls you "amazing" and a "genius."
    d. A person tries to smile although he feels depressed.

2. Homeostasis is a key concept in which theory of motivation?

    a. The instinct doctrine
    b. Arousal theory
    c. Incentive theory
    d. Drive reduction theory

3.   Charles wants his little boy to be motivated to be good at the store. When his little boy starts acting up and throwing a tantrum, Charles just keeps on trucking down the aisle. Charles thinks that to motivate his little boy to be good, he has to help him learn that bad behavior makes him lose dad's fun company. Charles's thinking reflects which theory of motivation?

    a.   Arousal theory
    b.   Drive reduction theory
    c.   Incentive theory
    d.   The instinct doctrine

4.   Allison is a 25-year-old woman who is interested in a long-term romantic relationship. According to the evolutionary approach, to which of the following people would Allison most likely be attracted?

    a.   Susan, a 25-year-old graduate student nearing completion of her degree
    b.   Tom, a 25-year-old artist who has a secretarial day job
    c.   Vic, a 33-year-old banker with a good salary and an interest in having children
    d.   Wally, an 18-year-old, good-looking waiter who likes movies, fast cars, and having fun at parties

5.   Anorexia nervosa is characterized by

    a.   eating more calories than are necessary for body maintenance.
    b.   self-starvation and weight loss.
    c.   overeating and self-induced vomiting.
    d.   None of these

6.   Jack was in training to lose enough weight to make a lighter class in wrestling. When his roommates invited him to join them for dinner at the Bavarian Buffet restaurant, Jack declined and ate alone at home. All else being equal and assuming it was the normal dinner hour, what may we suspect as the reason for Jack's refusal?

    a.   He had lost his appetite.
    b.   He was afraid he would overeat.
    c.   He was afraid his nutritional balance would be thrown off course.
    d.   It would violate his food culture.

7.   Ador has not eaten for several hours, and his body is letting him know it is hungry. This sense of being out of balance motivates him to eat to restore balance to his system. Ador's desire to seek equilibrium is known as

    a.   homeostasis.
    b.   an instinctive behavior.
    c.   an intervening variable.
    d.   a specific hunger.

8.   The principal example of an androgen is

    a.   estradiol.
    b.   progesterone.
    c.   testosterone.
    d.   CCK.

9. Julie, who has a high achievement motivation, is trying to decide where to work. Which job should she take?

   a. Company 1: high pay, little responsibility, great boss
   b. Company 2: low pay, lots of responsibility, mediocre boss
   c. Company 3: medium pay, lots of responsibility, chances for advancement, demanding boss
   d. Company 4: very high pay, easy work, not much chance for advancement, great boss

10. Marta claims that she will not be satisfied until she gets the respect she deserves for the job she does at work. According to Maslow's hierarchy of needs, Marta has

    a. given up her biological needs because she probably was unable to fulfill them.
    b. probably been poor all of her life.
    c. had her lower needs fulfilled to an acceptable degree.
    d. not had her lower needs fulfilled to an acceptable degree.

11. The board of trustees could not understand why faculty morale was so low and why so many faculty members were accepting positions at other colleges. Which of the following probably had the *least* negative effect on employee motivation?

    a. An article in the local paper quoted some board members as saying that the faculty members were getting lazy.
    b. Due to budgetary problems, the college canceled all raises for one year.
    c. When the college introduced a number of new web-based courses, no recognition was given to the faculty who had developed them.
    d. A new policy requires faculty members to fill out daily reports accounting for all content they cover in their classes and explaining how they spend their time between classes.

12. Lisa, a waitress, feels like screaming. One of her customers ordered steak and shrimp, but when she brought it to him, he said he had ordered steak and lobster. If she tells him that he is wrong, she could lose a big tip. If she takes the food back to the cook, he might get angry and make mistakes with her orders all night long, which would also ruin her tips. This is an example of which kind of motivational conflict?

    a. Approach-approach
    b. Approach-avoidance
    c. Avoidance-avoidance
    d. Multiple approach-avoidance

13. Research on subjective well-being suggests that

    a. event-related changes in mood persist for months, even years sometimes.
    b. trauma, like being imprisoned or the death of a spouse, is something that adversely affects your happiness level for extremely long periods.
    c. religious faith can hinder the level of happiness one is able to achieve.
    d. happiness has less to do with what happens to you and more to do with your baseline temperament.

14. When Harley received a letter from her fiancé that contained bad news, she experienced the fight-flight reaction. This means Harley's

    a. parasympathetic nervous system was activated.
    b. sympathetic nervous system was activated.
    c. digestion and salivation were stimulated.
    d. respiration and heart rate slowed.

15. Janet and Joan are experiencing identical patterns of physiological arousal: increased heart rate, sweaty palms, pupil dilation, and increased breathing rate. Janet feels happy, and Joan is very scared. Which of the following can explain the differences in their emotions?

    a.   James' peripheral theory
    b.   Schachter-Singer theory
    c.   Darwin's theory
    d.   Cannon's central theory

16. Which theory requires the existence of unique physiological states for every emotion?

    a.   James'
    b.   Cannon's
    c.   Schachter-Singer
    d.   Darwin's

17. Lori and Carol are discussing the places in town where they have met the best-looking men. Based on your knowledge of excitation transfer, which place do you think would be at the top of their list?

    a.   A men's clothing store
    b.   A laundromat
    c.   A local dance bar
    d.   A restaurant

18. The facial-feedback hypothesis is a variant of the _____ theory of emotion.

    a.   Schachter-Singer
    b.   Cannon central
    c.   James' peripheral
    d.   Maslow

19. People from many different cultures can recognize a smile as an indication of positive emotion. This suggests that at least some expressions of emotion are

    a.   innate.
    b.   culturally determined.
    c.   learned.
    d.   lateralized.

20. The fact that there is no English equivalent to certain words describing emotions in other countries illustrates differences in

    a.   social referencing.
    b.   attribution.
    c.   emotion culture.
    d.   excitation transfer.

Total Correct (See answer key) _____

ANSWERS TO FILL-IN-THE-BLANKS KEY TERMS

1.   Drive reduction (see Drive Reduction Theory)

2.   motive (see Concepts and Theories of Motivation)

3.   Instinctive behaviors (see The Instinct Doctrine and Its Descendants)

4.   homeostasis (see Drive Reduction Theory)

5.   Arousal (see Arousal Theory)

6.   Anorexia nervosa (see Unhealthy Eating)

7.   bulimia (see Unhealthy Eating)

8.   Androgens (see The Biology of Sex)

9.   bisexuality (see Sexual Orientation)

10.   estrogen; progestational hormones (see The Biology of Sex)

11.   homosexuality (see Sexual Orientation)

12.   attribution (see Cognitive Theories of Emotion)

13.   excitation transfer (see Cognitive Theories of Emotion)

14.   emotions (see Defining Characteristics)

15.   Satiety (see Biological Signals for Hunger and Satiation)

ANSWERS TO CONCEPTS AND EXERCISES

Theories of Motivation

1.   *The instinct doctrine.* Bill is asserting that his motivation to wear jewelry is genetically based and unlearned. (see The Instinct Doctrine and Its Descendants)

2.   *Arousal theory.* Veterans will become bored once they master a video game. Therefore, they will be motivated to seek out new challenges because their arousal will be below optimal level. (see Arousal Theory)

3.   *Drive reduction theory.* Salty snacks tend to make people thirsty. Taverns are trying to create a need for thirst-quenching drinks, which will increase their business. (see Drive Reduction Theory)

4.   *Opponent-process theory.* When Kelly first used the high board, her first reaction was fear, followed by the exhilaration of completing the dive safely. As time passed, the fear decreased and the exhilaration increased. (see Opponent Processes, Motivation, and Emotion)

5.   *Incentive theory.* Simon is motivated to do his homework well because if he does so, he will receive something he values. (see Incentive Theory)

Emotions at the Prom

1.   *James' peripheral theory.* This theory could explain Joya's emotional reaction since it is based solely on her physiological responses. She has decided that she is happy because she is experiencing all the physiological responses that occur with happiness. (see James's Peripheral Theory)

2.   *Excitation transfer.* Helen was probably still physiologically aroused from running into the school from the parking lot. She transferred this excitation to the anger she felt when she ripped her dress. This intensified her emotional reaction. (see Cognitive Theories)

3. *Cannon's central theory.* Cecelia is simultaneously experiencing the conscious emotion of being in love and a heightened physiological arousal. According to Cannon's central theory, cognition and physiological reactions to emotion occur at the same time. (see Cannon's Central Theory)

ANSWERS TO CRITICAL THINKING

1. Sam hypothesizes that Joey was motivated to kill Tony in order to avoid being killed himself. The incentive theory of motivation would support this hypothesis.

2. Martina hypothesizes that Joey was originally very fearful when killing someone but immediately felt the support and concern of the rest of the mob. Now, Joey is motivated to place himself in danger by killing someone, because the fear doesn't last long and it elicits the more important opposing reaction of relief and support from the group. The opponent-process theory of motivation would support this hypothesis.

3. Peter hypothesizes that since nothing was happening in the neighborhood, Joey killed Tony to increase his own level of arousal to an optimal level. The arousal theory of motivation would support this hypothesis.

ANSWERS TO MULTIPLE-CHOICE QUESTIONS

Circle the question numbers you answered correctly.

Quiz 1

1. c is the answer. Intervening variables help us understand why a given stimulus caused a given response. For example, hunger helps explain why someone ordered a pizza after hearing a pizza advertisement. The ad is the stimulus, and ordering the pizza is the response. The motive of hunger also explains why the person did not display some other response, such as ignoring the ad. (see Concepts and Theories of Motivation)

    a, b, d.   Motivation, motives, and needs are neither stimuli nor responses but can affect the responses made to stimuli.

2. d is the answer. Drive reduction theory is based on the concept of homeostasis. Homeostasis is the tendency for physiological systems to maintain a stable, steady level by constantly adjusting themselves in response to change. (see Drive Reduction Theory)

    a.   Incentives are the foundation of incentive theory, not drive reduction theory.

    b.   Subjective well-being is a combination of cognitive judgment of satisfaction with life, the frequent experiencing of positive moods and emotions, and the relatively infrequent experiencing of unpleasant moods and emotions.

    c.   Arousal theory is based on the concept of achieving an optimal level of arousal.

3. b is the answer. An incentive theorist would say that Stewart was behaving in a way that he thought would bring him closer to a goal or an incentive. (see Incentive Theory)

    a.   An instinct theorist would say that Stewart has an aggressive instinct.

    c.   An arousal theorist would say that Stewart has a very high level of optimal arousal.

    d.   A drive theorist would say that Stewart wants the job so that he will have enough money to buy food.

4. d is the answer. Although it is generally found that women prefer men who are mature and wealthy while men prefer women who are young and healthy, this is not true of the Zulu. Among

the Zulu, who have different gender roles, men value maturity and ambition in a mate more than women do. (see The Instinct Doctrine and Its Descendants)

a. No research has shown that men in the United States are more ambitious than men in Canada. Even if this were true, this evidence would not be as strong as that from the Zulu.

b, c. These behaviors both fit with the evolutionary view that men look for women who are able to bear children and women try to look like they can do so.

5. b is the answer. Arousal theory states that people try to maintain an optimal level of arousal. According to arousal theory, Dwayne will seek relaxation when overaroused. (see Arousal Theory)

a. This would fit with incentive theory.

c, d. These sound similar to Maslow's views; however, he did not directly address arousal in his hierarchy of needs.

6. a is the answer. Cholecystokinin is a chemical that is involved in the cessation of eating. (see Biological Signals for Hunger and Satiety)

b, c, d. Cholecystokinin is not involved in the regulation of thirst, sex, or arousal.

7. b is the answer. Leptin is a hormone that reaches receptors in the hypothalamus and provides information to the brain about increasing fat supplies. When leptin levels are high, hunger decreases, which in turn decreases food intake. Without leptin, hunger increases. (see Biological Signals for Hunger and Satiation)

a. Androgens are sex hormones that circulate in the bloodstream and regulate sexual motivation in both sexes.

c. Progestins are sex hormones that circulate in the bloodstream of both men and women.

d. Glucose is not a hormone. It is the main form of sugar used by body cells.

8. c is the answer. This 1994 survey found that people in the United States have sex less often and with fewer people than previously thought. Data also suggested that people in committed, monogamous relationships have the most frequent sex and the most satisfying sex. (see Focus on Research Methods: A Survey of Human Sexual Behavior)

a, b. People in committed, monogamous relationships reported the most frequent and most satisfying sex.

d. For most, sex occurs about once a week in monogamous relationships; about a third reported having sex only a few times or not at all in the past year.

9. a is the answer. Children whose parents encourage them to try new things and reward them for their successes develop a high achievement motivation. (see Need for Achievement)

b. Children with parents who interfered in their work would not develop a high achievement motivation.

c. Children with parents who let them give up would not develop a high achievement motivation.

d. A lack of praise would *not* encourage development of a high achievement motivation.

10. a is the answer. ERG theory does not assume that needs from various categories must be met in a particular order; rather, they each rise and fall over time and across situations. (see Relations and Conflicts Among Motives)

b.   Self-actualization is not more emphasized in ERG theory.

c.   Belongingness is not less emphasized in ERG theory.

d.   ERG theory has three categories of needs, which is fewer than Maslow specified.

11.   d is the answer. According to the opponent-process theory, an opposing reaction can eventually motivate a behavior. The parachutists' initial reaction was extreme fear, and the opposing reactions were relief and excitement. After repeated jumps, the initial reaction decreased and the opponent reaction of euphoria took over the motivation. (see Opponent Processes, Motivation, and Emotion)

a.   Arousal theory focuses on physiological arousal. Although the pilots were aroused by fear, they were overly aroused to the extent that they were urinating on themselves. Such an arousal is not strongly motivating. With repeated jumps, this arousal lessened.

b.   Drive reduction theory says we seek to satisfy a need created when we experience an imbalance in homeostasis. Diving out of an airplane is not a biological need, nor is it described as being associated with a primary drive.

c.   Incentive theory doesn't explain why parachutists would jump again after an initial harrowing experience. They would have no incentive to continue something that had caused fear and humiliation.

12.   b is the answer. Caitlin is trying to decide between two positive options. She would like to "approach" or do both, but can't. This is an approach-approach conflict. (see Linkages: Conflicting Motives and Stress)

a.   Approach-avoidance conflicts are those in which a person is presented with a single option to engage in or not. The option has both positive and negative aspects. In this case, Caitlin has two choices, both of which are positive.

c.   Avoidance-avoidance conflicts are those in which a person must choose between two negative alternatives.

d.   A multiple approach-avoidance conflict involves two situations, each of which has positive and negative features.

13.   b is the answer. The Hanley brothers' experience of emotion fits best with Cannon's central theory, which suggests that emotions take place in the brain but messages are simultaneously sent to the body. (see Cannon's Central Theory)

a.   Schachter-Singer theory suggests that physiological reactions can be labeled with different emotions, depending on the interpretation of the situation. In this scenario, immediate pleasurable emotion was experienced without interpretation.

c.   The thrust of James' peripheral theory is that there is no initial mental experience of emotion; rather, emotion is the result of the experience of bodily responses. In this scenario, the brain is primary in the experience of emotion.

d.   Arousal theory refers to motivation, not emotion.

14.   b is the answer. Innocent people usually react more strongly to control questions such as "Have you ever tried to hurt someone?" Therefore, Kurt should jam the tack in his toe after control questions in order to produce physiological arousal. (see James's Peripheral Theory)

a.   Questions about an alibi would not be good questions to seem upset about. Like questions that specifically refer to a crime, innocent people shouldn't react very strongly when asked about their whereabouts.

c.   Relevant questions are those that specifically refer to the crime. Guilty people react more strongly to relevant questions than to control questions.

d.   Reactions to relevant and control questions are compared in order to determine guilt or innocence. Questions about age, education, and income are neither control nor relevant questions.

15.   c is the answer. People remain physiologically aroused longer than they think they do. The woman at the gym will feel calm by the time she is toweling off, even though she will still be somewhat aroused. If Matt approaches her at this point, she will probably attribute any leftover arousal to him instead of to the exercise. (see Cognitive Theories of Emotion)

a.   The woman at the gym will experience very little physiological arousal while she is warming up. If she does experience any arousal, she will attribute it to exercising, not to Matt.

b.   Weightlifting and aerobics will cause physiological arousal. However, the woman will probably attribute her arousal to these activities instead of to Matt.

d.   By the time the woman has showered and gone to the parking lot, she will no longer be aroused.

16.   b is the answer. According to James' peripheral theory, there are unique changes in physiological arousal associated with each emotion. Frightened people do have cold feet because of decreased blood flow; therefore, fear may have a unique physiological response. (see James's Peripheral Theory)

a.   According to Cannon's central theory of emotion, physiological reactions do not play a role in the labeling of emotion because they occur at the same time as the emotion.

c.   Incentive theory is a theory of motivation.

d.   Schachter-Singer theory argues that a physiological reaction could be labeled with different emotions depending on a cognitive appraisal of the situation. Therefore, a unique physiological reaction is not necessary for each emotion.

17.   b is the answer. Subjective well-being is a combination of cognitive judgments of satisfaction with life, the frequent experiencing of positive emotions and moods, and the relatively infrequent experience of unpleasant emotions and moods. Ian is satisfied with his life and generally a positive person, which makes him likely to score high on measures of this variable. (see Achievement and Well-Being)

a.   Achievement motivation, or need for achievement, is a motive influenced by the degree to which a person establishes specific goals, cares about meeting them, and experiences feelings of satisfaction by doing so. This question says nothing about Ian's need for achievement.

c.   An emotion culture is a set of rules that govern what emotions are appropriate in what circumstances and what emotional expressions are allowed. This question only tells us about Ian's personal feelings, not about the social and cultural rules that govern the expression of his emotions.

d.   Social referencing refers to relying on cues from others when unsure of what is appropriate in ambiguous or strange situations. This question doesn't describe Ian as looking to others for what emotion to express.

18.   c is the answer. According to the Schachter-Singer theory, if we attribute arousal to a nonemotional cause (for example, caffeine), then the experience of emotion should be reduced.

Gloria was not experiencing any emotion. She simply thought she had too much coffee that morning. (see Cognitive Theories of Emotion)

a.   Darwin did not propose a theory of how we experience emotion.

b.   According to James's peripheral theory, Gloria should have interpreted her physiological arousal as resulting from an emotion.

d.   According to Cannon's central theory, Gloria should have cognitively experienced an emotion when she felt the physiological arousal. This cannot be the answer since Gloria felt the arousal but no emotion.

19.   c is the answer. James' peripheral theory suggests that we feel a physiological change and then perceive it as a specific emotion without considering the situation. (see James' Peripheral Theory)

a.   Arousal is a theory of motivation.

b.   Cannon's central theory states that the physiological reaction and emotion label will occur at the same time.

d.   Schachter-Singer theory proposes that we make an attribution about the situation before experiencing the emotion.

20.   b is the answer. Looking at another person to judge their emotional state as a guide for ours is social referencing. (see Social and Cultural Influences on Emotional Expression)

a.   The facial-feedback hypothesis says that our own facial muscles give us information about our emotional state.

c.   Attributions are the labels we assign to physiological arousal, according to the Schachter-Singer theory of emotion.

d.   Excitation transfer occurs when physiological arousal is unknowingly carried over into an unrelated situation.

Now turn to the quiz analysis table at the end of this chapter to find which areas you know well and which areas you need to work on. Circle the numbers in the table for items on Quiz 1 that you answered correctly.

Quiz 2

1.   b is the answer. Motivation is an intervening variable that explains the relationship between a stimulus and a response. Upon seeing a candy machine, a person makes one response if hungry and another if not hungry. Hunger is the intervening variable that explains the relationship between seeing the candy and buying it. (see Concepts and Theories of Motivation)

a.   Salivation following the sound of a bell could be caused by classical conditioning. The rat was not necessarily motivated to salivate; it was just a reflex.

c, d.   It isn't clear what the stimuli and responses are in either of these choices. A compliment or an attempt at cheerfulness may be motivated behavior, but it is unclear what the intervening variables would be.

2.   d is the answer. Homeostasis is the process of maintaining equilibrium in our physiological systems. Drives prompt us to behave in ways that maintain this balance or equilibrium. (see Drive Reduction Theory)

a.   The instinct doctrine said that our behavior occurs in response to specific stimuli rather than as a means of maintaining a balance in our systems.

    b.   Arousal theorists believe we behave in a certain way to maintain an optimal level of arousal, not to maintain a balance in our systems.

    c.   Incentive theorists believe we behave in ways that allow us to reach our goals of obtaining positive incentives and avoiding negative incentives.

3.   c is the answer. Incentive theory states that behavior is directed toward attaining desirable stimuli and avoiding unwanted stimuli. Charles thinks that if he removes a good stimulus (his fun company at the store) from his son when he behaves badly, his son will want to shape up so that he can get his daddy's attention back. (see Incentive Theory)

    a.   According to arousal theory, we behave in ways that maintain our optimal level of arousal.

    b.   According to drive theory, motivation arises from constant imbalances in homeostasis.

    d.   The instinct doctrine proposes that behavior is motivated by automatic, involuntary, and unlearned responses.

4.   c is the answer. Vic is the wealthiest, most mature male among the choices. (see The Instinct doctrine and Its Descendants)

    a.   The evolutionary approach emphasizes procreation. It hypothesizes that women seek a man with the ability to support children; therefore, a homosexual relationship would not be the best fit with this approach.

    b, d.   Tom and Wally do not have Vic's wealth and maturity; therefore, Tom and Wally are not as good a fit with the evolutionary approach to attraction and mating.

5.   b is the answer. People with anorexia starve themselves and lose weight, in some cases to the point of death. (see Unhealthy Eating)

    a.   Obesity is characterized by eating more calories than necessary for body maintenance.

    c.   Bulimia nervosa is characterized by overeating and then inducing vomiting.

    d.   b is the answer.

6.   b is the answer. Jack probably knew that most people consume 60 to 75 percent more food when they eat with others. Also, by definition a buffet would offer a variety of foods; Jack might also have known that he would probably eat more food if given more choices. (see Flavor, Sociocultural Experience, and Food Selection)

    a.   There is nothing in the question to suggest that Jack had lost his appetite. If anything, he would be hungry because he is on a restricted diet.

    c.   Jack would be able to select a balanced meal from the selection offered by the buffet.

    d.   Although culture influences our food preferences and eating habits, there is nothing in this question to suggest that Jack's cultural background would prevent him from dining with his roommates.

7.   a is the answer. Homeostasis is the tendency to keep physiological systems at a steady level, or equilibrium, by constantly making adjustments in response to change. (see Drive Reduction Theory)

    b.   An instinctive behavior is an innate, automatic response to a specific stimulus.

    c.   An intervening variable is something that is used to explain relations between environmental stimuli and behavioral responses. This question does describe a motive for eating, but the desire to achieve balance is the specific motive, so homeostasis is a better, more precise answer.

     d.   Specific hunger refers to a desire for a particular food at a particular time.

8.   c is the answer. Testosterone is the principal example of an androgen. (see The Biology of Sex)

     a.   Estradiol is the principal example of an estrogen.

     b.   Progesterone is the principal example of a progestin.

     d.   CCK stands for cholecystokinin, which is a neuropeptide that regulates meal size.

9.   c is the answer. It is important that Julie take the job that will yield the most satisfaction, which she will find in jobs that provide opportunities for advancement and individual responsibility. She should also take the job with the fewest dissatisfying characteristics, such as low pay and a mediocre boss. (see Need for Achievement)

     a.   Company 1 has very few dissatisfying characteristics but no satisfying characteristics either.

     b.   Company 2 offers a large amount of responsibility but several dissatisfying characteristics as well, such as low pay and a mediocre boss.

     d.   Company 4 has very few dissatisfying characteristics but no satisfying characteristics. The job carries no responsibility and does not provide any chances for advancement.

10.   c is the answer. Maslow's hierarchy of five types of needs begins with biological needs and progresses through safety needs, interpersonal needs, respect and self-esteem needs, up to self-actualization. According to Maslow, we will not be motivated to satisfy higher needs until the lower ones are met. Since Marta needs respect, her biological, safety, and intimacy needs must all have been satisfied. (see Relations and Conflicts Among Motives)

     a, b.   Marta is motivated to gain respect, so her biological needs must have been satisfied sufficiently so that being poor is not an issue.

     d.   If Marta had not had her lower needs satisfied, she would not be seeking respect, according to Maslow.

11.   b is the answer. Research suggests that extrinsic rewards like pay raises are not the key to job satisfaction. Morale would not necessarily suffer because of the wage freeze. When employees suspect that they are seen as lazy, are given little credit for their accomplishments, and feel heavily supervised with little control over their time, morale and motivation will suffer. (see Achievement and Success in the Workplace)

     a, c, d.   All of these will have a strong negative effect, leading to employee dissatisfaction and decreased motivation to do good work.

12.   c is the answer. Lisa is in a situation in which she faces two negative outcomes: The cook will probably be angry, and the customer will probably be irritated. This is characteristic of an avoidance-avoidance situation. (see Linkages: Conflicting Motives and Stress)

     a.   An approach-approach situation is a choice between two equally positive alternatives.

     b.   An approach-avoidance situation is a choice that has both a positive and a negative aspect.

     d.   A multiple approach-avoidance situation is a choice between two situations, each of which has a positive and a negative aspect.

13.   d is the answer. Research on subjective well-being indicates that how happy you are has less to do with what happens and is relatively stable throughout life in spite of significant circumstantial changes. (see Achievement and Well-Being)

    a.   Event-related changes in mood tend to subside within days or weeks—they don't usually persist for long periods.

    b.   Although trauma certainly has an impact on immediate levels of happiness, the effects tend not to last as long as most people expect, and most people return to their previous level of happiness.

    c.   Religious faith has actually been positively associated with happiness levels in general. It is not generally a hindrance to happiness.

14.   b is the answer. The fight-flight reaction is a pattern of increased blood pressure and heart rate, rapid breathing, and dry mouth, among other symptoms, that comes when the sympathetic nervous system has been activated. (see The Biology of Emotion)

    a.   The parasympathetic nervous system is responsible for calming the body. Its activity decreases during the fight-or-flight response.

    c, d.   When the sympathetic nervous system is activated, digestion and salivation decrease while respiration and heart rate increase.

15.   b is the answer. According to Schachter-Singer theory, our cognitive appraisals of situations can cause us to label identical physiological responses in several different ways. (see Cognitive Theories of Emotion)

    a.   According to James' peripheral theory, every emotion is associated with a unique physiological response.

    c.   Darwin did not address the mechanism that labels emotions. He said that emotional expressions are inherited.

    d.   Cannon thought the perception and experience of the emotion were simultaneous. He did not discuss cognitive appraisal.

16.   a is the answer. James' peripheral theory of emotion states that we experience emotion based on our physiological responses. If this is true, every emotion should be associated with a unique pattern of physiological arousal. (see James' Peripheral Theory)

    b.   According to Cannon's central theory, the thalamus is the core of emotion. Peripheral responses do not determine which emotion we are feeling.

    c.   According to the Schachter-Singer theory, the same pattern of physiological arousal can be attributed to different emotions based on our cognitive appraisal of the environment. Therefore, it is not necessary to have unique patterns of physiological arousal for every emotion.

    d.   Darwin discussed the functions that emotion serves in survival.

17.   c is the answer. Research has shown that, compared with people at rest, exercise-aroused people experience stronger feelings of attraction when they meet people of the opposite sex. When Lori and Carol get off the dance floor, they will transfer the excitation caused by dancing to the attractive men they see in the bar. (see Cognitive Theories of Emotion)

a, b, d.   A clothing store, laundromat, and restaurant do not offer any activity that causes an increase in physiological arousal.18.   c is the answer. The facial-feedback hypothesis is a variation on James' peripheral theory. It suggests that facial movements are information we interpret as part of our physiological response. According to James, we have a different set of facial expressions and bodily responses for each emotion. Some evidence shows that smiling will make a person feel happier. (see James' Peripheral Theory)

a. The Schacter-Singer theory proposes that emotion is determined by cognitive evaluation of physiological arousal, not that arousal or behavior determines emotion.

b. Cannon's central theory proposed that the thalamus is the seat of emotional experience, sending signals to the autonomic nervous system and cerebral cortex simultaneously. This theory proposes that in the cortex emotion becomes conscious.

d. Maslow's theory is a theory of motivation that specifies a hierarchy of motives.

19. a is the answer. Something innate should not be affected to any great degree by cultural influence. People from many different cultures all relate smiles to positive emotions. (see Innate Expressions of Emotion)

b, c. Events that are culturally determined or only learned are usually different in every culture. If expressions of happiness were culturally determined or learned, every culture would interpret a smile in a different way. However, this is not the case. All cultures relate smiling to positive emotion.

d. There is no causal relationship between universal recognition of emotion and the particular structure of the nervous system responsible for emotional recognition.

20. c is the answer. Emotion culture refers to the rules that govern what emotions are appropriate in various circumstances and what emotional expressions are allowed. Emotion cultures shape how we describe and categorize feelings. The fact that words for emotions occasionally do not translate effectively into another language illustrates emotion cultures. (see Social and Cultural Influences on Emotional Expression)

a. Social referencing involves using other people's emotions to guide one's behavior.

b. Attribution is the process of identifying the cause of an event.

d. Excitation transfer is the process of carrying over arousal from one experience to an independent situation.

Now turn to the quiz analysis table at the end of this chapter to find which areas you know well and which areas you need to work on. Circle the numbers in the table for items on Quiz 2 that you answered correctly.

For each question you answered correctly, circle its number. (Quiz 1 numbers are not shaded; Quiz 2 numbers are shaded.) Are there patterns in the types of questions or the topics you got wrong that could direct your further study? Did you improve from Quiz 1 to Quiz 2?

QUIZ REVIEW

Topic	Type of Question		
	Definition	Comprehension	Application
Concepts and Theories of Motivation		1	
			1
The Instinct Doctrine and Its Descendants			4
			4
Drive Reduction Theory		2	
		2	7
Arousal Theory			5
Incentive Theory			3
			3
Hunger and Eating			
Biological Signals for Hunger and Satiety		6	7
Flavor, Sociocultural Experience, and Food Selection			
			6
Unhealthy Eating			
	5		
Sexual Behavior			
Focus on Research Methods: A Survey of Human Sexual Behavior		8	
The Biology of Sex			
		8	
Achievement Motivation			
Need for Achievement			9
			9
Achievement and Success in the Workplace			
			11
Achievement and Well-Being			17
		13	
Relations and Conflicts Among Motives			10
			10

Topic	Type of Question		
	Definition	**Comprehension**	**Application**
Linkages: Conflicting Motives and Stress			12
			12
Opponent Processes, Motivation, and Emotion			11
The Nature of Emotion			
The Biology of Emotion			
		14	
Theories of Emotion			
James's Peripheral Theory			14, 16, 19
		16, 18	
Cannon's Central Theory			13
Cognitive Theories of Emotion			15, 18
			15, 17
Communicating Emotion			
Innate Expressions of Emotion			
		19	
Social and Cultural Influences on Emotional Expression			20
			20

Total correct by quiz:

Quiz 1:
Quiz 2:

CHAPTER 12

Human Development

Developmental psychology is the psychological subfield that documents the course and causes of people's physical, social, emotional, moral, and intellectual development throughout the life span.

OUTLINE

I.   EXPLORING HUMAN DEVELOPMENT
     Historically, researchers and scientists have argued about which governs development: nature or nurture. Is a person's development simply a process of maturation (nature)? Or are we shaped and molded by our surroundings (nurture)? Guided by research in *behavioral genetics*, today's psychologists recognize that both nature and nurture interact to influence the developmental process. The environment (nurture) can determine whether a genetic tendency (nature) is expressed, and genetic tendencies (nature) can evoke particular responses from the environment (nurture). Heredity and environment are correlated, as seen in cases where parents with special talents also nurture those talents in their children or children themselves use the environment to learn particular things when they have certain hereditary predispositions.

II. BEGINNINGS
     A.   Prenatal Development
          A zygote is the cell that forms when the father's sperm and mother's ovum merge.

          1.   *Stages of Development.* During *germinal stage* (the first and second weeks after fertilization), the cells divide to become the embryo. During the *embryonic stage*, all the organs form and cells differentiate into specialized functions. During the *fetal stage*, from week eight until birth, the organs of the fetus grow and function more efficiently.

          2.   *Prenatal Risks.* The *placenta* attaches itself to the mother via an *umbilical cord* to send nutrients to the fetus from the mother and waste away from the fetus. It also screens out harmful substances, but is an imperfect filter. Severe damage can occur if the mother takes certain drugs, is exposed to toxins, or contracts certain illnesses (such as rubella) during pregnancy. Teratogens, harmful external substances that result in birth defects, are especially dangerous during critical periods such as the embryonic stage. Babies whose mothers used cocaine are born premature, underweight, and fussy, and are at greater risk for learning and other severe developmental disabilities. Fetal alcohol syndrome is a pattern of defects that can occur as a result of maternal ingestion of even moderate amounts of alcohol. The effects that adverse substances will have depend upon genetic inheritance, their intensity, and the prenatal stage in which they occur.

     B.   The Newborn
          The study of newborns is extremely difficult due to how infrequently they are in a state of quiet alertness that allows assessment of their abilities. To learn what infants can see and hear, researchers commonly design studies that record infants' eye movements, heart rates, sucking rates, brain waves, movements, and skin conductance to learn what infants can see and hear.

1. *Vision and Other Senses*. Newborns have 20:300 sight. They prefer to look at objects that have contour, contrast, complexity, and movement. They experience some *size constancy* but it is a while before *depth perception* will develop. Within two to three days after birth, infants can hear soft voices and differentiate tones. They prefer to hear speech, especially speech that is high-pitched, exaggerated, and expressive. Newborns have a good sense of smell and taste and show a preference for the smell of their own mother's milk.

2. *Reflexes and Motor Skills*. <u>Reflexes</u> are swift and automatic movements that occur in response to external stimuli. Infants have more than twenty reflexes, including the *grasping*, *rooting*, and *sucking reflexes*. These reflexes tend to disappear around 3-4 months of age, and motor skills develop. Development of motor skills is a mix of maturation and experience. As muscle strength increases, infants try out various methods of crawling until they find the most efficient one.

III. INFANCY AND CHILDHOOD: COGNITIVE DEVELOPMENT

A. Changes in the Brain

Infants are born with their full quota of brain cells, but neural networks connecting these cells are immature. In the first few months, the cerebellum is the most mature area of the brain, but between six and twelve months the medial temporal lobe of the cortex develops to support the imitative skills infants display in this time frame. The frontal lobe develops later in childhood to support higher levels of thinking.

B. The Development of Knowledge: Piaget's Theory

According to Piaget, development proceeds in a series of distinct *stages* that occur in a specific order; each stage is *qualitatively* different from the next.

1. *Building Blocks of Development*. The movement through stages progresses as children develop <u>schemas</u> through their interaction with the environment. Schemas are elaborated through <u>assimilation</u>, during which information is added to existing schemas, and <u>accommodation</u>, during which existing schemas are modified according to new environmental information.

2. *Sensorimotor Development*. During Piaget's first cognitive development stage, the <u>sensorimotor stage</u>, infants' mental activity is confined to sensory and motor functions. As infants progress through this stage, they begin to learn <u>object permanence</u>: they become able to have *mental representations* of objects in their minds even when they cannot see or touch them. With object permanence, the infant moves into the next stage.

3. *Preoperational Development*. Lasting from age two to seven years, the <u>preoperational stage</u> is characterized by intuitive guesses. *Symbol* usage appears and children may attribute intent, feeling, and consciousness to inanimate objects (known as *animism*. In addition, they are highly *egocentric*, assuming everyone sees the same things that they do. Children in this stage do not have <u>conservation</u> skills because they do not understand the concepts of *complementarity* or *reversibility*.

4. *Concrete and Formal Operational Thought*. The <u>concrete operations</u> stage, from age seven to adolescence, is marked by the ability to conserve number and amount. However, children cannot think logically about abstract concepts during this stage. Abstract, hypothetical thinking occurs during Piaget's final development stage: the <u>formal operational stage</u>. Less than half of the population reach the formal operational level Piaget defined, although high school level training in math and science helps.

C. Modifying Piaget's Theory

Piaget's work has had a great influence on developmental psychology, but results of continued study suggest the theory needs some modification.

1. *New Views of Infants' Cognitive Development.* Psychologists using new research methods find that infants have more cognitive skills in the sensorimotor stage than Piaget acknowledged. Infants understand which soundtrack goes with a particular video, act surprised when they view a physically impossible event, and seem to develop some mental representations earlier than Piaget suggested. (See the Focus on Research Methods section for more information.)
2. *New Views of Developmental Stages.* Psychologists now view cognitive development as rising and falling in waves rather than moving in global, fixed stages. Evidence for this perspective comes from studies that reveal that not all preoperational children are egocentric and that they can be trained to develop conservation skills with specific experiences.

D. Information Processing During Childhood
From an <u>information-processing</u> approach, children are viewed as better able to absorb, remember, and store information in more organized ways as they grow older. Memory improves as children learn memory strategies, increase memory storage, and expand their knowledge. As short-term memory storage improves with age, children are better able to remember more complex/abstract information, such as the "gist" of a conversation. Both nature and nurture contribute to these advances, with familiarity promoting better performance on information-processing tasks.

E. Linkages: Development and Memory
Different hypotheses for why infantile amnesia occurs have been proposed. We may be unable to recall memories from before age three because of poor encoding and storage or because the memories are *implicit* rather than explicit. Lack of language skills during our early years may hamper our ability to solidify memories. Still another explanation is that early experiences are merged into generalized event representations (e.g., "going to Grandma's) rather than specific events to recall.

F. Culture and Cognitive Development
Children's interaction with their culture and language has significant effects on their development. Children form *scripts*, or mental representations of common cultural activities. A child will be much better able to perform a given task if it is presented in a familiar "script." The influence of language, teaching methods, and parental emphasis on education all contribute to cultural differences in cognitive development.

G. Improving or Endangering Cognitive Development
Cognitive development can be influenced to some degree by the environment. Stimulating surroundings and positive experiences tend to enhance a child's cognitive development. The case of Genie tragically illustrates the consequences of growing up in an impoverished environment. Less extreme conditions, like poverty as opposed to the emotional and physical abuse Genie endured, are still associated with diminished cognitive development. Music lessons, access to internet and even some electronic games have been associated with gains in cognitive development.

IV. INFANCY AND CHILDHOOD: SOCIAL AND EMOTIONAL DEVELOPMENT
Infants and parents *bond* during the first few months of life; infants respond to parental behavior, and parents respond to the infant. Infants are capable of *social referencing*, reacting with fear if they see their caregiver responding with fear. Infants also communicate feelings as well as recognize them.

A. Individual Temperament
<u>Temperament</u>, an individual's style and frequency of expressing needs and emotions, is genetically influenced and obvious at birth. But environment can influence temperament,

too. Babies tend to fall in one of three general categories of temperament: *easy, difficult,* or *slow-to-warm-up.* If the child's temperament matches the parents' expectations, the parent-child interaction will most likely be positive. Culture and innate tendencies interact in the development of temperament throughout childhood, creating observed differences between cultures and individual differences within cultures.

B. The Infant Grows Attached
    During the first year of life, infants form an <u>attachment</u> to their parents. <u>Attachment theory</u> was developed by John Bowlby.

1. *Motherless Monkeys and Children.* The Harlow attachment studies demonstrate that infant monkeys are motivated by contact comfort needs. Monkeys raised in isolation exhibit severe deficits in social and emotional development. Similar problems have been noted in abandoned and neglected children.

2. *Forming an Attachment.* In most cultures, the mother is the first person to whom the baby becomes attached. By six or seven months, most infants show a clear preference for their mother. Infants also become attached to fathers. Fathers are more likely to play with infants, while mothers are more likely to feed, cuddle, and talk with them.

3. *Variations in Attachment.* Many factors, including the infant's temperament, the caretaker's responsiveness, and cultural variability, can influence the development of <u>attachment behavior</u>. The *Strange Situation* helps researchers define what sort of attachment a child has. *Securely attached* children tend to be more socially and emotionally competent; more cooperative, enthusiastic, and persistent; better problem solvers; more compliant and controlled; and more playful and popular. There are three types of *insecure attachments—avoidant, ambivalent,* and *disorganized.* Patterns of attachment vary depending on what part of the world one studies, but almost always depends on the mother's attentiveness to the infant.

4. *Consequences of Attachment Patterns.* A secure attachment with a parent tends to be reflected in a child's relationships with others, even as they enter school age. Bowlby argues this is because the child develops an *internal working model* based on the type of attachment he or she has with a parent.

C. Does Day Care Harm the Emotional Development of Infants?
    What am I being asked to believe or accept?

Separation created by daycare can damage the mother-infant attachment and harm the child's emotional development.

What evidence is available to support the assertion?

While children who attend daycare do form attachments and prefer the company of their mothers, some research suggests that these children have a greater tendency to be insecurely attached.

Are there alternative ways of interpreting the evidence?

Infants in daycare may be more independent than those children who stay at home. In addition, mothers who work may reward more independent behavior in their children. Thus, they may be more tolerant of the separation the Strange Situation requires than children cared for at home.

What additional evidence would help to evaluate the alternatives?

Research must measure aspects of emotional adjustment other than secure attachments. Infant relationships with other caregivers in other situations must also be examined. Research that controls for factors such as parent education, income, and attitudes suggests that daycare in itself is not particularly damaging. However, Poor quality daycare combined with parental unresponsiveness is quite damaging to attachment.

What conclusions are reasonable?

According to a recent study, infants in quality daycare situations with sensitive and responsive mothers were no more likely to develop emotional or attachment problems than those not in daycare. So, daycare itself does not lead to problems, but poor quality daycare may interact with already risky home situations to have a negative effect on attachment.

C.   Relationships with Parents
1.   According to Erik Erikson's theory of social development, individuals pass through eight qualitatively different stages, each one associated with an issue that the individual must resolve. Positive resolution provides the basis for developing trust, autonomy, and initiative, whereas negative resolutions may leave a person psychologically troubled and less able to cope effectively with future situations.

2.   *Parenting Styles.* Socialization is the method by which authority figures teach children the skills and rules needed to function in their society. Socialization is seen in four distinct parenting styles.
   a)   Authoritarian parents are firm, punitive, and unsympathetic. Permissive parents give children complete freedom and use lax discipline. Authoritative parents are firm but understanding, increase children's responsibility as they grow older, and reason with their children. Uninvolved (rejecting-neglecting) parents are indifferent to their children.
   b)   Authoritarian parents tend to have children who are unfriendly, distrustful, and withdrawn. Permissive parents tend to have children who are immature, dependent, and unhappy, and who exhibit little self-control. Authoritative parents tend to have children who are friendly, cooperative, self-reliant, and socially responsible. Children of uninvolved parents tend to be more impulsive and aggressive, struggling with low self-esteem.
   c)   However, correlational socialization studies do not show causation, and their results are not strong. Hence, researchers cannot conclude that parental behavior *causes* a particular social outcome. Children's temperaments, physical health, and cultural environment influence social and scholastic development.
   d)   Parenting style interacts with culture and a major limitation on the research that found these styles is that it was conducted primarily with European American families. Collectivist cultures tend to have more authoritarian parenting styles without the negative consequences seen in European American families who use that style of parenting. It is important to evaluate parenting style within cultural context, rather than searching for the "best" style.
D.   Peer Friendships and Popularity
1.   Two-year-olds play with the same toys that their playmates do but do not interact with one another. By age four, children begin to interact socially through mutual play. In the final stages of the preschool years, children learn to cooperate or compete.
2.   Friends help children establish their sense of self-worth. *Popular children* tend to have the most friends and are good at communication, friendly and assertive. About 10 percent of school children to not have many friends and are either *rejected* (actively disliked) or *neglected* (isolated, but not disliked). These children tend to do poorly in school and have later psychological and behavioral problems. The most important factor in determining popularity is a child's *social skills.*

E.   Social Skills and Understanding

Social skills allow a child to sustain responsive interaction with peers. Cooperation, understanding, empathy, and self-regulation can be taught at home. Pretend play provides a good way to help teach children social skills. Siblings also provide a way to develop social skills, particularly if the siblings are close. Lack of social skills may lead to aggressive behaviors as well as lack of friends.

G.   Focus on Research Methods: Exploring Developing Minds

Researchers have questioned whether children under the age of four have a "theory of mind" that allows them to understand the perspective of others. Baillargeon argued that the research methods leading to these conclusions were not sensitive enough to measure children's theory of mind. She developed a method based on the premise that children look longer at events that violate their expectations. She then set up various situations that involved infants watching a woman put an object in one location and then leave the room. After she left, the object was moved to another location and the woman then returned. If infants expected her to look in the spot where she left it, they should stare longer at her if she looks in the new location for the object because it violates their expectation, which is exactly what happened. This sort of study and others raise the possibility that very young children are capable of theory of mind.

H.   Gender Roles

Through socialization, children learn the norms governing gender roles also known as sex roles) in their culture. Girls tend to speak and write earlier, read emotional signals better than boys, control their emotional responses better, and engage in more social conversation. Boys, on the other hand, have better spatial relations, are better at manipulating objects, are more physically active, and competitive.

1.   *Biological factors in gender roles.* Sex differences between boys and girls have some roots in anatomy, hormones, and brain organization and function. These differences emerge at an early age even in very different cultures.

2.   *Socialization of gender roles.* Sex differences are amplified by the ways parents interact differently with boys versus girls, conveying information about what is gender-appropriate.

3.   *Cognitive factors in gender roles.* Socialization processes lead to the development of gender schemas (cognitive factors), as boys and girls learn "appropriate" behaviors for boys and girls through modeling and encouragement (social factors).

I.   Risk and Resilience

Family instability, child abuse, homelessness, poverty, substance abuse, and domestic violence produce serious short- and long-term consequences for children. However, some children show resilience—successful development in the face of serious challenge. These children tend to be intelligent, easygoing, and self-confident, and they have a close, caring relationship with at least one adult. They also have genes that direct optimal regulation of serotonin, a neurotransmitter related to mood.

V.   ADOLESCENCE

Owing to the interplay of nature and nurture, adolescents experience changes in physical size, shape, and capacity. Changes also occur in social life, reasoning ability, and self-perception.

A.   Changes in Body, Brain, and Thinking

With the onset of puberty, sudden growth spurts occur, sexual characteristics develop, and sexual interest arises. The brain is pruned, and myelin develops, leaving fewer, but more efficient, neuronal connections. Dopamine, a neurotransmitter associated with pleasure, also becomes more prominent in this period. Changes in thinking are reflected in the ability to reason better, plan for the future, and foresee consequences, part of the *formal operational stage.*

B.   Adolescent Feelings and Behavior
Changes in adolescence are often difficult, especially for early maturing girls. Opportunities to do things increase, and moderate risk-taking is normal. Many problems that may arise are associated with *self-esteem*. The influence of peers increases, and this can cause tension with parents. Serious problems are most likely for teens who do not feel close to their parents, although parents who are too intrusive also increase the risk for problem behaviors in their children.

1.   *Love and Sex in Adolescence.* Dating usually begins in adolescence and can have a positive impact on sense of worth and belongingness. Half of teens in the U.S. have had sex by the age of 16. Teens who have sex are less conventional, have more unsupervised time, take greater risks, have peer groups that support risk taking, have parents with less education who talk to them less, and are more likely to have spent time without their childhood father. Sexual activity in adolescence brings a variety of risks, including sexually transmitted disease, pregnancy, and declining school achievement. Teen parents increase problems for themselves and for others in their family, with younger siblings being at greater risk for teen pregnancy and school problems if their older sibling gave birth. Children of teen parents tend to fare poorly compared to those of older parents in a variety of ways.

2.   *Violent Adolescents.* Violence in adolescence is rooted in genetics but also influenced by environment. Violent adolescents are more likely to be boys and to have displayed aggression, fearlessness, low intelligence, lack of empathy, and emotional self-regulation in childhood. These and other environmentally based risk factors can help predict who is likely to develop violent tendencies in adolescence. Many of these risk factors can be buffered by other factors such as religious beliefs or parental supervision.

C.   Identity and Development of the Self
A century ago, adulthood began at approximately fifteen years of age. Today, however, many people don't make the transition into adulthood until their early twenties in Western societies. Lengthened adolescence has created difficulties in identity formation. A person's sense of self develops throughout middle childhood, and then erupts during adolescence through self-consciousness and self-awareness. The personal identity is affected by ethnic identity, reflecting racial, religions, or cultural groups to which the person belongs.

D.   Moral Development
1.   *Kohlberg's Stages of Moral Reasoning.* Kohlberg studied moral development. He proposed that moral reasoning develops in six stages that progress from avoiding punishment and attaining pleasure (preconventional reasoning), to following rules as part of social duty (conventional reasoning), and finally to principles of justice, equality, and respect for human life (postconventional reasoning).

2.   *Limitations of Kohlberg's Stages.* Research generally supports the sequence of Kohlberg's stages, although in some cultures and studies postconventional reasoning does not appear. In addition, however, culture and gender influence people's definition of the moral "ideal." Males tend to focus on justice in their reasoning and females more on care.

3.   *Moral Reasoning and Moral Action.* The relationship between level of moral reasoning and moral action does occur, but not always. Delinquents tend to reason at Stage 1 compared to their non-delinquent counterparts who reason at Stage 4 more often. Yet, certain environmental conditions can reduce the likelihood of moral action regardless of level of moral reasoning attained.

E. Emerging Adulthood
Emerging adulthood lasts from 18-25 years of age, approximately.

1. *Facing the Identity Crisis*. Identity formation is the adolescent's central task, according to Erikson's psychosocial development theory. If the individual has developed trust, autonomy, and initiative in early childhood, the <u>identity crisis</u> will be positively resolved.

2. Psychological well-being tends to improve with resolution of the identity crisis. Failure to resolve it—either by accepting an identity from parents or remaining uncommitted—is associated with potential troubles ahead.

VI. ADULTHOOD
Development is a lifelong process. Adults are divided into early (20-39 years of age), middle (40-65 years of age) and late (66 years and older) adulthood periods.

A. Physical Changes
In early adulthood, shoulder width, height, and chest size increase, often a time considered to be the prime of life. The body begins to show signs of aging in middle adulthood. Sensory acuity begins to decrease, fertility declines (a process known as <u>menopause</u> in women), and susceptibility to heart disease is heightened. In late adulthood, the body continues to deteriorate and blood flow to the brain slows, although significant decline in late adulthood can be delayed by exercise and good nutrition.

B. Cognitive Changes
Cognitive abilities continue to improve until late adulthood. Because of years of experience and information accumulation, an older adult may be better able to handle complex situations than a younger adult.

1. *Cognitive Advances in Early, Middle, and Late Adulthood*. Cognitive abilities improve as young and middle-aged adults get new information, learn new skills, and refine old skills. Adults become more adept at problem solving and decision making; adult thought is more complex and adaptive than adolescent thought, moving beyond formal operational thinking to *dialectical* thought.

2. *Declining Cognitive Abilities in Late Adulthood*. After age sixty-five, the speed of information absorption slows and memory declines. Unfamiliar tasks, complex problems, and tasks that require divided attention are more difficult for older than for younger people. Given sufficient time for these intellectual tasks, older adults can perform as well as younger adults. Memory problems in late adulthood are typically seen in episodic, not semantic memory. One exception to this is that older adults are more likely to remember false information as being true, making them prone to victimization by scam artists. However, if mental faculties are used throughout the life span in activities that expose the older adult to a variety of people, cognitive skills are less apt to diminish. Alzheimer's disease poses the greatest threat to cognitive functioning in late adulthood.

C. Social Changes

1. *Early Adulthood: Work, Marriage, Parenthood*. In early adulthood (ages twenty to forty), people tend to gradually become more organized and focused on their career. Intimate relationships become more important and marriage may occur. The happiest adults marry rather than cohabit. Relationships may reflect earlier attachment patterns. Parenthood brings other challenges, and typically a decline in marital satisfaction follows the birth of a child. Because both parents tend to work, adapting to parenthood is somewhat more challenging than it was 40 years ago. Additionally, more gay men and lesbians are becoming parents, too, and may face special challenges because of

cultural hostilities. About half of married adults will have to face the challenges of divorce.

2. *Middle Adulthood*: *Reappraising Priorities*. Around age forty, many people become concerned with the crisis of generativity—that is, producing something that will outlast them, usually children or job achievements. People may experience a mid-life transition, when they feel compelled to reappraise or modify their lives in some way. Common stresses in middle adulthood include having to care for grandchildren and having children who are still financially dependent. Overall, the middle years are often a time of satisfaction and happiness when individuals feel they have control over their work, finances, marriage, children, and sex life, as well as other personality factors.

3. *Late Adulthood: Retirement and Restriction*. Most people in this age group consider themselves to be middle-aged. Retirement usually occurs and is a positive experience if viewed as a choice. In late adulthood, people become more reflective, cautious, and conforming, and they value relationships more.

D.   Death and Dying
A few years or months before dying, many people experience a sharp decline in mental functioning known as terminal drop. The awareness of impending death, according to Erikson, brings about the last social crisis. People reminisce and evaluate the meaningfulness of their lives, leading to a sense of either integrity or despair.

E.   Developmental Trajectories
Researchers who study developmental trajectories find a remarkable degree of stability from childhood through adulthood on many dimensions such as intelligence, memory, personality, and social competence.

F.   Longevity: The Length of Life
People want to live as long as possible. Longevity is greater among women, those without histories of heavy drinking or heart problems, and those who experience much *positive affect*. Longevity is also related to conscientiousness and curiosity, and a physically fit lifestyle that remains socially active.

KEY TERMS

1. **Developmental psychology** is the psychological specialty that documents the course of social, emotional, moral, and intellectual development over the life span. (see introductory section)

   Example: How do children learn to use language? Do infants respond to parents' emotional cues? Do cognitive changes occur during old age?

2. **Maturation** refers to natural growth or change that unfolds in a fixed sequence relatively independent of the environment. (see Exploring Human Development)

   Example: The development of secondary sexual characteristics occurs in a fixed sequence and is rarely affected by environmental conditions.

3. A **zygote** is a new cell formed from a father's sperm and a mother's ovum. (see Prenatal Development)

4. An **embryo** is the developing individual from the fourteenth day after fertilization until the end of the second month after conception. (see "Prenatal Development")

5. The **fetus** is the developing individual from the third month after conception until birth. (see Prenatal Development)

6. **Teratogens** are harmful substances that can cause birth defects. (see Prenatal Development)

7. **Critical period** refers to an interval during which certain kinds of growth must occur if development is to proceed normally. (see Prenatal Development)

   Example: If the heart, eyes, ears, hands, and feet do not appear during the embryonic period, they will not be formed at all.

8. **Fetal alcohol syndrome** is a pattern of physical and mental defects found in babies born to women who abused alcohol during pregnancy. (see Prenatal Development)

9. **Reflexes are** simple, involuntary, unlearned behavior directed by the spinal cord without instructions from the brain. (see The Newborn)

   Example: Babies exhibit a sucking reflex that occurs when anything touches a newborn's lips.

10. **Schemas** are generalizations based on experience that form basic units of knowledge. (see The Development of Knowledge: Piaget's Theory)

    Example: Sucking on a pacifier is a schema consisting of a pattern of action.

11. **Assimilation** is the process of trying out existing schemas on objects that fit those schemas. (see The Development of Knowledge: Piaget's Theory)

    Example: An infant who has learned to suck milk from a bottle will use the same sucking motion or schema when a pacifier is put in its mouth for the first time.

12. **Accommodation** is the process of modifying schemas when familiar schemas do not work. (see The Development of Knowledge: Piaget's Theory)

    Example: Infants who have become very good at sucking milk from a bottle and are given a cup must learn new patterns of motor behavior (modify the old sucking schema) to get the liquid out of the cup and into their mouth. Watch small children just learning how to drink from a cup. They suck and slurp the liquid instead of pouring it into their mouth and swallowing.

13. The **sensorimotor stage** is the first of Piaget's stages of cognitive development, when the infant's mental activity is confined to sensory perception and motor skills. (see The Development of Knowledge: Piaget's Theory)

    REMEMBER: Sensori means "sensory": vision, hearing, tasting, and so on. Motor means "movement": reaching, grasping, and pulling.

14. **Object permanence** is the knowledge that objects exist even when they are not in view. (see The Development of Knowledge: Piaget's Theory)

    Example: A child knows that a rattle exists when you put it behind your back, out of sight.

15. The **preoperational stage** is Piaget's second stage of cognitive development, during which children begin to use symbols to represent things that are not present. (see The Development of Knowledge: Piaget's Theory)

    Example: Elise likes to put on her big sister's dresses and makeup and pretend that she is going out shopping.

16. **Conservation** is the ability to recognize that the important properties of a substance remain constant despite changes in shape, length, or position. (see The Development of Knowledge: Piaget's Theory)

    Example: Eva, who is babysitting for a nine-year-old and a four-year-old, pours each child a glass of lemonade. She gives the older child a tall skinny glass and the younger child a short fat glass. The four-year-old insists that the short fat glass does not contain as much lemonade as the tall skinny glass (that is, she does not understand the logic of complementarity), even after Eva has poured the contents of the tall skinny glass into the short glass and back again (reversibility). The younger child, still in the preoperational stage, cannot conserve.

17. **Concrete operations** is Piaget's third stage of cognitive development, during which children's thinking is no longer dominated by visual appearances. (see The Development of Knowledge: Piaget's Theory)

    REMEMBER: During this stage, children can perform such operations as addition, subtraction, and conservation (reversibility, complementarity).

18. The **formal operational stage** is Piaget's fourth stage of cognitive development; usually beginning around age 11, when abstract thinking first appears. (see The Development of Knowledge: Piaget's Theory)

    Example: Children can think about abstract moral issues such as whether animals should be killed for fur or what the consequences of nuclear war might be.

    REMEMBER: During this stage, children can think and reason about abstract concepts, generate hypotheses, and think logically.

19. **Information processing** is the process of taking in, remembering or forgetting, and using information. (see Information Processing during Childhood)

    Example: Mariana is watching her brother play with a toy. She remembers how he does it and then mimics that behavior herself when it is her turn to play with the toy.

20. **Temperament** is an individual's basic disposition, which is evident from infancy. (see Individual Temperament)

    Example: When Sarah takes a bath, she squeals with delight, splashes in the water, and eagerly reaches for new toys. She has a very predictable schedule of eating and sleeping. Sarah is an easy baby. Franny, on the other hand, fusses all the time, cries very loudly whenever she encounters a new situation, person, or toy, and does not have a set schedule. Franny is a difficult baby.

21. **Attachment** is a deep and enduring relationship with a caregiver or other person with whom a baby has shared many early experiences. (see The Infant Grows Attached)

    Example: Johnny has an anxious insecure attachment; he is upset when his mother leaves but ignores or avoids her when she returns after a brief separation. Carl's attachment is secure; he may or may not protest when she leaves, but he greets her enthusiastically when she returns.

    REMEMBER: For a <u>secure attachment</u> to develop, the caregiver must not only provide adequate, consistent care, but must also be loving, supportive, helpful, sensitive, and responsive. If the care is inadequate or the relationship is distant, the child may develop an <u>anxious insecure attachment</u>.

22. **Attachment theory** is the idea that children form a close attachment to their earliest caregivers and that this attachment pattern can affect aspects of children's later life. (see The Infant Grows Attached)

    Example: Kiernan is securely attached to his mother. This provides a way for him to develop close romantic relationships in the future as he matures.

23. **Attachment behavior** refers to actions such as crying, smiling, vocalizing, and gesturing that help bring an infant into closer proximity to its caretaker. (see The Infant Grows Attached)

    Example: Baby Augie cries and reaches for his mother. She bends over and picks him up.

24. **Socialization** is the process by which parents, teachers, and others teach children the skills and social norms necessary to be well-functioning members of society. (see Relationships with Parents)

Example: Brady is whining about not getting his way. His mother says, "How sad that you are whining. It wears me out to hear that so I guess you will need to go to your room if you want to whine." She wants to teach him that whining is not a good way to function in society and is using time-out as a way to do it.

25. **Parenting styles** are the varying patterns of behavior that parents display as they interact with and discipline their children. (see Relationships with Parents)

Example: Ramona's mom consistently is pretty inattentive. Ramona is allowed to do what she wants when she wants and doesn't have much interaction with her mom. Her mom is displaying an uninvolved parenting style.

26. **Authoritarian parents** are firm, punitive, and unsympathetic parents who value obedience from the child and authority for themselves. (see Relationships with Parents)

Example: Armand told his father he wanted to study hair design at the local beauty college. Rather than discuss the advantages and disadvantages of the choice with Armand, his father forbade him to apply to that college and ordered him to work over the summer mowing lawns.

27. **Permissive parents** are parents who give their children freedom and lax discipline. (see Relationships with Parents)

Example: Penny could stay overnight at a friend's house without needing to ask permission.

28. **Authoritative parents** are parents who reason with the child, encourage give-and-take, and are firm but understanding. (see Relationships with Parents)

Example: Kiersten's mother is affectionate and encourages her to talk about anything. They have an agreement about what behaviors are acceptable, and recently they compromised on a later curfew.

29. **Uninvolved (rejecting-neglecting) parents** are parents who are indifferent to their children. (see Relationships with Parents)

Example: Joey's parents pretty much don't care what he does as long as he doesn't interfere with their plans.

30. **Self-regulation** is the ability to control one's emotions and behavior. (see Social Skills and Understanding)

Example: Jake is very mad that his friend won't share a toy, but he doesn't take the toy from the friend. He calms down and forces himself to choose a different toy, so he can move on and not feel so angry. He has regulated his emotion and his behavior in a positive way.

31 **Gender roles** or (**sex roles**) are patterns of work, appearance, and behavior that a society associates with being male or female. (see Gender Roles)

Example: In our society, some occupations have traditionally been considered more appropriate for men, others more appropriate for women. Men have been encouraged to become doctors and women to become nurses; men have been encouraged to become police officers, and women have not.

32. **Gender schemas** are the generalizations children develop about what toys, activities, and occupations are "appropriate" for males and for females. (see Gender Roles)

Example: Kate is watching a little boy play with a doll. "Hey," she says. "That is a toy for girls!" Kate is revealing her gender schema.

33. **Resilience** is a quality allowing children to develop normally in spite of severe environmental risk factors. (see Risk and Resilience)

Example: Although Nancy is from a poor home in which her parents paid little attention to her, she seems to function very well at school and is socially quite competent.

34. **Puberty** is the condition of being able, for the first time, to reproduce. (see Changes in Body Brain, and Thinking)

    REMEMBER: Its onset is characterized by menstruation in females and sperm production in males.

35. **Ethnic identity** is the part of a person's identity associated with the racial, religious, or cultural group to which the person belongs. (see Identity and Development of the Self)

36. **Preconventional moral reasoning** is moral reasoning that is not yet based on the conventions or rules that guide social interactions in society. (see Moral Development)

    Example: Morgan doesn't take cookies from the jar when she isn't supposed to because she doesn't want to be grounded.

    REMEMBER: According to Kohlberg's theory, preconventional moral reasongin is typical of children younger than nine years of age. Moral reasoning during this stage is directed toward avoiding punishment and following rules to one's own advantage.

37. **Moral development** refers to the growth of an individual's understanding of the concepts of right and wrong. (see Moral Development)

    Example: Leah is in first grade when she starts to understand that you should be good regardless of who is watching. Morally, she is developing from preconventional to conventional levels of reasoning.

38. **Conventional moral reasoning** is moral reasoning that reflects the belief that morality consists of following rules and conventions. (see Moral Development)

    Example: Juan doesn't take cookies from the jar when he isn't supposed to because it would disappoint his parents if he disobeyed them.

    REMEMBER: It is characterized by concern for other people due to social obligations such as caring for one's spouse and family.

39. **Postconventional moral reasoning** is moral reasoning in which judgments are based on personal standards or on universal principles of justice, equality, and respect for human life. (see Moral Development)

    Example: Underground resistance fighters during World War II disobeyed local and German laws in order to preserve the lives of fellow countrymen.

40. An **identity crisis** is a phase during which an adolescent attempts to develop an integrated self-image. (see Emerging Adulthood)

    Example: When Ray began college, he was rebellious and irresponsible at first. Eventually he settled down, chose a major, and became more conscientious again.

41. **Menopause** is the process whereby a woman's reproductive capacity ceases. (see Physical Changes)

42. **Generativity** refers to adult concerns about producing something that may be of benefit to others in the future. (see Social Changes)

    Example: David is undergoing a change in perspective. He has found a partner in life, and now he is concerned with having children.

43. **Terminal drop** is a sharp decline in mental functioning that tends to occur in late adulthood, a few months or years before death. (see Death and Dying)

   Example: Laurence is 95 years old. His son, his primary caretaker, has noticed a big difference in his dad's ability to remember things and take care of himself in the past year or so.

FILL-IN-THE-BLANKS KEY TERMS

This section will help you check your factual knowledge of the key terms introduced in this chapter. Fill in each blank with the appropriate term from the list of key terms in the previous section.

1. A(n) _____ is a substance that causes damage to the unborn child if it penetrates the womb.

2. A(n) _____ is the time within which a developmental process must occur if it is to occur at all.

3. The _____ is Piaget's first stage of cognitive development.

4. When children do not have to rely on sensory information to know that an object exists, they have developed _____.

5. When children first become able to solve basic math problems, they have reached the stage of _____.

6. _____ parents discourage independence and are harsh, demanding, and punitive.

7. The ability to use abstract reasoning and logic is a development of the _____.

8. _____ is the ability to know that when the shape of a given substance changes, its quantity remains the same.

9. Adults in their thirties who are concerned about being productive and contributing something they consider valuable are experiencing a crisis of _____.

10. The pattern of emotions that a newborn displays in response to the environment is called _____.

11. Object permanence is acquired during the _____ stage.

12. According to Piaget, the basic units of knowledge are _____.

13. The process in which existing schemas are changed to fit new information is called _____.

14. _____ parents are firm but understanding and encourage discussion.

15. Any developmental process that is entirely under genetic control is considered part of the _____ process.

Total Correct (See answer key) _____

LEARNING OBJECTIVES

1. Define <u>developmental psychology</u>. (see introductory section)

2. Discuss how the different historical views of human development explained the influences of nature and nurture. Define <u>maturation</u>. (see "Exploring Human Development")

3. Describe how modern psychologists view the contributions of nature and nurture to development. Explain why heredity and environment are correlated and mutually influential. (see "Exploring Human Behavior")

4. Describe the process of development in each of the prenatal stages. Define <u>zygote</u>, <u>embryo</u>, and <u>fetus</u>. (see "Prenatal Development")

5. Define <u>teratogen</u>. Define <u>critical period</u> and know the stage associated with it. Define <u>fetal alcohol syndrome</u>. (see "Prenatal Risks")

6. Describe the capacities of a newborn's senses. Define *reflexes*, and name three reflexes exhibited by newborns. Discuss how motor development is influenced by experimentation. (see "The Newborn")

7. Describe Piaget's theory of knowledge development. Explain why it incorporates both nature and nurture. Define <u>schemas</u>, <u>assimilation</u>, and <u>accommodation</u>. (see "The Development of Knowledge: Piaget's Theory")

8. Describe the development of mental abilities during the <u>sensorimotor stage</u>. Define <u>object permanence</u>. (see "Sensorimotor Development")

9. Explain how research has modified Piaget's description of infants in the sensorimotor stage. Discuss the experiments on object permanence and the role of experience in developing knowledge during infancy. (see "New View of Infants' Cognitive Development"; see also "Focus on Research Methods: Experiments on Developing Minds")

10. Describe the changes in cognition that occur during the <u>preoperational stage</u>.. Discuss the importance of symbol usage and imagination during this stage. Define <u>conservation</u>. (see "Preoperational Development")

11. Describe the changes in cognition that occur during Piaget's stage of <u>concrete operations</u>. (see "Concrete and Formal Operational Thought")

12. Describe the changes in cognition that occur during the <u>formal operational stage</u>.. (see "Concrete and Formal Operational Thought")

13. Discuss the criticisms of and alternatives to Piaget's theory of cognitive development. (see "Modifying Piaget's Theory")

14. Describe cognitive development from an information-processing approach. (see "Information Processing During Childhood")

15. Discuss the research on memory in early childhood. (see "Linkages: Development and Memory")

16. Describe the impact of culture on cognitive development. Define *scripts*. (see "Culture and Cognitive Development")

17. Describe the potential impact of the environment on cognitive development. (see "Improving or Endangering Cognitive Development")

18. Define <u>temperament</u>. Describe the three main temperament patterns discussed in the text. (see "Individual Temperament")

19. Define <u>attachment</u>. Describe the studies of motherless monkeys. Discuss the development of attachment, describe the four types of attachment, and explain the consequences of different attachment patterns. (see "The Infant Grows Attached")

20. Discuss the question of whether daycare damages the formation of a healthy mother-infant attachment. (see "Thinking Critically: Does Day Care Harm the Emotional Development of Infants?")

21.   Define *socialization*. Describe <u>authoritarian</u>, <u>permissive</u>, <u>authoritative</u>, and <u>uninvolved (rejecting-neglecting) parents</u>. Discuss the characteristics of children who have grown up under each of these styles. Explain the impact of the parents' culture and environment on the development of their parenting styles. (see "Relationships with Parents")

22.   Describe the importance of friendships and how popularity affects a child's social development. Discuss the development of social skills in children, including <u>self-regulation</u>. (see "Peer Friendships and Popularity"; see also "Social Skills and Understanding")

23.   Describe the environmental and biological factors that influence the development of <u>gender roles</u>. Discuss the influence of <u>gender schemas</u> on children. (see "Gender Roles")

24.   Describe the phenomenon of <u>resilience</u>. (see "Risk and Resilience")

25.   Define <u>puberty</u>, and discuss the physical, biological, and cognitive changes that occur during adolescence. Explain the development of love and sex during adolescence. Discuss the factors that affect violent behavior in adolescents. (see "Changes in Body, Brain, and Thinking"; see also "Adolescent Feelings and Behavior")

26.   Describe the development of both the personal identity and the <u>ethnic identity</u>. Define <u>identity crisis</u>. (see "Identity and Development of the Self")

27.   Describe the stages of moral reasoning suggested by Kohlberg. Define <u>preconventional</u>, <u>conventional</u>, and <u>postconventional</u> moral reasoning. Be able to discuss the cultural limitations of Kohlberg's stages. (see "Kohlberg's Stages of Moral Reasoning")

28.   Describe the relationship between moral reasoning and moral action. (see "Moral Reasoning and Moral Action")

29.   Define <u>identity crisis</u> and explain how identity development affects self-image and choice in an academic and career path. (see "Emerging Adulthood")

30.   Describe the physical changes that occur during adulthood. Define <u>menopause</u>. (see "Physical Changes")

31.   Describe the cognitive changes that occur during adulthood. Explain the development of *dialectical* thinking and *wisdom*. Discuss the cognitive decline that occurs in late adulthood, including *Alzheimer's disease*. (see "Cognitive Changes")

32.   Describe the social changes that occur during adulthood, including midlife transition and <u>generativity</u>. (see "Social Changes")

33.   Define <u>terminal drop</u>. Explain the factors that influence development and longevity of the lifespan. (see "Death and Dying"; see also "Developmental Trajectories"; see also "Longevity: The Length of Life")

CONCEPTS AND EXERCISES

Nature or Nurture

Today, developmental psychologists think that nature (genetic factors) and nurture (environmental factors) interact to produce an individual's characteristics. Below is a list of situations. After each description, decide whether nature or nurture had more influence on the final characteristics.

1.   Even though Pauline and Beth have spent just about the same amount of time lying in the sun, Pauline's tan is very dark and Beth's is a light brown. Pauline's ability to tan so darkly is probably a result of _____.

2.   Piano majors Yoko and Isabelle are very dedicated to practicing, and both work at it eight hours a day. Isabelle is very frustrated because her playing is not as musical as Yoko's, despite her long hours at the piano. Yoko's ability to play so musically is probably a result of _____.

3.   Estaban and Ricardo are identical twins. Their parents died in a car accident when they were nine weeks old. They had no other relatives, and separate adoptions were arranged. Estaban's adoptive parents are language professors at the local university, and Ricardo's are advertising executives. At age twelve, Estaban can speak three languages other than English; Ricardo is getting a D in English. The difference in their language abilities is probably due to _____.

4.   Tony was slight of build in high school. When he entered college, he started working out. The first time he returned home for the summer, his mother was surprised to see his well-developed muscles. Tony's new physique is probably due to _____.

The Toy Industry

Bill has just landed a job with a large toy company. His first assignment is to develop a new line of toys designed for children in each of Piaget's stages of cognitive development. Match each of Bill's ideas (listed below) to the appropriate stage of cognitive development.

1.   *A simple board game.* The winner is the first player to move a token completely around the board. The board itself is made of squares with pictures of animals, foods, family members (grandma, uncle, sister), and toys. Some of the squares have instructions to move ahead or fall back to the nearest square containing a picture of a certain animal, food, relative, or toy. For example, one square might instruct the player to move ahead to the nearest picture of a horn; and another, to move back to the nearest picture of a cow. To start, players roll a die and move the appropriate number of squares. A player's turn ends if he or she lands on a square with a picture. If the player lands on a square with instructions, he or she must follow them. The game is designed so that the players practice counting and recognizing different classes of objects. _____

2.   *A set of edible paints.* The paints come with a set of canvases that will not absorb paint. However, paint will adhere to the surface enough to remain in place. Each canvas contains an outline of a picture. The idea is for the child to paint a picture, then peel it off the board and eat it.

_____

3.   *A clown-face mobile painted in vibrant primary colors.* Each battery-operated clown face will, when pulled, emit a different melody or laugh, and the eyes in each face will light up.

_____

4.   *A board game called Planet Wars.* Each player receives a game piece in the shape of a planet. Some planets are more desirable than others, and a roll of the dice decides who gets which. Each planet comes with an army, several nearby star systems equipped with arsenals, an assortment of special weapons, and spy devices. The winner is the player who conquers the most planets. The players must generate hypotheses to help them form strategies for attack and must be able to logically anticipate the consequences of their own moves as well as those of their opponents.

_____

CRITICAL THINKING

Sam and Martina are working on a kidnapping case. Curiously, the biological mother has no pictures of the child to give to the two detectives. She has described her child, however, as five years old, male, blond, blue-eyed, smiley, and very typical. The child has been missing for over a week now. Sam and Martina feel sorry for the child; being kidnapped is a horrible ordeal. But since the mother is an alcoholic, they know that even if they find the boy, he won't come home to a very healthy situation.

Sam and Martina get a break. They receive a report from a homemaker, Ted, in a neighboring town. Ted says that a new child, Ritchie—five years old with blond hair and blue eyes—has suddenly appeared on the block and is living with a long-time neighbor of Ted's, whom he dislikes. The child doesn't seem to know his own name. Ted also mentions that he looks a little "funny" and appears to be mentally retarded. Ted knows that the neighbor is unable to have children and has wanted a child for quite some time. Also, as far as he knows, she doesn't have any relatives. In addition, she became extremely flustered when Ted asked her about Ritchie's origins. So where had the little boy come from?

Sam decides that Ritchie is not the child they are looking for. Ritchie fits the physical description given by the mother whose child had been kidnapped, but she specifically said the boy was healthy. She also didn't mention anything odd about his looks. However, Martina is sure they have found the child.

Using the five critical thinking questions in your text, the clues in the story, and what you have learned about human development, answer the following.

1.   What is Sam's hypothesis upon hearing about the "new kid on the block"?

2.   What evidence supports Sam's hypothesis?

3.   What is Martina's alternative hypothesis?

4.   What evidence supports Martina's alternative hypothesis?

5.   What conclusions can Sam and Martina draw?

PERSONAL LEARNING ACTIVITIES

1.   To see the development of the zygote into an embryo, then fetus, visit the following website: http://www.visembryo.com/baby/carnegiestages.html. Explore the visible changes in prenatal development, as well as the maternal symptoms of pregnancy. In terms of what you can see, how does the "look" of the developing infant change in the germinal versus embryonic versus fetal stages?

2.   To see some examples of the typical Piaget assessment for ability to conserve, visit these YouTube sites. First, try this one: http://www.youtube.com/watch?v=GLj0IZFLKvg. Then contrast the explanations the children in that video give to these conservation tasks to the explanations of older children in this second clip: http://www.youtube.com/watch?v=gA04ew6Oi9M. How does viewing these clips clarify for you the role of reversibility in the ability to conserve?

3.   To see an example of the Strange Situation, which is used to classify attachment type, visit the following YouTube site: http://www.youtube.com/watch?v=QTsewNrHUHU&feature=related. What sort of attachment do you think this child is displaying?

2.   Think back to a recent moral decision when you considered the reasons for and against doing something. List the reasons you gave at the time for the choice you made. What sorts of reasons did you give? Were they related to how other people would react, to what was legal, or to whether you might get punished, for example? At what stage of moral reasoning would Kohlberg place you based on this decision? Can you think of other decisions that would place you at a different level?

3.   Interview an elderly person in your life. Ask about what is important to him or her, what he or she is glad to have done, and what he or she would do differently. How does he or she view aging? How has he or she resolved Erikson's final crisis—in terms of integrity or despair?

MULTIPLE-CHOICE QUESTIONS

Quiz 1

1. Most contemporary developmental psychologists believe that development is guided by

    a. maturational processes.
    b. the influence of external conditions.
    c. the interaction of nature and nurture.
    d. biological processes.

2. Colleen is five years old, has mental retardation, and has a malformed face. What probably occurred during Colleen's prenatal development?

    a. Colleen was exposed to a teratogen.
    b. Her mother experienced severe stress.
    c. Colleen's mother did not provide a stimulating environment for her.
    d. Colleen's zygote period was skipped.

3. Penny is going to decorate her newborn's room and wants the baby to enjoy looking all around it. Which of the following will meet her decorating needs?

    a. Wallpaper covered with very small blue flowers
    b. A mobile with very small butterflies for the far end of the room
    c. Curtains with large smiling clown faces for the window right next to the baby's bed
    d. A wall hanging of gray and white checked fabric

4. Teratogens can be particularly harmful during the _____ stage of prenatal development, because it is then that the cardiovascular and nervous systems are beginning to develop.

    a. germinal
    b. embryonic
    c. fertile
    d. fetal

5. Why do infants have reflexes?

    a. They help babies survive.
    b. They are unnecessary evolutionary leftovers.
    c. They speed development.
    d. Psychologists are in serious disagreement on this issue.

6. Object permanence is acquired during Piaget's _____ stage of cognitive development.

    a. formal operational
    b. concrete operations
    c. preoperational
    d. sensorimotor

7. Gary's parents are constantly amazed at how their son has changed over the past year. Suddenly, he loves to study science, is a feminist, and wants to participate in an anti–nuclear-power demonstration. Gary has moved into the _____ stage of cognitive development.

    a. sensorimotor
    b. preoperational
    c. concrete operations
    d. formal operational

8. Jeffrey learned to pick up bits of cereal and push his fingers and the cereal into his mouth. Jeffrey discovered, however, that this method did not work for yogurt and eventually learned that yogurt is eaten with a spoon. Jeffrey's modified behavior shows

    a. accommodation.
    b. assimilation.
    c. conservation.
    d. object permanence.

9. One reason we may not remember things well prior to the age of three or so is because memories prior to that time tend to form automatically, without conscious recall. These memories are called _____ memories.

    a. explicit
    b. implicit
    c. language-based
    d. self-regulated

10. Claude pretends to be a baker while playing in the sand. He forms five sand cookie balls. Then he forms a sixth but flattens it into a pancake. "Wow!" he exclaims, "This is a much bigger cookie than the other ones!" According to Piaget, Claude is in the _____ stage of cognitive development.

    a. concrete operations
    b. formal operational
    c. preoperational
    d. sensorimotor

11. In assimilation,

    a. information is added to existing schemas.
    b. old schemas are modified.
    c. schemas are eliminated.
    d. None of these

12. An authoritative parent is

    a. firm, punitive, and unsympathetic.
    b. very lax about discipline and gives the child complete freedom.
    c. firm but reasonable and explains why a child's behavior is incorrect.
    d. one who demands obedience to authority.

13. It is interesting to watch nine-month-old P.J. react to a new object. He holds onto his mother very tightly for several long moments and then, using the furniture to steady himself, walks toward the object and warily checks it out. P.J. has a temperament that is typical of

    a. easy babies.
    b. difficult babies.
    c. slow-to-warm-up babies.
    d. exploratory babies.

14. Tyler wants to stay up late and watch a movie with his folks. They say, "Sure, we don't mind!" When Tyler wants to sleep in rather than get up because he stayed up late, his parents let him do that. "Tyler should be able to make all his own decisions," they say. "We don't want him to feel there is anything he can't do." Tyler's parents are displaying a(n) _____ parenting style.

    a. Authoritarian
    b. Authoritative
    c. Uninvolved
    d. Permissive

15. Gloria is forty years old and is beginning to feel the need to produce something that will outlast her, whether it be a child or an achievement at work. According to Erikson, Gloria is facing a(n) _____ crisis.

    a. intimacy
    b. integrity
    c. generativity
    d. autonomy

16. The Woodleys are concerned because both need to work and they must put their infant into daycare. What would you tell them?

    a. Their baby will be at risk for emotional problems.
    b. Their baby will be at risk for behavioral problems.
    c. If they are sensitive and responsive and it is a quality daycare situation, the child should not be at risk for any problems.
    d. They should not worry; infants are amazingly adaptable and will not develop problems, no matter what the situation.

17. Which of the following is not an example of self-regulation?

    a. Molly sucks her thumb when her mom puts her in her crib by herself.
    b. Noah takes deep breaths when he feels worried about taking a test.
    c. Cole screams at the top of his lungs when his dad sets him in his bouncy seat.
    d. Caden walks to the bus stop with friends to avoid a bully.

18. During Kohlberg's conventional level of moral reasoning, children

    a. consider what they will gain by the moral decision.
    b. choose an action that will bring approval.
    c. make decisions from a human rights perspective.
    d. make decisions based on their personal standards.

19. After the birth of a child, marital satisfaction tends to

    a. increase.
    b. decline.
    c. stay the same.
    d. increase, and then revert back to baseline.

20. Mark just turned forty-three. He reflects on how he has raised his boys and determines he should have spent more time with them, yelling less and communicating more. He feels he put too much time into work and makes arrangements to spend less time at the office and more time going camping with his teen-aged sons. Mark is likely experiencing (n)

    a. midlife transition.
    b. critical period.
    c. identity crisis.
    d. self-regulatory failure.

Total Correct (See answer key) _____

Quiz 2

Use this quiz to reassess your learning after taking Quiz 1 and reviewing the chapter.

1. In the context of the nature-nurture debate, nurture could be defined as

    a. a child's education.
    b. the sensitivity of the parent's care.
    c. a healthy diet.
    d. All of these

2. Lillian is not an alcoholic; she never drinks to excess. However, she does have wine with dinner every evening. Lillian, who is two weeks pregnant, has asked you whether this can injure her baby. What response could you correctly give her?

    a. Since Lillian is not an alcoholic, wine will probably not injure the baby.
    b. Since Lillian doesn't overindulge, wine will probably not injure the baby.
    c. Scientists still do not know the effects of wine drinking on unborn children.
    d. Even one glass of wine a day can cause damage to the unborn child.

3. Suppose a research team finds that an experimental drug causes heart abnormalities in rats, but only if it is given between day seven and day ten of gestation. These researchers have identified a(n) _____ period.

    a. germinal
    b. precocial
    c. critical
    d. artificial

4. What types of sounds do infants prefer?

    a. Soothing descending tones
    b. Low pitches
    c. Monotones
    d. High pitches

5.   Which of the following is NOT a risk associated with smoking during pregnancy.

    a.   Premature birth of the baby

    b.   Respiratory problems for the baby

    c.   Mental retardation

    d.   Irritability and attention problems

6.   Joey is six months old and loves to play "tug-of-war." When his dad leans over the crib with a toy in his hand, Joey grasps it and pulls on it. Joey's mom just got him a new toy—a little string of colored animals—to hang across his crib. She does not understand why Joey always reaches up and pulls down the string of colored animals. Joey is elaborating his schema of grasping and pulling through

    a.   accommodation.

    b.   integration.

    c.   assimilation.

    d.   anticipation.

7.   Stasha enjoys putting all kinds of objects, including bugs and dirt, in her mouth. She loses interest in playing with her toy train, however, when her babysitter hides it. Stasha is most likely in Piaget's _____ stage of cognitive development.

    a.   concrete operations

    b.   formal operational

    c.   preoperational

    d.   sensorimotor

8.   Susie is crying because her teddy bear, Boyd, has fallen off the kitchen table and landed on its face. She insists that her mother should put a bandage on Boyd's nose. Susie is in Piaget's _____ stage of cognitive development.

    a.   sensorimotor

    b.   preoperational

    c.   formal operational

    d.   concrete operations

9.   Understanding that a substance's quantity doesn't change, even when its form does, occurs during which of Piaget's developmental stages?

    a.   Sensorimotor

    b.   Preoperational

    c.   Concrete operational

    d.   Formal operational

10.   Egocentrism is one of the characteristics of the _____ stage of development.

    a.   sensorimotor

    b.   preoperational

    c.   concrete operational

    d.   formal operational

11. Temperament is first recognizable at what stage of development?

    a. Birth
    b. Preoperational stage
    c. Adolescence
    d. Middle childhood

12. Two mothers are assessing their children's abilities. One turns to the other and says, "Of course Juan is doing better at math. Now that he is older, his concentration is better and he can hold more chunks of information in his memory at the same time." _____ would agree with Juan's mom.

    a. Piaget
    b. Erikson
    c. An information-processing theorist
    d. Kohlberg

13. Pam is babysitting for Payton for the first time. When Payton's mom leaves, Payton cries. When her mom returns, Payton continues to cry as if she is mad at her mom for having left. Payton has a(n) _____ attachment.

    a. secure
    b. ambivalent
    c. avoidant
    d. disorganized

14. Betty is very careful to keep her new baby boy clothed and well-fed and to change his diaper when needed. She does not hold or touch him much because she thinks that this will spoil him and make him too dependent. Based on Harlow's studies, what should you tell Betty?

    a. Since humans are an intelligent species, their young can thrive well without being held much.
    b. Babies need to be touched and held to develop normally.
    c. Only a parent bonds with an infant, an infant does not bond with a parent.
    d. Humans do not usually form true attachments until they are eighteen months old.

15. Among European and European American parents, the parental socialization style that tends to be associated with the most positive outcomes is

    a. authoritative.
    b. permissive.
    c. uninvolved.
    d. authoritarian.

16. Which of these statements regarding children's social skills is *incorrect*?

    a. Parents can aid the development of cooperative interaction by initiating pretend play.
    b. Children who do not learn to detect others' emotional signals are often rejected by their peers.
    c. Children who cannot control their emotions are often unsympathetic and unhelpful.
    d. Empathy does not need to be learned; children develop it naturally.

17. Misha recently graduated from high school and is unsure about going to college. She hasn't picked out a career but wonders if taking courses would help her to decide who she is and what she wants to do. Erikson most likely would say Misha is in the midst of an
    a.   initiative conflict.
    b.   autonomy conflict.
    c.   integrity crisis.
    d.   identity crisis.

18. Jeanine and Helen are in a drugstore spending several weeks' worth of allowance on candy. Helen decides she wants to steal the candy, but Jeanine argues that they might get caught and put in jail. According to Kohlberg, Jeanine is at which level of moral reasoning?
    a.   Preconventional
    b.   Conventional
    c.   Concrete
    d.   Postconventional

19. Omar, a native of Nigeria whose family recently immigrated to the United States, has enrolled in ninth-grade classes. He is developing a sense of himself but is having concerns over his ethnic identity. What difficulty may Omar be experiencing?
    a.   He is unsure of what he wants to do in the future.
    b.   Although he is African, he does not identify with African American culture.
    c.   He is unsure of where he wants to live in the future.
    d.   He has been investigating various moral philosophies lately.

20. Dialectical thinking is
    a.   slower thinking that accompanies late adulthood.
    b.   understanding that knowledge is relative, not absolute.
    c.   having difficulty with multi-tasking.
    d.   wisdom.

Total Correct (See answer key) _____

ANSWERS TO FILL-IN-THE-BLANKS KEY TERMS

1.   teratogen (see Prenatal Development)

2.   critical period (see Prenatal Development)

3.   sensorimotor stage (see The Development of Knowledge: Piaget's Theory)

4.   object permanence (see The Development of Knowledge: Piaget's Theory)

5.   concrete operations (see The Development of Knowledge: Piaget's Theory)

6.   Authoritarian (see Relationships with Parents)

7.   formal operational stage (see The Development of Knowledge: Piaget's Theory)

8.   Conservation (see The Development of Knowledge: Piaget's Theory)

9.   generativity (see Social Changes)

10.   temperament (see Individual Temperament)

11.   sensorimotor (see The Development of Knowledge: Piaget's Theory)

12.   schemas (see The Development of Knowledge: Piaget's Theory)

13.   accommodation (see The Development of Knowledge: Piaget's Theory)

14.   Authoritative (see Relationships with Parents"

15.   maturation (see Exploring Human Development)

ANSWERS TO CONCEPTS AND EXERCISES

Nature or Nurture

1.   *Nature*. Pauline tans more easily than Beth, despite their spending the same amount of time in the sun, because Pauline's inheritance predisposes her pigmentation to be more reactive to the sun. (see Exploring Human Development)

2.   *Nature*. Yoko plays well because he has a genetic inheritance that predisposes him to be musical. (see Exploring Human Development)

3.   *Nurture*. Ricardo may not have been exposed to other languages in school or at home, but his poor performance in English indicates that he does not have a natural talent for languages. Estaban's parents have provided a multilingual environment for him, and this factor, rather than a genetic predisposition, is the likely reason he can speak three languages. (see Exploring Human Development)

4.   *Nurture*. Tony's genetic inheritance guided his physical development throughout high school. However, working out in the gym (an environmental factor, or nurture) was responsible for the changes in his muscles. (see Exploring Human Development)

The Toy Industry

1.   *Concrete operations*. During this stage of cognitive development, children learn how to do simple operations such as addition, subtraction, and conservation and to group objects into classes. (For example, cows, dogs, and rabbits are grouped as animals.) The board game encourages the child to practice counting and grouping objects into classes. (see The Development of Knowledge: Piaget's Theory)

2.   *Preoperational*. The ability to use symbols introduces the child to many new activities during this stage. Drawing involves creating a symbol of something in the real world. (see The Development of Knowledge: Piaget's Theory)

3.   *Sensorimotor*. During this stage, an infant loves to look at large objects that move and that feature lots of contrast and complexity—especially smiling faces. The mobile is perfect for this age: it moves, it consists of faces, and its colors, lights, and sounds provide contrast. (see The Development of Knowledge: Piaget's Theory)

4.   *Formal operations*. During this stage, adolescents learn to generate hypotheses and think logically about the outcome of events. To develop a strategy for the Planet Wars game, each player must create a plan (hypothesis) and think logically about the consequences of the plan's moves. (see The Development of Knowledge: Piaget's Theory)

ANSWERS TO CRITICAL THINKING

1.   Sam doesn't think they have solved the crime. His hypothesis is that Ritchie can't be the child they are looking for.

2. The evidence in support of Sam's hypothesis: Ted specifically said that Ritchie looked "funny" and appeared to be retarded, but the biological mother had described the child as very typical.

3. Martina's alternative hypothesis: Ritchie is the little boy they are looking for.

4. The evidence in support of Martina's alternative hypothesis: The biological mother is an alcoholic and her son may have fetal alcohol syndrome. That would explain Ted's description of odd-looking facial features and mental retardation. She thinks it's possible that, due to guilt, the biological mother didn't tell them about the fetal alcohol syndrome. Martina will want to collect additional evidence. She will want to know whether the mother was an alcoholic during her pregnancy and whether there are any medical records that discuss her son's health.

5. Martina thinks it may be reasonable at this point to conclude that they have the right child. (NOTE: Critical thinking is a constant process of hypothesizing, examining evidence, rehypothesizing, collecting more evidence, and so on. Martina may not be correct. Can you think of any other hypotheses that could explain these data?)

ANSWERS TO MULTIPLE-CHOICE QUESTIONS

Circle the question numbers you answered correctly.

Quiz 1

1. c is the answer. The nature of inherited genes can explain how people are alike in certain respects, and the nurture of widely different family and cultural environments produce differences among individuals. (see Exploring Human Development)

   a. Arnold Gesell in the early 1900s suggested that human development is determined by nature and is relatively unaffected by the environment.

   b. Early in this century John Watson believed that development is guided solely by learning.

   d. Biological processes would be synonymous with nature, or maturation.

2. a is the answer. Teratogens are harmful external substances that invade the womb and result in birth defects. (see Prenatal Development)

   b. Stress levels of the mother can affect the child, but they do so in more subtle ways that are reversible. There is no evidence that stress levels could cause these overt problems.

   c. If a pregnant woman maintains a healthy lifestyle and gets adequate prenatal care, the fetus will develop into a healthy baby. No extra stimulation of the unborn child is needed.

   d. If the zygote period was skipped, conception never occurred.

3. c is the answer. Infants can see large objects featuring lots of contrast, contour, complexity, and movement. They enjoy looking at faces. The clown faces are large and smiling and may move with the breeze. (see The Newborn)

   a. This wallpaper design may appeal to Penny, but her infant will not have the visual capability to see the small pattern.

   b. A mobile is a good idea because the parts move, but the infant will be unable to see it in the far corner.

   d. A wall hanging of brightly colored checks may provide enough contrast for the infant to see it. However, grey and white are not as contrasting as, say, blue and red.

4. b is the answer. Cardiovascular and nervous systems develop during the embryonic stage. A critical period exists: If certain systems and organs do not develop properly at this time, they

never will. So teratogens ingested during this period of prenatal development will interfere with this development, which makes them especially dangerous during this time period. (see Prenatal Development)

   a.   The germinal stage begins with fertilization and lasts for two weeks. This period has fewer critical periods in it. Although teratogens can be harmful anytime in pregnancy, ingestion during the embryonic stage would be more significant than during the germinal.

   c, d.   There is no such thing as the fertile stage in prenatal development. You may be thinking of the fetal stage. During this stage, systems integrate and the organs grow and begin to function more efficiently. Teratogens are certainly dangerous during the fetal stage, but this stage has fewer critical periods than the embryonic stage and so would have less significant of an impact.

5.   a is the answer. Because human babies are so helpless at birth, reflex movements help babies survive. Imagine trying to teach a day-old infant the mouth movements involved in sucking. By the time the baby learned, he or she would have starved. (see The Newborn)

   b.   Reflexes are necessary; they help babies survive.

   c.   Reflexes do not speed development, but they do help babies survive while their muscles are developing.

   d.   Psychologists agree on the role of reflexes.

6.   d is the answer. Object permanence is the ability to know that an object exists even when it is out of sight. Children acquire this ability during the sensorimotor stage, the first stage of cognitive development. (see The Development of Knowledge: Piaget's Theory)

   a.   An adolescent acquires the ability to think hypothetically and to imagine logical consequences of events in the formal operational stage.

   b.   A child learns to perform simple operations—subtraction, addition, classification, seriation, and conservation—during the concrete operational stage.

   c.   A child acquires the ability to use symbols during the preoperational stage.

7.   d is the answer. Studying science involves thinking logically and being able to generate hypotheses. Being involved with feminist movements and nuclear demonstrations requires the ability to question social institutions and to think about the world as it might be or as it ought to be. (see The Development of Knowledge: Piaget's Theory)

   a, b.   Children in the sensorimotor or preoperational stages do not have the ability to question social institutions. They may have some knowledge of feminism or nuclear power plants, but they cannot think about or accurately imagine the consequences of nuclear disasters or the treatment of women as inferior.

   c.   During the concrete operations stage, children can think logically about objects they directly experience.

8.   a is the answer. In accommodation, new information changes a schema. (see The Development of Knowledge: Piaget's Theory)

   b.   Assimilation is when new information is added to an unchanged schema.

   c.   Conservation is the ability to realize that the size, quantity, or mass of an object is the same although it looks different.

   c.   Children with object permanence know that an object exists even when it is hidden from view.

9. b is the answer. Implicit memories form automatically and can affect emotions and behavior even when we do not consciously recall them. (see Linkages: Development and Memory)

    a. Explicit memories are memories we purposely attend to recalling and usually can.

    c, d. There is no such term as a language-based memory or self-regulated memory.

10. c is the answer. Claude cannot perform the mental operations needed to conserve amounts (understand that although shapes may change, the amounts remain the same). Therefore, Claude is in the preoperational stage. (see The Development of Knowledge: Piaget's Theory)

    a. Concrete operations require the ability to conserve.

    b. The formal operational stage requires the ability to think about abstract concepts.

    c. Infants in the sensorimotor stage explore the world through their senses. They do not have object permanence until the end of the sensorimotor stage and cannot conserve amounts. Because Claude is pretending, however, we know that he has moved beyond the sensorimotor stage.

11. a is the answer. (see The Development of Knowledge: Piaget's Theory)

    b. In accommodation, old schemas are modified with new information.

    c. Schemas are enlarged in assimilation or are changed in accommodation, but they are not eliminated.

    d. a is the answer.

12. c is the answer. Authoritative parents are firm but reasonable and provide explanations when a child's behavior is incorrect. They encourage the child to take responsibility and to be independent. (see Relationships with Parents)

    a. Authoritarian parents are firm, punitive, and unsympathetic.

    b. Permissive parents are very lax about discipline and give their children complete freedom.

    c. Authoritarian parents demand obedience to authority figures.

13. c is the answer. Slow-to-warm-up babies take a while to explore the environment but eventually do. (see Individual Temperament)

    a. An easy baby has predictable cycles of eating and sleeping, reacts cheerfully to a new situation, and seldom fusses.

    b. A difficult baby is irritable and irregular.

    d. Although some infants are more exploratory than others, there is no category or classification termed "exploratory."

14. d is the answer. Permissive parents are less informed about their children's activities, set few rules, and use little discipline. Tyler's parents let him do pretty much what he wants, which suggests a lack of rules and a permissive style. (see Relationships with Parents)

    a. Authoritarian parents are strict and unyielding disciplinarians.

    b. Authoritative parents discuss rules with their children and then set them. Tyler's parents try not to have rules at all.

    c. Uninvolved parents are indifferent to their children. Tyler's parents appear to care but are just permissive.

15.   c is the answer. Erikson said that in middle adulthood people become concerned with generating or producing something that will outlast them. (see Social Changes)

   a.   Erikson said that concerns about intimacy are dealt with in early adulthood.

   b.   Integrity versus despair is the social conflict dealt with in late adulthood, according to Erikson.

   d.   Autonomy or independence is the challenge of the toddler, according to Erikson.

16.   c is the answer. Daycare by itself does not lead to insecure attachment or emotional harm. Responsive and caring parents and quality daycare should result in secure infant-adult attachments. (see Thinking Critically: Does Day Care Harm the Emotional Development of Infants?)

   a, b.   Daycare by itself does not lead to insecure attachments or emotional harm.

   d.   If daycare is of poor quality and caregivers are insensitive and unresponsive, infants will be less likely to develop secure attachments.

17.   c is the answer. Cole is unable to deal with his anxiety. Instead, he cries loudly to express it. (see Social Skills and Understanding)

   a.   Molly is regulating her anxiety about being along in her crib.

   b.   Noah is regulating his anxiety about the test.

   d.   Caden is avoiding anxiety by invoking social support.

18.   b. is the answer. Children at the conventional level make moral decisions based on other people's approval or on what everyone else says is right. (see Moral Development)

   a.   This is the preconventional level, which is basically characterized by selfishness.

   c, d.   Both of these choices describe reasoning at the postconventional level of moral reasoning, when decisions are based on personal standards or respect for human rights.

19.   b is the answer. Marital satisfaction tends to decline once a baby is born. (see Social Changes)

   a.   Marital satisfaction tends to decrease, not increase, after the birth of a child

   c.   Marital satisfaction tends to decrease, not stay equal, after the birth of a child.

   d.   Marital satisfaction does not initially increase and then revert—it declines after the birth of a child.

20.   a. is the answer. Mark is entering a period in which he reappraises his life and relationships. This period is known as a midlife transition. (see Social Changes)

   b.   A critical period is a stage of development in which something must occur, or it never will be able to develop outside of that time frame.

   c.   An identity crisis is a phase in adolescence. Mark is well past this period.

   d.   A self-regulatory failure would be a failure to manage one's own emotions. Mark is managing his emotions, although he is reflecting on what areas of life he would like to change.

Now turn to the quiz analysis table at the end of this chapter to find which areas you know well and which areas you need to work on. Circle the numbers in the table for items on Quiz 1 that you answered correctly.

Quiz 2

1. d is the answer. Nurture is anything in the environment that influences an organism, including education, parents' care, physical exercise, and diet. Nature is any characteristic resulting from inherited genetic material, such as eye color or a physical predisposition toward a disease, body type, or temperament. (see Exploring Human Development)

    a, b, c. Each of these choices is correct, but no one of them is the *best* answer.

2. d is the answer. Pregnant women who drink as little as a glass or two of wine a day can harm their infants' intellectual functioning. (see Prenatal Development)

    a, b, c. Only d is correct.

3. c is the answer. The critical period in prenatal development is the time when certain kinds of growth must occur if development is to proceed normally. If something happens during this time, abnormalities will result. The drug given to rats during that critical three-day period resulted in heart abnormalities. (see Prenatal Development)

    a. The germinal stage is a general term for the first two weeks of prenatal development. It does not refer to times when growth may be interrupted, as described in this question.

    b, d. These terms are not used in connection with periods of prenatal development in human beings.

4. d is the answer. (see The Newborn)

    a, b, c. Infants prefer ascending tones, spoken by a woman or a child. They like speech that is friendly, high-pitched, exaggerated, and expressive.

5. c is the answer. Mental retardation is not a risk directly associated with smoking during pregnancy. However, smoking is associated with premature delivery of the baby, and preemies are often at high risk for cognitive and behavioral problems throughout life. (see Prenatal Development)

    a., b, d. These are all risks directly associated with smoking during pregnancy.

6. c is the answer. Joey is assimilating because he is using the *same* schema of reaching and grasping to investigate a new object. (see The Development of Knowledge: Piaget's Theory)

    a. Accommodation occurs when a schema is modified or changed in response to acquiring new information. If the question stated that Joey learned to push the animals back and forth in the air instead of always reaching, grasping, and pulling them down, accommodation would have been the answer.

    b. Integration is the process of putting two schemas together. If the question stated that Joey learned that reaching and grasping can become a sequence of movements, this would be the correct answer.

    d. There is no anticipatory process in the elaboration of schemas.

7. d is the answer. Children in the sensorimotor stage, according to Piaget, are still acquiring object permanence. They often put things in their mouths to see how they feel. (see The Development of Knowledge: Piaget's Theory)

    a. Concrete operational children have acquired object permanence and do not explore the world by putting objects in their mouths.

    b. Adolescents or adults in the formal operational stage think abstractly.

    c. Preoperational children have object permanence.

8. b is the answer. Susie is probably between the ages of four and six and thinks that her bear, an inanimate (nonliving) object, is alive and feels pain because he fell on his face. Mom typically puts a bandage on Susie's cuts and bruises, and Susie wants the same treatment for Boyd. This behavior is characteristic of the preoperational stage. (see The Development of Knowledge: Piaget's Theory)

    a. Children in the sensorimotor stage do not recognize or label their own emotions and therefore cannot assume that their toys have emotions.

    c. Adolescents in the formal operational stage realize that inanimate (nonliving) objects do not feel pain.

    d. Children in the concrete operational stage realize that inanimate (nonliving) objects do not feel pain.

9. c is the answer. (see Linkages: Development and Memory)

    a. The sensorimotor stage starts with birth and extends through two years of age.

    b. Conservation—understanding that substances don't change in quantity even when their shape does—is an "operation." In the *pre*operational stage, children cannot perform this "operation."

    d. Adolescents in the formal operational stage already understand concrete operations.

10. b is the answer. Egocentrism, the belief that the way the world appears to you is how it appears to others, is a characteristic of the second half of the preoperational stage (age four through seven). (see The Development of Knowledge: Piaget's Theory)

    a. Object permanence is one of the principle cognitive developments that occur during the sensorimotor stage.

    c. Children are generally liberated from intuitive concepts like egocentrism during the concrete operational stage.

    d. When an adolescent reaches the stage of formal operations, he or she is capable of abstract reasoning, far beyond the simple use of symbols, and certainly beyond intuitive concepts like egocentrism.

11. a is the answer. (see Individual Temperament)

    b, c, d. While temperament is recognizable during the preoperational stage, adolescence, and middle childhood, it *first* appears at birth.

12. c is the answer. Developmental research based on information-processing theory focuses on the *quantitative* changes in children's mental capacities, rather than looking for qualitative advances or changes as Piaget did. *Better* concentration and retention of *more* chunks of information in memory at one time are all quantitative changes. Therefore, Johnny's mother is explaining her son's improvement as an information-processing theorist would. (NOTE: This approach focuses on quantitative changes. *Quantitative* pertains to number or amounts, so *bigger* or *more* ability accounts for a change, according to this view of cognitive development.) (see Information Processing During Childhood)

    a. Piaget explained that cognitive development pertains to a *different* kind of mental ability, not just an improved ability for the same cognitive skill. The use of symbols (acquired during the preoperational stage) is different from the ability to generate hypotheses (acquired during the formal operation stage). (NOTE: *Quality* is defined as "a distinguishing element or characteristic." And each stage of Piaget's cognitive development theory is distinguished by a *unique* characteristic or type of thinking.)

b.   Erikson studied the stages of emotional development.

d.   Kohlberg was interested in moral decision making—only one type of cognitive activity. His work does not provide a general theory about the development of cognitive abilities.

13.   b is the answer. A child with ambivalent attachment is upset when his or her mother leaves and vacillates between clinging to her and angrily rejecting her efforts at contact. (see The Infant Grows Attached)

a.   A secure attachment is evidenced by happiness upon the mother's return and receptivity to her contact.

c.   An avoidant attachment involves the infant avoiding the mother upon her return.

d.   A disorganized attachment revealed by inconsistent behavior that is disturbing.

14.   b is the answer. Betty's baby could experience dramatic problems due to developmental brain dysfunction and damage brought on by the lack of touch and body movement in infancy. (see The Infant Grows Attached)

a.   The need for comfort and connection has nothing to do with intelligence.

c, d.   Infants form attachments, or bonds, to caregivers during the first year of life.

15.   a is the answer. Authoritative parenting is associated with children being friendly, cooperative, and socially responsible. They also tend to achieve more in school, be more popular, and adjust better to divorce. (see Relationships with Parents)

b.   Permissive parenting tends to be associated with immaturity, dependence, and unhappiness in children. The children are more likely to have tantrums and need help when they encounter even slight difficulties.

c.   Uninvolved parenting is indifference to the children, and it not associated with favorable outcomes in any culture.

d.   Authoritarian parenting is associated with children being unfriendly, distrustful, and withdrawn. These children are more likely to cheat, be aggressive, be less empathic, and have difficulty accepting blame after doing something wrong.

16.   d is the answer. Social skills, like cognitive skills, must be learned. (see Social Skills and Understanding)

a, b, c.   All of these are true statements regarding children's social competencies and skills.

17.   d is the answer. Misha doesn't have the feeling that she is a unique person; she is still confused about her self-image and her role in life. (see Identity and Development of the Self)

a, b.   Conflicts dealing with initiative and autonomy occur during early childhood, according to Erikson.

c.   The issue of integrity is faced during late adulthood, according to Erikson.

18.   a is the answer. The preconventional level of reasoning is very self-serving. Moral decisions are made either to avoid punishment or to benefit the individual. The only reason Jeanine gives for not stealing the candy is avoiding potential punishment. (see Moral Development)

b.   At the conventional level of moral reasoning, Jeanine would be concerned with doing what attained the approval of others or with following the rules.

c.   There is no such level in Kohlberg's model. You may have been thinking of Piaget's concrete operational stage.

    d.   At the postconventional level of moral reasoning, Jeanine would be concerned with universal principles of human rights or with personal standards of justice.

19.   b is the answer. As part of the development of his personal identity as a unique individual, Omar must come to terms with that part that reflects his race, religion, and culture. Because his Nigerian culture differs not only from that of the majority culture in the United States, but also from that of the U.S. African American subculture, he may have difficulty figuring out what his ethnic identity is and feeling comfortable with it. (see Identity and Development of the Self)

    a, c, d.   None of these is particularly concerned with the particular question of ethnic identity as addressed in the question.

20.   b is the answer. Dialectical thinking is understanding that knowledge is relative, not absolute. It is in middle adulthood that this cognitive skill manifests itself. (see Cognitive Changes)

    a., c.   These are not the definitions of dialectical thinking. Dialectical thinking, which is understanding that knowledge is relative, has nothing to do with slow thinking or difficulty multi-tasking.

    d.   Although dialectical thinking may be part of wisdom, wisdom is defined as expert knowledge in the fundamental, practical aspects of life. Wisdom is a broader construct than dialectical thinking.

Now turn to the quiz analysis table at the end of this chapter to find which areas you know well and which areas you need to work on. Circle the numbers in the table for items on Quiz 2 that you answered correctly.

For each question you answered correctly, circle its number. (Quiz 1 numbers are not shaded; Quiz 2 numbers are shaded.) Are there patterns in the types of questions or the topics you got wrong that could direct your further study? Did you improve from Quiz 1 to Quiz 2?

QUIZ REVIEW

Topic	Type of Question		
	Definition	**Comprehension**	**Application**
Exploring Human Development		1	
			1
Beginnings			
Prenatal Development		4	2
		5	2, 3
The Newborn		5	3
		4	
Infancy and Childhood: Cognitive Development			
The Development of Knowledge: Piaget's Theory	11	6	7, 8, 10
		9, 10	6, 7, 8
Information Processing During Childhood			
			12
Linkages: Development and Memory		9	
Infancy and Childhood: Social and Emotional Development			
Individual Temperament			13
		11	
The Infant Grows Attached			
			13, 14
Thinking Critically: Does Day Care Harm the Emotional Development of Infants?			16
Relationships with Parents	12		14
		15	
Social Skills and Understanding			17
		16	
Adolescence			
Identity and Development of the Self			
			17, 19
Moral Development		18	
			18
Adulthood			
Cognitive Changes			
	20		
Social Changes		19	15, 20

Total correct by quiz:

| Quiz 1: | |
| Quiz 2: | |

CHAPTER 13

Health, Stress, and Coping

OUTLINE

The field of <u>health psychology</u> (also called <u>health care psychology</u>) investigates the psychological influence on how people stay healthy, why they become sick, and how they respond when they do get sick. This work is part of a larger field called *behavioral medicine*.

I. HEALTH PSYCHOLOGY

Scientific evidence supports that one's mental state, behavior, and health are linked. Part of the growth of the field of health psychology has to do with the changing nature of illness. For many years, infectious diseases were the primary causes of death and illness. But now, chronic disease (often associated with health-risk behavior) accounts for at least half of the deaths in the United States. A goal of the field is to help people understand the role they can play in controlling their own health and life expectancy by changing behavior.

II. UNDERSTANDING STRESS AND STRESSORS

<u>Stress</u> is the internal process that occurs when people try to adjust to events and situations. <u>Stressors</u> either disrupt, or threaten to disrupt, one's daily functioning and cause a person to make adjustments. <u>Stress reactions</u> are the physical, psychological, and behavioral responses that occur in the face of stressors. *Stress mediators* affect the severity of stress reactions. Examples of mediating factors include perceived control over stressors, the interpretation of the stressor, available social support, and quality of stress-coping skills.

A. Psychological Stressors

Pleasant and unpleasant events or situations can cause stress. Stressors that are perceived as negative or threatening are experienced as more stressful than events perceived as positive.

1. *Catastrophic events* that are life-threatening, such as assault, combat, fire, and tornadoes, can lead to serious psychological disorders.
2. *Life changes and strains* can be stressors, especially if they force a person to adapt. Examples of such changes include divorce, marriage, bad grades, graduation, a new job, a promotion, and death.
3. *Chronic problems* last for a long period and include things such as living in a high-crime neighborhood, experiencing discrimination over a lifetime, and so forth.
4. *Daily hassles*, such as minor irritations, pressures, and annoyances, when experienced regularly, can act as stressors.

B. Measuring Stressors

1. Several ways of measuring stress have been developed based on the premise that stress is a process that requires a person to make some sort of life adjustment. One instrument, called the *Social Readjustment Rating Scale (SRRS)*, measures stress in terms of *life-change units* (LCUs). Research suggests that people who experience a greater number of LCUs are more likely to suffer physical and mental illness.

2. The *Life Experiences Survey (LES)*, another instrument for measuring stress, also considers an individual's perceptions of the positive or negative impact of a given stressor. By examining perceptions of stress, the LES is able to measure the role that gender and cultural differences play in experiences of stress.

III.   STRESS RESPONSES
   A.   Physical Responses
       1.   *The General Adaptation Syndrome.* The <u>general adaptation syndrome (GAS)</u> is a stress response composed of three stages.
           a)   *Stage 1.* The fight-or-flight syndrome (FFS), or *alarm reaction*, is the first stage. The sequence of events causing the FFS is controlled by the *sympatho-adreno-medullary system (SAM)*; the hypothalamus triggers the sympathetic ANS, which stimulates the inner part of the adrenal gland, which in turn secretes *catecholamines* into the bloodstream. Catecholamines stimulate the heart, liver, kidneys, and lungs, thereby causing rapid breathing and increases in heart rate, blood pressure, blood sugar level, and muscle tension. Stressors also activate the *hypothalamic-pituitary-adrenocortical (HPA) system*. The hypothalamus triggers the pituitary to secrete adrenocorticotropic hormone (ACTH), which stimulates adrenal cortex *corticosteroid* secretion. Corticosteroids generate the emergency energy needed to handle stress.
           b)   *Stage 2.* If stressors persist, the *resistance stage* of the GAS begins. The energy drain is slower than that of Stage 1, but the body is still working hard physiologically to combat the stressor.
           c)   *Stage 3.* A continual depletion of energy eventually causes *exhaustion*, the third stage. The body eventually succumbs to <u>diseases of adaptation</u> caused by damaged heart and blood vessels, suppressed immune system functioning, and prolonged strain on systems that may have been weak even prior to the onset of the stressor.
   Psychobiological models have expanded Selye's theory of the GAS to include an individual's emotional state and perceptions of the stressor.

   B.   Psychological Responses
       1.   *Emotional Responses.* Most physical stress responses are accompanied by emotional stress responses. Emotional responses come and go with the onset and termination of stressors. Prolonged stress causes tension, irritability, sadness, and increased anxiety.
       2.   *Cognitive Responses.* An inability to concentrate, think clearly, or remember information accurately is a common cognitive reaction to stress. *Ruminative thinking*, the persistent interruption of thoughts about stressful events, is a cause of the reduction in thinking ability. When *catastrophizing*, a person tends to dwell on and overemphasize the potentially negative consequences of events. Overarousal causes the normal range of attention to narrow. People under stress are more likely to use *mental sets* and experience *functional fixedness*.
       3.   *Behavioral Responses.* Behavioral stress responses such as a shaky voice, changed body posture, and facial expressions provide clues about physiological and emotional stress responses. Some behaviors are aimed at helping one escape or avoid a stressor, such as alcohol abuse or late-night socializing. Aggression and suicide attempts are also examples of behavioral stress responses.
   C.   Linkages: Stress and Psychological Disorders
       1.   <u>Burnout</u> is a gradually intensifying pattern of physical, psychological, and behavioral dysfunction in response to a continual flow of stressors. Those experiencing burnout may become indifferent, impulsive, accident-prone, drug-abusing, suspicious, depressed, and withdrawn. It is particularly common among individuals involved in "people work."
       2.   <u>Posttraumatic stress disorder (PTSD)</u> is a pattern of adverse reactions following a traumatic event. The disorder may appear immediately or weeks to years after the event. Symptoms include anxiety, irritability, jumpiness, inability to concentrate or

work, sexual dysfunction, and difficulty in interpersonal relationships. In rare cases, *flashbacks* may occur. The most common symptom is re-experiencing the trauma through nightmares or vivid memories. PTSD may appear immediately after the trauma, but full symptoms may take weeks to develop.

3. Stress has also been implicated in other psychological disorders, including depression and schizophrenia. The *diathesis-stress model* sees certain people as predisposed to these problems, but the frequency, intensity, and nature of stressors encountered influences whether or not people actually develop these problems.

IV. STRESS MEDIATORS
Mediating factors include individual and stressor characteristics and the circumstances under which stressors occur.

A. How Stressors Are Perceived
Those who perceive a stressor as a challenge rather than a threat experience fewer and less intense negative stress consequences. The influence of cognitive mediating factors weakens as the intensity of a stressor increases.

B. Predictability and Control
Unpredictable stressors tend to have more negative impact than predictable ones. One's *perception of control* can dampen the effect of a stressor.

C. Coping Resources and Coping Methods
Coping resources include time and money to deal with stressors. *Coping methods* are either *problem-focused* or *emotion-focused*. Problem-focused coping involves efforts to eliminate or alter the stressor. Emotion-focused coping involves efforts to regulate the negative emotional consequences of the stressor. When a stressor is changeable, problem-focused coping is very effective. But when a stressor is difficult to control, it can be helpful to express and think about the emotion it has brought on.

D. Social Support
1. Social support—friends and family who lend support during stress—can greatly reduce the impact of stressors. It is associated with many health benefits.

2. Social support may work because it provides those under stress an opportunity to express pent-up emotions. It may also be the case that individual with good coping skills tend to get more social support. The quality of the social support matters—a social support network that is full of conflict will be less effective. Too much support (although well-intended), however, can inhibit a person's attempt to cope with stress. Finally, the type of stressor can also influence the degree to which social support is helpful as a mediating factor.

E. Stress, Personality, and Gender
1. Some personalities are more "disease-prone" than others, tending to ignore stressors as long as possible, see stressors as long-term catastrophic events brought on by oneself, and perceiving little control over stressors.

2. *Dispositional optimism*, or the expectation that things will work out well, is associated with fewer illnesses and faster healing. The impact of this personality is partly because optimists tend to take problem-focused coping methods to task on stressors they perceive as challenges (not threats).

3. In response to stress, men tend to get angry, avoid the stressor, or both. Females tend to utilize their social support network, instead. Men's tendency for "fight-or-flight" response to stressors as opposed to women's "tend-and-befriend" style may be in

response to hormonal differences between genders. Oxytocin is a hormone released during the GAS, but in men it tends to amplify stress responses while in women it tends to reduce those responses.

F.   Focus on Research Methods: Personality and Health
A study that followed gifted children for seventy years showed a relationship between *conscientiousness* and longer life. People whose parents had divorced or who had unstable marriages themselves died an average of four years earlier than those whose parents hadn't divorced or who had stable marriages. Because the data was correlational, we cannot know for certain that these personality traits or experiences caused longer life, just that they were associated with it. The study raised possible hypotheses for why this association exists, such as the possibility that conscientiousness promotes a healthier life style that in turn produces longer life expectancy.

V.   THE PHYSIOLOGY AND PSYCHOLOGY OF HEALTH AND ILLNESS
A.   Stress, Illness, and the Immune System
Psychoneuroimmunology is the field that studies the interaction of the psychological, social, behavioral, neural, hormonal, and immune system processes that affect the body's ability to defend itself against disease.

1.   *The Immune System and Illness*. The immune system defends the body against foreign substances and microorganisms. Problems with the immune system can either involve failure to defend the body from these substances, or an overactive immune system that attacks normal cells. The latter is called an *autoimmune disorder*. An active immune system has many components: the *leukocytes*, called *B-cells* and *T-cells*; the *antibodies* produced by B-cells; the *natural killer cells*; and *macrophages*. Stress-related psychological and emotional factors affect the immune system through the central and autonomic nervous systems and through the endocrine system.

2.   *The Immune System and Stress*. People who are stressed are more likely to develop infectious diseases and to show reactivation of latent viruses (such as AIDS) because of immune system suppression.

B.   Stress, Illness, and the Cardiovascular System
Heart disease is a major cause of death in most developed countries, including the United States. Repeated reactivation of the cardiovascular system in response to stress may increase risk for heart disease. This link is especially strong in people who show high physiological reaction to stressors. In particular, *hostility* (when accompanied by impatience and irritability) is associated with the appearance of coronary heart disease.

C.   Thinking Critically: Does Hostility Increase the Risk of Heart Disease?
What am I being asked to believe or accept?

People with hostility are more at risk for coronary heart disease and *myocardial infarction (MI)*, more commonly known as heart attack.

What evidence is available to support the assertion?

Hostility is associated with an increase in the time needed to return to a resting level of sympatho-adreno-medullary (SAM). Increased sympathetic nervous system activity causes the release of stress-related hormones that are damaging to the heart. Hostility may also have an indirect effect through social support. Hostile individuals may either receive less social support or use it less effectively.

Are there alternative ways of interpreting the evidence?

Genetically determined autonomic reactivity may make both hostility and heart disease more likely.

What additional evidence would help to evaluate the alternatives?

Further research has examined the effects of physiological arousal in hostile individuals when they are not angry. In circumstances such as surgery (a stressor but not one normally associated with anger or hostility), these individuals did show strong autonomic arousal, even when they were not conscious. This suggests that perhaps oversensitivity to stressors, not hostility, may be responsible for the risk for CHD.

What conclusions are most reasonable?

Although most researchers continue to find that hostile individuals have a higher risk of heart disease and heart attacks than nonhostile individuals, many interacting factors appear to affect the relationship between hostility and heart disease. And because this relationship is not universal, a more elaborate psychobiological model is needed to explain these relationships.

VI.   PROMOTING HEALTHY BEHAVIOR
Health promotion is the process of altering or eliminating behaviors that pose health risks and at the same time increase healthy behavior patterns.

A.   Health Beliefs and Health Behaviors
Irwin Rosenstock's health-belief model is based on the assumption that people's decisions about health-related behavior are guided by four main factors: perceived personal threat of illness; perceived seriousness of illness; belief that a particular behavior or health practice will reduce the threat; and balance between health practice cost and perceived benefits. In addition, people need to believe that they can change their behavior, which is known as *self-efficacy*. Related to self-efficacy is the *intention* to change.

B.   Changing Health Behaviors: Stages of Readiness
Successful adoption of health practices involves five stages: *precontemplation*, *contemplation*, *preparation*, *action*, and *maintenance*. These stages may overlap, with several "false starts" before permanent change is finally achieved.

C.   Programs for Coping with Stress and Promoting Health
1.   *Planning to Cope*. People who are able to adopt problem-focused coping skills and recognize which stressors can and can't be changed are better equipped to cope with stress and are more likely to escape its negative consequences. Those able to adjust their coping strategies to the stressor are most successful.
2.   *Developing Coping Strategies*. Strategies for coping with stress can be *cognitive* (such as *cognitive restructuring*), *emotional* (such as social support), *behavioral* (such as time management), and *physical* (such as progressive muscle relaxation training).

KEY TERMS

1.   **Health psychology (Health care psychology)** is a field in which psychologists conduct and apply research aimed at promoting human health and preventing illness. (see introductory section

2.   **Stress** describes the internal processes that occur as people try to adjust to events and situations, especially those that they perceive to be beyond their coping capacity. (see Understanding Stress and Stressors)

Example: Marcus is five years old. He has just started day care and has been exposed to many childhood diseases. He is under stress because his body must adjust to fighting off these diseases.

3. **Stressors** are events and situations to which people must adjust. (see Understanding Stress and Stressors)

    Example: Sharon has just been offered a new job. After graduation, she will move from a small town to a large city, have new responsibilities, and want to make new friends. Although these events are positive, they will involve big changes and therefore will be stressors.

4. **Stress reactions** are the physical, psychological, and behavioral responses that occur in the face of stressors. (see Understanding Stress and Stressors)

    Example: Sienna is really worried about her midterm exams. Her blood pressure is elevated (physical), she experiences anxiety and persistent thoughts of failing (psychological), and she bites her nails (behavioral).

5. The **general adaptation syndrome (GAS)** is a three-stage pattern of responses triggered by the effort to adapt to any stressor. (see Physical Responses)

    Example: To satisfy his intellectual curiosity, Bill is taking a full load of classes, teaching undergraduates, writing a book, and doing research for a professor in his department. At the beginning of the semester, Bill can feel his heart race as he hurries to make an appointment here or there on campus (alarm). During midterm exams, he is in a constant state of arousal but does not notice it. He is used to being busy all day (resistance). By the end of the semester, he has a constant cold, feels tired, and has high blood pressure (exhaustion). Bill's doctor tells him that he needs to take time to relax over term break. His body must have time to recuperate from trying to adjust to such an extraordinary level of stress.

    REMEMBER: The stages are the alarm reaction, the resistance stage, and the exhaustion stage.

6. **Diseases of adaptation** are illnesses promoted or caused by stressors. (see Physical Responses)

    REMEMBER: Diseases of adaptation are due to the body's efforts to adapt to stress.

7. **Burnout** is a gradually intensifying pattern of physical, psychological, and behavioral dysfunction in response to a continuous flow of stressors. (see Linkages: Stress and Psychological Disorders)

    Example: After years as an emergency room doctor, Coralette seems detached from her friends. She is increasingly irritable, depressed, and impulsive. Although Coralette has always been reliable, she now often oversleeps and misses the beginning of her shift.

8. **Posttraumatic stress disorder (PTSD)** is a pattern of adverse and disruptive reactions following a traumatic event. (see Linkages: Stress and Psychological Disorders)

    Example: After witnessing the murder of a close friend, Charles has recurring nightmares and trouble sleeping. Charles is uncharacteristically rude, nervous, and distracted at work.

    REMEMBER: It is characterized by anxiety, irritability, jumpiness, inability to concentrate or work productively, sexual dysfunction, emotional numbness, and difficulty getting along with others.

9. **Social support** refers to the network of friends and social contacts on whom one can depend for help in dealing with stressors. (see Social Support)

    Example: Ginetta and Tina are sisters and best friends. Whenever they have problems, they know they can count on each other or other family members to lend an ear or help in any way they can.

10. **Psychoneuroimmunology** is a field of research on the interaction of psychological, social, behavioral, neural, hormonal, and immune system processes that affect the body's defenses against disease. (see Stress, Illness, and the Immune System)

Example: Dr. Ramey is interested in understanding how the stress caused by a diagnosis of a chronic disease interacts with individual patients' coping strategies, and how those together influence the course of the disease.

11. **Immune system** is the body's first line of defense against invading substances and microorganisms. (see Stress, Illness, and the Immune System)

    Example: Mike has been exposed to a flu virus at school. His white blood cell (leukocytes) count increases as his body prepares to fight the virus.

12. **Health promotion** is the process of altering or eliminating behaviors that pose risks to health, as well as encouraging healthy behavior patterns. (see Promoting Healthy Behavior)

    Example: Kirk is trying to quit smoking. He is working with his doctor to identify options that will help him quit so that he won't have so many bouts of bronchitis next winter.

13. **Progressive muscle relaxation training** is a procedure for learning to relax that involves tensing muscles and then releasing tension in those muscles. (see Programs for Coping with Stress and Promoting Health)

FILL-IN-THE-BLANKS KEY TERMS

This section will help you check your factual knowledge of the key terms introduced in this chapter. Fill in each blank with the appropriate term from the list of key terms in the previous section.

1. The term for the stress reaction pattern that includes the alarm reaction is _____.

2. _____ work to understand the psychological and behavioral processes associated with achieving and maintaining health.

3. Illnesses caused, in part, by stressors are called _____.

4. _____ is the process of adapting to circumstances that threaten to disrupt one's physical or psychological functioning.

5. A person who is stressed to the point of not being able to function at work could be experiencing _____.

6. A coping method in which one seeks to reduce heart rate and blood pressure by training voluntary muscles to relax is called _____.

7. A _____ is the physical, psychological, or behavioral response that occurs in the face of a stressor.

8. Your group of friends or other social contacts whom can be relied upon to help during stressful situations are your _____.

9. The field that studies the interaction between psychological and physiological processes that affect the body's ability to defend itself against disease is _____.

10. _____ are situations or events that require adjustment.

11. After a devastating event, some people will experience a reaction characterized by lack of sleep, anxiety, irritability, and behavioral dysfunction called _____.

12. The process of altering or eliminating behaviors posing risks to health, as well as encouraging healthy behavior patterns, is called _____.

13. The _____ is the body's first line of defense against invading substances and microorganisms.

Total Correct (See answer key) _____

LEARNING OBJECTIVES

1. Define <u>health psychology</u>. List the objectives of health psychologists. (see introductory section; see also "Health Psychology")

2. Define <u>stress</u>, <u>stressors</u>, and <u>stress reactions</u>. Give examples of stressors. Be sure to include a *catastrophic event*, a *life change* or *strain*, a *chronic stressor*, an *acute stressor,* and a *daily hassle*. (see "Stress and Stressors")

3. Describe the Social Readjustment Rating Scale and the Life Experiences Survey. Explain how they are used to measure stress. (see Measuring Stressors)

4. Define <u>general adaptation syndrome</u>. Describe the three stages in this syndrome and discuss the physiological processes underlying it. Define <u>disease of adaptation</u>. (see "The General Adaptation Syndrome")

5. Discuss the major criticisms of Selye's model. (see "Psychological Responses")

6. Describe some common emotional, cognitive, and behavioral stress responses. Explain how *ruminative thinking*, *catastrophizing*, *mental sets*, and *functional fixedness* are linked to stress. (see "Psychological Responses")

7. Define <u>burnout</u> and <u>posttraumatic stress disorder</u>, and describe the conditions that can lead to both. (see "Linkages: Stress and Psychological Disorders")

8. Explain why the appraisal of stressors, their predictability, and a perception of control can reduce the impact of stressors. (see "How Stressors Are Appraised"; see also "Predictability and Control")

9. Discuss the role of coping resources and methods in combating stress. Give examples of *problem-focused* and *emotion-focused* coping strategies. (see "Coping Resources and Coping Methods")

10. Describe the effects of <u>social support</u> on the impact of stressful events. (see "Social Support")

11. Describe disease-resistant and disease-prone personalities. Define *dispositional optimism*. Discuss the quasi-experimental research on the relationship between personality and health. (see "Stress, Personality, and Gender"; see also "Focus on Research Methods: Personality and Health")

12. Define <u>psychoneuroimmunology</u>. (see "Stress, Illness, and the Immune System")

13. Describe the components of the immune system. Discuss the relationships among the immune system, the nervous system, the endocrine system, and stress. (see "Stress, Illness, and the Immune System")

14. Define hostility and outline the evidence relating hostility to heart disease. (see "Stress, Illness, and the Cardiovascular System"; see also "Thinking Critically: Does Hostility Increase the Risk of Heart Disease?")

15. List the health-endangering behaviors described in your textbook. (see "Risking Your Life: Health-Endangering Behaviors")

16. Define <u>health promotion</u>. Describe the four factors in Rosenstock's health-belief model. Explain the role of self-efficacy in altering behavioral health risks. (see "Promoting Healthy Behavior")

17. Describe the five stages in changing behavioral health risks. (see "Changing Health Behaviors: Stages of Readiness")

18. List the steps in a stress-coping program. Explain the importance of being able to recognize the difference between a changeable and a nonchangeable stressor. (see "Programs for Coping with Stress and Promoting Health")

19. Describe *cognitive coping strategies*. Define *cognitive restructuring*. (see "Developing Coping Strategies")

20. Describe some *emotional* and *behavioral coping strategies*. (see "Developing Coping Strategies")

21. Describe *physical coping strategies*. Explain the possible problems of using drugs to alter stress or stress responses. Explain how <u>progressive muscle relaxation training</u> can help people cope. (see "Developing Coping Strategies")

CONCEPTS AND EXERCISES

Recognizing Stressors

Following are several descriptions of people's daily lives. Underline all the stressors that you can find.

1. Maria and Juan have been married for ten years and have two children. This morning Maria got a run in her nylons just as she was on her way out the door to take the children to school. She was going to go up and change but remembered that she had to come back to the house anyway to pick up the dog for his veterinary appointment. When Maria did get back home, she started cleaning the house, only to find that the vacuum cleaner was broken. Sighing, she decided to scrub the bathrooms instead. By the time Juan came home, she had a headache from the children screaming, the dog whimpering, having to face dirty floors yet again, and struggling with dinner for the family.

2. Lee is trying to finish writing a grant proposal in the hopes of getting funding. The deadline for submitting the grant is in one week. Lee must also face a new crisis of some sort daily at work. His wife is starting to complain that he never spends time with her. Recently, he has started to have dizzy spells and can feel his heart pounding.

3. Jenny is five years old. Today is the first day of first grade. Jenny is horrified because she has to sit next to the neighborhood bully. He is always ramming his tricycle into hers or grabbing her swing on the playground and pushing it too high into the air. Jenny is spending the entire day imagining what he will do now that he sits next to her in class.

4. Akbar has just met his new roommate and cannot believe his bad luck. His roommate has told him that he goes to bed at 8:00 P.M., wants to study in the room every night until 7:45 P.M., must have complete quiet while he studies, and has some great posters of Bambi to hang on the walls. Akbar wants to do well in school; he was first in his high school class and wants to keep his ranking in college, but he is also worried about his social life.

Recognizing Stress Reactions

Following are several descriptions of stress reactions. Choose the name of the reaction from the list after the descriptions.

1. Boris's doctor has told him that he has an elevated level of corticosteroids. _____

2. Rosa's mother tells her that she constantly makes a mountain out of a molehill. _____

3. Lois, recently divorced, has been working three jobs for the past year to support her children. She is tired, irritable, and depressed. Her bosses are concerned because the quality of her work has gradually decreased. _____

4.   Nancy knows that her husband is drinking too much. His behavior bothers her so much that she has begun taking Valium daily. _____

   a.   Burnout

   b.   Physical coping strategy

   c.   Catastrophizing

   d.   Resistance stage of GAS

CRITICAL THINKING

Sam and Martina are at the gym working out. Pete, an ex-cop who retired from the force when he won the lottery, still works out with them. Pete was telling them stories about the people in his new, very expensive neighborhood.

Pete says, "So this lady down the street, her name is Rita, dies last week. A buddy of mine checked the pathologist's report; she had a massive heart attack. It's too bad. She was really nice. She was a high-priced lawyer, and her husband stayed home to take care of the kids. Now, he can afford to hire a new live-in nanny for each day of the week. I hear she was loaded and had a huge insurance policy. She had such a lousy life, though. Her husband, Jeff, treated her badly, even when he knew she had a heart condition."

Sam asks, "What do you mean, 'treated her badly'?"

"Well," Pete responds, "the team that cleans my house, Martha and Ed, also cleaned hers. Martha used to tell me all these stories about what Jeff used to do."

"Like what?" asks Martina.

"The usual stuff. He was having affairs. She knew because she would find women's things in the house. But Martha said he also did little things to drive her nuts all the time. For example, he would steal the papers out of her briefcase when he knew she had a big court case the next day. Martha said she heard him call her office one day, pretending to be drunk; he made up stories about how she mistreated the kids. He would ruin her favorite clothes or 'forget' to pick up her clothes from the dry cleaners. He actually called her up once and told her that one of the kids had died in an accident and then told her he was kidding. Martha said it had been going on for two years. The guy's a sicko."

Sam says, "Yeah, if she had to die, it's too bad he didn't kill her. We could have at least put him in jail."

Martina speaks up and says, "Maybe he did kill her."

Using the five critical thinking questions in your text, the clues in the story, and what you have just learned about stress, answer the following.

1.   What is Sam's hypothesis?

2.   What evidence supports Sam's hypothesis?

3.   What is Martina's alternative hypothesis?

4.   What evidence supports Martina's hypothesis?

PERSONAL LEARNING ACTIVITIES

1.   Visit the following website to learn more about the work of health psychologists: http://www.health-psych.org/AboutHowtoBecome.cfm. This is linked to the homepage for the division of the American Psychological Association devoted to Health Psychology. This particular

page tells you more about the work settings of, career opportunities for, and training required to become a health psychologist. What do you think the outlook is for careers in this field after reading this information?

2. Recall the last time you experienced the alarm reaction stage of the general adaptation syndrome. What was the cause? How did your body respond? How did you manage to calm yourself? Do you believe people are in control of "calming themselves" or that it just happens naturally as the stressor goes away?

3. Reflect over times in your life that have been particularly stressful for you. Did you notice that you seemed more susceptible to illness during those times? What are some coping strategies you could use, or work on developing, that might help buffer your immune system from the negative effects of stress the next time you have a stressful life event?

4. Take the coping skills test at the following website: http://discoveryhealth.queendom.com/coping_short_access.html. What does it tell you about your coping skills? Can you tell if the particular items on this short inventory are assessing different types of coping? Do some items seem more focused on cognitive or emotional responses, for example? What sorts of changes might you make if your coping skills seem to need improvement?

5. Describe some of your behaviors that are risks to your health. For example, do you smoke, overeat, or fail to exercise regularly? Have you tried to change any of these behaviors? If so, at which of the five stages of readiness are you for each behavior? For example, if you recently began walking two miles a day, four days a week, you are in the action stage of readiness. If it's a behavior that you want to change, but you are at the contemplation stage, perhaps you could try making specific plans and take the first step toward change (preparation stage). For some ideas on how to prepare for behavior change, visit the following website: http://www.valueoptions.com/spotlight_heart/html/pdfs/Articles/English/change_management/managing_change_preparing_to_change.pdf. Make sure you have a way to monitor your progress towards the goals you set as you enter the action stage.

MULTIPLE-CHOICE QUESTIONS

Quiz 1

1. Which of the following is true of stress measurement?
    a. Stressors always involve major life events.
    b. Major stressors have a greater impact than several minor stressors.
    c. Sometimes consistent daily hassles cause severe stress reactions.
    d. Only a combination of major and minor stressors causes a severe stress reaction.

2. Which of the following would NOT be considered a stressor?
    a. Taking a three-week vacation
    b. Planning a wedding reception for five hundred guests
    c. Being able to hear the neighbor's baby cry
    d. All of these are stressors.

3. The fight-flight reaction is part of the _____ stage of the GAS.
    a. resistance
    b. alarm
    c. exhaustion
    d. adaptation

4. Mario has been working two jobs for the past year and is taking a full load of classes. Mario is tired, irritable, and depressed. His bosses and teachers are concerned because the quality of his work has gradually decreased. Which of the following is Mario most likely experiencing?

   a. A behavioral stress response
   b. Burnout
   c. A disease of adaptation
   d. Posttraumatic stress disorder

5. Elenita is really worried about her grown child, who suffers from mental illness. She persistently thinks about him, frets incessantly, and pretty much chews on the same thoughts over and over, without working towards a solution. Elenita is engaged in

   a. catastrophizing.
   b. a mental set.
   c. functional fixedness.
   d. ruminative thinking.

6. Sally's dad just died. To cope, she and the rest of her family sit around at the dinner after the funeral and talk about her dad, share stories, and laugh and cry together. Even though it is still stressful, somehow things feel a little better. What stress mediator is helping to blunt the impact of Sally's loss?

   a. Social support
   b. Control
   c. Gender
   d. Dispositional optimism

7. Which of the following has been said of Selye's general adaptation syndrome?

   a. It underemphasizes the biological processes involved in stress response.
   b. It adequately explains the contribution of psychological factors in reactions to stress.
   c. It overemphasizes the contribution of psychological factors in the determination of stress responses.
   d. It underemphasizes the psychological processes involved in stress responses.

8. Melissa and Randy both have mountains of work on their desks. Melissa rolls up her sleeves in eager anticipation. She knows the project in front of her will earn her a promotion. Randy cringes every time he walks into his office and surveys the mess. He can think only of how long it is going to take him to finish. Which of them will experience the most stress?

   a. Melissa, because she is worried about getting promoted
   b. Randy, because he interprets the work as a stressor
   c. Melissa, because women are more prone to stress than men
   d. Randy and Melissa will both experience an equally large amount of stress.

9. Julie is feeling stress while completing a midterm exam. According to your text, which of the following would most likely reduce the amount of stress Julie is feeling?

   a. The teacher said the test would be true-false questions, but it is essay format.
   b. She thinks she is going to flunk the test.
   c. She knew that the test would be hard.
   d. She doesn't know anyone else in the class.

10. Wing knew he had to quit smoking because his breathing was painful and labored after climbing just a few stairs. Also, he had watched his favorite uncle suffer through lung cancer and die a horrible death. Wing knew that if he quit soon, many of the problems in his respiratory system would likely reverse themselves. Finally, he knew that the benefits of quitting would outweigh the discomfort. What did Wing still lack that would probably prevent him from trying to quit?

    a. Sufficient physical suffering and problems
    b. A belief that he could quit
    c. Fear of consequences
    d. Specific rewards for quitting

11. B-cells, T-cells, and natural killer cells are all examples of

    a. macrophages.
    b. leukocytes.
    c. antibodies.
    d. phagocytoses.

12. Hostility is characterized by

    a. patience.
    b. low levels of aggression.
    c. distrust of others.
    d. very few emotional stress reactions.

13. Which scale measures the amount of stress one experiences in terms of Life Change Units?

    a. Stages of Readiness Questionnaire
    b. Life Experiences Survey
    c. Social Readjustment Rating Scale
    d. Coping Styles Inventory

14. Eduardo is learning a coping technique. His instructor has told him to alternate between tensing and relaxing his muscles. Which method is he learning?

    a. Cognitive restructuring
    b. A behavioral coping method
    c. Progressive muscle relaxation training
    d. Stress reaction restructuring

15. The longitudinal quasi-experiment on the relationship between personality and health showed that participants who

    a. were impulsive were more likely to die from accidents.
    b. acted conscientiously were more likely to die of heart disease.
    c. ate more healthily were more likely to get divorced.
    d. stayed married were more likely to die young.

16. Brian and Sue are both encountering the exact same stressor—they are being laid off from their high paying jobs in a terrible economy. According to research on gender and stress mediators, Brian is likely to _____ and Sue is likely to _____.

    a.   engage in a fight-or-flight response pattern; engage in a fight-or-flight response pattern
    b.   engage in a tend-and-befriend response pattern; engage in a tend-and-befriend response pattern
    c.   engage in a fight-or-flight response pattern; engage in a tend-and-befriend response pattern
    d.   engage in a tend-and-befriend response pattern; engage in a fight-or-flight response pattern

17. Gary has developed a program to help people alter their diets and achieve healthier weights. Gary is engaged in what area related to health psychology.

    a.   Behavioral medicine
    b.   Health promotion
    c.   Progressive muscle relaxation training
    d.   All of these

18. A good stress-management program includes

    a.   systematic stress assessment.
    b.   goal setting.
    c.   effective plans for coping with stressors.
    d.   All of these

19. Cognitive restructuring is a(n)

    a.   emotional reaction to stress.
    b.   attempt to change stress-producing thought patterns.
    c.   plan to restructure the use of one's time.
    d.   process of systematic relaxation.

20. Which is better—problem-focused or emotion-focused coping?

    a.   It depends on the type of stressor. Changeable stressors tend to match better to emotion-focused coping and unchangeable ones to problem-focused.
    b.   It depends on the type of stressor. Changeable stressors tend to match better to problem-focused coping and unchangeable ones to emotion-focused.
    c.   Problem-focused is always better.
    d.   Emotion-focused is always better.

Total Correct (See answer key) _____

Quiz 2

Use this quiz to reassess your learning after taking Quiz 1 and reviewing the chapter.

1. Behavioral medicine is

    a.   an interdisciplinary field in which psychologists, doctors, nurses, and others pursue health-related goals.
    b.   the study of the interaction of psychological and physiological influences on defending against disease.
    c.   a field devoted to understanding psychological influences on health.
    d.   None of these

2. Glenda feels that she has had a rotten day. She got a run in her stocking before she left the house, slammed her finger in the car door, forgot to buy cat litter at the grocery store, and just missed a phone call from her boyfriend. Based on this information, what would her score on the Life Experiences Survey be?

    a. Low
    b. Moderate
    c. High
    d. Can't tell from this information.

3. When Caitlin did poorly on a midterm exam, she berated herself, saying, "You'll never do well. How did you ever get into this school? You'll probably flunk out because you're so stupid! Then you'll probably never be able to get a job." This is an example of

    a. cognitive restructuring.
    b. catastrophizing.
    c. trauma.
    d. fight-or-flight.

4. It is 2:00 A.M. and Aaron is lost in New York City with no money. His sympathetic nervous system has initiated the fight-flight reaction. What stage of the general adaptation syndrome (GAS) is he in?

    a. Alarm
    b. Resistance
    c. Exhaustion
    d. The fight-flight reaction is not part of the GAS.

5. Corticosteroids, which are released from the adrenal cortex,

    a. indirectly decrease the chance of developing arthritis.
    b. decrease the responsiveness of the immune system.
    c. increase the responsiveness of the immune system.
    d. reduce activation of the sympathetic nervous system.

6. Shane, a veteran, occasionally has flashbacks that are recollections of his experiences in Vietnam. This is a symptom of

    a. generalized anxiety disorder.
    b. posttraumatic stress disorder.
    c. the general adaptation syndrome.
    d. the fight-or-flightreaction.

7. Jaquan has arthritis and high blood pressure. Jaquan is experiencing

    a. the alarm reaction stage of the GAS.
    b. the exhaustion stage of GAS.
    c. diseases of adaptation.
    d. both the exhaustion stage of GAS and diseases of adaptation.

8. When Dr. Crusher went to the computer to explore ideas about the causes of an epidemic, she suddenly could not think. She stared at the computer screen, unable to formulate any ideas or even remember information about the illness. Dr. Crusher is experiencing a(n) _____ stress response.

    a. behavioral
    b. cognitive
    c. emotional
    d. problem-focused

9. Which of the following could reduce the impact of a stressor?

    a. Interpreting it as a threat
    b. Having a social support network
    c. Feeling an inability to control it
    d. All of these

10. Behavioral stress responses include

    a. a change in facial expression.
    b. feeling nervous.
    c. ruminative thinking.
    d. sweating.

11. Which of the following would cause the least stress?

    a. Pop quizzes scheduled by the teacher
    b. Quizzes prescheduled by the students' unanimous vote
    c. Quizzes given every Friday
    d. One quiz per month at an unannounced time

12. The head of human resources knows that the employees have very stressful jobs. One Friday afternoon each month he invites several employees who do not know one another to have lunch and spend the afternoon together. He has

    a. engaged his employees in cognitive restructuring.
    b. set up a social support network for his employees.
    c. provided his employees with a sense of control over their stress.
    d. All of these

13. _____ is the field that examines the interaction of psychological and physiological processes that affect the body's ability to defend itself against disease.

    a. Neurology
    b. Psychobiology
    c. Immunology
    d. Psychoneuroimmunology

14. John hasn't declared his major yet and feels that he has no time to think about it because he is overwhelmed by the workload of his general education courses. To cope with the stress and uncertainty, he begins a diary in which he writes quick notes about events, stress, and his reactions. John will probably _____ as a result of his _____.

   a.   improve his immune system functioning; disclosure
   b.   improve his immune system functioning; behavioral stress response
   c.   have no effect on his immune system; cognitive stress response
   d.   have no effect on his immune system; physical coping strategy

15. According to Rosenstock's health-belief model, which of the following would help Birgit quit smoking?

   a.   Perceiving a personal threat from her smoking behavior
   b.   Realizing that smoking can cause lung cancer
   c.   Believing that if she quits, she won't get lung cancer
   d.   All of these

16. Assume you are reading a science fiction story in which minds are able to visit the government biological bank and select body shells they wish to inhabit, along with physiological system packages. But government leaders have recently decided that budget cuts are necessary and funding for these packages will have to be reduced. If the immune system package is to be downsized, what part of it should *not* be eliminated?

   a.   Corticosteroids
   b.   Catecholamines
   c.   Leukocytes
   d.   The GAS

17. Carrie is a hard-working lawyer. She worries that her busy lifestyle might put her at risk for coronary heart disease. She is *most* at risk if she is also a(n) _____ person.

   a.   organized
   b.   hostile
   c.   competitive
   d.   assertive

18. Amanda loves chocolate chip cookies. She knows they aren't healthy foods and often thinks about limiting her intake of them or giving them up. However, Amanda has made no plans to change how often she eats them. Amanda is at the _____ stage of readiness.

   a.   precontemplation
   b.   contemplation
   c.   preparation
   d.   maintenance

19. Which of the following is a physical coping method?

   a.   Talking with your friends about the stressors you're encountering
   b.   Deciding to think that a stressor is a challenge rather than a threat
   c.   Progressive muscle relaxation training
   d.   Working on time management

20. Dink is away from his wife and kids for an extended training in a distant city. To cope with his loneliness, Dink goes out drinking every night. Dink is using a(n) _____ coping strategy.
    a. cognitive
    b. emotional
    c. physical
    d. behavioral

Total Correct (See answer key) _____

ANSWERS TO FILL-IN-THE-BLANKS KEY TERMS

1. general adaptation syndrome (see Physical Responses)
2. Health psychologists (Health care psychologists) (see introductory section)
3. diseases of adaptation (see Physical Responses)
4. Stress (see Understanding Stress and Stressors)
5. burnout (see Linkages: Stress and Psychological Disorders)
6. progressive muscle relaxation training (see Programs for Coping with Stress and Promoting Health)
7. stress reaction (see Understanding Stress and Stressors)
8. social support (see Social Support)
9. psychoneuroimmunology (see Stress, Illness, and the Immune System)
10. Stressors (see Understanding Stress and Stressors)
11. posttraumatic stress disorder (see Linkages: Stress and Psychological Disorders)
12. health promotion (see Promoting Healthy Behavior)
13. immune system (see Stress, Illness, and the Immune System)

ANSWERS TO CONCEPTS AND EXERCISES

Recognizing Stressors

1. Got a run in her nylons, picking up dog for his veterinary appointment, vacuum cleaner broken, children screaming, dog whimpering, dirty floors, struggling with dinner
2. Deadline, new crisis, wife starting to complain
3. First day of first grade, sit next to the neighborhood bully, ramming his tricycle into hers, grabbing her swing, pushing it too high, and imagining what he will do
4. New roommate, roommate goes to bed at 8 P.M., roommate wants to study in the room every night until 7:45 P.M., roommate must have complete quiet, roommate has some great posters of Bambi, wants to keep his ranking in college, worried about his social life.

Recognizing Stress Reactions

1. *Resistance stage of GAS.* Elevated levels of corticosteroids are associated with the resistance stage of the GAS. During this stage, a person may be unaware of the wear and tear his or her body is experiencing. (see Physical Responses)

2. *Catastrophizing*. A person who makes a mountain out of a molehill is overemphasizing the negative consequences of an event. (see Psychological Responses)

3. *Burnout*. The stress caused by a divorce and working three jobs has led to burnout for Lois. Burnout causes people to become less reliable workers and to become withdrawn, depressed, or accident-prone. (see Linkages: Stress and Psychological Disorders)

4. *Physical coping strategy*. Nancy is not making a logical response to her distress over her husband's use of a drug. Use of a drug is a physical coping strategy, but it can have extremely negative consequences. A person may become addicted to the drug and be unable to use other methods of coping. (see Programs for Coping with Stress and Promoting Health)

ANSWERS TO CRITICAL THINKING

1. Sam's hypothesis is that Rita died of a naturally occurring heart attack.

2. Sam is using the pathologist's report as evidence to support his hypothesis.

3. Martina hypothesizes that the husband, knowing his wife had a bad heart, behaved in ways that would expose her to very consistent and sometimes high levels of stress. Martina may think Jeff wants the insurance money all to himself.

4. Martina knows that ongoing little daily hassles can be just as stressful as major catastrophes. She also knows that consistent stress can lead to diseases of adaptation. The stress induced by Rita's husband may have caused her health to deteriorate to the point of her having a heart attack. (*NOTE:* Critical thinking is a constant process of hypothesizing, examining evidence, rehypothesizing, and collecting more evidence. Martina may not be correct.)

ANSWERS TO MULTIPLE-CHOICE QUESTIONS

Circle the question numbers you answered correctly.

Quiz 1

1. c is the answer. Often minor daily hassles have a larger impact than one or two major stressors. (see Psychological Stressors)

    a. Major life events, either positive or negative, are stressful, but small daily hassles are also stressful.

    b. Sometimes the cumulative effect of small but consistent stressors is larger than the effect of one or two major stressors.

    d. Even minor stressors alone can add up to major stress reactions.

2. d is the answer. Positive life events (marriage), any type of change (vacation), and consistent daily hassles (listening to a baby cry) are all stressors. (see Psychological Stressors)

3. b is the answer. (see Physical Responses)

    a. Resistance is the second stage of the general adaptation syndrome.

    c. Exhaustion is the third stage of the general adaptation syndrome.

    d. There is no such thing as the adaptation stage.

4. b is the answer. Burnout is a response to chronic stress in which a person becomes more and more irritable, indifferent, and unreliable. (see Linkages: Stress and Psychological Disorders)

a.   Behavioral stress responses are changes in the way people look, act, or talk. Aggression, dropping out of school, and strained facial expressions are examples. Mario is experiencing burnout, which is a pattern of physical, psychological, and behavioral stress responses.

c.   A disease of adaptation is an illness that occurs in the exhaustion stage of the general adaptation syndrome.

d.   Posttraumatic stress disorder is also a combination of physical, psychological, and behavioral stress responses, but it happens after a catastrophic event.

5.   d is the answer. Ruminative thinking involves recurring intrusion of thoughts about stressful events. Elenita keeps thinking about her son's mental illness. (see Psychological Responses)

a.   Catastrophizing is dwelling on and overemphasizing the consequences of negative events. Elenita is not described as magnifying any consequences.

b.   Mental sets involve using the same, though not the best, approaches to problem solving.

c.   Functional fixedness is the inability to think of novel uses for objects.

6.   a is the answer. Talking about how you feel and what you are going through is seeking social support. (see Social Support)

b.   Control is a stress mediator, but it involves feeling like you can control the stressor. Sally has no control over the fact that her dad is dead, and she doesn't appear to be trying to control anything in particular in this question.

c.   Gender is a stress mediator in that women are more likely to engage in a tend-and-befriend pattern of response to stress, and men tend to respond with fight or flight. Although Sally is engaged in social support, the question doesn't indicate that this is because she is female—it is just part of the funeral structure.

d.   Dispositional optimism is a personality characteristic. No description of Sally's personality is mentioned in this question.

7.   d is the answer. (see Physical Responses)

a.   Selye has been criticized for overemphasizing the role of biological factors in the determination of stress responses.

b, c.   People have commented that Selye did not focus on the role of psychological factors in the determination of stress responses.

8.   b is the answer. The way that people interpret their stress affects the impact of their stressors. Randy is interpreting his work as a stressor instead of as an opportunity. Melissa is thinking of her work as a vehicle for furthering her career. (see How Stressors Are Perceived)

a.   Melissa sees her workload in a positive way, so she will not experience as much stress.

c.   Women are no more prone to stress than men are.

d.   Randy will experience more stress than Melissa.

9.   c is the answer. If Julie knows the test will be hard, then she should be better able to deal with it. According to your text, stressors that are predictable have less impact than those that are unpredictable. (see Predictability and Control)

a.   If Julie is surprised by the format of the test, she will most likely experience more stress.

b.   If Julie believes she will fail the test, she may feel more stress.

    d.   If Julie doesn't know anyone in the class, she may receive less social support at the time of the test.

10.   b is the answer. People are unlikely to try to quit smoking unless they have a sense of self-efficacy, the belief that they can quit. (see Health Beliefs and Health Behaviors)

    a, c, d.   All of these are addressed in the question and can be matched to factors identified by Rosenstock. However, Wing will need to believe he can succeed before he will try to quit.

11.   b is the answer. Leukocytes are white blood cells and there are various types of them. B-cells, T-cells, and natural killer cells are all types of leukocytes. (see Stress, Illness, and the Immune System)

    a.   Macrophages are another type of immune system cell that engulf foreign cells and digest them.

    c.   Antibodies are produced by B-cells and T-cells.

    d.   There is no such thing as phagocytoses. You may be thinking of phagocytosis, which is the process by which macrophages "eat" other cells that are dangerous to one's health.

12.   c is the answer. People who exhibit hostility are suspicious, resentful, antagonistic, and distrustful of others. Hostility is a risk factor in heart disease. (see Thinking Critically: Does Hostility Increase the Risk of Heart Disease?)

    a, b.   People with hostility are unlikely to be patient and nonaggressive.

    d.   People who exhibit hostility are frequently angry.

13.   c is the answer. The Social Readjustment Rating Scale measures stress in terms of the Life Change Units a stressor requires. (see Measuring Stressors)

    a, d.   These are not scales that are mentioned in this chapter.

    b.   The Life Experiences Survey focuses not merely on the amount of change a stressor requires, but also on the appraisal of that stressor.

14.   c is the answer. Progressive muscle relaxation training is a physiological coping method in which people learn to completely relax their muscles, thus reducing heart rate and blood pressure. To learn this technique, people are told to alternately tense and relax their muscles in order to better recognize the feelings of relaxation. (see Programs for Coping with Stress and Promoting Health)

    a.   Cognitive restructuring involves replacing catastrophic thoughts with constructive thoughts.

    b.   Behavioral coping methods might involve taking a time-management course. Progressive muscle relaxation training is a physiological coping method.

    d.   There is no such method as stress reaction restructuring.

15.   a is the answer. People who were impulsive or low on conscientiousness were more likely to die from accidents or violence. (see Focus on Research Methods: Personality and Health)

    b.   In this study, those who were conscientious were more likely to stay married, eat healthily, and live longer. The study did not find that conscientious people were more likely to die from heart disease.

    b.   The study did not find that those who ate more healthily were more likely to get divorced.

    d.   The study did not find that those who stayed married were more likely to die young.

16. c is the answer. Men tend to engage in fight-or-flight responses involving anger and avoidance processes. Women tend to engage in tend-and-befriend response patterns that utilize social support networks. (see Stress, Personality, and Gender)

    a.   Brian would be likely to do this, but Sue as a female would not.

    b.   Sue would be likely to do this, but Brian as a male would not.

    d.   This is reversed—women are more likely to tend and befriend and men to fight or flee.

17. b is the answer. Gary is trying to help reduce behaviors that pose a health risk by helping people avoid obesity. Health promotion focuses on preventing, reducing, and eliminating behaviors that pose health risks, and increasing healthy behaviors. (see Promoting Healthy Behavior)

    a.   Behavioral medicine involves working with physicians, nurses, and public health workers. Gary is not described as doing so here.

    c.   Progressive muscle relaxation training is a physical coping strategy. It might be part of a health promotion initiative, but it is not described here.

    d.   b is the correct answer.

18. d is the answer. An effective stress-management program includes a systematic stress assessment. You have to know what the problem is before you can solve it. Setting goals helps you decide whether to eliminate the stressor or attempt to reduce the impact of that stressor. Finally, an effective plan must be made in order to deal with the stressors you face. (see Programs for Coping with Stress and Promoting Health)

19. b is the answer. Cognitive restructuring involves substituting constructive thoughts for stressful, destructive thoughts. (see Programs for Coping with Stress and Promoting Health)

    a.   Emotional stress reactions include frustration, anger, and depression.

    c.   Time management is important in reducing the stress caused by a tight schedule, but this coping method is behavioral, not cognitive.

    d.   Progressive muscle relaxation is the physiological coping method in which people are taught to completely relax their bodies.

20. b is the answer. Problem-focused coping tends to match well with stressors that can be changed, because these directly attack and change the source of stress. These do not work well with unchangeable stressors, because they only lead to frustration. Emotion-focused coping works better with unchangeable stressors. (see Coping Resources and Coping Methods)

    a.   This is reversed from what it should be.

    c.   Problem-focused coping is not always better, particularly if the stressor is an unchangeable one.

    d.   Emotion-focused coping is not always better, particularly if the stressor is something that you could alter or eliminate with problem-focused methods.

Now turn to the quiz analysis table at the end of this chapter to find which areas you know well and which areas you need to work on. Circle the numbers in the table for items on Quiz 1 that you answered correctly.

Quiz 2

1.   a is the answer. This is the definition of behavioral medicine. Physicians, psychologists, and others work together in this field to pursue health-related goals. (see Health Psychology)

b.   This is the definition of psychoneuroimmunology.

c.   This is the definition of health psychology, which is part of the field of behavioral medicine.

d.   a is the correct answer.

2.   d is the answer. The Life Experiences Survey measures not just what life events have occurred but also people's perceptions of how positive or negative those events are. This description tells us nothing about how Glenda perceives these events, so we don't know how she would score. Even though she has experienced only daily hassles (rather than huge events), if she appraises them as very negative she could still score high on the measure. (see Measuring Stressors)

a, b, c.   We can't tell how Glenda would score, because we are given no information about how she appraises the stressors she's encountered.

3.   b is the answer. Catastrophizing is an overemphasis of the negative consequences of an event. Although Caitlin has done poorly on only one test, she has inflated the negative consequences of that event until she thinks she will never amount to anything. (see Psychological Responses)

a.   Cognitive restructuring is a cognitive coping method. Positive, constructive thoughts are substituted for negative, destructive thoughts.

c.   Trauma is a major and shocking physical or emotional experience. Doing poorly on one test is not.

d.   Fight-or-flight is a term associated with the alarm reaction of the GAS.

4.   a is the answer. The fight-flight reaction is associated with the alarm reaction of the general adaptation syndrome. (see Physical Responses)

b, c.   The resistance and exhaustion stages of the GAS are not associated with the fight-or-flight syndrome.

d.   The fight-flight reaction is part of the alarm reaction of the general adaptation syndrome.

5.   b is the answer. High levels of corticosteroids are associated with decreased immune system functioning. (see Stress, Illness, and the Immune System)

a, c.   Corticosteroids suppress the functioning of the immune system, thereby promoting illnesses like heart disease, high blood pressure, and arthritis.

d.   When the sympathetic nervous system is activated, it causes surges of corticosteroids and catecholamines. Corticosteroids do not reduce the activation of the sympathetic nervous system.

6.   b is the answer. Posttraumatic stress disorder is a pattern of adverse and disruptive reactions following a traumatic event. In rare cases, flashbacks occur. (see Linkages: Stress and Psychological Disorders)

a.   Generalized anxiety disorder occurs when a person experiences constant emotional arousal with no identifiable cause.

c.   The general adaptation syndrome is a series of physiological adaptations to stress.

d.   The fight-or-flight syndrome is caused by an increase in adrenaline in response to a stressor. It prepares the body to either fight or flee.

7.   d is the answer. Jaquan's arthritis and high blood pressure are diseases of adaptation, according to the GAS. He is in the exhaustion stage. (see Physical Responses)

    a.   The alarm reaction stage is characterized by the fight-or-flight response.

    b.   Jaquan is experiencing the exhaustion phase, which is marked by the diseases of adaptation he has.

    c.   Jaquan has diseases of adaptation, which indicate he is in the exhaustion stage.

8.   b is the answer. (see Psychological Responses)

    a.   Behavioral stress responses are changes in appearance, such as shakiness or aggressive actions.

    c.   Emotional stress responses are changes in emotional state, such as fear, anger, irritability, and so on.

    d.   You may have been thinking of problem-focused coping; it is not a stress response, but it is an emphasis on changing or getting rid of a stressor.

9.   b is the answer. The existence of a social support network can reduce the impact of a stressor. (see Social Support)

    a.   Perceiving a stressor as a threat increases the negative impact of a stressor.

    c.   People who believe that they have the ability to control stressors generally experience less stress, even if they cannot control the stressor.

    d.   Only b is the answer.

10.   a is the answer. Facial expressions, shaking hands, and stuttering are examples of behavioral stress responses. (see Psychological Responses)

    b.   Feeling nervous is an emotional stress response.

    c.   Ruminative thinking is a cognitive stress response.

    d.   Sweating is a physical stress response.

11.   b is the answer. When one can predict and control the presence of a stressor, the impact of that stressor is usually reduced. To students, being able to control and predict the occurrence of a quiz will be much less stressful than any of the other alternatives. (see Predictability and Control)

    a.   Pop quizzes are not predictable and are therefore more stressful.

    c.   Even though quizzes given every Friday are predictable, students have no control over the scheduling of such quizzes.

    d.   One unannounced quiz per month is neither predictable nor controllable.

12.   b is the answer. By arranging for employees to get together and socialize, the human resources manager has created the potential for a social support network at work. (see Social Support)

    a.   Cognitive restructuring involves substituting constructive thoughts for negative, debilitating thoughts.

    c.   The head of human resources has not been able to give employees a sense of control over the stressful events at work. But he has provided employees with the beginnings of a social support network.

    d.   b is the answer.

13.   d is the answer. Psychoneuroimmunology is the study of the interaction of psychological and physiological processes that affect the body's ability to defend itself against disease. (see Stress, Illness, and the Immune System)

    a.   Neurology is the study of the nervous system.

    b.   Psychobiology is the study of the biological factors that underlie mental processes and behavior.

    c.   Immunology is the study of the physiological processes that affect the body's ability to defend itself against disease.

14.   a is the answer. Disclosure, even anonymously, has been shown to improve immune system functioning. (see Social Support)

    b.   John is expressing pent-up thoughts and feelings, which is disclosure. A behavioral stress response is a reaction like aggression, alcohol abuse, or avoidance of the stressful situation.

    c, d.   John is disclosing and it is likely to have a positive effect on his immune system.

15.   d is the answer. (see Health Beliefs and Health Behaviors)

16.   c is the answer. Leukocytes are an important component of the immune system; they serve as the body's defense system against foreign toxins. (see Stress, Illness, and the Immune System)

    a.   Corticosteroids are hormones released by the adrenal gland in reaction to persistent stress. This is not part of the immune system.

    b.   Catecholamines are hormones released by the adrenal gland when the sympathetic nervous system is activated in initial reactions to stress. This is not part of the immune system.

    d.   The GAS is a sequence of physical responses to stress. It is not part of the immune system.

17.   b is the answer. A link has been identified between hostility and risk for heart disease and heart attack. (see Thinking Critically: Does Hostility Increase the Risk of Heart Disease?)

    a, c, d.   All of these may be features of a person with a busy lifestyle, but none has been definitely linked with coronary heart disease.

18.   b is the answer. Being aware of a problem behavior and thinking of changing are part of the contemplation stage of readiness. (see Changing Health Behaviors: Stages of Readiness)

    a.   Precontemplation is the stage when a person does not perceive a problem and isn't considering change.

    c.   Preparation involves making plans.

    d.   Maintenance occurs after a person has successfully made a behavior change and kept it up for more than a few months.

19.   c is the answer. Physical coping methods involve attempting to directly alter physical responses before, during, or after stressors occur. (see Programs for Coping with Stress and Promoting Health)

    a.   This is an emotional coping method.

    b.   This is a cognitive coping method.

    d.   This is a behavioral coping method.

20.   c is the answer. Physical coping strategies change the body's response to stress, including loneliness, through drugs, exercise, meditation, and other means. Dink's use of alcohol to cope with is stress is a physical strategy. (see Programs for Coping with Stress and Promoting Health)

    a.   A cognitive coping method involves changing unconstructive thoughts to constructive ones.

b.   Emotional coping methods focus on buffering the ill effects of stressors.

d.   Behavioral coping strategies change actions in ways that minimize the impact of the stressors. Dink is going out drinking, which does not make the loneliness less; it just makes him less aware of it. It is a physical strategy, not a behavioral one. A behavioral one might involve seeking social support, which would actually affect his loneliness more directly.

Now turn to the quiz analysis table at the end of this chapter to find which areas you know well and which areas you need to work on. Circle the numbers in the table for items on Quiz 2 that you answered correctly.

For each question you answered correctly, circle its number. (Quiz 1 numbers are not shaded; Quiz 2 numbers are shaded.) Are there patterns in the types of questions or the topics you got wrong that could direct your further study? Did you improve from Quiz 1 to Quiz 2?

QUIZ REVIEW

Topic	Type of Question		
	Definition	Comprehension	Application
Health Psychology			
	1		
Understanding Stress and Stressors			
Psychological Stressors		1	2
Measuring Stressors		13	
			2
Stress Responses			
Physical Responses	3	7	
			4, 7
Psychological Responses			5
	10		3, 8
Linkages: Stress and Psychological Disorders			4
			6
Stress Mediators			
How Stressors Are Perceived			8
Predictability and Control			9
			11
Coping Resources and Coping Methods		20	
Social Support			6
		9	12, 14
Stress, Personality, and Gender			16
Focus on Research Methods: Personality and Health		15	
The Physiology and Psychology of Health and Illness			
Stress, Illness, and the Immune System	11		
	13	5	16
Thinking Critically: Does Hostility Increase the Risk of Heart Disease?	12		
			17
Promoting Healthy Behavior			17
Health Beliefs and Health Behaviors			10
			15
Changing Health Behaviors: Stages of Readiness			
			18
Programs for Coping with Stress and Promoting Health	19	18	14
			19, 20

Total correct by quiz:

Quiz 1:
Quiz 2:

CHAPTER 14

Personality

Personality is the unique pattern of enduring thoughts, feeling, and actions. Personality research focuses on the origins or causes of similarities and differences among people in their patterns of thinking, emotion, and behavior.

OUTLINE

I. THE PSYCHODYNAMIC APPROACH
    The psychodynamic approach, developed by Freud, emphasizes the interplay of unconscious psychological processes in determining human thought, feelings, and behavior.

    A. The Structure and Development of Personality
        According to Freud, personality develops out of each person's struggle to satisfy needs for food, water, sex, and aggression. Personality is reflected in how each person goes about satisfying these needs.

        1. *Id, Ego, and Superego*. Personality is composed of three structures: the id, the ego, and the superego. The id, which operates according to the pleasure principle, contains the life instincts, called *Eros*, and death instincts, called *Thanatos*. Libido, or *psychic energy*, is a product of the life instincts. The ego, which operates according to the reality principle, attempts to satisfy id impulses while obeying society's rules. As we *internalize* parents' and society's rules, the superego forms to tell us right from wrong.
        2. *Conflicts and Defenses*. The clashes among the three elements of the personality are called *psychodynamic conflicts,* or *intrapsychic conflicts*. The ego uses defense mechanisms to protect the individual from feeling anxious about id impulses.
        3. *Stages in Personality Development*. Freud believed in psychosexual development involving five stages. In each stage, a part of the body becomes the child's main source of pleasure. Failure to resolve conflicts at any stage can cause *fixation*, an unconscious preoccupation with the pleasure area associated with that stage. Personality characteristics are a reflection of each person's fixation(s).
            a. The oral stage occurs during the first year of life because the mouth is the center of pleasure. Early or late weaning can cause oral fixation.

            b. The anal stage occurs during the second year when toilet training begins. The ego evolves during this stage as the child vacillates between id impulses (defecation at will) and parental demands (only on the toilet).

            c. The phallic stage emerges at age three and lasts until age five. The boy experiences the Oedipal complex; he sexually desires his mother and wants to eliminate his father out of jealousy. To deal with this, he identifies with his father, and the superego develops out of this identification. In contrast, the girl begins this stage identifying with her mother, but develops *penis envy* and transfers her love to her father. To avoid maternal disapproval, she then returns to identify with and imitate her mother. This process is known as the Electra complex.

    d.   After age five, the <u>latency period</u> ensues, during which sexual impulses lie dormant, allowing the child to focus on social skills and education.

    e.   During the <u>genital stage</u>, which begins at adolescence and lasts until death, sexual desires reappear. The quality of relationships in this adult stage depends on how conflicts were resolved at earlier stages.

  B.   Variations on Freud's Personality Theory

Freud's ideas were very controversial, particularly his ideas about infant sexuality. *Neo-Freudian* followers maintained his basic ideas but developed their own approaches. Others shifted focus from the id to the ego, becoming known as *ego psychologists.*

    1.   *Jung's Analytic Psychology.* Jung viewed the libido as a general life force that included a productive blending of basic impulses and real-world demands of creativity and growth-oriented resolution of conflicts. Personality develops as the person tends toward *introversion* or *extraversion* and toward reliance on specific psychological functions (such as thinking versus feeling or vice versa). He also argued for a *collective unconscious* which served as a memory inherited from ancestors and motivated the innate tendencies we see in people.

    2.   *Other Neo-Freudian Theorists.* Several neo-Freudians, including Alfred Adler, Erik Erikson, Erich Fromm, and Henry Stack Sullivan, proposed that personality was determined by how social needs were met. Karen Horney was the first feminist personality theorist. She proposed that the inferiority that women may feel is caused by restrictions imposed by men, not penis envy, and that it is actually men who feel inferior when they experience *womb envy*. She argued for cultural factors' role in personality development over instinct.

  C.   Contemporary Psychodynamic Theories

Object relations theorists believe that the early relationships between infants and significant objects (such as primary caregivers) shape personality. Others focus more on the attachment process. *Attachment theory* sees the ideal pattern of development as starting with a close attachment to a mother figure, and then gradually gaining independence leading to a *secure attachment*. Other attachments may be *insecure*, leading to more anxiety and emotional difficulty.

  D.   Evaluating the Psychodynamic Approach

    1.   Freud developed one of the most influential personality theories ever proposed; his ideas shaped Western thinking from medicine to religion. Psychodynamic therapies introduced the use of personality assessments, including projective personality tests. Freud's ideas about defense mechanisms have also received some support from research on cognition.

    2.   Freud's theory is criticized for being based on an unrepresentative sample: his own patients, who were predominantly upper-class Viennese women with mental problems. Freud never examined patients from, or his theory with regard to, other cultures.

    3.   Freudian scholars acknowledge that Freud may have modified reports of therapy to fit his theory and that he may have asked leading questions during therapy. The theory also lacks scientific precision that would allow clear testing of his constructs. Finally, his belief that humans are driven mainly by instincts and the unconscious ignores the role of conscious drives and learning as important behavior determinants.

II.   THE TRAIT APPROACH

The trait approach has three basic assumptions: personality traits are relatively stable and therefore predictable; personality traits are consistent in diverse situations; and each person has a different set or degree of particular traits. The <u>trait approach</u> views personality as the combination of stable internal characteristics that people display consistently across time and across situations.

Traits vs. Types. Hippocrates suggested that a temperament, or personality type, is associated with a bodily fluid: blood, phlegm, black bile, or yellow bile. Other type theories have been proposed. Type theories focus on qualitative differences while trait theories focus on quantitative differences between individuals. Research has generally shown that personalities are much too varied to fit into type theories, although they have gained some acceptance.

A.   Allport's Trait Theory
Gordon Allport believed that there are usually about seven basic or *central traits*. *Secondary traits* are more specific to certain situations and have less control over behavior. His emphasis on the uniqueness of personality to individuals made it difficult to draw general conclusions about the structure of personality.

B.   The Five Factor Personality Model
More recently, trait theorists have focused on identifying a more universal underlying structure of personality through the use of *factor analysis*. Using this technique, Cattell identified 16 personality factors measured in the *Sixteen Personality Factor Questionnaire*. More recent research by Costa and McCrae identified five cross-cultural factors, known as the five factor personality model (or Big-Five model)—*Openness to Experience, Conscientiousness, Extraversion, Agreeableness*, and *Neuroticism*—that make up personality. The Big-Five model is supported by both Western culture and cross-cultural research.

C.   Biological Trait Theories
1.   Hans Eysenck also utilized factor analysis to identify two basic personality factors: *introversion-extraversion* and *emotionality-stability*, or *neuroticism*. Eysenck proposed that the ease with which the nervous system can be aroused relates to positions on these personality dimensions.
2.   Gray's reinforcement sensitivity theory has largely supplanted Eysenck's theory and suggests that these differences are due to biological differences in the sensitivity of brain systems involved with responsiveness to rewards (*behavioral approach system*) and punishments (*flight or freeze system*). This theory has gained wider acceptance than Eysenck because of its greater alignment to our understanding of brain structures, neurotransmitters, and how they operate.

D.   Thinking Critically: Are Personality Traits Inherited?
What am I being asked to believe or accept?

Core aspects of personality may be partly inherited.

What evidence is available to support the assertion?

Data from studies of twins and adoptive children show genetic basis for general predisposition and a few traits, including activity level, sociability, anxiety, and emotionality. An estimated 50 percent of variability in personality traits is due to genetics.

Are there alternative ways of interpreting the evidence?

A child's similarities to a parent could be due to social influence. For example, the child could model the parent and siblings. The fact that non-twins are less similar than twins could be due to *nonshared environment* factors. These include factors such as birth order, accidents, and illness.

What additional evidence would help to evaluate the alternatives?

Psychologists have studied infancy, a time period in which the environment hasn't yet had a chance to have an impact, and have found differences in infant *temperament*. This suggests biological and genetic influences. Studies examining adopted children have also supported the role of biology and genetics in the formation of personality. However, more research is needed.

What conclusions are most reasonable?

The evidence does suggest that genetic influences have a significant impact on personality. However, genetic makeup probably provides only a predisposition toward certain levels of activity, emotionality, and sociability. These factors then interact with the environment to produce specific personality features. *Epigenetics* studies how the environment may activate certain genes and how much those genes affect behavior.

E.   Evaluating the Trait Approach
Trait theories are better at describing behavior than at explaining it. Also, trait theories do not create a unique description of every individual, nor can they reflect changes in a person's behavior in different environments or situations.

III.   THE SOCIAL-COGNITIVE APPROACH
The social-cognitive approach to personality focuses on *conscious* thoughts and actions and is based on principles of learning. The founders of this approach were first called *social-learning theorists* because they focused on personality as the thoughts and actions we learn through observing and interacting with others.

A.   Roots of the Social-Cognitive Approach
B. F. Skinner employed functional analysis to understand behavior in terms of its function in obtaining rewards or avoiding punishment. As the social-cognitive approach developed, it went beyond focusing merely on behavior to include learned patterns of thought and feeling.

B.   Prominent Social-Cognitive Theories
1.   *Rotter's Expectancy Theory.* Julian Rotter suggested that behavior is determined by cognitive *expectancies*—that is, what a person expects to happen following behavior and the value the person places on the outcome. Rotter measured the degree to which people expect events to be controlled by their own *internal* efforts or by *external* forces over which they have no influence, and found these expectancies to be related to behavioral differences.
2.   *Bandura and Reciprocal Determinism.* Personality evolves as a result of the interaction among thought, the environment, and behavior through a process called *reciprocal determinism*. For example, Albert Bandura concludes that people's beliefs about the impact they have on the world and their self-efficacy (belief they will succeed) will determine emotions and behaviors.
3.   *Mischel's Cognitive/Affective Theory.* According to Walter Mischel, *cognitive person variables* are important in explaining behavior. The most important cognitive person variables are *encodings, expectancies, affects, goals and values,* and *competencies and self-regulatory plans.* These cognitive variables interact with situation to produce *behavioral signatures.*
Mischel's views sparked a debate that led to several conclusions (note the similarity to reciprocal determinism). First, traits influence behavior only in relevant situations. Second, traits can lead to behaviors that alter situations that, in turn, promote other behaviors. Third, people with different traits choose to be in different situations. Fourth, traits are more influential in some situations than in others.

C.   Evaluating the Social-Cognitive Approach
In its favor, this approach is objective, experimentally oriented, defined by operational concepts, and based on empirical data. Its concepts also translate well into treatments for psychological problems. However, some psychologists think that behaviorists' narrow focus

on behavior, the environment, and even cognitive factors still ignores other potential influences on behavior (subjective experiences, genetic and physiological factors).

IV. THE HUMANISTIC PSYCHOLOGY APPROACH

The humanistic psychology approach to personality focuses on the capabilities that set humans apart from other species. The primary human motivator is an innate drive toward growth that prompts people to fulfill their unique potential. To understand behavior in a particular situation, this approach focuses on one's unique view of the world rather than instincts, traits, or learning experiences, making this approach also known as the *phenomenological approach*. This approach has fueled the development of research in positive psychology with its focus on strengths rather than weaknesses.

A. Prominent Humanistic Theories
1. *Rogers's Self Theory*. Carl Rogers emphasized the concept of actualizing tendency, the innate inclination toward growth that motivates all human behavior. The self is what people come to identify as *I* or *me*. According to Rogers, the development of self-concept depends on self-evaluations and the *positive regard* shown by others. *Incongruities* between self-evaluations and others' evaluations cause anxiety and other problems. Whenever people, instead of their behaviors, are evaluated, conditions of worth are created. People come to believe that they are worthy only under certain conditions—those in which rewarded behaviors are displayed.
2. *Maslow's Growth Theory*. Abraham Maslow saw personality as the tendency to grow toward self-actualization, with people struggling to avoid distraction from needs lower than that on his hierarchy of needs. People can approach the satisfaction of their needs with a deficiency motivation (focus on material acquisition) or growth motivation (drawing satisfaction from what one has, which may lead to *peak experiences*).

B. Evaluating the Humanistic Approach

The humanistic approach has been instrumental in the development of many types of psychotherapy, short-term group experiences (such as encounter groups), and child-rearing practices. However, the belief that all humans are driven by a positive and innate growth potential may be naive. Also, this approach ignores potential genetic, biological, learning, social, and unconscious motivational influences on personality. Most humanistic assessment methods are better at describing behavior than explaining it. Also, many humanistic concepts are difficult to measure and define scientifically. The humanistic approach is culturally confined to North America and other Western cultures. The definition of self is very different in Japan, Africa, and other parts of the world.

C. Linkages: Personality, Culture, and Human Development

Recognition of the role of cultural factors in establishing ideals of personality development requires that various approaches to personality and to the achievement of self-esteem be evaluated in terms of the extent to which they apply to cultures different from the one in which they were developed. Individualist culture promotes an *independent self-system* while collectivist culture promotes and *interdependent-self system*. As a consequence, individualists' well being tends to be tied to having positive attributes, while collectivists' is more tied to having no negative attributes. Such cultural factors shape notions about ideal personality development. Gender-role differences must also be considered.

D. Focus on Research Methods: Longitudinal Studies of Temperament and Personality

In a longitudinal study of about 1,000 individuals, a significant but modest relationship was found between temperament at age three and personality and behavior at age twenty-one. However, individual differences in adult behavior within same-temperament groups suggest that long-term consistency in behavior results from the mutual influence that temperaments and environmental events have on one another.

V.   ASSESSING PERSONALITY
Psychologists usually describe personality using one of four main sources: *life outcomes, situational tests, observer ratings,* and *self-reports* (responses to interviews and personality tests). Personality tests are more standardized and economical than either observations or interviews. A test must be reliable and valid.

A.   Projective Personality Measures
Tests consisting of unstructured stimuli that can be perceived and responded to in many ways are called <u>projective personality measures</u>. The *Thematic Apperception Test (TAT)* and the *Rorschach Inkblot Test* are examples of this format. Responses to projective personality tests reflect many aspects of an individual's personality. These tests are relatively difficult to score and tend to be less reliable and valid than objective tests.

A.   Nonprojective Personality Measures
The typical <u>nonprojective personality measure</u> is a paper-and-pencil form containing clear, specific questions, statements, or concepts to which a person is asked to give yes-no, true-false, or multiple-choice answers. It is also known as an *objective personality measure.* Scores can be compared mathematically. The *Neuroticism Extraversion Openness Personality Inventory, Revised (NEO-PI-R)* is given to measure personality variables in normal populations. A widely used test for diagnosing disorders is the *Minnesota Multiphasic Personality Inventory (MMPI).*

B.   Personality Tests and Employee Selection
Personality tests do seem to be useful in screening prospective employees; however, the tests can lead to incorrect predictions. Some employees believe that utilizing personality tests in the selection process is a violation of their privacy. Their use is banned in selection of U. S. federal employees as a result of some lawsuits.

KEY TERMS

1.   **Personality** is the pattern of psychological and behavioral characteristics by which each person can be compared and contrasted with others. (see introductory section)

    REMEMBER: Those who study personality are interested in what makes each person unique.

2.   The **psychodynamic approach** was Freud's view that personality is based on the interplay of unconscious mental processes. (see The Psychodynamic Approach)

    REMEMBER: Freud introduced the idea that psychological activity plays a major role in behavior, mental processes, and personality. <u>Psych</u> refers to "mental," and <u>dynamic</u> pertains to "energy," "motion," and "forcefulness." Psychological factors have energy and play a forceful role in the determination of personality, behavior, and mental processes.

3.   The **id** is the unconscious portion of the personality that contains basic impulses and urges. (see The Structure and Development of Personality)

    Example: Freud might say that an infant cries whenever hungry, wet, bored, or frustrated because the infant's id wants instant fulfillment of every wish.

    REMEMBER: The id operates on the pleasure principle. Eros is the instinct for pleasure and sex. Thanatos is the death instinct, which can motivate aggressive and destructive behavior. The id seeks immediate gratification, regardless of society's rules or the rights and feelings of others.

4.   **Libido** is the psychic energy contained in the id. (see The Structure and Development of Personality)

5. The **pleasure principle** is the id's operating principle, which guides people toward whatever feels good. (see The Structure and Development of Personality)

    REMEMBER: The id operates on the pleasure principle, guiding people to do whatever gives them pleasure.

6. The **ego** is the part of the personality that mediates conflicts between and among the demands of the id, the superego, and the real world.   (see The Structure and Development of Personality)

    Example: Suppose Thanatos (part of the id) creates a desire to cut people with knives. The ego would consider society's rules and laws about this type of activity, which say that cutting other people is wrong. But a person can become a surgeon and cut people on a daily basis. Being a physician who cuts people does not violate society's rules and may symbolically satisfy the id's demands.

    REMEMBER: The ego operates according to the reality principle.

7. The **reality principle** is the operating principle of the ego that creates compromises between the id's demands and those of the real world. (see The Structure and Development of Personality)

    Example: Naomi's id wants her to eat an entire plate of donuts, but the ego suggests a more moderate response, which may partially satisfy the id. Naomi decides to have one donut (or two).

8. The **superego** is the component of personality that tells people what they should and should not do. (see The Structure and Development of Personality)

    Example: Suppose you are a small child in a candy store. Your id is "screaming" for candy. The conscience (part of the superego) is saying, "You know it is wrong to steal candy." The ego decides that the best way to handle this dilemma is for you to go home and ask your mother for your allowance. Then, you can go back and buy the candy, satisfying both the id and the superego.

    REMEMBER: The superego can be thought of as operating on the morality principle.

9. **Defense mechanisms** are psychological responses that help protect a person from anxiety and guilt. (see The Structure and Development of Personality)

    Example: Jansen has a new baby brother whom he dislikes for taking away his parents' attention. Jansen would be very upset about his intense dislike of his sibling if he were consciously aware of it; therefore, his ego employs a defense mechanism, reaction formation, to push the negative feelings into the unconscious. Now, Jansen is overly attentive and affectionate with his brother.

10. **Psychosexual development** occurs in periods of personality development in which, according to Freud, conflicts focus on particular issues. (see The Structure and Development of Personality)

    REMEMBER: Each period is distinguished by the part of the body from which a person derives dominant pleasure. The five stages are, in their respective order, <u>oral</u>, <u>anal</u>, <u>phallic</u>, <u>latent</u>, and <u>genital</u>. Failure to resolve the problems that occur during the oral, anal, or phallic stages can lead to fixation.

11. The **oral stage** is the first of Freud's psychosexual stages of personality development, in which the mouth is the center of pleasure and conflict. (see The Structure and Development of Personality)

    Example: Bill was weaned too early, thus depriving him of pleasure during the oral stage of personality development. As an adult, he talks quite a bit, is a heavy smoker, and loves to eat.

    REMEMBER: If a child is weaned too early or too late, problems that can lead to fixation may arise.

12. The **anal stage** is the second of Freud's psychosexual stages of personality development, in which the focus of pleasure and conflict shifts from the mouth to the anus. (see The Structure and Development of Personality)

    Example: Art was toilet trained at a very young age and is fixated at the anal stage. As an adult, he is very neat, orderly, and extremely organized.

    REMEMBER: If toilet training is too demanding or is begun too early or too late, problems that can lead to fixation may arise.

13. The **phallic stage** is the third of Freud's psychosexual stages of personality development, in which the focus of pleasure and conflict shifts to the genital area. (see The Structure and Development of Personality)

    Example: Eve hasn't had a long-term romantic relationship because she finds fault with each person she dates. Although Eve doesn't realize it, she wants people to match her unreasonably high expectations and becomes irritated when they don't.

    REMEMBER: During this stage, boys experience the Oedipal complex and girls experience the Electra complex. A fixation at the phallic stage could lead to problems with authority or difficulties maintaining love relationships.

14. The **Oedipal complex** is a pattern described by Freud in which a boy has sexual desire for his mother and wants to eliminate his father's competition for her attention. (see The Structure and Development of Personality)

    REMEMBER: The fear of retaliation causes boys to identify with their fathers and acquire male gender-role behaviors.

15. The **Electra complex** is pattern described by Freud in which a young girl develops an attachment to her father and competes with her mother for his attention. (see The Structure and Development of Personality)

    REMEMBER: To resolve this stage, girls identify with their mothers and acquire female gender-role behaviors.

16. The **latency period** is the fourth of Freud's psychosexual stages of personality development, in which sexual impulses lie dormant. (see The Structure and Development of Personality)

    Example: Will is excited about playing soccer on his grade-school team and works hard to do his homework well and on time.

17. The **genital stage** is the last of Freud's psychosexual stages of personality development, which begins during adolescence, when sexual impulses appear at the conscious level. (see The Structure and Development of Personality)

    Example: Penny began college this year and has made many new friends. Although she is not sexually active, Penny believes that her current romantic relationship is secure enough that it may eventually lead to a sexual relationship.

    REMEMBER: The genitals are once again the primary source of sexual pleasure. The satisfaction obtained during this stage is dependent upon the resolution of conflicts experienced in the earlier stages.

18. The **trait approach** is the view that personality is a combination of characteristics that people display over time and across situations. (see The Trait Approach)

    Example: When people say that a friend is sociable, understanding, and generous, they are using the trait approach to describing personality.

19. The **five factor personality model** (or **Big-Five model**) is a view based on factor-analytic studies suggesting the existence of five basic components of human personality: openness, conscientiousness, extraversion, agreeableness, and neuroticism. (see The Five Factor Personality Model)

20. The **social-cognitive approach** is the view that personality reflects learned patterns of thinking and behavior. (see The Social-Cognitive Approach)

    Example: Devorah explains that her friend has learned to be obnoxious at parties. Devorah believes they could shape her friend's behavior to be less obnoxious by rewarding her for more appropriate behavior.

21. **Functional analysis** consists of analyzing behavior by studying what responses occur under what conditions of operant reward and punishment. (see Roots of the Social-Cognitive Approach)

    Example: Brian, a seventeen-year-old, usually ends up denting or slightly damaging the family car whenever he drives it. Skinner would look for environmental consistencies every time this behavior appeared. As it turns out, Brian takes the car only when his usually inattentive father has gone out of town on business. When the father returns, he always spends time talking with Brian about his irresponsible behavior. Skinner might suggest that his father's attention is so reinforcing that Brian will even ruin the car to get it.

22. **Self-efficacy**, according to Albert Bandura, consists of learned expectations about the probability of success in given situations. (see Prominent Social-Cognitive Theories)

    Example: Jessica has low self-efficacy in interviewing situations and expects to do poorly. She can never think of answers to questions or creative solutions to the problems posed by the interviewer. Sandra, in contrast, has high self-efficacy in interviewing situations. Because she expects to do well, she is confident and approachable. Interviewers enjoy talking with Sandra because she is enthusiastic and energetic. The interviewers' responses further enhance Sandra's self-efficacy.

23. The **humanistic psychology approach** is the view that personality develops through an actualizing tendency that unfolds in accordance with each person's unique perceptions of the world. (see The Humanistic Psychology Approach)

    Example: Perry tells the jury that his client did not take her ill daughter, Sarah, to the hospital because she firmly believed that prayer would heal her and that taking Sarah to the hospital would show that she had no faith. In his summation, Perry argues that his client perceived that western medicine would not cure Sarah and might cause her death, because prayers from nonbelievers are not answered. Perry took a humanistic approach to explain that his client's view of reality influenced her behavior.

24. The **actualizing tendency,** according to Carl Rogers, is an innate inclination toward growth that motivates all people. (see Prominent Humanistic Theories)

    Example: Adam has wanted to be a nurse ever since kindergarten, when his younger sister was sick. In his nursing classes, Adam feels a sense of accomplishment and of motivation to learn more.

    REMEMBER: This concept is important in many humanistic personality theories. If growth toward self-actualization is not impeded, a person will tend to be happy and comfortable.

25. **Self-concept** is the way one thinks about oneself. It is influenced by self-actualizing tendencies and others' evaluations. (see Prominent Humanistic Theories)

Example: Lucy loves to bake in her play oven. Her whole family raves over how tasty her creations are, although Lucy's apple pie was a little chewy. Now, Lucy thinks that she's a fine baker and a nice person for treating her family to new desserts every day.

26. **Conditions of worth,** according to Carl Rogers, are the feelings an individual experiences when an evaluation is applied to the person rather than to the person's behavior. (see Prominent Humanistic Theories)

Example: Bruce sits on the desk folding all the papers into little squares, thinking that his mom would think it looked very neat. "No! Bad boy! Get down from there this instant!" yells Bruce's mom. Suddenly, Bruce doesn't feel that his ideas are good ones. If such incidents happen often enough, Bruce might come to believe he is a bad person.

27. A **deficiency motivation,** according to Abraham Maslow, is a preoccupation with perceived needs for things a person does not have. (see Prominent Humanistic Theories)

Example: Jacqueline is the chief executive officer of a major corporation. She has a beautiful house, a membership in the "right" country club, and a large salary. However, instead of being satisfied, Jacqueline is constantly worrying about what she does not have enough money to buy.

28. A **growth motivation,** according to Abraham Maslow, is a tendency to draw satisfaction from what is available in life, rather than to focus on what is missing. (see Prominent Humanistic Theories)

Example: Pedro is a developmental psychologist. He does not get paid as much as some people, but he loves his research. He also has a supportive family and a few very close friends. Pedro concentrates most of his effort on working and on enjoying his family to the fullest. He does not worry about what he cannot have. Instead, he derives a great deal of pleasure—indeed, joy—from what he does have.

29. **Projective personality measures** are personality assessments made up of ambiguous stimuli that can be perceived and responded to in many different ways. (see Projective Personality Measures)

Example: The TAT is a projective test that involves showing people pictures and asking them to tell a story about each picture.

REMEMBER: People who use these kinds of tests assume that responses will reflect aspects of personality. It is relatively difficult to transform these tests' responses into numerical scores.

30. **Nonprojective personality measures** are paper-and-pencil tests containing direct, unambiguous items relating to the personality of the individual being assessed. (see Nonprojective Personality Measures)

Example: The multiple-choice tests that you take in your classes are called objective tests because they can be graded objectively. Your score on a nonprojective personality measure can be compared mathematically with other students' scores.

REMEMBER: Nonprojective measures are scored objectively. The scorer has a key that shows how to assign scores, rather than each scorer choosing a way of interpreting responses.

FILL-IN-THE-BLANKS KEY TERMS

This section will help you check your factual knowledge of the key terms introduced in this chapter. Fill in each blank with the appropriate term from the list of key terms in the previous section.

1. _____ personality tests are written tests that contain clear, specific questions.

2. According to Freud, the _____ stage occurs during the second year of life, when children go through toilet training.

3. According to Freud, the basic instincts, desires, and impulses with which people are born are contained in the _____.

4. According to the psychodynamic approach, the _____ is the part of the personality that contains the conscience and that seeks to have the person behave in ways that are acceptable in society.

5. In psychodynamic theory, the ego seeks to meet the desires of the id by carefully balancing those desires with situations in the real world. This is called the _____ principle.

6. The _____ model of personality suggests that personality is based on five traits: neuroticism, extraversion, openness, agreeableness, and conscientiousness.

7. The psychoanalytical stage associated with dormant sexual impulses is called the _____ stage.

8. The _____ approach proposes that personality is a set of behaviors that a person acquires through learning.

9. People who, regardless of their success, focus on what they don't have follow a(n) _____.

10. The humanistic belief that all people are innately motivated to achieve their fullest potential is called the _____.

11. The _____ approach views personality as a unique combination of dispositions.

12. The focus of the _____ approach is on a person's unique view of self and world.

13. Tests of personality that contain ambiguous stimuli that allow the test taker to respond in many different ways are called _____ personality tests.

14. _____ is a humanistic concept that describes people who derive satisfaction in life by focusing on enjoying the situations they are in and the possessions they have.

15. Rogers defined the term _____ as the way in which one thinks about oneself.

Total Correct (See answer key) _____

LEARNING OBJECTIVES

1. Define personality. (see introductory section)

2. Describe the assumptions of Freud's psychodynamic approach to personality. (see "The Psychodynamic Approach")

3. Define and describe the nature and function of the id, ego, and superego. Define libido, the pleasure principle, and the reality principle. (see "Id, Ego, and Superego")

4. Define defense mechanism. Explain the purpose and give an example of each defense mechanism. (see "Conflicts and Defenses")

5. Name, define, and describe the psychosexual stages of personality development. Compare and contrast the Oedipal and Electra complexes. (see "Stages in Personality Development")

6. Explain some of the neo-Freudian variations on Freud's theory. Include Jung's, Adler's, and Horney's ideas. (see "Variations on Freud's Personality Theory")

7. Define object relations. Describe contemporary psychodynamic theory's emphasis on object relations to help explain personality development. (see "Contemporary Psychodynamic Theories")

8. Describe some applications and criticisms of the psychodynamic approach to personality. (see "Evaluating the Psychodynamic Approach")

9. Describe the three basic assumptions of the trait approach to personality. (see "The Trait Approach")

10. Distinguish between a trait and a type. (see "Traits Versus Types")

11. Compare and contrast Allport's trait theory and the five factor (Big-Five) model. Define Allport's *central* and *secondary traits* and the Big-Five dimensions of *openness to experience*, *conscientiousness*, *extraversion*, *agreeableness*, and *neuroticism*. (see "Allport's Trait Theory"; see also "The Big-Five Model of Personality")

12. Describe biological trait theories. Compare and contrast Eysenck's biological trait theory and Gray's approach-inhibition theory. Define Eysenck's dimensions of *introversion-extroversion* and *emotionality-stability* and Gray's *behavioral approach system* and *behavioral inhibition system*. (see "Biological Trait Theories")

13. Explain the controversy surrounding the role of heredity in personality development. Discuss the twin and adoptive children research. (see "Thinking Critically: Are Personality Traits Inherited?")

14. Describe some criticisms of the trait approach to personality. (see "Evaluating the Trait Approach")

15. Describe the basic assumption of the social-cognitive approach to personality. Define functional analysis. (see "The Social-Cognitive Approach")

16. Compare and contrast the operant approach (Skinner) and social-cognitive theories of personality. (see "Roots of the Social-Cognitive Approach")

17. Describe Rotter's expectancy theory, Bandura's *reciprocal determinism* and perceived self-efficacy, and Mischel's *cognitive person variables*. (see "Prominent Social-Cognitive Theories")

18. Describe some applications and criticisms of the social-cognitive approach to personality. (see "Evaluating the Social-Cognitive Approach")

19. Describe the humanistic approach to personality and how it has progressed research in positive psychology. (see "The Humanistic Approach")

20. Compare and contrast Rogers's self theory and Maslow's growth theory. Define Roger's use of actualizing tendency, positive regard, self-concept, congruence, and conditions of worth. Define Maslow's use of deficiency and growth orientation. (see "Prominent Humanistic Theories")

21. Describe some applications and criticisms of the humanistic approach. (see "Evaluating the Humanistic Approach")

22. Describe cultural differences in the concept of self. Explain how these differences shape the development of personality. (see "Linkages: Personality, Culture, and Human Development")

23. Discuss the longitudinal studies of personality and their conclusions about the continuity of personality across the lifespan. (see "Focus on Research Methods: Longitudinal Studies of Temperament and Personality")

24. Describe the four general methods of personality assessment. (see "Assessing Personality")

25. Discuss the difference between projective and nonprojective personality measures and give an example of each. (see "Assessing Personality")

26. Describe some of the applications of personality tests. (see "Personality Tests and Employee Selection")

CONCEPTS AND EXERCISES

Explaining Behavior

Jan's office is extremely neat and organized. His books are arranged alphabetically, and there is not a stray paper on the desk. His pencils, neatly arranged from shortest to longest, are so sharp that he could use them as weapons. Jan is a meticulous dresser. His clothes are never wrinkled, spotted, or torn. Match the following explanations of his behavior with the appropriate theorist or approach.

1.   Jan has learned that being organized and well dressed will further his career. _____

2.   Jan is fixated at the anal stage. _____

3.   Being organized is one of the central traits of Jan's personality. _____

4.   Jan may believe that he is worthwhile only if he displays neat and tidy behaviors. _____

    a.   Rogers

    b.   Social-cognitive

    c.   Allport

    d.   Freud

Treatment Goals

Bobbie is extremely anxious and unhappy. Using the list that follows the four statements, match each goal with the appropriate approach to personality.

1.   Bobbie should become aware of her unconscious conflicts and work to resolve them. _____

2.   Bobbie should become aware of her real feelings and beliefs instead of trying to fulfill the conditions of worth that her parents and others impose on her. _____

3.   Bobbie should learn to think positively and realize that she controls what happens to her. _____

4.   Bobbie should take some tests to assess her personality traits. If the tests show she has a disorder, she should go through some form of treatment. She can take the tests again later to monitor her progress. _____

    a.   Humanistic psychology

    b.   Social-cognitive

    c.   Psychodynamic

    d.   Trait

CRITICAL THINKING

Sam and Martina are discussing the use of character witnesses in violent crime court cases. Sam believes that people's personalities are very stable across diverse situations. Therefore, character witnesses who can describe personality traits should give a good indication of whether a person is capable of doing a violent crime. Martina says that people can act very differently when provoked by a situation, so character witnesses may not know everything about how likely a person is to behave in a violent manner.

Using the five critical thinking questions in your text, the clues in the story, and what you have learned about personality, answer the following.

1. What is Sam's hypothesis?

2. What is Martina's alternative hypothesis?

3. In any given case, what kinds of evidence do you think Martina would collect to support her alternative hypothesis?

PERSONAL LEARNING ACTIVITIES

1. Visit the following website to learn more about current research in personality: http://ipip.ori.org/ipip/. This site is a "collaboratory" that heavily emphasizes measuring aspects of personality. Does it seem to focus more on projective or nonprojective personality measures? In particular, look at the link that is labeled "warning." What would you conclude about people being able to "cheat" a personality test based on the information there? Do you think this site is predominantly influenced by the trait, psychodynamic, humanistic, or social-cognitive approach? Explain your answer.

2. To take a short measure of your locus of control, visit the following website: http://www.psych.uncc.edu/pagoolka/LocusofControl-intro.html. This 13-item measure will indicate if you are more of an "internal" or "external" locus of control. Do you agree that this scale accurately measures your locus of control? If not, why? Do you feel your locus of control may be more specific to certain situations than a general orientation?

3. There is an entire museum devoted to the life and work of Freud, the father of the psychodynamic approach. Visit its website at http://www.freud.org.uk/. Navigate around this site for a bit to get a better idea of the rich influence Freud has had on Western culture, not only in psychology but in areas such as art and literature, as well. Why do you think Freud's impact was so significant? Other information on Freud can be found at: http://users.rcn.com/brill/freudarc.html, a rich archive of material related to Freud and his work.

4. Describe your personality. How much do you think was inherited and how much was influenced by the environment? What sorts of experiences or perspectives do you think led to the personality characteristics you listed?

5. Learn more about the Rorschach Inkblot Test at: http://www.rorschach.org/. What was the history of this test's development and what were the intentions of the developer for its use? Does reading this information make you more open to what projective personality measures might reveal to us about a person?

MULTIPLE-CHOICE QUESTIONS

Quiz 1

1. The psychodynamic approach to personality is best characterized by which of the following statements?
    a. Consistent patterns of thought and behavior cause personality.
    b. Learning and cognition cause personality.
    c. Unconscious conflict causes personality.
    d. Personal growth and search for meaning determines personality.

2. The following is a conversation going on in someone's head:

    X: I am so mad that I could bash that person's skull in. I cannot believe he did that.

    Y: You know you are not supposed to hurt other people.

    Z: Why not tell him that his behavior is inappropriate so that he won't repeat it?

    X is the _____, Y is the _____, and Z is the _____.

    a. id; ego; superego
    b. ego; id; superego
    c. superego; id; ego
    d. id; superego; ego

3. Tom finds his wife stupid and sexually unattractive but doesn't tell her about these feelings. Instead, he criticizes his secretary for making mistakes and makes derogatory remarks about *her* appearance. This is an example of which defense mechanism?

    a. Rationalization
    b. Displacement
    c. Reaction-formation
    d. Projection

4. Eduardo believed that his poetry was not simply an expression of his personal feelings but rather a part of his being that represented the deepest feelings of all people. Eduardo's notion is similar to

    a. Jung's collective unconscious.
    b. Hippocrates's humors.
    c. Gray's Behavioral Approach System.
    d. Allport's central traits.

5. The Oedipus complex is experienced by _____; the Electra complex is experienced by _____.

    a. males; males
    b. females; females
    c. males; females
    d. females; males

6. Object relations are part of _____ theory.

    a. contemporary psychodynamic
    b. trait
    c. humanistic
    d. social-cognitive

7. Central traits

    a. were suggested by a social-cognitive theorist to explain behavior.
    b. organize and control behavior across many situations.
    c. are more situation-specific than are secondary traits.
    d. are seen in growth-oriented individuals.

8. Toni describes her best friend as intelligent, caring, extraverted, and lots of fun to be with. Which type of theorist would use the same type of description that Toni does?

   a. Trait
   b. Social-cognitive
   c. Psychodynamic
   d. Humanistic

9. Which of the following is an example of a person exhibiting a secondary trait?

   a. Amy, who is obnoxious and opinionated only when debating politics
   b. Arnold, whose entire life is devoted to ridding the world of thieves, murderers, and drug dealers
   c. Cathy, who usually sees the positive side of events
   d. Dave, who loves to help those less fortunate than himself

10. Jim is very easy to get along with and likes to make everyone happy. He is probably high on the Big-Five trait of

    a. openness to experience.
    b. agreeableness.
    c. extraversion.
    d. conscientiousness.

11. The best evidence that the dimensions of the Big-Five factors may represent the basic components of personality is that

    a. they were derived by using factor analysis techniques.
    b. some version of the Big-Five factors reliably appears in many countries and cultures.
    c. they do an excellent job of describing people.
    d. identical twins are no more alike in general temperament than are nonidentical twins.

12. The belief that behavior can be situation-specific is a main argument *against* which approach to personality?

    a. Psychodynamic
    b. Social-cognitive
    c. Humanistic
    d. Trait

13. Self-efficacy is

    a. our collection of learned expectancies for success in given situations.
    b. the efficiency with which we resolve unconscious conflicts.
    c. a secondary trait.
    d. a role of the ego.

14. Rotter's expectancy theory is part of the _____ approach to personality.

    a. trait
    b. humanistic
    c. social-cognitive
    d. psychodynamic

15. Colin is a high-functioning autistic child. His speech therapist has been working with him on making eye contact with people when he communicates. Colin has learned to make eye contact, but he only does so because he wants the reward of people listening to him, not because he finds eye contact rewarding in its own right. Understanding why Colin makes eye contact in terms of the purpose it serves for him is what Skinner would call

    a.   projective testing.
    b.   functional analysis.
    c.   a condition of worth.
    d.   a defense mechanism.

16. A deficiency motivation occurs when people

    a.   make do with less than perfect conditions.
    b.   focus on things they do not have.
    c.   attempt to fulfill their potentials.
    d.   have a trait missing from their personality.

17. Kareem is driven to achieve all that he can. He is constantly reading to learn more, and puts into practice what he learns. He just finished reading about gardening and is pursuing a master gardener class. He hopes to build a community garden to help feed the hungry in his city. Kareem's tendency toward growth and fulfillment is what Rogers would call

    a.   an actualizing tendency.
    b.   positive regard.
    c.   a deficiency motivation.
    d.   congruence.

18. Teddy had always been a well-adjusted child, but when he was thirteen, he got into trouble a few times. What is a likely prediction for Teddy's personality at age eighteen?

    a.   Teddy's personality was affected by hormonal changes during puberty, and he will continue to exhibit troubled behavior.
    b.   Teddy's personality was affected by the problems in puberty and will be unstable.
    c.   Teddy will probably be a well-adjusted adult because he was well-adjusted during most of his childhood.
    d.   No predictions can be made about Teddy's personality at age eighteen.

19. Which of the following would a humanistic psychologist use most frequently to assess personality?

    a.   Behavioral observations
    b.   Nonprojective personality measures
    c.   Assessments of physiological activity
    d.   Personal interviews

20. Tameka shows her clients a series of ambiguous pictures she painted and asks them to tell a story about each picture. Tameka hopes that her _____ personality test will uncover some of the unconscious thoughts of her clients.

    a. multiphasic
    b. nonprojective
    c. projective
    d. social-cognitive

Total Correct (See answer key) _____

Quiz 2

Use this quiz to reassess your learning after taking Quiz 1 and reviewing the chapter.

1. Lydia, a married woman, is incredibly attracted to her physician. Her _____ decides that the only way to see her doctor more often is to have more frequent physicals and have even the slightest symptom investigated immediately.

    a. id
    b. ego
    c. superego
    d. eros

2. Nathaniel can't stand his lab partner, Shelley. She is such a know-it-all. He absolutely hates her. Unconsciously, though, he actually feels attracted to her, which is why he hates her so much. This is an example of what defense mechanism?

    a. Creativity
    b. Projection
    c. Rationalization
    d. Reaction formation

3. Fixation occurs when

    a. psychosexual conflicts are not resolved.
    b. we use defense mechanisms to relieve anxiety.
    c. the rewards in a given situation fix our behaviors.
    d. our progress toward self-actualization is blocked at some stage.

4. Use the following conversation to answer the question: **Joe:** I don't think we should hire him. I saw him in a barroom brawl a few months ago. Why hire someone who is going to be aggressive in any given situation? -- **Kim:** His MMPI scores indicate that he isn't prone to violence. -- **Richard:** His self-concept may not include violence. -- **Erika:** Joe, how do you know that he's always going to be aggressive? Maybe the guy was just under stress at the time. Maybe he knows from past experience that a good fistfight relieves tension.

    Which of the following approaches is NOT represented in the above conversation?

    a. Social-cognitive
    b. Psychodynamic
    c. Humanistic
    d. Trait

5. Use the following conversation to answer the question: **Joe:** I don't think we should hire him. I saw him in a barroom brawl a few months ago. Why hire someone who is going to be aggressive in any given situation? -- **Kim:** His MMPI scores indicate that he isn't prone to violence. -- **Richard:** His self-concept may not include violence. -- **Erika:** Joe, how do you know that he's always going to be aggressive? Maybe the guy was just under stress at the time. Maybe he knows from past experience that a good fistfight relieves tension.

   Which two speakers agree with the trait approach to personality?

   a. Joe and Richard
   b. Erika and Kim
   c. Joe and Kim
   d. Richard and Erika

6. Sexual impulses lie dormant during the _____ period of the psychosexual stages of development.

   a. oral
   b. anal
   c. phallic
   d. latency

7. Dr. Lebryk believes Jack's romantic relationships are brief and unhappy because Jack had an anxious insecure attachment to his mother. Dr. Lebryk is most likely a(n) _____ theorist.

   a. Big-Five
   b. social-cognitive
   c. humanistic
   d. object relations

8. You describe your friend as outgoing, eccentric, generous, emotional, talkative, impulsive, and easygoing. Gordon Allport would say you have listed your friend's

   a. central traits.
   b. secondary traits.
   c. level of self-efficacy.
   d. level of externality.

9. Charlie acted the way he did because he saw life as a continual struggle. He felt that the world was against him and that everything he tried to do would be difficult and painful. This description of Charlie best fits with which approach to personality?

   a. Psychodynamic
   b. Trait
   c. Social-cognitive
   d. Humanistic

10. One of the criticisms of the humanistic approach is that it

   a. concentrates too much on what human beings have in common.
   b. is naive, romantic, and unrealistic.
   c. puts too much emphasis on explaining personality.
   d. puts undue emphasis on instincts.

11. Which theorist would most likely the statement "People are innately good"?
    a. Julian Rotter
    b. Sigmund Freud
    c. Carl Rogers
    d. Albert Bandura

12. Which of the following is NOT a criticism of the trait theories of personality?
    a. They describe behavior better than they explain it.
    b. They create descriptions that may be too general.
    c. They ignore situational influences on behavior.
    d. They place too much emphasis on the unconscious.

13. The learning process is most central to which personality theory?
    a. Psychodynamic
    b. Trait
    c. Social-cognitive
    d. Big-Five

14. Joe is an internal, according to Rotter's expectancy theory of personality. Therefore, you would expect Joe to
    a. ignore physical symptoms of illness.
    b. work on a factory assembly line.
    c. take a self-paced course at school.
    d. All of these

15. According to Bandura, a child could _____ through observational learning.
    a. learn to be truthful
    b. learn how to con Dad into giving up the car
    c. learn how to be assertive
    d. All of these

16. Martin was in his room reading contentedly when his father came in and told him that he was a bookworm and that if he were a real boy, he would be outside playing soccer. Martin's father may be creating a(n) _____, according to Rogers.

    a. deficiency motivation
    b. fixation
    c. interdependent self-system
    d. condition of worth

17. Grace tries not to stand out from the crowd. Not only does she describe herself in terms of her place in her family and work groups, but she also feels happiest when her interactions with her groups have gone well. Grace most likely

    a. has an independent self-system.
    b. has an interdependent self-system.
    c. is an internal.
    d. is an external.

18. A projective personality measure is usually

    a. reliable.
    b. valid.
    c. easy to score.
    d. None of these

19. Jay needs a reliable nonprojective personality measure to assist in a diagnosis of a client. Jay should use the

    a. NEO-PI-R.
    b. MMPI.
    c. TAT.
    d. Rorschach Inkblot Test.

20. Which personality test is most likely to be used in employee selection?

    a. NEO-PI-R
    b. MMPI
    c. TAT
    d. Rorschach Inkblot Test

Total Correct (See answer key) _____

ANSWERS TO FILL-IN-THE-BLANKS KEY TERMS

1. Nonprojective (see Nonprojective Personality Measures)

2. anal (see The Structure and Development of Personality)

3. id (see The Structure and Development of Personality)

4. superego (see The Structure and Development of Personality)

5. reality (see The Structure and Development of Personality)

6. Big-Five, or five factor (see Five Factor Personality Model)

7. latency (see The Structure and Development of Personality)

8. social-cognitive (see The Social-Cognitive Approach)

9. deficiency motivation (see Prominent Humanistic Theories)

10. actualizing tendency (see Prominent Humanistic Theories)

11. trait (see The Trait Approach)

12. humanistic psychology (see The Humanistic Psychology Approach)

13. projective (see Projective Personality Measures)

14. Growth orientation (see Prominent Humanistic Theories)

15. self-concept (see Prominent Humanistic Theories)

ANSWERS TO CONCEPTS AND EXERCISES

Explaining Behavior

1. *Social-cognitive.* A social-cognitive theorist would explain Jan's behavior by finding out what behaviors were rewarded in the past. (see The Social-Cognitive Approach)

2. *Freud.* Freud believed that an unresolved crisis during the psychosexual development would lead to fixation. Adults who are fixated at the anal stage are extremely neat and tidy. (see The Structure and Development of Personality)

3. *Allport.* Allport was a trait theorist. He believed that people have about seven central traits. (see Allport's Trait Theory)

4. *Rogers.* Rogers was a humanistic theorist. He said that many people display behaviors because they believe these are the only ways in which to gain approval and thus positive self-evaluation. (see Prominent Humanistic Theories)

Treatment Goals

1. *Psychodynamic.* Freud said that unconscious conflicts are the primary root of all mental disorders. In order to eliminate the anxiety these conflicts produce, patients should be made aware of them and work to resolve them. (see The Psychodynamic Approach)

2. *Humanistic Psychology.* Rogers said that unhappy people are out of touch with their true feelings. They are probably behaving according to others' values instead of according to their own feelings and values. (see The Humanistic Psychology Approach)

3. *Social-cognitive.* A social-cognitive approach suggests that Bobbie learn and practice more positive ways of thinking and behaving. (see The Social-Cognitive Approach)

4. *Trait.* A trait theorist might suggest that Bobbie take objective tests, such as the MMPI, to describe her personality and identify any type of possible personality disorders. (see The Trait Approach)

ANSWERS TO CRITICAL THINKING

1. Sam hypothesizes that if someone doesn't usually exhibit tendencies toward violence, then he or she probably didn't commit a violent crime.

2. Martina knows that trait theories have been criticized because they tend to ignore situational influences on behavior. She would therefore hypothesize that someone who is generally not violent could be provoked into violence by a particular situation.

3. Martina would probably want to investigate both the person's general personality traits and aspects of the situation that could explain the onset of violent behavior, consistent with the social-cognitive approach.

ANSWERS TO MULTIPLE-CHOICE QUESTIONS

Circle the question numbers you answered correctly.

Quiz 1

1. c is the answer. The psychodynamic approach assumes that personality is determined by unconscious mental processes that usually involve resolution of unconscious conflict. (see The Structure and Development of Personality)

    a. The statement characterizes the trait approach.

    b. This statement characterizes the social-cognitive approach.

    d. This statement characterizes the humanistic approach.

2. d is the answer. X wants to be aggressive. Y knows all the rules about what behaviors one should and should not display. Z will try to obey the rules of society as well as satisfy the id and superego. (see The Structure and Development of Personality)

3. b is the answer. Tom is displacing his feelings from the original source to an alternative source, his secretary. (see The Structure and Development of Personality)

    a. Rationalization is an attempt to explain away behavior. If this were the case, Tom might tell himself that all marriages have their low spots.

    c. Reaction-formation guides behavior in the direction opposite that of the unwanted impulse. If this were the case, Tom would shower his wife with attention and affection, telling her how intelligent and beautiful he thought she was.

    d. Projection is seeing unwanted impulses and desires in others. If this were the case, Tom might start noticing that his friends treat their wives very badly.

4. a is the correct answer. Jung defined the collective unconscious as the memories that each of us inherits from our human and nonhuman ancestors. So Eduardo's poetry would be influenced by that part of him that was connected to the feelings of all people who had ever lived. (see Variations on Freud's Personality Theory)

    b. Hippocrates suggested that personality was associated with differential amounts of four different humors, or bodily fluids. This would not explain how the feelings of all people wound up in Eduardo's poetry.

    c. Gray's Behavioral Approach System, or BAS, focuses on the sensitivity of the individual's brain to rewards.

    d. Allport's central traits focus on traits that describe individuals such that the individual is differentiated from others, not similar to others.

5. c is the answer. The Oedipus complex, according to Freud, involves boys' desire for their mothers and wishing to kill their fathers. The Electra complex is experienced by girls when they realize that they lack a penis and transfer their love from their mother to their father, according to the psychodynamic approach. (see The Structure and Development of Personality)

    a. Males experience only the Oedipus complex, not the Electra complex.

    b. Females experience only the Electra complex, not the Oedipus complex.

    d.   This is reversed—males experience the Oedipus complex and females the Electra complex.

6.   a is the answer. Object relations theorists study the relationship between people and significant objects. (see Contemporary Psychodynamic Theories)

    b.   Trait theorists study dispositions.

    c.   Humanistic theorists focus on people's perceptions of the world and their tendency toward reaching their potential.

    d.   Social-cognitive theorists focus on behaviors and learned thought patterns, which they believe influence personality.

7.   b is the answer. According to Allport's trait theory, about seven central traits guide our behavior in many situations. (see Allport's Trait Theory)

    a.   Central traits were proposed by Allport, who was a trait, not a social-cognitive, theorist.

    c.   Secondary traits are more situation-specific than are central traits.

    d.   Growth orientation is a humanistic concept proposed by Maslow.

8.   a is the answer. A trait theorist would describe a person in terms of such stable characteristics. (see The Trait Approach)

    b.   A social-cognitive theorist would describe a person in terms of behaviors and thought patterns.

    c.   A psychodynamic theorist would discuss the underlying unconscious conflicts that are responsible for a person's behavior.

    d.   A humanistic theorist would describe a person's perception of reality, values, and beliefs.

9.   a is the answer. A secondary trait, according to Allport, is one that is specific to certain situations. (see Allport's Trait Theory)

    b.   Arnold has a trait that affects his whole life; this would not be a secondary trait but a central trait.

    c, d.   Cathy sounds like she is optimistic in most situations and Dave sounds like he is often helpful; therefore, these are not secondary traits.

10.   b is the answer. Agreeableness is the Big-Five trait that involves being appreciative, forgiving, kind, trusting, noncritical, warm, compassionate, considerate, and straightforward. Jim's desire to get along with others probably reflects kindness, warmth, consideration, and being forgiving. (see The Five Factor Personality Model)

    a.   Openness to experience involves being artistic, curious, imaginative, insightful, and original. It does not specify how one interacts with others.

    c.   Extraversion involves being active, assertive, energetic, outgoing, talkative, gesturally expressive, and gregarious. It does not necessarily mean that you want to get along with others, just that you would like to be around others.

    d.   Conscientiousness involves being efficient, organized, planful, and reliable.

11.   b is the answer. If these factors appear in many situations in many countries and cultures, this suggests that they are universal and not just researchers' wishful thinking. (see The Five Factor Personality Model)

    a.   Factor analysis is the basic statistical technique that trait theorists use to cluster similar traits. Its use does not indicate evidence.

    c.   That traits describe people rather than explain them is one of the criticisms of the approach.

    d.   This statement is false. Identical twins are more alike in general temperament than fraternal twins are. But this statement provides no evidence for the Big-Five model.

12.   d is the answer. Trait theorists argue that behavior is a reflection of consistent and stable traits and that environmental or situational factors do not determine behavior. (see The Trait Approach)

    a.   Psychodynamic theorists have been criticized for adhering to Freud's emphasis on the unconscious and his use of patients' reports as a basis for psychosexual development theory. Freud was also accused of being sexist. But the belief in situation-specific behavior does not detract from the psychodynamic theory.

    b.   Social-cognitive theorists have been accused of overemphasizing overt behavior and the environmental factors of reward and punishment and not attending enough to the individual's perceptions, feelings, and thoughts.

    c.   Humanistic concepts are difficult to measure, more descriptive than explanatory, and naive since they are so optimistic about the nature of men and women.

13.   a is the answer. According to Bandura, a social-cognitive theorist, our learned expectations for success can influence our behavior. (see Prominent Social-Cognitive Theories)

    b.   Psychodynamic theorists, not cognitive behavioral theorists, focus on unconscious mental processes.

    c.   Self-efficacy is a social-cognitive phenomenon, not a trait or secondary trait.

    d.   The ego is a psychodynamic concept, not a social-cognitive concept.

14.   c is the answer. Rotter's expectancy theory is part of the social-cognitive approach. Rotter proposed that internals believe they control events and that externals believe that others (fate, other people, luck) control events. (see Prominent Social-Cognitive Theories)

    a.   Expectancies are not a trait or type, both of which are the foundation of the trait approach.

    b.   The humanistic approach doesn't emphasize expectancies in the development of personality.

    d.   Psychodynamic theories do not emphasize expectancies; they tend to focus on unconscious mental processes.

15.   b is the answer. Colin's eye contact serves the function of getting other people to listen to him. Functional analysis understands behavior in terms of the purpose it serves. (see Roots of the Social-Cognitive Approach)

    a.   A projective test is a type of personality test, not an analysis of the purpose a behavior serves.

    c.   A condition of worth is created when a person is evaluated rather than his or her behavior. If Colin's teacher told him he was a good boy for making eye contact, she would have created a condition of worth.

    d.   A defense mechanism is an unconscious tactic to protect against anxiety or guilt.

16.   b is the answer. A deficiency motivation, according to Maslow, occurs when individuals focus on what they do not have instead of on what they do have. (see Prominent Humanistic Theories)

    a.   If people focus on or derive satisfaction from what they have, they have a growth orientation.

c.   Humanistic theorists assume that we all attempt to fulfill our potentials.

d.   A deficiency motivation is a humanistic concept that is not related to traits.

17.   a is the answer. Kareem's tendency toward growth and fulfillment is an actualizing tendency. An actualizing tendency is an inclination to become more than one is through growth. (see Prominent Humanistic Theories)

b.   Positive regard is the approval of others.

c.   A deficiency motivation is a tendency to focus on what one lacks, rather than what one might achieve through growth.

d.   Congruence occurs when one's self-evaluations are consistent with the evaluations others provide.

18.   c is the answer. Longitudinal studies provide support for the idea that relatively accurate predictions can be made about an individual's personality as an adult on the basis of information about that person's temperament as a child. (see Focus on Research Methods: Longitudinal Studies of Temperament and Personality)

a, b.   There is no evidence that hormonal changes or problems during puberty will negatively affect an individual's personality.

d.   c is the answer; predictions can be made, based on information about childhood temperament.

19.   d is the answer. Those who take a humanistic view of personality believe that everyone sees a reality that is unique. Therefore, interviews, during which people can explain their points of view, would be the best method of assessment. (see Assessing Personality)

a.   A humanistic theorist would say that one cannot interpret someone's behavior without knowing that person's interpretation or perception of reality.

b.   A nonprojective measure assumes that people have the same general interpretation of the questions on it. If this were not the case, the questions could not be used to compare one person to another. Humanistic views assume that each person's view of anything, including a true-false or multiple-choice question, is unique.

c.   Humanistic theorists do not depend on physiological data in personality assessment; they are more interested in conscious experience.

20.   c is the answer. A projective test uses ambiguous stimuli to allow the taker to project unconscious conflicts and desires onto the test. If the picture of two people is unclear enough, for example, a person who has trouble with authority might make up a story about a person getting a reprimand. (see Projective Personality Measures)

a.   You may have been thinking of the Minnesota Multiphasic Personality Inventory (MMPI), which is an objective test.

b.   Nonprojective, or objective, tests have specific statements or questions to be read and responded to by the test taker.

d.   Social-cognitive theorists would not use ambiguous stimuli to test for personality. If they used a personality test at all, it would be one that looked for generalized expectancies or ideas about the self.

Now turn to the quiz analysis table at the end of this chapter to find which areas you know well and which areas you need to work on. Circle the numbers in the table for items on Quiz 1 that you answered correctly.

Quiz 2

1.   b is the answer. Lydia's ego has devised a solution that will let her spend more time with a man she is attracted to (thereby satisfying the id) without breaking the rules of society or doing something that the superego would disapprove of. (see The Structure and Development of Personality)

   a.   The id wants to have sex with the doctor and does not particularly care what rules are broken.

   c.   The superego would tell Lydia that she is married and cannot have sex with anyone but her husband.

   d.   Eros is the aggregate of life instincts.

2.   d is the answer. Reaction-formation guides behavior in the direction opposite to that of the unwanted impulse. Nathaniel feels hatred because he really likes her and feels threatened by that attraction. (see The Structure and Development of Personality)

   a.   Creativity is not a psychodynamic defense mechanism.

   b.   Projection involves projecting unwanted impulses onto other people, not displaying a behavior opposite from one's true feelings. Projection would involve Nathaniel saying that Shelley likes him, when he really is the one attracted to her.

   c.   Rationalization is an attempt to make your own behavioral actions or mistakes seem reasonable.

3.   a is the answer. Fixation occurs when we do not resolve psychosexual conflicts during development. For example, according to Freud, those who are weaned too early may engage in oral activities such as smoking, excessive talking, or overeating. (see The Structure and Development of Personality)

   b.   We use defense mechanisms to relieve anxiety, but this is not a fixation.

   c.   Fixation is not a part of behavioral theory.

   d.   Fixation is not part of humanistic theory.

4.   b is the answer. Psychodynamic views of personality are not represented by anyone. (see Variations on Freud's Personality Theory)

5.   c is the answer. Joe assumes that the man in question will always be aggressive. Trait theorists assume that people have several traits that will be present in many different situations. Kim is talking about the MMPI, a personality test developed by trait theorists. (see The Trait Approach)

   a.   Richard agrees with humanistic theorists.

   b.   Erika agrees with social-cognitive theorists.

   d.   Richard agrees with humanistic theorists, while Erika agrees with social-cognitive theorists.

6.   d is the answer. The latency period lasts from about age five until puberty. During this time, a child focuses on education and social development and sexual urges are dormant. (see The Structure and Development of Personality)

   a.   The oral stage involves the mouth as an erogenous zone.

   b.   The anal stage involves the anal area as an erogenous zone.

   c.   The phallic stage involves the genitalia as an erogenous zone.

7. d is the answer. Many current psychodynamic psychologists focus on object relations. Object relations theory suggests that people's relations to the mother or other primary caregivers shape a person's thoughts about social relationships later in life. Some research shows that early attachment styles are related to current relationship quality. (see Contemporary Psychodynamic Theories)

    a.   A Big-Five theorist would suggest that one of five traits is influencing Jack's troubles.

    b.   A social-cognitive theorist would probably hypothesize that Jack expects to fail or that Jack is being rewarded somehow for his present behavior.

    c.   A humanistic theorist would emphasize Jack's perceptions, not his attachment to his mother.

8. a is the answer. Most people can describe someone using about seven labels. Allport called these central traits. (see Allport's Trait Theory)

    b.   Allport also thought we had secondary traits, which are more tied to a situation. For example, a person who bluffs when playing cards might not bluff in other social situations.

    c, d.   Self-efficacy and expectancies (internal versus external) are social-cognitive concepts.

9. d is the answer. The humanistic approach maintains that the way people perceive and interpret the world forms their personalities and guides their behavior. (see Prominent Humanistic Theories)

    a.   The psychodynamic approach focuses on the struggle between unconscious impulses and society's rules.

    b.   The trait approach describes personality as a combination of stable internal characteristics that people consistently display.

    c.   The social-cognitive approach views personality as an array of behaviors that people acquire through learning and display in particular situations.

10. b is the answer. Because the humanistic approach suggests that all people are inherently good and growth-oriented, it has been criticized for being overly optimistic and unrealistic. (see Evaluating the Humanistic Approach)

    a.   The humanistic approach concentrates on the differences among individuals to understand personality.

    c.   Another criticism of the humanistic approach is that it seems to do a better job of describing personality than of explaining it.

    d.   The humanistic approach does not emphasize instincts. You might be thinking of the psychodynamic approach.

11. c is the correct answer. Rogers says we have an innate inclination toward growth and fulfillment—towards being the best we can. He has a positive view of human nature. (see Prominent Humanistic Theories)

    a, d.   These are both sociocognitive theorists. Sociocognitive theorists see humans as blank slates at birth—inclined neither towards goodness nor badness but towards whatever behaviors are rewarded.

    b.   Freud viewed humans as plagued by unconscious desires that were socially unacceptable. He had a more negative view of human nature.

12. d is the answer. Trait theories do not emphasize the unconscious as psychodynamic theories do. (see Evaluating the Trait Approach)

12.   d is the answer. Trait theories do not emphasize the unconscious as psychodynamic theories do. (see Evaluating the Trait Approach)

  a.   Traits are much better at describing than explaining behavior.

  b.   Many trait descriptions seem to fit a large number of people, thus reducing their value for describing a given person.

  c.   Trait descriptions do not explain situational influences on behavior. Trait theories imply stable behavior, driven by traits, in any situation.

13.   c is the answer. The social-cognitive approach is based on the assumption that people learn how to think and act. (see Roots of the Social-Cognitive Approach)

  a.   The psychodynamic approach focuses on the influence of unconscious mental processes on personality.

  b.   The trait approach attributes much of personality to inherent characteristics; it does not emphasize learning as much as the cognitive-behavioral approach does.

  d.   The Big-Five model is an example of a trait theory.

14.   c is the answer. Joe would be most likely to take a self-paced course because he would prefer being in control of his work pace. (see Prominent Social-Cognitive Theories)

  a, b.   Joe would probably not ignore physical symptoms of illness or work very well on an assembly line. Externals would be more likely to exhibit these types of behavior.

  d.   c is the answer.

15.   d is the answer. According to Bandura, we can learn new behaviors, learn to inhibit behaviors, and learn how to prompt or facilitate behaviors through observational learning. (see Prominent Social-Cognitive Theories)

16.   d is the answer. According to Rogers, parents may create a condition of worth when they lead a child to believe that his worth depends on displaying the right behaviors. In effect, Martin's father was suggesting that he would love Martin more or be more proud of him if Martin were doing "real" boy activities like playing soccer, rather than reading. (see Prominent Humanistic Theories)

  a.   A deficiency motivation is another humanistic concept, but it occurs when a person focuses on what is missing instead of on growth or satisfaction with current possessions.

  b.   A fixation will occur, according to Freud, if a person does not resolve conflicts at each stage of psychosexual development. Fixations are basically unrelated to parental reprimands.

  c.   Interdependent self-systems are more common in collectivist cultures, where one's place in groups is emphasized.

17.   b is the answer. People with an interdependent self-system see themselves as a fraction of a whole. They tend not to be happy when singled out for attention, even if it is for personal achievement. (see Linkages: Personality, Culture, and Human Development)

  a.   People with an independent self-system emphasize personal achievement rather than their place in a group.

  c.   This relates to Rotter's expectancy theory. Internals believe that they control events through their own efforts.

  d.   This is part of Rotter's expectancy theory. Externals believe that external forces control events.

18. d is the answer. Projective personality tests involve presenting a subject with an unstructured and ambiguous stimulus. Personality is supposedly reflected in the subject's response. Because the tasks are unstructured, they tend to be relatively difficult to score, unreliable, and not as valid as objective tests. (see Projective Personality Measures)

19. b is the answer. MMPI is a nonprojective personality measure. It is designed for use in diagnosing psychological disorders and is a reliable test. (see Nonprojective Personality Measures)

    a.   NEO-PI-R is a reliable, nonprojective personality measure, but it is not designed for use in diagnosing psychological disorders.

    c, d.   The TAT and the Rorschach Inkblot Test are projective measures, not nonprojective.

20. a is the answer. The NEO-PI-R measures the Big-Five personality dimensions, which are the most typically measured characteristics used in employment testing by large organizations. (see Personality Tests and Employee Selection)

    b, c, d.   These tests do not measure Big-Five dimensions and thus are not as likely to be used as the NEO-PI-R.

Now turn to the quiz analysis table at the end of this chapter to find which areas you know well and which areas you need to work on. Circle the numbers in the table for items on Quiz 2 that you answered correctly.

For each question you answered correctly, circle its number. (Quiz 1 numbers are not shaded; Quiz 2 numbers are shaded.) Are there patterns in the types of questions or the topics you got wrong that could direct your further study? Did you improve from Quiz 1 to Quiz 2?

QUIZ REVIEW

Topic	Type of Question		
	Definition	Comprehension	Application
The Psychodynamic Approach			
The Structure and Development of Personality	1	5	2, 3
	3	6	1, 2, 4
Variations on Freud's Personality Theory			4
Contemporary Psychodynamic Theories		6	
			7
The Trait Approach		12	8
			5
Allport's Trait Theory	7		9
			8
The Five Factor Personality Model		11	10
Evaluating the Trait Approach			
		12	
The Social-Cognitive Approach			
Roots of the Social-Cognitive Approach			15
		13	
Prominent Social-Cognitive Theories	13	14	
			14, 15
The Humanistic Psychology Approach			
Prominent Humanistic Theories	16		17
		11	9, 16
Evaluating the Humanistic Approach			
		10	
Linkages: Personality, Culture, and Human Development			
			17
Focus on Research Methods: Longitudinal Studies of Temperament and Personality			18
Assessing Personality		19	
Projective Personality Measures			20
		18	
Nonprojective Personality Measures			
			19
Personality Tests and Employee Selection			
		20	

Total correct by quiz:

Quiz 1:	
Quiz 2:	

CHAPTER 15

Psychological Disorders

Psychopathology (or *mental disorder*) involves patterns of thought, emotion, or behavior that result in personal distress or significant impairment in a person's social or occupational functioning. *Comorbidity* occurs when an individual is diagnosed with two or even three disorders simultaneously.

OUTLINE
I. DEFINING PSYCHOLOGICAL DISORDERS
   A. What Is Abnormal?
      There are several approaches to defining normality, but none are perfect.

      1. *Deviance.* Those behaviors displayed by the greatest number of people are considered normal. Statistical infrequency considers behavior that is atypical or rare to be abnormal. However, some behavior that is rare, such as creative genius or world-class athletic ability, is valued; therefore, statistical infrequency alone is not an adequate criterion. A related criterion is *norm violation,* which involves behavior that violates the cultural rules that tell us how to behave in certain situations. Yet, it is hard to use this criterion consistently because norms are variable across cultures and situations.
      2. *Distress.* Psychological problems causing distress require treatment. Because some people with disorders may not experience distress, *personal suffering* cannot be the only criterion for abnormality.
      3. *Dysfunction. Impaired functioning* involves difficulty fulfilling appropriate and expected roles in family, social, and work-related situations. Sometimes though, people with a dysfunction may not be abnormal but dealing with an overwhelming problem. Alternately, some people with a psychological disorder may be highly functional.
   B. Behavior in Context: A Practical Approach
      The *content* of behavior (whether behavior is bizarre, dysfunctional, or harmful), the sociocultural *context* in which the behavior occurs (where and when behavior occurs), and the *consequences* of behavior are all taken into consideration when judging whether behavior is abnormal in the *practical approach,* which is the approach most mental health professionals take.

II. EXPLAINING PSYCHOLOGICAL DISORDERS
   A. The Biopsychosocial Approach
      The biopsychosocial approach looks at abnormal behavior as caused by a combination and interaction of biological, psychological, and sociocultural factors.

      1. *Biological Factors.* The ancient Greek physician Hippocrates introduced the medical model, in which he explained that psychological disorders resulted from imbalances among four humors. The medical model eventually evolved into the concept of mental illness. The medical model is now termed the neurobiological model because it looks at problems in anatomy and physiology of the brain and other areas.
      2. *Psychological Processes.* In this view, mental disorders are caused by inner turmoil or other psychological events. Psychological models include the *psychodynamic, social-cognitive,* and *humanistic* approaches.

3. *Sociocultural Context.* The <u>sociocultural perspective</u> relies on <u>sociocultural factors</u> such as gender and age, physical and social situations, cultural values and expectations, and historical eras. *Culture-general* disorders appear in most societies, while culture-specific forms appear only in certain ones.

B. Diathesis-Stress as an Integrative Explanation
According to the <u>diathesis-stress model</u>, genetics, early learning, biological processes, and stress levels may all contribute to psychological disorders. The *diathesis* is the predisposition for a disorder, but it is triggered by stress.

III. CLASSIFYING PSYCHOLOGICAL DISORDERS
The classification system in the United States for psychological disorders is the *Diagnostic and Statistical Manual of Mental Disorder*, which is now in its latest edition known as the DSM-IV-TR. Outside the U.S., the manual used most frequently is World Health Organization's *International Classification of Diseases (ICD-10)*. Efforts are underway to make these two systems compatible.

A. A Classification System: DSM-IV-TR
DSM-IV-TR describes each form of disorder and provides criteria for diagnosis. DSM-IV-TR consists of a series of evaluations on five dimensions called *axes*. Every person is rated on each axis. Axis I comprises descriptive criteria of major mental disorders. Axis II contains personality disorders and mental retardation. Axis III comprises physical conditions or disorders. Axis IV has types and levels of stress. Axis V has a rating of the current level of functioning. (Neurosis, characterized by anxiety, and psychosis, whose symptoms include a break with reality, are no longer major diagnostic categories in DSM-IV-TR.) Revisions are underway to bring forth the next edition of the DSM (DSM-V) in 2013, and psychologists are arguing the benefits of various changes to introduce in that volume. The outcome will not be known for some time, however. *Positive psychology* argues that the DSM should include more emphasis on strengths, not just deficits.

B. Evaluating the Diagnostic System
The diagnostic system can be evaluated in terms of inter-rater reliability and validity. *Inter-rater reliability* is the degree to which different diagnosticians give the same label to one patient. Inter-rater reliability is stronger on Axis I, but weaker on Axis II, and is highest when semi-structured or structured interviews are used. The *validity* of the DSM-IV-TR is harder to establish because the accuracy of a diagnosis can be judged in many ways. The current system has certainly not satisfied everyone, but it probably is not possible to develop a system that could do so.

C. Thinking Critically: Is Psychological Diagnosis Biased?
What am I being asked to believe or accept?

Clinicians' diagnoses are biased by, for example, racial stereotypes.

What evidence is available to support the assertion?

African American people are more frequently diagnosed with schizophrenia than are European Americans. In addition, African Americans are overrepresented in facilities noted for higher incidences of more serious disorders (public mental health hospitals).

Are there alternative ways of interpreting the evidence?

Diagnostic differences by race may not reflect bias. There could very well be physiological or cultural differences that cause mental illness.

What additional evidence would help to evaluate the alternatives?

Studies that ask physicians to diagnose pairs of people with identical symptoms but different races could detect bias in diagnoses of mental illnesses. Some studies have failed to detect bias, but these were conducted with the physicians' knowledge of the research question. When the physicians were unaware of the question, some bias has been detected. Further, bias can result in either underdiagnosis or overdiagnosis. Therefore, ethnic bias is a factor in some diagnoses, particularly in mental hospital settings.

What conclusions are most reasonable?

Clinicians, because they are human, are prone to bias when diagnosing people who potentially have mental illness. However, bias can be minimized by becoming educated about a prospective patient's cultural background and its effect on behavior and mental processes and by relying less on clinical impressions and more on structured interviews and published diagnostic criteria.

IV. ANXIETY DISORDERS
    A. Types of Anxiety Disorders
        1. *Phobia.* A <u>phobia</u> is an <u>anxiety disorder</u> involving a strong, irrational fear of an object or situation that should not cause such a reaction. <u>Specific phobias</u> involve fear of specific physical objects, places, or activities. <u>Social phobias</u> involve fear of being negatively evaluated by others or publicly embarrassed by doing something impulsive, outrageous, or humiliating. <u>Agoraphobia</u> is a strong fear of being separated from a safe place like home or of being trapped in a place from which escape might be difficult.
        2. *Generalized Anxiety Disorder.* The condition called <u>generalized anxiety disorder (GAD)</u> involves milder but long-lasting feelings of anxiety, worry, dread, or apprehension that are not focused on any particular object or situation. *Free-floating anxiety* is a term sometimes used to describe the nonspecific nature of this anxiety.
        3. *Panic Disorder.* Periodic episodes of extreme terror (*panic attacks*) without warning or obvious cause are characteristic of people with <u>panic disorder</u>.
        4. *Obsessive-Compulsive Disorder.* The persistent intrusion of thoughts or images (<u>obsessions</u>) and a need to perform certain behavior patterns (<u>compulsions</u>) are symptoms of <u>obsessive-compulsive disorder (OCD)</u>. When the obsessive thinking or compulsive behaviors are interrupted, severe anxiety results.
    B. Causes of Anxiety Disorders
        1. *Biological Factors.* There is evidence of genetic contribution to anxiety disorders although study of *epigenetics* suggests that the gene by itself will not trigger the disorder. Rather, the gene is switched on or off by certain environmental conditions. Other biological explanations of anxiety disorders include abnormal levels of particular neurotransmitters and oversensitive brainstem mechanisms, especially the autonomic nervous system.
        2. *Psychological and Environmental Factors.* Families that don't socialize much and exaggerate everyday dangers may cause their children to learn anxiety and inadvertently promote anxiety disorders. A person suffering from an anxiety disorder may exaggerate the danger associated with certain stimuli and underestimate his or her coping skills, causing anxiety.
    C. Linkages: Anxiety Disorders and Learning
    Phobias start with distressing thoughts followed by operantly rewarded behaviors. Phobias can also be explained by classical conditioning. People may be *biologically prepared* to learn certain fears and avoid stimuli that had potential for harm to our evolutionary ancestors. Rare phobias may be a product of classical conditioning, but common ones such as snakes, fire, height, and insects may be due to a biological preparedness to react negatively to certain potentially hazardous things. However, biological preparedness

typically must encounter the right environmental stressor to trigger the disorder, as the diathesis-stress model suggests.

V. SOMATOFORM DISORDERS

Somatoform disorders are characterized by physical symptoms with no physical cause. In conversion disorder, a person appears to be, but is actually not, functionally impaired (for example, blind, deaf, or paralyzed). The physical symptoms often help reduce stress, and the person may seem unconcerned about them, but the person is generally not *malingering*. Hypochondriasis involves strong fears of a specific severe illness that are usually accompanied by complaints of many vague symptoms. In somatization disorder, a person makes dramatic but vague reports about a multitude of physical problems rather than any specific illness. Somatoform pain disorder is characterized by severe, often constant, pain with no apparent physical cause. Body dysmorphic disorder occurs when a person is intensely distressed about an imagined abnormality of the skin, hair, face, or other bodily area.

VI. DISSOCIATIVE DISORDERS

A. Dissociative disorders are characterized by a sudden, usually temporary, disruption in memory, consciousness, or identity. Fugue reaction (or dissociative fugue) is characterized by sudden memory loss and the assumption of a new identity in a new locale. In dissociative amnesia, a person has sudden memory loss without leaving home and creating a new identity. The most dramatic and least common dissociative disorder is dissociative identity disorder (DID), formerly known as multiple personality disorder (MPD), which involves having more than one identity, each of which speaks, acts, and writes differently. Psychodynamic theorists believe that dissociative disorders are methods of repressing (forgetting) unwanted impulses or memories. Social-cognitive theorists believe that dissociative disorders are examples of learned behavior patterns that have become so discrepant that a person may feel like and be perceived as a different person from time to time.

B. Recent studies have drawn several conclusions about people displaying multiple personalities: The memory loss and dissociation appears to be genuine phenomena; many people with dissociative disorders have experiences they would like to forget or avoid (such as child abuse); many are skilled at self-hypnosis; and most can escape trauma by creating "new personalities" to deal with the stress.

VII. AFFECTIVE DISORDERS

Affective disorders, or mood disorders, are characterized by persistent extreme mood swings that are inconsistent with environmental events.

A. Depressive Disorders

Major depression (or major depressive disorder) involves feeling sad and overwhelmed, loss of interest in activities or relationships, and taking pleasure in nothing. Also common are changes or disturbances in eating habits, sleep, decision making, and concentration. In extreme cases, depressed people exhibit delusions. A more common pattern of depression is dysthymic disorder, which involves symptoms similar to those of major depression but to a lesser degree and spread out over a longer time period.

1. *Suicide and Depression.* Depression is implicated in up to 70 percent of suicides. Hopelessness about the future is another predictor of suicide. Suicide rates differ depending on sociocultural factors. In the U. S., suicide is most common for males over 65 years of age, but it is the third leading cause of death among people aged 15-24. Women attempt suicide more often, but men who attempt suicide are more likely to succeed because they tend to choose more lethal methods. Suicide rates are highest among American Indians and lowest among Hispanic Americans. People who have a

specific plan, have given away possession, are impulsive, or have talked about suicide are at risk for committing suicide.

B.   Bipolar Disorders
Bipolar I disorder is characterized by alternating feelings of extreme depression and mania over a period of days, weeks, or years. *Bipolar I disorder* is relatively rare in comparison to major depression. Even less common is *bipolar II disorder*, which features major depressive episodes alternative with less severe manic episodes known as *hypomania*. Cyclothymic personality (or cyclothymic disorder) is a slightly more common pattern of less extreme mood swings.

C.   Causes of Affective Disorders
1.   *Biological Factors*. Genetics appear to play a role in affective disorders. Retions of the brain associated with mood such as the frontal lobes and the hippocampus have been implicated. Additionally, altered levels and possibly dysregulation of norepinephrine, serotonin, and dopamine (neurotransmitters), changes in the control of the stress-related hormone cortisol, abnormal biological rhythms, and genetic influences are causative factors in affective disorders. Thus, both the nervous system and the endocrine system are involved in affective disorders.
2.   *Psychological and Social Factors*. Most people recognize that biological explanations must be combined with psychological and social factors for a complete understanding. The biopsychosocial model sees affective disorders as a combination of the impact of anxiety, negative thinking, personality traits, family interactions with the biological factors, and environmental stressors. Social-cognitive theorists see *learned helplessness* as a factor in developing depression. Psychodynamic *object relations* theorists also see maladaptive childhood experiences as a contributing factor. A *negative attributional style* can lead to or sustain a depression, and women tend to develop a *ruminative style* that may add to this. Men, in contrast, use a *distracting style* that may mitigate the development of depression.

VIII. SCHIZOPHRENIA
Schizophrenic symptoms include severely disturbed thinking, emotion, perception, and behavior, which impair a person's ability to communicate and function on a daily basis. Schizophrenia is rare, occurring in only about 1 percent of the population. Improvement is more likely if a person had achieved a higher level of functioning before the symptoms appeared, referred to as *premorbid adjustment*.

A.   Symptoms of Schizophrenia
1.   People with schizophrenia often display incoherent forms of thought; for example, *neologisms*, *word salads*, *clang associations*, and *loose associations* are common symptoms. Schizophrenic thought content is equally disturbed; common symptoms include *delusions of influence, self-significant delusions,* and *delusions of persecution*.
2.   Symptoms of schizophrenia include an inability to focus attention or concentrate. Changes in perception of body parts or of other people may also occur. Many people with schizophrenia report hallucinations or false perceptions. Emotions are often absent ("flat affect") or inappropriate for a given situation. Movements may range from constant agitation to almost total immobility. Lack of motivation and social skills, deterioration in personal hygiene, and an inability to function from day to day are other common characteristics of schizophrenia.

B.   Categorizing Schizophrenia
The DSM-IV-TR lists five subtypes of schizophrenia: paranoid, disorganized, catatonic, undifferentiated, and residual. Many symptoms overlap, and no links are made to biological conditions thought to underlie schizophrenia. Instead, the focus is more on describing patients in terms of positive symptoms (additions of undesirable elements, such as

hallucinations) and <u>negative symptoms</u> (subtractions of normal elements of mental functioning, such as lack of emotion). There is also evidence for three separate dimensions of schizophrenia: psychotic (displaying hallucinations or delusions), disorganized (incoherence, inappropriate affect, and chaotic behavior), and negative (displaying negative symptoms).

   C.   Causes of Schizophrenia
      1.   *Biological Factors.* Possible biological causes of schizophrenia include inherited predispositions; oversensitivity to dopamine; loss, deterioration, or disorganization of certain brain cells; enlarged brain ventricles; reduced blood flow in certain parts of the brain; and abnormal brain lateralization. Not all persons with schizophrenia have all the biological problems listed here. Some symptoms, like enlarged ventricles, are associated more with negative symptoms than positive. Some researchers search for *neurodevelopmental abnormalities*, meaning that the brain problems stem from events that occurred while the brain was developing prior to birth and in childhood.
      2.   *Psychological and Sociocultural Factors.* Factors such as dysfunctional cognitive habits, the stress of urban living, being an immigrant, and exposure to stressful family communication patterns (such as *expressed emotion*) are associated with schizophrenia.
      3.   *Vulnerability Theory.* The vulnerability model takes a diathesis-stress approach. The vulnerability can be biological or psychological in nature.

IX. **PERSONALITY DISORDERS**
<u>Personality disorders</u>, which are less severe than psychological disorders, are lifestyles or ways of behaving that begin in childhood or adolescence and create problems, usually for others. Ten personality disorders are described in the DSM-IV-TR on Axis II. They are grouped into three clusters that share certain features. The *odd-eccentric* cluster features symptoms similar to but milder than schizophrenia and includes schizoid, schizotypal, and paranoid personality disorder. The *anxious-fearful* cluster includes dependent, obsessive-compulsive, and avoidant personality disorders. The *dramatic-erratic* cluster includes histrionic, narcissistic, borderline, and antisocial personality disorders. The main features of the dramatic-erratic disorders are extreme self-absorption and lack of empathy for others. <u>Antisocial personality disorder</u> is the most serious. It is characterized by a long-term pattern of irresponsible, impulsive, unscrupulous, and sometimes even criminal behavior. These individuals tend to become less active and dangerous after the age of 40 or so. Genetics, information processing deficits, and poor social environment (e.g., broken home, lack of attachment to caregiver) have all been implicated in antisocial personality disorder.

   A.   Focus on Research Methods: Exploring Links between Child Abuse and Antisocial Personality Disorder
      Using a prospective design, researchers compared 416 adults whose backgrounds included official records of abuse by age 11 to 283 adults without records of abuse. Although a minority of both groups showed criminal tendencies and incidence of antisocial personality, the rate of both was greater for the abused group. The two groups were matched on important variables such as socioeconomic status, but it is possible that abuse may indirectly cause criminality and antisocial personality disorder, as abused children are likely exposed to other risk factors such as poor role models. Future research should investigate this possibility more directly. It should also investigate why such a small percentage of abused children developed antisocial personality as a means of identifying the factors that protect abused children from developing the personality disorder.

X. A SAMPLING OF OTHER PSYCHOLOGICAL DISORDERS

A. Psychological Disorders of Childhood

Childhood disorders are unique because of the incomplete nature of children's development and their limited coping skills. Most childhood behavior problems can be categorized as either *externalizing* (lack of control) or *internalizing* (overcontrol) disorders. Common externalizing disorders include *conduct disorders* and *attention-deficit hyperactivity disorder* (ADHD). Internalizing disorders include *separation anxiety disorder*. *Pervasive developmental disorder* is diagnosed when children do not fall clearly into either the externalizing or internalizing categories but show clear communication difficulties and social impairments. The disorders in this group are also known as *autistic spectrum disorders* and range in severity. High-functioning autism is known as *Asperger's syndrome* which involves impaired relationships and repetitive behaviors, but fewer cognitive deficits associated with more severe *autistic disorder*. Disturbance in the function of *mirror neurons* may play a role in autistic spectrum disorders.

B. Substance-Related Disorders

Substance-related disorders are the result of the prolonged use of, or addiction (*physiological dependence*) to, psychoactive drugs, which can cause physical or psychological harm to the user and consequently to others around her or him.

1. *Alcohol Use Disorders*. *Alcohol abuse* (known as alcoholism) is a pattern of continual or intermittent drinking that may lead to *alcohol dependence* and almost always causes severe social, physical, and other problems. Prolonged use can lead to *Korsakoff's psychosis* and other physical ailments. The biopsychosocial model sees alcoholism as a result of a combination of genetic characteristics and what people learn in their social and cultural environments.

2. *Heroin and Cocaine Dependence*. Four percent of Americans are addicted to cocaine or heroin (estimate). Continued cocaine use or overdose can produce a range of symptoms: nausea, hyperactivity, paranoid thinking, sudden depressive "crashes," and even death. Both biological and psychological factors may be involved in the initial involvement with drugs.

XI. MENTAL ILLNESS AND THE LAW

People with mental illnesses are protected in two ways when accused of committing crimes. First, if a person can't understand the charges at the time of trial or assist in the defense, she or he is said to be *mentally incompetent*. Second, the person can be found *not guilty by reason of insanity* if, at the time of the crime, mental illness prevented the defendant from understanding what she or he was doing or that the act was wrong, or if it prevented the defendant from resisting the impulse to do wrong. These laws were designed to protect people with mental illnesses, but critics question the idea of protection. Others point to problems deciding who is insane and who is not when there is conflicting testimony.

Some states have abolished the insanity defense. Other states now permit a verdict of *guilty but mentally ill*. The *irresistible-impulse criterion* has been eliminated from the definition of insanity in federal courts, and the defense is now required to prove the defendant was insane at the time of the crime (the latter is also the case in some states).

KEY TERMS

1. **Psychopathology** involves patterns of thinking, feeling, and behaving that are maladaptive, disruptive, or uncomfortable for those who are affected or for those with whom they come in contact. (see introductory section)

REMEMBER: <u>Psych</u> refers to "mental" or "psychological," and <u>pathos</u> refers to "illness" or "sickness." <u>Psychopathology</u> means the study of mental illness or disorder.

2. The **biopsychosocial approach** is a view of mental disorders as caused by a combination of interacting biological, psychological, and sociocultural factors. (see Explaining Psychological Disorders)

3. The **medical model** (also called the **neurobiological model**) is a view in which psychological disorders are seen as reflecting disturbances in the anatomy and chemistry of the brain and in other biological processes. (see Explaining Psychological Disorders)

Example: Nora's doctor believes that her depression is caused by an imbalance of some neurotransmitter levels. Nora is taking an antidepressant to correct this physical problem.

4. The **psychological model** is a view in which mental disorder is seen as arising from psychological processes. (see Explaining Psychological Disorders)

REMEMBER: The psychodynamic, social-cognitive, and humanistic approaches are examples.

5. A **sociocultural perspective** is a way of looking at mental disorders in relation to gender, age, ethnicity, and other social and cultural factors. (see Explaining Psychological Disorders)

Example: The greater tolerance for excessive drinking in men may make alcohol abuse more likely in men than in women.

6. **Sociocultural factors** are characteristics or conditions that can influence the appearance and form of maladaptive behavior. (see Explaining Psychological Disorders)

Example: Because it is more acceptable in American culture for women to express their emotions, they are more likely to be diagnosed with depression because they are more likely to express negative emotions publicly.

2. The **diathesis-stress model** is the notion that psychological disorders arise when a predisposition for a disorder combines with sufficient amounts of stress to trigger symptoms. (see Diathesis-Stress as an Integrative Explanation)

Example: Frank has a biological susceptibility to stress. Entering the combined medical and doctoral program put him under a lot of stress. He was very depressed by the end of his first semester. Juan tends to be less stress-sensitive and is handling the same program with much less trouble.

3. **Anxiety disorders** are conditions in which intense feelings of apprehension are longstanding and disruptive. (see Anxiety Disorders)

REMEMBER: Anxiety disorders include phobias, generalized anxiety disorders, panic disorder, obsessive-compulsive disorders, and posttraumatic stress disorder.

4. A **phobia** is an anxiety disorder involving strong, irrational fear of an object or situation that does not objectively justify such a reaction. (see Types of Anxiety Disorders)

5. A **specific phobia** is an anxiety disorder involving fear and avoidance of heights, animals, or other specific stimuli and situations. (see Types of Anxiety Disorders)

Example: Claustrophobia is the fear of being in closed places.

6. A **social phobia** is an anxiety disorder involving strong, irrational fears relating to social situations. (see Types of Anxiety Disorders)

Example: Rosa is terrified of giving a speech to her class (social situation). She is afraid that she will be completely unable to speak and will embarrass herself by stammering until she blushes and has to run away.

7. **Agoraphobia** is an anxiety disorder involving strong fear of being alone or away from the security of home. (see Types of Anxiety Disorders)

Example: Eliza is afraid to leave her house. She cannot go shopping or out for an evening. She cannot hold a job or visit her friends and family. She cannot take her children to the doctor or drive them anywhere. Although she is less fearful when accompanied by her husband, she is still uncomfortable in any situation outside her home.

8. **Generalized anxiety disorder (GAD)** is a condition that involves relatively mild but long-lasting anxiety that is not focused on any particular object or situation. (see Types of Anxiety Disorders)

Example: Leslie has had a feeling of vague apprehension for about six weeks and always feels as though something bad is going to happen to her. She cannot sleep and is constantly tired and irritable.

9. **Panic disorder** is an anxiety disorder involving sudden panic attacks. (see Types of Anxiety Disorders)

Example: Akbar, a university professor, often experiences panic attacks. He can be in the middle of lecturing, driving his car, or browsing in a bookstore when he suddenly becomes terrified for no specific reason. He also experiences chest pain and dizziness during these episodes.

REMEMBER: Symptoms include heart palpitations, chest pain or pressure, dizziness, sweating, and a feeling of faintness.

10. **Obsessive-compulsive disorder (OCD)** is an anxiety disorder involving repetitive thoughts and urges to perform certain rituals. (see Types of Anxiety Disorders)

Example: Simon cannot enter a room and feel comfortable unless he touches all the walls first. If he cannot do this, he becomes very anxious and highly agitated.

16. **Obsessions** are persistent, upsetting, or unwanted thoughts that interfere with daily life and may lead to compulsions. (see Types of Anxiety Disorders)

Example: Collin cannot stop thinking about the germs he might have picked up when he shook hands with someone.

17. **Compulsions** are repetitive behaviors that interfere with daily functioning but are performed in an effort to prevent dangers or events associated with obsessions. (see Types of Anxiety Disorders)

Example: Uli keeps repeatedly washing his hands to get rid of germs that he is obsessing about.

18. **Somatoform disorders** are psychological problems in which symptoms of a physical disorder are present without a physical cause. (see Somatoform Disorders)

REMEMBER: Soma means "body." Somatoform disorders include conversion disorder, hypochondriasis, somatization disorder, somatoform pain disorder, and body dysmorphic disorder.

19. A **conversion disorder** is a somatoform disorder in which a person displays blindness, deafness, or other symptoms of sensory or motor failure without a physical cause. (see Somatoform Disorders)

REMEMBER: Conversion means a "change from one state to another." Think of a person experiencing a changed physical state (blindness, deafness) but without physical explanation. The imagined physical disabilities often help the person to be removed from the stressful situation.

Example: Joanie is a volunteer nurse on a cancer ward. She calls the hospital and calmly tells them that she cannot come to work because she cannot move her legs. There is nothing physically wrong, but the problem allows her to avoid dealing with patients who are in great pain and near death.

20. **Hypochondriasis** is a somatoform disorder involving strong, unjustified fear of having physical illness. (see Somatoform Disorders)

    REMEMBER: A person with this disorder makes frequent visits to doctors and will not be convinced that he or she is healthy.

21. **Somatization disorder** is a somatoform disorder in which there are numerous physical complaints without verifiable physical illness. (see Somatoform Disorders)

22. **Somatoform pain disorder** is a somatoform disorder marked by complaints of severe pain with no physical cause. (see Somatoform Disorders)

23. **Body dysmorphic disorder** is a somatoform disorder characterized by intense distress over imagined abnormalities of the skin, hair, face, or other areas of the body. (see Somatoform Disorders)

    Example: Chelsea is convinced that her eyes are droopy. She repeatedly seeks out plastic surgery, even though numerous physicians, and even surgeons, have told her there is nothing abnormal about her eyes.

24. **Dissociative disorders** are rare conditions that involve sudden and usually temporary disruptions in a person's memory, consciousness, or identity. (see Dissociative Disorders)

    Example: Bill, lost in New York City, does not remember his name, home address, or workplace. He cannot remember anything that will give him a clue to his identity. Bill is suffering from a dissociative disorder.

    REMEMBER: Dissociate means to "break a connection" or "disunite." Bill is disconnected from his past.

25. **Fugue reaction** (or **dissociative fugue**) is a dissociative disorder involving sudden loss of memory and possible assumption of a new identity in a new location. (see Dissociative Disorders)

    Example: Sabine's family frantically searches for her as she has been missing for weeks. They finally find her in a town 400 miles away, claiming a different identity and having no memory of her life as Sabine.

26. **Dissociative amnesia** is a dissociative disorder marked by a sudden loss of memory. (see Dissociative Disorders)

    Example: Mayumi cannot remember who she is or where she is from.

27. **Dissociative identity disorder** is a dissociative disorder in which a person reports having more than one identity. (see Dissociative Disorders)

    Example: Juan is talking to his therapist, when all of a sudden he insists that his therapist stop calling him Juan. He says he is "Charlize" and that Juan had to go away for a while.

28. **Affective disorders** (also called **mood disorders**) are conditions in which a person experiences extreme moods, such as depression or mania. (see Affective Disorders)

    REMEMBER: They include major depression, dysthymic disorder, mania, and the bipolar disorders.

29. **Major depression** (or **major depressive disorder**) is an affective disorder in which a person feels sad and hopeless for weeks or months. (see Depressive Disorders)

    Example: Shelly is depressed. She sits on the couch and watches television without enjoying the shows. She lacks the energy to clean the house or to care for the children. She cries frequently for no apparent reason other than that she feels life is pointless.

30. **Delusions** are false beliefs, such as those experienced by people suffering from schizophrenia or extreme depression. (see Depressive Disorders)

    Example: Regina believes that she has been selected by the government to take over the moon once it is colonized. She anxiously checks the mail each day to see if her instructions have arrived from the president.

31. **Dysthymic disorder** is an affective disorder involving a pattern of comparatively mild depression that lasts for at least two years. (see Depressive Disorders)

32. **Mania** is an elated, very active emotional state. (see Bipolar Disorders)

    Example: Lenny is a carpenter. While in a manic state, he decided to build a copy of the Empire State Building in his backyard. He called his office and quit his job, ordered supplies, and asked his neighbors to help him. When the people down the street tried to tell Lenny that he should check the city building codes before undertaking such an enormous task, he became belligerent. He stormed out of their house, accusing them of having no faith in the will, determination, and ability of American neighborhoods.

33. **Bipolar disorders** are affective disorders in which a person alternates between the emotional extremes of depression and mania. (see Bipolar Disorders)

    REMEMBER: Bi means "two," and polar means "extreme." A bipolar disorder is an affective disorder in which mood alternates between two opposite feelings: elation (mania) and extreme sadness (depression).

34. **Cyclothymic personality** (or **cyclothymic disorder**) is an affective disorder characterized by an alternating pattern of mood swings that is less extreme than that of bipolar disorders. (see Bipolar Disorders)

    Example: Dion is unpredictable. Some days he is really up and is like that for a week or so, then he can unexplainable shift into a sad frame of mind that will hang around for weeks, too. He is always one or the other—there's no middle ground with him!

35. **Schizophrenia** is a severe and disabling pattern of disturbed thinking, emotion, perception, and behavior. (see Schizophrenia)

    Example: Neologisms, an abnormality seen in the thinking, speaking, and writing of people with schizophrenia, are words that have meaning only to the person speaking them. For example, the word teardom in "I hereby teardom your happiness" is a neologism. There is no such word.

36. **Hallucinations** are a symptom of disorder in which people perceive voices or other stimuli when there are no stimuli present. (see Symptoms of Schizophrenia)

    Example: Many people with schizophrenia hear "voices" talking to them inside their heads. They may also report seeing things that don't really exist.

37. **Positive symptoms** are schizophrenic symptoms such as disorganized thoughts, hallucinations, and delusions. (see Categorizing Schizophrenia)

    REMEMBER: They are called positive symptoms because they are undesirable additions to mental processing.

38. **Negative symptoms** are schizophrenic symptoms such as absence of pleasure, lack of speech, and flat affect. (see Categorizing Schizophrenia)

    REMEMBER: They are called <u>negative</u> symptoms because they subtract elements from normal mental life.

39. **Personality disorders** are long-standing, inflexible ways of behaving that create a variety of problems. (see Personality Disorders)

    REMEMBER: There are several types of personality disorders, including schizotypal, avoidant, narcissistic, and antisocial.

40. **Antisocial personality disorder (APD)** is a personality disorder involving impulsive, selfish, unscrupulous, and even criminal behavior. (see Personality Disorders)

    Example: Andre, although quite charming, has been in trouble since his early teens. He has stolen cars, broken into people's homes, terrorized small children, and conned elderly people out of their social security checks. His parents and social worker have tried all sorts of remedies from punishment to counseling to no avail. Andre is now thirty and in prison for raping and murdering a teenage girl. The prison psychiatrist noted that Andre expresses no regret or remorse for his behavior.

    REMEMBER: People with antisocial personalities appear to have no morals and can be dangerous to the public because they very rarely experience deep feelings for anyone. Typically, they are smooth-talking, intelligent, charming liars who have no sense of responsibility.

41. **Substance-related disorders** are problems involving the use of psychoactive drugs for months or years in ways that harm the user or others. (see Substance-Related Disorders)

    Example: Carole's husband drinks so much each night that he isn't able to help her take care of the kids. She constantly feels alone and upset as a result.

42. **Addiction** is the development of a physical need for a psychoactive drug. (see Substance-Related Disorders)

    Example: Sheila takes heroin on a regular basis. Without the heroin, she experiences extreme nausea and vomiting and other physical symptoms. Sheila is addicted to heroin.

43. **Alcoholism** is a pattern of drinking that may lead to addiction and almost always causes severe social, physical, and other problems. (see Substance-Related Disorders)

    Example: Nancy has been an alcoholic for twenty years. She began drinking socially when she moved to the suburbs. Eventually, she drank every day to the point of being drunk, and she finally lost her job. Her children have suffered because they do not have regular meals, cannot bring their friends home, and often hear their parents argue about their mother's drinking.

FILL-IN-THE-BLANKS KEY TERMS

This section will help you check your factual knowledge of the key terms introduced in this chapter. Fill in each blank with the appropriate term from the list of key terms in the previous section.

1. _____ involves relatively mild but long-lasting anxiety not focused on any one thing.

2. _____ are long-standing maladaptive lifestyles or behavior patterns.

3. The _____ model attributes abnormal behavior to the interaction between a person's genetic predisposition and the environment.

4. A person with an intense fear of objects has a _____ phobia.

5. A person who becomes anxious when leaving her or his home has _____.

6. A person who suffers from constant but mild depression may have _____.

7. A person who appears to be paralyzed but really isn't may suffer from _____.

8. A person plagued by particular thoughts suffers from _____.

9. People with _____ are sure they are sick and report a variety of unrelated symptoms during frequent visits to the doctor.

10. Sudden and usually temporary disruptions in a person's memory, consciousness, or identity are symptoms of _____.

11. A person plagued by attacks of extreme fear could be diagnosed as having a _____.

12. A person who suffers from frequent and violent mood swings (extreme depression to mania) has _____.

13. Abnormalities in thought, perception, affect, motivation, and motor behavior are characteristic of _____.

14. In schizophrenia, additions of unpleasant elements such as hallucinations or delusions are called _____.

15. _____ is a physical need for a psychoactive drug.

Total Correct (See answer key) _____

LEARNING OBJECTIVES

1. Define <u>psychopathology</u> and *comorbidity*. Explain why psychopathology is a social as well as a personal matter. (see introductory section)

2. Describe the three criteria for abnormality. Discuss the advantages and disadvantages of using each criterion. Describe the *practical approach* and impaired functioning. (see "What Is Abnormal?")

3. Describe the following three explanations for psychological disorders: <u>neurobiological model</u>, <u>psychological model</u>, and the <u>sociocultural perspective</u>. Give an example of how each model would explain psychological disorders. Explain how each of these models fits into the <u>biopsychosocial approach</u>. (see "Explaining Psychological Disorders")

4. Define <u>diathesis-stress model</u> and explain how it integrates elements of the four other explanations for psychological disorders. (see "Diathesis-Stress as an Integrative Explanation")

5. Describe the contents of the Diagnostic and Statistical Manual of Mental Disorders (DSM-IV). List the five axes used in diagnosis based on DSM-IV. Explain the changes being discussed for the forthcoming DSM-V. (see "Classifying Psychological Disorders")

6. Explain why accurate and reliable diagnosis is important. Define *inter-rater reliability* and discuss its relationship to diagnosis. Discuss the research on the potential for psychological diagnoses to be biased. (see "Purposes and Problems of Diagnosis"; see also "Thinking Critically: Is Psychological Diagnosis Biased?")

7. Define <u>anxiety disorder</u>. Specify what disorders are classified as anxiety disorders. (see "Anxiety Disorders")

8. Define <u>phobia</u>, and give a brief description of <u>specific phobia</u>, <u>social phobia</u>, and <u>agoraphobia</u>. (see "Phobia")

9. Define <u>generalized anxiety disorder</u>, <u>panic disorder</u>, and <u>obsessive-compulsive disorder</u>. Explain the difference between *obsessions* and *compulsions*. (see "Generalized Anxiety Disorder"; see also "Panic Disorder"; see also "Obsessive-Compulsive Disorder")

10. State the causes, according to the various theoretical models, of anxiety disorders. (see "Causes of Anxiety Disorders")

11. Discuss how we are biologically prepared to learn certain phobias. (see "Linkages: Anxiety Disorders and Learning")

12. Define <u>somatoform disorder</u>. Give a brief description of <u>conversion disorder</u>, <u>hypochondriasis</u>, <u>somatization disorder</u>, and <u>somatoform pain disorder</u>. (see "Somatoform Disorders")

13. State the causes, according to various theoretical models, of somatoform disorders. (see "Somatoform Disorders")

14. Define <u>dissociative disorder</u>. Compare and contrast <u>fugue reaction</u> and <u>dissociative amnesia</u>. Describe <u>dissociative identity disorder</u>. (see "Dissociative Disorders")

15. State the causes, according to the various theoretical models, of dissociative disorders. (see "Dissociative Disorders")

16. Define <u>affective disorders</u>. Give a brief description of <u>major depression</u>, <u>delusions</u>, and <u>dysthymic disorder</u>. (see "Mood Disorders"; see also "Depressive Disorders")

17. Describe the relationship between depression and suicide. List the general guidelines for determining if a person might commit suicide. (see "Suicide and Depression")

18. Provide a brief description of <u>mania</u>, bipolar I disorder, bipolar II disorder, hypomania, and cyclothymic disorder. (see "Bipolar Disorders")

19. State the causes, according to various theoretical models, of affective disorders. Describe how learned helplessness and attributional style may contribute to depression. (see "Causes of Mood Disorders")

20. Define <u>schizophrenia</u>. Describe the disorganized thought and language characteristic of schizophrenia. Give examples of *neologisms, loose associations, clang associations*, and *word salad*. (see "Schizophrenia")

21. Describe the types of delusions and <u>hallucinations</u> common to schizophrenia. (see "Symptoms of Schizophrenia")

22. Name the five subtypes of schizophrenia. Describe the <u>positive symptoms</u> and the <u>negative symptoms</u> of schizophrenia. (see "Categorizing Schizophrenia")

23. State the possible causes of schizophrenia, according to various theoretical models. (see "Causes of Schizophrenia")

24. Define <u>personality disorder</u>. Give a brief description of schizotypal, avoidant, narcissistic, and <u>antisocial personality disorders</u>. (see "Personality Disorders")

25. Describe the possible causes of <u>antisocial personality disorder</u>, including research on childhood abuse. (see "Personality Disorders"; see also "Focus on Research Methods: Exploring Links Between Child Abuse and Antisocial Personality Disorder")

26. Describe the differences between *externalizing* and *internalizing* disorders of childhood. Define *conduct disorders, attention-deficit hyperactivity disorder, separation anxiety disorder*, and *autistic spectrum disorders*. (see "Psychological Disorders of Childhood")

27. Explain the symptoms and experiences related to substance-related disorders, including addiction. (see "Substance-Related Disorders")

28. Describe the problems associated with and the theoretical explanations for the development of alcoholism and heroin and cocaine dependence. (see "Substance-Related Disorders")

29. Discuss the laws designed to protect the rights of people with severe psychological disorders who are accused of a crime. (see "Mental Illness and the Law")

30. Describe the legal reform procedures regarding mental illness. (see "Mental Illness and the Law")

CONCEPTS AND EXERCISES

Choosing a Jury

Connie, a fifty-year-old woman, has killed her husband. She has pleaded not guilty and will stand trial. The prosecution and the defense lawyer are now in the process of selecting jurors. Connie's lawyer will attempt to convince the jury that, although she has committed a crime, the long-standing physical and mental abuse that she and her children endured makes her behavior understandable. She should, therefore, receive a lesser sentence.

Connie's lawyer will want jurors with a particular approach to defining abnormality. Each juror will be presented with the following list of behaviors and asked if he or she thinks that the behaviors are abnormal and why: getting drunk and singing at the top of your lungs; leading a hunger strike outside the White House; having a very high IQ; owning one hundred cats.

1. If you were Connie's lawyer, which of the following two prospective jurors would you choose?

Prospective juror one: I think there are times when the situation calls for a little celebration. I remember when my first grandchild was born. I whooped it up a little myself. As for a hunger strike, well, I think that some people, because of the circumstances in their lives, have been mistreated in this society. Someone should protest for them.

I knew this fella who is powerful smart, and he is a bit strange, but heck, if we didn't have people who were a little bit different, the world would be an awful boring place.

'Bout them cats. Hmmm. I had an aunt who had more cats than she did hairs on her head. She loved those varmints as if they were kids. She wasn't any stranger than the other folk that I knew. She just didn't have anybody living at home anymore, and the cats gave her something to care for and love. Everybody needs something to love.

Prospective juror two: The law strictly forbids drinking where I live, and based on that, I think people should not do it. Furthermore, if people want to change the system, they should do it through the proper channels. Holding a hunger strike is not the way to make a difference. People will only think you are a little weird if you sit on some steps and don't eat. I don't like very smart people. All the brainy people I knew in school were either uppity or nerds, not like everybody else. There are laws about the number of pets one is allowed to own, and I think that the law should be upheld at all times.

The Who's Who of Psychological Disorders

Ron, a hospital receptionist, is in trouble. He has several patients sitting in the reception room, and he has misplaced all the morning files. He does not know which patient is supposed to see which doctor.

He has written a list of everything he can remember in order to get each patient to the right doctor. See if you can help him match doctors to patients.

Doctor 1 has ordered a brain scan that would provide a view of the patient's ventricles.

Doctor 2 is putting out crayons and paper. This doctor wants to see if drawing will help the patient express why he is so fearful.

Doctor 3 is trying to figure out how not to pay too much attention to the patient's complaints while finding out if there has been severe stress in her life recently.

Doctor 4 is preparing a list of activities the patient can do that might take his mind off negative events in his life.

Doctor 5's initial conversation with the patient revolved around dirt and contamination and how one must continually try to keep clean.

1.   Doctor 1 is probably seeing patient _____.

2.   Doctor 2 is probably seeing patient _____.

3.   Doctor 3 is probably seeing patient _____.

4.   Doctor 4 is probably seeing patient _____.

5.   Doctor 5 is probably seeing patient _____.

   a.   **Patient A** does not answer when Ron asks him which doctor he is here to see.

   b.   **Patient B** is sitting next to the window, looking in her bag for a bottle of hand sanitizer.

   c.   **Patient C** seems to have numerous unrelated symptoms, including funny feelings in the stomach, oily and dry skin, and jumpy toes.

   d.   **Patient D's** clothes are hanging loose, suggesting dramatic weight loss. This patient seems exhausted and profoundly sad.

   e.   **Patient E** is clinging to the mother's neck. Every time the mother tries to get the patient to release her and sit on the seat next to her, Patient E begins crying uncontrollably.

CRITICAL THINKING

Centuries ago, people with abnormal behavior were thought to be witches possessed by demons. One of the standard methods for determining whether someone was a witch was to bind the suspect's hands and feet and then throw her into a lake. If she drowned, she was normal and therefore innocent. If she didn't drown and survived the ordeal, she was judged guilty and put to death.

1.   Using your critical thinking skills, explain what is wrong with this thinking.

PERSONAL LEARNING ACTIVITIES

1.   Write descriptions of behaviors you observed in the last month that you think are unusual. Evaluate them using each of the criteria (deviance, distress, or dysfunction). Was one criterion more likely than the others to be labeled abnormal? According to the practical approach, are the behaviors abnormal?

2.   Anxiety disorders are fairly common, and people with OCD can be highly functional and successful. To hear Howie Mandel talk about his experiences with OCD on television view the following YouTube clip: http://www.youtube.com/watch?v=eg14F72pY-4. To what extent do you think Mandel is able to be functional with this disorder because of his fame? Do you think this factor makes it easier, or harder, to deal with the obsessions and compulsions that plague him?

3. To learn more about depression—one of the more common psychological disorders, visit the following website: http://www.depression.com/. Here you can find information about how depression is understood and treated by psychologists. Do the treatments you learn about here fit with the explanations for depression you found in your textbook? Explain why or why not.

4. Your book talks about autism spectrum disorders, including high functioning autism, also known as Aspberger's disorder. To learn more about this disorder, visit the following site: http://www.aspergers.com/. After browsing the site, explain to a friend the difference between Asperger's and autistic disorder, and what biological factors may contribute to Asperger's. Asperger's is one of the disorders that may be removed from the next edition of the DSM (DSM-V). Read about this controversy here: http://aspergersatcollege.com/?p=21. What is your opinion on whether or not this disorder should remain or be removed in the DSM-V revision?

5. If a woman suffering from a severe psychological disorder loses touch with reality and commits a crime, should she be punished? Present arguments for and against punishment. What if a chemical imbalance in a man's brain is linked to his aggressive behavior, which later results in a homicide? Should that man be held accountable for his actions? What should happen to these people, and who should decide their fate? A jury? A judge? A clinical psychologist? Provide arguments supporting each of these three as the appropriate decision maker.

MULTIPLE-CHOICE QUESTIONS

Quiz 1

1. Who is abnormal according to the practical approach of defining abnormality?
    a. Jetta, who likes to ride horses bareback every morning before work
    b. Janiel, who likes to dance and sing in front of her mirror during her free time
    c. Keith, who rides the elevator facing the rear instead of the front
    d. Dieter, whose difficulty managing anger has lost him numerous jobs

2. Encouraging conformity is associated with which approach to defining normality?
    a. Practical
    b. Norm violation
    c. Statistical infrequency
    d. Both norm violation and statistical infrequency

3. Connor has symptoms associated with the autistic spectrum. His doctor believes that his symptoms are a result of a brain bleed he experienced when he was born. Connor's physician is using the _____ model to explain Connor's psychological disorder.
    a. diathesis-stress
    b. medical
    c. psychological
    d. sociocultural

4. Zelda's doctor told her that she has a genetic predisposition for depression, but that her recent job stress has brought on her latest episode of depression. Zelda's doctor takes the _____ approach to explaining Zelda's depression.
    a. sociocultural
    b. medical
    c. diathesis-stress
    d. humanistic

5. The DSM-IV-TR lists five axes for diagnosticians to use in evaluating people. Which of the following is NOT covered in one of the axes?
    a. Major psychological disorder description
    b. Physical condition
    c. Stress level
    d. Social status

6. Kat has dropped out of school. She cannot attend class because the thought of leaving her apartment leaves her feeling nauseated, anxious, and faint. Her symptoms suggest that she
    a. suffers from agoraphobia.
    b. has a phobia about classrooms.
    c. has panic attacks.
    d. has test anxiety.

7. Laurence is a psychotherapist. One of his patients, Heidi, complains of being very shy and lonely. She also says that she has a very intense need to touch repeatedly all four walls of any room she has never been in before. Laurence tells Heidi that she learned this compulsive behavior so that she could delay immediate social contact with anyone in the room, thereby avoiding the anxiety caused by her extreme shyness. Laurence adheres to the _____ model of abnormal behavior.
    a. psychodynamic
    b. humanistic
    c. social-cognitive
    d. medical

8. Ricky, a psychiatric intern, has just completed an evaluation of his new patient by using DSM-IV-TR. He writes: "The patient has a global assessment of functioning score of 50." This statement relates to which axis on the DSM-IV-TR?
    a. Axis I
    b. Axis II
    c. Axis IV
    d. Axis V

9. Fear of being embarrassed because you have food in your teeth and didn't realize it to the point where you won't eat in front of anyone is an example of
    a. a social phobia.
    b. a specific phobia.
    c. agoraphobia.
    d. panic disorder.

10. A conversion disorder is characterized by
    a. functional impairment of a limb or sensory ability with no apparent physical cause.
    b. severe pain with no apparent cause.
    c. a constant fear of becoming seriously ill.
    d. frequent vague complaints of physical symptoms.

11. Tomas has been suffering from severe chest pain for the past few weeks. His doctor has run extensive tests but can find no physical problem. Tomas may

    a. have a pain disorder.
    b. have hypochondriasis.
    c. have paranoia.
    d. suffer from somatization disorder.

12. "Massive repression of unwanted impulses or memories is responsible for dissociative disorders," is most likely a quote from a _____ theorist.

    a. social-cognitive
    b. humanistic
    c. psychodynamic
    d. sociocultural

13. Nuwanda and a classmate are talking when Mary approaches and calls Nuwanda "Paul." Although Nuwanda explains that he's from Dallas, Mary convincingly argues that he is Paul, her next-door neighbor in Chicago for twenty years. Nuwanda's identification card confirms that his name is Paul, but he insists that he has no memory of living in Chicago or of being called Paul. Nuwanda/Paul most likely has

    a. dissociative amnesia.
    b. fugue reaction.
    c. a conversion disorder.
    d. schizophrenia.

14. For the past three months, Beth has been sleeping twelve to sixteen hours a day and has gained thirty pounds. Gail can barely sleep at all and has lost fifteen pounds without trying; she just does not want to eat. Both women could be suffering from

    a. obsessive-compulsive disorder.
    b. major depression.
    c. hyperchondriasis.
    d. hypochondriasis.

15. Pam noticed during their daily tutoring sessions that Enya seemed unhappy for about a week, then happy for the next week. Sometimes the moods lasted longer, but Enya never settled into sadness or happiness for more than a few weeks at a time. Enya consulted a therapist, who suggested that since her mood swings were neither extreme nor debilitating, she most likely was experiencing

    a. depression.
    b. cyclothymic personality.
    c. dysthymic disorder.
    d. mania.

16. Sam displays the negative symptoms of schizophrenia when

    a. in his delusions, he thinks that he is being programmed to stop behaviors in others.
    b. he claims he is another person named Harry and acts totally unlike himself.
    c. he completely lacks emotional responses to anything he experiences.
    d. he keeps thinking he sees bugs moving all around him.

17. Juan has been diagnosed with schizophrenia. He is positive that all the students sitting around him during a test are cheating by reading his thoughts. Juan is experiencing a _____ symptom of schizophrenia.
    a. positive
    b. negative
    c. obsessive
    d. hallucination

18. Sean's roommate could be very charming, but he continually borrowed money without returning it and Sean often caught him telling lies. Sean finally moved out when his roommate borrowed his car, got into a serious accident, and then wondered why Sean was so upset. Sean's roommate is exhibiting symptoms of _____ disorder.
    a. antisocial personality
    b. manic
    c. dissociative identity
    d. conduct

19. Hope's dad has been an alcoholic for decades. He is now dying from liver failure, and worse, he isn't even himself anymore. He has experienced severe memory loss known as
    a. cluster A.
    b. cluster B.
    c. Korsakoff's psychosis.
    d. an autistic spectrum disorder.

20. Aaron is an infant who shows no signs of attachment to his parents. He doesn't like to be held and doesn't smile or laugh. Of the following, Aaron is most likely experiencing _____ disorder.
    a. infantile schizotypal
    b. autistic
    c. antisocial personality
    d. narcissistic personality

Total Correct (See answer key) _____

Quiz 2

Use this quiz to reassess your learning after taking Quiz 1 and reviewing the chapter.

1. According to the infrequency criterion, behavior would be considered abnormal if it
    a. caused discomfort.
    b. was uncommon.
    c. was bizarre but situationally appropriate.
    d. impaired a person's ability to function.

2. Stephen, a college student, drinks so much every weekend that he is barely able to function on Monday. Stephen's behavior would be labeled abnormal by the _____ approach.
    a. medical
    b. practical
    c. diathesis-stress
    d. logical

3. A woman disappeared during the Bosnian war, and two years later she showed up at home, with no memory for the time she was away. It was later discovered that she had created a whole new identity, living and working in another town under a different name. This woman may have suffered from

    a. dissociative amnesia.
    b. fugue reaction.
    c. dissociative identity disorder.
    d. conversion disorder.

4. Michael is homeless. He is very stressed that he never lived up to his now deceased parent's expectations. Ultimately, he ends up with a diagnosis of major depression. His sister says that he has that label because of the stress his parents put on him when they were living, and the general life stress associated with homelessness. Michael's sister is using the _____ model to explain his disorder.

    a. sociocultural
    b. diathesis-stress
    c. neurobiological
    d. medical

5. Mary Sue, a brilliant neurosurgeon, visits the local animal shelter every morning and lectures the animals on the dangers of ingesting poisonous microbes. Although her behavior is considered a bit strange, the shelter's workers like having someone lavish attention on the animals. Afterward, Mary Sue goes to work and starts her day on time. Mary Sue's behavior would be considered abnormal according to which approach or criterion?

    a. Statistical infrequency
    b. Psychopathological
    c. Logical
    d. Practical

6. Which of the following is NOT a problem with our present diagnostic system for psychological disorders?

    a. People's problems often do not fit neatly into a single category.
    b. The same symptoms may appear as part of more than one disorder.
    c. Inter-rater reliability is not very strong, except for personality disorder.
    d. Diagnoses are judgments, and personal biases may play a part.

7. Because Shantha has recurring thoughts about losing her belongings, she is continually checking the location of knickknacks and making sure her doors are locked. Shantha's strange behavior is most likely

    a. an obsession.
    b. a compulsion.
    c. due to mania.
    d. due to a conversion disorder.

8. Frank is so afraid of getting sick at the dinner table and being humiliated that he will not eat at a restaurant. Frank has

    a. a specific phobia.
    b. agoraphobia.
    c. a social phobia.
    d. an obsessive-compulsive disorder.

9. Myrnell is so freaked out about school. One day, she finds that she literally can't walk. When she goes to the doctor, the doctor can find no physical cause for her paralysis. A psychiatrist suspects that Myrnell's anxiety about school has literally paralyzed her and suggests that she has a(n) _____ disorder.

    a. anxiety
    b. somatoform
    c. dissociative
    d. personality

10. Hans, a police officer, was working the night shift when he came upon a young man who claimed that he could not remember his name, where he lived or worked, or anything else about himself. Most likely the mystery person displays

    a. dissociative disorder.
    b. antisocial personality disorder.
    c. dissociative identity disorder.
    d. schizophrenia.

11. Social-cognitive theorists would probably say that people who _____ are most likely to become depressed.

    a. exaggerate the dark side of events
    b. blame themselves when things go wrong
    c. jump to overly pessimistic generalizations
    d. All of these

12. Philip displays bipolar disorder. Which statement would best describe him?

    a. He is sometimes very depressed and sometimes in a pleasant mood.
    b. He is alternately severely depressed and wildly elated.
    c. He has sudden onsets of depression that last for a few hours and then he feels fine.
    d. His disorder is a very common one.

13. Mercedes has just brought home a dog from the pound. She was told that the dog's previous owners kept it on a leash and beat it daily for no reason. Mercedes notices that when the neighborhood kids bother the dog, it does not even try to run away. Mercedes's dog most likely has

    a. generalized anxiety.
    b. learned helplessness.
    c. hypersensitive brainstem mechanisms.
    d. enlarged ventricles.

14. Which of the following is a hallucination?
   a. Believing you are the President of the United States
   b. Hearing a voice tell you that people are out to get you
   c. Constantly worrying about coming into contact with germs
   d. Constantly checking your car to make sure the tires aren't flat

15. Childhood internalizing behavior problems include
   a. attention-deficit hyperactivity disorder.
   b. conduct disorder.
   c. separation anxiety disorder.
   d. All of these

16. Physical need for a substance is known as
   a. alcoholism.
   b. hallucination.
   c. autism.
   d. addiction.

17. What type of personality disorder would you expect to find among people in jail for fraud?
   a. Narcissistic
   b. Depressive
   c. Antisocial
   d. Mood

18. Which of the following is NOT suggested by the vulnerability model of schizophrenia?
   a. Vulnerability to schizophrenia is mainly biological.
   b. Cold, unresponsive parenting leads to a regression to childhood, which causes schizophrenia.
   c. Vulnerability is influenced partly by abnormalities associated with prenatal and birth complications.
   d. Inadequate coping skills may play a role in determining whether schizophrenia actually appears in a person.

19. Victor, a ten-year-old, tells a psychologist that he first came to the court system after setting a car on fire at age eight. In the numerous police contacts since then, he has been accused of theft, assault, and willful destruction of property. Victor most likely has _____ disorder.
   a. autistic
   b. narcissistic personality
   c. conduct
   d. schizotypal personality

20. Which of the following is NOT one of the criteria of the M'Naghton rule?
   a. Mental illness prevented one from understanding the legal proceedings in their case.
   b. Mental illness prevented one from understanding that what one did was wrong.
   c. Mental illness prevented one from knowing what one was doing.
   d. Mental illness prevented one from being able to resist the impulse do wrong.

Total Correct (See answer key) _____

ANSWERS TO FILL-IN-THE-BLANKS KEY TERMS

1. Generalized anxiety disorder (see Types of Anxiety Disorders)

2. Personality disorders (see Personality Disorders)

3. diathesis-stress (see Diathesis-Stress as an Integrative Explanation)

4. specific (see Types of Anxiety Disorders)

5. agoraphobia (see Types of Anxiety Disorders)

6. dysthymic disorder (see Mood Disorders)

7. conversion disorder (see Somatoform Disorders)

8. obsessive-compulsive disorder (see Types of Anxiety Disorders)

9. hypochondriasis (see Somatoform Disorders)

10. dissociative disorders (see Dissociative Disorders)

11. panic disorder (see Types of Anxiety Disorders)

12. bipolar disorder (see Affective Disorders)

13. schizophrenia (see Schizophrenia)

14. positive symptoms (see Categorizing Schizophrenia)

15. Addiction (see Substance-Related Disorders)

ANSWERS TO CONCEPTS AND EXERCISES

Choosing a Jury

1. Connie's lawyer wants jurors who define abnormal behavior from the practical approach. He wants jurors who think that her behavior is understandable given the context or situation of her home life. Connie's lawyer should choose prospective juror 1. When evaluating the abnormality of each behavior listed, this person considers the context as well as the content of the behavior. Prospective juror 2 is very concerned about the frequency of behaviors (the statistical infrequency criterion) and the social rules about behaviors based on the legal system (the norm violation criterion). (see What Is Abnormal?)

The Who's Who of Psychological Disorders

1. Doctor 1 is seeing Patient A with schizophrenia who is exhibiting negative symptoms. Recent research suggests that negative symptoms, such as lack of speech, are associated with abnormal brain structures, including enlarged ventricles. (see Categorizing Schizophrenia)

2. Doctor 2 is a child psychologist working with a boy (Patient E) who is displaying separation anxiety disorder. Children may not be able to verbalize how they feel but may be able to express their feelings in drawings. (see Psychological Disorders of Childhood)

3. Doctor 3's patient (Patient C) is probably suffering from somatization disorder, which is characterized by reports of many vague physical symptoms. Some patients may learn to exhibit symptoms to get attention. In other cases, severe stress may underlie the symptoms. (see Somatoform Disorders)

4. Doctor 4 follows a social-cognitive approach to treating the major depression of Patient D. She believes her patient keeps ruminating about things that go wrong in his life and that Patient D needs to distract himself from concentrating only on negatives. (see Causes of Affective Disorders)

5. Doctor 5 is seeing a woman with obsessive-compulsive disorder (Patient B). This patient is besieged by thoughts of germs and infections, and he must continually wash his hands to try to relieve these thoughts. (see Types of Anxiety Disorders)

ANSWERS TO CRITICAL THINKING

1. The hypothesis: The suspect is a witch. The evidence: Those who survive are witches and those who die are not. (NOTE: There was no attempt to formulate or test an alternative hypothesis, because the suspect was dead.)

ANSWERS TO MULTIPLE-CHOICE QUESTIONS

Circle the question numbers you answered correctly.

Quiz 1

1. d is the answer. The impaired functioning criterion, part of the practical approach, asks whether a person can display the behavior in question and still meet the demands of everyday life. Because Dieter's anger is interfering with his employment, it is impairing his ability to meet life's demands. (see Defining Psychological Disorders)

    a, b, c.   Although these behaviors are unusual (infrequency criterion), they are not interfering with life demands.

2. d is the answer. To conform, one follows the practices of the majority. Statistically, behaviors that are displayed by the majority of people are normal. According to the norm violation criterion, society determines which social rules to follow. Both criteria are problematic because some of the world's unique (nonconforming) people might thus be considered abnormal. (see Defining Psychological Disorders)

    a.   According to the practical approach, normal behavior can be unique (not seen frequently in other people) as long as the demands of everyday life are met and the behavior is situationally appropriate (approved of by others in that situation).

    b.   c is also correct.

    c.   b is also correct.

3. b is the answer. According to the medical model, problems in anatomy and physiology cause abnormal behavior. Connor's physician is explaining his autistic behavior as related to a brain trauma that occurred at birth. (see Explaining Psychological Disorders)

    a.   According to the diathesis-stress model, psychological disorders tend to manifest based on one's genetic predisposition and life stress. Connor's physician is not invoking life stress as part of this explanation.

    c.   The psychological model is rooted in psychodynamic thought and sees mind and the struggles within it as the root cause of abnormal behavior.

    d.   The sociocultural model sees factors outside of the person, such as social relationships and cultural expectations, as the cause of abnormal behavior.

4.   c is the answer. The diathesis-stress model proposes that genetic predispositions for abnormal behavior are not necessarily expressed, unless environmental stressors elicit them. (see Explaining Psychological Disorders)

     a.   The sociocultural model suggests that social factors alone can cause abnormal behavior.

     b.   The medical model argues that abnormal behavior is caused by physical problems.

     d.   The humanistic model emphasizes unique perceptions of reality, and failure to be in touch with one's true feelings can cause abnormal behavior.

5.   d is the answer. (see Classifying Psychological Disorders)

     a, b, c.   The five axes comprise major disorder description, mental retardation or personality disorders, physical condition, stress level, and highest functioning level.

6.   a is the answer. Kat becomes anxious when she thinks about leaving her home. This is a symptom of agoraphobia. (see Anxiety Disorders)

     b.   Being unable to attend class is a consequence of Kat's fear of leaving her apartment, but it is not the object of her phobia.

     c.   Panic attacks are characterized by extreme terror, racing heartbeat, and, sometimes, the feeling of going crazy. Kat did not experience any of these symptoms.

     d.   There is no mention of tests or test anxiety in the question. Kat is afraid of leaving her apartment.

7.   c is the answer. Social-cognitive theorists see compulsive behaviors as learned habits that allow a person to escape or avoid anxiety-provoking situations. For Heidi, who is painfully shy, new social situations cause extreme anxiety. (see Anxiety Disorders)

     a.   A psychodynamic therapist would look for unconscious conflicts. Laurence is focusing on the behavioral basis of Heidi's problem.

     b.   A humanistic therapist might suggest that Heidi's behavior is caused by her unique perceptions of social situations.

     d.   Those who view abnormal behaviors as symptoms of neurobiological or medical problems would look for physiological irregularities.

8.   d is the answer. Axis V evaluates the highest level of adaptive functioning over the previous year. (see Classifying Psychological Disorders)

     a.   Axis I lists descriptions of the major psychological disorders, not global assessment of functioning.

     b.   Axis II lists mental retardation and personality disorders, not global assessment of functioning.

     c.   Axis IV rates the level of stress experienced in the recent past, not global assessment of functioning.

9.   a is the answer. A social phobia is the fear of doing something that would cause embarrassment in public. (see Anxiety Disorders)

     b.   A specific phobia is the irrational and excessive fear of something in particular.

     c.   Agoraphobia is the fear of leaving home or being away from a loved one.

     d.   Panic disorder causes moments of terror in which the person believes he or she will die.

10.   a is the answer. Typical conversion disorders involve functional impairment, such as blindness, paralysis, or deafness, with no apparent physical cause. (see Somatoform Disorders)

    b.   Pain disorder is characterized by severe pain with no apparent cause.

    c.   Hypochondriasis is characterized by constant fear of becoming seriously ill.

    d.   People with somatization disorder or hypochondriasis have a tendency to complain of vague symptoms.

11.   a is the answer. Severe pain in the chest, neck, or back with no apparent physical cause is a classic symptom of the somatoform disorder called pain disorder. (see Somatoform Disorders)

    b.   A person with hypochondriasis worries about being stricken with a serious disease and often reports vague symptoms. Severe pain is not a vague symptom.

    c.   A person with paranoia usually worries about being persecuted by a particular person or group.

    d.   Somatization disorder involves vague reports of unrelated problems, but Tomas was quite specific about his chest pain.

12.   c is the answer. Dissociative disorders involve some degree of disruption in memory, consciousness, or personal identity. According to the psychodynamic model, psychological disorders are caused by unresolved unconscious psychological conflicts. When they threaten to become conscious and cause anxiety, the individual finds a way to keep them in the unconscious. To accomplish this, some people may forget not only unconscious material but also who they are or any of the personal bits of information that identify them. (see Dissociative Disorders)

    a.   A social-cognitive theorist would say that an individual has been rewarded in some way for dissociating. Perhaps distressing anxiety is removed when the person forgets her or his identity or escapes into another personality.

    b.   A humanistic theorist would say that an individual's multiple personalities actually represent the overt expression of dramatically conflicting perceptions of the world.

    d.   A sociocultural theorist would look to society, the environment, and social roles for the cause of a disorder.

13.   b is the answer. Paul has not only forgotten about his previous life, but he has moved to a new location and assumed a new identity as a student named Nuwanda. (see Dissociative Disorders)

    a.   Dissociative amnesia is forgetting personally relevant information, but one does not move to a new location and create a new identity.

    c.   Conversion disorders are a type of somatoform disorder in which people experience physical symptoms, like paralysis, that do not have a physical cause.

    d.   Schizophrenia is characterized by more disordered thoughts and perceptions.

14.   b is the answer. Weight loss or gain and sleep changes, including oversleeping or insomnia, are typical of depression. (see Affective Disorders)

    a, d.   Weight loss or gain and sleeping problems do not usually occur in obsessive-compulsive disorder or hypochondriasis.

    c.   There is no disorder known as hyperchondriasis.

15.   b is the answer. Cyclothymic personality is a less severe version of bipolar I disorder. Since Enya is still able to work, her swings are not as extreme as the swing from mania to depression. (see Affective Disorders)

    a.   Enya cycles between happiness and sadness; she is not just sad. In addition, major depression is more debilitating than what Enya is experiencing. People with major depression feel hopeless and worthless for weeks or months and lose interest in recreation, friends, and work.

    c.   Dysthymic disorder is a less severe form of depression in which people feel the sadness and lack of pleasure associated with depression, but less intensely and for a longer time.

    d.   Mania is an agitated, ecstatic, energetic state. Enya cycles between happiness and sadness.

16.   c is the answer. Negative symptoms are the absence of normal mental processes, in this case, emotional responses. (see Schizophrenia)
    a.   Delusions are positive symptoms, undesirable additions to one's mental life.

    b.   The adoption of another personality is a symptom of dissociative identity disorder.

    d.   Hallucinations are positive symptoms, undesirable additions to one's mental life.

17.   a is the answer. Juan is having persistent, unfounded beliefs that people around him are capable of reading his thoughts, which is a delusion. A delusion is a positive symptom because it is an undesirable addition to his experience. (see Schizophrenia)
    b.   Negative symptoms involve loss of desirable parts of experience.

    c.   Obsessions are persistent, unwanted ideas that cannot be dispelled by reasoning. Juan is being governed by his unfounded beliefs, not by unwanted ideas. This is not generally part of schizophrenia.

    d.   Hallucinations are false perceptions, not false beliefs.

18.   a is the answer. Sean's roommate displays symptoms of antisocial personality disorder through his cold, unthinking, and unscrupulous behaviors. (see Personality Disorders)
    b.   There is no such thing as manic disorder. Mania is a very agitated, usually elated, emotional state that is one part of bipolar I disorder.

    c.   Dissociative identity disorder is characterized by the display of more than one personality. Sean's roommate does not fit this description.

    d.   Conduct disorder is a childhood disorder typified by aggressive, disobedient, and destructive behaviors.

19.   c is the answer. Korsakoff's psychosis is severe memory loss associated with vitamin deficiency due to prolonged overuse of alcohol. (see A Sampling of Other Psychological Disorders)
    a.   Cluster A is a clustering of personality disorders that are odd-eccentric in nature.

    b.   Cluster B is a clustering of personality disorders that are dramatic-erratic in nature.

    d.   Autistic spectrum disorders are a group of disorders that involve communication problems and impaired social relationships.

20.   b is the answer. Autistic disorder is a type of childhood disorder. Children with autistic disorder are not attached to caregivers, do not make eye contact, and are generally unable to be social. They may rock themselves and play with objects endlessly. (see A Sampling of Other Psychological Disorders)

    a.   There is no such thing as infantile schizotypal disorder.

    c.   Antisocial personality disorder is a long-term pattern of irresponsible, rash, unprincipled behavior.

d.   Narcissistic personality disorder is characterized by an exaggerated sense of self-importance and a need for attention.

Now turn to the quiz analysis table at the end of this chapter to find which areas you know well and which areas you need to work on. Circle the numbers in the table for items on Quiz 1 that you answered correctly.

Quiz 2

1.   b is the answer. The statistical infrequency criterion says that a behavior is normal if many people in a given population display it and abnormal if few people display the behavior. (see Defining Psychological Disorders)

   a.   The practical approach considers the discomfort that a particular behavior causes as a factor for defining abnormality.

   c.   Content and appropriateness are evaluated by the practical approach to defining abnormality.

   d.   Meeting the demands of everyday life is part of the impaired functioning criterion, an important feature of the practical approach.

2.   b is the answer. Stephen's behavior prevents him from meeting the demands of his everyday life. Therefore, his behavior meets the impaired functioning criterion in the practical approach. (see Defining Psychological Disorders)

   a.   The medical model is an explanation of abnormal behavior that emphasizes problems in anatomy and physiology.

   c.   The diathesis-stress model is also used to explain behavior. It proposes that people with disorders may have had a genetic predisposition to develop the disorder, but that environmental stressors brought it on. The item doesn't say that Stephen has an inherited tendency toward alcoholism or another disorder.

   d.   There is no such thing as the logical approach to defining abnormality.

3.   b is the answer. Fugue reaction is characterized by sudden loss of personal memory and the adoption of a new identity in a new locale. (see Dissociative Disorders)

   a.   Dissociative amnesia involves sudden memory loss, but the person does not leave home or create a new identity.

   c.   Dissociative identity disorder is characterized by the seeming existence of more than one personality in a single individual.

   d.   Conversion disorder is a somatoform condition in which people are dissociated from a part of their body.

4.   a is the answer. The sociocultural model looks to individual difference variables (such as age, gender, marital status) and contextual variables (such as economic conditions, family conditions) as explanations for psychological disorders. (see Explaining Psychological Disorders)

   b.   The diathesis-stress model argues that psychological disorders manifest when there is both genetic predisposition and sufficient life stress.

   c, d.   The neurobiological model explains psychological problems as due to problems in anatomy and physiology. The medical model is what the neurobiological model used to be called.

5.   a is the answer. According to the statistical infrequency criterion, behaviors are abnormal unless displayed by a large number of people. Few, if any, neurosurgeons lecture animals on the dangers of ingesting dangerous microbes. (see Defining Psychological Disorders)

   b.   There is no such thing as the psychopathological approach to defining abnormality.

   c.   There is no such thing as the logical approach to defining abnormal behavior.

   d.   The practical approach evaluates behavior content in the context of a situation. Mary Sue's behavior is not harmful and does not interfere with her everyday functioning, although it is a bit bizarre. However, this approach states that if everyone in the situation approves, even a bizarre behavior may not be considered abnormal. The shelter's workers like to see Mary giving the animals attention every day. Her behavior is not abnormal in this context.

6.   c. is the answer. Since the adoption of DSM-IV-TR, interrater reliability has *improved,* except for personality disorders and other complex conditions. (see Classifying Psychological Disorders)

   a, b, d.   These are all problems with DSM-IV-TR, the present diagnostic system.

7.   b is the answer. Compulsions are behaviors that the person thinks will keep harm from coming to him or herself, family, or friends. (see Anxiety Disorders)

   a.   An obsession is an unwanted, persistent thought.

   c, d.   Mania and conversion disorder do not cause unwanted, persistent thoughts and repetitive behaviors.

8.   c is the answer. Never displaying a behavior in public, such as eating or writing, for fear of humiliation is called a social phobia. Frank is afraid that he will embarrass himself by getting sick in public, so he refuses to eat at restaurants. (see Anxiety Disorders)

   a.   Specific phobias include fear of objects or situations, such as heights, dogs, or air travel, but do not include any social factors. In other words, people may have a fear of spiders and not feel worried that their fear will humiliate them.

   b.   Agoraphobia is a fear of leaving one's home and, sometimes, of being alone.

   d.   Obsessive-compulsive disorder is characterized by taking great pains to be organized, neat, clean, or particular about details or by recurring, unpleasant thoughts.

9.   b is the answer. Conversion disorders are physical symptoms, like paralysis or blindness, without physical causes. Anita probably has a conversion disorder, which is a type of somatoform disorder. (see Somatoform Disorders)

   a.   Anita has a conversion disorder, which is not an anxiety disorder.

   c.   Anita has a conversion disorder, which is not a dissociative disorder.

   d.   Anita has a conversion disorder, which is not a personality disorder.

10.   a is the answer. A dissociative disorder is characterized by disruptions in memory, consciousness, or identity. (see Dissociative Disorders)

   b.   Someone with antisocial personality disorder usually displays a pattern of impulsive, selfish, and even criminal behavior. However, the symptoms associated with personality disorders do not usually include memory loss.

   c.   Symptoms of dissociative identity disorder may include blackouts or a loss of memory over a certain period of time when an alternate personality takes over, but do not include a loss of personal information, such as one's name.

d.   A person with schizophrenia experiencing thought blocking or withdrawal may feel as though he or she is being prevented from remembering his or her own name, job, or family, but there are no specific symptoms of memory loss typical of schizophrenia.

11.   d is the answer. A social-cognitive theorist would say that our thinking, positive or negative, or our blaming ourselves instead of the environment can lead to depression. (see Affective Disorders)

12.   b is the answer. Bipolar disorder involves extreme changes in mood and, consequently, behavior. (see Affective Disorders)

a, c.   A pleasant mood is normal, so there is only one symptom present in each answer: depression. Both mania and depression must be present before a bipolar disorder is suspected.

d.   Bipolar disorders are very rare.

13.   b is the answer. Mercedes's dog has learned helplessness; it has learned or come to believe that its actions—barking and growling—will not control its environment by scaring the children away. (see Affective Disorders)

a.   Generalized anxiety is worry and fear detached from any specific cause.

c.   Hypersensitive brainstem mechanisms are associated with panic disorder in humans.

d.   Enlarged ventricles are associated with schizophrenia in humans.

14.   b is the answer. A hallucination is a false perception. Hearing voices that are not there is a false perception. (see Schizophrenia)

a.   Believing you are President is a false belief. A false belief is a delusion.

c.   Constantly worrying about something specific is an obsession.

d.   A repetitive behavior, like constant checking, is a compulsion.

15.   c is the answer. Internalizing disorders include separation anxiety disorder and pervasive developmental disorders such as autism. All of these disorders involve distress within the child. (see A Sampling of Other Psychological Disorders)

a.   This is an externalizing disorder of childhood.

b.   Autistic disorder fits neither the internalizing nor the externalizing categories.

d.   Only c is the answer.

16.   d is the answer. Addiction is the physical need for a substance. (see A Sampling of Other Disorders)

a.   Alcoholism may involve addiction, but addiction is more general, involving need for any substance, not just alcohol.

b.   Hallucinations are false perceptions.

c.   Delusions are false beliefs.

17.   c is the answer. People with antisocial personality disorder display a long-term, persistent pattern of impulsive, selfish, unscrupulous, and even criminal behavior. (see Personality Disorders)

a.   The main characteristic of narcissistic personality disorder is an exaggerated sense of self-importance. Although these people may be annoying in their constant quest for attention from the right people, they usually are not free of guilt, nor do they tend to commit crimes.

b. Depression is a mood disorder, not a personality disorder, involving feelings of sadness and hopelessness and a loss of self-worth.

c. A mood disorder is not a personality disorder. Mood disorders, such as depression or mania, involve changes in emotions.

18. b is the answer. Poor parenting and regression to childhood are psychological theories for schizophrenia that have not received strong research support. Psychological factors alone are no longer considered to be the primary causes of schizophrenia. (see Schizophrenia)

a, c, d. These are all part of the integrative view of the vulnerability model.

19. c is the answer. Conduct disorder falls under the externalizing category. Its primary features are aggressive, destructive, disobedient behaviors. (see A Sampling of Other Psychological Disorders)

a. Autistic disorder is neither an externalizing nor internalizing disorder. It is a severe condition usually diagnosed in the first thirty months of life and is characterized by ritualistic play, lack of attachment to caregivers, and lack of positive emotional expressions.

b. Narcissistic personality disorder is not a disorder of childhood and is identified when a person is egotistical, overly sensitive to criticism, and in need of attention.

d. Schizotypal personality disorder is similar to schizophrenia, but not as severe. People with this disorder may have odd beliefs, but they do not hallucinate.

20. a is the answer. This is not part of the M'Naghton rule. If one is unable to understand the proceedings and assist in one's defense, one will indeed be judged mentally incompetent to stand trial until one is competent. The M'Naghton rule has to do with the not guilty by reason of insanity plea, not whether or not one stands trial. (see Mental Illness and the Law)

b, c, d. All three of these criteria are part of the M'Naghton rule.

Now turn to the quiz analysis table at the end of this chapter to find which areas you know well and which areas you need to work on. Circle the numbers in the table for items on Quiz 2 that you answered correctly.

For each question you answered correctly, circle its number. (Quiz 1 numbers are not shaded; Quiz 2 numbers are shaded.) Are there patterns in the types of questions or the topics you got wrong that could direct your further study? Did you improve from Quiz 1 to Quiz 2?

QUIZ REVIEW

Topic	Type of Question		
	Definition	**Comprehension**	**Application**
Defining Psychological Disorders		2	1
	1		2, 5
Explaining Psychological Disorders			3, 4
			4
Classifying Psychological Disorders		5	8
		6	
Anxiety Disorders			6, 7, 9
			7, 8
Somatoform Disorders	10		11
			9
Dissociative Disorders		12	13
			3, 10
Affective Disorders			14, 15
		11	12, 13
Schizophrenia			16, 17
		18	14
Personality Disorders			18
			17
A Sampling of Other Psychological Disorders			19, 20
	15, 16		19
Mental Illness and the Law			
	20		

Total correct by quiz:

Quiz 1:	
Quiz 2:	

CHAPTER 16

Treatment of Psychological Disorders

Psychotherapy is used by those who take a psychodynamic, humanistic, or social-cognitive (behavioral) approach to the treatment of psychological disorders. The biological approach uses drugs and other physical treatments.

OUTLINE

I. BASIC FEATURES OF TREATMENT
    All methods of treatment share certain basic features, including a *client* or patient seeking relief from problems; a *therapist* who is accepted as one who can help the client because of training or experience; a *special relationship* between client and therapist, which helps ease the client's problems; and a *theory* of what caused the patient's problems.

    Clients can be categorized as *inpatients* or *outpatients*. Psychiatrists are medical doctors who specialize in the treatment of mental disorders and can prescribe medications. Psychologists who do psychotherapy usually have a doctoral degree in clinical or counseling psychology, but only in New Mexico and Louisiana can they prescribe drugs. The main goal of psychotherapists is to help people change their thinking, feeling, and behavior so that they will be happier and higher functioning. Although this chapter discusses different treatment method separately, most therapists consider themselves to be *eclectic* or *integrative therapists*, drawing on a variety of approaches.

II. PSYCHODYNAMIC PSYCHOTHERAPY
    Freud's method of treatment, psychoanalysis, attempts to help the patient understand unconscious conflicts and wishes and work through their implications for everyday life.

    A. Classical Psychoanalysis
        Free association consists of asking a client to verbalize all thoughts, feelings, and memories that come to mind. The content and pattern of associations contain clues to unconscious material so that clients can gain *insight* into their problems and subsequently *work through* them. In the interpretation of dreams, a patient reports the *manifest content* (the surface story) of a dream and works to understand its *latent content* (the unconscious meaning), as represented by the dream's symbols. The psychoanalyst looks for evidence that the feelings, reactions, and conflicts the client experiences toward others have been transferred onto the therapist. *Transference* may help the client reenact and resolve old conflicts.

    B. Contemporary Variations on Psychoanalysis
        Psychoanalysis requires much time, money, verbal skill, and abstract thinking ability; these requirements limit its use. Variations on psychoanalytic treatments, such as *ego analysis* and *individual analysis*, are based on neo-Freudian theories. More recent variations have become less expensive, less intense, and more appropriate for a broader range of clients. These are termed *short-term psychodynamic therapy*.

        Object relations therapy is one of these newer approaches. Therapists using this approach believe that personality and the arising conflicts that cause problems stem from the need for supportive human relationships, such as the mother-child bond. The therapist takes an active role in therapy and tries to establish a supportive and nurturing relationship with the client so that she or he can experience what may have been missed as an infant. *Interpersonal therapy* focuses on exploring and overcoming problematic events that occurred after childhood.

Other variations on psychodynamic therapy look for core conflicts that appear repeatedly across a variety of relationships, including the therapeutic one, and try to work through those.

III.   HUMANISTIC PSYCHOTHERAPY

Humanistic psychologists (also called *phenomenologists*) believe that behavior is shaped by an innate drive toward growth that is guided by an individual's interpretation of the world. Humanistic treatment is based on the following assumptions: Treatment is a human encounter between equals, not a cure; clients will improve on their own, given the right conditions; an accepting and supportive relationship will support clients' growth; and clients must remain responsible for choosing how to feel and think.

    A.   Client-Centered Therapy
         Carl Rogers's <u>client-centered therapy</u>, or <u>person-centered therapy</u>, is based on creating a relationship characterized by <u>unconditional positive regard</u> or <u>acceptance</u>, <u>empathy</u>, and <u>congruence</u>.

         1.   *Unconditional Positive Regard.* The therapist must show that he or she genuinely cares about and accepts the client as a person without *conditions of worth*.
         2.   *Empathy.* The therapist must appreciate how the world looks from the client's point of view. Empathy is communicated through a technique called <u>active listening</u> or <u>reflection</u>.
         3.   *Congruence.* Sometimes called *genuineness,* congruence conveys that the way the therapist feels is consistent with the way he or she acts toward the client. The therapist's unconditional positive regard and empathy are real, not manufactured. This experience should help promote congruence in other relationships the client experiences.

    B.   Gestalt Therapy
         The goal of Frederick and Laura Perls' <u>Gestalt therapy</u> is to help clients become more unified, self-aware, and self-accepting so that they can begin growing again in their own unique, consciously guided directions. Gestalt therapists encourage clients to become aware of real feelings that they have denied and to discard foreign feelings, ideas, and values. They pay special attention to body language, and engage the client in role play and imaginary dialogues.

IV.   BEHAVIOR THERAPY

Therapists who use behavior therapies assume that problems are *learned* patterns of thinking and behaving that can be changed without looking for the meanings behind them. Basic features of behavioral treatment include the development of a productive client-therapist relationship, a list of behaviors and thoughts to be changed, a therapist who acts as a teacher by setting and implementing specific treatment plans, and ongoing evaluation of the effects of therapy. Treatments that utilize classical conditioning principles are referred to as <u>behavior therapy</u>; those utilizing operant conditioning are called <u>behavior modification</u>. Therapies that focus on changing thinking patterns as well as overt behavior are called <u>cognitive behavior therapy</u>.

    A.   Techniques for Modifying Behavior
         1.   *Systematic Desensitization Therapy.* During <u>systematic desensitization therapy</u>, a client practices *progressive relaxation* while imagining fear-provoking situations from a *desensitization hierarchy*. The process of remaining calm while thinking about something feared weakens the learned association between anxiety and the feared object or situation. It is not practiced as often as it used to be because of research

indicating real (rather than imagined) presentation of the items on the hierarchy were more effective, *in vivo* desensitization. Now, *virtual reality graded exposure* is used so that the client can experience vivid and precise versions of the feared stimulus in the absence of real exposure.

2. *Modeling.* Through participant <u>modeling</u>, a client can learn about or get comfortable displaying desirable behaviors. The therapist demonstrates desirable behaviors, and the client gradually practices them. The clients can learn to be more appropriately self-expressive and more comfortable in social situations through <u>assertiveness training</u> and <u>social skills training</u>, both of which also rely on modeling.

3. *Positive Reinforcement.* A therapist systematically uses <u>positive reinforcement</u> to alter problematic behaviors. The receipt of rewards or tokens is *contingent* upon a client's display of desirable behaviors. In institutions, behavior therapists sometimes establish a <u>token economy program</u>.

4. *Extinction.* <u>Extinction</u> modifies behavior by removing reinforcers that normally follow a particular response. A procedure called <u>flooding</u> relies on extinction by keeping a patient in a feared but harmless situation. As a result, the client who is deprived of the normally rewarding escape pattern has no reason for continued anxiety. Because flooding and similar methods continuously expose the client to feared stimuli, they are called <u>exposure therapy</u>.

5. *Aversion Therapy.* <u>Aversion conditioning</u> uses classical conditioning to reduce undesirable behavior by associating it with some psychological or physical discomfort. Because it is uncomfortable, may not work for all clients, and may have only temporary effects, it is only used rarely.

6. *Punishment.* <u>Punishment</u> eliminates a dangerous or disruptive behavior by presenting an unpleasant stimulus after the behavior, which reduces its occurrence. Punishment is appropriate in some treatment settings, but only after a careful review of ethical and legal questions such as: Is the client's life in danger without treatment? Have other treatment methods failed? Has an ethics committee reviewed the treatment procedure? Has the client (or a close relative) agreed to the treatment? Punishment works best when it is combined with treatments that reinforce the appropriate behavior.

B. Cognitive Behavior Therapy
Cognitive behavior therapy can help people change behavior and negative thoughts, which can induce depression, anger, or anxiety.

1. *Rational-Emotive Behavior Therapy.* <u>Rational-emotive behavior therapy (REBT)</u> tries to identify and eliminate self-defeating thoughts. *Cognitive restructuring, self-instruction*, and *stress inoculation training* can teach a client new and calming thoughts to help her or him cope with stressful or anxiety-provoking situations.

2. *Beck's Cognitive Therapy.* <u>Cognitive therapy</u> rests on the assumption that a client has *cognitive distortions* about the self and the world such as *catastrophizing, all-or-none thinking,* and *personalization.* Treatment involves demonstrating the inaccuracy of these thoughts by testing them. Clients are then given homework that will help to challenge the false belief. Some cognitive therapists use *mindfulness-based cognitive therapy*, which uses practices such as meditation to help monitor problematic thoughts.

V. GROUP, FAMILY, AND COUPLES THERAPY
A. Group Therapy
<u>Group therapy</u> is the simultaneous treatment of several unrelated clients by one therapist who facilitates helpful interactions amongst the clients. Groups are organized around either one type of problem or one type of client. Group therapy has several advantages: The therapist can observe clients' personal interactions; clients realize that they aren't the only people with a particular problem; clients support one another, which increases self-esteem;

clients learn from one another; through mutual modeling, clients become more willing to share feelings and more sensitive to others; and clients have a safe environment in which to try out new behaviors. Some of these advantages are put to use in *self-help organizations*.

B. Family and Couples Therapy
Family therapy is based in part on the idea that a patient's problems stem from early family relationships and problems, and that problems are multifaceted and must be dealt with in the family system in which they are maintained. In family therapy, the entire family is the "client," and the therapist attempts to create harmony within the family by facilitating each member's understanding of the family's interactions and how they relate to problems. *Structural family therapy* aims to identify communication patterns that create unhealthy *alliances* in the family.

Couples therapy focuses on communication between partners. Therapists and clients often set "rules for talking" to improve communication skills. Emphasis may be on making five times as many positive statements as negative ones during interactions.

VI. EVALUATING PSYCHOTHERAPY
Eysenck conducted research which found that untreated clients often had better outcomes than clients who received therapeutic intervention. Critics cited a number of reasons this result was unpersuasive, and offered their own evidence to contradict it. The question of the effectiveness of therapy is difficult for several reasons. First, it is not straightforward how to define "effective" in this context. Secondly, therapy involves such a broad range of clients, therapists, and treatments. The question of whether therapy "works" in a broad sense is difficult, then, to answer scientifically. Some reviews, however, do suggest it can be effective.

A. Thinking Critically: Are All Forms of Therapy Equally Effective?
What am I being asked to believe or accept?

Different forms of therapy are equally effective, independent of theoretical approach or methods. This is called the Dodo Bird Effect.

What evidence is available to support the assertion?

Meta-analyses combine the results of a large number of therapy studies and have shown psychodynamic, humanistic, and behavioral therapies to be equally effective.

Are there alternative ways of interpreting the evidence?

Meta-analyses may be unable to detect the effect of different therapies for different problems. Differences between the therapies may be overshadowed by *common factors* to all therapy. Also, experimental methods and conclusions may not take into account the personal qualities of psychotherapists practicing in the "real world" and how these may interact with clients.

What additional evidence would help to evaluate the alternatives?

Research that focuses on which combinations of therapists, clients, and treatments produce the most successful results still needs to be conducted. The "ultimate question" to ask is: what treatment, by whom, is most effective for this individual with that specific problem under these specific circumstances?

What conclusions are most reasonable?

Caution should be used when drawing conclusions about the relative superiority of different approaches to therapy. As we gain a better understanding of the answer to the "ultimate question", we will be able to develop evidence-based practice in which decisions about which treatment method to use will be based on empirical evidence about the effectiveness of it. This evidence should speak to both the *clinical* and *statistical significance* of the treatment method.

B.   Focus on Research Methods: Which Therapies Work Best for Which Problems?
A task force examined the outcomes of thousands of experiments evaluating psychotherapy methods used to treat different disorders. They found that certain therapies were identified as effective for particular problems. These are called <u>empirically supported therapies (ESTs)</u>. This study, however, focused on the therapeutic method only, rather than on the characteristics and interaction of the therapists and clients, which could affect the therapy outcome. Future research should include this facet in both laboratory and naturalistic studies.

When choosing a type of therapy, a person should give careful consideration to not only empirical evidence of an approach's effectiveness, but also what approach he or she finds appealing, the therapist's "track record," and the potential for forming a productive client-therapist relationship.

C.   Sociocultural Factors in Psychotherapy
Cultural differences may lead a client and therapist to have different expectations and goals about the outcome of therapy and the approach and methods used. In the United States, sociocultural clashes may explain underuse or withdrawal from therapy in certain minority populations. Currently, psychologists are working to align cultural influence and choice of a specific treatment. For example, some evidence suggests that clients from collectivist cultures prefer a more directive approach than traditional "client-centered" methods would allow. In addition to diversity training that will sensitize therapists to these issues, mental health training programs need to recruit more students from varying cultures.

D.   Rules and Rights in the Therapeutic Relationship
The ethical standards of the American Psychological Association forbid a sexual relationship between therapist and client and for two years after the therapy has ended. A therapist must also hold whatever the client says in complete confidentiality. Exceptions to this rule include situations in which the client's current or historical condition is used as part of a civil or criminal defense, the client is so severely disturbed or suicidal that hospitalization is required, the therapist must defend against a malpractice suit, the client reveals information about sexual or physical abuse of a child or incapacitated adult, or the therapist believes that the client may commit a violent act against another person.

Clients are also protected against being placed or kept in an institution unnecessarily. A person threatened with commitment must have written notice, a chance to prepare a defense with an attorney, a court hearing (with a jury if the client wishes), and the right to take the Fifth Amendment. Furthermore, the prosecution must prove that the client is mentally ill *and* poses a danger to himself or herself and others. Once in an institution, a client may refuse certain treatments, and states are required to review every case periodically to determine if the client should be released. While hospitalized, clients have the right to treatment, and the right to refuse certain forms of treatment. There is a tension between keeping someone unnecessarily confined and releasing someone too soon, which some states have begun to develop legislature to deal with.

VII. BIOLOGICAL TREATMENTS
Biological treatments for psychological disorders have been in existence since the time of Hippocrates. Methods used in the sixteenth through eighteenth centuries included laxative purges, bleeding of "excess" blood, induced vomiting, cold baths, hunger, and other physical discomforts, all of which were designed to shock the patient back to normality. Biological treatments have advanced considerably since that time.

A.   Psychosurgery
Psychosurgical techniques, including *prefrontal lobotomies*, were once used to treat problems involving strong emotional responses, such as schizophrenia, depression, anxiety, aggressiveness, and obsessive-compulsive disorders. Today, psychosurgery is done only as a last resort and involves the destruction of only a tiny amount of brain tissue.

B.   Electroconvulsive Shock Therapy
Electroconvulsive shock therapy (EST) was used in the 1940s and 1950s to treat schizophrenia, depression, and sometimes mania. Today, EST is used primarily to treat severe depression in patients who don't respond to psychoactive drugs and are at risk for suicide. EST procedures have changed; today, shock is applied to one hemisphere and patients are given a deep muscle relaxant prior to treatment. Why EST works is unclear. EST is one of the most controversial biological treatments. Safer versions of it are being investigated, including *magnetic seizure therapy, repetitive transcranial magnetic stimulation,* and *deep brain stimulation.*

C.   Psychoactive Drugs
Psychoactive drugs have largely replaced EST and psychosurgery.
1.   *Neuroleptics*. Neuroleptic drugs (antipsychotic drugs) are effective in reducing delusions, hallucinations, paranoid suspiciousness, and other severe forms of disturbed thought and behavior. Phenothiazines and haloperidol are common neuroleptic drugs that produce improvement in 60 to 70 percent of patients. However, these drugs produce side effects such as tardive dyskinesia. Clozapine, a new antipsychotic drug, is equally effective and does not cause movement disorders. It comes with the risk of a fatal blood disorder, though, so it is typically only used when a patient fails to respond to the other neuroleptic drugs. Newer neuroleptic drugs have been introduced, but their effectiveness in comparison to older ones is still under scrutiny.
2.   *Antidepressants*. By increasing the amount of serotonin or norepinephrine available at synapses, antidepressant drugs such as *monoamine oxidase inhibitors, tricyclic antidepressants*, and *fluoxetine* (which affects serotonin) can produce a gradual lifting of depression, allowing the person to return to normal life. About 50 to 60 percent of patients taking an antidepressant experience improvement, although the benefits are seen more rarely in the severely depressed population. Some research suggests the effectiveness of antidepressants is largely a placebo effect.
3.   *Lithium and Anticonvulsants*. *Lithium*, although associated with severe side effects, is helpful in reducing and even preventing both the depression and the mania associated with the bipolar disorders. *Anticonvulsants* are becoming more popular in treating mania, but carry a risk of suicide and their long-term benefits are questionable. They are still compared to lithium as the drug of choice in treating bipolar disorder and mania.
4.   *Tranquilizing Drugs (Anxiolytics)*. Tranquilizing drugs, also called anxiolytics, are the most widely used of all legal drugs. They relieve anxiety and tension. Some of them, however, are potentially addictive and, when mixed with alcohol, can have fatal consequences.
5.   *Human Diversity and Drug Treatment*. Drugs can have varying effects on different ethnic groups and genders.

D.   Evaluating Psychoactive Drug Treatments
Although drugs can at times be very useful in the treatment of mental disorders, enthusiasm about drugs is not universal. Anxiolytics, in particular, may be overrelied on by physicians and therapists. At least three limitations apply: Drugs may cover up the problem without permanently curing it; drugs carry the potential for abuse, resulting in physical or

psychological dependence; and many drugs have undesirable side effects. There is added concern that the drugs may not be as effective as once thought and that their popularity is due to research done by drug companies rather than independent scientists.

E. Drugs and Psychotherapy
It is unclear which is more effective in treating psychological disorders: drugs or psychotherapy. It has been suggested that, where indicated, treatment begin with some form of psychotherapy and that drug treatments be added only if psychotherapy is ineffective.

F. Linkages: Biological Aspects of Psychology and the Treatment of Psychological Disorders
Therapeutic drugs alter neurotransmitter activity by enhancing or inhibiting the binding of neurotransmitters to receptors; acting as receptor *antagonists* by blocking neurotransmitters' receptor sites and, as a result, inhibiting action potential activity; or increasing the amount of neurotransmitter available at the synapse by stimulating neurotransmitter production or blocking *reuptake*. Prozac, for example, is a *selective serotonin reuptake inhibitor*.

VIII. COMMUNITY PSYCHOLOGY: FROM TREATMENT TO PREVENTION
Community psychology is a movement that attempts to increase early detection of problems and minimize or prevent mental disorders by making social and environmental changes (e.g., addressing poverty, substandard housing, and so forth). Community psychology emerged in part because of a *deinstitutionalization* movement in the 1960s and 1970s that aimed to reduce the number of inpatient treatment beds. People who once would have been institutionalized may now live in community-based facilities and work on *psychosocial rehabilitation*. The emphasis is independent living, but the down side is that those who do not benefit from these services often end up in the homeless population. Early detection of psychological problems may help fewer people reach this extreme situation.

KEY TERMS

1. **Psychotherapy** is the treatment of psychological disorders through talking and other psychological methods. (see introductory section)

   Example: Psychoanalysis, client-centered therapy, Gestalt therapy, rational-emotive therapy, and cognitive-behavior therapy are all examples of psychotherapy.

2. **Psychiatrists** are medical doctors who have completed special training in the treatment of psychological disorders. (see Basic Features of Treatment)

   Example: Tim is a psychiatrist who primarily sees patients who are in need of a drug treatment, but does a little bit of therapy with them.

3. Among therapists, **psychologists** are people who have completed a master's or (usually) doctoral degree in clinical or counseling psychology and who may have received additional specialty training. (see Basic Features of Treatment)

   Example: Russ is a clinical psychologist who works with clients on stress management using meditation in combination with behavioral techniques.

4. **Psychoanalysis** is a method of psychotherapy that seeks to help clients gain insight by recognizing and understanding unconscious thoughts and emotions. (see Psychodynamic Psychotherapy)

   Example: Jane is a psychoanalytic therapist. She has her client free associate—tell her everything that is on his mind without editing himself. She then helps provide insight into the unconscious problems that she sees in the content of his free association.

5. **Client-centered** (or **person-centered**) **therapy** is a therapy that allows the client to decide what to talk about, without direction, judgment, or interpretation from the therapist. (see Client-Centered Therapy)

   Example: Karl actively listens to his client, repeating back to him in paraphrase form what is said to demonstrate active listening and to convey he understands. He does not provide "solutions" to the client's problems, but validates that the problems are real and that he respects the client's intellect and ability to choose a path to solve the problem.

   REMEMBER: Developed by Carl Rogers, this therapy assumes that a client has a drive toward self-actualization. It is based on a relationship between client and therapist that is characterized by unconditional positive regard, empathy, and congruence.

6. **Unconditional positive regard**, or **acceptance** refers to a therapist attitude that conveys caring for and recognition of the client as a valued person. (see Client-Centered Therapy)

   REMEMBER: The therapist communicates acceptance *without conditions;* even if the client admits to socially undesirable behaviors or views, the therapist is encouraging and respectful.

7. **Empathy** is the therapist's attempt to appreciate and understand how the world looks from the client's point of view. (see Client-Centered Therapy)

   Example: Yvonne came into therapy because she resented having to care for her younger sisters even though she knew that her mother was working three jobs. Yvonne's therapist must try to see the world from Yvonne's point of view and can accomplish this by understanding the constraints that Yvonne feels as a result of such tremendous responsibility.

8. **Active listening** or **reflection** is a method for conveying empathy on the part of the therapist by paraphrasing a client's statements and noting accompanying feelings. (see Client-Centered Therapy)

   Example: Read the example for Key Term 7. The therapist might respond to Yvonne by saying, "You're tired of doing so much around the house with your sisters, which prevents you from going out and doing what you want. You're angry at your mom." The therapist has reflected what Yvonne has said, thus also demonstrating empathy.

9. **Congruence** (sometimes called **genuineness**) refers to a consistency between a therapist's feelings and the therapist's behavior towards clients. (see Client-Centered Therapy)

   Example: Read the examples for Key Terms 7 and 8. The therapist must genuinely feel empathy and unconditional positive regard for Yvonne. She cannot think to herself that Yvonne is spoiled and selfish. The therapist must actually accept Yvonne's feelings with unconditional positive regard for her worth as a person.

   REMEMBER: The therapist's behavior toward the client must be a reflection of how he or she really feels; it cannot be an act. Ideally, the client will learn that openness and honesty can be the foundation of a human relationship.

10. **Gestalt therapy** is an active treatment designed to help clients get in touch with genuine feelings and disown foreign ones. (see Gestalt Therapy)

    Example: When Renee describes how angry she became when her boss asked her to stay late, the therapist suggests they role-play the conversation between Renee and her boss. Renee finds that it really wasn't the request that made her the most angry; it was her perception that the boss assumed she had nothing better to do.

    REMEMBER: A Gestalt therapist takes an active and directive role in helping a client become aware of denied feelings and impulses and learn how to discard foreign feelings, ideas, and values. Also, the therapist helps the client become more self-accepting. Methods used include dialogues with people, inanimate objects, and various body parts.

11. **Behavior therapy** describes treatments that use classical conditioning principles to change behavior. (see Behavior Therapy)

    Example: Flooding and aversive conditioning are examples of behavior therapies. (See Key Terms 21 and 23.)

12. **Behavior modification** describes treatments that use operant conditioning methods to change behavior. (see Behavior Therapy)

    Example: Modeling is an example of behavior modification therapy. (See Key Term 15.)

13. **Cognitive behavior therapy** consists of learning-based treatment methods that help clients change the way they think, as well as the way they behave. (see Behavior Therapy)

    Example: Rational-emotive behavior therapy is an example of cognitive behavior therapy. (See Key Term 25.)

14. **Systematic desensitization therapy** is a behavioral treatment for anxiety in which clients visualize a graduated series of anxiety-provoking stimuli while remaining relaxed. (see Techniques for Modifying Behavior)

    Example: Carlos is terrified of heights. His therapist asks him to create a desensitization hierarchy. He lists several "height" experiences from the least to the most frightening.

    a.   Standing on a small step stool

    b.   Standing on the bottom rung of a ladder

    c.   Looking out the top-floor window of a three-story building

    d.   Standing on the middle rung of a ladder

    e.   Standing on the top rung of a ladder

    f.   Standing and peering into an empty ten-story elevator shaft

    g.   Standing on the edge of Niagara Falls

    h.   Standing on the edge of the lookout tower over the Grand Canyon

    i.   Riding in a helicopter

    Carlos's therapist will gradually work through each of these scenes using systematic desensitization.

15. **Modeling** involves demonstrating desirable behaviors as a way of teaching them to clients. (see Techniques for Modifying Behavior)

    Example: Kip is afraid of snakes. Modeling therapy might include having him watch films of people handling snakes. Then, he might be present in the same room while others are handling.

16. **Social skills training** is a method for teaching clients the behaviors they need in order to interact with others more comfortably and effectively. (see Techniques for Modifying Behavior)

    Example: John was so timid that he didn't know how to make conversation with others. He worked with his therapist to practice strategies for making small talk, and this increased his confidence in social situations.

17. **Assertiveness training** is a form of social skills training that focuses on teaching clients to express themselves in ways that are clear and direct. (see Techniques for Modifying Behavior)

Example: Nan, a very shy woman, was constantly being taken advantage of despite her knowledge of auto mechanics. Every time she took her car to a mechanic, the garage overcharged her or did unnecessary work. She knew this but just could not bring herself to say something about it until she had gone through assertiveness training.

REMEMBER: People are taught how to be assertive, not aggressive. Nan does not have to be aggressive in order to express herself effectively in the auto shop. Instead, she simply needs to be direct in her demand for fair service.

18. **Positive reinforcement** is a therapy method that uses rewards to strengthen desirable behaviors. (see Techniques for Modifying Behavior)

Example: A therapist who is assisting a client with a weight problem may give the client lots of praise (positive reinforcement) when the client loses one pound in the hopes that the praise will motivate the client to continue to follow the program. Praise is contingent on weight loss; that is, if the client loses no weight, no praise is given.

19. **Token economy programs** are systems for improving the behavior of institutionalized clients in which desirable behaviors are rewarded with tokens that can be exchanged for desired items or activities. (see Techniques for Modifying Behavior)

Example: Tony and his therapist have decided that he should be able to complete his daily homework and keep his room neat. For every completed homework assignment, he receives two tokens. When he makes his bed, picks up his clothes, and keeps his dresser organized, he receives three tokens. Tony exchanges his tokens for field trips to local museums or for dinner in town.

REMEMBER: Eventually social reinforcements, such as smiles of approval and encouragement, come to replace tokens.

20. **Extinction** is the gradual disappearance of a conditioned response or operant behavior through nonreinforcement. (see Techniques for Modifying Behavior)

Example: By having Maggie flooded with a room full of friendly golden retrievers, she does initially experience her intense phobic fear of dogs. However, she is no longer able to escape from the dogs and be reinforced with the removal of that fear. As time passes, she realizes that nothing bad has happened in the presence of the dogs, and that her fear response has subsided even in their presence.

21. **Flooding** is an exposure technique for reducing anxiety that involves keeping a person in a feared, but harmless situation. (see Techniques for Modifying Behavior)

Example: Clint was extremely afraid of riding on buses. He and his therapist rode a city bus for an hour. Clint was very frightened at first, but then he calmed down, and eventually he lost his fear. Clint realized that the bus ride (CS) did not predict any catastrophic event (UCS).

22. **Exposure therapy** refers to behavior therapy methods in which clients remain in the presence of strong anxiety-provoking stimuli until the intensity of their emotional reactions decrease. (see Techniques for Modifying Behavior)

Example: Flooding is an example of an exposure therapy. (see Key Term 21.)

15. **Aversion conditioning** is a method that uses classical conditioning to create a negative response to a particular stimulus. (see Techniques for Modifying Behavior)

Example: In the movie *A Clockwork Orange,* the main character spends most of his time raping and beating women. Later he is forced to watch movies of these types of behaviors while experiencing the effects of a nausea-producing drug. After the treatment, the mere thought of violent actsmakes him experience nausea.

24. **Punishment** is a therapy method that uses operant conditioning to weaken undesirable behavior by following it with an unpleasant stimulus. (see Techniques for Modifying Behavior)

    Example: Peter is seven years old and lives in an institution. He climbs on the roofs of the buildings in the development. He has already fallen and broken his legs and arms three times. Despite repeated attempts to stop this behavior using a token economy, Peter still climbs on the roofs. His therapist has decided that punishment is the only way to keep Peter from putting himself in an extremely dangerous situation.

    REMEMBER: Usually, punishment is used as a last resort to eliminate problem behaviors.

25. **Rational-emotive behavior therapy (REBT)** is a treatment designed to identify and change self-defeating thoughts that lead to anxiety and other symptoms of disorder. (see Cognitive Behavior Therapy)

    Example: Brady is a personnel administrator. He feels uncomfortable because he is often faced with disciplinary decisions that result in angry employees. His therapist has pointed out that it is unrealistic to think that everyone will like him and be happy with his decisions all the time. Brady learns to treat people fairly and not to expect them to like all of his decisions.

26. **Cognitive therapy** is a treatment in which the therapist helps clients notice and change negative thoughts associated with anxiety and depression. (see Cognitive Behavior Therapy)

    Example: Leslie is convinced that she will never be successful on her new job. As a result, she is very anxious. Her therapist helps her list the skills she will need on the new job. Then Leslie and the therapist recall past jobs where Leslie performed very well using just those skills. Leslie's therapist helps her see that her anxiety-producing thoughts about her performance are wrong.

27. **Group therapy** is psychotherapy involving several unrelated clients. (see Group Therapy)

    Example: Misha is in a support group for teen mothers. The group members meet with a therapist once a week to discuss how things are going and to offer each other support.

    REMEMBER: The therapist can observe clients interacting with one another in real social situations; clients feel less alone when they realize that other people are struggling with similar problems; and clients can learn from one another.

28. **Family therapy** involves treatment of two or more individuals from the same family. (see Family and Couples Therapy)

    Example: Robert has been hostile and depressed lately, but he is not attending therapy alone. Robert's parents and sometimes his siblings go to sessions with him. The therapist observes how the family members interact and tries to help them see how they affect each other.

    REMEMBER: The real client in family therapy is the family, and the goal of family therapy is to create harmony within the family by helping each member better understand the family's interactions and the problems they create.

29. **Couples therapy** is a form of therapy focusing on improving communication between partners. (see Family and Couples Therapy)

    Example: Daniel and Mara bicker constantly. Their couples' therapist observes that the ratio of positive to negative things they say to one another is about 1:2. She assigns that in the coming week they work on reversing that so it is 5:1. In therapy, they work on identifying positive sorts of behaviors they could focus on to fuel this change.

30. **Evidence based practice** is the selection of treatment methods based mainly on empirical evidence of their effectiveness. (see Thinking Critically: Are All Forms of Therapy Equally Effective?)

Example: Joshua knows that empirical evidence suggests that cognitive behavior therapy has been demonstrated to work for depression. Therefore, when a client comes to him and is diagnosed with depression, he employs cognitive therapy.

31.   **Empirically supported therapies (ESTs)** are treatments whose effects have been validated by controlled experimental research. (see Focus on Research Methods: Which Therapies Work Best for Which Problems?)

Example: Behavioral family therapy has been empirically supported as specific and efficacious in the treatment of schizophrenia.

32.   **Psychosurgery** involves surgical procedures that destroy tissue in small regions of the brain in an effort to treat psychological disorders. (see Psychosurgery)

REMEMBER: Psychosurgery treats <u>psychological</u> problems through <u>surgical</u> techniques. This treatment is used as a last resort in treating problems involving strong emotional reactions.

33.   **Electroconvulsive therapy (EST)** involves brief electrical shock administered to the brain, usually to reduce depression that does not respond to drug treatments. (see Electroconvulsive Shock Therapy)

RMEEMBER: Today, shock is applied to only one brain hemisphere, and patients are given a deep muscle relaxant prior to treatment to prevent injury.

34.   **Neuroleptic drugs** (also called antipsychotic drugs) are medications that alleviate the symptoms of severe disorders such as schizophrenia. (see Psychoactive Drugs)

Example: Clozapine (clozaril) is an example of a neuroleptic drug.

REMEMBER: These drugs are effective in reducing hallucinations, delusions, paranoid suspiciousness, and incoherence. Unfortunately, neuroleptic drugs such as chlorpromazine and haloperidol can cause severe side effects, such as tardive dyskinesia.

35.   **Antidepressant drugs** are medications that relieve depression. (see Psychoactive Drugs)

Example: Prozac is an example of an antidepressant drug.

REMEMBER: Drugs which increase levels of serotonin and norepinephrine, are useful in treating depression. This class of drugs includes monoamine oxidase inhibitors, tricyclic antidepressants, and fluoxetine.

36.   **Tranquilizing drugs (anxiolytics**) are drugs that reduce feelings of anxiety. (see Psychoactive Drugs)

Example: Buspiron (BuSpar) is an example of an anxiolytic drug.

REMEMBER: Tranquilizing drugs include Librium and Valium and may also be used to treat agoraphobia (Xanax) in some cases. These drugs can be addictive and should not be combined with alcohol.

37.   **Community psychology** is an approach to minimizing or preventing psychological disorders through changes in social systems and through community mental health programs. (see Community Psychology: From Treatment to Prevention)

Example: Sally tries to reduce mental health problems by reducing the stress some families feel in finding adequate housing. She works with struggling families to place them in stable housing situations and believes that the reduced stress will decrease their risk for depression, marital discord, and other problems.

FILL-IN-THE-BLANKS KEY TERMS

This section will help you check your factual knowledge of the key terms introduced in this chapter. Fill in each blank with the appropriate term from the list of key terms in the previous section.

1. _____ are physicians who have received special training in the treatment of mental disorders.

2. When a therapist communicates that he or she understands how a client feels, the therapist is showing _____.

3. In client-centered therapy, it is important that the way a therapist feels and behaves toward a client be consistent; in other words, the therapist must show _____.

4. _____ is a set of techniques designed to help clients be direct and expressive in situations that involve other people.

5. A therapeutic technique that associates unpleasant feelings with undesirable behaviors and thereby causes a client to discontinue the undesirable behaviors is called _____.

6. Identifying and eliminating thought patterns that lead to depression, anger, or anxiety are the goal of _____.

7. _____ is a technique in which small amounts of brain tissue are destroyed in order to alleviate a psychological disorder.

8. _____ increase the amount of serotonin or norepinephrine available at synapses.

9. _____ focuses on the prevention of psychological disorders.

10. _____ block the action of dopamine and are used to treat severe mental disorders such as schizophrenia.

11. _____, developed by Carl Rogers, is based on the humanistic approach.

12. _____ is a cognitive-behavior therapy technique in which clients are taught to recognize self-destructive thought patterns and replace them with constructive ways of thinking.

13. _____ focuses on communication between partners.

14. _____ uses the principles of classical conditioning to change behavior.

15. Learning new behaviors by imitating others is called _____.

Total Correct (See answer key) _____

LEARNING OBJECTIVES

1. Define psychotherapy. Describe the approach of an eclectic therapist. (see introductory section)

2. Describe the common features of treatments. Define and distinguish between a psychiatrist and a psychologist. Describe other types of therapists. (see "Basic Features of Treatment")

3. Define psychoanalysis and describe the goals of a psychoanalyst. (see "Psychodynamic Psychotherapy"; see also "Classical Psychoanalysis")

4. Define *free association*, *manifest* and *latent contents* of dreams, and *transference*. Discuss the ways in which these methods of psychotherapy reveal clues about unconscious mental processes. (see "Classical Psychoanalysis")

5. Describe the difference between Freud's original psychoanalysis and modern variations. Describe some of the methods used in contemporary psychoanalysis. Discuss the criticisms of psychoanalysis. (see "Contemporary Variations on Psychoanalysis")

6. Describe the theoretical basis of the humanistic approach to therapy. List the four assumptions on which phenomenological therapists operate. (see "Humanistic Psychotherapy")

7. Describe <u>client-centered therapy</u>, or <u>person-centered therapy</u>. Define and discuss the importance of <u>acceptance</u>, <u>empathy</u>, <u>active listening</u> (<u>reflection</u>), and <u>congruence</u> in this therapy. (see "Client-Centered Therapy")

8. Explain the basic assumptions of <u>Gestalt therapy</u>. Discuss how this approach differs from client-centered therapy. (see "Gestalt Therapy")

9. Define <u>behavior therapy</u>. Describe its basic features and the assumptions on which it is based. (see "Behavior Therapy")

10. Explain the differences among <u>behavior therapy</u>, <u>behavior modification</u>, and <u>cognitive-behavior therapy</u>. (see "Behavior Therapy")

11. Define <u>systematic desensitization</u>, <u>flooding</u> and other <u>exposure therapies</u>, <u>modeling</u>, <u>social skills training and assertiveness training</u>, <u>positive reinforcement</u>, <u>token economy programs</u>, <u>extinction</u>, <u>punishment</u>, and <u>aversion conditioning</u>. Give an example of each. Specify the type of learning (classical or operant conditioning) each method is based on. (see "Techniques for Modifying Behavior")

12. Define and discuss <u>rational-emotive behavior therapy</u>, *cognitive restructuring*, *stress inoculation training*, Beck's <u>cognitive therapy</u>, *cognitive distortions*, and *mindfulness-based cognitive therapy*. (see "Cognitive-Behavior Therapy")

13. Define <u>group</u>, <u>family</u>, and <u>couples therapy</u>. Discuss the advantages and disadvantages of each. (see "Group, Family, and Couples Therapy")

14. Discuss the results of research that has attempted to evaluate psychotherapy's effectiveness. (see "Evaluating Psychotherapy"; see also "Thinking Critically: Are All Forms of Therapy Equally Effective?")

15. Discuss the following questions: Is there one form of psychotherapy that is best? What should a person look for when seeking psychotherapy? Define <u>empirically-supported therapies</u>. (see "Focus on Research Methods: Which Therapies Work Best for Which Problems?"; see also "Choosing a Therapist")

16. Discuss the cultural influences on the choice of psychotherapy, its goals, and its expectations. (see "Cultural Factors in Psychotherapy")

17. Describe a client's rights in a therapeutic relationship. (see "Rules and Rights in the Therapeutic Relationship")

18. Define <u>psychosurgery</u>. Describe the historical and present use of the prefrontal lobotomy. (see "Psychosurgery")

19. Describe the historical and present use of <u>electroconvulsive shock therapy (ECT)</u>. (see "Electroconvulsive Therapy")

20. Define <u>neuroleptic</u> (antipsychotic), <u>antidepressant</u>, *lithium*, and <u>anxiolytic</u>. Specify the psychological problems each group of drugs is used to treat. Explain the side effects of these drugs and how each works within the nervous system. (see "Psychoactive Drugs")

21. Describe how differences in ethnicity and gender may result in different responses to psychoactive drugs. (see "Human Diversity and Drug Treatment")

22. Explain the criticisms of using psychoactive drugs to treat psychological disorders. Discuss the combined use of drugs and psychotherapy. (see "Evaluating Psychoactive Drug Treatments"; see also "Drugs and Psychotherapy")

23. Describe the ways that psychoactive drugs affect neurotransmitters. Define receptor *antagonists* and the process of *reuptake*. (see "Linkages: Biological Aspects of Psychology and the Treatment of Psychological Disorders")

24. Define <u>community psychology</u>. Describe the types of work involved in community psychologists' attempts to treat and prevent mental illness. (see "Community Psychology: From Treatment to Prevention")

CONCEPTS AND EXERCISES

Differentiating Approaches to Therapy

Several psychotherapists have met at a convention to have dinner. Over coffee they argue about the various causes of abnormal behavior and mental processes. Decide what type of therapy each therapist probably practices.

1. *Patricia:* Clearly, thoughts in the unconscious drive behavior. If unconscious thoughts are revealed, the client can understand and possibly change the problematic behavior. You, on the other hand, Eliot, treat only the behavior and not the cause. _____

2. *Eliot:* What does it matter if I treat only the behavior? My goal is to create new behaviors that allow people to function in their environment. If they are functional, they will probably be successful and receive positive reinforcement, making them feel good about themselves.
   _____

3. *Carlos:* She has a point, Eliot. If you would try to alter conscious thought patterns as I do, replacing problematic ones with functional ones, then many behaviors associated with those thoughts might change as well. _____

4. *Ida:* I think you are all a bit manipulative. We are therapists, but our clients have the ability to grow and change on their own. They just need to get in touch with their feelings. All we have to do is step back, accept them as people, and show them it's okay to accept themselves just as they are. _____

5. *Lana:* Pretty soon, you folks are going to be out of a job. When we understand how the brain works, we will be able to treat most psychological problems with drugs or corrective surgery.
   _____

Identifying Methods of Therapy

Following are several descriptions of treatments given to various clients. Read each description, and then answer the question following it.

1. Clarice, who has schizophrenia, takes a drug that blocks the action of dopamine in her brain. What type of drug is she taking? _____

2. Cal is afraid of writing his name in public. His therapist has taken him to a busy shopping mall and asked him to write his name until he has covered several pieces of paper. What is this behavioral method? _____

3. Lisa is being treated for alcohol dependence. Her therapist has given her a drug that will make her nauseated if she drinks alcohol. What is this behavioral method? _____

4. Flora has received almost every treatment available for depression. Her doctor has suggested a drastic method as a last resort. What is this method? _____

5. Antero is painfully shy. His teacher has devised a new system to prompt Antero to participate in group discussions at school. Every time Antero speaks, he will receive ten points. At the end of the day, he can cash in his points for special privileges, such as going to the library or choosing the book the teacher will read to the class. What behavioral method is his teacher using? _____

CRITICAL THINKING

A concerned neighbor, Aida Schultz, calls the precinct with reports of an old man walking around the block. He appears to be slightly spastic and a bit dizzy and has odd dark spots on his arms and hands. She also says that the man keeps sticking his tongue out, whether there is someone in front of him or not. Other reports from this same neighborhood have been coming in regarding an old man who is scaring children. Sam and Martina go to check these reports out.

When they arrive at Aida Schultz's house, they ask where she last saw the man. She points down the block. Sam and Martina slowly cruise the street and then turn the corner.

"There he is!" cries Sam. "I bet he's the one who's been scaring all the kids around here. Let's go pick him up."

"Not so fast. There may be a reason for his symptoms," Martina remarks.

Using the five critical thinking questions in your text, the clues in the story, and what you have learned about psychotherapy, answer the following:

1. What is Sam's hypothesis?

2. What evidence supports Sam's hypothesis?

3. What is Martina's alternative hypothesis?

4. What evidence supports Martina's hypothesis? What other evidence might Martina need?

5. What conclusions are reasonable?

PERSONAL LEARNING ACTIVITIES

1. Stop by your local campus counseling center and see what materials and services they have available. Do they seem to emphasize one treatment strategy over another? Or are they fairly eclectic? What are the educational backgrounds of the people who provide counseling services there?

2. To see an example of client-centered therapy conducted by the Carl Rogers, view the following clip on YouTube: http://www.youtube.com/watch?v=ZBkUqcqRChg. This is one clip from a series of the "Gloria" tapes that have been used to illustrate his client-centered techniques. Can you identify examples of unconditional positive regard, empathy, reflection, and congruence?

3. In recent years, online psychotherapy has grown, but is it effective? Visit the following website to read an article suggesting it is: http://www.psychologytoday.com/blog/the-mindfulness-approach/200911/online-psychotherapy-is-effective. What do you think would be the pros and cons of online psychotherapy? Which therapeutic techniques would work best in this medium? Which would not work at all?

4. Think of a situation in which a cognitive-behavior technique could improve your reaction. Write the thing you usually say to yourself during the event and then write an alternative reaction. For example, if you tend to get nervous during exams, you could imagine what you usually say to yourself during testing situations and try to identify self-defeating thoughts. What would a rational-emotive therapist suggest that you say to yourself instead? You could write the alternatives to your usual thinking style in your notebook and look at it before your next test begins.

5. Explore community psychology more at the website for the Society for Community Research and Action: http://www.scra27.org/. This is a division of the American Psychological Association. Look through both the "Research" and "Practice" links on this homepage. Do you see continuity between the research and practice involved in community psychology?

MULTIPLE-CHOICE QUESTIONS

Quiz 1

1. A psychiatrist has what kind of training?
    a. A degree in psychology
    b. A Ph.D. in Clinical Psychology
    c. An M.D.
    d. An M.D. plus specialty training in treating psychological disorders

2. Sayumi is a licensed psychologist. In which state can she prescribe medication for her clients?
    a. New Mexico
    b. Missouri
    c. Georgia
    d. Psychologists cannot prescribe medication because they lack a medical degree.

3. The focus of Freudian psychoanalysis is on
    a. getting the client in touch with his or her present feelings.
    b. helping the client gain insight into unconscious problems.
    c. replacing problematic behaviors with desirable behaviors.
    d. teaching the client new ways of thinking.

4. Carl Rogers developed _____ therapy.
    a. client-centered
    b. rational-emotive
    c. cognitive behavior
    d. object relations

5. Individual analysis, object relations, and ego analysis are all variations of
    a. client-centered therapy.
    b. psychoanalysis.
    c. cognitive restructuring.
    d. behavior modification.

6.   As Dwayne prepares for an exam, he comments to his friend, Rerun, "This test is gonna be a seize." Rerun says, "A seize? Don't you mean 'a breeze?'" A _____ therapist would be most likely to think that Dwayne's comment indicates that he unknowingly fears freezing up during the exam and can't admit to it consciously.

   a.   behavioral
   b.   community
   c.   humanistic
   d.   psychodynamic

7.   Vivian is distressed because she has lost custody of her children due to drug problems. As she pours her heart out to her pastor, he responds to her by saying, "Everyone makes mistakes. It doesn't define you. You are a terrific person with wonderful qualities, and I'm glad to know you." Vivan's pastor is using which humanistic technique?

   a.   Sympathy
   b.   Acceptance
   c.   Reflection
   d.   Modeling

8.   Pat is afraid of using a computer. To counteract Pat's misconceptions about what could happen if she used a computer, her therapist suggests a dialogue exercise. Pat is to imagine that she is talking to a computer and fill in what the computer would "say" to her. Pat's therapist is using _____ therapy.

   a.   client-centered
   b.   Gestalt
   c.   psychoanalysis
   d.   systematic desensitization

9.   A _____ therapist would use rational-emotive behavior therapy.

   a.   psychoanalytic
   b.   humanistic
   c.   cognitive behavior
   d.   biological

10.   In behavioral therapy, associating an unpleasant stimulus with the simultaneous occurrence of an undesirable behavior is called

   a.   aversion conditioning.
   b.   object relations therapy.
   c.   flooding.
   d.   building a desensitization hierarchy.

11.   Harvey is a psychotherapist. In treating his clients, he uses systematic desensitization and participant modeling in cases of phobia. What type of therapist is Harvey?

   a.   Behavioral
   b.   Psychoanalytic
   c.   Humanistic
   d.   Biological

12. Bonnie fears driving in the mountains. Her therapist has suggested that they take a ride into the mountains for several hours. What method is the therapist proposing?
    a. Aversive conditioning
    b. Modeling
    c. Punishment
    d. Flooding

13. Kevin is at his therapy session. He is really lonely and as part of the therapy, he has to learn to role-play making small talk with strangers in various common situations. Sometimes he has to role-play with the therapist that he is purchasing an item at a checkout line and make small talk with the cashier. Other times he has to role-play going out with a peer to a ball game or concert. He and his therapist talk about what kinds of comments are "appropriate" versus "inappropriate" in such settings. Kevin is receiving
    a. systematic desensitization.
    b. group therapy.
    c. social skills training.
    d. assertiveness training.

14. Group therapy is associated with which theoretical approach?
    a. Group therapy has no particular theoretical approach.
    b. Humanistic
    c. Behavioral
    d. Psychoanalytical

15. When Shau-Jin is angry with Wendy, he often says things like, "Why do you always criticize me?" and "You're such a nag!" The therapy that would focus most on their communication pattern would be
    a. couples therapy.
    b. extinction.
    c. rational-emotive behavior therapy (REBT).
    d. psychoanalysis.

16. According to the *Ethical Principles of Psychologists and Code of Conduct* of the American Psychological Association, a therapist may disclose information mentioned by a client during therapy when
    a. the client is applying for a job and the employer asks for information.
    b. the client ends therapy.
    c. defending herself or himself against a malpractice charge.
    d. Any of these

17. In the past, broken bones, memory loss, speech disorders, and even death were associated with which type of treatment?
    a. Family therapy
    b. Lithium
    c. Electroconvulsive shock therapy
    d. Punishment

18. Raoul has been taking drugs for schizophrenia for years. His family notices that he seems to be developing some strange tics. He nods his head uncontrollably and his eyes twitch. At first his family is concerned that his schizophrenic symptoms have returned, but after examination, his physician says that Raoul has developed

    a. symptoms to an overdose of lithium.
    b. an anxiety disorder.
    c. Tourette's syndrome
    d. tardive dyskinesia.

19. Which of the following is NOT a criticism of drug therapy?

    a. Drug therapy may treat only symptoms, not the problem itself.
    b. Drug therapy may make patients depend on the drug, instead of on their own efforts, for improvement.
    c. Many drugs have unwanted side effects.
    d. Drug therapy is more expensive than any other kind of therapy.

20. A community psychologist

    a. treats clients by providing therapy in an inpatient setting.
    b. treats troubled people in their home situations and focuses on prevention.
    c. does a lot of treatment with drugs such as neuroleptics and anxiolytics.
    d. None of these

Total Correct (See answer key) _____

Quiz 2

Use this quiz to reassess your learning after taking Quiz 1 and reviewing the chapter.

1. Which of the following professionals can provide therapy for psychological disorders?

    a. Psychiatrists
    b. Psychologists
    c. Licensed Professional Counselors
    d. All of these

2. Simone asks her clients to remember their childhood experiences in order to gain insight into unconscious processes and thoughts. Simone is probably a _____ therapist.

    a. behavioral
    b. Gestalt
    c. client-centered
    d. psychodynamic

3. Which of the following would a psychoanalyst be *least* likely to use in therapy?

    a. Dream interpretation
    b. Ego analysis
    c. Free association
    d. Modeling

4.   Acceptance in client-centered therapy is
    a.   perceiving a client's view of reality.
    b.   restating or paraphrasing a client's words.
    c.   unconditional positive regard.
    d.   consistency between a therapist's words and actions.

5.   Which of the following describes flooding?
    a.   A client is gradually exposed to a feared stimulus.
    b.   A client is placed in a harmless but fearful situation and not allowed to escape.
    c.   A client learns not to let negative thoughts overwhelm or flood the mind.
    d.   A client receives a negative stimulus following an undesirable behavior.

6.   Mac is a therapist who relies on his clients' natural drive toward growth. Marcia tells him that she thinks she's so ugly it is not worth it to exercise or to dress nicely, and she asks him if he thinks she is ugly. Rather than interpreting Marcia's behavior, Mac discloses his honest reaction, saying, "Right now you think it is futile to try to improve your looks. Although I think you are attractive, what *you* think is much more important and it seems you are discouraged." Mac is exhibiting _____, which is associated with _____ therapy.
    a.   analysis of transference; psychodynamic
    b.   congruence; client-centered
    c.   reflection; cognitive behavioral
    d.   sympathy; humanistic

7.   In psychoanalysis, transference occurs when
    a.   unconscious thoughts become conscious.
    b.   a client transfers feelings about a significant person onto a therapist.
    c.   the manifest content of a dream is translated into latent content.
    d.   free association reveals unconscious conflicts.

8.   Aversion conditioning is
    a.   based on operant conditioning.
    b.   based on classical conditioning.
    c.   used to increase a behavior's occurrence.
    d.   based on reward and punishment.

9.   Li is frightened to leave his apartment. His therapist has instructed him to make a list of progressively frightening thoughts about leaving home. Li is constructing a(n) _____ as part of _____.
    a.   desensitization hierarchy; systematic desensitization
    b.   fear manifest; cognitive restructuring
    c.   desensitization hierarchy; flooding
    d.   fear manifest; psychoanalysis

10. Amy has been sent to a camp for children with behavior disorders. On her first day, she and her counselor decide what behaviors Amy will learn to do on a daily basis. These include playing cooperatively, speaking respectfully to the counselors, and helping clean the dining hall after dinner. Immediately following the successful display of a behavior, Amy receives a pink piece of cardboard. Each day she can trade these pieces of cardboard for special activities and privileges. This is an example of

    a.   aversion conditioning.
    b.   flooding.
    c.   a token economy program.
    d.   cognitive restructuring.

11. Virtual reality has been successfully used to treat

    a.   schizophrenia.
    b.   conduct disorder.
    c.   posttraumatic stress disorder.
    d.   phobia.

12. Chung Wa has gone to see a therapist because she is very depressed and dislikes herself. She doesn't get perfect grades and is not the most popular person on her dorm floor. What kind of therapy do you think would be best for Chung Wa?

    a.   Antidepressant drugs
    b.   Rational-emotive behavior therapy
    c.   Aversive conditioning
    d.   Token economy program

13. Roberto has a dog phobia. He and his therapist go for a walk, and Roberto watches from across the street as his therapist approaches people who are walking their dogs. The therapist asks the owner if the dog is friendly, lets the dog sniff his hand, and gently pats the dog. The therapist is using _____ to help Roberto.

    a.   token economies
    b.   modeling
    c.   flooding
    d.   classical conditioning

14. Sixteen-year-old Micah has been diagnosed with anorexia nervosa. As part of her treatment, she meets with her therapist, her mom and dad, and her siblings to talk about feelings. During one session, Micah says, "I have so many rules that tell me what to do, but no one can make me eat. I like being thin because it is the one thing I feel I have a say-so about." Through discussion, her parents learn that they need to give Micah more choices to help her recover. The therapist's goal is that they all together identify the factors in their relationships that need to change for Micah to recover. Micah is in

    a.   group therapy.
    b.   family therapy.
    c.   psychoanalysis.
    d.   social skills training.

15. In which of the following scenarios may a therapist NOT reveal confidential information?

    a.   When discussing a case with a family member

    b.   When defending herself or himself against a malpractice charge

    c.   When a client requires hospitalization

    d.   When a therapist feels a client may physically harm another person

16. Who would be the most likely candidate for electroconvulsive shock therapy?

    a.   Jackson, who just received his diagnosis of depression

    b.   Jonna, who is completely depressed and has not responded to medications

    c.   Marta, who has been diagnosed as manic and has not responded to medications

    d.   Taylor, who has recently been diagnosed as manic

17. Most of the therapies identified as ESTs are from which approach to personality?

    a.   Humanistic

    b.   Psychodynamic

    c.   Social-cognitive

    d.   Trait

18. Nina has been experiencing moods of extreme elation alternating with severe depression. What kind of drug will her doctor most likely prescribe?

    a.   Tricyclics

    b.   Phenothiazines

    c.   Monoamine oxidase inhibitors

    d.   Lithium

19. When Terence takes fluoxetine (Prozac), serotonin remains in the synapse rather than flowing back into the presynaptic terminal. The antidepressant is

    a.   acting as a receptor antagonist.

    b.   blocking reuptake.

    c.   causing tardive dyskinesia.

    d.   preventing anxiolytic action.

20. Michel has spent the morning teaching preschool teachers the early signs of psychological problems, hoping that children can be helped before their problems become severe. What kind of psychologist is Michel?

    a.   Biological

    b.   Rational-emotive

    c.   Community

    d.   None of these

Total Correct (See answer key) _____

ANSWERS TO FILL-IN-THE-BLANKS KEY TERMS

1. Psychiatrists (see Basic Features of Treatment)

2. empathy (see Client-Centered Therapy)

3. congruence (see Client-Centered Therapy)

4. Assertiveness training (see Techniques for Modifying Behavior)

5. aversion conditioning (see Techniques for Modifying Behavior)

6. cognitive behavior therapy (see Behavior Therapy)

7. Psychosurgery (see Psychosurgery)

8. Antidepressant drugs (see Psychoactive Drugs)

9. Community psychology (see Community Psychology: From Treatment to Prevention)

10. Neuroleptic drugs (see Psychoactive Drugs)

11. Client-centered therapy (see Client-Centered Therapy)

12. Rational-emotive behavior therapy (see Cognitive Behavior Therapy)

13. Couples therapy (see Family and Couples Therapy)

14. Behavior therapy (see Behavior Therapy)

15. modeling (see Techniques for Modifying Behavior)

ANSWERS TO CONCEPTS AND EXERCISES

Differentiating Approaches to Therapy

1. *Psychoanalysis.* Patricia believes that unconscious mental processes cause behavior. Methods such as free association, dream analysis, transference, and analysis of everyday behaviors are designed to bring unconscious material into conscious awareness. (see Psychodynamic Psychotherapy)

2. *Behavior therapy.* Eliot's goal is to change behavior, not mental processes. Methods such as token economies, flooding, and aversive conditioning are designed to change behavior. (see Behavior Therapy)

3. *Cognitive behavior therapy.* Carlos believes that behavior can be changed by altering harmful conscious thought patterns. Cognitive restructuring and rational-emotive therapy are methods designed to alter thought patterns. (see Behavior Therapy)

4. *Humanistic therapy.* Ida believes that her clients have a natural tendency toward growth and change. Clients simply need to get in touch with their feelings. Empathy, reflection, congruence, and unconditional positive regard help clients achieve this goal. (see Humanistic Psychotherapy)

5. *Biological therapy.* Lana believes that altering the nervous system's chemical activity will change behavior. (see Biological Treatments)

Identifying Methods of Therapy

1. *A neuroleptic drug.* These drugs are used to treat severe disorders such as schizophrenia. Their antipsychotic effects are due to their receptor antagonist action. (see Psychoactive Drugs)

2. *Flooding.* Cal is being exposed to the object or event that he fears, and he will not be allowed to escape. He will eventually realize that there is nothing to fear. (see Techniques for Modifying Behavior)

3. *Punishment.* Remember from the chapter on learning, this is an operant conditioning technique. Lisa will suffer unpleasant consequences if she drinks. Therefore, her drinking behavior should decrease. (see Techniques for Modifying Behavior)

4. *Electroconvulsive shock therapy.* This is a last-resort treatment for depression. (see Electroconvulsive Shock Therapy)

5. *Token economy program.* The points act as tokens, which can later be exchanged for whichever positive reinforcement Antero chooses. (see Techniques for Modifying Behavior)

ANSWERS TO CRITICAL THINKING

1. Sam believes that this is the old man who has been scaring the neighborhood children.

2. The evidence is that the man matches the description called in by several neighbors.

3. Martina hypothesizes that the man may be suffering from tardive dyskinesia.

4. The evidence is that the old man appears to be dizzy and has odd pigmentation on his arms. He also exhibits tongue thrusting, which is another common symptom of tardive dyskinesia. Martina may want to find where the man has been staying and ask those caring for him if he is taking neuroleptic drugs.

5. Martina can't draw any conclusions until she obtains additional evidence.

ANSWERS TO MULTIPLE-CHOICE QUESTIONS

Circle the question numbers you answered correctly.

Quiz 1

1. d is the answer. A psychiatrist is a medical doctor with specialty training in treating psychological disorders. (see Basic Features of Treatment)

    a. A psychiatrist may or may not hold a degree in psychology, but they by definition must hold an M.D.

    b. An individual with a Ph.D. in Clinical Psychology is a psychologist.

    c. A psychiatrist does have an M.D. but has also had specialty training in treating psychological disorders, which makes "d" the better answer.

2. a is the answer. Psychologists have recently earned the privilege of prescribing medication for clients in New Mexico and in Louisiana. (see Basic Features of Treatment)

    b, c. Psychologists practicing in New Mexico and Louisiana can prescribe medication for clients, not in any other states.

    d. Although it used to be true that psychologists could never prescribe medicine because they did not possess a medical degree, at least two states now permit it. Others may follow in the future.

3.   b is the answer. The focus of psychoanalytic therapy is to reveal and work through unconscious conflicts. (see Psychodynamic Psychotherapy)

    a.   Humanistic therapies help clients get in touch with and express their present feelings.

    c.   Behavior therapies usually focus on replacing undesirable behaviors with new ones.

    d.   Cognitive-behavior therapies focus on teaching the client new and more constructive ways of thinking.

4.   a is the answer. Carl Rogers developed the humanistic methods of client-centered therapy (or person-centered therapy). (see Humanistic Psychotherapy)

    b.   Albert Ellis developed rational-emotive therapy.

    c.   Rational-emotive therapy is a type of cognitive behavior therapy.

    d.   Object relations therapy is a variation on psychoanalysis.

5.   b is the answer. All of these are contemporary variants of classical psychoanalysis. (see Psychodynamic Psychotherapy)

    a, c, d.   Only b is the answer.

6.   d is the answer. A psychodynamic therapist would be likely to find unconscious meaning in behaviors. (see Psychodynamic Psychotherapy)

    a.   A behavioral therapist would focus on learning of behaviors, not unconscious meanings.

    b.   A community psychologist works to prevent disorders.

    c.   Humanistic therapists are interested in a client's viewpoint but would be unlikely to assume that Dwayne could not become aware of his fear.

7.   b is the answer. Vivian's pastor is showing her acceptance (also known as unconditional positive regard). (see Humanistic Psychotherapy)

    a.   Sympathy involves expressing concern for someone else.

    c.   Reflection involves paraphrasing the client's statements and noting accompanying feelings. The pastor is actually stating his perspective, not just reflecting hers.

    d.   Modeling is a technique of imitating positive behaviors used in behavioral therapy.

8.   b is the answer. Gestalt therapy, a form of humanistic therapy, uses more dramatic methods to help clients become more self-accepting. Clients might carry on imaginary conversations with people, parts of themselves, or objects. (see Humanistic Psychotherapy)

    a.   Client-centered therapy is a type of humanistic therapy, but it allows the client to direct the course of a session.

    c.   Psychoanalysis seeks to uncover unconscious conflicts by interpreting transference, free association, and dreams.

    d.   Systematic desensitization is a behavioral treatment for phobias; however, it involves visualizing progressively more frightening situations while remaining calm.

9. c is the answer. Rational-emotive behavior therapy is a cognitive- behavior therapy. Clients are taught to recognize damaging thoughts and to replace them with more positive and functional thoughts. (see Behavior Therapy)

   a. Psychoanalysts focus on revealing a person's unconscious thoughts and conflicts.

   b. Humanistic therapists focus on a person's feelings and drive toward growth.

   d. Biological therapists use biological treatments either alone or in conjunction with other forms of therapy to cause changes in nervous system functioning.

10. a is the answer. Aversion conditioning is used to decrease a behavior's occurrence. An unpleasant stimulus is experienced every time an undesirable behavior is displayed. (see Behavior Therapy)

    b. Object relations therapy is a type of psychoanalytic therapy.

    c. Flooding is based on extinction. A client is exposed to the entire object, situation, or event that he or she fears. Since the client cannot escape, he or she has the chance to realize that the fear is unfounded.

    d. A desensitization hierarchy is used in systematic desensitization.

11. a is the answer. Harvey is a behavioral therapist because he uses methods based on learning theory. (see Behavior Therapy)

    b. A psychoanalyst would be far more likely to use free association, dream analysis, and other methods aimed at revealing unconscious material.

    c, d. A humanistic or biological therapist would probably not use systematic desensitization.

12. d is the answer. To use the flooding method, a client is placed in a feared but harmless situation and not allowed to escape. The person soon realizes that he or she has nothing to fear. Exposing Bonnie to the situation she fears and not allowing her to escape may help her overcome her fear of driving in the mountains. (see Behavior Therapy)

    a. Aversive conditioning is also used to decrease behavior. However, a client experiences a negative stimulus when she or he engages in the undesirable behavior.

    b. Modeling involves teaching a client desirable behaviors by demonstrating those behaviors and showing the client how to behave more calmly in feared situations. However, the client is not actually in the feared situation.

    c. Punishment, a procedure used to decrease a behavior, involves presenting a negative stimulus following an undesirable behavior.

13. c is the answer. Social skills training involves teaching clients how to interact with people more comfortably and effectively. Kevin's therapist is using role-play to help teach him these skills. (see Behavior Therapy)

    a. Systematic desensitization is a technique used to treat phobias. There is no indication in this question that Kevin is afraid of social situations, just that he is lonely and needs to learn how to interact more effectively.

    b. Group therapy involves interacting with a group of people who share a similar problem. Although social skills training certainly can be done in a group, this question describes interaction between a therapist and client only.

    d. Assertiveness training focuses on helping clients learn to be more direct and expressive in social interaction. Kevin's therapist is not teaching him these skills.

14.   a is the answer. Group therapy has no particular theoretical assumptions underlying it. Instead, groups are organized around a specific type of problem (such as alcoholism) or client (such as teenagers). (see Group, Family, and Couples Therapy)

    b, c, d.   Group therapies are not associated with a particular theoretical approach.

15.   a is the answer. Therapists often recommend couples therapy if communication with a partner seems to be a major problem. In couples therapy, people practice more constructive ways of getting ideas across. Rather than calling Wendy names or overgeneralizing, for example, Shau-Jin probably would be encouraged to say something about how he feels in the present situation. (see Group, Family, and Couples Therapy)

    b.   Extinction removes the reinforcers that usually follow a behavior. It is a behavior therapy that doesn't work on communication skills.

    c.   Rational emotive behavior therapy would concentrate on irrational ideas, not communication.

    d.   Psychoanalysis would focus on unconscious conflicts rather than on communication.

16.   c is the answer. Confidentiality is a critical aspect of therapy that is seldom violated. However, if a client brings a malpractice suit against the therapist, the records of their sessions could be important evidence of the therapist's efforts to help. (see Evaluating Psychotherapy)

    a.   Employers do not have a right to information about confidential therapy sessions.

    b.   The end of therapy does not signal the end of the obligation to protect a client's right to privacy.

    d.   Only c is correct.

17.   c is the answer. In the past, ECT did have serious side effects. However, now it is much more precise and less hazardous. (see Biological Treatments)

    a.   Family therapy does not cause such problems, although it might be used to halt or prevent physical abuse among family members that may cause them.

    b.   Lithium treatment for the bipolar disorders can be problematic, but the side effects mentioned in this question are not associated with this therapy.

    d.   Punishment as used by ethical behavioral therapists would never have such results.

18.   d is the answer. Schizophrenia is treated with neuroleptic drugs. One of the side effects of neuroleptic drugs that can occur after years of use is tardive dyskinesia. It is an irreversible disorder of the motor system that involves uncontrollable, repetitive movements of the body. (see Biological Treatments)

    a.   Lithium is not used to treat schizophrenia, and disordered movement is not one of the side effects associated with lithium anyway.

    b.   An anxiety disorder involves symptoms of anxiety in different forms such as a phobia (fear) or panic (panic attacks). Raoul is showing no symptoms of anxiety.

    c.   Tourette's syndrome does sometimes involve tic-like movements, but it is caused by something other than neuroleptic drug use.

19. d is the answer. Drugs are not necessarily the most expensive form of therapy. Freudian psychoanalytic therapy, because it can take several years, is very expensive. (see Biological Treatments)

   a, b, c.   These are all problems with drug therapy.

20. b is the answer. Prevention of problems such as psychological disorders and treatment in home communities is the focus of community psychologists. (see Community Psychology: From Treatment to Prevention)

   a.   Inpatient treatment is probably provided by a clinical psychologist or a psychiatrist.

   c.   Drug treatments are usually provided by psychiatrists, and in some states clinical psychologists.

   d.   b is the correct answer.

Now turn to the quiz analysis table at the end of this chapter to find which areas you know well and which areas you need to work on. Circle the numbers in the table for items on Quiz 1 that you answered correctly.

Quiz 2

1.   d is the answer. All of these individuals are trained as treatment providers. (see Basic Features of Treatment)

2.   d is the answer. Psychodynamic therapists (or psychoanalysts) believe that exploring childhood experiences and thereby gaining understanding of unconscious processes are the keys to resolving mental illness. (see Psychodynamic Psychotherapy)

   a.   Behavioral therapists may focus on past learning experiences, but they usually deal with current behaviors, not unconscious processes and thoughts.

   b.   Gestalt therapists concentrate on identifying the problematic ways in which people may be behaving so that they live according to the expectations of others, not according to their true selves. Therapists may focus on the incorrect thought patterns that clients possess and the ways in which they defend against self-exploration.

   c.   Client-centered therapists focus on creating a therapeutic environment in which clients can explore the reasons for their problems and get themselves back on the track toward fulfillment and self-actualization.

3.   d is the answer. Modeling is a behavior modification technique. (see Psychodynamic Psychotherapy)

   a, c.   Dream interpretation and free association are part of classical psychoanalysis.

   b.   Ego analysis is a contemporary psychodynamic treatment.

4.   c is the answer. Acceptance, or unconditional positive regard, is accepting each statement a client makes as reflecting the client's view of the world. It involves treating a person as valued no matter what. (see Humanistic Psychotherapy)

   a.   This is empathy.

   b.   This is reflection.

   d.   Congruence, or genuineness, is consistency between a therapist's feelings and actions.

5.   b is the answer. A client is exposed to the feared situation, object, or event and is not allowed to escape. Since the person cannot escape, he or she can come to realize that there is nothing to fear. (see Behavior Therapy)

    a.   Gradual exposure to a feared stimulus takes place in systematic desensitization or participant modeling.

    c.   Cognitive restructuring can teach a client to replace destructive thoughts with more effective or constructive ones.

    d.   Presenting an unpleasant stimulus after an undesirable behavior is called punishment.

6.   b is the answer. Congruence between thoughts and actions is part of client-centered therapy. (see Humanistic Psychotherapy)

    a.   Analysis of transference is a psychodynamic technique in which the client's reaction to the therapist is compared to conflicts with significant others in childhood.

    c.   Reflection is a client-centered therapy technique.

    d.   You may have been thinking of empathy, which is a client-centered technique.

7.   b is the answer. Psychoanalysts believe that if they reveal nothing about themselves, clients will begin to transfer onto them many feelings and attitudes about conflicts experienced with significant people in their lives. (see Psychodynamic Psychotherapy)

    a, d.   Free association does help reveal unconscious conflicts, making them conscious, but this process is not called transference.

    c.   Interpreting a dream's manifest content in order to understand its symbolic or latent content is part of psychoanalytic treatment. This process is not called transference.

8.   b is the answer. Aversion conditioning is based on classical conditioning. (see Behavior Therapy)

    a, d.   Methods such as token economies and punishment are based on operant conditioning principles.

    c.   Aversive conditioning is used to decrease the occurrence of a specific behavior.

9.   a is the answer. A desensitization hierarchy is a list of fear-producing situations that is constructed for use in systematic desensitization. (see Behavior Therapy)

    b, d.   There is no such thing as a fear manifest. (You may have been thinking of manifest content, which is used in psychodynamic dream analysis.)

    c.   Li has constructed a desensitization hierarchy, but this hierarchy is a part of systematic desensitization, not flooding. Flooding is a behavioral technique in which a person is repeatedly put into the fear-producing situation until the conditioned fear response is extinguished.

10.   c is the answer. The camp has set up a type of economic system in which campers receive tokens when they display behaviors they have agreed to work on. The campers can exchange their tokens for various forms of positive reinforcement. In Amy's case, her tokens are exchanged for special activities and privileges. Token economy programs serve to increase the occurrence of desirable behaviors. (see Behavior Therapy)

    a.   Aversion conditioning is used to decrease, not increase, a behavior's occurrence.

    b.   Flooding is used to decrease a behavior, usually avoidance.

d.   Cognitive restructuring involves replacing negative and damaging thoughts with more constructive ones.

11.   d is the answer. Used as part of systematic desensitization, virtual reality graded exposure has enabled clients to experience and work through vivid and intensely feared situations without actually being exposed to them. (see Behavior Therapy)

a, b, c.   This technique has been used as part of treatments to help clients overcome specific unrealistic fears. Specific fears are not a primary component of these disorders.

12.   b is the answer. Chung Wa's ideas about having everyone like her and being a perfect student are probably at the root of her depression. Rational-emotive therapy will help her recognize and eliminate these unhealthy thoughts. (see Behavior Therapy)

a.   Chung Wa's depression might be alleviated by antidepressants, but it is obvious that her thought patterns about being liked and perfect will continue to cause her problems. Changing her thinking should alleviate her depression on a long-term basis.

c.   Aversive conditioning is used to decrease a specific behavior. Chung Wa needs to change her thought patterns, not a specific behavior.

d.   Token economy programs are used to increase the occurrence of desired behaviors. Chung Wa needs to change her thought patterns, not her overt behavior.

13.   b is the answer. Modeling involves teaching a client desirable behaviors by demonstrating those behaviors and showing the client how to behave more calmly in feared situations. (see Behavior Therapy)

a.   Token economies involve receiving tokens for demonstrating desirable behaviors. The tokens can later be traded in for rewards or privileges. Roberto is not performing any behaviors; he is watching how his therapist behaves with dogs.

c.   Flooding involves placing a client in a feared but harmless situation. Once deprived of his or her normally rewarding escape pattern, the client has no reason for continued anxiety. If Roberto and his therapist had shut themselves in a small room with a gentle, friendly dog, this would have been the answer.

d.   Classical conditioning is a part of aversive conditioning and flooding. Modeling is based on operant conditioning.

14.   b is the answer. Family therapy involves treatment of a problem, like anorexia, as reflecting problems in the functioning of the entire family. A therapist meets with two or more individuals from the same family system, even though only one member of the family may have a diagnosis. (see Group, Family, and Couples Therapy)

a.   Group therapy involves treating a group of people who are not part of the same family system but who share similar problems.

c.   Psychoanalysis is an individual therapy.

d.   Social skills training is often done in groups but would not focus on sharing concerns about how the family dynamic supports a disease like anorexia.

15. a is the answer. A therapist is bound by law to keep strictly confidential any information revealed by a client. He or she can discuss a case with a client's family only if the client gives permission. (see Evaluating Psychotherapy)

    b, c, d. These are all situations in which a therapist may release information given by a client.

16. b is the answer. Electroconvulsive shock therapy is currently used to treat depression that has not responded to other treatments. (see Biological Treatments)

    a. Therapists would probably try drug treatments on Jackson before subjecting him to EST.

    c, d. Lithium is used to treat mania, not EST.

17. c is the correct answer. The social-cognitive approach to personality, which is rooted in behavioral approaches to psychology, is responsible for producing the behavioral, cognitive, and cognitive-behavioral therapies. These therapies are the main ones identified as ESTs. (see Evaluating Psychotherapy)

    a. The humanistic approach to personality is seen in client-centered therapy techniques. Most of the ESTs are not client centered.

    b. Although some psychoanalytic therapies have been identified as empirically supported, these are not the dominant ones on the list.

    d. The trait approach corresponds mainly to drug or other biological treatments. The task force that developed the list of ESTs mainly looked at psychotherapy, not biological treatments.

18. d is the answer. Lithium is used to treat bipolar disorders. (see Biological Treatments)

    a, c. Tricyclics and MAO inhibitors are used to treat depression.

    b. Phenothiazines are used to treat severe disorders such as schizophrenia.

19. b is the answer. Blocking reuptake keeps a neurotransmitter from returning to the presynaptic cell. (see Biological Treatments)

    a. A receptor antagonist does block neurotransmitters, but it blocks them from binding to a postsynaptic cell.

    c. Tardive dyskinesia is a side effect caused by neuroleptic drugs after years of use.

    d. Anxiolytics are anti-anxiety drugs.

20. c is the answer. Community psychologists seek both to treat and to prevent psychological problems. Michel believes that if psychological problems are detected in their early stages, treatment will be shorter, less expensive, and possibly more effective. (see Community Psychology: From Treatment to Prevention)

    a, b, d. Michel could believe in a psychoanalytic, humanistic, biological, or behavioral approach to treating psychological problems. However, those who work to reduce stressors in the environment and in public domains such as schools are called community psychologists.

Now turn to the quiz analysis table at the end of this chapter to find which areas you know well and which areas you need to work on. Circle the numbers in the table for items on Quiz 2 that you answered correctly.

For each question you answered correctly, circle its number. (Quiz 1 numbers are not shaded; Quiz 2 numbers are shaded.) Are there patterns in the types of questions or the topics you got wrong that could direct your further study? Did you improve from Quiz 1 to Quiz 2?

QUIZ REVIEW

Topic	Type of Question		
	Definition	Comprehension	Application
Basic Features of Treatment		1	2
		1	
Psychodynamic Psychotherapy	3	5	6
	7	3	2
Humanistic Psychotherapy		4	7, 8
	4		6
Behavior Therapy	10	9	11, 12, 13
	5	8, 11	9, 10, 12, 13
Group, Family, and Couples Therapy		14	15
			14
Evaluating Psychotherapy		16	
		15, 17	
Biological Treatments		17, 19	18
		19	16, 18
Community Psychology: From Treatment to Prevention	20		
			20

Total correct by quiz:

Quiz 1:	
Quiz 2:	

CHAPTER 17

Social Cognition

Social psychology is the study of how people influence and are influenced by other people. The mental processes associated with how people perceive and react to other individuals and groups are called social cognitions.

OUTLINE

I. SOCIAL INFLUENCES ON THE SELF
    Two important components of the self are self-concept, the beliefs we have about our characteristics, and self-esteem, our evaluation of ourselves.

    A. Social Comparison
        1. According to the theory of social comparison, people use other people as a basis of comparison for self-evaluation when no objective criteria exist.
        2. Social comparisons involve comparing oneself to groups of other people called reference groups. Temporal comparisons involve comparing one's own past state to a present state.
        3. As changes occur over the course of life, people change reference groups. People may find their self-evaluations to be poor in comparison to others in the new group, an *upward social comparison*, and begin to experience relative deprivation. *Downward social comparisons* usually produce more favorable self-evaluations.
        4. Usually people do not compare themselves to others who are not in their immediate reference group, and an upward comparison may be ameliorated if one indicates that the person compared to is *not* in the reference group.
        5. Chronic use of extreme reference groups can lead to depression and anxiety. When larger groups experience relative deprivation, political unrest may follow.

    B. Focus on Research Methods: Self-esteem and the Ultimate "Terror"
        Terror management theory proposes that humans cope with anxiety, especially anxiety related to knowledge that death will eventually occur, by establishing and maintaining high self-esteem. To test whether high self-esteem indeed buffers anxiety, researchers had 150 North American students participate in studies in which self-esteem was manipulated by having participants take a test and providing either positive or neutral feedback on it. Next, participants were placed in either an anxiety-provoking or neutral situation. Afterwards, anxiety was measured. High self-esteem participants were less anxious in the anxiety-provoking situation than neutral self-esteem participants. Researchers concluded that the results supported terror management theory. Future research must examine other ways people manage anxiety, with particular emphasis on the role of one's values.

    C. Social Identity Theory
        Many people form a social identity (also known as group identity), which may create associations based on nationality, gender, or religion. These identities help us feel part of a larger whole. However, social identities can foster prejudice, discrimination, and intergroup conflict based on the "us versus them" phenomenon.

II. SOCIAL PERCEPTION
Social perception refers to the processes through which people interpret information about others, form impressions of them, and draw conclusions about the reasons for their behavior.

A. The Role of Schemas
People often use *schemas*, or mental representations, to perceive and interpret new information. Schemas influence our processing, retention, and judgment of new information, including the way we perceive people. This top-down processing can influence, and bias, person perception.

B. First Impressions
Schemas allow us to quickly categorize a person we have just met. The first impression is formed quickly and is difficult to change, becoming the lens through which we view all future behavior of that person.

1. *Forming Impressions.* We tend to expect people we meet to have attitudes and values similar to our own, and this schema predisposes us to like others. If they violate this and do something unlikeable, we particularly notice because it violates our schema. Thus, negative information is given more weight than positive information in first impressions.

2. *Lasting Impressions.* First impressions are difficult to change because they shape interpretations of new information. People tend to remember their initial general impressions better than later corrections, and to interpret new information as consistent with the first impression.

3. *Self-Fulfilling Prophecies.* An initial impression can create a self-fulfilling prophecy. With the impression formed, we behave in ways that cause others to confirm our first impression. This can also occur in our perception of groups as well as individuals.

C. Explaining Behavior: Attribution
We form *implicit theories* about why people behave as they do. We then make attributions about a person's behavior according to the internal characteristics of a person or to the external characteristics of the situation.

1. *Sources of Attributions.* How people go about making attributions depends on *consensus*, *consistency*, and *distinctiveness*. An *internal attribution* is made if consensus is low, consistency is high, and distinctiveness is low. An *external attribution* is made if consistency and consensus are both either low and distinctiveness is high.

2. *Culture and Attribution.* Individuals from different cultures tend to make different kinds of attributions. People from the United States have a tendency to make internal attributions. Differences in tendencies to make internal versus external attributions may contribute to misunderstandings across cultures.

D. Biases in Attribution
1. *The Fundamental Attribution Error.* Attributional biases are tendencies to systematically distort one's view of behavior. The fundamental attribution error is the tendency to attribute other people's behavior to internal causes. The *ultimate attribution error* takes attributional bias to the group level: it is the tendency to attribute positive behavior by an outgroup member to external causes, but their negative behavior to internal causes. Yet, when we view positive behavior by an ingroup member, we do the opposite, attributing it to internal causes and negative behavior to external causes. People from collectivist cultures are less prone to the fundamental attribution error. Additionally, it may not always prove to be an error, as sometimes behavior is due to internal causes.

2.   *Other Attributional Biases.* The <u>actor-observer effect</u> is the tendency to attribute others' behavior to internal causes and our own behavior to external causes, especially when the behavior is inappropriate or involves failure. This bias mainly occurs because we have different types of information available to us when we are the actor versus the observer. The <u>self-serving bias</u> is the tendency to take credit (make an internal attribution) for success and blame external causes for failures. This tendency is more pronounced in individualistic cultures.

E.   The Self-Protective Functions of Social Cognition

As in the self-serving bias, people are often motivated to think in ways that protect them from upsetting or threatening conclusions. Many people exhibit a pattern of *unrealistic optimism*; they believe that positive events are more likely and negative events less likely to happen to them than to others, even in the face of strong evidence otherwise.

III.   ATTITUDES

An <u>attitude</u> is a tendency to think, feel, or act positively or negatively towards an object in our environment.

A.   The Structure of Attitudes

Attitudes have three components: cognitive (belief), affective (emotional), and behavioral (way of acting). These three components are not always strongly aligned. Four factors determine whether behavior will be consistent with other attitude components: if the attitude is important in one's life, if the behavioral component is consistent with *subjective norms*, if we have *perceived control* of the behavior, and if we have *direct experience* with the attitude object. Another theory suggests that behavior will be affected by how easily interconnected evaluations and beliefs come to mind.

B.   Forming Attitudes

Learning plays an important role in attitude formation. Social learning is especially important; classical and operant conditioning can also produce positive or negative attitudes. The *mere exposure effect* plays a role in attitude formation; all else being equal, positive attitudes are positively correlated with exposure frequency.

C.   Changing Attitudes

Persuasive communications can change attitudes, depending on several factors.

1.   *Two Routes to Attitude Change.* Attitude change depends on three things: characteristics of the communicator, message content, and audience. According to the <u>elaboration likelihood model</u> of attitude change, messages can change attitudes through two routes: *peripheral* (generally ignores content and focuses on *persuasion cues* such as confidence or attractiveness of the person delivering the message) and *central* (focuses on logic and content of the message itself). The peripheral route is more likely when a person is busy thinking about something else. The central route is more likely if someone is personally involved in the attitude issue or has a high *need for cognition.*

2.   *Cognitive Dissonance Theory.* <u>Cognitive dissonance theory</u> holds that when attitudes and behaviors are inconsistent (or "dissonant"), people feel uneasy and are motivated to make them consistent. One way to do so is to change the inconsistent attitude. Based on this theory, if someone is persuaded to behave inconsistently with their attitude, then that will motivate them to change their attitude to be in line with their behavior. This may occur as a way to maintain self-concept, which work on *self-affirmation* suggests. Culturally, individualists tend to experience dissonance when they behave inconsistently with their own beliefs. But collectivists tend to experience dissonance when they behave inconsistently with the values of the groups they belong to, not necessarily inconsistently with their personal beliefs.

3.   *Self-Perception Theory*. The <u>self-perception theory</u> suggests that when situations occur in which people are unsure about their attitudes, they will observe their own behavior and infer what their attitudes must have been. This suggests that tension or discomfort of "dissonance" is unnecessary as an explanation. However, brain imaging studies suggest that internal tension, or dissonance, does occur. Further, people adjust their attitudes to match their behavior even when they are not given opportunity to reflect on their behavior and make an inference. Self-perception theory appears to apply best when a person had no pre-existing attitude.

D.   Linkages: Biological and Social Psychology
Social neuroscience (or *social cognitive neuroscience*) is an emerging field that focuses on the influence of social processes on biological phenomenon, and vice versa. Research showing stress' health consequences points to the importance of this field. New research shows that the amygdala is more active when a European American prejudiced person looks at a picture of an African American than at a picture of a European American. Though still in its infancy, social cognitive neuroscience shows promise for illuminating links between cognitive, social and biological phenomena.

IV. PREJUDICE AND STEREOTYPES
<u>Stereotypes</u> are general impressions or schemas of members of a group of people. They are often so deeply ingrained their effects are automatic and unconscious. Stereotyping may lead to <u>prejudice</u>, a positive or negative attitude toward a person based on their group membership. The behavioral component of prejudice is often <u>social discrimination</u>.

A.   Theories of Prejudice and Stereotyping
1.   *Motivational Theories*. People with *authoritarian* personalities tend to accept traditional values and unquestioningly follow orders of authority figures. To protect themselves from threats, they strongly identify with their own ethnic, cultural, or social group—known as their ingroup—and they develop negative stereotypes of people in their outgroups. Social identity theory sees the tendency to favor one's ingroup as independent of the authoritarian personality trait and more a function of using group membership to maintain and elevate one's own self-esteem.
2.   *Cognitive Theories*. Given the complexity of the world, people tend to categorize others in groups. Grouping people into *social categories* can result in stereotypes and *illusory correlations* between behavior and an ethnicity.
3.   *Learning Theories*. Children often learn stereotypes from their parents, their peers, and others. *Biopreparedness* may even lead us to be likely to learn to fear those who look different than us. The ways different races or ethnic groups are portrayed on television can also promote learning of stereotypes and prejudice.

B.   Reducing Prejudice
The <u>contact hypothesis</u> states that stereotypes and prejudices about a group should be reduced as friendly contact between members of equal standing in the two groups is increased. Research suggests that intergroup contact has positive effects when members have equal social and economic status, are in a situation that demands interdependence and cooperation, interact on a one-on-one basis, and are perceived as typical of that group. Intergroup contact without these features may merely reinforce existing stereotypes.

C.   Thinking Critically: Is Ethnic Prejudice Too Ingrained Ever to Be Eliminated?
What am I being asked to believe or accept?

People who deny having prejudices still have negative stereotypes about and show discrimination toward ethnic out-groups. These negative attitudes run so deep in all of us that ethnic prejudice can never be eliminated.

What evidence is available to support the assertion?

The theory of *aversive racism* suggests that although many European Americans find ethnic prejudice aversive, they will still display it, especially when they don't have to admit that they are prejudiced. Several studies show that people who consider themselves unprejudiced are inclined to discriminate. Priming studies show that negative stereotypes can be activated even among people who believe they are free of prejudice.

Are there alternative ways of interpreting the evidence?

If people are unaware of their prejudices, such views will be difficult to change. But unconscious stereotypes may not affect everyone in the same way.

What additional evidence would help to evaluate the alternatives?

Responses of prejudiced and nonprejudiced people need to be compared in different experimental situations. One study found that when unconscious stereotypes are activated in nonprejudiced people, the effects are more subtle.

What conclusions are most reasonable?

Prejudice may be subconscious in some people. Although it is deeply ingrained, evidence suggests it can be reduced.

V. INTERPERSONAL ATTRACTION
   A. Keys to Attraction
       1. *The Environment.* Proximity is an important predictor of attraction. The more often people interact, the more they tend to like each other. The situation in which people meet also influences attraction. If people meet others in positive circumstances, they are more likely to be attracted to each other.
       2. *Similarity.* People tend to like others who have attitudes similar to their own, especially attitudes about other people because this promotes *balanced* relationships. We like similar others also because we expect that they will like us.
       3. *Physical Attractiveness.* People tend to like attractive people. But, according to the matching hypothesis, people tend to form committed relationships with people who are similar in physical attractiveness.
   B. Intimate Relationships
       1. *Intimate Relationships. Interdependence* and *commitment* to the relationship are the key components of intimate relationships.
       2. *Analyzing Love.* Sternberg's triangular theory of love suggests that love is a function of *intimacy*, *passion*, and *commitment*. *Romantic love* is characterized by passion and intimacy. *Companionate love* is marked by commitment and intimacy. The most complete and satisfying love is *consummate love*, which includes a high level of passion, intimacy, and commitment. The success of a relationship depends on these characteristics, as well as how well the relationship fits with the partners' "ideal" love stories. The importance of love to a relationship varies across cultures.
       3. *Strong and Weak Marriages.* A close, intimate dating relationship between two people with similar attitudes is predictive of the success of the future marriage between the two. People report high levels of marital satisfaction when the relationship is perceived as equitable. Marriages that end in early divorce have both positive and negative feelings but struggle to communicate the negative ones in a non-hurtful way, leading to a communication breakdown. Marriages that last longer but ultimately end in divorce have a different pattern: the spouses simply communicate less and less about anything over time.

KEY TERMS

1. **Social psychology** is the study of how people's thoughts, feelings, and behavior influence and are influenced by the behavior of others. (see introductory section)

2. **Social cognition** refers to the mental processes associated with people's perceptions of and reactions to other people. (see introductory section)

3. One's **self-concept** is the way one thinks of oneself. (see Social Influences on the Self)

   Example: Mimi believes she is a responsible student, a caring friend, and a somewhat shy person.

4. **Self-esteem** consists of the evaluations one makes about how worthy one is as a human being. (see Social Influences on the Self)

   Example: Although Juan recently failed a thermodynamics quiz, he knows that he is smart and a good person.

5. **Social comparison** is using other people as a basis of comparison for evaluating oneself. (see Social Comparison)

   Example: If you want to know how athletic you are, you might compare yourself to friends of the same sex.

6. **Reference groups** are the categories of people to which people compare themselves. (see Social Comparison)

   Example: Jerome is an undergraduate student at a major university. He would probably consider his reference group to be other students; therefore, he would not compare his attractiveness or wardrobe to that of models he sees in magazines.

7. **Relative deprivation** is the belief that, in comparison to a reference group, one is getting less than is deserved. (see Social Comparison)

   Example: Rachel has just graduated with a Ph.D. in biology and taken a new job. At the university, she was considered one of the best students in her department. At her new job, she must start over and earn the respect of her superiors and peers. She experiences relative deprivation as she begins her new job.

8. **Social identity** consists of the beliefs we hold about the groups to which we belong. (see Social Identity Theory)

   Example: Karl says he is a German American Lutheran farmer.

9. **Social perception** refers to the processes through which people interpret information about others, draw inferences about them, and develop mental representations of them. (see Social Perception)

10. A **self-fulfilling prophecy** is a process through which our expectations about another person cause us to act in ways that lead the person to behave as we expected. (see First Impressions)

    Example: Jayne believed that she would never succeed in college. During her first semester, she found that she had to study much harder than she did in high school and decided it was a sign that she was stupid. Jayne quit studying, thinking that it was of no use, and flunked out of college.

11. **Attribution** is the process of explaining the causes of people's behavior, including our own. (see Explaining Behavior: Attribution)

    Example: How would you respond to an inquiry about the causes of your grades? Would you say that you are smart and work hard (internal causes) or that you are lucky and consistently end up with easy professors (external causes)?

REMEMBER: Internal or external causes can account for behavior.

12. The **fundamental attribution error** is a bias toward overattributing the behavior of others to internal causes. (see Biases in Attribution)

    Example: Latanya's brother calls and tells her that he has just flunked an algebra exam. Before he can speak another word, Latanya is telling him that he is either lazy or stupid or both. She thinks that her brother's behavior, not situational factors, caused him to flunk his algebra test.

13. An **outgroup** refers to those whom we perceive as being different from ourselves. (see Biases in Attribution)

    Example: Sandra is very politically conservative. She perceives Democrats as "liberals" and considers them part of her outgroup.

14. An **ingroup** refers to those whom we perceive as being similar to ourselves. (see Biases in Attribution)

    Example: Marsha has joined a predominantly African American sorority. She is an African American. She perceives her sorority sisters as part of her ingroup.

5. The **actor-observer effect** is the tendency to attribute other people's behavior to internal causes while attributing our own behavior (especially errors and failures) to external causes. (see Biases in Attribution)

    Example: When John failed to stop at a stop sign, he attributed his behavior to the sun in his eyes and poor placement of the sign (external factors). When someone else runs a stop sign, however, John thinks they did so because of carelessness or lack of attention (internal factors).

6. The **self-serving bias** is the tendency to attribute our successes to internal characteristics while blaming our failures on external causes. (see Biases in Attribution)

    Example: Jerry has noticed that whenever his company wins a big account with a new client, each person claims responsibility for the success. However, when a client decides to take its business elsewhere, everyone denies responsibility for the problems that precipitated the client's departure. People like to take credit for success but do not like to take the blame for failure.

7. An **attitude** is a predisposition toward a particular cognitive, emotional, or behavioral reaction to objects. (see Attitudes)

    Example: Sima joins the marching band because she believes it challenges its members to become better musicians (cognitive component). She practices her clarinet nearly every day (behavioral component) and enjoys band practices and performances (affective component).

8. The **elaboration likelihood model** suggests that attitude change can be driven by evaluation of the content of a persuasive message (central route) or by irrelevant persuasion cues (peripheral route). (see Changing Attitudes)

    Example: Matthew chose to purchase a generic medication after reading an informational pamphlet and discussing it with his doctor (central route). Jennifer chose to buy generic medicines after seeing a television commercial with a trustworthy, confident person describing their advantages (peripheral route).

9. The **cognitive dissonance theory** asserts that attitude change is driven by efforts to reduce tension caused by inconsistencies between attitudes and behaviors. (see Changing Attitudes)

    Example: Jan is an advertising executive. She is working on a cigarette company's account, but she thinks that cigarettes should not be advertised to teenagers. Her attitudes and behavior are inconsistent. She will have to change her attitude about cigarette advertising or change jobs in order to reduce cognitive dissonance and the psychological tension it causes.

REMEMBER: People prefer that their cognitions about themselves and the rest of the world be consistent with one another. When cognitions are inconsistent, or dissonant, people feel uneasy and are motivated to make them more consistent.

10. **Self-perception theory** suggests that attitudes can change as people consider their behavior in certain situations and then infer what their attitude must be. (see Changing Attitudes)

Example: To be initiated into his boyhood group of friends, Gabriel was required to eat a worm, a live goldfish, and the head of a bumblebee. After eating these, Gabriel liked the group even more than he did before. He inferred that he must really like the group because he was able to overcome his loathing of worms, live fish, and bugs.

11. **Stereotypes** are false assumptions that all members of some group share the same characteristics. (see Prejudice and Stereotypes)

Example: Jai is interviewing candidates for a position in his company. He has decided not to hire anyone with a Ph.D. He has been told by his peers that people with Ph.D.s are flaky, absent-minded, and socially inept.

REMEMBER: This can lead to prejudice.

12. **Prejudice** is a positive or negative attitude toward an entire group of people. (see Prejudice and Stereotypes)

Example: Isa, an American, went to study in Russia for a year. She met a child on the street one day who asked her why Americans wanted to destroy the world with nuclear bombs. The child had never been exposed to Americans before but had prejudged them based on information from the press, her parents, and her peers.

13. **Social discrimination** is the differential treatment of various groups; the behavioral component of prejudice. (see Prejudice and Stereotypes)

Example: Eva has brought her date, an artist, to meet her parents. She is very embarrassed because her father will not even speak to him. Later, she asks her father to explain his extremely rude behavior. He remarks that all artists are shiftless and no good and forbids her to see her friend again.

14. The **contact hypothesis** is the idea that stereotypes and prejudice toward a group will diminish as contact with the group increases. (see Reducing Prejudice)

Example: Anna grew up in the East. Her parents always told her that people who spoke with a southern accent were stupid and lazy. When Anna's company relocated her to Texas, she eventually came to enjoy interacting with other employees and found them to be competent at their jobs.

15. The **matching hypothesis** is the notion that people are most likely to form relationships with those who are similar to themselves in physical attractiveness. (see Keys to Attraction)

Example: As you walk around your campus or neighborhood, look at the couples you see. They will often be about equal in attractiveness.

FILL-IN-THE-BLANKS KEY TERMS

This section will help you check your factual knowledge of the key terms introduced in this chapter. Fill in each blank with the appropriate term from the list of key terms in the previous section.

1. The mental processes with which we think about others are called _____.

2. After moving into a new reference group, a person sometimes feels inadequate; this phenomenon is called _____.

3. Those whom we perceive as being similar to ourselves are called our _____.

4. The process of explaining the causes of behavior is called _____.

5. The people to whom we compare ourselves are called a _____.

6. The tendency for people to be attracted to those of similar physical attractiveness is described in the _____.

7. A(n) _____ can cause behavior that confirms an original hypothesis.

8. The _____ bias says that we usually attribute other people's behavior to internal factors, especially when the behavior is negative.

9. The _____ bias says that we attribute our successes to internal factors, and our failures to external factors.

10. Schemas of entire groups of people that assume that all members share the same characteristics are called _____.

11. The _____ model of attitude change states that a message may change a person's attitude through a peripheral or central route.

12. The notion that group stereotypes should be reduced by members of different groups getting to know one another is part of the _____.

13. _____ consists of the evaluations we make about how worthy we are as human beings.

14. The _____ is the tendency to see the behavior of others as a function of internal personality factors.

15. According to _____, people determine what their attitudes are by examining past behavior.

Total Correct (See answer key) _____

LEARNING OBJECTIVES

1. Define social cognition and social psychology. (see introductory section)

2. Compare and contrast self-concept and self-esteem. (see "Social Influences on the Self")

3. Discuss the difference between temporal and social comparisons. Describe the relationship of reference groups to the process of self-evaluation, including *upward* and *downward social comparison*. Define relative deprivation. (see "Social Comparison")

4. Describe the importance of self-esteem in managing negative emotion. (see "Focus on Research Methods: Self-esteem and the Ultimate Terror")

5. Define social identity. Discuss the theory of social identity. (see "Social Identity Theory")

6. Discuss how self-schemas affect our feelings and actions. (see "Self-Schemas")

7. Define <u>social perception</u>. Describe the influences, including the role of schemas, on impression formation. Explain why impressions are difficult to change. (see "Social Perception")

8. Define <u>self-fulfilling prophecy</u>. Discuss the relationship between self-fulfilling prophecies and impressions. (see "Self-Fulfilling Prophecies")

9. Define <u>attribution</u>. Describe the three criteria (*consensus*, *consistency*, and *distinctiveness*) used in making attributions and explain how they influence whether we make an *internal* or *external attribution*. (see "Explaining Behavior: Attribution")

10. Describe the cross-cultural experiment on attribution and its outcome. (see "Culture and Attribution")

11. Define the <u>fundamental attribution error</u> and the *ultimate attribution error* and give examples. Define the <u>actor-observer effect</u> and the <u>self-serving bias</u> and give examples of each. (see "Biases in Attribution")

12. Define *unrealistic optimism* and *unique invulnerability*. Describe the ways in which social cognition is self-protective. (see "The Self-Protective Functions of Social Cognition")

13. Define <u>attitudes</u>. Describe the cognitive, affective, and behavioral components of attitudes and give an example of each. (see "Attitudes")

14. Discuss the factors that promote attitude-behavior consistency. (see "The Structure of Attitudes")

15. Discuss how attitudes are formed and changed. Include the *mere exposure effect* and the <u>elaboration likelihood model</u> of attitude change. (see "Forming Attitudes"; see also "Changing Attitudes")

16. Define <u>cognitive dissonance</u>, and describe the process of reducing cognitive dissonance. (see "Cognitive Dissonance Theory")

17. Define <u>self-perception theory</u>. Describe the influence of past behavior on attitudes, according to the self-perception theory. (see "Self-Perception Theory")

18. Discuss the growing field of social neuroscience and how it contributes to the understanding of the interactions between biological, cognitive, and social phenomena. (see "Linkages: Biological and Social Psychology")

19. Define <u>stereotype</u>, <u>prejudice</u>, and <u>social discrimination</u>. (see "Prejudice and Stereotypes")

20. Compare and contrast the motivational, cognitive, and learning theories of stereotypes and prejudice. Define the *authoritarianism*, *social categories*, and *illusory correlation*. (see "Theories of Prejudice and Stereotyping")

21. Describe the <u>contact hypothesis</u>. Discuss the specific conditions necessary for the contact hypothesis to hold true. (see "Reducing Prejudice")

22. Discuss the studies on the possibility of eliminating prejudice. Define aversive racism. (see "Thinking Critically: Is Ethnic Prejudice Too Ingrained Ever to Be Eliminated?")

23. Describe the influences of the environment, similarity, and physical attractiveness on attraction. Define the <u>matching hypothesis</u>. (see "Keys to Attraction")

24. Describe the most important components of an intimate relationship. (see "Intimate Relationships")

25. Describe Sternberg's triangular theory of love. Discuss the differences among romantic love, companionate love, and consummate love. Describe the predictors of strong versus weak marriages. (see "Analyzing Love"; see also "Strong and Weak Marriages")

CONCEPTS AND EXERCISES

Persuasive Advertising

For each of the following advertising campaigns, use the list below to suggest a reason for the chosen method.

1. A company is selling herbal supplements as memory enhancers. Because clinical evidence for their claims is very weak, they have hired as spokesman for the product an actor who plays a respected doctor in a hit TV series. _____

2. An ad designed to increase Red Cross blood donations opens with a woman stating that it is everyone's moral duty to donate blood. The camera returns to the woman later as she self-defensively explains to her coworkers, who have stopped at the Red Cross booth, that she's too busy to donate. She begins to walk away uncomfortably; then she turns and imagines a scene at a hospital where a young boy dies because of a lack of blood. She begins smiling and rolling up her sleeve as she walks back to the booth. _____

3. A drug company places advertisements in medical journals. Each is a full page and contains many details about the drug, its dosage, advantages, and side effects. Why would the company put so much information in their advertisement? _____

4. During a televised movie, a beverage company arranges to have its products advertised in eight spots of fifteen seconds each, rather than two spots of sixty seconds each. _____

    a. Mere exposure effect

    b. Peripheral route

    c. Central route

    d. Cognitive dissonance

Prejudice

For each of the descriptions, decide which of the theories or concepts below best fit the situation:

1. To lessen racial tensions among twelve-year-old boys in a community youth home, the director introduced uniforms, instituted two-person teams who room and work together, and held recreational activities that involved all the boys in popular group sports. _____

2. Stereotyping and prejudice are logical by-products of our perceptual tendency to simplify complexity by grouping like stimuli together. Rather than individually remembering people who resemble one another, we group them together and assume they are alike in everything.

    _____

3. The *Journal of the American Medical Association* reported a study that found that physicians were 40 percent less likely to order sophisticated cardiac tests for women and African Americans who complained of chest pain than they were for men and whites with the same symptoms. When interviewed, these doctors were shocked by the findings because they sincerely believed that they were not prejudiced. _____

4. When Dino's parents saw people who appeared to be from a different racial or ethnic group, they looked at each other and then watched the people as long as they were in the neighborhood. Dino noticed their behavior and now feels suspicious of anyone who appears different from him.

    _____

    a. Motivational theories

  b.   Learning theories

  c.   Cognitive theories

  d.   Contact hypothesis

  e.   Aversive racism

  f.   Jigsaw technique

CRITICAL THINKING

Sam and Martina are trying to discover the motive for a murder. When questioned, the killer, a forty-year-old man named Brian Canton, said he just felt like killing the victim even though he didn't know him. Sam decides that Brian has an antisocial personality and leaves the interrogation room. Martina is not so sure and continues to talk to Brian.

Later, Sam is incredibly frustrated. "Look, Martina, the guy is admitting to a classic symptom of antisocial personality. He just *felt like it*. He hasn't shown any signs of remorse. This is an easy one. We finally have a break here."

Martina snaps, "If you had stayed in the room for a little while longer, you would have picked up some information that would have led you to an alternative hypothesis."

"Oh yeah, like what?" asks Sam.

Martina replies, "He kept telling me how much he hated killing that guy. And he kept wanting to know if anything bad would happen to his family. Doesn't sound like an antisocial personality to me. Besides, do you know how rare antisocial personalities are? The guy would have a criminal record a mile long." Martina thinks for a minute. "I've got it. That guy was a paid assassin. I'll be right back. I need to ask some more questions. Sam, you go take care of the paperwork on this one. We'll meet later."

That afternoon Sam and Martina get together again. Sam sighs and says, "Okay, I know you've got it figured out. Let's hear the answers to those questions you always use."

Using the five critical thinking questions in your text, the clues in the story, and what you have learned about cognitive dissonance, answer the following.

1.   What is Sam's hypothesis?

2.   What evidence supports Sam's hypothesis?

3.   What is Martina's alternative hypothesis?

4.   What additional evidence supports Martina's hypothesis?

5.   What conclusions are reasonable?

PERSONAL LEARNING ACTIVITIES

1.   Answer the following questions. Are you attractive? Are you extremely intelligent? Do you dress well? Are you well educated? The individuals or groups of people to whom you compare yourself when answering these questions are your reference groups. Who made up your reference groups? Were the groups different for each question? Think about where you will be in ten years. How might your reference groups change? In what situations could you experience relative deprivation?

2.   Can you think of a time you felt something akin to unrealistic optimism. How did things turn out? Do you think the self-protective functions of cognition lessen with age?

3.   Consider any political advertisement (many of these are archived on YouTube if they aren't currently running on television). Watch it and analyze the content to see what elements contribute to the two routes of persuasion. What sorts of peripheral persuasion cues are there? How strong is the logic of the argument (the main contribution to the central route)? What factors about yourself determine if you would be more influenced by the peripheral cues or the central route?

4.   To see an example of how unconscious prejudice might be measured, visit this website that has the implicit association test available: https://implicit.harvard.edu/implicit/. Try out the demonstration there, and see what it tells you about your own unconscious prejudices. Do you agree that the methodology is a good way to measure unconscious prejudice?

5.   A great deal of research has been done on differentiating between strong and weak marriages. John Gottman has done a great deal of work on this matter. To see a short synopsis of his work, watch the following YouTube clip: http://www.youtube.com/watch?v=CbJPaQY_1dc&NR=1. If you are interested in the findings he reports there, you can learn more about his work at The Gottman Relationship Institute website at: http://www.gottman.com/. How does the information you learned in this clip and on that site fit with what your textbook says about strong versus weak marriages? What does this research suggest that you can do to be a better relationship partner?

MULTIPLE-CHOICE QUESTIONS

Quiz 1

1.   _____ is the study of the mental processes associated with the ways in which people perceive and react to other individuals and groups.
    a.   Social cognition
    b.   Social psychology
    c.   Social influence
    d.   Social identity

2.   The belief that you are getting less than you deserve in terms of recognition, status, money, and so on is
    a.   cognitive dissonance.
    b.   the fundamental attribution error.
    c.   relative deprivation.
    d.   self-fulfilling prophecies.

3.   Those whom we perceive as being different from ourselves are called our
    a.   ingroup.
    b.   outgroup.
    c.   subjective norm.
    d.   contacts.

4.   Jodee is in an experiment. She is asked to complete the statement, "I am…" in any way she chooses. She says "Chinese." Her response reflects her
    a.   self-esteem.
    b.   schema.
    c.   social identity.
    d.   social perception.

5. On Gena's first day at work, she felt her boss didn't like her because he was short-tempered and gruff with her. From then on she was constantly prepared for more nasty comments. Gena's defensiveness irritated her boss further and caused him to be even more short-tempered. When Gena's boss gave her a negative six-month evaluation, it was most likely due to

    a.   a stereotype.
    b.   prejudice.
    c.   a self-fulfilling prophecy.
    d.   discrimination.

6. Carol goes to a party to meet people. While there, she is introduced to Rico, an attractive man about her age. During their conversation, Rico is rude several times. Based on what you know about impression formation, which of the following is likely to be her response?

    a.   Carol will assume that Rico is rude because he had a bad day.
    b.   Carol will assume that Rico is a rude person.
    c.   Carol is experiencing a self-fulfilling prophecy.
    d.   Carol will assume that Rico is similar to her and form a positive impression.

7. An attributional bias in which we attribute our failures to external causes and our successes to internal factors is called the

    a.   actor-observer effect.
    b.   fundamental attribution error.
    c.   self-fulfilling prophecy.
    d.   self-serving bias.

8. Nicole just graduated from college and secured her first teaching position. She didn't make even $5,000 annually while in college, but her first year teacher salary is $26,000. Even though that salary is not lucrative, to Nicole it feels like big money because it is so much more than she made previously. Nicole's sense of "wealth" is due to the _____ she is making.

    a.   temporal comparison
    b.   social comparison
    c.   reference group
    d.   schema

9. The fundamental attribution error is to attribution about _____ while the ultimate attribution error is attribution about _____.

    a.   individuals; individuals
    b.   groups; groups
    c.   individuals; groups
    d.   groups; individuals

10. Julia is proud to be dating Vernon because he is thoughtful and considerate to everyone. He always sends her flowers and is willing to help his friends. Julia's friends are envious; none of their boyfriends is as considerate as Vernon. Vernon's behavior demonstrates _____ consensus, _____ consistency, and _____ distinctiveness. Julia will attribute his behavior to an _____ cause.

    a.   high; high; high; external
    b.   high; low; high; internal
    c.   low; high; low; internal
    d.   high; high; low; external

11. Bridget and Jay just got into the car to go to lunch. Bridget asks Jay to wear his seatbelt, but he ignores her because he never gets into accidents. Which of the following best explains Jay's behavior?
    a. Cognitive dissonance
    b. Unrealistic optimism
    c. Self-handicapping strategy
    d. Self-serving bias

12. When Rosa heard the knock on her door, she looked out and saw a young man laughing heartily. She thought he must be good natured and friendly, and she opened the door to him. Rosa didn't know that the reason he was laughing was that he had just conned her neighbor out of $500. Rosa had
    a. cognitive dissonance.
    b. a faulty schema.
    c. a fundamental attribution error.
    d. a self-serving bias.

13. Erik always says that looks are not important to him when he asks a woman out; however, recently he did not invite either of two women he liked to a dance because he didn't think they were attractive. When his friend points out the difference between what Erik said was important and what was really influencing him, Erik most likely experienced
    a. the actor-observer effect.
    b. cognitive dissonance.
    c. deindividuation.
    d. the mere exposure effect.

14. Renato says that stereotyping occurs because people group others into social categories and see all members of a category as similar. Renato agrees with the _____ theory of prejudice.
    a. motivational
    b. cognitive
    c. contact
    d. learning

15. Discomfort caused by attitude-behavior inconsistency tends to be
    a. influenced more by individual differences than by culture.
    b. greater in collectivist cultures.
    c. greater in individualist cultures.
    d. about equal in all cultures.

16. Members of hate groups often act aggressively toward individuals whom their leaders identify as representing threats to the group's ideals. The members' behavior is best explained by _____ theories of prejudice.
    a. motivational
    b. aversive racism
    c. learning
    d. cognitive

17. Which of the following is a good predictor of whether people will form a committed relationship?
    a. Similar attitudes
    b. Similar degrees of attractiveness
    c. Lack of conflict and anger
    d. Similar attitudes and similar degrees of attractiveness

18. Susan has just moved into a new dormitory. She will most likely become good friends with the women
    a. on the floor above hers.
    b. in the dorm next door.
    c. in the room next door.
    d. at the other end of the hall.

19. Which new marriage is least likely to end in divorce, based on the research cited in your text?
    a. Brad and Delanie, who rarely communicate about feelings at all
    b. Phil and Renee, who have difficulty expressing negative feelings about each other
    c. Joe and Kacie, who agree on politics and religion
    d. There is an equal probability that these three marriages will end in divorce.

20. George and Louise share their thoughts, hopes, and daily worries and plan to stay married until death parts them. They enjoy an active and creative sex life. According to Sternberg's theory, George and Louise have _____ love.
    a. consummate
    b. companionate
    c. fatuous
    d. romantic

Total Correct (See answer key) _____

Quiz 2

Use this quiz to reassess your learning after taking Quiz 1 and reviewing the chapter.

1. Jack is depressed. He took a job in the city after completing graduate school on a scholarship and graduating with honors. Now that he is in the city, it seems that everyone is older, richer, and wiser than he is. Jack is experiencing
    a. cognitive dissonance.
    b. relative deprivation.
    c. role isolation.
    d. a self-fulfilling prophecy.

2. If Jack (see question 1) would compare his new job to the minute amount of money he made in graduate school rather than to other people, he might be less depressed. Jack needs to make a _____ rather than a _____.
    a. temporal comparison; social comparison
    b. social comparison; temporal comparison
    c. internal attribution; external attribution
    d. external attribution; internal attribution

3.   Our social identity is our
   a.   desire to be like our peers.
   b.   desire to be like our idols.
   c.   belief about our self-worth.
   d.   belief about the groups to which we belong.

4.   High self-esteem is predicted to be a buffer against anxiety brought on by thoughts of pain and death according to which theory?
   a.   Social identity theory
   b.   Terror management theory
   c.   Attributional theory
   d.   Cognitive dissonance theory

5.   Wenlan is highly religious and a member of a small Christian denomination. When she meets others who are members of that denomination, she perceives them to be part of her
   a.   ingroup.
   b.   outgroup.
   c.   self-concept.
   d.   self-esteem.

6.   When Lance introduced himself to Nathan, he mentioned that he worked as a cashier in a supermarket. Nathan remembered all of Lance's comments about food and car repairs and remembered none of his comments about English poets and politics. Nathan's perception was most likely biased by
   a.   discrimination.
   b.   a schema.
   c.   social comparison.
   d.   the actor-observer effect.

7.   According to the fundamental attribution error, we
   a.   always attribute our behavior to internal causes.
   b.   always make an internal attribution for our successes.
   c.   usually attribute others' behavior to external causes.
   d.   usually attribute others' behavior to internal causes.

8.   People attribute behavior to an external cause when it has _____ consistency, _____ distinctiveness, and _____ consensus.
   a.   high; low; low
   b.   high; high; low
   c.   high; low; high
   d.   low; high; high

9. While finishing an exam, Sal looks around the room and notices that there are just two other students left. Though he has taken extra time because he is double-checking his answers, he assumes that the two students still working must not be very smart. The different explanations Sal uses for his own and for others' behavior illustrates

    a. the fundamental attribution error.
    b. the actor-observer effect.
    c. unrealistic optimism.
    d. self-perception theory.

10. While talking about her daughter Nicole, Clarissa says, "I have taught Nicole to be considerate, thoughtful, and moral, but Nicole's father is responsible for her inability to manage her money." This is an illustration of

    a. the fundamental attribution error.
    b. the self-serving bias.
    c. the actor-observer effect.
    d. relative deprivation.

11. Discrepancies between what we do and what we believe lead to

    a. prejudice.
    b. cognitive dissonance.
    c. the fundamental attribution error.
    d. relative deprivation.

12. George was in New Orleans for Mardi Gras. He had never eaten raw oysters before and visited an oyster bar with his friends. When George discovered that he had eaten more than anyone else, he concluded that he must really like oysters. Which theory best explains George's attitude?

    a. Cognitive dissonance theory
    b. Elaboration likelihood model
    c. Social learning theory
    d. Self-perception theory

13. When Mark sees a television commercial that shows a couple meeting and falling in love, he immediately phones the number they list to sign up for the dating service. Mark most likely used _____ to change his attitude.

    a. a central route
    b. a peripheral route
    c. cognitive "busyness"
    d. cognitive dissonance

14. Margie wants to reduce children's prejudices; therefore, she decides to run an after-school program in her grade school to bring together students of different backgrounds for games, study sessions, and snacks. Based on the description of successful intergroup contact given in the text, which of the following would bring Margie the most success?

    a. Allow the children to choose sides for a game of basketball
    b. Have the different ethnic groups describe their families' customs
    c. Design a project that will require all the children to cooperate in order to succeed
    d. Point out the errors of the high-status children

15. Cognitive dissonance and the self-perception theory differ in that
    a. cognitive dissonance involves attitudes, whereas self-perception involves attribution.
    b. cognitive dissonance involves attitude change, whereas self-perception involves social facilitation.
    c. cognitive dissonance involves the reduction of internal tension, whereas self-perception does not.
    d. None of these

16. Someone studying _____ would be most likely to use EEGs and MRIs in their research.
    a. social cognitive neuroscience
    b. attitude change and persuasion
    c. social identity
    d. prejudice and discrimination

17. Prejudice is to _____ as stereotype is to _____.
    a. behavior; attitude
    b. attitude; behavior
    c. attitude; belief
    d. belief; attitude

18. Ryan believes, and generally behaves, as though he is not prejudiced against African Americans. But when he interacts with African Americans, the length of his interaction is briefer than when he interacts with people who are European American, like himself. This pattern of interaction supports the theory of
    a. triangular love.
    b. aversive racism.
    c. cognitive dissonance.
    d. elaboration likelihood.

19. Shelly and Eric share everything with each other and are very committed to each other for life. They share a
    a. romantic love.
    b. consummate love.
    c. companionate love.
    d. All of these

20. Russ and Sarah just had their first baby. What may happen to their marital satisfaction, based on research cited in your text?
    a. Russ's marital satisfaction will decline.
    b. The baby will increase their mutual marital satisfaction.
    c. Sarah's marital satisfaction will decline.
    d. Sarah's marital satisfaction will increase.

Total Correct (See answer key) _____

ANSWERS TO FILL-IN-THE-BLANKS KEY TERMS

1. social cognition (see introductory section)
2. relative deprivation (see Social Comparison)
3. ingroup (see Biases in Attribution)
4. attribution (see Explaining Behavior: Attribution)
5. reference group (see Social Comparison)
6. matching hypothesis (see Keys to Attraction)
7. self-fulfilling prophecy (see First Impressions)
8. actor-observer (see Biases in Attribution)
9. self-serving (see Biases in Attribution)
10. stereotypes (see Prejudice and Stereotypes)
11. elaboration likelihood (see Changing Attitudes)
12. contact hypothesis (see Reducing Prejudice)
13. Self-esteem (see Social Influences on the Self)
14. fundamental attribution error (see Biases in Attribution)
15. self-perception theory (see Self-Perception Theory)

ANSWERS TO CONCEPTS AND EXERCISES

Persuasive Advertising

1. *Peripheral route.* The company probably hopes that viewers will use the peripheral route to attitude change by focusing attention on the confident, persuasive message from the famous star who plays a doctor on TV rather than on the objective features of the supplement itself. (see Changing Attitudes)

2. *Cognitive dissonance.* This ad demonstrates cognitive dissonance by featuring a woman who feels discomfort because her behavior does not match her expressed attitude about blood donation. The woman feels better only when she acts in accordance to her belief by donating blood. The Red Cross is hoping that viewers have been in similar situations, will recognize the discomfort, and will model the solution to it. (see Cognitive Dissonance Theory)

3. *Central route.* By giving so much information, a company may be hoping that people will use critical thinking to consider the advantages and disadvantages of the product. (see Changing Attitudes)

4. *Mere exposure effect.* People tend to like things they have seen more often. Advertisers try to take advantage of this tendency by showing their advertisements repeatedly. (see Forming Attitudes)

Prejudice

1. *Contact hypothesis.* Prejudice will diminish as contact increases if certain social conditions are created: equality in social and economic status, cooperation and interdependence, one-on-one contact, and the belief that members are typical of their group. (see Reducing Prejudice)

2. *Cognitive theories.* This is a Gestalt-type explanation that parallels the social category idea of grouping people on certain superficial similarities and then assuming they must be similar in beliefs and values. (see Theories of Prejudice and Stereotyping)

3. *Aversive racism.* This study, published in March 1999 in JAMA, is a startling, real-world example of aversive racism. Although these highly educated and humane white physicians sincerely believed they did not have a prejudiced bone in their bodies, they unconsciously displayed prejudice in their behavior. (see Thinking Critically: Is Ethnic Prejudice Too Ingrained Ever to Be Eliminated?)

4. *Learning theories.* Dino learned discriminatory behaviors from his parents through observational learning. Although Dino may have had very little contact with the ethnic group, he now has suspicions about anyone from the group. (see Theories of Prejudice and Stereotyping)

ANSWERS TO CRITICAL THINKING

1. Sam hypothesizes that Brian has an antisocial personality.

2. The evidence is Brian's remark that he just felt like killing the guy.

3. Martina hypothesizes, based on cognitive dissonance theory, that Brian got paid to do the killing but didn't really want to do it.

4. Martina probably wants to find out if Brian or any member of his family needed money.

5. What conclusions are most reasonable? If Brian answered yes, Martina could conclude that Brian was a paid assassin. But she probably shouldn't form a conclusion just yet. What else could Martina ask Brian that would support her hypothesis?

ANSWERS TO MULTIPLE-CHOICE QUESTIONS

Circle the question numbers you answered correctly.

Quiz 1

1. a is the answer. Social cognition is the study of how others influence our mental processes. (see introductory section)

    b. Although the definition in this question is part of what comprises social psychology, social psychology also includes the study of how others influence our behavior, not just mental processes.

    c. Social influence is the study of how others influence our behavior.

    d. Social identity is an area of study within social cognition, but social cognition is a broader construct than just social identity.

2. c is the answer. Relative deprivation is the belief that you are getting less than you deserve. (see Social Comparison)

    a. Cognitive dissonance is experienced when components of attitude(s) and behavior(s) are not in line with each other.

    b. The fundamental attribution error is the tendency to believe that others' behaviors are caused by their personal characteristics rather than by the environment.

    d. Self-fulfilling prophecies occur when we allow our expectations to influence our actions, which, in turn, influence those around us into behaving as we expected.

3.   b is the answer. Outgroup refers to those whom we see as different from ourselves. (see Biases in Attribution)

   a.   Ingroup refers to those whom we see as similar to ourselves.

   c.   Our subjective norm refers to what the important others in our lives think about particular behaviors we should or shouldn't do. It influences the consistency of our attitudes with our behaviors.

   d.   Contacts is not a term in this chapter. You may be thinking of the contact hypothesis, which specifies the conditions under which intergroup contact can reduce prejudice.

4.   c is the answer. A social identity is our set of beliefs about the groups to which we belong. Those groups may be religions, nationalities, or ethnic groups, to name a few. (see Social Identity Theory)

   a.   Self-esteem is a positive or negative evaluation of how worthwhile we are. If Jodee had said, "I'm a worthless idiot" or "Gosh, I am a great gal," she would be showing her level of self-esteem.

   b.   A schema is a mental representation that can be quite general and not necessarily about oneself.

   d.   Social perception is a rather general term for how we interpret information about others and make inferences based on that information. It includes a mental representation of other people but does not include the groups to which we personally belong.

5.   c is the answer. Gena fulfilled her own prophecy. She was defensive because she expected her boss to be gruff. As a result, she elicited the boss's irritability and was given a negative evaluation. (see First Impressions)

   a.   A stereotype is an impression of a group of people. Gena has formed a first impression about only one person: her boss.

   b.   Prejudice is a preformed negative or positive judgment about a group of people. This would have been the correct answer only if Gena's first impression had led her to believe that all bosses were gruff and nasty.

   d.   Discrimination is the differential treatment of certain groups or individuals. If Gena's boss treated her negatively because she was female, black, lesbian, or pregnant, this example would demonstrate discrimination.

6.   b is the answer. Negative acts such as being rude tend to heavily influence first impressions. Also, people assume that negative behavior reflects undesirable characteristics. Therefore, Carol will form a negative impression of Rico and probably assume that he is a rude person. (see First Impressions)

   a.   In forming first impressions, people tend to assume that negative acts are due to some undesirable characteristic of the person being evaluated. Carol is likely to assume that Rico is rude, rather than believe his behavior is the result of a bad day.

   c.   A self-fulfilling prophecy occurs when an already-formed first impression of another person elicits behavior that confirms that impression. Carol had no impression of Rico prior to their conversation at the party.

   d.   All else being equal, people assume that others are similar to themselves. Since people usually evaluate themselves positively, they also evaluate others positively. However, all else is not equal in this situation. Rico is rude to Carol. Since negative acts usually carry a lot of weight and are assumed to reflect negative characteristics, Carol will form a negative impression of Rico.

7.   d is the answer. The self-serving bias is the belief that our behavior is responsible for our successes but not for our failures. (see Biases in Attribution)

    a.   The actor-observer effect is the tendency to attribute our own behavior to external causes and others' behavior to internal causes.

    b.   According to the fundamental attribution error, we are more likely to attribute other people's behavior to internal causes.

    c.   A self-fulfilling prophecy is not an attributional bias but a situation in which one person behaves toward another in a manner that elicits a response consistent with the person's initial expectations of the other.

8.   a is the answer. Temporal comparisons involve comparing the way we are now to the way we were in the past. Nicole is comparing her new salary to her previous one. (see Social Comparison)

    b.   Social comparisons involve comparing yourself to other people. Nicole is not doing that.

    c.   Reference groups are the people we *refer,* or compare, to in the social comparison process.

    d.   Schema are our mental representations based on prior knowledge.

9.   c is the answer. The fundamental attribution error occurs when we make internal attributions for an individual person's behavior. The ultimate attribution error occurs when we make internal or external attributions for a person based on their group membership. (see Biases in Attribution)

    a.   Only the fundamental attribution error concerns attributions about individuals.

    b.   Only the ultimate attribution error concerns attributions based on group membership.

    d.   The correct answer is the reverse of this.

10.   c is the answer. Vernon's behavior has a low degree of consensus because not everyone is considerate and thoughtful. His behavior has a high degree of consistency because he is always considerate and thoughtful. His behavior has a low degree of distinctiveness because he is considerate and thoughtful toward all his friends. (see Explaining Behavior: Attribution)

    a, b, d.   Vernon's behavior could be attributed to external factors only if everyone was considerate and thoughtful (high consensus), if he was considerate only in a specific situation (high distinctiveness), and if he was not consistently considerate (low consistency).

11.   b is the answer. Jay is unrealistically optimistic that he will not be involved in an accident. (see The Self-Protective Functions of Social Cognition)

    a.   Cognitive dissonance occurs when components of an attitude do not match up and cause discomfort. There is nothing in the story to suggest that Jay feels uncomfortable, for example, because his cognitive component doesn't match his behavioral component.

    c.   People using the self-handicapping strategy behave in a less than efficient or healthy way so that they have an excuse when they fail.

    d.   The self-serving bias is manifested when a person takes credit for success but not for failure.

12.   c is the answer. Rosa attributed the man's behavior to internal factors, such as personality traits. She did not consider external reasons for his laughter. (see Biases in Attribution)

a.   This is a theory of attitude change. Rosa was explaining the cause of a behavior.

b.   A schema would consist of Rosa's mental representations based on prior knowledge. This was the first time Rosa had seen this man.

d.   The self-serving bias is a tendency to take personal credit for success but to blame external causes for failure. It does not apply here.

13.   b is the answer. When our behavior doesn't match our beliefs (cognitive component), we feel uncomfortable and motivated to change either the attitude or the behavior. (see Changing Attitudes)

a.   The actor-observer effect has to do with attributing behavior to external versus internal causes; it doesn't deal with disagreement between components of an attitude.

c.   Deindividuation, which is discussed in Chapter 18, is the feeling of losing oneself in a crowd.

d.   The mere exposure effect occurs when people who see each other often are more likely to become friends.

14.   b is the answer. The cognitive theory of prejudice suggests that we use schemas and cognitive shortcuts such as social categories. (see Theories of Prejudice and Stereotyping)

a.   The motivational theory of prejudice proposes that people with authoritarian personalities have a tendency to obey people of higher status and discriminate against people of lower status.

c.   The contact hypothesis is not a theory of prejudice, but it is based on the cognitive and learning theories.

d.   Learning theory emphasizes that observational learning and operant conditioning can teach children about stereotypes and prejudice.

15.   c is the answer. Individualist cultures encourage consistency between self-concept and behavior. If this consistency is not demonstrated, one may be derogatorily labeled a hypocrite. (see Changing Attitudes)

a, d.   Research suggests that there are cross-cultural differences.

b.   Collectivist cultures may exhibit less discomfort because behaving differently than one feels is acceptable if it contributes to group harmony.

16.   a is the answer. Motivational theories suggest that people with the trait of authoritarianism act aggressively toward those who are identified as threats by authority figures. (see Theories of Prejudice and Stereotyping)

b.   Aversive racism suggests that negative attitudes toward out-groups may be expressed even by those who do not consider themselves prejudiced. Members of hate groups would not fall into this category.

c.   Learning theories, which propose that people learn prejudice by watching others, is not demonstrated in this question.

d.   Cognitive theories emphasize that the cognitive structures we use to make sense of our social world can contribute to prejudice.

17.   d is the answer. Frequent contact, similar attitudes, and similar attractiveness are associated with positive relationships. (see Keys to Attraction)

    a.   b is also the answer.

    b.   a is also the answer.

    c.   Conflict and anger are part of any relationship. The successful resolution of conflict and anger is indicative of a positive relationship.

18.   c is the answer. Research has shown that next-door neighbors are more likely to become good friends than are people who live at opposite ends of the hall or farther away. (see Keys to Attraction)

    a, b, d.   People tend to like those with whom they have the most contact. Susan will probably have more contact with the women living next door.

19.   c is the answer. Joe and Kacie's similarity in attitudes and values are likely to buffer them from the risk of divorce. (see Intimate Relationships and Love)

    a.   Brad and Delanie's inability to communicate about feelings puts them at risk for divorce later into their marriage.

    b.   Phil and Renee's difficulty discussing negative feelings will put them at risk for divorce early in their marriage.

    d.   Similarity tends to promote longevity in marriage, and communication difficulties increase the risk of divorce.

20.   a is the answer. George and Louise's relationship has a high level of intimacy, commitment, and passion. (see Intimate Relationships and Love)

    b.   Companionate love is low on passion but high on intimacy and commitment.

    c.   Fatuous love is high on passion and commitment but low on intimacy.

    d.   Romantic love is high on passion and intimacy but low on commitment.

Now turn to the quiz analysis table at the end of this chapter to find which areas you know well and which areas you need to work on. Circle the numbers in the table for items on Quiz 1 that you answered correctly.

Quiz 2

1.   b is the answer. Although Jack isn't truly "deprived," he is experiencing deprivation compared to what he was used to before. (see Social Comparison)

    a.   Cognitive dissonance is the product of conflicting attitudes.

    c.   There is no such thing as role isolation.

    d.   A self-fulfilling prophecy is an impression that elicits behavior confirming the impression. Jack's impressions are not making him depressed. His standing in comparison to others in his new reference group is making him unhappy.

2.   a is the answer. Jack needs to make a temporal comparison, relating his new salary to his smaller graduate school earnings. If he would do this instead of engaging in the social comparison to others who make more, he might feel better about his salary. (see Social Comparison)

    b.   The social comparison is what Jack is already doing, and it is contributing to his depressed mood. He needs to focus more on a temporal comparison instead.

c, d.　Attributions are explanations for behavior. Jack is not trying to explain behavior.

3.　d is the answer. Our social identity is our belief about our membership in groups. (see Social Identity Theory)

　　a, b.　We may want to be like our peers or idols, but d is the best answer.

　　c.　Self-esteem is our belief about our self-worth.

4.　b is the answer. Terror management theory predicts and has found some evidence to suggest that high self-esteem can buffer one from anxiety brought on by thinking about pain and death. (see Focus on Research Methods: Self-Esteem and the Ultimate Terror)

　　a.　Social identity theory sees our group memberships as governing the way we process information about others who are ingroup versus outgroup members, the way we are motivated to share resources with those persons, and so forth.

　　c.　Attributional theory has to do with the way we explain our own and other's behavior.

　　d.　Cognitive dissonance theory is a theory about attitude change, not self-esteem and anxiety.

5.　a is the answer. Wenlan sees the other members of her denomination as similar to herself, and thus they are part of her ingroup. (see Biases in Attribution)

　　b.　Outgroup members are people one perceives as different from oneself. Wenlan might have seen Christians from a different denomination as outgroup members.

　　c.　Self-concept refers to the way one thinks about oneself, not about others.

　　d.　Self-esteem refers to the way one evaluates how worthy one is as a human being. This question does not mention Wenlan engaging in evaluation of her own worth.

6.　b is the answer. When Nathan thought about Lance's job, it most likely activated a schema for cashiers or supermarket workers that didn't include interests in poetry and politics. (see The Role of Schemas)

　　a.　Discrimination is the behavioral component of a prejudicial attitude, but it does not bias memory.

　　c.　Social comparison is the process by which we compare ourselves to others. Nathan may have been comparing himself to Lance, but it was not an influence on his memory.

　　d.　The actor-observer effect relates to internal versus external attributions, not memory for personal information.

7.　d is the answer. According to the fundamental attribution error, we usually attribute others' behavior to internal causes. (see Biases in Attribution)

　　a.　According to the fundamental attribution error, we attribute others' behavior to internal causes.

　　b.　According to the self-serving bias, we attribute our successes to internal causes.

　　c.　According to the fundamental attribution error, we usually attribute others' behavior to internal, not external, causes.

8.　d is the answer. Low consistency, high consensus, and high distinctiveness would lead to an external attribution. (see Explaining Behavior: Attribution)

　　a, b, c.　High consistency means that a person always behaves in a similar manner. Low consensus means that not many people display a particular behavior. Low distinctiveness means that the behavior occurs in many situations. These features would lead one to attribute someone's behavior to an internal cause; that person often displays the behavior in many situations, whereas other people do not. The behavior is probably due to a characteristic of the person, not to an external cause.

9.   b is the answer. The actor-observer effect occurs when we make a comparison. We attribute our own behavior to external factors (just checking) but assert that others' behavior is due to internal factors (not being very smart). (see Biases in Attribution)

   a.   The fundamental attribution error does not involve an attribution about ourselves. It is a tendency to ascribe others' behavior to internal factors. If Sal simply made an observation about the other students and did not explain his own behavior in terms of external causes, this answer would apply.

   c.   Unrealistic optimism is the tendency to believe that positive events are more likely to happen to oneself than to others. It does not apply here.

   d.   Self-perception involves determining attitudes from behaviors. This question concerns differential explanations for a behavior.

10.   b is the answer. According to the self-serving bias, we take credit for success but blame external causes for failure. Nicole's mother is taking credit for Nicole's good habits and qualities but not for her bad ones. (see Biases in Attribution)

   a.   According to the fundamental attribution error, Nicole's mother should attribute Nicole's behavior to Nicole's internal characteristics. Instead, she believes that the causes of Nicole's behavior are her and her husband's style of raising their daughter (characteristics that are external to Nicole).

   c.   The actor-observer effect is the tendency to attribute our own behavior to an external cause. Nicole's mother is making attributions about Nicole's behavior, not her own.

   d.   People experience relative deprivation when they compare themselves to others who have a higher standard of living.

11.   b is the answer. Cognitive dissonance is internal tension due to conflicting attitudes or components of attitudes. (see Changing Attitudes)

   a.   Prejudice is a preformed negative or positive attitude toward an entire group of people. Stereotypes can lead to prejudice.

   c.   The fundamental attribution error refers to mistakes made in explaining the causes of behavior.

   d.   Relative deprivation occurs when, as a new member of a reference group, a person's standing in comparison to others is low.

12.   d is the answer. According to self-perception theory, we look for clues in our actions when we have no attitude about something. Since George had eaten so many oysters, he concluded that he must like them. (see Changing Attitudes)

   a.   Cognitive dissonance results from inconsistency between belief and behavior. An attitude must already exist before there can be cognitive dissonance.

   b.   The elaboration likelihood model provides an explanation for attitude change. George is forming a new attitude in this question, not changing an old one.

   c.   Social learning theory from the chapter on learning suggests that we learn much by observing the behavior of others. (See Chapter 6 to review this topic.)

13. b is the answer. Mark is not thinking critically about the dating service. He is using appearances (happy couples) to make his decision. (see Changing Attitudes)

    a.   A central route would be one that considers the content of the message to be more important than the communicator.

    c.   Cognitive "busyness" occurs when we are involved in thinking about something other than the decision to be made. It makes a peripheral route to decision-making more likely. Mark is not described as being busy thinking about something else.

    d.   Cognitive dissonance occurs when thoughts, behaviors, and attitudes are inconsistent with one another.

14. c is the answer. Cooperation is an important factor in determining the success of contact in reducing prejudice. Activities like the jigsaw technique often help reduce prejudice. (see Reducing Prejudice)

    a, d.   A sports competition or the singling out of a few individuals will probably not reduce prejudices and, in fact, may worsen them.

    b.   A presentation of information may help students understand each other, but it won't be as effective as having the students cooperate.

15. c is the answer. Cognitive dissonance, unlike self-perception, involves internal tension caused by discrepant or conflicting attitudes. According to self-perception theory, people who are unsure about their attitudes examine their past behavior. This does not involve any uneasiness or internal tension. (see Changing Attitudes)

    a.   Cognitive dissonance and self-perception theory both involve attitudes.

    b.   Self-perception does not involve social facilitation.

    d.   c is the answer.

16. a is the answer. Social cognitive neuroscience is the study of the reciprocal influence of social processes on biological processes. It often involves the use of an MRI to determine how social interaction influences brain activity, or EEG technology to determine how social activity influences, and is influenced by, nervous system activity. (see Linkages: Biological and Social Psychology)

    b, c, d.   Attitude change, social identity, and prejudice could be studied using these technologies, but wouldn't have to be. Social cognitive neuroscientists need these technologies to answer their research questions.

17. c is the answer. Prejudice is a positive or negative attitude toward an individual based on the individual's group membership. Stereotypes are beliefs about members of groups. (see Prejudice and Stereotypes)

    a.   Behavior would correspond to discrimination, not prejudice; attitude would correspond to prejudice.

    b.   Although it is true that attitude corresponds to prejudice, behavior does not correspond to stereotype—belief does.

    d.   This is reversed. Attitude corresponds to prejudice, and belief to stereotype.

18. b is the answer. Aversive racism is the theory that even though many European Americans consider ethnic prejudice to be unacceptable, they will still sometimes display it, especially when they can so do without admitting they are prejudiced. Ryan's shorter interaction time with African

Americans suggests some discomfort and prejudice, but he is probably not even aware of this pattern. (see Thinking Critically: Is Ethnic Prejudice Too Ingrained Ever to Be Eliminated?)

    a.   Sternberg's triangular theory of love classifies different types of relationships.

    c.   Cognitive dissonance is a theory of attitude change.

    d.   The elaboration likelihood model is a theory of attitude change.

19.   c is the answer. Companionate love is characterized by intimacy and commitment, but lacks passion. This question describes high intimacy and high commitment, but says nothing about passion between Shelly and Eric. (see Intimate Relationships and Love)

    a.   Romantic love is composed of high levels of passion and intimacy but low levels of commitment. Shelly and Eric are high on intimacy, but not on passion. They also have high commitment, which romantic love lacks.

    b.   Consummate love is characterized by high levels of intimacy, commitment, and passion. The relationship described here does not appear high on passion.

    d.   Only c is the answer.

20.   c is the answer. Often when the first child is born, the wife experiences more work than anticipated, and if the husband does not share in the work, Sarah's marital satisfaction will decline. (see Intimate Relationships and Love)

    a.   Russ's satisfaction may decline, but more evidence suggests that the wife's will decline.

    b.   The birth of the first child rarely increases marital satisfaction initially.

    d.   Sarah's satisfaction is more likely to decline than increase.

Now turn to the quiz analysis table at the end of this chapter to find which areas you know well and which areas you need to work on. Circle the numbers in the table for items on Quiz 2 that you answered correctly.

For each question you answered correctly, circle its number. (Quiz 1 numbers are not shaded; Quiz 2 numbers are shaded.) Are there patterns in the types of questions or the topics you got wrong that could direct your further study? Did you improve from Quiz 1 to Quiz 2?

QUIZ REVIEW

Topic	Type of Question		
	Definition	Comprehension	Application
Introductory Section	1		
Social Influences on the Self			
Social Comparison	2		8
			1, 2
Focus on Research Methods: Self-Esteem and the Ultimate Terror		4	
Social Identity Theory			4
	3		
Social Perception			
The Role of Schemas			
			6
First Impressions			5, 6
Explaining Behavior: Attribution			10
		8	
Biases in Attribution	3, 7	9	12
	7		5, 9, 10
The Self-Protective Functions of Social Cognition			11
Attitudes			
Changing Attitudes		15	13
		11, 15	12, 13
Linkages: Biological and Social Psychology			
		16	
Prejudice and Stereotypes			
		17	
Theories of Prejudice and Stereotyping			14, 16
Reducing Prejudice			
			14
Thinking Critically: Is Ethnic Prejudice Too Ingrained Ever to Be Eliminated?			
			18
Interpersonal Attraction			
Keys to Attraction		17	18
Intimate Relationships and Love			19, 20
			19, 20

Total correct by quiz:

Quiz 1:	
Quiz 2:	

CHAPTER 18

Social Influence

OUTLINE

Social influence is the process by which one's thoughts, feelings, and behaviors are directly or indirectly affected by the words or actions of other people.

I. SOCIAL INFLUENCE
Social norms are learned social rules that prescribe what people should or should not do in various situations. *Descriptive norms* communicate what other people do. *Injunctive norms* tell us what others would approve or disapprove of. The *reciprocity norm* is a powerful injunctive norm. The social influence exerted by norms creates orderly social behavior. We learn them from parents, teachers, clergy, peers, and other cultural agents.

Social influences also create deindividuation, a personal loss of individuality that occurs as people become "submerged" within a group. A deindividuating experience can cause people to perform acts they normally wouldn't because personal accountability is diminished and attention shifts from internal behavioral standards to the external group standards.

A. Linkages: Motivation and the Presence of Others
Social factors often influence motivation. Social facilitation occurs when the presence of another person improves performance, and social interference occurs when another's presence harms performance. Levels of arousal, task complexity, the expectations of peer evaluation, and increased self-evaluation interact to produce these phenomena. Social loafing occurs when people in a group exert less effort than they would when performing alone. People engage in social loafing for three reasons: it is harder to evaluate individual performance in a group context, rewards come to the group whether or not every member exerts maximum effort, and those rewards are usually divided equally regardless of member effort. Social loafing is less common in Eastern cultures where *social striving* may be observed.

II. CONFORMITY AND COMPLIANCE
Conformity results from unspoken group pressure, real or imagined. Compliance occurs when people adjust their behavior in response to a request.

A. The Role of Norms
Group norms tend to affect people's behavior even after the people are no longer members of that group. Conformity is especially likely in collectivist cultures.

B. Why Do People Conform?
Norms provide information about what is correct, and people like to be correct. Thus. they tend to conform to social norms. Conforming to group norms also can increase one's sense of personal worth. Norms may also influence the distribution of rewards and punishment, so conforming to norms may increase one's potential reward in a situation.

C. When Do People Conform?
1. *Ambiguity of the Situation*. The more uncertain the situation, the more people rely on the opinions of others.

2. *Unanimity and Size of the Majority.* Conformity is greatest when a group decision is unanimous. The larger the size of the majority, the more conformity is observed, generally speaking. *Social impact theory* argues that increasing the size of the majority will have impact on the level of conformity, but that impact depends on the size the majority was in the first place.

3. *Minority Influence. Minority influence* is less common than conformity to a majority opinion. When they are persistent and united, minorities can influence the behavior or beliefs of a majority, especially on private acceptance.

4. *Gender.* Gender differences in public conformity stem from men's desire to be seen as independent and women's desire to be seen as cooperative—not on genuinely different reactions to social pressure.

D. Creating Compliance

People can be induced to comply with requests by starting with small requests, as in the *foot-in-the-door technique*; by starting with an unreasonable request, as in the *door-in-the-face technique*; or by gaining verbal agreement for one request and then demonstrating the need to escalate the cost of the original commitment, as in the *low-ball technique*.

III. OBEDIENCE

Obedience is a behavioral change in response to a demand from an authority figure. Stanley Milgram created a procedure to measure obedience. He developed a situation in which participants thought they were delivering shocks to a person, but the person was never actually shocked. When confederates complained about the pain of the shock they were supposedly receiving, Milgram demanded that the participants continue to deliver the shocks. Despite feeling stressed, 65 percent of the participants delivered the full 450 volts of shock possible.

A. Factors Affecting Obedience

1. *Experimenter Status and Prestige.* When the status and legitimacy of the experimenter were reduced, obedience decreased, but only from 65 to 48 percent.

2. *The Behavior of Other People.* The presence of others who disobeyed decreased obedience to 10 percent. Further, the behavior of the victim matters—when the victim escalated protests of pain it did *not* affect obedience, but when the victim asked to be released from the experiment people did seem more likely to respond with disobedience at that point.

3. *Personality Characteristics.* Although social influences are the strongest factor in obedience, people high in *authoritarianism* were more likely than others to shock the learner. People with high levels of *empathy* were less likely to continue to shock the learner.

B. Evaluating Milgram's Studies

Recent tragedies that occurred as a result of unquestioning obedience to authority suggest that Milgram's findings are still relevant and important.

1. *Questions about the Ethics of Milgram's Research.* Some observers say that the experiment was unethical. However, Milgram argued that his debriefing procedure and continued contact with his participants showed that it was a positive experience. Ethical questions are difficult ones. Milgram's study would probably not be approved by today's ethics committees.

2. *Questions about the Meaning of Milgram's Research.* It has been suggested that alternative explanations could account for the participants' behavior. However, most psychologists believe that, under certain circumstances, human beings are capable of extreme acts of brutality toward other humans.

IV. AGGRESSION

<u>Aggression</u> is an act intended to harm another person. Nearly 1.4 million violent crimes are committed each year in the United States.

A. Why Are People Aggressive?

According to Freud, aggression is an inborn instinct that needs release in behavior. Evolutionary psychologists believe that aggression aided the survival of gene pools and was passed down through generations. Aggressive behavior results from a nurture/nature interaction.

1. *Genetic and Biological Mechanisms.* Research demonstrates hereditary influences on aggressive behavior. Lesions within certain brain areas like the limbic system can lead to *defensive aggression*, and male hormones such as testosterone (especially in the prenatal environment) are associated with higher levels of aggression. Drugs may also affect aggression, as can neurotransmitters. Lower levels of serotonin are linked with higher levels of impulsive aggression.

2. *Learning and Cultural Mechanisms.* Aggression is more common in individualistic than collectivistic cultures. Even within a country, aggression varies. More males in the southern United States commit homicide than males from the northern states, which has been attributed to endorsement of the *culture of honor.* People learn to be aggressive by watching others or by being reinforced for aggressive acts, which is especially clear from studies of the impact of violent television on aggressive behavior.

B. Thinking Critically: Do Violent Video Games Make People More Aggressive?

What am I being asked to believe or accept?

That exposure to violent video games increases the frequency of aggressive thoughts, feelings, and actions in people who play them.

What evidence is available to support the assertion?

Correlational studies show that the more time people spent playing violent video games, the more aggressive they tended to be. In laboratory experiments on violent video games, researchers found that participants expressed more hostility and aggressive intentions when they were able to "be" characters in the game and when their victims bled when wounded.

Are there alternative ways of interpreting the evidence?

Correlational studies do not speak to causation—it is possible that people who are more aggressive choose to play more violent video games, rather than the games causing the aggression. Laboratory results may not generalize to the real world—artificial measures of aggression may not really tell us about aggression in daily life. Finally, although there is a statistically significant relationship between violent video games and aggression, it is not a strong one, particularly in comparison to other influences.

What additional evidence would help to evaluate the alternatives?

Studies that track the behavior of people who choose to engage in varying amounts of violent game-playing at different ages of development would help to clarify the causal mechanisms. It would also be useful to know what happens in the brains of people who play violent video games.

What conclusions are most reasonable?

Violent video games probably have at least some short-term effects on the people who play them. Questions about how strong the causal relationship is and how long it might last have not yet been answered.

C.   When Are People Aggressive?
1.   *Frustration and Aggression.* According to the modified <u>frustration-aggression hypothesis</u>, stress produces a readiness to respond aggressively, but aggression is displayed only if there are environmental cues associated with an aggressive response. The direct cause of most kinds of aggression is negative affect (emotion).
2.   *Generalized Arousal.* In *transferred excitation*, an internal characteristic and environmental conditions interact to produce aggression. Generalized arousal is most likely to produce aggression when the situation contains some reason, opportunity, or target for aggression.
3.   *Environmental Influences on Aggression.* <u>Environmental psychology</u> is the study of how people's behavior is affected by the environment in which they live. Hot weather, noise, and crowding can all lead to increased aggression.

V.   ALTRUISM AND HELPING BEHAVIOR
<u>Helping behavior</u> (also called <u>prosocial behavior</u>) is any act that is intended to benefit another person. <u>Altruism</u> is an unselfish concern for another's welfare.

A.   Why Do People Help?
1.   *Arousal: Cost-Reward Theory.* The <u>arousal: cost-reward theory</u> suggests that people feel upset when they see a person in need and are motivated to do something to reduce the unpleasant arousal. People then weigh the costs of helping versus not helping. The *clearer* the need for help, the more likely people are to help. The *presence of others* inhibits helping behavior due to *diffusion of responsibility*, a belief that someone else will help. This phenomenon is known as the <u>bystander effect</u>. Environmental and personality characteristics also influence helping. But the arousal: cost-reward theory does not explain environmental influences such as differential helping rates between urban and rural settings very effectively, nor does it address how one will handle situations when the cost of helping and not helping are both high.
2.   *Empathy-Altruism Theory.* According to the <u>empathy-altruism theory</u> (also called <u>empathy-altruism helping theory</u>), helpfulness is seen in those who have empathy with the person in need. Critics argue that it is not empathy that promotes helping, but a desire to relive one's negative emotional state that occurs when one sees someone in need of help.
3.   *Evolutionary Theory.* Evolutionary theories propose that people help others to ensure the survival of their genes, at the risk of endangering themselves. *Kin selection* (helping a relative to survive) has evolutionary benefit.

B.   Focus on Research Methods: Does Family Matter?
Researchers cannot ethically put people in danger to see who will help them; therefore, researchers used a laboratory simulation, or analogue. Participants were asked to imagine situations in which they could help only one of three people. The outcome of the experiment indicates that people describe themselves as more likely to save the life of, or do a favor for, a close relative than an unrelated friend in a hypothetical situation. However, since this was a laboratory situation, caution must be used in making generalizations to the real world.

VI.   COOPERATION, COMPETITION, AND CONFLICT
<u>Cooperation</u> is any type of behavior in which people work together to attain a goal. <u>Competition</u> exists whenever people try to attain a goal for themselves while denying that goal to others. <u>Conflict</u> results when people believe that another stands in the way of achieving a goal.

A.   Social Dilemmas
<u>Social dilemmas</u> are situations in which an action that is most rewarding for each individual will, if adopted by all, become negative or even catastrophic for the group.

1. *The Prisoner's Dilemma.* Researchers have created a <u>prisoner's dilemma game</u> in which cooperation guarantees the best mutual outcome but in which there are incentives to compete. Players cannot be certain that their partners will cooperate. This makes it a *mixed- motive conflict* because there are good reasons to both cooperate and compete. Research shows that people tend to respond competitively because winning is rewarding and competition seems to beget more competitive behavior.
2. *Resource Dilemmas.* When people share a common resource, conflicts exist between the individual and the group, and between short- and long-term interests.

B. Promoting Cooperation
Cooperation increases when non-threatening and relevant communications increase. Playing tit-for-tat, or rewarding cooperative responses with cooperation, and punishing exploitative strategies with like actions, produces a high degree of overall cooperation.

C. Interpersonal Conflict
When one person can win only at another's expense, it is a <u>zero-sum game</u>, which can lead to interpersonal conflict. There are four major causes: compromise may seem too costly after investing so much, attributing another's motives to selfishness or unfriendliness, faulty communication, and the belief that the other side is uninterested in reaching compromise.

1. *Managing Conflict.* Conflict can lead to beneficial changes. It is much better to manage conflict than to eliminate it. *Bargaining*, *third-party interventions*, and the introduction of *superordinate goals* are all methods of managing conflict.

VII. GROUP PROCESSES
A. Group Leadership
In general, good leaders are agreeable, conscientious, extraverted, and emotionally stable. Leadership ability also depends on the situation and on the person's style of handling it. Both the <u>task-motivated leaders</u> and the <u>relationship-motivated leaders</u> are effective, depending on the structure of the group's task and the time pressure the group is under. *Transactional leaders* lead in ways that depend on follower actions, rewarding those who behave as they wish and punishing those who don't. *Transformational leaders* focus on creating a vision and giving their followers a reason to respect them. Research has uncovered gender differences in leadership. Initial findings suggested that men tend to be more successful when the task calls for a task-motivated leader, but women tend to be more successful leaders when the situation calls for a relationship-motivated leader. Alice Eagly's recent work suggests that women may have a slight edge over men in leadership, however.

B. Groupthink
In small, closely-knit groups, decisions can reflect a process called <u>groupthink</u>, a pattern of thinking that renders members unable to evaluate decisions realistically. Groupthink occurs when the group feels isolated from outside forces, intense stressors are experienced, and the leader has already made up his or her mind. Assigning someone a "devil's advocate" role and arranging ways to gather opinions anonymously can help avoid groupthink.

KEY TERMS

1. **Social influence** is the process whereby one person's behavior is affected by the words or actions of others. (see introductory section)

    Example: Kelly is talking to her friends, who all say they love sushi. Even though she doesn't, she chimes in about how great sushi is, too.

2. **Social norms** are socially based rules that prescribe what people should or should not do in various situations. (see Social Influence)

Example: Many of your daily behaviors follow the social norms present in our culture. Sometimes it is easier to understand norms by thinking about what would happen if they were broken. Think, for instance, what would happen if you broke the social norm dictating that you may not go shopping wearing only your underwear.

REMEMBER: Norms vary with the culture, subculture, and situation.

3. **Deindividuation** is a psychological state occurring in group members that results in loss of individuality and a tendency to do things not normally done when alone. (see Social Influence)

   Example: Molly is usually a very quiet individual. However, when in the crowd at a football game, she joined others in jeering and booing the officials.

4. **Social facilitation** is a phenomenon in which the presence of others improves a person's performance. (see Linkages: Motivation and the Presence of Others)

   Example: Jon doesn't run as fast by himself as he does when in a race.

5. **Social interference** is a reduction in performance due to the presence of other people. (see Linkages: Motivation and the Presence of Others)

   Example: Tony has practiced the song "Mad Man" on his bongo drums only a few times and is now playing it for his instructor. He is making even more mistakes than he did when he practiced by himself.

   REMEMBER: Usually, new, complex, or difficult tasks are most vulnerable to social interference.

6. **Social loafing** is exerting less effort when performing a group task than when performing the same task alone. (see Linkages: Motivation and the Presence of Others)

   Example: Helmut is a bright but lazy individual. In work groups at the office, he goes to all the meetings on his projects but exerts very little effort, knowing that nobody will really be able to measure his personal performance in the group.

7. **Conformity** refers to changing one's behavior or beliefs to match those of others, generally as a result of real or imagined, though unspoken, group pressure. (see Conformity and Compliance)

   Example: Jill wears a suit to the office because all her coworkers wear suits.

8. **Compliance** is adjusting one's behavior because of an explicit or implicit request. (see Conformity and Compliance)

   Example: Carlotta, Cecelia, and Carmen are sisters. Their mother tells them that if they want to go swimming, they must all clean their rooms. Carlotta and Cecelia hurry to straighten their rooms, but Carmen at first refuses to touch the mess in her bedroom. After Carlotta and Cecelia repeatedly ask Carmen to help, Carmen finally complies and cleans her room.

9. **Obedience** is changing behavior in response to a demand from an authority figure. (see Obedience)

   Example: Carlotta's mother tells her that she must clean her room, and Carlotta obeys.

10. **Aggression** is an act intended to cause harm to another person. (see Aggression)

    Example: Ned is playing in the sandbox at the playground when other children begin to insult him. He retaliates by throwing sand in their faces with the express purpose of hurting them.

11. The **frustration-aggression hypothesis** is a proposition that frustration always leads to some form of aggressive behavior. (see When Are People Aggressive?)

Example: After attempting nine slam dunks of the basketball and missing them all, Kimberly is in a bad mood. She notices a bully shoving her brother around the park. Although not usually violent, she reacts by punching the bully in the stomach.

12. **Environmental psychology** is the study of the relationship between behavior and the physical environment. (see When Are People Aggressive?)

    Example: Heat, air pollution, noise, and overcrowding are environmental factors that contribute to aggression. Bill is a paramedic in Chicago. He hates the summer because the number of violent calls his ambulance receives increases dramatically as the temperature rises in June, July, and August.

13. **Helping behavior** (or **prosocial behavior**) is any act that is intended to benefit another person. (see Altruism and Helping Behavior)

    Example: Sophie knows that one of her best friends is working extremely hard and has barely enough time to clean, cook, and do laundry. Sophie, an excellent cook, prepares three weeks' worth of dinners for her friend.

14. **Altruism** is an unselfish concern for another person's welfare. (see Altruism and Helping Behavior)

    Example: People who sacrifice their own lives in order to save others' are acting altruistically.

15. The **arousal: cost-reward theory** attributes people's helping behavior to their efforts to reduce the unpleasant arousal they feel in the face of someone's need or suffering. (see Why Do People Help?)

    Example: Juan feels terrible when he sees that Mary's fall on the sidewalk has injured her and scattered her packages everywhere. He knows that he'll be late to work if he helps, but after a moment he decides that his guilt over not helping would be worse than having to explain his late arrival.

    REMEMBER: People will help if the costs of not helping outweigh the costs of helping.

16. The **bystander effect** is a phenomenon in which the chances that someone will help in an emergency decrease as the number of people present increases. (See Why Do People Help?)

    Example: Lori's car breaks down on a busy highway, and no one stops to help. She thinks it is odd, because last time she had car trouble, the first person who went by stopped to help. Of course, last time she broke down she was in the middle of a rural area that was not very well traveled.

17. The **empathy-altruism theory** (also known as **empathy-altruism helping theory**) suggests that people help others because of empathy with their needs. (see Why Do People Help?)

    Example: Sandeep knows what it feels like to be totally confused about a homework assignment, so he feels badly for his classmate Randy and stays after class to clarify the directions. Other students who don't feel empathy for Randy leave the two to work out the problem together.

18. **Cooperation** is any type of behavior in which people work together to attain a goal. (see Cooperation, Competition, and Conflict)

    Example: Claudia and Missy are sisters. Until they were teenagers, they could not stand each other. However, once they realized that they were interested in breaking the same parental rules, they began to cooperate and cover for each other.

19. **Competition** is behavior in which individuals try to attain a goal for themselves while denying that goal to others. (see Cooperation, Competition, and Conflict)

Example: James is very intelligent. He knows that he can win a scholarship given to the highest-ranking student at the end of the year. He formulates a competitive strategy and stops tutoring his classmates.

20. **Conflict** is the result of a person's or group's belief that another person or group stands in the way of their achieving a valued goal. (see Cooperation, Competition, and Conflict)

21. A **social dilemma** is a situation in which actions that produce rewards for one individual will produce negative consequences if adopted by everyone. (see Social Dilemmas)

    Example: If one person in a residence hall chooses to litter the hallway with unwanted papers, the behavior may be rewarded by its ease in ridding the person of garbage. If everyone chooses to litter the hallways, however, the hallways will eventually be too full of garbage to walk through.

22. The **prisoner's dilemma game** is a social dilemma scenario in which mutual cooperation guarantees the best mutual outcome. (see Social Dilemmas)

    Example: Alison's video game gives the greatest number of total points when both players press the "buddies" button. Alison gets more points individually, however, when the other player presses the "buddies" button and Alison presses the "rivals" button. The risk is that if they both push the "rivals" button, they lose their points, but neither knows what the other will do. Alison thinks that getting the same number of points as the other player by pressing the "buddies" button is not very interesting; therefore, she decides to press the "rivals" button once in a while.

    REMEMBER: Pairs of subjects are presented with a choice of behaviors. One choice does nothing for either subject; another choice moderately rewards both subjects; and a third rewards one subject and does nothing for the other subject.

23. **Zero-sum games** are social situations in which one person's gains are subtracted from another person's resources so that the sum of the gains and losses is zero. (see Interpersonal Conflict)

    Example: At a swim meet, one person is declared the winner of each race. The other swimmers may place second or third in a race, but they cannot win.

24. **Task-motivated leaders** are leaders who provide close supervision, lead by directives, and generally discourage group discussion. (see Group Leadership)

    Example: Rebecca knows that to get the construction estimate out by noon, she'll need to give each worker a job. As they work on their separate contributions, she'll track their progress to ensure that each can accomplish her or his part. Rebecca doesn't think it's necessary to get the workers' opinions, especially since there is not much time.

25. **Relationship-motivated leaders** are leaders who provide loose supervision, ask for group members' ideas, and are concerned with subordinates' feelings. (see Group Leadership)

    Example: Each time his group has a new project, Lorcan first asks group members to contribute ideas without censoring them. Eventually the group works together to choose the best ideas and Lorcan tries to ensure that everyone is in agreement.

26. **Groupthink** is a pattern of thinking in which group members fail to evaluate realistically the wisdom of various options and decisions. (see Groupthink)

    Example: The union leaders discussing the latest contract proposal tend to ignore any suggestion that it is fair. The head of the union does not believe they should accept any contract that gives them a cut in pay. The small group discussing it is unaware that some union members are willing to make that sacrifice; therefore, they keep rejecting the company's offers.

FILL-IN-THE-BLANKS KEY TERMS

This section will help you check your factual knowledge of the key terms introduced in this chapter. Fill in each blank with the appropriate term from the list of key terms in the previous section.

1.   A change in behavior that occurs in response to unspoken pressure from a group is called
     _____.

2.   _____ occurs when people comply with a demand because they think they must do so.

3.   When a person changes his or her behavior in response to a spoken request, it is called
     _____.

4.   Any act that is intended to harm another person is considered _____.

5.   _____ are social rules that indicate correct and incorrect behavior in various social situations.

6.   When individuals working in a group don't work as hard as they would if they were working alone, _____ has occurred.

7.   The study of how a person's surroundings affect his or her behavior is part of _____.

8.   Concern for another's welfare above and beyond one's own is called _____.

9.   People who believe that helping behavior occurs because people are upset by a person's misfortune and think the price of helping is not too high would agree with the _____ theory.

10. _____ is any type of behavior in which people work together to attain a goal.

11. Behaviors that reward each individual but would harm the group if everyone did them lead to a
     _____.

12. Sometimes in a crowd people do things they wouldn't normally do. They are probably experiencing _____.

13. _____ leaders provide close supervision, suggest behavior, and discourage group discussion.

14. _____ proposes that people will help others when they can relate to the problems of the person in need.

15. A person whose performance was improved by the presence of other people has experienced
     _____.

Total Correct (See answer key) _____

LEARNING OBJECTIVES

1.   Define social norms (including *descriptive* and *injunctive norms*) and describe their influence on social behavior. (see "Social Influence")

2.   Define deindividuation and describe the factors that cause it. (see "Social Influence")

3.   Define and give examples of social facilitation and social interference. Describe the social factors that influence motivation and define social loafing. (see "Linkages: Motivation and the Presence of Others")

4. Compare and contrast <u>conformity</u> and <u>compliance</u>. Describe the role of norms in conformity and compliance. (see "Conformity and Compliance")

5. Describe the factors that lead to conformity. Explain how factors of ambiguity, unanimity, minority influence, and gender affect when people conform. (see "Why Do People Conform?"; see also "When Do People Conform?")

6. Explain the strategies for inducing compliance, including *foot-in-the-door technique*, *door-in-the-face procedure*, and *low-ball approach*. (see "Inducing Compliance")

7. Define <u>obedience</u>. Describe Milgram's study and his findings on obedience. (see "Obedience")

8. Name and describe the factors that influence obedience. (see "Factors Affecting Obedience")

9. Discuss the ethical considerations in carrying out an experiment like Milgram's. (see "Ethical Questions")

10. Define <u>aggression</u>. Describe the Freudian and evolutionary theories of aggression. (see "Aggression"; see also "Why Are People Aggressive?")

11. Describe the genetic and biological influences on aggression. Discuss the roles of areas of the brain, hormones, and drugs in aggressive behavior. (see "Genetic and Biological Mechanisms")

12. Describe the role of learning and cultural mechanisms, including *culture of honor* and observational learning, in aggression. (see "Learning and Cultural Mechanisms")

13. Discuss the question of whether exposure to violent video games leads to an increase in aggression. (see "Thinking Critically: Do Violent Video Games Make People More Aggressive?")

14. Define the <u>frustration-aggression hypothesis</u>. Describe the role of generalized arousal and *excitation transfer* in aggression. (see "Frustration and Aggression")

15. Define <u>environmental psychology</u> and describe the environmental influences on aggression. (see "Environmental Influences on Aggression")

16. Define <u>helping behavior</u> and <u>altruism</u>. Describe the development of helping behavior. (see "Altruism and Helping Behavior")

17. Discuss how the <u>arousal: cost-reward theory</u> explains helping behavior. Describe the characteristics of situations in which people would or would not be likely to display helping behavior. Define <u>bystander effect</u> and *diffusion of responsibility*. (see "Arousal: Cost-Reward Theory")

18. Describe the <u>empathy-altruism</u> and evolutionary theories of helping. Discuss the study of helping behavior through a laboratory analogue experiment. Explain what conclusions are reasonable. (see "Empathy-Altruism Theory"; see also "Evolutionary Theory"; see also "Focus on Research Methods: Does Family Matter?")

19. Define <u>cooperation</u>, <u>competition</u>, and <u>conflict</u>. (see "Cooperation, Competition, and Conflict")

20. Define <u>social dilemmas</u> and the tit-for-tat strategy. Describe the research findings from experiments with <u>prisoner's dilemma games</u>. Explain the two types of resource dilemmas. (see "Social Dilemmas")

21. Describe ways to foster cooperation. (see "Promoting Cooperation")

22. Define <u>zero-sum games</u>. Describe the four main causes of interpersonal conflict. Explain why managing conflict effectively is better than trying to eliminate it. (see "Interpersonal Conflict")

23. Describe the personality characteristics of a good leader. Define the <u>task-oriented</u> and <u>person-oriented</u> *transactional* and *transformational leaders*. Explain the research on gender and leadership styles. (see "Group Leadership")

24. Define <u>groupthink</u>. What can be done to minimize or prevent it from happening? (see "Groupthink")

CONCEPTS AND EXERCISES

Group Decision Making

Shereif is the president of a major corporation. He wants to give a problem to three different groups of his top management people. Match the descriptions of each group's interaction with the appropriate term from the list below.

1. Group 1, a very tightly knit group, made a decision that surprised everyone. Consultants had even been called in, but the group disagreed with their suggestions. Finally, the leader made the decision and asked the "troops to rally 'round." _____

2. Gordon spent an hour at the beginning of the meeting gathering the opinions of all group members. At the end of four hours, the group agreed on a plan of action that incorporated many of the members' opinions. _____

3. Angela spent the first thirty minutes delegating jobs for individuals to carry out. At the end of four hours, each individual presented his or her results. Angela did not encourage group discussion. _____

   a. Groupthink

   b. Task-motivated leadership

   c. Relationship-motivated leadership

Sales Training

George fits the stereotype of a particularly sleazy used car salesman, but he sells new cars. He trains his new staff by telling them about some of the successful strategies he has used in the past. Use the following list to name the strategies that George is describing: *low-ball; foot-in-the-door; door-in-the-face; reciprocity norm.*

1. "To get people to spend money on cars, especially on the extras, you gotta get 'em warmed up to the idea a little at a time. First, get them to buy the inexpensive extras, like power locks. Then you can move up to the medium-priced gadgets, like a better-than-average stereo. When they agree to buy the car and all the gadgets you've sold so far, go for the big, expensive ones, like a sunroof." _____

2. "Guys come in here all the time lookin' for a car that basically does the same thing, ya know. I mean he has to drive to work, the wife goes to the grocery store, and he takes the kids to baseball practice. Ninety percent of the guys coming in here will tell ya the same thing. But we got a problem. We have to sell a variety of cars. Sometimes it's easy 'cause this guy likes the red one and that guy likes the blue one. But if you have to move inventory, get a guy to agree to buy a moderately priced car. Get him all excited about how great that car is, how good he is going to look in it, and on and on. Then tell him, oops! you forgot; it isn't available anymore. Then show him one that is even more expensive. I guarantee you, nine times outta ten, he's gonna buy it." _____

3. "So you got a customer who is worried about spending too much money. So show him all the really expensive cars that are definitely out of his price range. When he starts to get a little fussy, tell him he's right; you shouldn't have been trying to sell him an expensive car. Then start showing him the price range he can afford. After seein' all those big price tickets on the fancy cars, the one he buys will seem small in comparison. You'll probably even be able to get an extra thousand or so outta him for the car." _____

CRITICAL THINKING

Several days ago, there was an assault on a woman during a huge demonstration against nuclear weapons. Those responsible for the attack ran off before the police got there. Martina and Sam have obtained a list of anti-nuclear weapons members who were supposed to have been at the demonstration. They are pulling all twenty-three in for possible identification by the victim. Martina is waiting for the twenty-first individual on the list when Sam hauls a big burly guy into the office. "Martina," he says with a smug grin, "this is our guy!"

Martina looks up and says, "So this is number twenty-one, huh?"

"Nah," Sam replies. "This is number twenty-two, Bruce Robe. I checked on twenty-one, a guy named Mikey Smitt. What a loser. He's this timid little pip-squeak of a guy. No way he could have landed the punches that made the bruises on that woman's face."

Martina looks at Robe and asks, "Do you have an alibi for the date in question?" Robe, looking furious, says, "You bet I do. I've been trying to tell that to this monkey of a partner of yours ever since he yanked me away from my breakfast this morning."

Martina patiently listens to Robe's story, then makes a few phone calls and verifies his alibi. Martina says gruffly to Sam. "Go get number twenty-one. I think he is our guy."

Sam is angry. "No way. This is our guy. He's lyin' about where he was. That other guy is this timid mouse. I bet he doesn't even know how to throw a punch, let alone have the guts to do it!"

Martina sighs. "Just go and bring Mikey Smitt in for questioning. NOW!"

Using the five critical thinking questions in your text, the clues in the story, and what you have learned about behavior, answer the following.

1. What is Sam's hypothesis?

2. What evidence supports Sam's hypothesis?

3. What is Martina's alternative hypothesis?

4. What evidence supports Martina's hypothesis?

5. What conclusions are reasonable?

Personal Learning Activities

1. Visit the following website to learn how social norms can be used to promote healthy behavior at the following site: http://www.socialnorm.org/. Here, you can see how social influence provides a way to promote desirable behaviors in situations where information alone does not persuade people to behave rationally. Do you think this approach will be effective? Better than persuasion based on information and argument? Why or why not?

2. Violate a norm as an experiment. (Don't do anything dangerous or illegal, of course!) Perhaps you could stand at a door and open it for each approaching person or make a paper hat and walk around in public wearing it. It would also violate a norm if you sat right next to someone when

there were many empty seats on a bus. How did other people react to you? How did it make you feel? Based on your experience, outline some of the reasons people generally follow norms.

3. Try to get someone to comply with a request by using the foot-in-the-door technique, the door-in-the-face procedure, or the low-ball approach. For example, you might see if someone is more likely to photocopy notes for you, help you pick up litter, or carry your backpack if you try one of the above methods rather than just asking.

4. To see a modern version of Milgram's experiments, watch the following YouTube clip: http://www.youtube.com/watch?v=HwqNP9HRy7Y. What does this suggest about the meaning behind Milgram's results? Do you think that his results were realistic?

5. To play a prisoner's dilemma game online, visit the following site: http://www.gametheory.net/Web/PDilemma/default.htm. Here you can play the game with five different personalities. How do the different personalities approach this situation? Does it affect your willingness to cooperate with them? How could this information be used to promote cooperation in situations like public goods dilemmas or resource dilemmas?

MULTIPLE-CHOICE QUESTIONS

Quiz 1

1. People sometimes behave with fewer inhibitions when they are in a group than when they are alone. This phenomenon is called
    a. diffusion of responsibility.
    b. deindividuation.
    c. situation ambiguity.
    d. social facilitation.

2. Everyone felt very uncomfortable when Ashley kept smiling during a funeral. Ashley's smiling defied
    a. deindividuation.
    b. social facilitation.
    c. social loafing.
    d. a social norm.

3. Nina's auto racing time has not improved in days. Although she knows the course well, she is no longer improving. To increase her speed, Nina should
    a. have someone race against her.
    b. eject her staff and race the course without anyone recording times.
    c. combat deindividuation.
    d. reduce the bystander effect.

4. Shawn's instructor doesn't observe or grade student study group behavior; therefore, Shawn sits back and listens to the other students. Shawn is exhibiting social
    a. facilitation.
    b. interference.
    c. loafing.
    d. penalty.

5. Conformity is highest
    a.   when the stimulus is unambiguous.
    b.   when unanimity exists.
    c.   in men.
    d.   in women.

6. Robert is in an experiment. He is in a pitch-dark room except for one point of light that is projected onto the wall opposite him. There are several other people there. They have to report out loud how far the light moved on repeated trials. Robert's estimate will probably
    a.   converge with the others' estimates over time.
    b.   stay the same over time.
    c.   diverge from the others' estimates over time.
    d.   fluctuate randomly over time.

7. In the door-in-the-face technique,
    a.   larger and larger requests are made.
    b.   a straightforward request is made.
    c.   a very large request is made, followed by a smaller one.
    d.   the original commitment is devalued, and a request is made for more.

8. Ian has just joined a new group of friends. They want to steal the school mascot from a neighboring high school. Ian listens as they plot, then voices reservations about pulling the prank. His friends say, "Won't you come with us? Think of the memories you'll be missing out on if you stay home for this one!" Ian relents and goes with them. Ian has
    a.   conformed.
    b.   complied.
    c.   obeyed.
    d.   competed.

9. Diane is in a faculty meeting. Everyone is discussing whether or not students in the psychology undergraduate degree program should have to pass every class with a C or better to graduate. All the faculty seem to agree that this would be a good idea. Diane is the lone voice that speaks up to say the idea might be problematic, "Hey, you guys, this could really put some pressure on us… A lot of times, these sorts of changes lead to grade inflation!" The group dismisses her and moves on, but Diane keeps bringing up her point. Diane's influence on the final decision will
    a.   depend on how far away in time the decision is—if it is close in time she will have more impact than if it is further away.
    b.   depend on how far away in time the decision is—if it is close in time she will have less impact than if it is further away.
    c.   be inconsequential—she is merely one voice out of the whole faculty.
    d.   be powerful no matter what.

10. Obedience is
    a.   conformity to a request.
    b.   private acceptance of a suggestion.
    c.   yielding to a command from an authority figure.
    d.   a response to aggressive behavior.

11. Diffusion of responsibility occurs when

    a. many people are present when someone needs help.
    b. groups try to make decisions.
    c. a leader divides work equally among his or her staff.
    d. people do not take responsibility for aggressive acts.

12. Which is NOT true of the relationship between playing violent video games and aggression?

    a. People who spend more time playing violent video games tend to be more aggressive.
    b. Playing violent video games in the lab increases aggressive thoughts and feelings.
    c. Playing violent video games has some short term influence on individuals who play them.
    d. Violent video games are a significant cause of aggressive behavior.

13. Agatha is moving to Miami Beach, Florida, to begin her career. She wants to find a very safe apartment to live in. Which of the following should she choose?

    a. An area near the airport because her job requires her to travel quite a bit
    b. An area that has zoning laws restricting the number of occupants per building
    c. An apartment building with no air conditioning
    d. An area near the plant where she works, despite the smell

14. According to the arousal: cost-reward theory, Darlene will be most likely to help the lost child crying in the mall if she

    a. is related to the child.
    b. is very worried for the child's safety and has the time to help.
    c. has been to the mall many times.
    d. knows what it feels like to be a lost child.

15. Dean doesn't properly maintain his car's exhaust system due to the expense. If everyone behaved like Dean, the air pollution would become unbearable; therefore, Dean's situation is an example of a(n)

    a. analogue experiment.
    b. prisoner's dilemma.
    c. social dilemma.
    d. zero-sum game.

16. In an analogue experiment, when people were asked whom they would save in a life-or-death situation, researchers found that

    a. the older, most helpless individuals would be saved.
    b. the younger individuals would be saved.
    c. the closest related person would be saved.
    d. the closest related person who is still reproductively fit would be saved.

17. Tim and Jill are medical students. At the beginning of the semester, Tim does not let Jill borrow his notes. When Tim asks Jill for her notes, she won't let him borrow them. Before the midterm exam, though, he calls her and offers his notes and assistance. Before the final exam, Jill offers her notes and assistance. Tim and Jill are employing which strategy?

    a. Tit-for-tat
    b. Low-ball
    c. Altruism
    d. Foot-in-the-door

18. Darrell and Tomer's softball teams have a friendly rivalry. Because only one team can win, they often try to distract each other while competing. Darrell and Tomer are participating in a(n)

    a. injunctive norm.
    b. prisoner's dilemma.
    c. tit-for-tat strategy.
    d. zero-sum game.

19. Bernadette is a task-motivated leader. This means she will

    a. provide loose supervision.
    b. ask for group members' ideas.
    c. be concerned with subordinates' feelings.
    d. probably not be terribly well liked by subordinates.

20. Wing, the president of the student council, wants to reduce the likelihood of groupthink. In order to be successful, he should

    a. isolate the group from other student groups.
    b. forcefully explain his position before allowing others to contribute ideas.
    c. suggest that everyone contribute suggestions anonymously.
    d. use task-motivated leadership.

Total Correct (See answer key) _____

Quiz 2

Use this quiz to reassess your learning after taking Quiz 1 and reviewing the chapter.

1. Why do social norms influence behavior to such a great degree?

    a.   They allow us to predict the behavior of others.
    b.   They let us know which behaviors will be rewarded.
    c.   They let us know how to behave in new situations.
    d.   All of these

2. At the football game, Luis felt swept up in the excitement and rushed onto the field with the rest of the fans. If Luis had thought things through, he would not have helped the mob push over the goal posts, but he experienced

    a.   deindividuation.
    b.   diffusion of responsibility.
    c.   social facilitation.
    d.   compliance.

3. Claudette is a piano major. She has been practicing for her end-of-the-semester performance for four months and has the music memorized. At her lessons, however, she plays lackadaisically. Her teacher wants to prepare her for her performance and arranges to have a few faculty members come to Claudette's next lesson to hear her play. Claudette plays flawlessly. What do you think happened?

    a.   Social facilitation
    b.   Social interference
    c.   Social enhancement
    d.   Social diffusion

4. Lori's bridesmaids like the pink backless dress, but Lori does not. Although no one actually asks her to concede, she decides to go along with the crowd and choose that dress. Lori has exhibited

    a.   conformity.
    b.   compliance.
    c.   consensus.
    d.   None of these

5. Ambiguous social situations facilitate which of the following?

    a.   Diffusion of responsibility
    b.   Conformity
    c.   Use of norms to guide behavior
    d.   All of these

6. Myron wants his secretary to stay late. He gets her to agree to stay until 7 P.M. and then tells her that it will not do him any good unless she stays until 10 P.M. This is called the

    a.   foot-in-the-door technique.
    b.   door-in-the-face technique.
    c.   low-ball technique.
    d.   tit-for-tat strategy.

7. Sherry is in a jam. She needs a place to stay in New York while she looks for a job. Several weeks before her trip, she calls a friend and asks if she can stay for a night. Once Sherry arrives, she asks if she can stay for several days. On the second day, she asks if she can stay for an entire week. Sherry is employing which method of compliance?

    a. Zero-sum game
    b. Tit-for-tat strategy
    c. Low-ball technique
    d. Foot-in-the-door technique

8. Mai Ling is a veteran emergency room nurse. The doctor in charge, who has been on duty for twenty-four hours without a break, has ordered her to administer the wrong drug to a patient. She knows that if she obeys the doctor's order, the patient will die. Under which circumstances will she be *least* likely to obey?

    a. If the doctor is high in prestige at the hospital
    b. If there are other nurses in the room watching
    c. If there are other nurses in the room who will also disobey
    d. If she has an authoritarian personality

9. Which of the following conclusions was derived from Milgram's studies of obedience?

    a. Even ordinary people, with no particular hostility, under certain circumstances are capable of brutal acts toward other people.
    b. Most people are able, under the proper circumstances, to suppress their natural aggressiveness.
    c. The need to be accepted by others is a powerful motivating force.
    d. When individuals lose their sense of identity in a group, they often become more aggressive.

10. Jayson is walking along and someone "accidentally" bumps into him. What really happened was the other person purposefully didn't get out of Jayson's way. Jayson reacts very angrily and shoves the other student back. Jayson probably endorses

    a. minority influence.
    b. the frustration-aggression hypothesis.
    c. a culture of honor.
    d. the Freudian perspective of aggression.

11. Dana had to wait longer at the checkout line than she wanted—and she was already running late. When she leaves the store, she rushes out, pushing a pokey person in front of her out of the way. Dana's behavior is consistent with which perspective on aggression?

    a. Biological
    b. Learning
    c. Frustration-aggression hypothesis
    d. Instinct

12. Environmental psychology is

    a. the study of cooperative behavior.
    b. the study of relationships between people's physical environment and their behavior.
    c. the study of social influence.
    d. the practice of working to prevent psychological disorders.

13. What is the difference between altruism and helping behavior?
    a.   They are opposites—altruism is aggressive behavior and helping behavior is assistive.
    b.   They are interchangeable terms—there is no difference.
    c.   Altruism is the beneficial action itself; helping behavior is the motive for the action.
    d.   Altruism is a motive for helping and helping behavior is the beneficial action itself.

14. Which of the following is an example of a resource dilemma?
    a.   If not enough people watch a television program, advertisers will no longer sponsor it.
    b.   If everyone watches noncommercial public television but no one contributes money for its support, it will go off the air.
    c.   Apartment dwellers need to pitch in to buy a high-powered television antenna for their building.
    d.   If two people keep competing instead of cooperating, they will both lose.

15. The shelter for homeless people has a large number of volunteers who were once homeless. When such volunteers are asked why they contribute so much to the shelter, they often say it's because they know what it feels like to be without a home. Their explanation fits best with the _____ theory of helping.
    a.   arousal: cost-reward
    b.   empathy-altruism
    c.   environmental
    d.   evolutionary

16. The tit-for-tat strategy involves being competitive
    a.   in response to competition.
    b.   in response to cooperation.
    c.   after initiating cooperation.
    d.   after initiating competition.

17. If two community service organizations want to reduce the conflict between them, the best course of action would be to
    a.   find a common community service goal.
    b.   ensure that each individual's contributions are noted and rewarded.
    c.   keep members from discussing issues outside of meetings.
    d.   start a contest to see which group can raise the most money for their projects.

18. Jim is the president of a university. He focuses a lot on defining the vision for where the school should go and is highly respected by students, faculty, and staff. Jim is a _____ leader.
    a.   transactional
    b.   transformational
    c.   task-motivated
    d.   relationship-motivated

19. Who is most likely to display a transformational leadership style?

    a.   Joe, who is task-motivated
    b.   Karen, who is relationship-motivated
    c.   Jack, who is relationship-motivated
    d.   They are all equally likely to display a transformational leadership style.

20. The phenomenon of poor decision making in closely knit groups with strong leaders is called

    a.   deindividuation.
    b.   groupthink.
    c.   social loafing.
    d.   social interference.

Total Correct (See answer key) _____

ANSWERS TO FILL-IN-THE-BLANKS KEY TERMS

1.   conformity (see Conformity and Compliance)

2.   Obedience (see Obedience)

3.   compliance (see Conformity and Compliance)

4.   aggression (see Aggression)

5.   Social norms (see Social Influence)

6.   social loafing (see Linkages: Motivation and the Presence of Others)

7.   environmental psychology (see When Are People Aggressive?)

8.   altruism (see Altruism and Helping Behavior)

9.   arousal: cost-reward (see Why Do People Help?)

10. Cooperation (see Cooperation, Competition, and Conflict)

11. social dilemma (see Social Dilemmas)

12. deindividuation (see Social Influence)

13. Task-motivated (see Group Leadership)

14. Empathy-altruism theory (see Why Do People Help?)

15. social facilitation (see Linkages: Motivation and the Presence of Others)

ANSWERS TO CONCEPTS AND EXERCISES

Group Decision Making

1.   *Groupthink.* This group is very close, disregards outside counsel, and is heavily influenced by a leader who makes a surprising decision and then asks for or expects support. (see Groupthink)

2.   *Relationship-motivated leadership.* This group leader is asking for the opinions of all the members, a characteristic of this style of leadership. (see Group Leadership)

3.   *Task-motivated leadership.* Angela is almost dictatorial. She makes a list of tasks, hands them out to the group, and does not ask for any opinions. And, she makes the final decision on her own. (see Group Leadership)

Sales Training

1. *Foot-in-the-door.* Once George gets a customer to buy the less expensive options, the customer has let George get his foot in the door and may be more easily convinced that more expensive options are worthwhile. (see Creating Compliance)

2. *Low-ball.* After a customer has agreed to buy a car, the customer is unlikely to back out of the deal completely when told that the car is unavailable. George used low-ball to gain compliance by getting the person to agree to buy one car, preventing the purchase, and then getting the customer to buy a more expensive car. (see Creating Compliance)

3. *Door-in-the-face.* A customer who was shown many unaffordably expensive cars may be relieved when George finally shows the affordably priced cars. After continually saying "no" to the expensive cars (like slamming the door in George's face), the customer may feel that buying a less expensive car is a compromise. (see Creating Compliance)

Critical Thinking

1. Sam's hypothesis is that Robe led the assault.

2. Robe's size and Sam's stereotype of the small, timid-looking man support his hypothesis.

3. Martina hypothesizes that Mikey Smitt could have led the assault.

4. The possibility of deindividuation and the fact that compact, sinewy guys can do some damage if they want to, are Martina's evidence.

5. Martina can't conclude anything at this point. She will probably ask Smitt for an alibi and put him in a line-up for identification by the victim.

ANSWERS TO MULTIPLE-CHOICE QUESTIONS

Circle the question numbers you answered correctly.

Quiz 1

1. b is the answer. Deindividuation occurs because people feel they won't be held accountable for their actions. (see Social Influence)

    a. Diffusion of responsibility means that the more people there are in a crowd, the less likely each individual is to help someone in need.

    c. There is no such phenomenon as situation ambiguity.

    d. Social facilitation occurs when the presence of others increases performance.

2. d is the answer. When Ashley violated a social norm, it made the people around her uncomfortable. Usually the person breaking the social rule also feels uneasy. (see Social Influence)

    a. Deindividuation is losing oneself in the group action, as in a mob.

    b. A person experiencing social facilitation performs better while people are around than when alone.

    c. Social loafing occurs when a person in a group doesn't do his or her share of the work.

3.　a is the answer. When a task is well-rehearsed, people often perform better with others present. If Nina knows the course well, then having someone race her may be the motivation she needs to push herself to drive her best. (see Social Influence)

　　b.　A well-rehearsed activity is not usually harmed by the presence of others; therefore, such social impairment shouldn't be a factor for Nina.

　　c.　Deindividuation is feeling "swept up" by the mood of a crowd.

　　d.　The bystander effect is related to diffusion of responsibility, which is the hesitance of people to help when others are around. Each person puts the responsibility of helping on the other bystanders.

4.　c is the answer. Shawn is not making much of an effort because he doesn't believe his behavior in the group is being monitored. (see Social Influence)

　　a, b.　Social facilitation and social interference relate to behaviors on which we think we might be evaluated. Social facilitation is when others' presence improves performance; social interference is when others' presence worsens performance.

　　d.　Social penalty is not one of the concepts discussed in this chapter.

5.　b is the answer. When everyone else has the same view, it is more likely that another person will conform. (see Conformity and Compliance)

　　a.　An unambiguous stimulus would be less likely to cause conformity, because people would be more certain of their decisions and not have to rely on others for cues.

　　c, d　No gender differences in conformity have been found when the situations were equally familiar.

6.　a is the answer. This question is describing Sherif's study of conformity using the autokinetic phenomenon. Sherif found that people's estimates tended to converge over time as they established a group norm. (see Conformity and Compliance)

　　b, c, d.　Sherif found that estimates tend to converge in this situation, not diverge, remain stable, or fluctuate randomly.

7.　c is the answer. The door-in-the face technique involves making a large request, having it denied, and then making a smaller request. (see Conformity and Compliance)

　　a.　This is the foot-in-the-door technique.

　　b.　Asking for something is a request, not a technique for inducing compliance.

　　d.　This is the low-ball approach, which occurs when a person claims the original commitment won't work and asks for more.

8.　b is the answer. Ian is changing his behavior in response to expressed (spoken) social influence. (see Conformity and Compliance)

　　a.　Conformity occurs when people change their behavior in response to real or imagined unspoken peer pressure.

　　c.　Ian's friends are not authority figures who demanded that he go along with them; they just applied social pressure.

　　d.　Ian was not in competition with his friends; they were asking him to go with them.

9.   b is the answer. Diane's remarks are examples of minority influence. Minority influence tends to be indirect and delayed, so her remarks will have more influence if the group decision is further away from when she first makes her comments. (see Conformity and Compliance)

   a.   This is reversed—though it is true her impact depends on the timing of the group decision, minority influence like Diane tends to have greater impact if the group decision is further away in time.

   c.   Minority influence is not inconsequential; it is delayed and indirect in nature.

   d.   Minority influence is not necessarily powerful, but it does have impact on groups over time and in an indirect manner.

10. c is the answer. Obedience occurs when people yield to a demand, rather than a request, because they think they must. (see Obedience)

   a.   Conformity results from unspoken group pressure, not a request.

   b.   People can and do comply without accepting or agreeing with the suggestion.

   d.   Obedience is not a response to aggression.

11. a is the answer. When many people are present, diffusion of responsibility occurs and helping behavior is reduced. (see Altruism and Helping Behavior)

   b.   Diffusion of responsibility is unrelated to group decision making. (You may be thinking of groupthink, the inability of a small, closely knit group to evaluate realistically the decisions it makes.)

   c.   Diffusion of responsibility is related to helping behavior, not to leadership styles.

   d.   Diffusion of responsibility is related to helping behavior, not to aggression.

12. d is the answer. Playing violent video games has some influence, but it is unclear as to how strong or how long-lasting that influence is. Other influences seem to be more significant. (see Aggression)

   a.   Correlational studies support this conclusion. It is correct.

   b.   Laboratory studies support this conclusion. It is correct.

   c.   Short-term effects have been documented by laboratory research.

13. b is the answer. As crowding increases, so does aggression. Living in an area where zoning laws limit crowding would be safer than living in any of the other alternatives. (see Aggression)

   a.   Living near the airport will increase the noise in Agatha's neighborhood. Unwanted noise has been associated with increases in aggression.

   c.   High temperature is correlated with aggression. Miami Beach, which normally has a warm climate, can become oppressively hot during the summer months. If people have no way to escape the heat, they may behave aggressively.

   d.   Air pollution raises levels of aggression.

14. b is the answer. Once a person is upset by another's misfortune, the person will weigh the costs of helping versus not helping. Darlene is upset, and the cost of helping is not very high. (see Altruism and Helping Behavior)

   a.   This would be an evolutionary view of why people help.

   c.   Being familiar with an area may increase helping behavior, but this is not part of the arousal: cost-reward theory.

   d.   The empathy-altruism model proposes that helping is often a result of empathy.

15. c is the answer. What is economically beneficial for Dean would be terrible for the environment if everyone did it. (see Cooperation, Competition, and Conflict)

    a. An analogue experiment was used to study the evolutionary approach to helping behavior. It was called analogue because the people were asked to imagine their reactions to hypothetical situations, rather than being placed in those situations. Dean is not in an analogue experiment.

    b. A prisoner's dilemma occurs when two people are differentially rewarded for cooperating or competing. The greatest number of individual wins results from one person choosing a competitive response and the other person choosing a cooperative response. The greatest number of overall wins results from cooperation. The smallest number of overall wins results from both people making a competitive response.

    d. In a zero-sum game, only one person can win. If Dean were to properly maintain his car, other people would *not* automatically have something taken away; therefore, this is not a zero-sum game.

16. d is the answer. Individuals were most likely to save the closest relative to them who would be able to bear children. (see Altruism and Helping Behavior)

    a. Older individuals might be likely to get a favor, but in a life-or-death situation they are less likely to be saved, particularly if they are distantly related to the person responding to the question.

    b. Younger individuals are likely to be saved, but not necessarily. It depends on how closely related they are to the person in question.

    c. The closest relative is likely to be saved, but they are most likely to be saved if they are still able to bear children.

17. a is the answer. The tit-for-tat strategy involves punishing competitive moves with competition and rewarding cooperative moves with cooperation. (see Cooperation, Competition, and Conflict)

    b. The low-ball technique is used to increase compliance by first getting a commitment and then devaluing that commitment and making an even larger request.

    c. Altruism is the desire to help someone without an external incentive. Neither Tim nor Jill freely shares notes; they are making an exchange.

    d. The foot-in-the-door technique involves making gradually larger and larger requests.

18. d is the answer. In a zero-sum game, when one person wins, the other must lose. (see Cooperation, Competition, and Conflict)

    a. An injunctive norm is a guide to what a person should do. An example of following the injunctive norm of reciprocity is giving a present to someone in return for a present.

    b. In the prisoner's dilemma, a person can gain by cooperating. It is not a situation where only one can win at the others' expense.

    c. The tit-for-tat strategy may be used when cooperation is possible, unlike this game, where only one team can win.

19. d is the answer. The task-motivated style of leadership may not endear a leader to his or her followers. (see Group Processes)

    a. Loose supervision is a characteristic of relationship-motivated leadership.

    b. Asking for member ideas is a characteristic of relationship-motivated leadership.

    c.   Being concerned with subordinates' feelings is a characteristic of relationship-motivated leadership.

20.   c is the answer. When people hear others all pushing for the same idea, they are more hesitant to disagree. If suggestions were made anonymously, perhaps more ideas would be proposed. (see Group Processes)

    a, b.   Group isolation and leaders who take a firm stand contribute to groupthink.

    d.   Task-motivated leadership would mean that Wing would give instructions rather than consult the group, but it would not improve the choices made, nor would it make groupthink unlikely. Wing might still feel he had the support of the group for the ideas he was directing them to carry out.

Now turn to the quiz analysis table at the end of this chapter to find which areas you know well and which areas you need to work on. Circle the numbers in the table for items on Quiz 1 that you answered correctly.

Quiz 2

1.   d is the answer. Social norms make us more comfortable because we know what to expect from others and how to behave. (see Social Influence)

2.   a is the answer. Much of mob behavior can be explained by the loss of personal identity that comes with getting caught up in the group mentality. (see Social Influence)

    b.   Diffusion of responsibility is the spreading around of responsibility for helping when many people see someone in need.

    c.   Social facilitation occurs when our performance benefits from the presence of other people. Luis is just going along with the mob, not improving a personal performance.

    d.   Luis is not complying with a request; he is conforming to the riotous behavior of others.

3.   a is the answer. We become aroused in the presence of others. Dominant or well-rehearsed behaviors are usually performed better under these circumstances. (see Social Influence)

    b.   If Claudette were playing a particularly difficult piece that she did not know well, this would have been the answer.

    c, d.   There is no such thing as social enhancement or social diffusion.

4.   a is the answer. Conformity occurs when people, in the face of unspoken peer pressure, change their behavior to match that of other group members. (see Conformity and Compliance)

    b.   Compliance occurs when people change their behavior because of expressed social influence.

    c.   When people's behavior is based on their beliefs and happens to match that of other people, consensus exists.

    d.   a is the answer.

5.   d is the answer. (see Conformity and Compliance)

    a, b, c. In an ambiguous situation, people let norms guide their behavior, tend to conform, and are less likely to help because they do not clearly recognize the need for help.

6.   c is the answer. Myron first got his secretary to agree to stay late. Then he said staying late would do him no good unless she stayed very late. (see Conformity and Compliance)

    a.   The foot-in-the-door technique involves starting out with a small request, which is complied with, and then making larger and larger ones. The secretary did not have a chance to comply with the first request; instead, it was labeled as unhelpful.

    b.   The door-in-the-face technique involves first making a very large request, which is usually refused, and then making a smaller request. The smaller request is usually granted.

    d.   The tit-for-tat strategy rewards cooperation with cooperation but punishes competition with competition.

7.   d is the answer. Sherry is gradually making larger and larger requests, which represents the foot-in-the-door technique. (see Conformity and Compliance)

    a, b.   The tit-for-tat strategy and zero-sum game are competitive. Sherry is not competing with her friend.

    c.   The low-ball technique involves getting an original commitment, not allowing compliance by devaluing that commitment, and asking for more. Instead, Sherry is gradually asking for more and more after her friend has complied with previous requests.

8.   c is the answer. The presence of others who will also disobey would be the most powerful factor in reducing obedience in this example. (see Obedience)

    a.   If the doctor is of high prestige, Mai Ling will be more likely to obey, not less.

    b.   If others are watching is not a factor that Milgram tested, so we cannot be certain how this would affect her tendency to obey.

    d.   People high in authoritarianism are more likely than others to obey.

9.   a is the answer. (see Obedience)

    b, c.   Both of these statements are true, but they do not derive from Milgram's studies of obedience.

    d.   This describes deindividuation, a phenomenon not examined in Milgram's studies.

10.   c is the answer. People who endorse a culture of honor tend to react more angrily, and aggressively, to perceived insults. Jayson's reaction to the insult of being bumped into suggests he is defending his honor. (see Aggression)

    a.   Minority influence is influence of a smaller faction on a larger one.

    b.   The frustration-aggression hypothesis proposes that frustration can lead to aggression. There is no information to suggest whether Jayson believes this or not.

    d.   The Freudian view of aggression is that it is innate and builds up over time, finally leaking out when the pressure is too great. We can't tell whether or not Jayson would agree with Freud.

11.   c is the answer. According to the frustration-aggression hypothesis, aggression is displayed if a person is frustrated and there are aggressive cues in the environment. Dana was frustrated. (see Aggression)

    a.   According to the biological viewpoint, aggression is caused by physical factors. This question describes a frustrating situation, not a biological cause.

    b.   According to the learning approach, we can learn aggression by watching others' aggressive behavior. Dana did not see anyone acting aggressively at the store in this question.

    d.   Instinct theory proposes that aggression is natural, not learned.

12.   b is the answer. Environmental psychologists try to understand how the physical environment influences people's behavior. (see Aggression)

    a.   The study of social dilemmas is the study of cooperation (and competition).

    c.   Social influence is the study of how social factors influence human behavior.

    d.   This is what community psychologists do, not environmental.

13.   d is the answer. Altruism is unselfish concern for another and viewed as a motive for actual helping behavior, which is action intended to benefit another. (see Altruism and Helping Behavior)

    a.   They are not opposites; they are related in that altruism is a potential motive for actual helping behavior.

    b.   They are not interchangeable. Altruism is a motive while helping behavior is an action.

    c.   This is reversed. Altruism is a motive, not an action. Helping behavior is an action, not a motive.

14.   b is the answer. This is a particular type of resource dilemma involving public goods. In the short run, the individual benefits by watching public television without contributing. But if no one contributes, there will be no revenue to keep this kind of TV on the air. (see Cooperation, Competition, and Conflict)

    a.   Advertisers spend money to sponsor a program based on its ratings. This is a business practice; there is no common resource involved.

    c.   This option could be an example of a superordinate goal but not of a resource dilemma.

    d.   This statement describes potential results of the prisoner's dilemma.

15.   b is the answer. According to the empathy-altruism theory of helping behavior, if people know what the person in need feels like, they will be more likely to help. (see Altruism and Helping Behavior)

    a.   The arousal: cost-reward theory doesn't focus on empathy for the person in need; it focuses on the upset of the helper. If the person is upset enough by the other person's plight, he or she is likely to evaluate the price of helping.

    c.   There is no environmental theory of helping behavior, although population density and noise do influence helping.

    d.   The evolutionary theory states that we are more likely to help relatives. Evolutionary theorists do not take empathy or arousal into account.

16.   a is the answer. When the tit-for-tat strategy is used, presumably to increase cooperation, competitive maneuvers are punished with competitive maneuvers. (see Cooperation, Competition, and Conflict)

    b.   If cooperative moves are punished with competitive moves, cooperation will decrease.

    c, d.   The tit-for-tat strategy involves responses to the other player's move. There are no strategies based on a pattern of cooperation or competition on the part of just one player.

17. a is the answer. When superordinate goals are emphasized, people feel like part of the same group" and usually work together better. (see Cooperation, Competition, and Conflict)

   b. Recognizing individual contributions would probably create more competition and conflict.

   c. Communication generally has a positive impact. Often when people discuss issues further, they can correct misperceptions or attributional errors.

   d. A contest would most likely increase competition, thereby increasing conflict.

18. b is the answer. Transformational leaders focus on creating vision and inspiring others to pursue it. They give followers reasons to respect and admire them. (see Group Processes)

   a. Transactional leaders tend to punish those who fail to follow their directives and reward those who do follow them.

   c. A task-motivated leader gives directives without input from the group.

   d. A relationship-motivated leader seeks group input and is concerned with subordinate feelings.

19. b is the answer. Women are more likely to display a transformational leadership style. Karen is the only woman listed here. (see Group Processes)

   a. Joe, as a man, and particularly as a task-motivated leader, is less likely to display a transformational style.

   c. Jack, although relationship-motivated, as a male is less likely to display a transformational style in comparison to Karen. He may do so, but he is less likely to than she.

   d. Karen is most likely to display a transformational leadership style.

20. b is the answer. Small, closely knit groups with strong, opinionated leaders tend to lose the ability to evaluate their decisions realistically. (see Group Processes)

   a. Deindividuation is the tendency of people to behave in a less inhibited way when in a crowd.

   c. Social loafing is working less hard in a group than when alone. In closely knit groups, social loafing would be reduced because members identify with the group.

   d. Social interference occurs when a person performs more poorly while others are present.

Now turn to the quiz analysis table at the end of this chapter to find which areas you know well and which areas you need to work on. Circle the numbers in the table for items on Quiz 2 that you answered correctly.

For each question you answered correctly, circle its number. (Quiz 1 numbers are not shaded; Quiz 2 numbers are shaded.) Are there patterns in the types of questions or the topics you got wrong that could direct your further study? Did you improve from Quiz 1 to Quiz 2?

QUIZ REVIEW

Topic	Type of Question		
	Definition	**Comprehension**	**Application**
Social Influence		1	2, 3, 4
		1	2, 3
Conformity and Compliance	7	5, 6	8, 9
			4, 5, 6, 7
Obedience	10		
		9	8
Aggression		12	13
	12		10, 11
Altruism and Helping Behavior	11	16	14
		13	15
Cooperation, Competition, and Conflict			15, 17, 18
	16	14	17
Group Processes			19, 20
	20		18, 19

Total correct by quiz:

Quiz 1:	
Quiz 2:	

CHAPTER 19

Industrial and Organizational Psychology

OUTLINE

I. AN OVERVIEW OF INDUSTRIAL AND ORGANIZATIONAL PSYCHOLOGY
   <u>Industrial and organizational (I/O) psychology</u> is the science of behavior and mental processes in the workplace. Such scientists engage in both research and practice with two main goals: (1) promoting effective job performance and (2) improving the health, safety, and well-being of employees. Forty-one percent work as professors in college or university departments of psychology, business, or related fields. Twenty-four percent work as consultants, and the same percentage work in corporate positions. A smaller 7percent work in the public sector.

II. ASSESSING PEOPLE, JOBS, AND JOB PERFORMANCE
   A. Knowledge, Skills, Abilities, and Other Characteristics
      Knowledge, skills, abilities, or other characteristics (*KSAOs*) are the human attributes needed to do a job successfully. *Knowledge* refers to what one knows. *Skill* refers to how good a person is at doing something. *Ability* is a person's potential for learning a skill. *Other personal characteristics* might be anything else relevant to the job, such as an attitude or personality trait.

   B. Job Analysis
      1. <u>Job analysis</u> involves collecting information about jobs and job requirements. The *job-oriented approach* to this describes tasks involved in doing a job. The *person-oriented approach* describes the KSAOs needed to do the job. The *personality-oriented approach* focuses on the specific personality characteristics associated with success in a job.

      2. Job analysis is used by organizations to guide hiring decisions and help define what training needs exist.

      3. The most common method of job analysis is to ask *job incumbents* to fill out questionnaires about what they do in the workplace. Sometimes, instruments like the *Position Analysis Questionnaire* are used to collect the information.

      4. The Occupational Information Network (or O*NET) compiles analyses of thousands of jobs.

   C. Measuring Employee Characteristics
      1. *Psychological Tests.* A *psychological test* is a systematic procedure for observing behavior in a standard situation and describing it on a number scale or a system of categories. I/O psychologists use standard IQ tests, *situational judgment tests (SJTs)*, personality tests as well as *integrity tests*.
      2. *Job Applicant Interviews.* A job applicant interview is designed to determine an applicant's suitability for a job. *Structured interviews* involve a prepared list of questions the interviewer asks in a particular order. *Unstructured interviews* are more spontaneous and variable. Research has consistently found structured interviews to be related to better hiring decisions than unstructured.

3.   *Assessment Centers.* An <u>assessment center</u> is an extensive set of exercises designed to determine an individual's suitability for a particular job. They are most often used to hire or promote managers, though they can be used for other positions. The *in-basket* task is a typical assessment center exercise that involves working through an overflowing in-basket left by a "previous manager." Performance is graded on a variety of dimensions. Other exercises measure interpersonal skills. Scores on all exercises are then compiled to predict an individual's suitability for a particular position. Assessment centers are valuable, but they can be expensive and time-consuming to operate.

D.   Measuring Job Performance
<u>Job performance</u> appraisal provides an evaluation of how one is doing in various aspects of one's work. To conduct an appraisal, one needs to first have an idea of the criteria of "good" performance.

1.   *Establishing Performance Criteria. Criteria* define what is meant by good or bad performance in an organization. A *theoretical criterion* is a statement of what good or poor performance is, in theory. An *actual criterion* specifies what should be measured to tap whether the theoretical criterion has been met. The match between theoretical and actual criteria is imperfect, however, and often several actual criteria are needed.

E.   Methods of Performance Appraisal
1.   *Objective Measures. Objective measures* of job performance include counting the frequency of particular behaviors or the results of those behaviors. These are useful for some jobs, but not all, as some jobs do not have "countable" criteria.

2.   *Subjective Measures. Subjective measures* involve supervisor judgments about employees' work. *Graphic rating forms* list several dimensions of job-performance and provide a space for a rating (for example, on a scale from one to ten). Such judgments are prone to a variety of errors such as the *leniency* and *halo errors*. To minimize these errors, I/O psychologists recommend *behavior-focused rating forms*, which ask supervisors to rate specific behaviors rather than dimensions of performance. Additionally, using "360 degree" ratings can also help manage the error associated with graphic rating forms.

III.   RECRUITING AND SELECTING EMPLOYEES
A.   Recruitment Processes
The first step in recruitment is to determine what employees are needed. Next, organizations need to persuade people with the right kinds of KSAOs to apply for the open positions using a variety of methods, such as newspaper advertising, internet postings, interviewing graduating college seniors on campus, collecting information from current employees about potential candidates, working with employment agencies, and relying on walk-in applications. Walk-in applicants may be a successful strategy for lower-skilled positions, but higher skilled positions usually require more elaborate strategies and effort.

B.   Selection Processes
<u>Validation</u> studies are used to determine how well a particular test, interview, or other assessment method predicts an employee's job performance. A large body of evidence is available in I/O psychology to tell organizations which types of tests or assessments are valid in predicting performance in particular jobs.

C.   Legal Issues in Recruitment and Selection
Laws have been designed to protect employees and job candidates from discrimination. Special safeguards exist for *protected classes*—age, ethnicity, gender, national origin, disability, and religion. In some states and other countries, sexual orientation is also a protected class. I/O psychologists helped the U.S. government create the Uniform

Guidelines on Employee Selection Procedures to help assure fairness in hiring. The most important element of these guidelines is that hiring decisions be based solely on job-related criteria.

IV. TRAINING EMPLOYEES
  A. Assessing Training Needs
      A *training needs assessment* helps organizations identify which employees need what kind of training. Other strategies, such as a *personal development plan*, allow employees and their supervisors to identify the kinds of training employees would like to have. These plans involve evaluating strength and weaknesses of an employee and using the weaknesses to determine where training is needed.

  B. Designing Training Programs
      Successful training programs attend to several design issues.

      1. *Transfer of Training. Transfer of training* involves teaching knowledge and skills that are generalizable, or transferable, to the workplace.
      2. *Feedback. Feedback* involves a trainer or fellow trainees telling someone how they are doing with constructive suggestions following error or failure, and reinforcement following progress.
      3. *Training in General Principles. Training in general principles* involves putting new information in broader context so that it fits into a bigger picture.
      4. *Overlearning. Overlearning* allows trainees to practice using information and skills until they reach a high level of performance, often to the point of using the information and skills automatically.
      5. *Sequencing. Sequencing* refers to the timing of the training. *Massed training* is cheaper and less disruptive to an employee's schedule, but not as effective as *distributed training*.

  C. Evaluating Training Programs
      I/O psychologists need to determine if a training program produced enough benefits to make it worth the time and money it cost. Although an experimental design would best answer the question of how effective a training program is, most organizations rely on nonexperimental method. Several types of criteria are used to evaluate training programs.

      1. *Evaluation Criteria. Training-level criteria* include data collected immediately after a training session about how much trainees liked or perceived value in the training. *Trainee learning criteria* involve information about what trainees actually learned from the program. *Performance-level criteria* evaluate the degree to which transfer-of-training occurred. Programs may have high ratings on one type of criteria with low ratings on others.

V. EMPLOYEE MOTIVATION
  A. ERG Theory
      Existence, relatedness, growth (ERG) theory places human needs into three categories. *Existence needs* are things required for survival. *Relatedness needs* include need for social contact. *Growth needs* involve the development and use of capabilities. ERG theory suggests that the strength of people's needs in each category is rising and falling from time to time and from one situation to another. It is applied by helping organizations recognize that employees may not be as motivated to pursue job-related growth needs if other categories are frustrated or unfulfilled.

  B. Expectancy Theory
      Expectancy theory assumes that employees behave in accordance with the results they expect their actions to bring (expectancy) and how much they value those results (value).

Strong empirical support exists for this theory, and this theory is applied through helping organizations make high performance worthwhile to their employees.

C.   Goal Setting Theory
Goal setting theory proposes that performance at work is influenced by employees' intentions to achieve specific goals. Employees are expected to choose, engage in, and persist at behaviors that take them closer to their goals. Goals that are most motivating are chosen by employees, difficult but not impossible, and specific rather than vague.

VI.   JOB SATISFACTION
Job satisfaction is the degree to which people like or dislike their jobs. It comprises cognitive, affective, and behavioral components.

A.   Measuring Job Satisfaction
Some scales take a *global approach* toward measuring job satisfaction, while others take a *facet approach*. A global approach measures attitudes toward a job in general; a facet approach measures assess various aspects of work separately. Most often, job satisfaction is measured using questionnaires such as the *Job in General Scale* (global approach) or the *Job Satisfaction Survey* (facet approach).

B.   Factors Affecting Job Satisfaction
1.   *Job Requirements.* In general, people tend to be more satisfied with work that is more complex. However, individuals who lack the knowledge and skills to do complex work may not experience increased satisfaction with increased complexity.
2.   *Salary.* Higher salaries alone do not increase job satisfaction. Knowing that salary decisions are made in a fair way may be more important than the salary itself. Knowing others are paid more for the same work leads to the experience of relative deprivation.
3.   *Work-Family Conflict.* Needing to care for a sick child or attend a school play are examples of this conflict. Many organizations deal with this by developing *family-friendly work policies* such as *flextime*.
4.   *Gender, Age, and Ethnicity.* Gender has not been found to impact job satisfaction, but age has. Older workers tend to be more satisfied than younger workers, perhaps because older workers have the education and experience to be involved in more complex, highly paid jobs. Research on ethnicity and job satisfaction has produced mixed results.

C.   Thinking Critically: Is Job Satisfaction Genetic?
What am I being asked to believe or accept?

Differences in job satisfaction reflect genetic predispositions toward liking or not liking a job.

What evidence is available to support the assertion?

Research has shown that genetically influenced personality traits are related to job satisfaction. Also, a study directly examined this assertion using the following method. Thirty-four pairs of identical twins who had been separated and raised in different environments completed a job satisfaction questionnaire. The results showed a strong positive correlation between the twins' responses.

Are there alternative ways of interpreting the evidence?

Although the positive correlation is supportive of the assertion, it is merely a correlational study and factors other than genetic predisposition could have influenced job satisfaction. It may be that genes don't shape job satisfaction itself but do shape the characteristics that influence people's access to satisfying work.

What additional evidence would help to evaluate the alternatives?

Information about the impact of job characteristics on the high correlation between twins' job satisfaction ratings would be helpful. Researchers did examine this and found that the twins tended to hold very similar jobs in terms of complexity. A more complete assessment of the jobs and job environments would be helpful.

What conclusions are most reasonable?

There is no single reason why people differ in job satisfaction. The results suggest a strong genetic influence, but this influence could be indirect by affecting worker characteristics that in turn determine access to jobs that tend to be more satisfying.

- D. Consequences of Job Satisfaction
    1. *Job Performance.* Satisfied workers tend to be more motivated, work harder, and perform better than dissatisfied ones.
    2. *Organizational Citizenship Behavior.* Organizational citizenship behavior (OCB) is a willingness to go beyond formal job requirements to help coworkers and the organization. High satisfaction increases the probability of an employee showing high OCB, but it may be that personality influences both satisfaction and OCB, or that OCB influences job satisfaction.
    3. *Turnover.* High satisfaction is not always related to low job *turnover*. Employees tend not to leave one job until they have another, so dissatisfied workers tend not to leave until they have an alternative. Thus, turnover is more closely related to job satisfaction when jobs are plentiful. Organizations may use *mentors* with *protégés* t try to reduce turnover problems.
    4. *Absenteeism.* The correlation between job satisfaction and absenteeism is weak. Other factors, such as work-family conflicts, however, are more predictive of absenteeism.
    5. *Aggression and Counterproductive Work Behavior.* Job dissatisfaction is one cause of workplace aggression and other forms of *counterproductive work behavior (CWB)*. Stress at work tends to lead to dissatisfaction and negative emotions, which in turn can result in CWB, especially when employees feel that they have been treated unfairly or have little control over the stressors.
- E. Linkages: Aggression in the Workplace
    Most workplace homicides are committed by strangers, in contrast to other murder victims, who generally know their attackers. Most homicides at work involve *instrumental aggression*—meaning the aggressor's intent is not to injure but to achieve a goal such as getting money. Most cases of injury at work occur under stressful circumstances that foster aggression, such as an emergency room. In these situations, the aggressor generally intends to injure the employee victim. These are examples of aggression between employees and non-employees. Aggression between employees is more often verbal than physical.

VII. OCCUPATIONAL HEALTH PSYCHOLOGY
Occupational health psychology is concerned with psychological factors that affect the health, safety, and well-being of employees in the workplace.

- A. Physical Conditions Affecting Health
    The Occupational Safety and Health Administration (OSHA) establish guidelines to minimize employees' exposure to hazards. *Universal precautions* in medical care would be an example of a guideline. Such guidelines and the procedures they advocate can be useful in reducing risk, but often workers do not follow the guidelines because of lack of

encouragement from supervisors. I/O psychologists try to design ways to increase compliance with guidelines. *Repetitive strain injuries* such as *carpal tunnel syndrome* are one of the common stressors from certain types of jobs. *Engineering psychologists* (also called *human factors psychologists*) try to design tools that will reduce these kinds of physical stressors associated with work.

B. Work Schedules, Health, and Safety
1. *Rotating Shift Work.* Employees whose shifts change week to week experience disruption in their *circadian rhythms* that can cause fatigue, irritability, and reduced cognitive functioning.
2. *Long Shifts and Long Weeks.* Although employees often like long shifts because they result in greater blocks of time off, extended work days may create health and performance problems for some. Workweeks that last over forty-eight hours can be especially problematic and are associated with health problems such as heart disease.

C. Stress, Accidents, and Safety
Longer-than-normal work shifts and extended workweeks are one source of occupational stress that contributes to the fatigue, inattention, cognitive impairment, and sleepiness that elevate the risk of accidents at work. Other factors include the *climate of safety*—how much training and supervisory emphasis there is on workplace safety.

VIII. WORK GROUPS AND WORK TEAMS
A work group is at least two people who interact as they perform different tasks. A work team is a special kind of work group in which (1) members activities are coordinated with and depend on one another, (2) each member has a specialized role, and (3) members share a common goal. Promoting efficiency in work teams, especially those from diverse backgrounds and perspectives, is a goal of I/O psychologists. I/O psychologists distinguish between "surface" and "deep" diversity in doing so.

A. Autonomous Work Groups
Autonomous work groups (AWG) manage themselves and do not report to anyone for routine daily supervision. Members of such groups tend to report higher job satisfaction levels and often perform better than members of more traditional arrangements. AWGs often cost less because fewer supervisors are needed.

B. Group Leadership
1. *What Makes a Good Leader?* Intelligence, trustworthiness, and being team-oriented have been identified as important traits of good leaders. In some countries, a willingness to take risks is identified as a positive leader trait; in other countries that same trait is viewed negatively.
2. *How Do Good Leaders Behave?* Good leaders tend to be high on both *consideration* and on *initiating structure*. Consideration is concern for the welfare of employees. Initiating structure is the degree to which a leader coordinates employee efforts by assigning tasks and clarifying expectations. Leaders who are high on initiating structure and low on consideration tend to fare the worst in ratings from subordinates and other measures of leadership effectiveness.
3. *Leader-Member Interactions.* Leader-member exchange (LMX) theory suggests that most leaders tend to adopt different styles with two kinds of subordinates. The most consideration and best treatment is given to the *in-group*, and the *out-group* employees are given less consideration. In-group members experience more job satisfaction and less occupational stress. Research suggests that LMX theory may not adequately explain interaction between leaders and subordinates in virtual teams, as it was designed to capture face-to-face interactions between leaders and subordinates.

C.   Focus on Research Methods: Can People Learn to be Charismatic Leaders.
A *charismatic leader* is one who inspires followers to embrace a vision of success and make extraordinary efforts to achieve things they wouldn't have done on their own. I/O psychologists wondered if one could be trained to be charismatic. A study of twenty branches of a large banking organization randomly assigned branch managers to either a charisma training group or a no-training group. After training, results showed that the charisma training program had a positive impact on managers' charisma as rated by their employees. The trained managers had higher job satisfaction after training than untrained managers. Financial performance of trained managers' branches increased; untrained managers' branch performance decreased somewhat. Charisma can be taught to some extent, but future research needs to determine if the results are due to placebo effects and how long the effects last over time.

KEY TERMS

1.   **Industrial and organizational (I/O) psychology** is the science of behavior and mental processes in the workplace. (see An Overview of Industrial and Organizational Psychology)

Example: Jenna is employed by a consulting firm. She travels all around the world visiting various clients and helping them to measure their employees' current job satisfaction, then identifies ways for the organizations to improve employee job satisfaction.

2.   **Job analysis** is the process of collecting information about jobs and job requirements that is used to guide hiring and training decisions. (see Job Analysis)

Example: Wendy, an I/O psychologist, is watching a professor do her job. She notes that the job requires the following knowledge, skills, abilities, and other characteristics: organization, communication skills, analytical skills, interpersonal skills, and reliability. She is performing a person-oriented job analysis. Other job analyses take a job-oriented approach, in which the job analyst notes the actual tasks involved in doing the job.

3.   An **assessment center** is an extensive set of exercises designed to determine an individual's suitability for a particular job. (see Measuring Employee Characteristics)

Example: Bruce is trying to get promoted to the director level in the company he works for. As part of that process, he goes to a separate site for several days and participates in activities there. One day he has to pretend he is a new manager going through the previous manager's overflowing in-basket. Another day he has to role-play a manager firing an incompetent employee. Experts observe his work in each exercise, score it, and provide him feedback so that he will know what areas he needs to work on to improve his chances of being promoted.

4.   **Job performance** is a measure of how well employees are doing in various aspects of their work, usually recorded annually. (see Measuring Job Performance)

Example: Kirby appraises the performance of the employees on her sales team once each month. She uses objective measures like how frequently the employee was absent or late to work, how many contacts the employee made to potential consumers, and how many actual sales were made. Other supervisors might use more subjective measures of performance appraisal.

5.   **Validation** in I/O psychology is the effort to determine how well a test, interview, or other assessment method predicts job performance. (see Selection Processes)

Example: Josh wants to find out if an intelligence test is a valid method for selecting upper-level managers. He gives the intelligence test to all job applicants but then makes his hiring decisions without it. Later, once the actual hires have been on the job long enough to have several performance appraisals, Josh correlates the intelligence test score with the job performance appraisals. He finds out that they don't seem related to each other at all. Josh has conducted a validation study.

6. **Existence, Relatedness, Growth (ERG) theory** is a theory of motivation that focuses on employees' needs at the level of existence, relatedness, and growth. (see ERG Theory)

Example: Marta's dad, with whom she was quite close, just died. Marta throws herself into her work. According to ERG theory, Marta is throwing herself into work to focus on her growth needs because her relatedness are frustrated by the death of her father.

REMEMBER: ERG theory is an attempt to address some of the problems in Maslow's hierarchy of needs theory, which you learned about in Chapter 8. Existence needs are things necessary for survival, relatedness needs refer to the need for social contact, and growth needs involve the development of one's capabilities. Unlike Maslow's theory, however, ERG theory does not specify a particular order in which these three needs must be satisfied.

7. **Expectancy theory** is a theory of workplace motivation in which employees act in accordance with expected results and how much they value those results. (see Expectancy Theory)

Example: Dannette's boss tells her that if she performs really well, then she will be promoted. But Dannette does not want a promotion, because that would mean she would have to work longer hours. Even though Dannette expects that she *could* perform well if she tried, and thereby obtain the promotion, she doesn't value that outcome, so her motivation remains unchanged.

8. **Goal setting theory** is a theory of workplace motivation focused on the idea that employees' behavior is shaped by their intention to achieve specific goals. (see Goal Setting Theory)

Example: Phil is trying to increase his employees' motivation at the construction firm he runs. As part of this effort, he sits down with each employee, and together they develop a list of specific and challenging goals. For a site supervisor, one of the goals might be "I will reduce the number of injuries experienced on my site by half in the next year."

9. **Job satisfaction** is the degree to which people like or dislike their jobs. (see Job Satisfaction)

Example: Mike is unhappy with his job. The pay is really good, but the work hours mean he can rarely be home with his family, and the work environment is really high pressure.

10. **Organizational citizenship behavior (OCB)** is a willingness to go beyond formal job requirements in order to help coworkers or the organization as a whole. (see Consequences of Job Satisfaction)

Example: Shannon, an executive secretary in a trust office, does a lot more on the job than her job description actually requires. If the corporate kitchen has dirty dishes, she jumps right in and washes them. If a coworker is behind schedule, Shannon will stay late to help her with the project.

11. **Occupational Health Psychology** is a field concerned with psychological factors that affect the health, safety, and well-being of employees. (see Occupational Health Psychology)

Example: Vicki is an I/O psychologist who has been hired to evaluate the physical conditions of a regional hospital. She reads the hospital regulations for wearing gloves and handling hazardous material, observes how well employees follow these regulations, and examines the physical space to determine if there are possible hazards such as cords one could trip over, poor lighting, and so on.

12. A **work group** is two or more people who interact as they perform workplace tasks. (see Work Groups and Work Teams)

Example: The counter at the local bank has three teller lines. The tellers work side by side as they serve the bank's clientele, but they do not depend on each other, nor do they have specialized functions. They all do the exact same work at their stations.

13. A **work team** is a work group in which the members' specialized activities are coordinated and interdependent as they work toward a common goal. (see Work Groups and Work Teams)

Example: At a vacation resort, the entire staff functions as a work team. Some employees are to clean guest cabins, others are to prepare meals, some serve the food, still others clean dishes or perform maintenance, and so on. But all employees share the same goal of making each guest's vacation so excellent that they will want to return the next year. And all employees depend on each other to make that happen—the servers depend on the cooks, the dishwashers depend on the servers to bring the dishes, and so on.

14. **Autonomous work groups (AWGs)** are self-managed employee groups that do not report to anyone for routine daily supervision. (see Autonomous Work Groups)

Example: John works in a factory where he and his co-workers are responsible for assembling entire automobiles. They rotate among jobs so that each team member performs each job occasionally.

15. **Leader-member exchange (LMX) theory** is a theory suggesting that leaders tend to supervise ingroup and outgroup employees in different ways. (see Group Leadership)

Example: Cheryl is a manager in a marketing department. She has three staff members who work for her: Lia, Lindsay, and Lauren. She spends a lot of time with Lia, helping Lia with her professional development and visibility within the corporation. She often asks Lia's opinion and listens to it, incorporating it in her planning. With Lindsay and Lauren, though, Cheryl rarely spends one-on-one time, and never asks their opinions. Lia is an ingroup subordinate, while Lindsay and Lauren are outgroup subordinates.

FILL-IN-THE-BLANKS KEY TERMS

This section will help you check your factual knowledge of the key terms introduced in this chapter. Fill in each blank with the appropriate term from the list of key terms in the previous section.

1. A measure of how well employees are doing in various aspects of their work is _____.

2. _____ is a willingness to go beyond formal job requirements in order to help coworkers and/or the organization.

3. The theory of workplace motivation focused on the idea that employees' behavior is shaped by intention to achieve specific goals is _____.

4. A(n) _____ is at least two people who interact with one another as they perform the same or different workplace tasks.

5. An extensive set of exercises designed to determine an individual's suitability for a particular job is part of a(n) _____.

6. The idea that leaders tend to supervise in-group and out-group employees in different ways is part of _____.

7. An effort to determine how well a test, interview, or other assessment method predicts job performance is called _____.

8. The field concerned with behavior and mental processes in the workplace is known as _____.

9. _____ are self-managed employee groups that do not report to anyone for routine daily supervision.

10. The degree to which people like or dislike their jobs is _____.

Total correct (See answer key) _____

LEARNING OBJECTIVES

1. Define <u>industrial and organizational (I/O) psychology</u>. Discuss the two main goals of I/O psychologists. Describe the types of employment held by I/O psychologists. (see "An Overview of Industrial and Organizational Psychology")

2. Describe the human attributes collectively referred to as KSAOs. Define <u>job analysis</u>, and describe the *job-oriented* and *person-oriented approaches* to job analysis. Discuss the three main methods of job analysis. (see "Assessing People, Jobs, and Job Performance")

3. Describe the various types of psychological tests employed by I/O psychologists. Describe selection interview, and compare and contrast structured and unstructured interviews. Define <u>assessment center</u>, and describe the types of exercises that make up assessment centers. (see "Assessing People, Jobs, and Job Performance")

4. Define and describe the purposes of <u>job performance</u> appraisals. Describe and give examples of *theoretical criteria* and *actual criteria*. Discuss the limitations of using actual criteria. (see "Measuring Job Performance")

5. Describe and give examples of *objective* and *subjective measures* of job performance. Describe *graphic rating forms*, and discuss the tendency for graphic ratings to reflect *leniency error* and *halo error*. Describe the use of critical incidents on behavior-focused rating forms. (see "Methods of Performance Appraisal")

6. Discuss the steps involved in the recruitment process. List the six most common methods for identifying and attracting job candidates. (see "Recruiting and Selecting Employees")

7. Define <u>validation</u> studies, and discuss how they are used by I/O psychologists. Discuss the legal issues involved in employee recruitment and selection. (see "Selection Processes"; see also "Legal Issues in Recruitment and Selection")

8. Discuss the aspects involved in a training needs assessment. Discuss the importance of the following in training program design: *transfer of training*, *feedback*, *training in general principles*, *overlearning*, and *sequencing*. (see "Training Employees")

9. Describe the use of experiments, *training-level criteria*, *trainee learning criteria*, and *performance-level criteria* in evaluating training programs. (see "Evaluating Training Programs")

10. Describe the following theories and discuss their applications to employee motivation: <u>Existence, Relatedness, Growth (ERG) theory</u>, <u>expectancy theory</u>, and <u>goal setting theory</u>. (see "Employee Motivation")

11. Define <u>job satisfaction</u>, and give examples of its cognitive, emotional, and behavioral components. (see "Job Satisfaction")

12. Describe the ways in which I/O psychologists measure job satisfaction. Discuss the environmental and personal factors that influence employee satisfaction. (see "Job Satisfaction")

13. Discuss the research examining the role of genetics in job satisfaction. (see "Thinking Critically: Is Job Satisfaction Genetic?")

14. Describe the relationship between job satisfaction and job performance. Define <u>organizational citizenship behavior (OCB)</u>, and describe its relationship to job satisfaction. (see "Consequences of Job Satisfaction")

15. Describe the relationship between job dissatisfaction and each of the following: turnover, absenteeism, aggression, and *counterproductive work behavior* (CWB). Discuss the research on aggression in the workplace. Describe *instrumental aggression*. (see "Consequences of Job Satisfaction"; see also "Linkages: Aggression in the Workplace")

16. Define <u>occupational health psychology</u>. Describe the physical conditions in the workplace that may cause illness and injury, and discuss the various procedures employed to minimize the effects of such conditions. (see "Occupational Health Psychology")

17. Discuss the effects that rotating shift work, long shifts, and long workweeks can have on health and safety. Describe other factors affecting workplace safety, including an organization's *climate of safety*. (see "Occupational Health Psychology")

18. Compare and contrast <u>work groups</u> and <u>work teams</u>. Define and describe <u>autonomous work groups (AWGs)</u>. (see "Work Groups and Work Teams")

19. Discuss the personality characteristics and behaviors of effective leaders. Describe the leadership dimensions of consideration and initiating structure, and discuss their relationship to employee satisfaction. (see "Group Leadership")

20. Define and describe <u>leader-member exchange (LMX) theory</u>. (see "Leader-Member Interactions")

21. Discuss the research examining whether people can learn to become charismatic leaders. (see "Focus on Research Methods: Can People Learn to Be Charismatic Leaders?")

CONCEPTS AND EXERCISES

Assessment Methods

Following are several descriptions of assessment methods. Choose the name of the assessment method from the list after the descriptions.

1. Lena is trying to find a job as a district manager. She has applied to a large transportation company for this type of role. As part of the company's evaluation of Lena, she must go to a site for two or three days in a row. At the site she participates in a variety of activities. One day, she has to sit at a desk and role-play a manager going through a new in-basket. Another day, she has to play the role of a manager with an irate customer. _____

2. Carson is applying to work as a loan officer at a bank. As part of the hiring process, Carson is asked to fill out a paper-and pencil assessment. On the assessment, he is asked questions that seem to be related to how reliable and industrious he is. _____

3. Cooper wants to be a human resource representative at a large telecommunications company. He has applied for a job. The hiring decision maker has called him back and scheduled a time to go through a prepared list of specifically worded questions face-to-face. _____

4. Joseph wants to be a sales clerk at a local department store. He is talking with the manager about the job as part of the hiring process. The course of the conversation is really relaxed and easy. They discuss a variety of topics and seem to spontaneously change topics as the whim hits them.

_____

   a. Intelligence test
   b. Personality test

    c.   Structured interview

    d.   Unstructured interview

    e.   Assessment center

Designing and Evaluating a Training Program

Following is a conversation among human resource employees who are trying to develop and evaluate a new training program for how to log information into the new company database. Each employee describes either an element that should be present in training or a strategy for evaluating training. After each speaker's turn, fill in the blank for the concept the speaker just described. You may choose from the list below.

1. *Troy:* I think we should try to make sure the employees get the "big picture" in our training program. We should relate how the new program works to how other programs they already know about work. And we should explain why this program is better, and the purpose of each step in the process. _____

2. *Melinda:* Right, Troy. But I also think we need to make them really practice using the new program, too. We want them to have it down automatically before they leave. _____

3. *Brenda:* OK, but what we really want is for them to use these skills back on the job. I think we need to assess how the training impacts their workplace behavior. _____

4. *Brad:* You're absolutely right, Brenda. And I think they are more likely to use the training on-the-job if we make the training sessions shorter, but spread them out over several weeks rather than cramming it all into a two-hour session. _____

    a.   Massed training

    b.   Distributed training

    c.   Overlearning

    d.   Performance-level criteria

    e.   Training-level criteria

    f.   Training in general principles

CRITICAL THINKING

Sam and Martina are investigating a workplace homicide at a local convenience store. The clerk working the late night shift was found by the morning shift to have been shot point-blank. All of the money in the cash register—only about $200 according to records—is missing. After interviewing fellow employees of the victim, Sam and Martina meet to go over their notes.

Sam tells Martina excitedly, "Man, this is the easiest case we've had in a long time. It's so obvious. The manager just fired someone last week for stealing from the cash register on the sly. I'm sure that guy is totally hacked about losing his job—not to mention his 'extra' source of income. I'll bet he came here in a rage and just shot whoever was on duty, then helped himself to the cash!" "I don't know, Sam," Martina said slowly. "That seems pretty unlikely to me. Don't you remember in the academy how they taught us that 85 percent of workplace homicides are committed against employees by strangers?" "Yeah," Sam said, "but what about the cash being gone? That was exactly what that former employee used to do all the time. The profile totally fits!" "Oh, Sam," Martina sighed, "I really don't think the perpetrator *meant* to kill anyone. Let's find the videotape and see what that reveals."

1. What is Sam's hypothesis?

2. What evidence supports Sam's hypothesis?

3. What is Martina's alternative hypothesis?

4. What evidence supports Martina's hypothesis?

5. What conclusions are most reasonable? What additional evidence is needed to reach a conclusion?

PERSONAL LEARNING ACTIVITIES

1. Go online to http://online.onetcenter.org. Once at that site, find the job or career group that you intend to go into once you complete your higher education. What types of knowledge, skills, or abilities are required for that profession? How can you tailor your college career to maximize your chance of success in that profession?

2. Look at recruitment ads for job openings on websites like www.hotjobs.com, www.careerbuilder.com, or www.monster.com. How do the advertisements vary for different types of positions? Can you tell from the postings which jobs are more competitive and difficult to land? How many jobs are posted in the area in which you eventually hope to work? What kinds of skills are employers looking for?

3. One area of employee training that is very important right now is to manage the diversity of having four different generations collaborating in the workplace. To see an overview of the challenges these four generations face when working together, visit http://www.fdu.edu/newspubs/magazine/05ws/generations.htm. Then, to see a training product designed to assist with this issue, visit http://www.generationsatwork.com/. What sorts of training evaluation information is available on the website? Based on what your text says about training, do you think there is sufficient information on the site to determine if the training program is effective or not?

4. Visit the following website: http://www.osha.gov/ to learn more about the Occupational Safety and Health Administration. What sorts of guidelines do they have in place for the kind of work you do, or hope to do? Look around your workplace, or a place you spend a lot of time at school, if you do not work. What health and safety mechanisms are in place there? Are the computer keyboards ergonomically correct? How about the chairs? How are you protected from hazardous material? How well do these protections match what the OSHA website indicates is appropriate for that setting?

5. To see a talk by Colin Powell on leadership, visit the following site: http://www.youtube.com/watch?v=T21HBWxBd-U. How do the ideas he articulates here fit with the theories of motivation in your text? How does he promote goal setting theory? Does he apply elements of expectancy theory at all? What elements of charisma does he display or promote in this brief talk? Can you see those elements in other clips you might find from current world leaders such as President Barack Obama? Why or why not?

MULTIPLE-CHOICE QUESTIONS

Quiz 1

1. Which of the following is an I/O psychologist least likely to do?
   a. Help a company develop new selection tools
   b. Identify ways to reduce occupational stress and fatigue
   c. Develop ways for organizations to exploit employees
   d. Measure employee job satisfaction

2. Kylie just did a job analysis of a secretary's position. Her write-up includes the following: "answers telephones, greets customers, types documents." Kylie has performed a
_____ job analysis.
   a. job-oriented
   b. person-oriented
   c. personality-oriented
   d. theoretical

3. Christopher is trying to select a new accountant. He has five applicants for his open position. To select a new employee, Christopher invites each applicant to come to the office for a visit. During each visit, Christopher chats with each applicant about a wide variety of topics. What he discusses with each person varies. Christopher is using which of the following assessment tools?
   a. Psychological tests
   b. Structured interviews
   c. Unstructured interviews
   d. Assessment centers

4. Which of the following is true of the assessment method Christopher is using in Question 3?
   a. It is an excellent assessment method as it is.
   b. It would be more valid if Christopher would ask totally different questions for each applicant.
   c. It will allow personal bias to enter the hiring decision.
   d. It will help Christopher focus only on the objective qualifications of the candidate.

5. Dena is a professor. Almost everyone in her class gets A's on papers. Dena shows the
_____ in her grading.
   a. halo error
   b. leniency error
   c. theoretical criterion
   d. actual criterion

6. Matt is trying to determine if a test he has ordered for a company is actually related to sales clerks' performance. Matt gives the tests to all the sales clerks in his store, then correlates their test scores with their performance appraisals. Matt is
   a. identifying the theoretical criterion.
   b. identifying the actual criterion.
   c. doing a job analysis.
   d. conducting a validation study.

7. Which of the following is an actual criterion for a car salesperson?
   a. Has good customer relations
   b. Meets or exceeds sales quota each month
   c. Works well with co-workers
   d. Is responsible and hardworking

8. Jerome is running a training program for the customer service representatives at a catalog sales company. He asks that each employee attend one training session per month. Jerome is using _____ in his training program.

   a. massed training
   b. distributed training
   c. overlearning
   d. general principles

9. After each training session, Kirk asks employees to fill out a questionnaire that measures how much they liked the training and how valuable they felt it was. Kirk is using _____ criteria to evaluate his training program.

   a. training-level
   b. trainee learning
   c. performance-level
   d. both trainee learning and performance-level

10. According to expectancy theory of motivation, who is most likely to be motivated to work the hardest?

   a. Martin, who values a promotion, but thinks that it doesn't matter how hard he works
   b. Brian, who doesn't care if he is promoted or not
   c. Cleo, who values a promotion, but doesn't believe that her boss will ever choose her
   d. Gary, who wants to be promoted and believes that if he works hard his boss will promote him

11. Mariah believes that job satisfaction should be measured in general. Paul believes one should measure how satisfied employees are with pay, hours, benefits, and coworkers separately. Mariah takes the _____ approach to measuring job satisfaction, while Paul takes the _____ approach.

   a. global; facet
   b. facet; global
   c. global; global
   d. facet; facet

12. Shahariah always gets to work a little early and often agrees to do more than her share of a project. She works hard to be supportive of her coworkers—sending gifts when one has a baby or flowers if there is a death in the family. She volunteers to help at charitable events that will allow the company to promote a good image in the community. All of this is in addition to doing a great job on her actual job duties. Shahariah is demonstrating

   a. counterproductive work behavior.
   b. work-family conflict.
   c. instrumental aggression.
   d. organizational citizenship behavior.

13. Jobs that require performing specific movements in the same way over long periods of time can create

    a. carpal tunnel syndrome.

    b. human factors injuries.

    c. repetitive strain injuries.

    d. disruptions in circadian rhythms.

14. At least two people working together as they perform the same or different tasks constitutes a(n)

    a. autonomous work group.

    b. work team.

    c. ingroup.

    d. work group.

15. Leaders who show lots of concern for the welfare of their employees are high on the dimension of

    a. initiating structure.

    b. ingroup leadership.

    c. outgroup leadership.

    d. consideration.

16. Dr. Arnold has an interesting strategy for supervising his subordinates at work. For Kelly, Phil, and Evelyn, he is always available and interested in what they have to say. For Sharon, Nan, and Joan, he is rarely available and doesn't listen to them very well when he is interacting with them. Dr. Arnold's leadership behaviors are consistent with the ideas in _____ theory.

    a. leader-member exchange

    b. expectancy

    c. ERG

    d. goal setting

17. Research in your text on training leaders to be charismatic best supports which of the following conclusions?

    a. Charisma is something you are born with; it cannot be trained.

    b. Charisma is completely trainable with astonishing results.

    c. Charisma training can increase charisma to some extent.

    d. Charisma does not impact employee job satisfaction.

18. Jon works for a construction company. His supervisor scoffs at safety rules, and Jon and his colleagues routinely break those rules. Jon's company has

    a. instrumental aggression.

    b. universal precautions.

    c. disruptive circadian rhythms.

    d. a poor climate of safety.

19. Wafah and Noor are identical twins who have been raised in different environments. Wafah is very satisfied with her job as an adult. Noor is probably
    a. also very satisfied with her job.
    b. very dissatisfied with her job.
    c. We cannot predict how Noor feels about her job because they were raised separately.
    d. not employed.

20. Instrumental aggression is
    a. aggression without the intent to injure.
    b. a poor climate of safety.
    c. a willingness to go beyond formal job requirements.
    d. attempts to injure a coworker.

Total Correct (See answer key) _____

Quiz 2

Use this quiz to reassess your learning after taking Quiz 1 and reviewing the chapter.

1. The science of behavior and mental processes in the workplace is known as _____ psychology.
    a. industrial and organizational
    b. occupational health
    c. engineering
    d. human factors

2. Although Kathy does not know how to run the new computer program at work, her boss thinks that she has the potential for learning to do so. Kathy's boss believes in her
    a. knowledge.
    b. skill.
    c. ability.
    d. None of these

3. Tests that measure the likelihood that someone might steal or engage in disruptive acts at work are known as _____ tests.
    a. intelligence
    b. personality
    c. integrity
    d. structured

4. Diane, a professor, has a list of ways she might respond to a student with whom she has a disagreement. At one end of the list is "tell the student to shut up and leave," in the middle of the list is "try to bend rules to compromise with student," and at the other end of the list is "listen patiently to student and finds ways to accommodate their concerns without bending the rules." Diane has a list of
    a. behavior-focused rating forms.
    b. critical incidents.
    c. leniency errors.
    d. halo errors.

5. One is most likely to be able to rely on walk-in applicants for which of the following jobs?
    a. Teaching at a college
    b. Receptionist at a bank
    c. Nurse in the ER
    d. Accountant at a tax firm

6. When an I/O psychologist is trying to help an organization identify which employees need what kind of training, the I/O psychologist is performing a
    a. training needs assessment.
    b. job analysis.
    c. job satisfaction measurement.
    d. None of these

7. Throughout Beth's training session, she gets lots of constructive comments from her trainer on how to do better. Her fellow trainees also encourage her to overcome mistakes and point out her positive efforts. Beth is receiving _____ as part of her training.
    a. general principles
    b. transfer of training
    c. overlearning
    d. feedback

8. Micha has just been given an eviction notice from her apartment. Now she finds it difficult to concentrate on her friendships or on her work because she is scrambling to find a place to live. According the ERG theory, Micha is focusing on her _____ needs.
    a. existence
    b. relatedness
    c. growth
    d. self-actualization

9. According to goal setting theory, which of the following is the best-stated goal?
    a. Sell more cars than I did last month.
    b. Keep up the good work.
    c. Quadruple the number of cars I sold last month.
    d. Increase the number of cars I sell by 50 percent over the next month.

10. Which of the following is a *personal* factor that can affect one's job satisfaction?
    a. Pay
    b. Job requirements
    c. Flexibility
    d. Gender

11. The research on job satisfaction and genetics discussed in your text concludes that
    a. genetics are a direct cause of job satisfaction.
    b. genetics have no influence on job satisfaction.
    c. genetics influence worker characteristics that in turn influence job satisfaction.
    d. no conclusions are possible at this time.

12. Which of the following is true of workplace homicides?
     a.   They are overwhelmingly committed by former employees.
     b.   They are overwhelmingly committed by strangers.
     c.   They are typically a result of intent to harm the victim.
     d.   They are rarely in places where people deal directly with the public and handle money.

13. The field that is concerned with psychological factors that affect the health, safety, and well-being of employees in the workplace is _____ psychology.
     a.   industrial and organizational
     b.   occupational health
     c.   engineering
     d.   human factors

14. When a person undergoes surgery, there are several people present for the process, each serving a different function: the surgeon, the anesthesiologist, a couple of residents to assist, and one or two nurses. These individuals are part of a(n)
     a.   work group.
     b.   work team.
     c.   autonomous work group.
     d.   outgroup.

15. According to LMX theory, leaders supervise out-group members by giving them _____ structure and _____ consideration.
     a.   high; low
     b.   low; high
     c.   high; high
     d.   low; low

16. When conducting a job analysis, one can ask the people currently in the job, known as _____, to fill out questionnaires about what they do in the workplace.
     a.   I/O psychologists
     b.   occupational health psychologists
     c.   position analysts
     d.   job incumbents

17. Which of the following is a good theoretical criterion for the position of college student?
     a.   Studies four hours a day
     b.   Participates in at least one student activity club each year
     c.   Makes a 3.5 grade-point average or higher
     d.   Seeks intellectual stimulation and growth

18. Naija works for a large transportation company in the marketing department. Even though it is not part of her job description, she participates in the organization's Corporate Challenge competitions, walks for March of Dimes in WalkAmerica (the company's official charity), and cleans up the break room routinely. Naija is high on
    a. organizational citizenship behavior.
    b. counterproductive work behavior.
    c. overlearning.
    d. job satisfaction.

19. Which of the following is the best example of an autonomous work group?
    a. A professional football team
    b. A work crew at the typical McDonalds franchise
    c. A team responsible for assembling Saturn automobiles
    d. A group of people taking customer service calls in a call center

20. Yeslam is interested in using a paper-and-pencil test of leadership skills to select new managers for his organization. Before investing a lot of money in the test, though, he does some research to see if any studies have correlated the test scores with managerial success. Yeslam is looking for
    a. climate of safety.
    b. transfer of training.
    c. validation studies.
    d. halo error.

Total Correct (See answer key) _____

ANSWERS TO FILL-IN-THE-BLANKS KEY TERMS

1. job performance (see Measuring Job Performance)

2. Organizational citizenship behavior (see Consequences of Job Satisfaction)

3. goal setting theory (see Employee Motivation)

4. work group (see Work Groups and Work Teams")

5. assessment center (see Measuring Employee Characteristics)

6. leader-member exchange theory (see Group Leadership)

7. validation (see Selection Processes)

8. industrial and organizational psychology (see An Overview of Industrial and Organizational Psychology)

9. Autonomous work groups (see Autonomous Work Groups)

10. job satisfaction (see Job Satisfaction)

ANSWERS TO CONCEPTS AND EXERCISES

Assessment Methods

1. *Assessment center.* An assessment center routinely uses in-basket exercises and exercises designed to test interpersonal skill, like the two exercises described here. Typically, assessment centers require two to three days to complete. (see Measuring Employee Characteristics)

2.   *Personality test.* Carson's test is probably trying to measure her level of conscientiousness, a personality trait that has been linked to job performance across a variety of occupations. (see Measuring Employee Characteristics)

3.   *Structured interview.* Cooper's interview sounds like it will be very structured, with a set list of questions or topics to cover. He and the interviewer will not be allowed to discuss just any old topic that arises. (see Measuring Employee Characteristics)

4.   *Unstructured interview.* Joseph's interview sounds unstructured. The manager doesn't seem to have a preset list of questions or topics, and they just discuss whatever topic comes up. Typically, this type of interview is not nearly as predictive of good job performance as the structured interview, and in fact, it will allow more bias to enter the hiring process. (see Measuring Employee Characteristics)

Designing and Evaluating a Training Program

1.   *Troy: Training in general principles.* Troy wants to make sure that the employees understand the general principles of how the new program works. (see Designing Training Programs)

2.   *Melinda: Overlearning.* Melinda wants to make sure the employees have the opportunity to practice using the new program over and over until they can use it automatically. (see Designing Training Programs)

3.   *Brenda: Performance-level criteria.* Brenda wants to measure how the training impacts employees' actual job performances. (see Evaluating Training Programs)

4.   *Brad: Distributed training.* Brad thinks that the team should develop a distributed training program, as opposed to a massed training program that would compress the training into a single shorter period of time. (see Designing Training Programs)

ANSWERS TO CRITICAL THINKING

1.   Sam's hypothesis is that a disgruntled former employee shot the clerk and then robbed the store.

2.   Sam is using fellow employees' testimony as evidence to support his hypothesis.

3.   Martina hypothesizes that the perpetrator was a stranger committing a random robbery rather than a fellow employee.

4.   Martina knows that most workplace homicides are committed by strangers, especially in this type of setting. Disgruntled employees typically resort to verbal assault, not physical.

5.   Martina needs to view the videotape to see if it recorded the crime as it happened. If the former employee is responsible for the shooting, that person probably knew where the camera was and deactivated it before committing the crime. A random robber who got too nervous and shot the clerk would not know the location of the camera and how to deactivate it. In that case, the camera may have recorded the crime in action. (*NOTE:* Critical thinking is a constant process of hypothesizing, examining evidence, rehypothesizing, and collecting more evidence. Martina may not be correct.)

ANSWERS TO MULTIPLE-CHOICE QUESTIONS

Circle the question numbers you answered correctly.

Quiz 1

1.   c is the answer. An I/O psychologist tries to improve work life for employees, not help exploit them. (see An Overview of Industrial and Organizational Psychology)

a, b, d.   All of these are activities an I/O psychologist would participate in.

2.   a is the answer. A job-oriented job analysis yields a list of tasks the job requires. (Assessing People, Jobs, and Job Performance)

   b.   A person-oriented job analysis yields a list of KSAOs, not a list of tasks that the job requires.

   c.   A personality-oriented job analysis identifies the personality traits needed to perform a particular job well.

   d.   There is no such thing as a theoretical job analysis.

3.   c is the answer. An unstructured interview allows the interviewer to ask a variety of questions without worrying about consistency of questions or topics between interviewees. (see Assessing People, Jobs, and Job Performance)

   a.   A psychological test would likely be a paper-and-pencil tool, not an interview.

   b.   A structured interview requires consistency among the topics discussed and questions asked between the interviewees.

   d.   An assessment center is a series of exercises in which experts rate the applicant's performance.

4.   c is the answer. Christopher was conducting an unstructured interview in Question 3. An unstructured interview allows personal bias to enter the hiring decision. (see Assessing People, Jobs, and Job Performance)

   a.   A structured interview would be a better assessment method than an unstructured interview.

   b.   Asking totally different questions for each applicant would make the interview less valid, not more.

   d.   A structured interview would help Christopher focus on the objective qualifications of candidates, but an unstructured interview would not.

5.   b is the answer. The tendency to give all papers high scores is known as the leniency error, because the rater is being generally very lenient. (see Assessing People, Jobs, and Job Performance)

   a.   The halo error is the tendency to rate a person very similarly across all dimensions.

   b.   The theoretical criterion is statement of what is meant by good performance in theory.

   d.   The actual criterion specifies what should be measured to determine if the theoretical criterion has been met.

6.   d is the answer. A validation study attempts to relate an assessment method, such as a test, to actual performance on the job. Matt does this by correlating the test to his employees' performance appraisals. (see Recruiting and Selecting Employees)

   a.   Identifying the theoretical criterion involves stating what one believes theoretically reflects good performance.

   b.   Identifying the actual criterion involves specifying how one will measure the theoretical criterion.

   c.   Doing a job analysis involves identifying either the tasks a job requires or the KSAOs necessary to do the job.

7.   b is the answer. An actual criterion should be something clear and measurable. Only "meets or exceed sales quota each month" is clearly measurable. (Assessing People, Jobs, and Job Performance)

    a, c, d.   Each of these is more abstract and is a theoretical criterion.

8.   b is the answer. Distributed training involves spacing training out in shorter sessions over a span of time. (see Training Employees)

    a.   Massed training involves compressing the training into a single, longer time period.

    c.   Overlearning means trainees are allowed to practice and learn a new skill until it is automatic.

    d.   Training in general principles involves teaching the employee why a certain skill or procedure is important and helping them see it as part of a bigger picture.

9.   a is the answer. Training-level criteria are measures taken at the end of a training session that indicate how enjoyable and valuable the employees perceived the training to be. (see Training Employees)

    b.   Trainee learning criteria measure what the trainee learned in the training, typically in the form of a test.

    c.   Performance-level criteria measure how well the trainee transfers the training back to on-the-job performance.

    d.   Neither trainee learning criteria nor performance-level is correct.

10.   d is the answer. According to expectancy theory, both the expectation that one can perform well if he or she tries and the expectation that good performance will result in a valued outcome are important. Gary values a promotion (the outcome) and believes that his hard work will pay off. (see Employee Motivation)

    a.   Martin does not have the expectancy that hard work will result in the desired promotion; therefore, he is not likely to be motivated to work for it.

    b.   Brian does not value the promotion, so he will not be motivated.

    c.   Cleo values the promotion but does not expect that her behavior will result in her boss's selection of her, so she will not be motivated.

11.   a is the answer. The global approach to job satisfaction argues that one should measure job satisfaction at a very general level; the facet approach argues one should measure satisfaction with various facets of the job. (see Job Satisfaction)

    b.   This answer is backwards from the correct one (see explanation above).

    c.   Only Mariah takes the global approach.

    d.   Only Paul takes the facet approach.

12.   d is the answer. Organizational citizenship behavior involves going above and beyond one's actual duties to promote the well-being of the organization and one's coworkers. (see Job Satisfaction)

    a.   Counterproductive work behavior involves doing things that harm the organization. Shahariah is not harming the organization.

    b.   Work-family conflict occurs when one's job responsibilities interfere with one's family responsibilities.

c.   Instrumental aggression involves aggression without the intent to harm—aggression as a means to achieve another goal.

13.   c is the answer. Repetitive strain injuries occur when a job requires performing a specific movement in the same way over long time periods. Eventually these movements cause joints to become inflamed—a repetitive strain injury. (see Occupational Health Psychology)

a.   Carpal tunnel syndrome is a specific type of repetitive strain injury, but there are many other kinds of repetitive strain injuries.

b.   There is no such thing as a human factors injury. Human factors is a subfield of psychology that focuses on creating tools and equipment that will help prevent repetitive strain injuries and other problems.

d.   Disruptions in circadian rhythms occur when one's work schedule involves shift changes that disrupt the employee's pattern of eating, sleeping, and wakefulness.

14.   d is the answer. A work group is at least two people working together on the same or different tasks. (see Work Groups and Work Teams)

a.   An autonomous work group is a self-managed employee work group that does not report to anyone for routine daily supervision.

b.   A work team is a work group in which members' specialized activities are coordinated and interdependent as they work towards a common goal.

c.   An in-group is a group in which one is a member. In LMX theory, the in-group is the group of employees that the leader treats more favorably than others—asking their opinion and including them in decision making.

15.   d is the answer. Leaders who are high on consideration show concern for the welfare of their employees, including friendly, supportive behavior that makes working more pleasant. (see Work Groups and Work Teams)

a.   Initiating structure is a dimension of leadership behavior, but it involves different kinds of behavior. Leaders high on initiating structure spend a lot of time coordinating employee efforts by assigning tasks and clarifying expectations.

b.   Ingroup leadership does tend to be high on consideration, but ingroup leadership is not a dimension of leader behavior. It just describes the setting in which a leader behaves with high consideration behaviors.

c.   Outgroup leadership tends to be high on initiating structure. Leaders also tend to give outgroup employees less opportunity to influence decisions (low consideration).

16.   a is the answer. Leader-member exchange theory proposes that leaders supervise in-group and out-group members differently. Dr. Arnold treats Kelly, Phil and Evelyn as ingroup members, showing them high consideration. The others he treats as outgroup members. (see Work Groups and Work Teams)

b, c, d.   These are all theories of motivation, not leadership.

17.   c is the answer. Managers who received charisma training were perceived by their employees as more charismatic after training as compared to a control group. (see Work Groups and Work Teams)

a.   Although it is likely that charisma comes more naturally to some than to others, it does appear somewhat teachable.

    b.   Although charisma appears to be teachable, more research is needed to determine the extent to which it is teachable and the magnitude of the training's impact.

    d.   Leaders who had charisma training had subordinates who showed an increase in job satisfaction following the leader's charisma training, as compared to controls.

18.   d is the answer. A poor climate of safety is evidenced by lack of safety training, little supervisor emphasis on following safety rules, and worker tendency to ignore safety rules. (see Occupational Health Psychology)

    a.   Instrumental aggression occurs when the purpose of the aggressive act is not to injure, but to accomplish something else through the "instrument" of aggression.

    b.   Universal procedures are safeguards taken by the healthcare community.

    c.   Disrupted circadian rhythms occur when shifts are rotated.

19.   a is the answer. There is a strong correlation between job satisfaction ratings by identical twins, even when they have been raised apart. If Wafah is satisfied, it is likely that Noor feels similarly. (see Job Satisfaction)

    b.   Noor probably feels similarly to Wafah, not the opposite.

    c.   Noor's job satisfaction can be predicted based on Wafah's, because identical twins' job satisfaction ratings are highly positively correlated.

    d.   We cannot predict if Noor is employed or not based on the evidence in your text regarding job satisfaction and genetics.

20.   a is the answer. Instrumental aggression involves aggressive behavior without the intent to injure. Rather, the aggressor seeks to attain some other goal (money or valuables) and the aggression is simply a means to that end. (see Job Satisfaction)

    b.   A poor climate of safety involves a workplace with little safety training, supervisors who do not emphasize safety rules, and worker disregard of such rules.

    c.   This is organizational citizenship behavior, not instrumental aggression.

    d.   Instrumental aggression does not involve the intent to injure.

Now turn to the quiz analysis table at the end of this chapter to find which areas you know well and which areas you need to work on. Circle the numbers in the table for items on Quiz 1 that you answered correctly.

Quiz 2

1.   a is the answer. Industrial and organizational psychologists study behavior and mental processes in the workplace. (see An Overview of Industrial and Organizational Psychology)

    b.   Occupational health psychology is the study of psychological factors that affect the health, safety, and well being of employees in the workplace.

    c.   Engineering psychology focuses on creating tools and equipment that are less physically stressful to use.

    d.   Human factors psychology is the same thing as engineering psychology (see c).

2.   c is the answer. Ability refers to one's potential for learning a skill. Running a computer program is a skill, and Kathy's boss believes she has the potential to do it; therefore, he believes in her ability. (see Assessing People, Jobs, and Job Performance)

    a.   Knowledge refers to what a person already knows. Kathy does not know how to run the new program, so her boss does not believe in her knowledge.

    b.   Skill refers to how good a person is doing at a particular task. Kathy does not yet know how to do the task of running the program, therefore her boss does not believe in her skill.

    d.   c is the correct answer.

3.   c is the answer. Integrity tests are a special type of test related to personality tests. They are used to identify people who have tendencies that might lead them to steal or engage in disruptive acts at work. (see Assessing People, Jobs, and Job Performance)

    a.   Intelligence tests (also called IQ tests) measure general skill and ability, not one's tendency to steal or be disruptive.

    b.   Personality tests assess a wide variety of employee characteristics, providing information about personality dimensions that may be relevant to hiring decisions. They are more general than just measuring tendencies to steal or be disruptive.

    d.   An integrity test may well be structured, but lots of tests can be very structured.

4.   b is the answer. Critical incidents illustrate different levels of performance—ranging from extremely good performance to extremely poor—on various job dimensions. Diane's list of possible responses includes poor, moderate, and good performance exemplars. (see Assessing People, Jobs, and Job Performance)

    a.   Behavior-focused rating forms contain lists of critical incidents for a variety of job dimensions. Diane's list does not make a complete rating form because it has only critical incidents related to a single situation and because it does not involve a supervisor rating the employee.

    c.   Leniency errors mean a supervisor tends to use only the top of a scale, giving all employees high (positive) ratings.

    d.   Halo errors occur when a supervisor tends to give the same rating to an employee across all dimensions being evaluated.

5.   b is the answer. Jobs that can typically be filled with just walk-in applicants are typically low-level positions in an organization and require few skills. A position as a receptionist doesn't involve any degree or special training beyond high school, and it is not a high-level position in a bank, so it can rely on walk-ins. (see Recruiting and Selecting Employees)

    a, c, d.   Being a college teacher, a nurse, or an accountant all require some kind of advanced schooling. Jobs that require advanced training typically cannot rely on walk-ins and demand the use of many different recruitment methods.

6.   a is the answer. Training needs assessments are performed by I/O psychologists to help organizations take into account the organizations job categories, its work force, and its goals. The purpose of identifying these is to use the information to determine which employees are in need of what kind of training. (see Training Employees)

    b.   A job analysis is the process of collecting information about jobs and job requirements that is used to guide hiring and training decisions.

    c.   Measuring job satisfaction involves determining the degree to which people like or dislike their jobs.

    d.   a is the correct answer.

7. d is the answer. Feedback in training means telling someone how he/she is doing. This can take the form of reinforcement following progress, constructive suggestions following errors, and encouragement to continue to learn. Beth's trainer and fellow trainees are all providing her with feedback. (see Training Employees)

    a. Training in general principles involves providing the trainee with the big picture so they understand how and why the new skill they are learning is important and fits in with other skills they may already have. Beth's training may have general principles, but they are not described here.

    b. Transfer of training refers to the goal of making sure that training is transferred from the training session and site to be used on the job. We do not know if Beth will transfer her training to her actual work setting.

    c. Overlearning means a training session provides the trainee with enough practice opportunities so that her or she can reach a high level of performance—at which point the new skill can be used almost automatically. Although Beth's training may involve overlearning, this question describes only how she receives feedback.

8. a is the answer. Existence needs in ERG theory are things that are necessary for survival, such as food, water, and shelter. Micha is concentrating on finding shelter, so she is focused on existence needs. (see Employee Motivation)

    b. Relatedness needs in ERG theory are needs for social contact and satisfying relationships and interactions. Micha is having trouble concentrating on friendships, so she is not focused on relatedness needs.

    c. Growth needs in ERG theory are needs for developing and using one's capabilities. Micha is not concentrating on her work and how to develop herself there, so she is not focused on growth needs.

    d. Self-actualization needs are the highest level of need in Maslow's hierarchy of needs. Within ERG theory, self-actualization is included in growth needs, which Micha is not focused on (see above).

9. d is the answer. According to goal-setting theory, the most motivating goals are challenging but not impossible and specific enough to allow progress to be tracked. A 50 percent increase is difficult, but not impossible, and is specific enough to track progress. (see Employee Motivation)

    a. "Sell more cars than I did last month" is not very specific and may not be challenging enough.

    b. "Keep up the good work" is also not specific or challenging enough.

    c. Quadrupling the number of cars sold may be too challenging of a goal.

10. d is the answer. Personal factors that affect job satisfaction are gender, age, and ethnicity— qualities that are tied to the person. (see Job Satisfaction)

    a, b, c. These are all environmental factors that affect job satisfaction because they are tied to the job, not the person.

11. c is the answer. Individual differences in job satisfaction are probably related to workers' characteristics, some of which are influenced by genetics. (see Job Satisfaction)

    a. We do not yet know the precise mechanisms through which genetics might affect job satisfaction, and direct cause has not yet been adequately demonstrated.

    b. This statement is false. Genetics *do* have some influence on job satisfaction.

     d.   We can conclude that genetics influence characteristics that in turn influence job satisfaction. Future research, however, may lead us to revise this conclusion.

12.   b is the answer. Eighty-five percent of workplace homicides are committed against employees by strangers. (see Occupational Health Psychology)

     a.   Only 15 percent of workplace homicides are committed by disgruntled employees or former employees.

     c.   Most aggression at work is instrumental aggression, with the intent not necessarily to injure but to achieve a goal such as getting money or valuables.

     d.   Employees who deal with the public, handle money, and work alone at night are at particular risk for aggression and workplace homicide, not lower risk.

13.   b is the answer. Occupational health psychology is the study of psychological factors that affect health safety, and well being at work. (see Occupational Health Psychology)

     a.   Industrial and organizational psychology is the study of behavior and mental processes at work, not just health, safety, and well being.

     c.   Engineering psychology focuses on creating tools and situations at work that will cause less physical stress as they are used.

     d.   Human factors psychology is the same thing as engineering psychology.

14.   b is the answer. A work team is a special kind of work group in which the members' activities are coordinated with and depend on one another, each member has a specialized role, and members work to accomplish a shared goal. In surgery, the goal is to effectively help the patient (shared goal), but each member on the team has a different role. (see Work Groups and Work Teams)

     a.   A work group is at least two people who interact with one another as they perform the same or different tasks. Although a set of people involved in surgery are a work group, they are a special kind of work group—the work team.

     c.   An autonomous work group is a special type of group that manages itself and does not report to anyone for routine daily supervision. Although the surgery team may have some autonomy, there is not enough information here to demonstrate that it is an autonomous work group.

     d.   An outgroup refers to a set of people who are not members of one's own group (the in-group).

15.   a is the answer. LMX theory postulates that leaders provide outgroup members high structure and low consideration. (see Work Groups and Work Teams)

     b.   Leaders provide ingroup members with low structure and high consideration, according to LMX theory.

     c.   Leaders provide only high structure, not high consideration, to outgroup members.

     d.   Leaders provide only low consideration, not low structure, to outgroup members.

16.   d is the answer. Job incumbents are the individuals currently holding the job in question. (see Assessing People, Jobs, and Job Performance)

     a.   I/O psychologists study behavior and mental processes in the workplace.

     b.   Occupational health psychologists study factors affecting the health, safety, and well-being of employees.

c.   You may be thinking of the Position Analysis Questionnaire, which is a method of job analysis described in your text. A position analyst is not described in your text.

17.   d is the answer. A theoretical criterion is abstract idea of what constitutes good performance. This is the only abstract description. (see Assessing People, Jobs, and Job Performance)

a, b, c.   These are all concrete, measureable features of student performance. They are actual criteria, not theoretical.

18.   a is the answer. Organizational citizenship behavior is the willingness to go beyond formal job requirements. Naija is doing that by cleaning the break room, walking for charity, and so forth. (see Job Satisfaction)

b.   Counterproductive work behavior is a variety of negative behavior at work, including theft, aggression, computer hacking, and so forth.

c.   Overlearning is a desired element of a training program. It involves learning the new skill or behavior to the point of automaticity.

d.   Job satisfaction is the degree to which one likes or dislikes their job. This question does not tell us how Naija feels about her job.

19.   c is the answer. Saturn is a company that uses AWGs in vehicle assembly. Such teams make their own decisions (including hiring and firing) and manage themselves. (see Work Groups and Work Teams)

a.   A professional football team is usually hierarchically organized, with the head coach and others at the top of the organization determining hiring and firing of players, what plays to run, and so forth.

b.   The typical McDonald's crew is directed by a manager, or assistant manager.

d.   Taking calls in a call center typically involves a manager who will deal with complaints that the front-line customer service representative cannot resolve.

20.   c is the answer. Validation studies document the relationship (typically using correlations) of predictors, such as tests, with work outcomes. (see Recruiting and Selecting Employees)

a.   Climate of safety refers to the degree to which supervisors and employees and the organization as a whole support safety rules and training.

b.   Transfer of training occurs when the skills learned in the training sessions transfer and are used in actual work situations.

d.   Halo error occurs when one is unable to distinguish between differences in dimensions being rated.

Now turn to the quiz analysis table at the end of this chapter to find which areas you know well and which areas you need to work on. Circle the numbers in the table for items on Quiz 2 that you answered correctly.

For each question you answered correctly, circle its number. (Quiz 1 numbers are not shaded; Quiz 2 numbers are shaded.) Are there patterns in the types of questions or the topics you got wrong that could direct your further study? Did you improve from Quiz 1 to Quiz 2?

Topic	Type Of Question		
	Definition	**Comprehension**	**Application**
An Overview of Industrial and Organizational Psychology		1	
	1		
Assessing People, Jobs, and Job Performance		4	2, 3, 5, 7
	3	16	2, 4, 17
Recruiting and Selecting Employees			6
		5	20
Training Employees			8. 9
		6	7
Employee Motivation			10
			8, 9
Job Satisfaction	20		11, 12, 19
		10, 11	18
Occupational Health Psychology		13	18
	13	12	
Work Groups and Work Teams	14	15, 17	16
		15	14, 19

Total correct by quiz:

Quiz 1:	
Quiz 2:	

CHAPTER 20

Neuropsychology

OUTLINE

I. FOUNDATIONS OF NEUROPSYCHOLOGY
    Neuropsychology is the study of the relationships among brain processes, human behavior, and
    psychological functioning. It rests on two assumptions: (1) Complicated mental tasks can be
    tested and studied separately and (2) Different psychological processes are controlled by different
    regions (or combinations of regions) in the brain. *Experimental neuropsychologists* study
    primarily people with brain damage to understand brain function better (but may study people
    with normal brains), while clinical neuropsychologists use this knowledge to help treat individuals
    with brain damage or dysfunction.

    A. A Brief History of Neuropsychology
        Localization of function is the idea that specific psychological functions can be affected by
        damage to a specific brain area. In the early 1800s, this was not a commonly accepted
        notion. Franz Gall proposed it but had also mistakenly believed in a variety of other ideas
        about brain science that turned out to be false (including *phrenology*). Later, Paul Broca,
        who had higher status in the scientific community, studied a patient who had a history of
        stroke, more officially known as a cerebrovascular accident (CVA). He found that certain
        speech difficulties were related to brain lesions in specific locations. This finding ultimately
        led to the acceptance, and broader support, of the notion of localization of function.

    B. Modules and Networks
        Modules are discrete brain regions that perform their own kinds of unique analysis.
        Somewhat like a circuit board, each module adds a required piece of the puzzle that allows
        speech, or some other complex function, to occur. Teams of modules form networks, which
        are collectively responsible for more global functions. *Disconnection syndromes* illustrate
        what happens when modules remain intact but are unable to interact in a network. One such
        example is *alexia without agraphia* (the ability to write but not read).

    C. Lesion Analysis
        Lesion analysis is the study of localization of function by looking at the results of brain
        damage. To do this, experimental neuropsychologists must know what precise ability, or
        psychological function, has been damaged. They must identify what a brain regions are
        involved in that ability, and which ability is *disassociated* because it is based in a different
        brain module. Such assessments are made through neuropsychological testing.

    D. Neuropsychological Assessment
        Neuropsychological assessment can either be individually tailored or involve a standardized
        test battery. Standardized batteries have the advantage of giving the same test in the same
        way to all patients, but they are unable to be tailored to a particular patient's problem. Most
        clinical neuropsychologists start with a standardized test battery and then follow up with
        individual tests that look relevant. To interpret test results, neuropsychologists rely on norms
        to reveal if a particular result is abnormal or normal.

E.   Training for Neuropsychology
Training in neuropsychology focuses on learning about a large number of different neuropsychological tests, including how to give and score them and interpret results. Usually, training involves earning a Ph.D. in clinical psychology with a focus on neuropsychology, followed by an internship under the supervision of a licensed clinical neuropsychologist. Clinical neuropsychologists are employed by hospitals or specialty clinics. Experimental neuropsychologists are usually employed in a university setting where they teach, conduct research, and test patients as time permits.

II.   MECHANISMS OF BRAIN DYSFUNCTION
A.   Cerebrovascular Accidents
Disruption of behavior and mental processes due to loss of blood supply in some part of the brain is known as a stroke or cerebrovascular accident (CVA). They are the third leading cause of death in the United States. Because there are no pain receptors in the brain, strokes usually involve no pain, which can lead to costly delay in medical treatment as the victim may not realize anything is wrong. The degree of recovery possible with a stroke depends on the quality and speed of the medical treatment, the size and location of the stroke, the health of the remaining blood vessels and brain tissue, the degree to which the remaining nervous system can reorganize along its original lines, and the nature of the rehabilitation program. Scientists are experimenting with chemicals that may help the brain to heal itself after a CVA.

B.   Traumatic Brain Injury
Traumatic brain injury (also known as trauma) is damage to the brain due to sudden impact. This impact may involve an object striking the head, or the head suddenly stopping or starting movement. It occurs because the brain floats in cerebrospinal fluid, and as an object strikes the head or the abrupt head movement occurs, the brain slides around in its bony case. As it bumps and bounces against bone, nerve fibers are damaged. The amount of damage depends on the degree of force, and damage in trauma tends to be more widespread compared to strokes.

C.   Neurodegenerative Diseases
Neurodegenerative diseases cause *neurodegeneration*, the gradual process of cell damage in the brain. Notable examples include Alzheimer's disease, Parkinson's disease, and Huntington's disease. Each of these diseases affects a particular kind of brain cell (or cells in a particular location), causing specific loss of function. Causes of neurodegeneration are largely unknown, although infection, nutritional deficiency, and genetic abnormalities have been known to cause it.

III. NEUROPSYCHOLOGICAL DISORDERS
Patterns of symptoms typically observed in individuals with stroke, trauma, or neurodegeneration are known as syndromes.

A.   Amnestic Disorders
1.   Amnestic disorders involve memory loss. Examples include anterograde amnesia and Korsakoff's psychosis (or Korsakoff's syndrome).

2.   Anterograde amnesia involves damage to the hippocampus and results in inability to form new memories.

3.   Korsakoff's psychosis can be caused by vitamin B1 deficiency or by alcoholism resulting in damage to the medial dorsal thalamus. Such damage yields anterograde amnesia with confabulation, the creation of false memories.

B. Consciousness Disturbances

1. <u>Consciousness disturbances</u> involve impairment of the ability to accurately be aware of the world. For example, damage to the <u>reticular formation</u>, or *reticular activating system* (RAS), can result in a *coma* (severe damage) or a *persistent vegetative state* (lesser damage). Chances of recovery are low following significant damage to the RAS.

2. Damage to both sides of the cerebral cortex can also result in impairment to consciousness. This can occur with drugs or alcohol.

3. <u>Delirium</u>, the waxing and waning of consciousness, can be caused by fever, poisoning, infection, or side effects from medication. It is usually not permanent.

4. *Anosognosia*, the absence of the knowledge of disease, is possible when damage occurs to the right side of the brain. Anosognosia can lead to delay in seeking medical treatment, as the patient does not realize there is a problem.

C. Thinking Critically: Can Someone Be Partially Paralyzed and Not Know It?
What am I being asked to believe or accept?

Patients with *hemiparesis* (paralysis on one side of the body) are genuinely unaware of their partial paralysis.

What evidence is available to support the assertion?

Hemiparesis patients seem aware of other areas of weakness and potentially upsetting occurrences, which is unlikely if they were simply using ego defense mechanisms to avoid coping with the hemiparesis. Furthermore, hemiparesis is more likely with right hemisphere brain damage than left—unlikely if ego defenses are the underlying explanation for the lack of awareness. Finally, using the *Wada technique,* scientists have demonstrated that hemiparesis patients show anosognosia even when the paralysis is known to be temporary. Together, these finding suggest that hemiparesis patients are not using ego defenses to avoid awareness of their paralysis but indeed are genuinely unaware of their condition.

Are there alternative ways of interpreting the evidence?

One problem with the Wada technique is that it is retrospective—it requires patients to describe their experience while "paralyzed" after the fact. Recalled answers may differ from those that might be given while actually under paralysis. Family studies suggest that individuals who tended to use denial as a coping mechanism before their hemiparesis occurred were most likely to experience anosagnosia as compared to those individuals who tended to not use denial as a coping tool.

What additional evidence would help to evaluate the alternatives?

Retrospective bias makes the interpretation of the Wada technique results and the family studies difficult. One solution would be to conduct a *prospective study* in which individuals were identified and their stress-coping techniques assessed. They could then be followed for a period of time to determine whether those individuals who used denial most consistently were more likely to experience anosagnosia following a stroke.

What conclusions are most reasonable?

Until prospective studies have been conducted, it is most reasonable to conclude that at least some of the anosagnosia that occurs with hemiparesis is indeed genuine unawareness.

D.   Perceptual Disturbances
1.   Damage to perceptual systems in the brain causes <u>perceptual disturbances</u>. In the visual system, such damage can occur in the "what" and in the "where" neural pathways.

2.   "What" neural pathways, so named because they help us determine what we are seeing, are in the cortical region leading to the ventrolateral temporal lobe. Damage to the "what" systems can result in *visual agnosia*, a condition in which one is unable to identify objects. *Prosopagnosia* is a more specific visual agnosia which involves the inability to recognize faces. *Capgras syndrome* is another facial recognition disorder in which the patient can recognize the face, but believes the person has been replaced by an imposter. It tends to occur after temporal lobe damage.

3.   "Where" neural paths are the cortical regions leading to the parietal lobe. Damage to these paths can yield *simultanagnosia* (difficulty perceiving a whole scene) or *hemineglect* (difficulty responding to information from one side of the world). An interesting feature of hemineglect is that it cannot be explained as due to lack of sensation from one side of the world or another. Rather, patients with hemineglect are more likely to pay attention to one side of the world. Some hemineglect patients do also experience sensory loss in addition to their perceptual disturbances.

E.   Focus on Research Methods: Studying Hemineglect
It is difficult to know if hemineglect is a perceptual problem or a sensory problem, because one can't report on a perception unless it originated with a sensation. Bisiach proposed that if it is perceptual, then the neglect of a side of the world will occur in imagination as well as raw sensations. To test this idea, he created stimuli and presented them to participants with hemineglect through a "slit" so that the participants had to imagine the whole. Even in these imagined representations, participants displayed hemineglect. However, these patients all had damage in the parietal lobes, so damage in other parts of the brain need to be studied as well.

F.   Linkages: Language Disorders and the Brain
1.   Damage to the brain that results in difficulty speaking, reading, writing, and understanding language is known as a <u>language disorder</u>, or <u>aphasia</u>.

2.   Most aphasias result from damage to the left side of the brain, often stroke or trauma. Neurodegenerative processes such as *frontotemporal degeneration* (*FTD*) can also produce aphasia known as *primary progressive aphasia*.

3.   <u>Broca's aphasia</u> is the loss of the ability to produce language fluently. They tend to retain the ability to speak of concrete objects, but struggle to express abstract ideas. Their speech leaves out abstract articles, adverbs, and adjectives, making it telegraphic. They also may make mistakes in naming objects based on how a word sounds, which is called *phonemic paraphasia*. They also struggle with understanding subtle rules of grammar, a problem called *agrammatism*.

4.   <u>Wernicke's aphasia</u> is difficulty understanding language and sensations more generally. These patients speak fluently but make *semantic paraphrasias* in which they use words that have the wrong meaning. Their speech tends to use lots of adverbs, adjectives, and articles, but few nouns and verbs. They do not recognize their errors and are surprised when others do not understand them.

5.   *Aprosodia* is the inability to use tone to communicate meaning or to understand the meaning of what someone else is saying. *Expressive aprosodia* involves speaking in a dull monotone. *Receptive aprosodia* involves the inability to understand the meaning of other people's tone.

G. Movement Disorders

When learned motor skills are disrupted due to brain damage or dysfunction, one is said to have a <u>movement disorder</u>, or <u>apraxia</u>. *Ideational apraxia* occurs when movements are performed correctly but in the wrong sequence. *Ideomotor apraxia* occurs when the sequence of movements is correct but the performance of skilled movements is poor.

H. Dementia

1. <u>Dementia</u> is diagnosed when a person has notable impairment of memory along with at least one other impairment of psychological function, and the impairments have significant impact on daily living requirements. It is usually gradual, progressive, and irreversible.

2. *Mild cognitive impairment (MCI)* may precede the appearance of some kinds of dementia. *Amnestic MCI* involves well-below-average scores on neuropsychological tests of memory but no other deficits. Such an indicator is helpful, as medication may be given at this point to ward off full scale dementia.

3. Dementia is often caused by neurodegenerative disease such as *Alzheimer's disease*. Alzheimer's disease involves microscopic abnormalities in the brain, including *neurofibrillary tangles* and *amyloid plaques*. The disease mainly damages neurons using the neurotransmitter *acetylcholine*, especially in the parietal and medial temporal lobes of the brain. Because parietal lobes deal with locating objects in space, Alzheimer's patients may easily get lost. Because the left parietal lobe is involved in naming objects and performing learned movements, patients may also struggle with *anomia* and apraxia. Finally, because the medial temporal lobes contain the hippocampus, one of the main symptoms of Alzheimer's disease is difficulty forming new memories.

4. <u>Vascular dementia</u> is caused by restrictions in blood supply to the brain, but the hippocampus is relatively well-preserved. Patients with vascular dementia can form new memories but have difficulty retrieving them, making neuropsychological assessment critical to discerning the difference between vascular dementia and Alzheimer's disease so that proper medication may be prescribed.

5. Giving the right drug at the right time can help delay the impact of the dementia, but a major challenge is patient compliance. The patient must take the medication as prescribed to reap the benefit, and many dementia patients do not comply. Some pharmaceutical companies now offer medication in a patch that is not dependent on patient memory to take the medication.

KEY TERMS

1. **Neuropsychology** is the subfield of psychology whose goal is to explore and understand the relationships among brain processes, human behavior, and psychological functioning. (see Foundations of Neuropsychology)

Example: Scientists who study consequences of brain injuries, such as shaken baby syndrome, are working in the field of neuropsychology.

2. **Clinical neuropsychologists** are neuropsychologists who use tests and other methods to try to understand neuropsychological problems and intact functions in individual patients. (see Foundations of Neuropsychology)

Example: Irene works with individuals who have experienced head trauma and brain injury of some sort. She sees patients and tests them; she tries to reach a diagnosis and, if possible, plan treatment. She is rarely, if at all, involved in conducting research, although she reads published research frequently and uses the results to guide her diagnosis and treatment of patients.

3. **Localization of function** is the idea that specific psychological functions can be affected by damage to specific brain areas. (see A Brief History of Neuropsychology)

   Example: A person who has experienced damage to Broca's area in his or her brain loses the ability to speak clearly, although he or she can understand language and other brain functions remain intact.

4. A **cerebrovascular accident (CVA),** or **stroke,** is a loss of blood supply to some part of the brain, resulting in disruption of some aspect of behavior or mental processes. (see A Brief History of Neuropsychology)

   Example: Dan's dad is visiting his family over the winter holiday when he suddenly starts to have trouble remembering words and seems confused. Dan takes his dad to the emergency room, and testing reveals that he has had a small stroke.

5. A **lesion** is an area of damaged tissue in the brain. (see A Brief History of Neuropsychology)

   Example: Marie is studying a man with damage (a lesion) in his left temporal lobe. She is testing him to find out precisely what cognitive deficits he displays.

6. **Modules** are regions of the brain that perform their own unique kind of analysis of the information they receive. (see Modules and Networks)

   Example: To perceive objects accurately, one must be able to see, detect features of an object, remember objects like it that one has previously seen, and correctly categorize or label what the object is. Each of the regions of the brain that perform these functions is not solely responsible for the complex ability to perceive and label objects accurately, but the regions responsible for these functions make up a complex network of modules that together make it possible to perceive an object as a car, for example.

7. **Neuropsychological assessment** involves testing a patient's intelligence, memory, reading, motor coordination, and other cognitive and sensory functions in an effort to locate problems in the brain responsible for neuropsychological symptoms. (see Neuropsychological Assessment)

   Example: Dr. Shin is testing a man who claims his wife has been replaced by an imposter to find out what area of the brain may not be functioning properly.

2. **Traumatic brain injury (trauma)** is an impact on the brain caused by a blow or a sudden, violent movement of the head. (see Traumatic Brain Injury)

   Example: Heather is in a car accident in which her head slams into the headrest behind her and then strikes the windshield. She survives the incident, but she has severe brain injuries as a result of her brain striking the inside of the skull because of its movement against the headrest and windshield.

9. **Cerebrospinal fluid** is a clear liquid that surrounds and buffers the brain against vibration. (see Traumatic Brain Injury)

   Example: Demi is in an accident that causes her brain to move so forcefully around that it hits her skull as it moves through her cerebrospinal fluid.

10. **Neurodegenerative diseases** are conditions in the brain that result in a gradual loss of nerve cells and of the cognitive or other functions in which those cells are normally involved. (see Neurodegenerative Diseases)

Example: Charlotte has Alzheimer's disease. Her brain cells are gradually damaged over time. Her symptoms, which were mild at first, worsen as the damage progresses.

11. **Syndromes** are patterns of symptoms associated with a specific disorder. (see Neuropsychological Disorders)

Example: The inability to form new memories is an amnestic disorder (anterograde amnesia), which is a syndrome. It appears in cases where a patient has suffered hippocampal damage.

12. **Amnestic disorders** are neuropsychological disorders that involve memory loss. (see Amnestic Disorders)

Example: Korsakoff's psychosis can result in an amnestic disorder. Korsakoff's psychosis involves depletion of thiamine due to poor nutrition or alchoholism. This deficiency causes cells in the medial dorsal thalamus to be damaged or to die, and the result is anterograde amnesia with confabulation (creation of false memories).

13. **Anterograde amnesia** is a loss of memory for events that occur after a brain injury. (see Amnestic Disorders)

Example: Sarai has injured her hippocampus. She cannot form new memories and seems to live in an "eternal present."

14. **Korsakoff's psychosis** (or **Korsakoff's syndrome**) is an amnestic condition in people whose thiamine (vitamin B1) level is depleted by inadequate nutrition or alcoholism. (see Amnestic Disorders)

Example: Manute is talking to his neuropsychologist. He asks where she is from, and when she says "Cleveland" he says, "I lived there for many years!" They proceed to have a conversation about his life in Cleveland and what people they know in common. When he leaves the room, his neuropsychologist tells her staff that Manute has never lived in Cleveland and was engaged in confabulation, and he will not remember the conversation.

15. **Confabulation** is a characteristic of some neuropsychological disorders in which patients report false memories. (see Amnestic Disorders)

Example: Sade's neuropsychologist asks her what she did this weekend. Sade says that she just returned from Europe and tells an elaborate, interesting story about her vacation there. Sade's mom indicates this is completely false, but Sade insists that it is true.

16. **Consciousness disturbances** are neuropsychological disorders in which there are impairments in the ability to be accurately aware of the world. (see Consciousness Disturbances)

Example: Lisa's brain was injured when she fell rock climbing. Her reticular formation was severely damaged, and she is in a coma.

17. **Reticular formation** is a collection of cells and fibers in the hindbrain and midbrain that are involved in arousal and attention. (see Consciousness Disturbances)

Example: Philip has sustained damage to his reticular formation and is now in a persistent vegetative state.

18. **Delirium** refers to periods of abnormally impaired or abnormally elevated levels of consciousness. (see Consciousness Disturbances)

Example: Blessing has a very high fever. She babbles incoherently. She is experiencing delirium.

19. **Perceptual disturbances** are neuropsychological disorders in which there are impairments in the ability to organize, recognize, interpret, and make sense of incoming sensory information. (see Perceptual Disturbances)

Example: Visual agnosia is a perceptual disturbance that involves the inability to know what objects are based on their appearance.

20. **Language disorders**, also called **aphasias**, are neuropsychological disorders in which there are disruptions in the ability to speak, read, write, and understand language. (see Linkages: Language Disorders and the Brain)

    Example: Expressive aprosodia is a language disorder resulting from damage to the right frontal lobe. It involves the inability to use tone to express meaning.

21. **Broca's aphasia** is a language disorder in which there is a loss of fluent speech. (see Linkages: Language Disorders and the Brain)

    Example: Leah has experienced damaged to Broca's area. Now, when she wants to communicate, she uses telegraphic speech, saying things like "Go store" instead of "We need to go to the store today."

22. **Wernicke's aphasia** is a language disorder in which there is a loss of the ability to understand written or spoken language and to produce sensible speech. (see Linkages: Language Disorders and the Brain)

    Example: Zachary's Wernicke's area has been damaged. He often uses the wrong word to name objects, although his speech appears to come effortlessly. He is perplexed when people do not seem to understand what he is saying because he isn't aware of the mistakes he makes.

23. **Movement disorder** (or **apraxia**) refers to neuropsychological disorders in which there are impairments in the ability to perform or coordinate previously normal motor skills. (see Movement Disorders)

    Example: Joe has ideomotor apraxia as a result of damage to the motor pathways in his brain. He struggles to use tools he once used effortlessly. For example, he can't figure out how to use his spoon to feed himself, and he tries to use it inappropriately.

24. **Dementia** refers to neuropsychological disorders in which there are significant and disruptive impairments in memory, as well as in perceptual ability, language, or learned motor skills. (see Dementia)

    Example: Michaela has serious problems with memory, and she also seems to be unable to perform basic tasks like communicating effectively what she needs to her family and taking a bath.

25. **Vascular dementia** is a form of dementia caused by multiple restrictions of the brain's blood supply. (see Dementia)

    Example: Collin has vascular dementia that resulted when the blood supply to his brain was restricted. He has trouble remembering recent events. For example, when he goes to the zoo with his grandchildren, he can't remember what they did there. He is able to form the memory of going to the zoo, but he is unable to retrieve it.

FILL-IN-THE-BLANKS KEY TERMS

This section will help you check your factual knowledge of the key terms introduced in this chapter. Fill in each blank with the appropriate term from the list of key terms in the previous section.

1. _____ is the subfield of psychology that explores the relationship between brain processes, human behavior, and psychological functioning.

2. Disorders that involve memory loss are _____.

3.   Sudden impact on the brain by a blow or violent movement of the head is known as _____.

4.   A neuropsychogical disorder with significant memory impairment along with perceptual, language, and motor problems is known as _____.

5.   A(n) _____ uses tests and other methods to try to understand neuropsychological problems and remaining functions in individual patients.

6.   A _____ is an area of damaged tissue in the brain.

7   The idea that a specific psychological function can be affected by damage to a specific brain area is _____.

8.   _____ are disruptions in the ability to speak, read, write, and understand language.

9.   _____ are regions of the brain that perform their own unique kind of analysis of the information they receive.

10. The loss of the ability to produce fluent speech is known as _____.

11. _____ are impairments in the ability to perform or coordinate previously normal motor skills.

12. A _____ is a loss of blood supply to some part of the brain, resulting in disruption of some aspect of behavior or mental processes.

13. Conditions in the brain that result in the gradual loss of nerve cells and the cognitive or other functions in which those cells are normally involved are called _____.

14. _____ are patterns of symptoms associated with a specific disorder.

15. Neuropsychological disorders in which there are impairments in the ability to organize, recognize, interpret, and make sense of incoming sensory information are _____.

LEARNING OBJECTIVES

1.   Define neuropsychology. (see "Foundations of Neuropsychology")

2.   Describe the work of experimental and clinical neuropsychologists and how they use the knowledge of the field in their careers. (see "Foundations of Neuropsychology")

3.   Explain the history of neuropsychology as it relates to localization of function, including the contributions of Franz Gall and Paul Broca. (see "A Brief History of Neuropsychology")

4.   Define and describe the function of modules in the brain. Explain how *disconnection syndrome* affects the ways that modules interact. (see "Modules and Networks")

5.   Describe how lesion analysis works in localizing brain functions and identifying what functions have been damaged. (see "Lesion Analysis")

6.   Discuss the benefits and limitations of the two main types of neuropsychological tests: tests that are uniquely tailored to each patient and standardized test batteries. (see "Neuropsychological Testing")

7.   Describe the education required to become a neuropsychologist. Discuss the various work settings held by neuropsychologists. (see "Training for Neuropsychology")

8.   Define cardiovascular accident, traumatic brain injury, and neurodegenerative disease. Explain the symptoms of each, how they cause brain damage and dysfunction, and the likelihood of recovery from each condition. (see "Mechanisms of Brain Dysfunction")

9. Define neurological disorders. (see "Neuropsychological Disorders")

10. Define the symptoms of <u>amnestic disorders</u>. Describe the causes and common features of *anterograde amnesia* and *Korsakoff's psychosis*. (see "Amnestic Disorders")

11. Define <u>consciousness disturbances</u>. Describe the common features and causes of disruption to the *reticular activating system* (RAS), *delirium*, and *anosognosia*. Explain why treatment is often difficult to obtain for each of these disorders. (see "Disorders of Consciousness")

12. Discuss the research on anosognosia and *hemiparesis*. Describe the evidence that anosognosia reflects a true lack of awareness and the evidence for a patient's use of denial. Explain the conclusions that seem most reasonable. (see "Thinking Critically: Can Someone Be Paralyzed and Not Know It?")

13. Explain the relationship between <u>perceptual disturbances</u> and the "what" and "where" neural pathways. Describe how *visual agnosia* and *prosopagnosia* result from damage to the "what" system and how *simultanagnosia* and *hemineglect* result from damage to the "where" system. (see "Disorders of Perception")

14. Discuss research on hemineglect. Describe how the use of a patient's memory and imagination help researchers understand the nature of this disorder. Discuss the limitations of this study. (see "Focus on Research: Studying Hemineglect")

15. Define <u>language disorders</u>, or <u>aphasias</u>. Discuss the causes of aphasias. (see "Linkages: Language Disorders and the Brain")

16. Describe how <u>Broca's aphasia</u> and <u>Wernicke's aphasia</u> affect an individual's language use and comprehension. (see "Linkages: Language Disorders and the Brain")

17. Discuss how damage to the right hemisphere, such as with *aprosodia*, affects an individual's communication ability. (see "Linkages: Language Disorders and the Brain")

18. Define <u>movement disorder</u>. Explain the symptoms of *ideational apraxia* and *ideomotor apraxia*. (see "Disorders of Movement")

19. Describe the symptoms and causes of <u>dementia</u>. Explain how dementia can result in Alzheimer's disease and how Alzheimer's disease affects the brain. Explain how <u>vascular dementia</u> differs from neurodegenerative diseases. (see "Dementia")

CONCEPTS AND EXERCISES

In the Emergency Room

Frank works in an emergency room in a large urban hospital. He often sees patients with brain dysfunction and has to not only treat the pattern of symptoms but also determine what might be the underlying reason for the dysfunction. Below are some cases he has had to deal with during the past work week. Choose from the list of terms below what might be the mechanisms behind the brain dysfunction he is observing in each patient.

1. Ava comes into the ER after sustaining injuries in a high-impact car collision on the freeway. Of course, the actual injuries to the brain are not visible without special tools, but Frank can clearly see that her head has been injured just by looking at the exterior. The injuries look very painful.

   _____

2. Andrew has been brought to the ER by his family because he suddenly seems very confused to the people around him. When the family has asked him what is wrong, he is puzzled and can't understand why they think he is sick. He doesn't feel any pain and isn't aware that he is behaving

in a confused fashion. The onset of these behaviors was very sudden, and his family is quite concerned. _____

3. Carolyn is a sixty-year-old patient whose husband has finally brought her to the ER because he didn't know what else to do. Like Andrew in Question 2 above, she is very confused and clearly some brain dysfunction has occurred. But Carolyn seems more aware of her own confusion than Andrew, and she is frustrated by it. When Frank questions Carolyn's husband, he learns that this pattern of symptoms started over five years ago and has simply gotten worse over time, until the husband could no longer cope with it, at which point he brought Carolyn to the ER.
_____

   a. Cerebrovascular accident

   b. Traumatic Brain Injury

   c. Neurodegenerative disease

Neuropsychological Disorders

Dr. Lettinger is a neuropsychologist. When she first meets a patient, she tries to examine the pattern of symptoms the patient is presenting and determine which class of neuropsychological disorders the diagnosis might fall into. Below are some descriptions of patients Dr. Lettinger has met recently. Select from the list what class of disorder you suspect she should categorize each patient as having. You may use a term more than once, or not at all.

1. *Clay.* Clay has been referred to Dr. Lettinger. He seems to be completely coordinated and able to do a variety of activities, but he keeps doing them in the wrong order. When he tries to drive, for example, he goes to the car and attempts to put it in gear before putting the keys in the ignition.
_____

2. *Shauna.* Dr. Lettinger sees Shauna in the long-term-care facility that she visits on weekends. Shauna seems very unaware of her surroundings, although she opens her eyes during the day and appears to "look around" and then goes to sleep at night. But she doesn't interact with her environment. _____

3. *Karl.* Karl comes to Dr. Lettinger because he seems to constantly ignore things on the left side of his world. He doesn't shave the left side of his face, doesn't eat food on the left side of his plate, and so on. _____

4. *Jamel.* Dr. Lettinger sees Jamel as part of her treatment plan for recovering from alcoholism. After years of heavy drinking, Jamel seems to have trouble forming new memories. In addition, she reports all kinds of memories of events that have never even happened to her. She seems convinced these experiences were real, however. _____

   a. Amnestic disorders

   b. Consciousness disturbances

   c. Perceptual disturbance

   d. Apraxia

   e. Dementia

CRITICAL THINKING

Sam and Martina are investigating a homicide. Upon entering the apartment, they find a deceased woman on the floor who has clearly been killed in a physical attack. The apartment also appears to have been burglarized, with thousands of dollars in jewelry having been taken. Her husband, who called 911, is nearby. He seems to be paralyzed on the left side of his body from the neck down, but he is able to gesture and move with the right side of his body. When Sam and Martina interview him, he describes the burglar and attack on his wife. When they ask him why he didn't intervene to help her, he is unable to explain why. Sam suggests that perhaps it is because of his physical paralysis that he was unable to intervene, but the man acts like he doesn't know what Sam is talking about. "I'm not paralyzed, you idiot!" he exclaims.

After the interview, Sam and Martina compare notes. Sam remarks, "Martina, this is so obvious. Those jewels were insured for thousands, and they were all his wife's family heirlooms, not his. I bet he just knocked his wife off himself and disposed of the jewels to make an insurance claim. And now he is trying to blame the whole thing on a burglar!"

"I'm not so sure," Martina responds carefully. "I mean, he really does seem to be paralyzed on his left side, and I think it would be pretty hard for him to kill his wife with that sort of physical challenge."

"C'mon," says Sam, "did you notice the paralysis was on only half his body? And then he is pretending to not even know he is paralyzed? He is just trying to fake the paralysis, or maybe he's even trying to act crazy in case we figure out it was him. That way he'll have the perfect insanity defense!"

Martina looks incredulously at Sam and shakes her head. "Sam, you just don't remember a thing from introductory psychology, do you?"

1.   What is Sam's hypothesis?

2.   What evidence supports Sam's hypothesis?

3.   What is Martina's alternative hypothesis?

4.   What evidence supports Martina's hypothesis?

5.   What conclusions are most reasonable? What additional evidence is needed to reach a conclusion?

PERSONAL LEARNING ACTIVITIES

1.   Division 40 of the American Psychological Association is devoted to clinical neuropsychology. Visit the following area of their site to explore training programs in clinical neuropsychology: http://www.div40.org/training/index.html. Are there training programs in your region of the country? Are these programs located in psychology departments or medical schools, or both? Do any of these programs also offer an experimental neuropsychology track? What are the admission criteria for the programs?

2.   See if you can find a local neuropsychologist who might be willing to do an informational interview with you. Ask about his or her training and what the day-to-day work is like. Does he or she seem more clinical or experimental in orientation? Does he or she have a specialty within neuropsychology? What are the traits that he or she thinks are important to being a good neuropsychologist? What are the downsides to the career? If you can't find someone in your area to interview, then check out the following online transcript of an interview with a clinical neuropsychologist: http://www3.nsta.org/main/news/stories/science_teacher.php?news_story_ID=53149.

3.   To view some neuropsychological case studies, visit the following site: http://www.neuropsychflorida.com/Casestudies.html. As you read a case, see if you can identify the mechanisms behind the brain dysfunction described in the case (cerebrovascular accident, traumatic brain injury, or neurodegenerative diseases). Also determine what category of neuropsychological disorder the diagnosis provided falls into (consciousness disturbance, apraxia, perceptual disturbance, amnestic disorder, or dementia).

4. Many neuropsychological disorders, such as Alzheimer's disease, have foundations that promote research and family support for individuals with that particular problem. Select a disease that you found particularly interesting in this chapter and go online to the foundation for that disease to learn more about it. For example, the Alzheimer's Association site is at: http://www.alz.org/index.asp. Many of these foundations also sponsor fundraising walk-a-thons, jail-and-bail events, and so forth to raise funds. See if these or any other programs might be an interesting service-learning project for you and a group of friends to do together.

5. Do a family history of disease and try to determine if any neuropsychological disorders have occurred in your family tree. Note if they were of the sort that are likely to increase your own risk for such disorders (for example, a history of stroke or Huntington's disease), and if there is any kind of lifestyle change you could make now that would reduce your risk or not.

MULTIPLE-CHOICE QUESTIONS

Quiz 1

1. Who is least likely to be a neuropsychologist?
    a. John, who conducts research on brain injuries resulting from shaken baby syndrome
    b. Sarah, who tests patients to try to determine exactly what their neuropsychological deficits are
    c. Mike, who works in a research hospital studying the causes and consequences of stroke
    d. Kayla, who treats patients with schizophrenia

2. The idea that a specific psychological function can be affected by damage to a specific brain area is called
    a. modularity.
    b. localization of function.
    c. lesion analysis.
    d. phrenology.

3. Dr. Wyatt studies visual agnosia. He is very interested in determining what parts of the brain are responsible for the losses he sees in his patients. To try to sort this out, he determines where the brain damage is located and then engages his patients in a series of neuropsychological assessments that show exactly what functions the individuals have lost. He then tries to determine the correspondence between where the brain was damaged and the function(s) the patient has lost. Dr. Wyatt is using
    a. autopsy analysis.
    b. phrenology.
    c. lesion analysis.
    d. None of these

4. What is the benefit of standardized batteries of tests as compared to individualized testing?
    a. They are uniquely tailored to each patient.
    b. They measure the specific problems that a given patient is most likely to have.
    c. They are given to all patients the same way, making it easier to determine norms for comparison.
    d. They are more flexible in the administration strategies.

5.   Laura's doctor is trying to determine the reason for the brain dysfunction Laura is experiencing. Her husband is concerned because she suddenly seems rather confused but at the same time is relatively unaware of the problems he is observing. Furthermore, she claims to be experiencing no pain even when her symptoms are at their height. This all has happened rather suddenly, within the last two hours. What is the likely cause for Laura's brain dysfunction?

   a.   Cerebrovascular accident
   b.   Traumatic brain injury
   c.   Neurodegenerative disease
   d.   Amnesia

6.   Alzheimer's disease is caused by which mechanism of brain dysfunction?

   a.   Cerebrovascular accident
   b.   Traumatic brain injury
   c.   Neurodegenerative disease
   d.   Hemineglect

7.   The case of H. M. discussed in your text involves which amnestic disorder?

   a.   Confabulation
   b.   Visual agnosia
   c.   Korsakoff's psychosis
   d.   Anterograde amnesia

8.   Damage to the _____ results in a coma or persistent vegetative state.

   a.   reticular formation
   b.   hippocampus
   c.   medial dorsal thalamus
   d.   thalamus

9.   Which of the following is a reason for discrediting the ego defense mechanism explanation of anosognosia, according to "Thinking Critically: Can Someone Be Paralyzed and Not Know It?"

   a.   Anosognosia does not operate in a general way—it seems specific to the particular deficit.
   b.   Anosognosia occurs even when there is no threat of permanent paralysis.
   c.   Anosognosia is more likely to occur with right hemisphere damage than with left hemisphere damage.
   d.   All of these

10. The perceptual disturbance involving the inability to recognize faces is known as

   a.   visual agnosia.
   b.   prosopagnosia.
   c.   simultanagnosia.
   d.   hemineglect.

11. It is difficult to demonstrate that hemineglect is due to damage in the parietal lobes' "where" system, not just sensory problems, because

　　a.　the brain damage that causes hemineglect also causes a loss of sensation from the same side.

　　b.　most tests for hemineglect rely on giving a person some kind of sensation to respond to.

　　c.　Both the brain damage that causes hemineglect also causes loss of sensation from the same side AND most tests for hemineglect rely on giving a person some kind of sensation to respond to.

　　d.　It is not difficult to show that hemineglect is more than sensory problems.

12. Amy has experienced brain damage to the left side of her brain. She speaks in a halting manner and with great effort. Her vocabulary mainly refers to concrete items such as *house*, *door*, *cat*. She often makes mistakes when naming objects. Amy probably has which language disorder?

　　a.　Wernicke's aphasia

　　b.　Broca's aphasia

　　c.　Expressive aprosodia

　　d.　Receptive aprosodia

13. Movement disorders are known as

　　a.　apraxia.

　　b.　aphasia.

　　c.　agnosia.

　　d.　amnesia.

14. Studying the brains of deceased Alzheimer's patients shows that the anatomical basis of the disease is mainly in the neurons that use

　　a.　dopamine.

　　b.　seratonin.

　　c.　acetylcholine.

　　d.　endorphins.

15. Sherril's grandmother is showing signs of dementia. She seems to have trouble remembering things, but testing reveals that the underlying cause of her dementia is mainly that she can't retrieve recently formed memories, not that she can't form those memories in the first place. Sherril's grandmother probably has

　　a.　Alzheimer's disease.

　　b.　anomia.

　　c.　ideational apraxia.

　　d.　vascular dementia.

16. Brain damage due to sudden impact on the brain by being struck by an object or by abruptly stopping or starting movement is known as

　　a.　traumatic brain injury.

　　b.　cerebrovascular accident.

　　c.　neurodegenerative disease.

　　d.　dementia.

17. What training is typically required to become licensed clinical neuropsychologist?
    a. A Ph.D. in clinical psychology with emphasis in neuropsychology
    b. An internship with a licensed clinical neuropsychologist supervising
    c. An M. D. with further specialty training in neuropsychology
    d. Both a Ph.D. in clinical psychology with emphasis on neuropsychology and an internship with a licensed clinical neuropsychologist supervising

18. Regions of the brain responsible for performing unique sorts of analysis on the information received are known as
    a. networks.
    b. modules.
    c. lesions.
    d. None of these

19. Chantal is really annoyed at her roommate for leaving the door unlocked. Chantal sarcastically comments, "Thanks a lot for taking such good care of our stuff!" Chantal's roommate doesn't even notice Chantal's tone, and politely says, "You're welcome." Chantal's roommate may have
    a. aprosodia.
    b. expressive aprosodia.
    c. receptive aprosodia.
    d. ideational apraxia.

20. Brad, an alcoholic, has difficulty forming new memories. But he can weave colorful descriptions of "memories" that his friends and family report never even happened. When Brad tells these tales as if they actually happened, he is engaged in
    a. lesion analysis.
    b. confabulation.
    c. phrenology.
    d. disconnection syndrome.

Total Correct (see Answers to Multiple-Choice Questions) _____

Quiz 2

Use this quiz to reassess your learning after taking Quiz 1 and reviewing the chapter.

1. Which scientist was responsible for the more recent belief in localization of function that neuropsychologists accept today?
    a. Franz Gall
    b. Paul Broca
    c. June Wada
    d. Edoardo Bisiach

2. Alexia without agraphia is an example of a(n) _____, which results from a modularly organized neurological system.
    a. disconnection syndrome
    b. lesion analysis
    c. amnestic disorder
    d. language disorder

3. The method used to study the intricacies of localization of function by looking at the results of brain damage is known as
    a. the Wada technique.
    b. neuropsychological testing.
    c. phrenology.
    d. lesion analysis.

4. In which setting is an experimental neuropsychologist most likely to work?
    a. A hospital
    b. A specialty clinic
    c. A private practice
    d. A university setting

5. When blood supply to part of the brain is blocked, a person is said to have experienced
    a. neurodegenerative disease.
    b. traumatic brain injury.
    c. a cerebrovascular accident.
    d. None of these

6. Which mechanism behind brain dysfunction would occur most slowly?
    a. Neurodegenerative disease
    b. Traumatic brain injury
    c. Cerebrovascular accident
    d. Aphasia

7. Jenna has an amnestic disorder, and she is malnourished. One of the major vitamins she lacks is thiamine. Which amnestic disorder does Jenna most likely have?
    a. Anterograde amnesia
    b. PVS
    c. Delirium
    d. Korsakoff's psychosis

8. Mei has a high fever and has been acting strangely lately. She appears sleepy one minute and then overly attentive the next. When doctors try to test her, she isn't able to cooperate very well with the testing process, and it appears that every brain function is somewhat impaired. Which disorder of consciousness does Mei likely have?
    a. PVS
    b. Delirium
    c. Anosognosia
    d. Hemiparesis

9. What sort of research would help scientists better understand anosognosia's causes better, given the current state of the literature?
    a. Retrospective studies
    b. More use of the Wada technique
    c. Prospective studies
    d. No additional research is needed to clarify this matter.

10. Matt is looking at a T-shirt design for his senior class logo. The names of all the seniors are on the T-shirt, and they are organized such that they collectively make the pattern of the numbers '11 which is the year they graduate. He shows it to his dad, who says he doesn't see an '11 on the design, just the names. Matt's dad may have the perceptual disorder known as

    a. visual agnosia.
    b. prosopagnosia.
    c. simultanagnosia.
    d. hemineglect.

11. The patients that Bisiach used in his research on hemineglect all had damage in their _____ lobes, and the stimuli used in his study were all _____.

    a. parietal; visual
    b. parietal; auditory
    c. occipital; visual
    d. occipital; auditory

12. Which language disorder is *not* due to damage in the left hemisphere of the brain?

    a. Aprosodia
    b. Broca's aphasia
    c. Wernicke's aphasia
    d. Semantic paraphasia

13. Lisa has trouble positioning her hand to feed herself, holding a pencil to write, and so forth. Which movement disorder does she most likely have?

    a. Ideational apraxia
    b. Ideomotor apraxia
    c. Dementia
    d. Delirium

14. To receive a diagnosis of dementia, a person must have

    a. developed a notable impairment of memory.
    b. a notable impairment in memory plus an impairment of some other area of function.
    c. impairments significant enough to affect everyday living.
    d. All of these are necessary for a diagnosis of dementia.

15. _____ explain why a pattern of symptoms has occurred; _____ is the term we use for the actual pattern of symptoms itself.

    a. Mechanisms of brain dysfunction; neuropsychological disorders
    b. Neurological disorders; mechanisms of brain dysfunction
    c. Strokes; trauma
    d. Strokes; neurodegenerative disease

16. In trauma patients, functional deficits are often diffuse, while in stroke patients, functional deficits are often very specific. Therefore,

    a. we know more about the symptom patterns associated with trauma than stroke.
    b. we know more about the symptom patterns associated with stroke than trauma.
    c. trauma is easier to treat than stroke.
    d. trauma patients have greater chance of recovery than stroke patients.

17. A large deviation from the average score on a neuropsychological test indicates
    a. everything is probably all right.
    b. something significant is probably wrong.
    c. the test was given incorrectly.
    d. we need to know more about the norms to know what a large deviation means.

18. Cleve is feeling his brother's skull. He comments, "I see you have a large knot near the back of your skull, which indicates you probably are very insightful. But the slight indentation near your temple probably suggests you are not a very good listener." Cleve is using principles of _____ to assess his brother's personality.
    a. phrenology
    b. lesion analysis
    c. the Wada technique
    d. reticular activating system

19. Which of the following is NOT an assumption on which neuropsychology rests?
    a. Complicated mental tasks can be studied separately.
    b. Different psychological processes are controlled by different brain regions.
    c. Feeling the skull can help you interpret problems in the brain.
    d. All of these are principles on which neuropsychology rests.

20. Errors in naming an object, such as calling a pencil a tree, are known as
    a. aprosodia.
    b. paraphasias.
    c. semantic paraphasias.
    d. phonemic paraphasias.

Total Correct (see Answers to Multiple-Choice Questions) _____

ANSWERS TO FILL-IN-THE-BLANKS KEY TERMS

1. Neuropsychology (see Foundations of Neuropsychology)

2. amnestic disorders (see Amnestic Disorders)

3. traumatic brain injury (see Traumatic Brain Injury)

4. dementia (see Dementia)

5. clinical neuropsychologist (see Foundations of Neuropsychology)

6. lesion (see A Brief History of Neuropsychology)

7. localization of function (see A Brief History of Neuropsychology)

8. Language disorders or Aphasias (see Linkages: Language Disorders and the Brain)

9. Modules (see Modules and Networks)

10. Broca's aphasia (see Linkages: Language Disorders and the Brain)

11. apraxia (see Movement Disorders)

12. cerebrovascular accident (see A Brief History of Neuropsychology)

13.   neurodegenerative diseases (see Neurodegenerative Diseases)

14.   Syndromes (see Neuropsychological Disorders)

15.   perceptual disturbances (see Perceptual Disturbances)

ANSWERS TO CONCEPTS AND EXERCISES

In the Emergency Room

1.   *Traumatic Brain Injury.* The fact that Ava's injuries were sustained in a high-impact car collision immediately suggests traumatic brain injury—the sudden impact on the brain caused when the skull is struck or the head suddenly and violently accelerates or decelerates. Such injuries would be likely to occur when a car suddenly stops (head decelerates while the brain is still moving in the skull) and in the resultant impact the skull might make with a dashboard or the oncoming car that is striking the vehicle. The fact that Ava's injuries look painful also suggests trauma because the other possibilities, cerebrovascular accident and neurodegenerative diseases, are less likely to involve painful-looking external wounds. (see Traumatic Brain Injury)

2.   *Cerebrovascular accident.* Several clues allow Frank to determine quickly that Andrew is likely experiencing or has just experienced a cerebrovascular accident, or stroke. The fact that Andrew is confused but feels like nothing is wrong is one tip-off. Second, the fact that his family reports the onset of this behavior as sudden is another clue that allows Frank to rule out neurodegenerative diseases, which would have a much slower onset. Finally, Andrew's lack of pain is consistent with a stroke experience because the brain contains no pain receptors. Had Andrew reported a lot of pain, Frank might investigate the possibility of traumatic brain injury more closely. (see Cerebrovascular Accidents)

3.   *Neurodegenerative diseases.* The first clue to Frank that Carolyn is experiencing neurodegenerative diseases—as opposed to a cerebrovascular accident—is that the onset of her symptoms has been gradual. This gradual onset has also helped Carolyn to become more aware over time of her own worsening condition, so she is much more frustrated with and aware of her own confusion than Andrew, who had a stroke. (see Neurodegenerative Diseases)

Neuropsychological Disorders

1.   *Apraxia.* Clay's symptoms center around ordering movements rather than actually doing the movements. This is known as ideational apraxia, which is an example of a movement disorder. (see Movement Disorders)

2.   *Consciousness disturbance.* Shauna's symptoms correspond to the description of a persistent vegetative state (PVS) in your text. PVS is an example of a consciousness disturbance. (see Consciousness Disturbances)

3.   *Perceptual Disturbance.* Karl's symptom pattern appears to be hemineglect, which is a perceptual disturbance. (see Perceptual Disturbances)

4.   *Amnestic disorder.* Jamel's inability to form new memories (anterograde amnesia) and memory for events that never happened (confabulation), along with her history of alcoholism, suggest *Korsakoff's psychosis.* Korsakoff's psychosis is an example of an amnestic disorder. (see Amnestic Disorders)

ANSWERS TO CRITICAL THINKING

1.   Sam's hypothesis is that the husband killed the wife and disposed of the jewels to make an insurance claim, and that he is trying to act crazy to get an insanity plea.

2. Sam is using the fact that the jewels are gone, the large insurance policy, and the unusual pattern of symptoms (partial paralysis accompanied by unawareness) as evidence for his view.

3. Martina hypothesizes that the perpetrator was actually a burglar and that the husband's unusual pattern of symptoms is actually hemiparesis (partial paralysis affecting just one side of the body) accompanied by anosognosia (lack of awareness of a neurological deficit).

4. Martina knows hemiparesis and anosognosia are real neuropsychological disorders that can co-occur. If the husband really has these conditions, then it would be very hard for him to kill his wife in a physical attack or even protect her from a burglar who was doing her harm. His lack of awareness of his condition might not be an attempt to act crazy but a genuine lack of awareness.

5. Martina needs to dig into the husband's medical records to determine if he really has hemiparesis and anosognosia. She also needs to look for evidence of the timeline of events in the apartment. If she can determine that the husband discovered the burglar and tried to protect his wife, he might have injuries himself supporting that hypothesis. His lack of awareness of his paralysis should make it likely he did so, because he wouldn't have known about his weakness and therefore he would have thought he could help her. (*Note:* Critical thinking is a constant process of hypothesizing, examining evidence, rehypothesizing, and collecting more evidence. Martina may not be correct.)

ANSWERS TO MULTIPLE-CHOICE QUESTIONS

Circle the question numbers you answered correctly.

Quiz 1

1. d is the answer. Although schizophrenia patients may have some underlying neuropsychological issues, treating schizophrenia is more likely to be done by a clinical psychologist than a neuropsychologist. (see Foundations of Neuropsychology)

   a, b, d. All of these are activities in which a neuropsychologist would participate.

2. b is the answer. Localization of function is the idea that specific psychological abilities, or functions, can be affected by damage in a corresponding specific brain region. (see Foundations of Neuropsychology)

   a. Modules are discrete regions of the brain. Each module performs its own unique analysis of information it receives.

   c. Lesion analysis is a way neuropsychologists study localization of function.

   d. Phrenology is the idea that parts of the brain grow larger with use and that corresponding bumps on the head can be used to determine what parts of the brain are related to different traits.

3. c is the answer. Lesion analysis helps neuropsychologists study the intricacies of localization of function. Dr. Wyatt is using lesion analysis to study localization of function in visual agnosia patients. (see Foundations of Neuropsychology)

   a. An autopsy is conducted on deceased patients, not live ones.

   b. Phrenology is a method of study from the early 1800s.

   d. Lesion analysis is the correct answer.

4. c is the answer. Because standardized tests are given to each patient the same way, they are easier to use for normative comparisons between a specific patient and a "normal" population. (see Foundations of Neuropsychology)

    a.   Standardized tests are not uniquely tailored to specific patient needs.

    b.   Standardized tests do not address specific problems a given patient might have.

    d.   Standardized tests have many guidelines for how they should be administered. They are not flexible.

5.   a is the answer. A cerebrovascular accident, or stroke, is the likely cause, given the sudden onset, lack of pain, and relative unawareness of the neuropsychological deficit. (see Foundations of Neuropsychology)

    b.   Traumatic brain injury would typically involve pain, and Laura would likely be very aware of the problems, if she were even still conscious.

    c.   Neurodegenerative disease has a slow onset, so as a cause for her problems, it is unlikely.

    d.   Amnesia is a neuropsychological disorder, or pattern of symptoms, not a cause for brain dysfunction. Laura's symptom pattern is not described well enough here to determine if she is experiencing amnesia.

6.   c is the answer. Alzheimer's disease develops through a gradual process of cell damage in the brain, which is known as neurodegeneration. It is a neurodegenerative disease. (see Mechanisms of Brain Dysfunction)

    a.   Cerebrovascular accident, or stroke, occurs when the blood supply to the brain is blocked, and usually this is a sudden effect, not a gradual effect as in Alzheimer's disease.

    b.   Traumatic brain injury is caused by impact to the brain.

    d.   Hemineglect is a pattern of symptoms resulting from damage to the brain, not a mechanism behind brain damage.

7.   d is the answer. H. M. had difficulty forming new memories, which is anterograde amnesia. (see Neuropsychological Disorders)

    a.   Confabulation is a characteristic of Korsakoff's psychosis, which is also an amnestic disorder. It involves forming memories of events that never occurred.

    b.   Visual agnosia is not an amnestic disorder. Although it involves difficulty remembering the names of familiar objects, it is a problem of visual recognition, not memory.

    c.   Korsakoff's psychosis is an amnestic disorder, but H. M. did not have this particular problem.

8.   a is the answer. Damage to the reticular formation, or the reticular activating system, can result in coma if the damage is severe. Lesser amounts of damage there may result in a persistent vegetative state. (see Neuropsychological Disorders)

    b.   Damage to the hippocampus tends to result in anterograde amnesia, not coma or PVS.

    c.   Damage to the medial dorsal thalamus is implicated in Korsakoff's psychosis, which is an amnestic disorder. Coma and PVS are consciousness disturbances.

    d.   The thalamus is the sensory relay station. Damage to it would not necessarily result in a coma or PVS.

9.　d is the answer. Each of these is a reason anosognosia is more likely to be due to genuine unawareness than the ego defense mechanism explanation. (see Thinking Critically: Can Someone Be Partially Paralyzed and Not Know It?)

　　a, b, c.　All three of these are correct; therefore, d is the correct answer.

10.　b is the answer. Prosopagnosia is the inability to recognize faces, even very familiar ones. (see Neuropsychological Disorders)

　　a.　Visual agnosia involves the inability to recognize objects in the world based on their appearance.

　　c.　Simultanagnosia is a condition in which a person can see parts of a visual scene but has difficulty perceiving the whole.

　　d.　Hemineglect involves difficulty seeing, responding to, or acting on information coming from either the right, or more often left, side of the world.

11.　c is the answer. Both of these are reasons it is challenging to demonstrate that hemineglect is more than just sensory problems. (see Focus on Research Methods: Studying Hemineglect)

　　a, b.　Both of these are reasons; therefore c is the answer.

　　d.　It is challenging to demonstrate that the reasons for hemineglect are more than sensory problems.

12.　b is the answer. Broca's aphasia results in loss of language fluency. Amy's speech is no longer fluent. (see Linkages: Language Disorders and the Brain)

　　a.　Wernicke's aphasia results in an ability to speak fluently, although the content of speech is odd, relatively free of content.

　　c, d.　These language disorders result from damage to the right side of the brain, not the left. Expressive aprosodia results in a person speaking in a dull monotone, while receptive aprosodia results in difficulty understanding the meaning of other people's tone.

13.　a is the answer. Apraxia refers to movement disorders. (see Neuropsychological Disorders)

　　b.　Aphasia refers to language disorders.

　　c.　Agnosia refers to perceptual disturbances.

　　d.　Amnesia refers to memory loss.

14.　c is the answer. The anatomical basis of Alzheimer's is largely due to neurons using acetylcholine, particularly those neurons in the parietal and medial temporal lobes on both sides of the brain. (see Neuropsychological Disorders)

　　a, b, c.　Neurons using these neurotransmitters are not mainly involved in Alzheimer's disease.

15.　d is the answer. Vascular dementia is caused by restricted blood supply to the brain. Over time, small tissue death results in a cumulative effect of dementia. The result looks very similar to Alzheimer's but the hippocampus stays largely intact in these patients, making it possible for them to form new memories but difficult for them to retrieve them. (see Neuropsychological Disorders)

　　a.　Alzheimer's patients have difficulty forming new memories, not just difficulty retrieving them.

　　b.　Anomia is a condition that some Alzheimer's patients develop. It involves difficulty naming objects, even if the patient knows what those objects are.

　　c.　Ideational apraxia is a movement disorder, not dementia.

16. a is the answer. Brain damage caused by sudden impact is traumatic brain injury. (see Mechanisms of Brain Dysfunction)

    b. Cerebrovascular accident, or stroke, occurs when the blood supply to an area of the brain is cut off.

    c. Neurodegenerative diseases are gradual, not a sudden, in the symptoms they produce.

    d. Dementia is a neurological disorder, not a mechanism of brain dysfunction.

17. d is the answer. Most clinical neuropsychologists complete a Ph.D. in clinical psychology (with specialty training in neuropsychology). Then, to practice, they must complete a year-long internship with a licensed professional supervising them. (see Foundations of Neuropsychology)

    a, b. Both of these are correct.

    c. Medical doctors are not typically trained extensively in neuropsychological testing.

18. b is the answer. Modules are the regions of the brain that perform specific analyses on information received. (see Foundations of Neuropsychology)

    a. Networks are teams of modules, responsible for complex functions.

    c. Lesions are areas of brain damage.

    d. b is the answer.

19. c is the answer. Receptive aprosodia is the inability to use tone to understand language others produce. (see Linkages: Language Disorders and the Brain)

    a. Chantal's roommate has aprosodia, but receptive aprosodia is a better, more precise description of her symptoms, as the question describes the roommate as being unable to understand tone.

    b. Expressive aprosodia is the inability to use tone to express oneself. We do not know how Chantal's roommate uses tone herself; only about how she uses tone that others produce.

    d. Ideational apraxia is the inability to correctly sequence movements.

20. b is the answer. Confabulation is the creation of false memories. Brad likely has Korsakoff's psychosis as a result of his alcoholism. (see Neuropsychological Disorders)

    a. Lesion analysis is the study of localization of function through analysis of areas of brain damage.

    c. Phrenology is the practice of using bumps on the head to assess a person's psychological make-up.

    d. Disconnection syndrome occurs when modules in a network are prevented from interacting.

Now turn to the quiz analysis table at the end of this chapter to find which areas you know well and which areas you need to work on. Circle the numbers in the table for items in Sample Quiz 1 that you answered correctly.

Quiz 2

1. b is the answer. Paul Broca's work on localization of function in 1861 led to the upsurge of scholarly interest in that topic still seen today. (see Foundations of Neuropsychology)

   a. Franz Gall was responsible for phrenology in the early 1800s. Although phrenology also emphasized localization of function, the results of this idea were not supported and interest in localization of function waned until Broca's later work.

   c. June Wada's research occurred in the 1980s—well after the modern interest in localization of function had been revived. She studied anosognosia.

   d. Edoardo Bisiach's research was done in the late 1970s, after interest in localization of function had revived. He focused on hemineglect.

2. a is the answer. Disconnection syndromes occur when various modules in a network, though themselves intact, are prevented from interacting. In patients with alexia without agraphia (inability to read while still being able to write), the damage is to the left occipital lobe, resulting in loss of vision in the right visual field. When this co-occurs with damage to the corpus callosum, the information from the pathway is blocked and the two abilities, so seemingly related, do not both function. (see Foundations of Neuropsychology)

   b. Lesion analysis is a method used to study localization of function.

   c. Amnestic disorders involve memory loss, not an inability to read.

   d. Language disorders involve an inability to produce or understand language. Alexia without agraphia is a perceptual disorder because the problem is in perceiving the written work, not in understanding it.

3. d is the answer. Lesion analysis is the method used to examine the intricacies of localization of function by looking at the results of brain damage. (see Foundations of Neuropsychology)

   a. The Wada technique is used to study anosognosia, a specific disorder, not localization of function generally.

   b. Neuropsychological testing may be used to supplement lesion analysis, but it does not involve directly examining where brain damage has occurred. It focuses on loss of function.

   c. Phrenology is an earlier, discredited idea about localization of function that examined bumps on the head and tried to relate their size and location to personality traits and other characteristics.

4. d is the answer. Experimental neuropsychologists focus on teaching students, conducting their own research, and testing patients as time permits. They do not see patients in a clinical setting, typically. (see Foundations of Neuropsychology)

   a, b, c. These are all settings in which a clinical neuropsychologist, not an experimental neuropsychologist, would likely work.

5. c is the answer. Cerebrovascular accident occurs when blood supply to part of the brain is blocked. (see Mechanisms of Brain Dysfunction)

   a. Neurodegenerative diseases involve a gradual process, not a sudden blockage.

   b. Traumatic brain injury results from a sudden impact to the brain, not a sudden blockage.

   d. c is the correct answer.

6.   a is the answer. Neurodegenerative diseases involve the *gradual* process of cell damage in the brain. (see Mechanisms of Brain Dysfunction)

    b, c.   Both traumatic brain injury and cerebrovascular accident (stroke) occur suddenly.

    d.   Aphasia is the term for a language disorder, not a mechanism behind brain dysfunction.

7.   d is the answer. Korsakoff's psychosis involves anterograde amnesia with confabulation. It results from thiamine deficiency, which can occur with inadequate nutrition or with alcoholism. (see Neuropsychological Disorders)

    a.   Anterograde is an amnestic disorder, but it has a broader array of possible causes than thiamine deficiency.

    b.   PVS, or persistent vegetative state, is a disorder of consciousness, not an amnestic disorder.

    c.   Delirium is a disorder of consciousness, not an amnestic disorder.

8.   b is the answer. Delirium does involve variability in consciousness, and it is often caused by fever. It is particularly hard to test patients with this because they are unable to cooperate with the testing due to short attention spans. (see Neuropsychological Disorders)

    a.   PVS, or persistent vegetative state, does not involve waxing and waning of consciousness. Patients with this remain unaware of their environment.

    c.   Anosognosia is lack of awareness of impairment, typically partial paralysis.

    d.   Hemiparesis is partial paralysis, not a disorder of consciousness.

9.   c is the answer. Prospective studies would better help evaluate the underlying causes of anosognosia because the existing studies are plagued by retrospective bias. (see Thinking Critically: Can Someone Be Partially Paralyzed and Not Know It?)

    a.   Retrospective studies are all that have been done to examine this issue. Prospective studies are needed to balance out the bias inherent in such approaches.

    b.   The Wada technique is a retrospective technique.

    d.   More research is needed to clarify the explanation for anosognosia.

10.   c is the answer. Simultanagnosia is a condition in which a person can see parts of a visual scene (that is, the names) but has difficulty perceiving the whole scene (the '09). (see Neuropsychological Disorders)

    a.   Visual agnosia is the inability to recognize objects based on their appearance.

    b.   Prosopagnosia is the inability to recognize faces.

    d.   Hemineglect is difficulty seeing, responding to, or acting on information from either the right or left side of the world.

11.   c is the answer. Bisiach's studies all used patients with damage to their parietal lobes and all presented visual stimuli. (see Focus on Research Methods: Studying Hemineglect)

    a.   Although Bisiach's participants did have damage to their parietal lobes, they were not presented with auditory stimuli.

    b.   Although Bisiach's participants were presented with visual stimuli, their damage was in the parietal, not occipital, lobes.

    d.   Participants in Bisiach's research did not have damage in the occipital lobe, nor were they presented with auditory stimuli.

12. a is the answer. Aprosodia occurs with right hemisphere damage, not left, and results in difficulty using tone to express or deduce meaning. (see Linkages: Language Disorders and the Brain)

   b, c. Both of these language disorders are due to damage in the left hemisphere of the brain.

   d. Semantic paraphasias occur with Wernicke's aphasia, and they involve using words that have the wrong meaning (using the word *dog* when one means *patio*, for example).

13. b is the answer. Ideomotor apraxia is difficulty in performing skilled movements. Lisa is having trouble with skills such as self-feeding, writing, and so forth. (see Neuropsychological Disorders)

   a. Ideational apraxia is difficulty not in actually performing skilled movements, but sequencing them.

   c. Dementia is a not a movement disorder.

   d. Delirium is a disorder of consciousness, not movement.

14. d is the answer. All three of these are required for a dementia diagnosis. (see Neuropsychological Disorders)

   a. Impairment in memory is necessary, but not sufficient, for a dementia diagnosis.

   b. Although impairment in both memory and some other area of function are required for a dementia diagnosis, these alone do not address the severity of the impairments, which is also necessary.

   c. This addresses the severity of the impairments, but it does not specify that memory must be one of them and that one additional area of impairment is needed to qualify for a diagnosis.

15. a is the answer. Mechanisms of brain dysfunction (cerebrovascular accident (stroke), traumatic brain injury (trauma), neurodegenerative diseases) explain how brain damage occurred; neuropsychological disorders describe the pattern of symptoms actually observed as a result of the damage. (see Mechanisms of Brain Dysfunction)

   b. The reverse is true.

   c. Both stroke and trauma are ways that brain damage can occur, but they do not describe a pattern of symptoms.

   d. Both stroke and neurodegenerative diseases are ways that brain damage can occur, but they do not describe a pattern of symptoms.

16. b is the answer. When deficits following brain dysfunction are diffuse, hard to specify, and involve multiple aspects of functioning, studying them is more complex than when the deficits are very specific and easily isolated. Consequently, we know more about the symptom pattern following stroke than trauma. (see Mechanisms of Brain Dysfunction)

   a. We know more about the neuropsychological symptom patterns following stroke than we do about those following trauma.

   c. Trauma is not necessarily easier to treat than stroke.

   d. Trauma patients do not necessarily have a greater chance of recovery relative to stroke patients.

17.   d is the answer. To interpret results of neuropsychological tests, one must know what the normative data are. In some cases, even a small deviation can indicate a problem, while in others, a large deviation may be within the bounds of normal functioning. Without the norms, the size of the deviation is difficult to interpret. (see Foundations of Neuropsychology)

    a, b.   Without the norms, these interpretations cannot be made.

    c.   The size of the deviation does not tell you about the procedure used during testing administration.

18.   a is the answer. Cleve is using phrenology. Phrenology is the idea (now refuted) that by feeling bumps on the skull you can assess personality. (see Foundations of Neuropsychology)

    b.   Lesion analysis is the study of localization of function through the study of brain damage.

    c.   The Wada technique is a research method that involves temporarily inducing hemiparesis through anesthetizing one side of the brain.

    d.   The reticular activating system is a brain structure responsible for regulating arousal and consciousness.

19.   c is the answer. Feeling bumps on the skull is phrenology, which has been discredited. Neuropsychology does not rely on this idea. (see Foundations of Neuropsychology)

    a, b.   Both of these are principles on which neuropsychology rests.

    d.   c is not a principle of neuropsychology.

20.   c is the answer. Semantic paraphasias are errors in naming objects in which that you use a true word to label something, but it is the wrong word. (see Linkages: Language Disorders and the Brain)

    a.   Aprosodia is the inability to use tone to understand and/or express meaning in language.

    b.   Paraphasias are naming errors, but this question describes a specific type—semantic paraphasias.

    c.   Phonemic paraphasias are naming errors that involve using an incorrect label that is not a word. For example, calling a pencil a pekel.

Now turn to the quiz analysis table at the end of this chapter to find which areas you know well and which areas you need to work on. Circle the numbers in the table for items in Sample Quiz 2 that you answered correctly.

For each question you answered correctly, circle its number. (Sample Quiz 2 numbers are shaded; Sample Quiz 1 numbers are not.) Are there patterns in the types of questions or the topics you got wrong that could direct your further study? Did you improve from Sample Quiz 1 to Sample Quiz 2?

QUIZ REVIEW

Topic	Type of Question		
	Definition	Comprehension	Application
Foundations of Neuropsychology	2, 18	4, 17	1, 3, 5
	3, 5	1, 4, 17, 19	2, 18
Mechanisms of Brain Dysfunction	16	6	5
		6, 15, 16	
Neuropsychological Disorders	10, 13	8, 14	7, 15, 20
		14	7, 8, 10, 13
Thinking Critically: Can Someone Be Partially Paralyzed and Not Know It?		9	
		9	
Focus on Research Methods: Studying Hemineglect		11	
		11	
Linkages: Language Disorders and the Brain			12, 19
	20	12	

Total correct by quiz:

Quiz 1:	
Quiz 2:	

APPENDIX A

Behavioral Genetics

Behavioral genetics is the study of how genes affect behavior. Behavioral genetics researchers look at the impact of genetics and environment on behavior.

OUTLINE

I. THE BIOLOGY OF GENETICS AND HEREDITY
   <u>Genetics</u> is the biology of inheritance. <u>Chromosomes</u> are long, thin structures composed of <u>genes</u>. Genes, which are made up of <u>DNA</u> (deoxyribonucleic acid), provide instructions for the synthesis of proteins. Proteins are the basis of physical traits, such as eye color. Male sperm cells and female egg cells are formed by meiosis, which leaves them with twenty-three single chromosomes. The twenty-three single chromosomes are combined in conception to form a new cell, called a zygote. Many traits are <u>polygenic traits</u>—that is, influenced by many genes. The forty-six chromosomes contain the genes, which are the individual's <u>genotype</u>. An individual's <u>phenotype</u> is the set of observable characteristics resulting from an interaction between heredity and environment.

II. A BRIEF HISTORY OF GENETIC RESEARCH IN PSYCHOLOGY
   Sir Francis Galton first suggested that family, twin, and adoption studies be used to study the link between heredity and human behavior. Galton referred to genetic influences as "nature" and environmental influences as "nurture." Although a genetic contribution to intelligence was supported by studies in 1924, research on genetic influences was inhibited by behaviorism and the association of genetics research with the views of the Nazis. The work of Arthur Jensen and Richard Herrnstein angered people because of its focus on ethnic and class differences.

III. THE FOCUS OF RESEARCH IN BEHAVIORAL GENETICS
   Behavioral genetics is the study of differences in a given trait in a population, not the study of the development of that trait for an individual. Average differences in height in a specific population are influenced primarily by genetics, for example; however, we cannot say that a specific person's height was influenced primarily by genetics. Genes can affect a trait without completely determining whether or not it will appear.

IV. THE ROLE OF GENETIC FACTORS IN PSYCHOLOGY
   A. Genetic Influences over the Life Span
      Genetic influences on mental ability apparently increase throughout the life span. A possible reason for this is that inherited predispositions may lead people to choose environments that are favorable to the development of a particular ability.

   B. Genes Affecting Multiple Traits
      Genes that influence one characteristic may also influence others. Anxiety and depression may be affected by some of the same genetic factors.

   C. Identifying Genes Related to Behavior
      Huntington's disease, which leads to a loss of motor control, personality changes, and forgetfulness, is caused by a single dominant gene. Several genes have now been linked to Alzheimer's disease. These and other advances flowing from the Human Genome Project will continue to help identify genes related to human behavior. Thus far, the most surprising

finding of the project is that the number of genes in the human genome is much smaller than expected. New techniques help to illuminate gene-environment interactions.

V. BEHAVIORAL GENETICS AND ENVIRONMENTAL INFLUENCES

While genetic causes of schizophrenia have been supported with evidence from behavioral genetics research, environmental factors can be just as important. Often 50 percent or more of the variance among individuals is due to nongenetic factors. One goal of psychologists is to study the "nonshared" aspects of the environment to see how the different environments of family members influence the appearance of traits. Events and others' behavior can be experienced differently by children in the same family.

A current hypothesis to be investigated is that genetic differences between siblings can contribute to differences in how they are treated. Research so far indicates that parents' responsiveness is related to children's mental abilities and that children choose playmates partly based on genetically influenced traits such as temperament. Nature and nurture, therefore, are interacting to influence a person's characteristics.

KEY TERMS

1. **Genetics** is the biology of inheritance. (see The Biology of Genetics and Heredity)

2. **Chromosomes** are long, thin structures in every biological cell that contain genetic information. (see The Biology of Genetics and Heredity)

    REMEMBER: Chromosomes are made up of genes. Each sperm and ovum contains twenty-three single chromosomes. Fertilization results in twenty-three pairs of chromosomes.

3. **Genes** are the biological instructions, inherited from both parents and located on the chromosomes, that provide the blueprint for physical development. (see The Biology of Genetics and Heredity)

4. **DNA** is the molecular structure of a gene that provides the genetic code. (see The Biology of Genetics and Heredity)

    REMEMBER: The arrangement of these molecules determines which protein a gene will produce. Thus, DNA provides the individual's genetic code, a blueprint for constructing the entire human being.

5. **Polygenic traits** are characteristics that are determined by more than one gene. (see The Biology of Genetics and Heredity)

    Example: Height is influenced by more than one gene.

    REMEMBER: Poly means "more than one." Polygenic means "more than one gene."

6. **Genotypes** are the full set of genes, inherited from both parents, contained in twenty-three pairs of chromosomes. (see The Biology of Genetics and Heredity)

    REMEMBER: A genotype will tell you what type of genes someone has.

7. **Phenotypes** are how an individual looks and acts, which depends on how inherited characteristics interact with the environment. (see The Biology of Genetics and Heredity)

    REMEMBER: You can see a person's phenotype. A photograph shows you the same information as a phenotype.

    Example: Rick was a calm, happy baby and became an easygoing, happy child. Part of his phenotype is his calm personality. (No one knows how much of his personality is genetically, and how much is environmentally, influenced.)

FILL-IN-THE-BLANKS KEY TERMS

This section will help you check your factual knowledge of the key terms introduced in this appendix. Fill in each blank with the appropriate term from the list of key terms in the previous section.

1. _____ is the study of the biology of inheritance.

2. Characteristics that are influenced by more than one gene are called _____.

3. Genes are composed of _____.

4. _____ are made up of genes.

5. The interaction of a person's genotype and the environment produces the person's _____.

Total Correct (See answer key) _____

LEARNING OBJECTIVES

1. Explain how behavioral genetics is a study of both environment and heredity. (see introductory section)

2. Define genetics. (see The Biology of Genetics and Heredity)

3. Define chromosomes, genes, and deoxyribonucleic acid (DNA). (see The Biology of Genetics and Heredity)

4. Define mitosis. Name the elements involved in meiosis and describe the process itself. (see The Biology of Genetics and Heredity)

5. Explain how dominant and recessive genes affect the expression of a trait. Define polygenic. (see The Biology of Genetics and Heredity)

6. Define genotype and phenotype. (see The Biology of Genetics and Heredity)

7. Discuss the history of behavioral genetics, including studies by Galton and the factors that inhibited research in behavioral genetics. (see A Brief History of Genetic Research in Psychology)

8. Describe some of the misunderstandings about behavioral genetics. Define heritability. (see The Focus of Research in Behavioral Genetics)

9. Describe the results of research on genetic influences over the life span and the genetic influence of multiple traits. Discuss the studies of the genes responsible for Huntington's and Alzheimer's diseases. (see The Role of Genetic Factors in Psychology)

10. Discuss how nonshared environmental factors may explain differences between siblings. (see Behavioral Genetics and Environmental Influences)

11. Discuss the influence of genetics on environmental events. (see Behavioral Genetics and Environmental Influences)

CONCEPTS AND EXERCISES

A person's phenotype comes from the interaction of genetics (nature) and environment (nurture). For the situations listed below, decide whether nature or nurture had more influence on the person's phenotype.

1. Nina and Maria swim together every day for the same amount of time. Although they've done the same workout for years, Nina is still a much better swimmer than Maria. Nina's higher level of swimming skill is most likely a result of _____.

2. Ken and Ben are identical twins. Ever since their grandmother bought him an electronics set, Ken was interested in how electronic appliances ran. Ken took apart toasters, radios, and a computer to see if he could figure them out and talked with his grandmother about her job as an electrical engineer. Ben, meanwhile, was interested in becoming a drummer with a rock band. The difference in Ken and Ben's interests is most likely the result of _____.

PERSONAL LEARNING ACTIVITIES

1. Think of an example of a way a natural ability could influence a person's environment.

2. What if you could have your DNA analyzed to determine your susceptibility to Alzheimer's disease, bipolar I disorder, and schizophrenia—all of which are incurable and not totally controllable with current treatments? Assume you chose to have these tests, and your results indicated that it is highly likely that you will develop one of these diseases before age forty. What would you do?

3. Suppose that researchers identified a gene associated with violent behavior and, therefore, could diagnose in childhood those who would be likely to become violent. What are the advantages and disadvantages of such research? What are the ethical considerations?

4. Recently it has become possible for parents who are doing in vitro fertilization to request preimplantation genetic testing. For a brief explanation, visit the following site: http://www.rrc.com/pgd_program.html. Do you want the ability to select a genetically normal child? What effect might preimplantation genetic testing it have on future generations? Although most physicians use this technique to try to prevent miscarriage, what other ways might this be used? What ethical questions does it raise for you?

MULTIPLE-CHOICE QUESTIONS

Quiz 1

1. Genes are made up of
   a. zygotes.
   b. chromosomes.
   c. ribonucleic acid.
   d. deoxyribonucleic acid.

2. A person's height is influenced by more than one pair of genes; therefore, height is a _____ characteristic.
   a. dominant
   b. recessive
   c. polygenic
   d. dizygotic

3. Long thin structures in every biological cell that contain different genetic information are
   a. genotypes.
   b. chromosomes
   c. heritabilities.
   d. degrees of freedom.

4. Which of the following people most stimulated research in the field of behavioral genetics?

    a. Francis Galton
    b. John B. Watson
    c. Arthur Jensen
    d. Richard Herrnstein

5. A person with the single gene responsible for Huntington's disease is likely to experience _____ in adulthood.

    a. personality changes and loss of motor control
    b. an increase in intelligence
    c. a decrease in intelligence
    d. no problems or symptoms

6. Suppose a large-sample twin study showed that about 40 percent of the variance in sociability can be accounted for by genetic factors. The researchers should conclude that

    a. nongenetic factors are unimportant.
    b. nongenetic factors are at least as important as genetic factors.
    c. most of the time, if one fraternal twin is sociable, the other will be too.
    d. most of the time, if one identical twin is sociable, the other will be too.

7. Thomas has a low IQ. His brother, Chris, has a relatively high IQ. Compared to Chris, Thomas tends to make friends with children with low IQs. In addition, their parents often pay more attention to Chris because he asks so many questions. Unlike Chris' experiences, Thomas' interactions with his peers and his parents do not encourage his cognitive development. Thomas and Chris's experiences are an example of how

    a. genetics may influence the environment.
    b. the environment may influence genetics.
    c. genetics determines intelligence.
    d. the environment determines intelligence.

Total Correct (See answer key) _____

Quiz 2

Use this quiz to reassess your learning after taking Quiz 1 and reviewing the appendix.

1. Cell division is known as

    a. ovum.
    b. polygenic.
    c. mitosis.
    d. meiosis.

2. Kathleen's mom used cocaine while pregnant with her. As a result, Kathleen is small for her age, has malformed kidneys, is unable to concentrate, and is irritable. Her mom influenced Kathleen's _____ by using cocaine.

    a. genotype
    b. phenotype
    c. blood type
    d. polytype

3. Sir Francis Galton's most famous behavioral genetics study showed that
   a. personality is environmentally influenced.
   b. personality is genetically influenced.
   c. genius runs in families.
   d. the environment influences intelligence.

4. Imagine that researchers discover that activity level is highly heritable, and that about 75 percent of the differences among people can be explained by genetic differences. Twenty-year-old Randy is extremely active. He can't stand to sit still for long and is constantly in need of stimulation from other people, the television, or the stereo. We can conclude that Randy
   a. inherited 75 percent of his activity level, and the environment added the other 25 percent.
   b. inherited an unusually high level of activity.
   c. is more active than average due to environmental effects.
   d. is more active than average for unknown reasons.

5. Marcus and Craig are identical twins; their sisters, Ashley and Tanya, are fraternal twins. As they age from childhood through late adulthood, we should expect the correlation between the IQs of _____ to increase.
   a. Marcus and Craig
   b. Ashley and Tanya
   c. Ashley and Marcus
   d. Craig and Tanya

6. Which of the following is most likely caused by a nongenetic factor?
   a. Huntington's disease
   b. Phenylketonuria
   c. Eye color
   d. Measles

7. Researchers reported the discovery of a gene linked to novelty-seeking behavior. If you found out you had the gene associated with high novelty-seeking, you could conclude that
   a. you are very likely to be bored when alone.
   b. you are very unlikely to be bored when alone.
   c. you may or may not show novelty-seeking behavior.
   d. your risky behaviors are genetically caused.

Total Correct (See answer key) _____

ANSWERS TO FILL-IN-THE-BLANKS KEY TERMS

1. Genetics (see The Biology of Genetics and Heredity)

2. polygenic (see The Biology of Genetics and Heredity)

3. deoxyribonucleic acid (DNA) (see The Biology of Genetics and Heredity)

4. Chromosomes (see The Biology of Genetics and Heredity)

5. phenotype (see The Biology of Genetics and Heredity)

ANSWERS TO CONCEPTS AND EXERCISES

1. *Nature.* Nina's higher level of swimming skill is most likely an inherited talent, because she and Maria have similarly practiced swimming for years.

2. *Nurture.* Because Ken and Ben are identical twins, the difference in their interests is most likely the result of environmental influence.

ANSWERS TO MULTIPLE-CHOICE QUESTIONS

Circle the question numbers you answered correctly.

Quiz 1

1. d is the answer. Genes are composed of DNA, or deoxyribonucleic acid. (see The Biology of Genetics and Heredity)

   a. Zygotes are the one-celled organism that results from conception.

   b. Chromosomes are composed of genes, not the other way around.

   c. It is through the production of RNA (or ribonucleic acid) that the proteins each gene will produce are determined.

2. c is the answer. A characteristic influenced by many genes is polygenic. (see The Biology of Genetics and Heredity)

   a. Dominant genes are phenotypically expressed when present in the genotype.

   b. Recessive genes need to be paired with a similar recessive gene in order to be expressed in the phenotype.

   d. Dizygotic (fraternal) twins are no more similar than any other two siblings, because they come from two separate egg cells. Monozygotic twins are genetically identical because they come from a single fertilized egg.

3. b is the answer. Chromosomes are long thin structures made up of thousands of genes. Most human cells contain forty-six chromosomes that are arranged in twenty-three matching pairs. (see The Biology of Genetics and Heredity)

   a. Genotypes are the full set of genes, inherited from both parents, contained in twenty-three pairs of chromosomes.

   c. Heritability estimates give researchers an idea of how much of the variation of a trait in a population is due to genetic variation.

   d. Degrees of freedom is a concept relating to statistics, not behavioral genetics.

4. a is the answer. Francis Galton was a pioneer in the field of behavioral genetics. He suggested several types of studies for investigating the influence of genetic and environmental effects. Although Galton overstated the influence of inherited characteristics, his work did create interest in the field. (see A Brief History of Genetic Research in Psychology)

   b. Watson was a behaviorist who promoted the idea that a person's capacities, temperament, and talents are due to training rather than genetics. This inhibited research on behavioral genetics.

   c, d. Arthur Jensen proposed that differences between blacks and whites were caused by genetics; Richard Herrnstein thought social class differences were influenced by genetics. The publication of these views had a negative effect on research.

5. a is the answer. Huntington's disease is caused by a single dominant gene; the symptoms of deterioration of the central nervous system, loss of motor control, and personality changes are likely to appear in adulthood. (see The Role of Genetic Factors in Psychology)

   b, c. Huntington's disease is not characterized by a change in level of intelligence, although it can cause forgetfulness.

   d. Because the gene responsible for Huntington's disease is dominant, it will be expressed outwardly whenever present.

6. b is the answer. If 40 percent of variance is accounted for genetically, then 60 percent is due to environmental factors. (see Behavioral Genetics and Environmental Influences)

   a. Nongenetic factors account for more of the variability in this case than do the genetic factors.

   c. Fraternal twins, like other nonidentical twin siblings, share only 50 percent of their genes; therefore, they may or may not be similar on sociability.

   d. Identical twins are genetically the same. However, only 40 percent of the variance in sociability in our hypothetical study is accounted for by genetic factors; therefore, more than half of the time, identical twins may have different levels of sociability.

7. a is the answer. Although Thomas and his parents may be unaware of the differences, Thomas' level of intelligence appears to be influencing his environment. He chooses less intelligent friends than Chris does, and he gets less attention from his parents. (see Behavioral Genetics and Environmental Influences)

   b. The environment is not changing Thomas' genotype.

   c. Genetics has an influence on intelligence but does not completely determine it. The story shows how a person's environment may or may not encourage cognitive development.

   d. The environment has an influence on intelligence but does not completely determine it. The story shows how a person's level of intelligence may influence his environment.

Now turn to the quiz analysis table at the end of this appendix to find which areas you know well and which areas you need to work on. Circle the numbers in the table for items on Quiz 1 that you answered correctly.

Quiz 2

1. c is the answer. Cell division is known as mitosis. (see The Biology of Genetics and Heredity)

   a. An ovum is a woman's unfertilized egg.

   b. Polygenic refers to characteristics that are determined by more than one gene.

   d. Meiosis occurs when a male's sperm cells and a female's egg cells are formed and involves chromosome pairs not being copied but being randomly split and rearranged. This leaves each new sperm and egg cell with just one member of each chromosome pair, no two of which are quite the same.

2. b is the answer. Although Kathleen could have been genetically susceptible to harm from a foreign substance during the critical period of embryonic development, it was her phenotype that was affected by her mother's drug use. (see The Biology of Genetics and Heredity)

   a. Kathleen's genotype is the set of genes that she inherited from her parents. Her mother, of course, was one influence on Kathleen's genotype; however, her mother's drug use was unlikely to have affected Kathleen's genotype.

c.   Again, Kathleen's parents influenced her blood type, but her mother's drug use did not.

d.   Polytype is not a term. Perhaps you were thinking of polygenic. A trait that is polygenic is controlled by many genes.

3.   c is the answer. Galton's family study showed that genius ran in families. Although Galton made the extreme interpretation that genetics was a much more powerful influence than the environment, his work awakened interest in the field of behavioral genetics. (see A Brief History of Genetic Research in Psychology)

a, b.   Galton's most famous study did not address personality traits.

d.   Galton concluded that genetics caused genius to run in families, although intelligence is certainly influenced by the environment.

4.   d is the answer. Even with highly heritable traits, we can make no conclusions about an individual's amount of inherited trait. Randy may be more active than average because of genetics, but knowledge of a trait's heritability allows only generalizations about people on average, not about one person. (see The Focus of Research in Behavioral Genetics)

a.   In our imaginary example, 75 percent of the activity-level differences between people are explained by genetics. This is not the same as saying that an individual inherited 75 percent of a characteristic.

b.   Randy may indeed have inherited an unusually high level of activity, but we cannot say that with any certainty.

c.   The environment could have caused Randy's high activity level, but we cannot say that with any certainty.

5.   a is the answer. The IQ scores of identical twins become more similar over the life span. (see The Role of Genetic Factors in Psychology)

b, c, d.   We don't have any reason to expect increases in IQ correlations among siblings who are not identical twins; indeed, such correlations may actually decrease.

6.   d is the answer. Measles is an illness caused by a virus. Even if you weren't sure what measles were or what caused them, you could have arrived at this answer through the process of elimination. (see Behavioral Genetics and Environmental Influences)

a.   Huntington's disease is caused by a single dominant gene.

b.   Phenylketonuria occurs when the two recessive genes responsible for it are inherited.

c.   Eye color is caused by more than one pair of genes.

7.   c is the answer. Knowing that a gene is associated with a behavior does not allow us to know whether a particular person will exhibit that behavior—unless the behavior is completely determined by the gene. (see Behavioral Genetics and Environmental Influences)

a, b.   Boredom when alone may occur for a person high on the novelty-seeking trait, but we cannot predict such a specific feeling from a person's genotype.

d.   As with other traits, it is highly likely that 50 percent or more of the variance associated with novelty-seeking is environmentally caused; therefore, risky behaviors are more likely to have been influenced by the environment than by a person's genotype.

Now turn to the quiz analysis table at the end of this appendix to find which areas you know well and which areas you need to work on. Circle the numbers in the table for items on Quiz 2 that you answered correctly.

For each question you answered correctly, circle its number. (Quiz 1 numbers are not shaded; Quiz 2 numbers are shaded.) Are there patterns in the types of questions or the topics you got wrong that could direct your further study? Did you improve from Quiz 1 to Quiz 2?

QUIZ REVIEW

Topic	Type of Question		
	Definition	Comprehension	Application
The Biology of Genetics and Heredity	3	1, 2	
	1		2
A Brief History of Genetic Research in Psychology		4	
		3	
The Focus of Research in Behavioral Genetics			
			4
The Role of Genetic Factors in Psychology		5	
		5	
Behavioral Genetics and Environmental Influences			6, 7
		6	7

Total correct by quiz:

Quiz 1:	
Quiz 2:	

APPENDIX B

Statistics in Psychological Research

Statistics are used to understand and interpret psychological research results.

OUTLINE

I.   DESCRIBING DATA
     Researchers engage in <u>null hypothesis testing</u>, which evaluates the assertion that the independent variable will have no effect on the dependent variable.

   A. The Frequency Histogram
       <u>Histograms</u>, graphic descriptions of data, are useful for visualizing and better understanding the "shape" of research data.

   B. Descriptive Statistics
       The numbers that summarize a pool of data are called <u>descriptive statistics</u>. The four basic categories measure the number of observations, summarize the typical value of the data set, summarize the variability of the data set, and express the correlations.

       1. *N*. The easiest statistic to compute is *N*, the number of observations in the data set.
       2. *Measures of Central Tendency*. Three statistical measures describe the typical value of a data set. The mode is the score that occurs most often in the data set. The median is the halfway point in the data set: half of the scores fall above the median, and half fall below it. The mean is the arithmetic average of all the scores in the data set.
       3. *Measures of Variability*. There are two statistical measures that indicate the dispersion of scores in a data set, or that measure variability. The <u>range</u> describes the distance between the highest score and the lowest score. The <u>standard deviation</u> measures the average difference between each score and the mean of the data set.
       4. *The Normal Distribution*. When most of the scores in a data set fall in the middle of a distribution that has few extreme scores, the data resemble a bell-shaped curve called the <u>normal distribution</u>. In this case, the mean, median, and mode all have the same value. The normal distribution is the basis for percentiles and standard scores. A <u>percentile</u> score indicates the percentage of subjects or observations that fall below a given score. <u>Standard scores</u> express distance in standard deviations from the mean.
       5. *Correlation*. The relationship between two variables is described by a correlation. The statistical measures that represent this relationship are called correlation coefficients.

II. INFERENTIAL STATISTICS
     <u>Inferential statistics</u> provide a measure of confidence or probability that conducting the same experiment again would yield similar results.

   A. Differences Between Means: The *t* Test
       The *t* test, a type of inferential statistic, assesses whether differences between two means occurred because of chance or because of the effect of an independent variable. Results that show a low probability of chance effects are statistically significant. Performing a *t* test requires using (a) the difference between the means, (b) the standard deviation, and (c) the number of observations or subjects. The researcher also takes the <u>degrees of freedom</u> and *p* value into account.

B. Beyond the *t* Test

Other statistical tests are used to analyze data from experiments that are more complex than comparisons between two groups. An analysis of variance analyzes the effects of more than one variable on a dependent variable.

KEY TERMS

1. **Null hypothesis testing** evaluates whether the independent variable manipulated by the experimenter will have no effect on the dependent variable measured by the experimenter. (see Describing Data)

2. A **histogram** is a graphic presentation of data that consists of a set of bars, each of which represents how frequently different scores or values occur in a data set. (see The Frequency Histogram)

    REMEMBER: Frequency means "how often." This graph tells you how often various scores occurred.

3. **Descriptive statistics** are numbers that summarize a set of data. (see Descriptive Statistics)

4. The **range** is a measure of variability that is the difference between the highest and lowest values in a data set. (see Measures of Variability)

5. The **standard deviation (SD)** is a measure of variability that is the average difference between each score and the mean of the data set. (see Measures of Variability)

6. **Normal distribution** describes a dispersion of scores such that the mean, median, and mode all have the same value. When a distribution has this property, the standard deviation can be used to describe how any particular score stands in relation to the rest of the distribution. (see The Normal Distribution)

    REMEMBER: If you are having problems understanding what a normal distribution is, be sure to do the exercise "A Statistical Report Card."

7. A **percentile** is a value that indicates the percentage of people or observations that fall below a given point in a normal distribution. (see The Normal Distribution)

    Example: If your psychology exam score is at the 95th percentile, you know that you did better than 95 percent of the people who took the test. It does not mean that you answered 95 percent of the questions correctly.

8. **Standard scores** are values that indicate the distance, in standard deviations, between a given score and the mean of all scores in a data set. (see The Normal Distribution)

    Example: A standard score of +1.5 means that the score is 1.5 standard deviations above the mean of the distribution.

9. **Inferential statistics** are a set of procedures that provide a measure of how likely it is that research results came about by chance. (see Inferential Statistics)

10. **Degrees of freedom (df)** are the total sample size or number of scores in a data set, less the number of experimental groups. (see Differences Between Means: The *t* Test)

FILL-IN-THE-BLANKS KEY TERMS

This section will help you check your factual knowledge of the key terms introduced in this chapter. Fill in each blank with the appropriate term from the list of key terms in the previous section.

1. A(n) _____ states that the independent measure will not affect the dependent measure.

2. A(n) _____ is a graphic display of data.

3. In a(n) _____, scores fall symmetrically around the mean.

4. The value that denotes the percentage of people or observations that fall below a given score is called a(n) _____.

5. The _____ score indicates the value of a score by measuring its distance in standard deviations from the mean.

6. A(n) _____ is used to evaluate the differences between two means in a data set.

Total Correct (See answer key) _____

LEARNING OBJECTIVES

1. Describe the differences between <u>descriptive</u> and <u>inferential statistics</u>. (see introductory section; see also Descriptive Statistics and Inferential Statistics)

2. Define <u>null hypothesis testing</u>. (see Describing Data)

3. Describe a <u>histogram</u>, and explain why it is used. (see The Frequency Histogram)

4. Name the four basic categories of descriptive statistics. (see Descriptive Statistics)

5. Define measure of central tendency, and describe the three measures of central tendency. (see Measures of Central Tendency)

6. Explain how to calculate the mean, median, and mode for a given data set. (see Measures of Central Tendency)

7. Define measure of variability, and describe the two measures of it. (see Measures of Variability)

8. Discuss the features of a <u>normal distribution</u>. (see The Normal Distribution)

9. Define <u>percentile</u> and <u>standard scores</u>, and explain how to use each one. (see The Normal Distribution)

10. Define correlation. Specify the formula for computing a correlation coefficient. (see Correlation)

11. Define <u>t test</u>. Specify the formula for calculating a t value as well as the procedures for interpreting it. (see Differences Between Means: The t Test)

12. Define <u>degrees of freedom</u>. (see Differences Between Means: The t Test)

13. Define analysis of variance, and explain when this statistic is used. (see Beyond the t Test)

CONCEPTS AND EXERCISES

Statistics and the Consumer

Ricardo has just won the lottery and has hired you to help him spend his money. He has given you a stack of statistical documentation on the qualities of all the brand-name items he wants to buy. Because Ricardo knows nothing about statistics, you must choose the best brand for the money.

1. Ricardo wants a sports car and cares only about its maximum speed. Your information says that the mean maximum speed of car A is 180 mph; the standard deviation for all the speed trials is 32

mph. The mean maximum speed of car B is 173 mph, with a standard deviation of 5 mph. Which car should Ricardo buy? _____

2. Ricardo wants to buy and sell property to make a profit. Therefore, he needs to know which areas contain properties that will increase quickly in value. In the last five years, Brentwood Oaks has had a mean increase in value of 15 percent and a standard deviation of 2 percent. Redwood Estates has had a mean increase of 18 percent and a standard deviation of 0.5 percent. In which area should Ricardo buy? _____

3. Ricardo is overweight and wants to get in shape. Clients at the Body Beautiful Fitness Center have achieved a mean loss of 35 pounds with a standard deviation of 20 pounds. Clients at the Bare Bones Fitness Center have achieved a mean loss of 25 pounds with a standard deviation of 4 pounds. At which center can Ricardo be more certain of losing 20–25 pounds? _____

4. Ricardo and one of his new friends want to bet on the season performance of various football teams. Each man will pick the team that he thinks has the chance of scoring the most points in the upcoming season. Whoever picks the highest-scoring team will win. Team A has a mean point total of 355 for the past five seasons, with a standard deviation of 15 points, and team B has a mean point total of 370 for the past five seasons and a standard deviation of 5 points. Which team should Ricardo pick? _____

Choosing the Correct Statistical Method

Pick the most appropriate statistical method for analyzing the data from the following three experiments.

1. A psychologist believes that environment affects the development of connections among nerve cells in the brain. She raises two groups of rats. Rats in group 1 live together in a cage filled with toys. Rats in group 2 are housed in separate steel cages with no toys. After several months, the psychologist examines the brains of the rats to see if there are differences between the two groups in the number of nerve cell connections. _____

2. Some psychologists believe that genetic factors determine intelligence. Others believe that environmental factors, such as educational opportunities, nutrition, and the quality of care received during childhood, determine intelligence. To test this hypothesis, a psychologist looks for a relationship between IQ scores and socioeconomic status. _____

3. A psychologist believes that the different types of therapy used to treat abnormal behavior are not really different from one another. To test this, he chooses three different therapies and divides his group of subjects, all of whom are suffering from severe depression, into three groups. Each group receives one type of therapy. After all the subjects have been treated for six months, their level of depression is measured. _____

PERSONAL LEARNING ACTIVITIES

1. Take a survey and compute measures of central tendency on your data. For example, you could find out at what age people first got a job, drove a car, or had a date. You might find that the modal age for a first date is higher than the mean or median age.

2. For the survey data you collected in Personal Learning Activity 1, compute a correlation coefficient following the instructions in the section on correlations in your text. For example, are people who first drove at an older age also likely to have had their first date at an older age? If this were the case, you would find a positive correlation between "drive age" and "date age."

3. Go online and find an archival news report based on a survey. It may be a political survey or a health/medical related survey. What sorts of statistics are being reported? Are they being used appropriately? When should one report the mean, as opposed to the median or mode? Are correlations being discussed as measures of relation, or (erroneously) as assessments of cause.

MULTIPLE-CHOICE QUESTIONS

Quiz 1

Part I

1. Which is the easiest statistic to compute?
    a. N
    b. Frequency histogram
    c. Mean
    d. Range

2. The frequency histogram is
    a. a graphic representation of data.
    b. a measure of central tendency.
    c. a measure of variability.
    d. a measure of relationship between two variables.

Part II

Donald is a high school football coach. He has kept track of the number of touchdowns his players have made during every game. Using the data that he has collected, answer questions 3, 4, and 5.

Data: 1, 2, 3, 3, 8, 10, 7, 6, 5

3. What is the mode?
    a. 3
    b. 4
    c. 5
    d. 6

4. What is the median?
    a. 3
    b. 4
    c. 5
    d. 6

5. What is the mean?
    a. 3
    b. 4
    c. 5
    d. 6

6. Which of the following data sets would best fit the definition of a normal distribution?
    a. 1, 6, 6, 12, 100, 100, 200
    b. 1, 2, 3, 4, 5, 5, 5, 6, 7, 8, 9
    c. 2, 4, 6, 8, 10, 10, 11

7. Jean Luc completed a study of music tastes. He found a significant correlation of .51 between the amount of milk people drink and the amount of jazz they listen to. The correct interpretation of this correlation is that in Jean Luc's sample
   a. people who drink more milk tend to listen to more jazz.
   b. people who drink more milk tend to listen to less jazz.
   c. listening to jazz music causes people to drink milk.
   d. drinking milk causes people to listen to jazz music.

8. Researchers use _____ statistical methods to summarize and present their data.
   a. descriptive
   b. significant
   c. inferential
   d. standard

9. Phil is comparing two sections of introductory psychology to each other. In one class, he is using PowerPoint to present his lectures. In the other class, he uses old-fashioned blackboard techniques. He is going to compare the classes' exam scores. Which statistic will he need for this comparison?
   a. Frequency histogram
   b. Correlation coefficient
   c. ANOVA
   d. t test

10. Cheryl designed an experiment to find out how the loudness of her music affects her fans' enjoyment of her concerts. One group in Cheryl's experiment is assigned to the "ears ring for two days" condition, where the music is very loud. Another group hears the same music at a loud but nondamaging level, and a third group hears it at a low level. She then has them complete a questionnaire to rate their enjoyment. Cheryl should use _____ to determine if there is a significant difference between the three groups.
    a. an analysis of variance
    b. a correlation coefficient
    c. the median
    d. a t test

Total Correct (See answer key) _____

Quiz 2

Part I

Use this quiz to reassess your learning after taking Quiz 1 and reviewing the appendix.

1. In order to best illustrate the differences in the weekly sales figures for each type of fat-free cookie, the "Cookie Man" should show
   a. the median overall cookie sales.
   b. a histogram indicating the weekly sales of each variety of cookies.
   c. the range of weekly sales figures for each cookie type.
   d. the standard deviation for each cookie type.

2. *N* is equal to the number of

    a. subjects in an experiment.
    b. observations in a data set.
    c. independent variables in an experiment.
    d. dependent variables in a data set.

3. You have decided to buy a certain kind of car because you heard that it gets great gas mileage. According to a consumer magazine, the mean gas mileage obtained during testing was 30, the median was 26, and the mode was 25. If you purchase this kind of car, the gas mileage you are likely to get will most likely

    a. be more than 30 miles per gallon.
    b. vary from 20 to 40 miles per gallon.
    c. be less than 30 miles per gallon.
    d. be 28 miles per gallon.

4. Phani is a nutritionist. She measured the number of protein grams ingested and the reported level of satiety in a sample of 1,000 people. She found a correlation of +.70 between those two variables. Phani should conclude that

    a. eating more protein causes satiety.
    b. reports of satiety tend to be higher for people who eat more protein.
    c. reports of satiety tend to be lower for people who eat more protein.
    d. protein ingestion and satiety are nearly unrelated.

5. Maxine found that she scored at the 93rd percentile on her calculus exam. This means that

    a. she got 93 percent of the problems correct.
    b. seven other people in the class scored higher than Maxine.
    c. she scored higher than 93 percent of the calculus class on the test.
    d. she did 93 problems correctly.

6. The mean is a poor descriptive measure of central tendency when

    a. the standard deviation is very small.
    b. it is very large.
    c. the range is very small.
    d. there are extreme or unrepresentative scores in the data set.

Part II

When Vitus asked his psychology and rhetoric classmates to rate his personality on a scale from 1 (irritating) to 10 (extremely pleasant), he received the following data:

Psychology class:	1	9	4	6	3	3	9
Rhetoric class:	8	7	7	8	8	9	9

Using these data, answer questions 7 and 8.

7. What are the mean and median ratings of his psychology class?

    a. 3, 6
    b. 5, 4
    c. 5, 6
    d. 6, 5

8. Which of the following statements best describes the sets of ratings in Vitus's two classes?

   a. The rhetoric class has extremely high variability.
   b. The rhetoric class has more variability than the psychology class.
   c. The psychology class has more variability than the rhetoric class.
   d. The psychology class has extremely high variability.

Part III

9. Pierre has been computing *t* values for statistical analysis of his data. He has discovered a mistake in his calculation of the standard deviations for his data groups. They are much higher than he originally thought. The recalculated *t* values will be

   a. higher, thereby increasing his chances of getting statistically significant results.
   b. higher, thereby decreasing his chances of getting statistically significant results.
   c. lower, thereby increasing his chances of getting statistically significant results.
   d. lower, thereby decreasing his chances of getting statistically significant results.

10. Chris has done an experiment that involves two independent variables. Which inferential statistical measure should she use to analyze her data?

    a. Mean
    b. Standard deviation
    c. *t* test
    d. Analysis of variance

Total Correct (See answer key) _____

ANSWERS TO FILL-IN-THE-BLANKS KEY TERMS

1. null hypothesis (see Describing Data)

2. frequency histogram (see The Frequency Histogram)

3. normal distribution (see The Normal Distribution)

4. percentile score (see The Normal Distribution)

5. standard (see The Normal Distribution)

6. *t* test (see Differences Between Means: The *t* Test)

ANSWERS TO CONCEPTS AND EXERCISES

Statistics and the Consumer

1. *B*. Ricardo wants to buy a car that is consistently fast. Car A has a higher mean speed than car B over all the time trials. However, the standard deviation is very large. This indicates that car A is fast but not consistently fast, and that there was much variation in the data from the time trials. Car B's speed is 7 miles per hour slower than car A's, but the variation is low. Therefore, Ricardo should buy car B since he can depend on it to be more consistently fast. (see Measures of Variability)

2. *Redwood Estates.* To make money quickly but with very low risk, Ricardo must buy property that will increase in value consistently and at a fairly fast rate. Redwood Estates has a higher mean increase in property value and a small standard deviation, which indicate that the mean is a good description of the increase in the property's value. Ricardo should buy land in Redwood Estates. Brentwood Oaks not only has a lower mean value increase but also has a great deal of variability in the increase. (see Measures of Central Tendency; see also Measures of Variability)

3. *Bare Bones.* If Ricardo wants to be sure to lose weight, he should go to the Bare Bones Fitness Center. Even though the mean weight loss there is lower by 10 pounds, the variability is low, which means that most people who have gone there have lost close to 25 pounds. The Body Beautiful Fitness Center has a higher mean weight loss but also a higher variability, which means that some people have lost a lot of weight there, while others have lost very little. (see Measures of Central Tendency; see also Measures of Variability)

4. *B.* Team B has consistently scored close to 370 points for the past five years. Team A has a mean of 355 points but has not been consistent. This means that some years it scored well above 355 points and some years well below 355 points. Team B's mean point total is higher and more consistent than team A's mean point total. Therefore, Ricardo should bet on team B. (see Measures of Central Tendency; see also Measures of Variability)

Choosing the Correct Statistical Method

1. *t test.* This psychologist is going to compare the mean number of nerve cell connections in rats from group 1 to the mean number of nerve cell connections in rats from group 2. She will use a *t* test, which will tell her how likely it is that the differences between the means of the two groups are due to the effects of the different environments or to chance. If her results are significant, then she can conclude that the housing did indeed cause changes in the number of nerve cell connections in the brains of the rats. (see Differences Between Means: The *t* Test)

2. *Correlation coefficient.* This psychologist is looking at the relationship between two variables: level of intelligence and environmental conditions. Therefore, she will find the correlation coefficient that represents this relationship. Remember, even if the correlation is very high, the psychologist can conclude only that these variables are related. She cannot conclude that environmental conditions cause changes in the level of intelligence. Correlation does not imply causation. (see Correlation)

3. *Analysis of variance.* This psychologist is interested in the effect of therapy (independent variable) on depression (dependent variable). He wants to know if there are any differences in the effectiveness of three different types of therapy. Therefore, there are three levels of the independent variable. These data require an analysis of variance. (see Beyond the *t* Test)

ANSWERS TO MULTIPLE-CHOICE QUESTIONS

Circle the question numbers you answered correctly.

Quiz 1

1. a is the answer. *N* is the easiest statistic to compute—it is simply the number of observations in the data set. (see Descriptive Statistics)

    b. A frequency histogram is a graphic description of data—not a statistic in itself.

    c. A mean is a measure of central tendency that is the sum of all the scores in the data set, divided by the number of scores in the data set (the arithmetic average). It is more complex than simply counting the number of observations.

    d.   The range is the distance between the highest and lowest scores in the data set. It is more complex to compute than N because you have to sort the scores in the data set to identify highest and lowest before you can calculate.

2.   a is the answer. A frequency histogram is a graphic representation of data that allows you to see the "shape" of the data set. (see The Frequency Histogram)

    b.   Mean, median, and mode are examples of measures of central tendency.

    c.   Range and standard deviation are examples of measures of dispersion.

    d.   The correlation coefficient, or r, stands for the relationship between two variables.

3.   a is the answer. The mode is the most frequently occurring score, which is 3. (see Descriptive Statistics)

4.   c is the answer. To find the median, rearrange the scores from lowest to highest and then find the score that splits the data in half. The data from lowest to highest: 1, 2, 3, 3, 5, 6, 7, 8, 10. There are nine scores, so the fifth score will split the set such that half the scores (four) are below it and half (four) are above it. The value of the fifth score is 5. (see Descriptive Statistics)

5.   c is the answer. The mean is 5. It is calculated by adding all the scores and then dividing by the number of scores. The sum of all the scores is 45, which, divided by 9 (the total number of scores), is 5. (see Descriptive Statistics)

6.   c is the answer. The mean, median, and mode are equal in a normal distribution. (see Descriptive Statistics)

    a, b, d.   None of these data sets has a mean, a median, and a mode that are all equal.

7.   a is the answer. A significant positive correlation coefficient indicates that as one variable increases, the other tends to increase. As milk drinking increases, jazz listening increases. (see Descriptive Statistics)

    b.   In a negative correlation, as one variable increases, the other decreases. Jean Luc found a positive correlation.

    c, d.   A correlation indicates only a relationship; therefore, Jean Luc cannot conclude that either of these is true.

8.   a is the answer. (see Descriptive Statistics)

    b.   There is no such thing as a "significant statistical" method. Researchers use inferential statistics to conclude from data that experimental results are statistically significant.

    c.   Inferential statistics are the mathematical procedures psychologists use to draw conclusions from data and make inferences about what they mean.

    d.   There is no such thing as a standard statistic.

9.   d is the answer. A t test is used to compare the difference between two means. Phil is comparing two section means, so he will need the t test. (see Differences Between Means: The t Test)

    a.   The frequency histogram is a graphic representation of the data—it will not help Phil compare means.

    b.   The correlation coefficient is a measure of the relationship between two variables. It does not assess the differences between means, as Phil would like to do.

    c.   The analysis of variance, or ANOVA, is used to compare three or more means. Phil is comparing only two means, so he just needs the t test.

10. a is the answer. An analysis of variance is the inferential statistic that is used when comparing more than two groups. (see Beyond the *t* Test)

   b.   A correlation coefficient indicates the strength and direction of the relationship between two variables. Cheryl cannot infer from a correlation coefficient whether her three groups are different.

   c.   One median will not allow for comparisons between groups. Even if we found different medians for each group, it would not allow us to infer that they were significantly different.

   d.   A *t* test is an inferential statistic, but it only compares two groups.

Now turn to the quiz analysis table at the end of this appendix to find which areas you know well and which areas you need to work on. Circle the numbers in the table for items on Quiz 1 that you answered correctly.

Quiz 2

1.   b is the answer. A frequency histogram would show visually how the weekly sales figures differed. (see The Frequency Histogram)

   a.   The median overall cookie sales would be one number indicating how sales generally have gone.

   c.   The range of sales figures would show how large the variation in cookie sales have been each week but would not be a good illustration of how many cookies were sold each week. After all, if 10,000 boxes of Cookie One were sold one week, and the next week 20,000 were sold, that would be a range of 10,000. If we compared the weekly sales of Cookie Two—50,000 and 60,000 (a range of 10,000)—we would see no difference in the figures for cookie types one and two.

   d.   Like the range, the standard deviation describes variability rather than general sales figures.

2.   b is the answer. Observations or scores are numerical representations of the measurement of the dependent variable. The total number of observations is called *N*. (see Descriptive Statistics)

   a.   If each subject gives two responses or answers in an experiment, then the total number of observations, *N*, will be equal to twice the size of the sample. Therefore, counting the number of subjects will not always give the value of *N*.

   c, d.   The number of independent or dependent variables will not tell you how many observations a data set has.

3.   c is the answer. Since the mode and median are both below 30, you should suspect that the mean has been artificially inflated by a few extreme, unrepresentative scores. Therefore, the gas mileage will probably be lower than 30 miles per gallon. (see Descriptive Statistics)

   a, b, d.   The mean has been inflated by a few extreme unrepresentative scores. The car's mileage will be lower than 30 miles per gallon. However, you cannot predict on the basis of the data given just how much lower it will be, nor can you predict what the range of performance will be.

4.   b is the answer. A positive correlation indicates that as the number of protein grams ingested increased, reports of satiety also increased. (see Descriptive Statistics)

   a.   Correlations show relationships between variables. A high correlation indicates a stronger relationship, but cannot indicate if one variable causes the other—or if a third variable causes both of them.

c.   If the correlation were negative, then this would be the correct answer.

d.   The correlation is fairly high, so the variables are not unrelated. If the absolute value of the correlation were closer to zero, then this might be true.

5.   c is the answer. A percentile score indicates the percentage of people or observations that fall below a given score in a normal distribution. Therefore, 93 percent of Maxine's calculus class received scores that were lower than hers. (see Descriptive Statistics)

a.   A percentile does not show how many problems Maxine answered correctly. It does show how well Maxine did relative to the other people in her class.

b.   How many people did better or worse than Maxine cannot be calculated unless the number of people in her class is known.

d.   The percentile is not related to the number of problems on the test.

6.   d is the answer. The mean is an average of the values of all the scores in a data set. Extremely low or extremely high scores can have a huge effect on the value of the mean, and it will not provide an accurate description of where most of the scores tend to fall. (see Descriptive Statistics)

a.   If the standard deviation is small, most of the scores in the data set cluster around the mean, and the mean accurately represents the central tendency of the data.

b.   The size of the mean does not make it a better or worse measure of central tendency. A large mean could accurately indicate a predominance of large scores in the data set or the presence of very large unrepresentative scores.

c.   If the range is small, there may not be much variability in the data. The less variability there is, the more accurate the mean is in conveying where the scores had a tendency to center.

7.   b is the answer. The mean is calculated by adding the scores and dividing by the number of observations. $35 \div 7 = 5$. To find the median, you must put the scores in order (1, 3, 3, 4, 6, 9, 9) and choose the middle one (4). (see Descriptive Statistics)

8.   c is the answer. Even without calculating a standard deviation, one can see that the ratings of the rhetoric class are all within one point of the mean, which is 8. The rhetoric class has a range of 2, and the psychology class has a range of 8. (see Descriptive Statistics)

a, d.   Neither class has extremely high variability.

b.   The ratings of Vitus's psychology classmates vary more than those of his rhetoric classmates.

9.   d is the answer. If you look at the formula for a *t* test, you will see that increasing the standard deviation will decrease the overall value of the equation, or *t*. The lower the value of *t* is, the more likely it is to be smaller than the *t* values listed in a *t* table and, hence, statistically insignificant. (see Differences Between Means: The *t* Test)

a, b.   A larger standard deviation will result in a smaller *t* value.

c.   A larger standard deviation will result in a smaller *t* value. But the obtained *t* value must still be equal to or larger than the *t* values listed in a *t* table for the data to be considered statistically significant.

10.   d is the answer. In an experiment with two or more independent variables, the results may be due to either of the independent variables or the interaction between them. An analysis of variance can measure the size and source of these effects. (see Beyond the *t* Test)

   a, b.   The mean and standard deviation are necessary to compute inferential statistics (such as the *t* test and analysis of variance), but they are descriptive statistics.

   c.   A *t* test is an inferential statistic, but it is used to test the difference between two means in an experiment that uses only one independent variable.

Now go to the quiz analysis table below to find which areas you know well and which areas you need to work on. Circle the numbers in the table for items on Quiz 2 that you answered correctly.

For each question you answered correctly, circle its number. (Quiz 1 numbers are not shaded; Quiz 2 numbers are shaded.) Are there patterns in the types of questions or the topics you got wrong that could direct your further study? Did you improve from Quiz 1 to Quiz 2?

QUIZ REVIEW

Topic	Type of Question		
	Definition	Comprehension	Application
Describing Data			
The Frequency Histogram	2		
			1
Descriptive Statistics	8	1	3, 4, 5, 6, 7
	2	6	3, 4, 5, 7, 8
Inferential Statistics			
Differences Between Means: The *t* Test			9
			9
Beyond the *t* Test			10
			10

Total correct by quiz:

Quiz 1:	
Quiz 2:	